THE
INVESTOR'S
INFORMATION
SOURCEBOOK

A Quick Reference to Investment Information and Advice

Spencer McGowan

NEW YORK INSTITUTE OF FINANCE

NEW YORK • TORONTO • SYDNEY • TOKYO • SINGAPORE

10   9   8   7   6   5   4   3   2   1

Library of Congress Cataloging-in-Publication Data

McGowan, Spencer.
   The investor's information sourcebook : a quick reference to investment
information and advice / Spencer McGowen
      p.   cm.
   Includes bibliographical references and index.
   ISBN 0-13-125162-7 (paper)
   1. Investments—Information services.
HG4515.9.M35 1995
016.3326—dc20   94-38182
                                           CIP

ISBN 0-13-125162-7

 NEW YORK INSTITUTE OF FINANCE
Englewood Cliffs, NJ 07632

Simon & Schuster, A Paramount Communications Company

Printed in the United States of America

Contents

ACKNOWLEDGMENTS

Special thanks to Dean McGowan, who served as our technical advisor; Ruth Bison for her expertise as our publishing consultant; Laura Hooper for a tremendous effort as research coordinator; Stephen Montalvo for in-depth computer research; Daniel Flores for his diligence in newsletter research; and Charles and Judy Taylor of Computer Magicians for amazing database and typesetting support.

PREFACE

Investors need information. The good news is that there is a wealth of investment information available in every shape and size. The bad news is that you could spend a lifetime sorting through all the available sources of information in order to determine which ones best fit your individual needs. That's why *The Investor's Information Sourcebook* was created.

Before selecting information or advice, it's worth exploring the many choices available to accomplish your investment goals. We hope you find *The Investor's Information Sourcebook* to be a high quality, user friendly tool—a one stop, overall view of what's available with a concise description of each source.

Only investment sources focused on publicly or exchange-traded securities are listed: bonds, mutual funds, stocks, options, and futures/commodities. Collectibles and non-exchange traded real estate investments are excluded so the *Sourcebook* can focus on uniformly traded instruments.

The Investor's Information Sourcebook is setup as a comprehensive menu of investment information sources. The chapters are organized by source type:

Newsletter and Chart Services

Computer and Quote Services

Performance Ranking Services

Stock and Bond Research Publications

Brokerage Research Publications

Free Brochures and Pamphlets on Investing

Magazines, Newspapers, and Periodicals

Financial Television Programs

Books and Tapes on Investing

General References

All of the sources within each chapter are listed alphabetically with complete information regarding their content, cost, and ordering instructions. By using the index an investor can quickly scan a list of sources by title. For example, if you are searching for a book to explain more about corporate bonds, a quick scan of the index will provide a list of potential titles.

The *Sourcebook* will help you find the information appropriate to your situation, regardless of the size of your portfolio or the sophistication of your investment strategies. Some sources give extremely detailed looks at specific investments; others provide quick overviews of a broad spectrum of investments. While most of the items described have costs attached, some are available free to all investors. Because the *Sourcebook* has everything available gathered in one place, you're sure to find exactly what you're looking for.

Every source entry includes designations indicating the level of sophistication: Beginning, Individual, or Professional. Each entry also notes the risk level of the strategies suggested by the source: Conservative, moderate, or aggressive. Conservative refers to investments with an orientation towards yield or income. Moderate refers to growth and income goals. Aggressive refers to trading or growth strategies.

Most of the sources listed in the *Sourcebook* have been contacted to edit their own entries for accuracy. Further, each entry has been telephoned to verify its continued operation. However, the accuracy and reliability of the sources listed are in no way endorsed or assured.

NEWSLETTERS AND CHART SERVICES

Newsletter and chart services provide an excellent source of frequently updated investment advice, suggestions, and market information. But with so many choices available, how do you find the services that will fill your particular needs?

This chapter includes most newsletters and chart services focused on investing in marketable securities, stocks, bonds, mutual funds, options and futures/commodities. It is organized to speed your search for useful newsletters by putting pricing, descriptions, date of first issue and author information at your fingertips. The convenience of comparing newsletters and chart services without having to sift through pounds of mail and advertisements allows you to concentrate on improving returns.

Many newsletters offer a hotline service which allows investors to call in for information that is updated even more frequently. The advantage offered by these "telephone newsletters" is that market and trading information can be dispersed in a timely manner and accessed when an investor has the time to act on information provided.

Bear in mind that the listed publications are not necessarily recommended and the accuracy and quality of advice is certainly not assured. In particular, if you are a trader, you may want to test the recommendations of a newsletter hypothetically before committing real dollars to trading systems or trade ideas.

1-900-HOT-WIRE

Dow Jones & Company, Inc.
P.O. Box 300
Princeton, NJ 08543-0300

PH: (900) HOTWIRE
Cost: $2.00 for the first minute,
 $1.00 thereafter
Started in 1990

Telephone newsletter. Rumors, recommendations, buyouts, buybacks. . . .the hottest news on companies experiencing unusual trading, from the Dow Jones Professional Investor Report.

AUDIENCE: Individual, Professional   RISK LEVEL: Aggressive
TOPICS: Stocks, Options

13D Small Cap Opportunities Report

13-D Research Services
100 Executive Drive
Southeast Executive Park
Brewster, NY 10509

PH: (914) 278-6500
FAX: (914) 278-6797
Cost: $6,500.00 annually
Frequency: Every 2 weeks
Date of first issue: 1983

Includes fundamental analysis. Covers: stocks. Screens 13D filings to discover the investment opportunities in the small cap universe. You will receive 50-55 investment ideas per year along with timely updates on previous company reports and a complete listing of all 13D filings that have occurred during the preceding 2 week period. Several other services available.

AUDIENCE: Individual   RISK LEVEL: Aggressive
TOPICS: Stocks

5 Star Investor

Morningstar
225 West Wacker Drive
Chicago, IL 60606-1228

PH: (312) 696-6000
(800) 876-5005
FAX: (312) 427-9215
Cost: $65.00/yr
Published: Monthly
Fundamental Analysis

"Teaches the fundamentals of constructing a solid mutual-fund portfolio." Explains how funds are analyzed, how portfolios are created and how the market operates. Each issue covers the following
TOPICS: Lead Articles which affect mutual fund investments, the basics of investing, portfolio building tips and ideas, spotlight on a particular fund, top-performers, the Morningstar 500 performance reports and a candid editorial on a broad range of market subjects.

AUDIENCE: Beginning, Individual   RISK LEVEL: Moderate, Aggressive
TOPICS: Mutual Funds

AAII Journal

American Association of Individual
Investors
625 N. Michigan Avenue
Chicago, IL 60611-3110

PH: (312) 280-0170
Cost: $45.00
Free to members of American
Association of Individual Investors
Frequency: 10 times a year
Date of first issue: 1978

Covers stocks, bonds, mutual funds. Provides a continuing stream of information on investment theory and practice. Includes practical explanations of investment mathematics, interviews with leading professional money managers, and columns on financial planning, stock screening, insurance products and taxes. AAII Quoteline is free to members to obtain real-time quotes on stocks, options, and mutual funds.

AUDIENCE: Individual   RISK LEVEL: Conservative, Moderate, Aggressive
TOPICS: Bonds, Mutual Funds, Stocks

Acker Letter, The

Bob Acker
2718 E. 63rd St.
Brooklyn, NY 11234

PH: (718) 531-8981
Cost: $59.00/yr

Focuses on under researched companies for the middle income investor. Recurring features include coverage of the American stock exchange, the New York stock exchange and the over-the-counter market.

AUDIENCE: Individual, Professional   RISK LEVEL: Moderate, Aggressive
TOPICS: Stocks

Addison Report, The

Addison Investment Management Company
P.O. Box 402
Franklin, MA 02038-0402

PH: (617) 528-8678
Cost: $140.00 (17 issues)
Frequency: Every 3 wks
Date of first issue: June 1980

Includes technical and fundamental analysis. Covers stocks, commodities, mutual funds, municipal, corporate, and government bonds. Stock, bond, and commodity market overview. 30-40 stock recommendations per issue. Mutual fund switch advice, conservative and speculative monitored lists and special quarterly reports focusing on technical analysis of the Dow.

AUDIENCE: Individual, Professional   RISK LEVEL: Conservative, Moderate, Aggressive
TOPICS: Bonds, Mutual Funds, Stocks, Asset Allocation

Adrian Day's Investment Analyst

Agora, Inc.
824 E. Baltimore Street
Baltimore, MD 21202

PH: (800) 433-1528
(410) 234-0515
Cost: $49.00 annually
Frequency: Monthly
Date of first issue: 1981

Covers stocks, mutual funds, bond (municipal, corporate, and government), and precious metals. Gives economic and market commentary and forecasts, along with specific recommendations, investment, and financial planning advice. Includes hotline.

AUDIENCE: Individual   RISK LEVEL: Conservative, Moderate, Aggressive
TOPICS: Bonds, Mutual Funds, Stocks

Advisor Line

Investor Link
PH: (900) 446-1111 to bill calls to your phone;
(800) 395-4400 to bill calls to a major credit card
Cost: 95 cents per minute

Provides today's investment recommendations. Quotes from Martin J. Pring, Pring's Market Review; Al Frank, The Prudent Speculator; Andy Addison, The Addison Report.

AUDIENCE: Individual, Professional   RISK LEVEL: Moderate, Aggressive
TOPICS: Stocks

AIC Investment Bulletin

AIC Investment Advisors, Inc.
440 South St.
Pittsfield, MA 01201

PH: (413) 499-1111
FAX: (413) 499-1127
Cost: $60.00/yr
Frequency: semi-monthly
Date of first issue: 1934
Individual Portfolio analysis
  available for $250.00

Includes fundamental analysis. Covers stocks, charts and graphs, bonds, precious metals. "Serves investors by covering current business conditions, gold, and silver. Also covers securities markets, interest rates, bonds, and domestic common stocks. Analyzes industries and individual securities on an approved list, and discusses general economic conditions and special factors that influence security values." Richard F. Maloney, Editor.

AUDIENCE: Individual, Professional   RISK LEVEL: Moderate, Aggressive
TOPICS: Bonds, Mutual Funds, Stocks, Options, Futures/Commodities

AIMR Newsletter, The

Association for Investment
Management and Research
P.O. Box 3668
Charlottesville, VA 22903

PH: (804) 977-6600
Cost: $25.00/yr
Frequency: 6/yr
Date of first issue: 11/64

Covers educational programs. "Offers articles about the ongoing activities and educational programs of the Association. Recurring features include news of upcoming educational opportunities for members and the investment community, examination, information, and announcements of recent publications by the Association."

AUDIENCE: Professional   RISK LEVEL: Conservative, Moderate, Aggressive
TOPICS: All

AL HANSON'S ECONOMIC NEWSLETTER

Allen D. Hanson
P.O. Box 9
Ottertail, MN 56571

PH: (218) 367-2404
COST: $40.00/yr
Date of first issue: 1981
Frequency: Monthly
Fundamental and Technical
  Analysis

Offers advice on trading stocks, bonds, and commodities. Discusses the ramifications of tax law changes, U.S. economic policy, and foreign economic news for professional traders. Recurring features include news of research and a calendar of events.

AUDIENCE: Professional   RISK LEVEL: Conservative, Moderate, Aggressive
TOPICS: Bonds, Stocks, Futures/Commodities

All- Scenario Database

Money Power
4257 46th Ave. N.,#207
P.O. Box 22586
Minneapolis, MN 55422

Cost: $24.00/yr
Frequency: Monthly
Technical and Fundamental
  Analysis

Subtitled: "Opposite-Mode Investment Strategy." Tracks and analyzes the most potentially profitable up cycle/down cycle "opposite pairs." Identifies mutual funds and single stocks and specifies switch timing.

AUDIENCE: Individual   RISK LEVEL: Moderate, Aggressive
TOPICS: Bonds, Mutual Funds, Stocks

American Abroad

AMAB
PF249
Villach, Austria A-9500

PH: 43-4254-3985
FAX: 43-4254-3985
Cost: $195.00
Frequency: 12-18 times per year

Includes fundamental analysis. Covers European stocks and mutual funds. "Investment advice for Americans working and investing abroad. European stock market review and forecast." Includes a model portfolio and recommendations.

AUDIENCE: Beginning, Individual, Professional   RISK LEVEL: Conservative, Moderate, Aggressive
TOPICS: Bonds, Mutual Funds, Stocks, Options, Futures/Commodities, Asset Allocation, Investment Planning, General Reference

American Shareholders Management Report

Terrence H. Laundry
Three Thurston's Court
Nantucket, MA 02554

PH: (508) 228-2995
Cost: $520/yr
Frequency: Monthly
Date of first issue: 1974
Fundamental Analysis

Provides management's view of stock, gold, and bond funds.

AUDIENCE: Individual, Professional   RISK LEVEL: Moderate, Aggressive
TOPICS: Mutual Funds

APM Global Report

Thomas E. Aspray
P.O. Box 2141
Spokane, WA 99210-2141

PH: (509) 838-0434
Cost: $900.00/quarter
Frequency: Three times/month

Covers commodities. Includes technical analysis. Twelve page newsletter of unique technical analysis with charts of many CompuTrac derived technical indicators for most markets. Hotline includes specific recommendations. Covers the global bond and equity markets.

AUDIENCE: Professional   RISK LEVEL: Moderate, Aggressive
TOPICS: Bonds, Stocks

Argus Viewpoint

Argus Research Corporation
17 Battery Place
New York, NY 10004

PH: (212) 425-7500
Cost: $390.00
Frequency: Monthly
Date of first issue: 1934

Includes fundamental analysis. Covers stocks. "Defines Argus' investment policy and its relationship to economic, political and market developments. The report discusses investment strategies for the stock and bond markets and also incorporates a tabular update of the stock recommendations."

AUDIENCE: Individual, Professional   RISK LEVEL: Moderate, Aggressive
TOPICS: Stocks

Armstrong Report

Princeton Economic Consultants,
Inc.
P.O. Box 7227
Princeton, NJ 08543-7227

PH: (609) 987-0600
Cost: $295.00/yr
Published monthly
Technical Analysis

Provides market and economic analysis of North America.

AUDIENCE: Individual, Professional   RISK LEVEL: Moderate, Aggressive
TOPICS: Futures/Commodities

Astro-Investor, The

Mull Publications
P.O. Box 11133
Indianapolis, IN 46201-0133

Cost: $45.00/yr.
Frequency: Monthly
Date of first issue: May 1986
Technical and Fundamental Analysis

Daily market forecasts; describes at least 6 different stocks, book reviews and general investment news.

AUDIENCE: Individual, Professional   RISK LEVEL: Moderate, Aggressive
TOPICS: Stocks

Astute Advisory, The

Astute Publishing
P.O. Box 291
Draper, UT 84020

PH: (801) 272-2113
FAX: (801) 272-2557
Cost: 95.00/yr
Fundamental Analysis
Frequency: 9 issues/yr

"Recommends stocks that are long-term holds."

AUDIENCE: Individual   RISK LEVEL: Moderate
TOPICS: Stocks

Astute Investor, The

Charles E. Cardwell, Ph.D.
135 Beechwood Lane
Kingston, TN 37763

PH: (615) 376-2732
Cost: $30.00 annually
Frequency: Monthly
Date of first issue: 1982

Covers stocks. A monthly summary of 4-6 pages, plus reference lists of addresses and phone numbers of all the companies mentioned, discussions of investing philosophies, and reviews of other writings. Proprietary value-based stock lists.

AUDIENCE: Individual, Professional   RISK LEVEL: Moderate
TOPICS: Stocks

Astute Speculator, The

Astute Publishing
P.O. Box 291
Draper, UT 84020

PH: (801) 272-2113
FAX: (801) 272-2557
Cost: $95.00/yr
Fundamental Analysis
Frequency: 9 issues/yr

"Recommends quality stocks selling for under 50 cents a share."

AUDIENCE: Individual   RISK LEVEL: Aggressive
TOPICS: Stocks

ASUI Newsletter

American Society of Utility
  Investors (ASUI)
P.O. Box 342
New Cumberland, PA 17070

PH: (717) 774-8434
Cost: $190.00/yr
Frequency: Quarterly
Date of first issue: 1980
Fundamental Analysis

Supplies stock market statistics reports relating directory to electric and gas utilities. Reviews pertinent news events, including a focused analysis on government and regulatory agency activities and legislation where it affects member interests. Washington, utility briefs, and utility statistics.

AUDIENCE: Individual, Professional   RISK LEVEL: Moderate
TOPICS: Bonds, Stocks

At the Helm

Michael Paladini
175 Federal St.
Boston, MA 02110-2267

PH: (617) 295-1000
Cost: Free to Investors of
  Scudder Funds
Frequency: Quarterly
Fundamental Analysis

Provides information on news offerings and explains new government regulations. Covers stock exchanges, bonds, currencies, estate and retirement planning, business and economics, precious metals and stones, securities, taxes and tax shelters, treasury bills, and mutual funds.

AUDIENCE: Beginning, Individual   RISK LEVEL: Conservative, Moderate, Aggressive
TOPICS: All

Bahamas Dataline

Carribbean Dateline Publications,
  Ltd.
P.O. Box 23276
Washington, D.C. 20026

Cost: $36.00/yr
Frequency: Monthly
Date of first issue: 1976
Fundamental Analysis

Provides information on investments, tourism business, and real estate in the Bahamas for foreign investors. Recurring features includes news of research, a periodic directory of properties for sale or rent, and a column titled review of the news.

AUDIENCE: Individual, Professional   RISK LEVEL: Moderate, Aggressive
TOPICS: Stocks, Investment Planning, General Reference

Bank Stock Analysis

Growth Stock Outlook Inc.
P.O. Box 15381
Chevy Chase, MD 20825

PH: (301) 654-5205
Cost: included as a supplement to
  growth stock outlook
Frequency: Semi Annually
Fundamental Analysis

Risks and rewards of investing in bank stocks. 6-year summary of earnings, four-year compound growth rate of earnings, price-earnings and price book value ratios, return on assets and equity, percentage nonperforming loans, and shares outstanding and total assets.

AUDIENCE: Individual, Professional   RISK LEVEL: Moderate, Aggressive
TOPICS: Stocks

Bartlett Letters, The

John W. Bartlett
P.O. Box 465
Audra, IL 60507

PH: (312) 896-3143
Cost: $475.00/yr
Frequency: Weekly
Fundamental Analysis
Date of first issue: November 1953

Serves as a weekly investment advisory service for investors hopeful of capital gains. Carries weekly recommendations based on a supervised list of about ten model fund stocks. Recurring feature includes statistics.

AUDIENCE: Individual   RISK LEVEL: Moderate, Aggressive
TOPICS: Mutual Funds, Stocks

Baxter

William J. Baxter/Baxter World
  Economic Service
1300 E. Putnam Avenue
Greenwich, CT 06830

PH: (203) 637-4559
Cost: $175 annually
Frequency: Monthly
Date of first issue: 1924

Fundamental analysis. Stocks and treasuries. Review of business and economic developments, continuing study of monetary conditions, domestic and abroad, specific stock recommendations, special situations, follow-up of recommendations, regular analysis of U.S. Treasury securities.

AUDIENCE: Individual   RISK LEVEL: Conservative, Moderate
TOPICS: Bonds, Stocks, Asset Allocation, General Reference

Bench Investment Letter, The

Bench Corp.
222 Bridge Plaza, S.
Ft. Lee, NJ 07024

PH: (201) 585-2333
Cost: $120.00/yr
Frequency: Monthly
Technical and Fundamental
  Analysis

Evaluates dividends plus capital gains plus options premium. Forecasts the long and short-term conditions of the economy, and makes specific recommendations. A list of favorable securities, mutual fund digest, follow up of recommendations, and total return strategies. Tables and graphs.

AUDIENCE: Individual   RISK LEVEL: Moderate, Aggressive
TOPICS: Bonds, Mutual Funds, Stocks, Options, Futures/Commodities

BI Research

Thomas C. Bishop, Editor
Bi Research, Inc.
P.O. Box 133
Redding, CT 06875

PH: (203) 270-9244
Cost: $90.00 per year
Frequency: every 6 weeks
Date of first issue: 2/81

Covers stocks, mutual funds. "Contains 5-8 in-depth investment recommendations per year, featuring common stocks judged likely to at least double over the next 1-3 years. Updates each open recommendation in detail approximately every 6 weeks."

AUDIENCE: Individual	RISK LEVEL: Moderate, Aggressive
TOPICS: Mutual Funds, Stocks	

Blue Book of CBS Stock Reports, The

Canadian Business Service (CBS)
Marpep Publishing Limited
133 Richmond Street West
Suite 700
Toronto, Ontario, Canada M5H3M8

PH: (416) 869-1177
FAX: (416) 869-0456
Cost: $245.00
Frequency: Every two weeks
Date of first issue: 1941

Includes fundamental analysis and technical analysis. Covers: Canadian stocks, charts. Statistical financial analysis on Canadian stocks. Provides buy, sell, hold recommendations as well as five year performance data and company description.

AUDIENCE: Individual, Professional	RISK LEVEL: Moderate, Aggressive
TOPICS: Stocks	

Blue Chip Barometer

Blue Chip Barometer
P.O. Box 42023
Philadelphia, PA 19101

Cost: $195.00
Frequency: Twice monthly

Technical analysis. Stocks, market timing. "Uses a highly accurate econometric model to generate statistically reliable forecast of the Dow and 26 key industry groups over the next 6 months, and which stocks in each industry group should perform best over the next 6 months."

AUDIENCE: Individual	RISK LEVEL: Moderate, Aggressive
TOPICS: Stocks	

Blue Chip Stocks

Elton Stephens
4016 S. Michigan St.
South Bend, IN 46614-3823

PH: (219) 291-3823
(800) 553-5866
FAX: (219) 291-3823
Frequency: Annual
Cost: $45.00/yr
Date of first issue: 1982
ISSN: 0869 4904

Recommends blue chip stocks that have good earnings and dividends.

AUDIENCE: Beginning, Individual	RISK LEVEL: Moderate
TOPICS: Stocks	

Bob Black's Taking Stock

Taking Stock, Inc.
1400 Temple Bldg.
Rochester, NY 14604

PH: (716) 232-4268
FAX: (716) 232-1736
Cost: $95.00/yr
Date of first issue: May 1983
Frequency: 24/yr
Technical and Fundamental
  Analysis

In-depth research report on undervalued stocks, which it defines as "stocks selling at a distress level; includes sections titled Aggressive Investment Monitor Portfolio, In Situation, Industrial Outlook Monitor, Informed Perspective, Long-Term Value Portfolio, Market Opportunities.

AUDIENCE: Individual   **RISK LEVEL: Moderate, Aggressive**
TOPICS: Stocks

Bob Brinker's Marketimer

Robert J. Brinker Investment
  Advisory Services, LTD.
P.O. Box 321580
Coco Beach, FL 37932

PH: (407) 784-5003
(800) 700-1030
Cost: $185.00 annually
Frequency: Monthly
Date of first issue: January 1986

Mutual funds, stocks, treasuries, gold, interest rates, and market timing. No-load mutual fund recommendation list, model portfolios, The Fed's monetary policy, business cycle, supply/demand and technical market condition, individual stock selections, interest rate and gold updates, asset allocation, U.S. Treasury note offering details.

AUDIENCE: Individual   **RISK LEVEL: Conservative, Moderate, Aggressive**
TOPICS: Bonds, Mutual Funds, Stocks

Bob Nurock's Advisory

Bob Nurock
Box 988-B
Paoli, PA 19301

PH: (800) 227-8888
(215) 296-2411
Cost: $247.00 annually
Frequency: Every three weeks
Date of first issue: Early 80's

Includes economic, fundamental and technical analysis. Covers stocks, mutual funds, bonds and gold comments. Includes thought provoking comments on the economy, rates, stocks, sectors/groups, funds, bonds and gold. All with specific buy/sell ideas. Technical market index.

AUDIENCE: Individual, Professional   **RISK LEVEL: Conservative, Moderate, Aggressive**
TOPICS: Bonds, Mutual Funds, Stocks

Bond Buyer

American Banker - Bond Buyer
1 State St. Plaza
New York, NY 10004

PH: (212) 943-8341
(800) 407-8241
Cost: $1,400.00
Fundamental analysis
Frequency: Daily

Covers the following markets: corporate and treasury bonds, municipal bonds, mortgage-backed securities, futures and taxable issues.

AUDIENCE: Individual, Professional   **RISK LEVEL: Conservative, Moderate, Aggressive**
TOPICS: Bonds, Futures

Bond Buyer, The

American Banker-Bond Buyer
1 State Street Plaza
New York City, NY 10004

PH: (212) 943-8200;
(800) 982-0633
Cost: $1,897.00 annually; discounts
  available
Date of first issue: 1892
Frequency: Daily
Fundamental Analysis

"Covers national municipal bond market." The Bond Buyer is news for investors, tax-exempt issuers, lawyers, and finance professionals. Contents include: daily financial news, market review, investing, state budgets, public finance, law, issuers, local economic trends, opinion and editors' comments.

AUDIENCE: Individual, Professional   RISK LEVEL: Conservative, Moderate
TOPICS: Bonds, Investment Planning

Bondweek

Institutional Investor Systems
488 Madison Avenue
New York, NY 10022

PH: (212) 303-3300
FAX: (212) 421-7038
Cost: $12.75/yr.
Frequency: Monthly
Date of first issue: 1975

Corporate, government, and foreign bonds. Bondweek covers the major taxable debt markets - treasuries and foreign sovereigns, mortgages, and investment-grade and high-yield corporates. Its chief function is to provide institutional fixed-income investors with information.

AUDIENCE: Professional   RISK LEVEL: Conservative, Moderate, Aggressive
TOPICS: Bonds

Bowser Directory of Small Stocks, The

Cindy Bowser, Editor
P.O. Box 6278
Newport News, Virginia 23606

PH: (804) 877-5979
FAX: (804) 595-0622
Cost: $89.00; $138.00 outside of
  US, Canada, & Mexico
Frequency: Monthly

"Includes 14 fields of information, on over 700 low priced stocks on the NYSE, ASE, OTC for use by the do it yourself researcher." Information is kept current and indicates whether the issue has gone up or down.

AUDIENCE: Individual, Professional   RISK LEVEL: Aggressive
TOPICS: Stocks

Bowser Report, The

R. Max Bowser
Box 6278
Newport News, VA 23606

PH: (804) 877-5979
FAX: (804) 595-0622
Cost: $39.00 annually
Frequency: Monthly
Date of first issue: November 1976
ISSN: 0738-7288

Includes fundamental analysis, covers stocks. Ten page report specializes in analyzing stocks that sell for $3 per share or less. Each month contains a "Company of the Month." The Bowser Report follows its recommendations very closely. Max Bowser, Editor.

AUDIENCE: Individual, Professional   RISK LEVEL: Aggressive
TOPICS: Stocks

Braun's System Newsletter

Braun's Systems
317 Wynt Field Dr.
Lewisville, NC 27023

PH: (919) 945-9110
FAX: (408) 243-7645
Cost: $295.00/yr
Date of first issue: 1981
Frequency: Weekly
Fundamental Analysis

Robert F. Braun, Editor. Advises investor specializing in stocks, options, bonds, futures, and precious metal. Covers stock index futures, T-bond futures, and yen, gold, soybean, and porkbellies futures. AUDIENCE: Professional and general investors.

AUDIENCE: Individual, Professional   RISK LEVEL: Conservative, Moderate, Aggressive
TOPICS: All

Broadcast Investor

Paul Kagan Associates, Inc.
126 Clock Tower Place
Carmel, CA 93923-8734

PH: (408) 624-1536
FAX: (408) 625-3225
Cost: $675.00 annually
Frequency: Monthly
Date of first issue: 1975
ISSN: 0146-0110

Includes fundamental and technical analysis, and uses charts. Covers investments in private radio, TV stations, and public broadcast companies. Newsletter on investments in private radio and TV stations plus public broadcast companies. Analysis of cash flow multiple, valuations of stations and companies. Paul Kagan, Editor.

AUDIENCE: Individual   RISK LEVEL: Moderate, Aggressive
TOPICS: Bonds, Stocks

Broadcast Investor Charts

Paul Kagan Associates, Inc.
126 Clock Tower Place
Carmel, CA 93923-8734

PH: (408) 624-1536
FAX: (408) 625-3225
Cost: $395.00 annually
Frequency: Monthly
Date of first issue: 1983
ISSN: 0736-9069

Includes technical analysis and charts. Covers stocks. A monthly chart service showing stock price movements of 48 publicly held broadcast companies for the past two years. Paul Kagan, Editor.

AUDIENCE: Individual, Professional   RISK LEVEL: Moderate, Aggressive
TOPICS: Bonds, Stocks

Browning Newsletter, The

Fraser Management Associates, Inc.
309 S. Willard Street
Burlington, VT 05402

PH: (802) 658-0322
FAX: (802) 658-0260
Cost: $225.00/yr
Date of first issue: 1976
Frequency: Monthly

"Dr. Iben Browning, a climatologist, was an early and correct forecaster in stating the proposition that the earth's climate has entered a period of sharp change....Extensive studies of physical data and phenomena make for intriguing reading. Emphasis is on climate, behavior, commodities, along with original papers and historical perspectives."

AUDIENCE: Individual, Professional   RISK LEVEL: Conservative, Moderate, Aggressive
TOPICS: All

BSMA: Bill Staton's Money Advisory

Bill Staton Enterprises, Inc.
2113 E. 5th Street
Charlotte, NC 28204

PH: (704) 335-0276
FAX: (704) 332-0427
Cost: $89.00
Frequency: 3 times a month
Date of first issue: January 20, 1986

Includes fundamental analysis. Covers stocks, mutual funds, municipal bonds, corporate bonds, and government bonds. "The smart guide for you and your money." A general financial newsletter. Investing, insurance matters and taxation and provides minimal recommendations.

AUDIENCE: Beginning, Individual   RISK LEVEL: Conservative, Moderate, Aggressive
TOPICS: All

Bullion Advisory, The

Money Power
4257 46th Avenue N., #207
P.O. Box 22586
Minneapolis, MN 55422

PH: (612) 537-8096
Cost: $36.00/yr US and Canada;
  $45.00/yr elsewhere
Published monthly
Technical and Fundamental
  Analysis

James H. Moore, editor. Advises on investments in gold, silver, and platinum, including which metal is at a bargain price, when to buy, when to exchange for other bullion to multiply ounces free, reputable dealers, safe storage, and fair prices. Illustrations: tables and charts.

AUDIENCE: Individual, Professional   RISK LEVEL: Aggressive
TOPICS: Options, Futures/Commodities

Bullish Consensus, The

Market Vane, Inc.
P.O. Box 90490
Pasadena, CA 91109-0490

PH: (818) 395-7436
(900) 990-4266 (telephone
  newsletter)
Cost: $395.00 with weekly hotline
$695.00 with daily hotline Annually
Frequency: Weekly
Date of first issue: 1964

Includes sentiment analysis. Covers commodities. The Bullish Consensus is a unique tool for trading stocks, bonds, mutual funds, indexes, foreign currencies, precious metals, options and futures based on the degree of bullish sentiment on a particular market.

AUDIENCE: Individual, Professional   RISK LEVEL: Aggressive
TOPICS: Options, Futures/Commodities

Burning Match, The

J.F. (Jim) Straw
301 Plymouth Drive N.E.
Dalton, GA 30721-9983

PH: (404) 259-6035
Cost: $48.00/yr
Frequency: Monthly

Each issue explains in detail how to use The Burning Match principle to make money. Gives inside information about the "hot" investment opportunities you should buy and those to avoid and why.

AUDIENCE: Beginning, Individual   RISK LEVEL: Moderate, Aggressive
TOPICS: Stocks

Cable TV Investor

Paul Kagan Associates, Inc.
126 Clock Tower Place
Carmel, CA 93923-8734

PH: (408) 624-1536
FAX: (408) 625-3225
Cost: $795.00/yr
Frequency: Monthly
Date of first issue: 1969

"The most comprehensive source of information on investments in cable TV systems and public cable stocks. Exclusive databases. Develops research methods values systems and companies."

AUDIENCE: Beginning, Individual, Professional   RISK LEVEL: Moderate, Aggressive
TOPICS: Stocks

Cable TV Investor Charts

Paul Kagan Associates, Inc.
126 Clock Tower Place
Carmel, CA 93923-8734

PH: (408) 624-1536
FAX: (408) 625-3225
Cost: $395.00/yr
Frequency: Monthly

"Your road map to cable stock trends. Chart services tracking stock price movements of 37 publicly-held cable TV companies. Each graph shows two years of stock price activity."

AUDIENCE: Beginning, Individual, Professional   RISK LEVEL: Moderate, Aggressive
TOPICS: Stocks

Cabot Market Letter, The

Cabot Heritage Corp., Publisher
P.O. Box 3067
Salem, MA 01970

PH: (508) 745-5532
FAX: (508) 745-1283
Cost: $270.00
Frequency: Bimonthly
Date of first issue: 1970

Carlton G. Lutts and Timothy W. Lutts, editors. The Cabot Market Letter combines technical and fundamental analysis of common stocks. It covers buying and selling stocks and uses long-term market timing. The Letter recommends and follows growth stocks.

AUDIENCE: Individual, Professional   RISK LEVEL: Aggressive
TOPICS: Stocks, Asset Allocation

Cabot's Mutual Fund Navigator

Cabot Heritage Corp.
P.O. Box 3067
Salem, MA 01970

PH: (508) 745-5532
FAX: (508) 745-1283
Cost: $96.00/yr individual
Frequency: Monthly
Date of first issue: 1988

Timothy W. Lutts, Editor. Cabot's Mutual Fund Navigator is your guide to investing profitably and safety in the best low and no-load mutual funds. For bigger profits and greater safety, the Navigator also uses long-term market timing. Funds in our three portfolios, one for income, one for growth and income, and one for aggressive growth.

AUDIENCE: Beginning, Individual   RISK LEVEL: Moderate, Aggressive
TOPICS: Mutual Funds

California Municipal Bond Advisor

California Municipal Bond Advisor
1750 E. Arenas Rd.
Suite 25
Palm Springs, CA 92262

PH: (619) 320-7997
FAX: (619) 323-4912
Cost: $125.00/yr
Date of first issue: 1984
Frequency: Monthly
Technical and Fundamental Analysis

Provides analysis on California bonds and bond funds. Includes graphics and charts.

AUDIENCE: Individual, Professional   **RISK LEVEL: Conservative, Moderate**
TOPICS: Bonds

California Public Finance

American Banker - Bond Buyer
1 State St. Plaza
New York, NY 10004

PH: (212) 943-8351
(800) 407-8241
Cost: $545.00
Date of first issue: January 1991
Frequency: Weekly
Fundamental Analysis
Available on-line

Covers developments affecting municipal bonds and public finance in California.

AUDIENCE: Individual, Professional   **RISK LEVEL: Conservative, Moderate**
TOPICS: Bonds

California Technology Stock Letter

Michael Murphy
P.O. Box 308
Half Moon Bay, CA 94019

PH: (415) 726-8495
FAX: (415) 726-8494
Cost: $295.00 annually
Frequency: Biweekly
Date of first issue: 1982

Includes fundamental analysis. Covers stocks. Concentrates on the computer, electronics, and biotechnology industries. Each letter contains specific stock recommendations. Subscriptions include a hotline service.

AUDIENCE: Beginning, Individual, Professional   **RISK LEVEL: Aggressive**
TOPICS: Stocks

Called Bond Record

Standard & Poor's Corporation
25 Broadway
New York, NY 10004

PH: (212) 208-8000
(212) 208-1199
FAX: (212) 514-7016
Frequency: Semi-weekly
Cost: $1,500.00/yr.
Editor: Vito Calbi

Provides information on calls, defaults and payments.

AUDIENCE: Individual, Professional   **RISK LEVEL: Conservative, Moderate**

Cambridge Financial Manager

Cambridge Commodities Corp.
55 Cambridge River Front
No. 2
Cambridge, MA 02142

PH: (617) 621-8500
Cost: $349.00/yr
Frequency: Monthly
Technical and Fundamental
  Analysis
Date of first issue: Fall 1977

Dr. James T. Kneafsey, Editor. Provides in-depth analysis of futures markets, with special emphasis on foreign currencies and stock indices. Offers advice on investing in stocks, bonds, and mutual funds. Illustrations: Includes charts. Subscription includes a telephone hotline.

AUDIENCE: Individual   RISK LEVEL: Conservative, Moderate, Aggressive
TOPICS: Bonds, Mutual Funds, Stocks

Canadian High-Growth Investment Letter

Graeme Kirkland
12 Sheppard St.
Suite 422
Toronto, ON, Canada M5H 3A1

PH: (416) 364-4949
FAX: (416) 890-7784
Cost: $245.00/yr
Date of first issue: 1982
Frequency: Monthly
Fundamental Analysis

Graeme Kirkland, Editor. Offers investment advice on the Toronto Stock Exchange, listed technology, and other high growth companies.

AUDIENCE: Individual, Professional   RISK LEVEL: Moderate, Aggressive
TOPICS: Stocks

Canadian Market Confidential

Phoenix Communications Group,
  Ltd.
P.O. Box 670
Colorado Springs, CO 80901-0670

PH: (719) 576-9200
Cost: $79.00/yr
Frequency: Monthly
Technical and Fundamental
  Analysis
Date of first issue: 1980

J.C. Katz, Editor.

AUDIENCE: Individual   RISK LEVEL: Moderate, Aggressive
TOPICS: Stocks

Canadian Resources and Pennymines Analyst

MPL Publishing
133 Richmond St., W.
Suite 700
Toronto, ON, Canada M5H 3M8

PH: (416) 869-1177
Cost: $157.00/yr
Published monthly
Technical Analysis

Glenn Tetu, Editor. Covers Canadian penny stocks. Offers model portfolio and recommendations.

AUDIENCE: Individual   RISK LEVEL: Aggressive
TOPICS: Stocks

Capital Growth Letter

Bollinger Capital Management
P.O. Box 3358
Manhattan Beach, CA 90266

PH: (310) 798-8855
Frequency: Monthly
Date of first issue: January 1987
Cost: $225.00/yr
Technical Analysis

"Technical analysis, commentary and charts on stocks, precious metals, international markets, bonds and energy. Twice-a-week hotline. Daily Bollinger Bond updates for the stock and bond markets."

AUDIENCE: Individual, Professional   RISK LEVEL: Conservative, Moderate, Aggressive
TOPICS: Bonds, Stocks

Caribbean Dateline

Caribbean
P.O. Box 23276
Washington, D.C. 20026

Cost: $95.00/yr U.S. and Canada
$101.00/yr elsewhere
Frequency: Monthly
Fundamental Analysis
Date of first issue: May 1980

N. Poteat Day, Editor. Subtitled: Events, Trends, Opportunities for investors in the Caribbean and Central America. Highlights investment opportunities, business, tourism, real estate, and IRS rulings relevant to foreign investors in that area.

AUDIENCE: Individual   RISK LEVEL: Moderate, Aggressive
TOPICS: Bonds, Stocks, Investment Planning, General Reference

Carol Mull's Market Forcaster

Mull Publications
P.O. Box 11133
Indianapolis, IN 46201-0133

PH: (317) 357-6855
Cost: $45.00/yr
Published monthly
Date of first issue: May 1986
Technical and Fundamental
  Analysis

Employs Gann techniques, Fibonacci ratios, Elliott Wave theory, planetary angles, economic cycles and the author's own research to forecast market trends. Covers individual stocks and industries as well as the market as a whole.

AUDIENCE: Individual, Professional   RISK LEVEL: Aggressive
TOPICS: Stocks

Cash Rich Companies

Charles E. Cardwell, Ph.D.,
  Editor/Publisher
135 Beechwood Lane
Kingston, TN 37763

PH: (615) 376-2732
Cost: $24.00 annually
Frequency: Monthly
Date of first issue: 1991

Provides investors with significant financial facts on the 40 widely traded stocks which have the highest ratio of NetNetQuickAssets (i.e., quick assets less all liabilities) to market price. Often, such stocks present significantly above-average potential for price appreciation.

AUDIENCE: Beginning, Individual, Professional   RISK LEVEL: Moderate, Aggressive
TOPICS: Stocks

Charles Cummings K.I.$.$.

Chas. C. Cummings, Jr.
R. R. 6
Guelph, Ontario Canada N1H6J3

Cost: $144.00
Frequency: Timely 13+ issues
Date of first issue: 1988

Private investor Charles Cummings's market analysis reflects 44 years investment experience. Additionally, his US $100,000 North American portfolio model trades some of the very stocks managed for his own family's needs. Guest guru comments, too.

AUDIENCE: Beginning, Individual RISK LEVEL: Moderate, Aggressive
TOPICS: Bonds, Stocks, Asset Allocation, Investment Planning, General Reference

Chartcraft Commodity Service

Chartcraft, Inc.
30 Church Street
P.O. Box 2046
New Rochelle, NY 10801

PH: (914) 632-0422
Cost: $224.00/yr
Published weekly
Technical and Fundamental Analysis

Commodity price charts covering 50 domestic commodity markets.

AUDIENCE: Individual, Professional RISK LEVEL: Aggressive
TOPICS: Futures/Commodities

Chartcraft Hot Line

Chartcraft, Inc.
30 Church Street
P.O. Box 2046
New Rochelle, NY 10801

PH: (900) 990-0909 ext 31
(914) 632-0422
Cost: per minute $2.00
24 Hour service
Frequency of update: Daily

Covers stocks. Technical figures are Wednesdays at 11AM, other days there is a "Chart of the Day" featured at 11AM except Mondays which is at 9AM.

AUDIENCE: Beginning, Individual RISK LEVEL: Moderate, Aggressive
TOPICS: Mutual Funds, Stocks, Options

Chartcraft, Inc.

Chartcraft, Inc.
30 Church Street
P.O. Box 2046
New Rochelle, NY 10801

PH: (914) 632-0422
FAX: (914) 632-0335
Cost: $360.00 annually
Frequency: Monthly
Date of first issue: 1983

Chart service. Includes technical analysis. Covers stocks. 50 technical indicator charts, 88 industry charts, 20 x 60, 10 x 30, 5 x 15, DJIA Technical Chart, 200 NYSE/ASE stocks with top/bottom Relative Momentum, Option Indexes, world markets, Technical Indicator Review, Introduction to Charting. Includes toll-free hotline.

AUDIENCE: Individual, Professional RISK LEVEL: Moderate, Aggressive
TOPICS: Stocks, Mutual Funds, Asset Allocation, Investment Planning, General Reference

Chartcraft Long Term Individual Charts

Chartcraft, Inc.
30 Church St.
New Rochelle, NY 10801

PH: (914) 632-0422
FAX: (914) 632-0335
Cost: $3.50 per single chart, with
quantity discounts available, faxing
at a slight additional fee.

"Available for all common stocks on the NYSE, ASE and
NASDAQ OTC system, charts are 8 1/2 x 11, 3-hole punched and
loaded with history. Also available for Mutual Funds, Commodity
Futures, Indexes @ Indicators, etc."

AUDIENCE: Beginning, Individual, Professional   RISK LEVEL: Moderate, Aggressive
TOPICS: Stocks

Chartcraft Monthly P & F Chartbook on NYSE/ASE

Chartcraft, Inc.
30 Church St.
New Rochelle, NY 10801

PH: (914) 632-0422
FAX: (914) 632-0335
Frequency: Monthly
Cost: $402.00/yr (13 issues)
1 issue $41.00

"A big 400+ page volume with P & F charts on all NYSE and ASE
common stocks and over 480 OTC issues. Through the last
Tuesday of each month and mailed FIRST CLASS on Thursday.
The latest price history lets you visualize the trends of each stock -
its direction, buy/sell signals, supports and resistance area,
trendlines penetrated, etc."

AUDIENCE: Beginning, Individual, Professional   RISK LEVEL: Moderate, Aggressive
TOPICS: Stocks

Chartcraft O-T-C Point and Figure Chart Book

Chartcraft, Inc.
30 Church Street
P.O. Box 2046
New Rochelle, NY 10801

PH: (914) 632-0422
FAX: (914) 632-0335
Cost: $100.00 annually
Frequency: Quarterly

Chart service. Includes technical analysis. Covers stocks. More
than 1,350 OTC stocks, NASDAQ composite chart and
introduction to P&F charting. Each large grid chart is 2" x 3" with
9 charts to the page.

AUDIENCE: Beginning, Individual, Professional   RISK LEVEL: Moderate, Aggressive
TOPICS: Stocks

Chartcraft Quarterly Mutual Funds P & F Chartbook

Chartcraft, Inc.
30 Church St.
New Rochelle, NY 10801

PH: (914) 632-0422
FAX: (914) 632-0335
Frequency: Quarterly
Cost: $104.00/yr (4 issues)
Current issue: $30.00

"This 100 plus page book has charts of all the Mutual Funds in the
Weekly Mutual Funds Breakout service. Most charts cover 2-4
years and show buy/sell signals and stoploss points. They are
adjusted for capital gains distributions. Charts are arranged by
investment objective."

AUDIENCE: Beginning, Individual   RISK LEVEL: Moderate, Aggressive
TOPICS: Mutual Funds

Chartcraft Quarterly Options P & F Chartbook

Chartcraft, Inc.
30 Church St.
New Rochelle, NY 10801

PH: (914) 632-0422
FAX: (914) 632-0335
Frequency: Quarterly
Cost: $160.00/yr (12 sections)
Single issue of 3 sections: $46.00

"This 620+ page book has long-term charts on all underlying stocks. Designed for use with the Weekly Options Service or to Update from any newspaper, this book illustrates long-term trends, showing support and resistance. Two charts fill an 8 1/2 x 11 page."

AUDIENCE: Individual, Professional   RISK LEVEL: Aggressive
TOPICS: Options

Chartcraft Quarterly Options Relative Strength Chartbook

Chartcraft Inc.
30 Church St.
New Rochelle, NY 10801

PH: (914) 632-0422
FAX: (914) 632-0335
Frequency: Quarterly
Cost: $104.00/yr (4 issues)
Current issue - $30.00

"This volume has Relative Strength charts of all underlying stocks. These P & F charts compare each stock to the DJIA. RS help identify MAJOR trends in individual stocks which usually last many years. They help eliminate "whipsaws" and pick out market leaders. The book is designed for easy updating from the Weekly Options Service or Weekly NYSE/ASE Service."

AUDIENCE: Beginning, Individual, Professional   RISK LEVEL: Conservative,
                                                             Moderate, Aggressive
TOPICS: All

Chartcraft Technical Indicator Review

Chartcraft, Inc.
30 Church Street
P.O. Box 2046
New Rochelle, NY 10801

PH: (914) 834-5181
(914) 632-0335
Cost: $72.00 per year
Frequency: Biweekly
Date of first issue: 1961

Chart service for stocks. "Provides a concise review of the stock market. Each stock in the Dow Jones Industrial Averages is listed and marked bullish or bearish. Industry group trends, relative strength, and bullish percentage." Includes fundamental analysis. Covers stocks, charts and graphs.

AUDIENCE: Individual, Professional   RISK LEVEL: Moderate, Aggressive
TOPICS: Stocks

Chartcraft Weekly Breakout Service

Chartcraft, Inc.
30 Church St.
New Rochelle, NY 10801

PH: (914) 632-0422
FAX: (914) 632-0335
Frequency: Weekly
Technical Analysis
Cost: $168.00/yr

Contains P&F charts of all NYSE stocks with new breakouts. Each chart includes 30 week moving averages, P/E and yield, Bullish/Bearish price objectives, and a current relative strength signal. Also available for ASE and OTC stocks combined for $168 per year.

AUDIENCE: Individual, Professional   RISK LEVEL: Moderate, Aggressive
TOPICS: Stocks

Chartcraft Weekly Futures Service

Chartcraft, Inc.
30 Church St.
New Rochelle, NY 10801

PH: (914) 632-0422
FAX: (914) 632-0335
Frequency: Weekly
Technical Analysis
Cost: $256.00/yr

Point and figure charts on all domestic futures listed in The Wall Street Journal. Includes a twice weekly hotline.

AUDIENCE: Individual, Professional   RISK LEVEL: Aggressive
TOPICS: Futures

Chartcraft Weekly Mutual Funds Breakout Service

Chartcraft, Inc.
30 Church St.
New Rochelle, NY 10801

PH: (914) 632-0422
FAX: (914) 632-0335
Frequency: Weekly
Cost: $154.00/yr

"Covers 450 funds giving point and figure price changes, last buy or sell, signal and stoploss point. Charts of BREAKOUTS are included. Funds are listed by investment objective for easy use."

AUDIENCE: Beginning, Individual   RISK LEVEL: Moderate, Aggressive
TOPICS: Mutual Funds

Chartcraft Weekly Options Service

Chartcraft, Inc.
30 Church St.
New Rochelle, NY 10801

PH: (914) 632-0422
FAX: (914) 632-0335
Frequency: Weekly
Date of first issue: 1974
Cost: $168.00/yr
Technical Analysis

"Point and figure change and relative strength data is given for all underlying stocks as is 10 week and 30 week. Moving averages. DJIA charts & technical indicators are included."

AUDIENCE: Individual, Professional   RISK LEVEL: Aggressive
TOPICS: Options

Chartcraft Weekly Service

Chartcraft, Inc.
30 Church Street
New Rochelle, NY 10801

PH: (914) 632-0422
(914) 632-0335
Cost: $224.00/yr
Frequency: Weekly
Date of first issue: February 1949

Includes technical analysis. Covers stocks, charts and graphs. "Offers recommendations to investors in New York, American Stock Exchange and O.T.C. securities, including buy and sell signals and relative strength. Discusses industry groups and options indexes. Lists more than 1,400 stocks, and includes point and figure data for each stock covered."

AUDIENCE: Beginning, Individual, Professional   RISK LEVEL: Moderate, Aggressive
TOPICS: Mutual Funds, Stocks, Options, Futures/Commodities

Chartist Mutual Fund Timer, The

Dan Sullivan
P.O. Box 758
Seal Beach, CA 90740

PH: (213) 596-2385
(213) 493-5906
Cost: $100.00 annually
Frequency: Monthly
Date of first issue: 1988

Includes technical analysis. Covers mutual funds and market timing. Publishes an "Actual Cash Account" which mirrors Dan Sullivan's own fund portfolio. Question and Answer section for subscribers. Includes Hotline with daily updates of "actual cash account" recommendations.

AUDIENCE: Beginning, Individual   RISK LEVEL: Aggressive
TOPICS: Mutual Funds, Asset Allocation

Chartist, The

The Chartist
P.O. Box 758
Seal Beach, CA 90740

PH: (213) 596-2385
Cost: $150.00/yr
Frequency: Twice a month
Date of first issue: 1969

Includes technical analysis. Covers stocks. Stock advisory service, publishes an actual "Trader's Portfolio with current results and mental stop recommendations for more speculative traders and an 'Actual Cash Account' which mirrors his own personal portfolio. Provides general financial information, including the ratings of over 2,000 stocks."

AUDIENCE: Beginning, Individual, Professional   RISK LEVEL: Aggressive
TOPICS: Stocks, Asset Allocation

Cheap Investor, The

Mathews & Associates, Inc.
2549 W. Golf Road
Suite 350
Hoffman Estates, IL 60194

PH: (708) 830-1345
FAX: (708) 830-5797
Cost: $98.00/yr
Frequency: Monthly
Date of first issue:1981

Bill Mathews, editor. Includes fundamental analysis. Covers stocks. Each issue includes 3 or 4 buy recommendations on quality, low-priced stocks along with updates on recommendations. The Cheap Investor searches for and finds small, quality stocks under $5 on the OTC, ASE, and NYSE and new issues with growth potential for a 50-100 % stock price move.

AUDIENCE: Beginning, Individual   RISK LEVEL: Moderate, Aggressive
TOPICS: Stocks

CIS Cattle Hotline

Commodity Information Systems,
  Inc.
210 Park Avenue
Suite 2970
Oklahoma City, OK 73102

PH: (800) 231-0477 (Credit card
  orders only)
Cost: $600.00/yr
Frequency of update: daily

Telephone newsletter. Covers cattle. Designed specifically for the professional cattle trader that keeps you up-to-date with statistics, and all other major aspects of the cattle market. Direct trade volume and prices, packer break-even levels, what the feedlot sources expect, closing beef prices, closing cutout values and boxed beef volume, special analysis.

AUDIENCE: Individual, Professional   RISK LEVEL: Aggressive
TOPICS: Futures/Commodities

Clean Yield, The

Clean Yield Publications Ltd.
P.O. Box 1880
Greensboro Bend, VT 05842

PH: (802) 533-7178
Cost: $95.00 annually
Frequency: Monthly
Date of first issue: March 1985

Includes fundamental and technical analysis. Covers stocks and market timing. Specializes in socially responsible companies providing unhedged advice and recommendations on when and at what price to buy and sell their stocks. Rian Fried & Doug Fleer, Editors. ISSN: 0882-3820

AUDIENCE: Beginning, Individual, Professional   RISK LEVEL: Moderate
TOPICS: Stocks, Asset Allocation

College of Common Sense Bulletin

Steve Garrett & Associates
P.O. Box 66115
Arcadia, CA 91066

PH: (818) 355-7666
FAX: (818) 355-8260
Cost: $48.00/yr
Fundamental Analysis
Frequency: Monthly

Provides economic commentary and forecasts along with specific stock and bond recommendations. Also provides general investment and financial planning information.

AUDIENCE: Individual   RISK LEVEL: Conservative, Moderate, Aggressive
TOPICS: Bonds, Stocks, Investment Planning

Commodex Daily Signals

Equidex, Inc.
7000 Blvd. East
Guttenberg, NJ 07093-4808

PH: (900) 234-7777
Cost: per minute $2.00
24 Hour service
Frequency of update: Twice daily

Covers commodities. Follow the commodity on financial futures contracts you need - up to 45 different futures with as many as 100 contract months. Your complete daily self management system.

AUDIENCE: Individual, Professional   RISK LEVEL: Aggressive
TOPICS: Futures/Commodities

Commodex Signals

Eqidex, Inc.
7000 Blvd. East
Guttenberg, NJ 07093-4808

PH: (800) 336-1818
(201) 868-2600
Cost: $1,695.00 Annually
Frequency: Twice daily

Fax service. Covers commodities. Each bulletin includes more than 45 commodity and financial futures with up to 100 contract months. The easy to use signal codes tell you exactly what to trade. Special "Turbo-Fax" sends latest bulletin in less than two minutes.

AUDIENCE: Individual, Professional   RISK LEVEL: Aggressive
TOPICS: Futures/Commodities

Commodities Law Letter

Commodities Law Press Associates
900 3rd Ave.
New York, NY 10022

PH: (212) 935-0638
Cost: $245.00/yr U.S. and Canadian
$255.00 elsewhere
Date of first issue: March 1981
Frequency: Monthly
Technical and Fundamental
　Analysis
ISSN: 8 0277-2930

Editor: Richard A. Miller. Subtitled "Financial Futures and Options on Futures." Description: Monitors legal and regulatory developments affecting commodities and securities industries, including information on litigation, legislation, taxation, pensions, and banking. Analyzes the impact of specific cases and decisions. Recurring features include book reviews.

AUDIENCE: Professional	RISK LEVEL: Aggressive
TOPICS: Futures/Commodities	

Commodities Litigation Reporter

Andrews Publications, Inc.
P.O. Box 1000
Westtown, PA 19395

PH: (215) 394-6600
Cost: $980.00/yr
(800) 345-1101
FAX: (215) 399-6610
Date of first issue: July 1985
Frequency: Semi monthly, indexed
　Semi annually
Technical and Fundamental
　Analysis
ISSN: 8 0887-784X

Editor: Barbara Pizzirani. Reports on the rights and responsibilities of customers and futures commission merchants under Commodity Exchange Act and Commission rules. Monitors commodities market related litigation at the pretrail, trial, and appellate levels and reprints texts of key decisions and pleadings.

AUDIENCE: Professional	RISK LEVEL: Aggressive
TOPICS: Futures/Commodities	

Commodity Common Sense

Commodity Sense, Inc.
1009 Camden
Coffeyville, KS 67337

PH: (316) 251-4422
Cost: $4,285.00/yr U.S. and Canada
Frequency: Weekly
Technical Analysis

Editor: Steven R. Myers. Provides technical analysis of commodity futures for commodity future traders.

AUDIENCE: Individual, Professional	RISK LEVEL: Aggressive
TOPICS: Options, Futures/Commodities	

Commodity Futures Forecast

Equidex, Inc. - Philip Gotthelf
7000 Blvd. East
Guttenberg, NJ 07093-4808

PH: (800) 336-1818
(201) 868-2600
Cost: $350.00 annually
Frequency: Weekly
Date of first issue: 1956

Includes fundamental and technical analysis used for timing. Provides complete trading details for carefully selected commodity, financial, and energy futures. Incorporates latest charts, weather-fax, government reports and confidential information Recommendations are clear, concise, and easy to use. Periodic special reports.

AUDIENCE: Individual, Professional	RISK LEVEL: Aggressive
TOPICS: Futures/Commodities	

Commodity Information Systems

Bill Gary, Commodity Information
 Systems, Inc.
P.O. Box 690652
Houston, TX 77269-9974

PH: (800) 231-0477
(713) 890-2700
FAX: (713) 890-4938
Cost: $360.00 annually
Frequency: Bimonthly

Includes fundamental analysis. Covers commodities. Fundamental analysis of all major commodity and financial markets. Also includes special reports on outstanding developing trades, situation analysis of major economic changes, specific long-term trading strategies, graphics and commentary that make fundamental factors easy to understand.

AUDIENCE: Individual, Professional   RISK LEVEL: Aggressive
TOPICS: Options, Futures/Commodities

Commodity Price Charts

Oster Communications
219 Parkade
Cedar Falls, IA 50613

PH: 800-221-4352 ext 750
FAX: (319) 277-7896
Cost: $450.00/yr
Frequency: Weekly
Date of first issue: 1975

Chart service for technical analysis. Covers commodities. In addition to weekly charts, 6 times a year receive long term historical charts, 10 & 20 year charts. 49 commodities covered, 255 charts in each issue. Large charts - 14 1/2 x 22 3/4 give you up to fifteen months of price history on each major commodity. Shipped Friday.

AUDIENCE: Individual, Professional   RISK LEVEL: Aggressive
TOPICS: Futures/Commodities

Commodity Timing

Larry Williams
140 Marine View Drive #102T
Solana Beach, CA 92075

PH: (800) 800-8333
Cost: $200.00 annually
Frequency: Annually
Date of first issue: 1969

Timing recommendations.

AUDIENCE: Individual, Professional   RISK LEVEL: Aggressive
TOPICS: Futures/Commodities

Complete Strategist, The

Howard Young
Wall Street On-Line Publishing
P.O. Box 6
Riverdale, NY 10471

PH: (212) 884-5408
Cost: $50.00/yr
Frequency: Monthly
Date of first issue: 1991

Includes fundamental and technical analysis. Covers stocks, futures and commodities, mutual funds, options, interest rates, precious metals, municipal bonds, corporate bonds, government bonds. "Monthly advisory newsletter. Predicts market direction. Illustrates and explains indicators. Includes Model Portfolio, with buy/sell range for stocks."

AUDIENCE: Individual, Professional   RISK LEVEL: Moderate, Aggressive
TOPICS: Mutual Funds, Stocks, Options, Futures/Commodities

Computerized Investing

American Association of Individual Investors
625 N. Michigan Avenue
Chicago, IL 60611-3110

PH: (312) 280-0170
Cost: $60.00 annually
$30.00 for members of American
   Association of Individual Investors
Frequency: 6 times a year
Date of first issue: 1978

Covers computerized investing. Keeps investors abreast of the latest investment related computer developments. Includes comprehensive investment software reviews, news of developments in software and database services, as well as how-to-do-it articles on using computers to assist in investment analysis and valuation.

AUDIENCE: Beginning, Individual, Professional	RISK LEVEL: Conservative,
TOPICS: All	Moderate, Aggressive

Concordia Letter, The

The Concordia Letter
656 Harbor Rd.
Southport, CT 06490

PH: (203) 227-0856
Cost: $140.00/yr
Frequency: Biweekly
Date of first issue:1982
Technical and Fundamental
   Analysis

Editor: Jack P. Phelan. Contains recommendations on specific companies for investors seeking "maximum capital gains potential." Service also includes a confidential telephone hotline with the latest in stock market information and advice. Current reviews of recommended stocks, analysis of the current market situation, and charts.

AUDIENCE: Beginning, Individual	RISK LEVEL: Moderate, Aggressive
TOPICS: Stocks	

Consensus of Insiders

Consensus of Insiders, Inc.
P.O. Box 24349
Ft. Lauderdale, FL 33307-4349

PH: (305) 772-7186
FAX: (305) 783-0097
Cost: $72.00/yr
Date of first issue: 1962
Frequency: Quarterly
Technical and Fundamental
   Analysis

Editor: Barry Unterbrink. Acts as a stock market advisory, based upon analysis of transactions by members of the stock exchanges, specialists, and trades. Provides advice on market timing and put-to-call ratios. Evaluates the effect of mutual, pension, and foreign funds and the activities of institutions and funds on the stock market.

AUDIENCE: Individual, Professional	RISK LEVEL: Moderate, Aggressive
TOPICS: Stocks	

Conservative Speculator

Guidera Publishing Corporate
3 Myrtle Bank Road
Hilton Head, SC 29926

PH: (803) 681-3399
Cost: $198.00/yr
Published monthly
Date of first issue: February 1988
Technical and Fundamental
   Analysis

Larry C. Oakley, editor. Covers small cap companies. Provides three to five in-depth reviews each month as well as updates on previous recommendations, and a model portfolio.

AUDIENCE: Beginning, Individual, Professional	RISK LEVEL: Aggressive
TOPICS: Stocks	

Contrary Investor Follow-up, The

Fraser Management Associates, Inc.
309 S. Willard St.
P.O. Box 494
Burlington, VT 05402

PH: (802) 658-0322
Cost: $65.00/yr.
Frequency: Biweekly
Date of first issue: 1963

Contains analysis and regular reports on all stock selections found in The Contrary Investor until each has closed at a definite selling price. James L. Fraser, Editor.

AUDIENCE: Individual   RISK LEVEL: Moderate, Aggressive
TOPICS: Bonds, Stocks, Asset Allocation, Investment Planning, General Reference

Contrary Investor, The

Fraser Management Associates, Inc.
P.O. Box 494
309 S. Willard St.
Burlington, VT 05402

PH: (802) 658-0322
Cost: $95.00 annually
Frequency: 26 issues annually

Includes fundamental analysis. Covers stocks. "Ponders the stock market passing on brain work in the field of investment and speculation. Lists specific securities with contrary speculative possibilities most likely to succeed." Concentrates on value versus fashion, discovering unusual situations with superior profit potential.

AUDIENCE: Individual   RISK LEVEL: Moderate, Aggressive
TOPICS: Bonds, Stocks, Asset Allocation, Investment Planning, General Reference

Corporate Financing Week

Institutional Investor Systems
488 Madison Avenue
New York, NY 10022

PH: (212) 303-3300
Cost: $1,150.00 annually
Frequency: Weekly
Date of first issue: 1975

Includes fundamental analysis. Covers stocks and bonds. The mission of CFW is to inform all finance officials at corporations on innovations, trends, and ways to save money on new debt and equity issues, private placements, mergers, and acquisitions, leveraged buyouts, venture capital, and tax and accounting issues.

AUDIENCE: Professional   RISK LEVEL: Moderate, Aggressive
TOPICS: Bonds, Stocks

Corporate Governance Bulletin

Investor Responsibility Research
  Center, Inc.
1755 Massachusetts Ave., N.W.
Suite 600
Washington, DC 20036

PH: (202) 332-8570
Cost: included in membership
$225.00/yr. for non-members
Frequency: 6 issues per year

Monitors policy developments in Congress, federal regulatory agencies, the courts, and other government bodies affecting institutional and corporate investing. Highlights significant actions by companies and major institutional investors. Mary W. Cohn, Editor.

AUDIENCE: Professional   RISK LEVEL: Conservative, Moderate, Aggressive
TOPICS: All

Corporate Growth Report Weekly, The

Quality Services Company
5290 Overpass Road
Santa Barbara, CA 93111

PH: (805) 964-7841
FAX: (805) 964-1073
Cost: $795.00/yr
Frequency: Weekly
Date of first issue: 7/80

Reports and forecasts merger, acquisition, and divestiture activity, including in-depth analysis of major transactions. Publishes statistics on seller's and buyer's sales, profits, net worth, book value and earnings per share, and multiples of earnings, sales, and net worth compared with purchase price.

AUDIENCE: Professional   RISK LEVEL: Moderate, Aggressive
TOPICS: Bonds, Stocks

Corporate Transfer Agents Association-Output

Corporate Transfer Agents
Association, Inc.
c/o Santa Fe Southern Pacific Corp.
120 Broadway
Suite 2905
New York, NY 10005

PH: (212) 902-3111
Cost: included in membership
Date of first issue: 1971
Frequency: Monthly
Fundamental Analysis

Editor: D. Klippel. Reports on topics related to securities affecting corporations, transfer agents, and proxy activities. Covers procedures and happenings in the field, from Securities and Exchange Commission regulation to changes in the uniform code.

AUDIENCE: Professional   RISK LEVEL: Conservative, Moderate, Aggressive
TOPICS: All

Cotton Trade Report

New York Cotton Exchange
Four World Trade Center
New York, NY 10048

PH: (212) 938-7909
FAX: (212) 839-8061
Cost: $80.00/yr
Date of first issue: 1924
Frequency: Weekly
Technical and Fundamental
   Analysis

Editor: Tom Bertolini. Contains analysis of conditions, trends, and prospects in the cotton trade; domestic cotton crop progress during the growing season; U.S. Government activities in the cotton trade; and economic conditions affecting the cotton trade and market. Charts showing daily and weekly fluctuation of spot and futures cotton prices.

AUDIENCE: Individual, Professional   RISK LEVEL: Aggressive
TOPICS: Options, Futures/Commodities

Crawford Perspectives

Arch Crawford
205 E. 78th Street
New York, NY 10021

PH: (212) 628-1156
Cost: $250.00 annually
Frequency: Monthly
Date of first issue: 1977

Includes technical analysis. Covers market timing. General stock market timing with astronomical cycles and technical analysis. Also includes short summary on gold and bond markets.

AUDIENCE: Individual, Professional   RISK LEVEL: Moderate, Aggressive
TOPICS: Bonds, Stocks, Options, Futures/Commodities

CRB Commodity Index Report

Commodity Research Bureau (CRB)
Knight-Ridder Business
Information Services
75 Wall St., 22nd Flr.
New York, NY 10005

PH: (212) 504-7754
FAX: (212) 809-5442
Frequency: Weekly
Cost: $175.00/yr
Date of first issue: July 29, 1981
Technical and Fundamental
  Analysis

A comprehensive weekly report on commodity indices and cash prices." Carries the CRB Futures Price Index and the CRB Spot Market Index. Provides statistics for the last five business days and for the previous week, month, and year. Tables and graphs.

AUDIENCE: Individual, Professional   RISK LEVEL: Aggressive
TOPICS: Options, Futures/Commodities

CRB Futures Market Service

Commodity Research Bureau (CRB)
Knight-Ridder Business Information
  Service
75 Wall St., 23rd Floor
New York, NY 10005

PH: (212) 504-7754
(800) 621-5271
Frequency: Weekly
Cost: $150.00/yr
Date of first issue: 1934

Discusses developments that will affect the future status of supply, demand, and price movements for the different commodities traded on the futures markets.

AUDIENCE: Individual, Professional   RISK LEVEL: Aggressive
TOPICS: Futures/Commodities

Crisis Investing

Agora, Inc.
824 E. Baltimore St.
Baltimore, MD 21202-4799

PH: (800) 433-1528
FAX: (410) 837-3879
Frequency: Monthly
Cost: $97.50
Date of first issue: 1981

Advisory letter concentrating on mining commodities, precious metals and technological innovative forms.

AUDIENCE: Individual   RISK LEVEL: Moderate, Aggressive
TOPICS: Futures/Commodities

CTCR Commodity Traders Consumer Report

Bruce Babcock
1731 Howe Avenue, Suite 149
Sacramento, CA 95825

PH: (916) 677-7562
(800) 999-CTCR
FAX: (916) 672-0425
Cost: $198.00 annually
Frequency: Bimonthly
Date of first issue: 4/83

Covers commodities. Monitors major commodity trading advisory services - both their letters and hotline and summarizes the results of their recommendations. Designed to make you a smarter consumer and better trader in the exciting world of commodity trading.

AUDIENCE: Individual, Professional   RISK LEVEL: Aggressive
TOPICS: Futures/Commodities, General Reference

Current Yield

Ostrander Asset Management
711 N.E. Windrose Ct.
Suite A
Kansas City, MO 64155

PH: (816) 468-7521
Cost: $79.95
Frequency: Monthly

Includes fundamental analysis. Covers municipal bonds and corporate bonds. Focuses on vesting. Each issue contains a rate forecast, bond valuations, list showing the highest yields and which ones to purchase or avoid, short-term and asset allocation and much more; including bond funds, annuities, GNMA's and others.

AUDIENCE: Beginning, Individual   RISK LEVEL: Conservative, Moderate
TOPICS: Bonds

CUSIP Master Directory

Standard & Poor's Corporation
25 Broadway
New York, NY 10004

PH: (212) 208-8000
Cost: $1,975.00/yr.
Frequency: Annual
Includes weekly and quarterly
  updates

Covers all municipal issues, corporate bonds and warrants and their issuers.

AUDIENCE: Individual, Professional   RISK LEVEL: Conservative, Moderate
TOPICS: Bonds

Cycles Research

Advertising and Marketing
  Strategies
1314 Alps Drive
McLean, VA 22102

PH: (703) 448-3358
FAX: (703) 448-0814
Cost: $200.00
Frequency: approximately every
  month

Includes technical analysis. Covers stocks, municipal bonds, corporate bonds and gold. Identifies and interprets financial market cycles providing valuable recommendations to keep investors ahead of the pack. Service includes 10 reports and interim news flashes. Hotline available for $144 for subscribers or $233 for non-subscribers.

AUDIENCE: Individual, Professional   RISK LEVEL: Moderate, Aggressive
TOPICS: Bonds, Stocks, Futures/Commodities

Cyclewatch

Walter Bressert
6987 North Oracle Road
Tucson, AR 85704

PH: (800) 677-0120
Cost: $179.00/yr
Frequency: Monthly
Date of first issue: 7/91

Includes technical analysis and Oscillator/Cycle Charts with commentary. Covers stocks, market timing, charts, government bonds. Cyclewatch uses cycles to forecast time and price moves in the S&P Index, Bonds, Gold and DJIA, plus Oscillator/Cycle Combinations to mechanically identify cycle tops and bottoms as they appear. Cyclewatch Hotline for $2 for the first minute.

AUDIENCE: Individual, Professional   RISK LEVEL: Moderate, Aggressive
TOPICS: Bonds, Stocks, Options, Futures/Commodities

Czeschin's Mutual Fund Outlook and Recommendations

Robert W. Czeschin, Editor
Walter Bonner, Publisher
Agora, Inc.
824 E. Baltimore Street
Baltimore, MD 21202

PH: (301) 234-0691
Cost: $147.00/yr
Frequency: Monthly
Date of first issue: 1987

Includes fundamental analysis. Covers stocks. "Includes commentary on the stock market outlook and specific recommendations for one or more of three model portfolios: the income, the long-term growth, and the jaguar portfolios."

AUDIENCE: Beginning, Individual   RISK LEVEL: Moderate, Aggressive
TOPICS: Mutual Funds

Daily Bulletin

Vancouver Stock Exchange
P.O. Box 10333
609 Granville St.
Vancouver, B.C. V7Y1H1

PH: (604) 689-3334
FAX: (604) 688-6051
Cost: $785/yr USA & Canada,
  $1,180/yr overseas
Frequency: Daily - each trading day

"Contains a breakdown of trading in all issues, including volume, value, high, low, close, price changes, closing market, advances & declines, large transactions, new highs and lows, VSE listing notices, company meeting dates, short politions, dividends, indices & options."

AUDIENCE: Individual, Professional   RISK LEVEL: Moderate, Aggressive
TOPICS: Stocks, Options

Daily Graphs

William O'Neil & Co., Inc
P.O. Box 66919
Los Angeles, CA 90066

PH: (310) 448-6843
Costs and frequencies: NYSE
$429.00 (weekly)
$305.00 (biweekly)
$203.00 (monthly)
AMEX/OTC $719.00 (weekly)
$549.00 (biweekly)
$345.00 (monthly)
Date of first issue: 1974

Chart service. Includes fundamental and technical analysis. Covers 2500 NYSE, AMEX & OTC Companies arranged by industry groups. Includes 41 fundamental and 26 technical factors in every chart.

AUDIENCE: Beginning, Individual, Professional   RISK LEVEL: Moderate, Aggressive
TOPICS: Stocks, Options

Daily Graphs Option Guide

William O'Neill and Company, Inc.
P.O. Box 24933
Los Angeles, CA 90024

PH: (213) 820-2583
Cost: $229.00/yr
Frequency: Weekly

Covers chart service and options. Graphic and statistical data on active CBOE, AMEX, PSE, PHIL, NYSE options and underlying issues. It also includes a weekly listing of quarterly earnings due, stocks going x-dividend, short term technical indicators, computer selected call writes, yearly graphs of market averages with 50 and 200-day moving averages.

AUDIENCE: Individual, Professional   RISK LEVEL: Aggressive
TOPICS: Options

Daily Market Comment - Market Fax, The

Market Mani, Inc.
P.O. Box 1234
Pacifica, CA 94044

PH: (415) 952-8853
FAX: (415) 952-0844
Cost: $150.00/month per fax
Frequency of update: Daily - one
  page format

Types of investments: Stocks and chart service. Since late 1987, Glenn Cutler has written the Market Fax, a one-page analysis of the day's happenings in the markets, including comments and ideas for the coming day. Each night prior to trading days, it is faxed directly to your office.

AUDIENCE: Individual, Professional   RISK LEVEL: Aggressive
TOPICS: Stocks

Daily Market Report

Coffee, Sugar and Cocoa Exchange,
  Inc.
Four World Trade Center
New York, NY 10048

PH: (212) 938-2800
Cost: $110.00/month
Frequency: Daily

Includes technical analysis. Covers commodities. Trading prices, open interest and volume for coffee, sugar and cocoa, spot prices for sugar, warehouse stocks for coffee and cocoa, opening and closing prices for London coffee and sugar, and Paris cocoa.

AUDIENCE: Individual, Professional   RISK LEVEL: Aggressive
TOPICS: Options, Futures/Commodities

Daily Stockwatch, The

Canjex Publishing, Ltd.
700 W. Georgia St.
Box 10371, Pacific Centre
Vancouver, BC, Canada V7Y 1J6

PH: (604) 687-1500
Cost: $395.00/ yr
Date of first issue: 1984
Frequency: Daily; indexed: weekly
  and monthly
Technical and Fundamental Analysis

Various reports published by companies on the Vancouver Stock Exchange such as reviews of annual and semi-annual reports, shareholder control changes, regulatory notices and more. Also provides a market summary.

AUDIENCE: Individual, Professional   RISK LEVEL: Moderate, Aggressive
TOPICS: Stocks

Daily Stockwatch Revised, The

Canjex Publishing, Ltd.
700 W. Georgia St.
Box 10371
Pacific Centre
Vancouver, BC, Canada V7Y 1J6

PH: (604) 687-1500
Cost: Contact vendor
Date of first issue: 1984
Frequency: Daily; indexed: weekly
  and monthly
Technical and Fundamental Analysis

Various reports published by companies on the Vancouver Stock Exchange such as reviews of annual and semi-annual reports, shareholder control changes, regulatory notices and more. Also provides a market summary.

AUDIENCE: Individual, Professional   RISK LEVEL: Moderate, Aggressive
TOPICS: Stocks

Dallas Morning News Stock/Business Hotline, The

The Dallas Morning News Stock
Business Hotline

PH: (900) 990-9900 (then enter 195)
(214) 977-8809
Cost: $.95 per minute
24 Hour service
Frequency of update: Every 15
minutes

Telephone newsletter includes stocks and covers business news.
Use your touchtone phone to get timely stock quotes (15 minutes
delayed) on more than 9,000 publicly traded issues and concise
hourly business news updates prepared by business experts from
the Associated Press.

AUDIENCE: Beginning, Individual   RISK LEVEL: Moderate, Aggressive
TOPICS: Mutual Funds, Stocks

Derivatives Week

Institutional Investor, Inc.
488 Madison Avenue
New York, NY 10022-5782

PH: (800) 543-4444
(212) 303-3233
FAX: (212) 303-3353
Cost: $1,295.00/yr
Date of first issue: 4/92
Frequency: Weekly

coverage of who's using derivatives and how. With stories from
London, Tokyo and New York, it provides competitive intelligence
and reports on the instruments linked to equities, interest rates,
commodities and currencies."

AUDIENCE: Professional   RISK LEVEL: Aggressive
TOPICS: Bonds, Stocks, Futures/Commodities

"Get the only weekly comprehensive

Dessauer's Journal of Financial Markets

John P. Dessauer
P.O. Box 1718
Orleans, MA 02653

PH: (508) 255-1651
(800) 272-7550
FAX: (508) 255-9243
Cost: $195.00 annually
Frequency: Twice a month
Date of first issue: Fall 1980

Includes fundamental Analysis. Covers stocks and the world
financial markets. Dessauer's Journal provides analysis and advice
on world trade trends. Mr. Dessauer believes it is futile to determine
investment strategies while watching only the U.S. financial
markets.

AUDIENCE: Individual, Professional   RISK LEVEL: Moderate, Aggressive
TOPICS: Stocks

Dick Davis Digest

Dick Davis Publishing Company
Steven Halpern
P.O. Box 9547
Ft. Lauderdale, FL 33310-9547

PH: (305) 771-7111
FAX: (305) 771-1756
Cost: $140.00 annually
Frequency: Bimonthly
Date of first issue: 1982

Includes fundamental analysis. Covers stocks, and mutual funds.
Investment ideas from the best minds on Wall Street. Presents news
and information to convey helpful, factual information which may
include the views, opinions, and recommendations of individuals or
organizations whose thoughts are deemed of interest.

AUDIENCE: Beginning, Individual, Professional   RISK LEVEL: Moderate, Aggressive
TOPICS: Bonds, Mutual Funds, Stocks

Dines Letter, The

James Dines
P.O. Box 22
Belvedere, CA 94920

PH: (800) 84-LUCKY
Cost: $195.00
Frequency: Twice monthly
Date of first issue: 1960

Includes technical analysis. Covers stocks, precious metals. Explicit buy/sell advice, information on precious metals markets and hedging strategies, futuristic predications for long-term investors, market analysis and commentary. Comments: Fax interim warning bulletins available to subscribers only for $224 per year.

AUDIENCE: Individual, Professional   RISK LEVEL: Moderate, Aggressive
TOPICS: Stocks, Options, Futures/Commodities

Directory of Bond Agents

Standard & Poor's Corporation
25 Broadway
New York, NY 10004

PH: (212) 208-8000
Cost: $1,310.00/yr.
Frequency: Bimonthly
Editor: Vito Calbi

Names, addresses and phone numbers of all registered corporate and municipal bond agents. Also updates new issues and redemptions.

AUDIENCE: Professional   RISK LEVEL: Conservative, Moderate
TOPICS: Bonds

Directory of Institutional Investors

Vickers Stock Research Corp.
226 New York Ave.
Huntington, NY 11743

PH: (516) 423-7710
(800) 645-5043
Cost: $225.00/yr
Editor: Jim Van Dyke
Frequency: Semi-annual

Lists Domestic and Canadian and foreign institutional investors. Provides addresses, phone numbers, types of institution, asset information.

AUDIENCE: Individual, Professional   RISK LEVEL: Conservative, Moderate, Aggressive
TOPICS: All

Directory of Mutual Funds

Investment Company Institute
1401 H St., NW
Suite 1200
Washington, DC 20005

PH: (202) 326-5800
Cost: $8.50/yr.
Frequency: Annual
Editor: Arlene Zuckerberg

Provides directory of members of the Institute and asset information on the funds themselves. Includes addresses and phone numbers, investment advisors, total assets and more.

AUDIENCE: Beginning, Individual   RISK LEVEL: Moderate, Aggressive
TOPICS: Mutual Funds

Directory of Registered Investment Advisors

Money Market Directories
320 E. Main St.
Charlottesville, VA 22902-5234

PH: (804) 977-1450
FAX: (804) 979-9962
Cost: $325.00
Date of first issue: 1986
Frequency: Annual

Provides names, addresses, FAX #, SEC#, dates of registration, total assets under management, key people and titles, asset allocation by tax status and investment strategies of advisors registered with the securities and exchange commission.

AUDIENCE: Beginning, Individual, Professional	RISK LEVEL: Conservative,
TOPICS: All	Moderate, Aggressive

Doane's Agricultural Report

Doane's Information Services
Paul Justis
11701 Borman Dr.
St. Louis, MO 63146

PH: (314) 569-2700
(800) 535-2342
FAX: (314) 569-1083
Cost: $84.00/yr
Frequency: Weekly
Date of first issue: 1938

Includes fundamental analysis. Covers commodities. Marketing and management information for the agricultural market. Gives world news relevant to the agricultural market. "When to Sell and Buy" section gives investment recommendations on individual commodities. Last page titled "From Washington" brings you the latest government information.

AUDIENCE: Individual, Professional	RISK LEVEL: Moderate, Aggressive
TOPICS: Options, Futures/Commodities	

Dohmen Mutual Fund Strategy

Wellington Financial Corp.
6600 Kanalianole Hwy.
No. 144-C
Honolulu, HI 96825

PH: (808) 396-2220
(800) 992-9989
FAX: (808) 528-5016
Cost: $140.00/yr US and Canada
Date of first issue: June 1989
Frequency: Monthly

Editor: Bert Dohmen-Ramirez. Provides analysis of the stock market from fundamental and technical viewpoints and gives recommendations on individual mutual funds and mutual fund sectors. Gives specific buy and sell signals, includes tables and graphs.

AUDIENCE: Individual	RISK LEVEL: Moderate, Aggressive
TOPICS: Mutual Funds	

Donoghue's Money Fund Directory

IBC/Donoghue, Inc.
290 Eliot St.
Box 91004
Ashland, MA 01721-9104

PH: (508) 881-2800
FAX: (508) 881-0982
Frequency: Annual
Cost: $27.95
Date of first issue: 1990
Editor: Daniel Bates

Provides statistical information on over 1,000 money funds such as: 10 yr. performance data, expense rates, total assets, minimum/subsequent investments and more.

AUDIENCE: Beginning, Individual, Professional	RISK LEVEL: Conservative
TOPICS: Bonds	

Donoghue's Money Fund Report

The Donoghue Organization, Inc.
3290 Eliot Street
P.O. Box 9104
Holliston, MA 01721-9104

PH: (800) 343-5413
FAX: (508) 429-2452
Cost: $195.00/yr
Frequency: Weekly
Date of first issue: 10/75

Includes fundamental analysis. Covers mutual funds, tables. "Publishes weekly and monthly statistics on 351 taxable and tax-free money funds. Provides information and commentary on net assets; 7- and 30-day yields, average maturity, valuation method, number of share holdings, and sales and redemptions."

AUDIENCE: Beginning, Individual, Professional   RISK LEVEL: Conservative
TOPICS: Bonds

Donoghue's Moneyletter

The Donoghue Organization, Inc.
290 Elliot St.
Ashland, MA 01721-9104

PH: (800) 343-5413
(508) 429-5930
FAX: (508) 429-2452
Cost: $89.00/yr
Frequency: Bimonthly
Date of first issue: 3/80

Includes fundamental analysis. Covers mutual funds. "Explains high-interest money market investment options and strategies in clear, easy-to-read terms. Offers investment advice and options for the do-it-yourself investor. Lists top-performing money market funds and includes coverage of no-load mutual fund switch families."

AUDIENCE: Beginning, Individual   RISK LEVEL: Moderate, Aggressive
TOPICS: Mutual Funds

Dow Theory Forecasts

Chuck Carlson
7412 Calumet Avenue
Hammond, IN 46324

PH: (219) 931-6480
FAX: (219) 931-6487
Cost: $233.00 annually
Frequency: Weekly
Date of first issue: 1946

Includes technical analysis. Covers stocks and market timing. Information and analysis of stocks; uses Dow Theory as primary investment tool, Dow & transportation index, most subscribers in 50's & 60's - conservative approach to investing in equities.

AUDIENCE: Individual   RISK LEVEL: Moderate
TOPICS: Mutual Funds, Stocks, Asset Allocation

Dow Theory Letters

Richard Russell
P.O. Box 1759
La Jolla, CA 92038

PH: (619) 454-0481
Cost: $250.00/yr
Frequency: Every two weeks
Date of first issue: 1958

Includes technical analysis. Covers stocks, mutual funds, charts, precious metals. Primarily an investment theory/trend letter. Focuses on the Primary Trend Index. Provides some general investment recommendations.

AUDIENCE: Individual   RISK LEVEL: Moderate, Aggressive
TOPICS: Mutual Funds, Stocks, Futures/Commodities

Dowbeaters

Peter DeAngelis, C.F.A.
P.O. Box 284
Ionia, NJ 07845

PH: (201) 543-4860
Cost: $100.00 annually
Frequency: Monthly

Includes fundamental analysis. Covers stocks. Looks for obscure, overlooked situations and emerging growth stocks of low price with good fundamentals. Each issue has 1 or 2 specific recommendations and market evaluations.

AUDIENCE: Beginning, Individual   RISK LEVEL: Moderate, Aggressive
TOPICS: Stocks

Dowphone

Dow Jones & Co., Inc.
P.O. Box 300
Princeton, NJ 08543-0300

PH: (800) 345-NEWS
Cost: Peak hours: 95 cents /minute
Off peak hours: 75 cents/minute
$15 sign up fee refunded in the form
of a usage credit
24 Hour service
Frequency of update: Constantly

Covers stocks. A voice information service providing alerts to company news, market updates and the day's top stories. Real time stock and investment opinions.

AUDIENCE: Individual, Professional   RISK LEVEL: Moderate, Aggressive
TOPICS: Stocks

DRIP Investor

Charles B. Carlson, Editor
Dow Theory Forecasts, Inc.
7412 Calumet Ave.
Hammond, IN 46324

PH: (800) 962-4369
Cost: $79.00/yr
Date of first issue: 8/92
Frequency: Monthly
Fundamental Analysis

Focuses on stocks that offer dividend reinvestment. Different topics are "DRIPS in the news," "Market Capsule," "Readers' TALK," "The DRIP Analyst," and "The Model Portfolio."

AUDIENCE: Beginning, Individual   RISK LEVEL: Moderate, Aggressive
TOPICS: Stocks

Dunn & Hargitt Commodity Service

Dunn & Hargitt, Inc.
22 N. 2nd St.
P.O. Box 1100
Lafayette, IN 47906

PH: (317) 423-2624
Cost: $245.00/yr
Frequency: weekly
Technical and Fundamental Analysis
Date of first issue: 1965

Comprehensive charts on 35 commodities providing daily high/low/close data weekly volume, open interest and point and figure charts as well as market forecasts and trading information for the coming week.

AUDIENCE: Individual, Professional   RISK LEVEL: Aggressive
TOPICS: Commodities

Dynamic Investor, The

The Dynamic Investor
8010 S. Highway 101
Ukiah, CA 95482

PH: (800) 743-6960
FAX: (707) 462-2905
Cost: $158.00/yr
Date of first issue: 1988
Frequency: Monthly
Technical and Fundamental
  Analysis

"Your pioneer guide for tapping into the wealth building profit dynamics of small cap growth stocks." Gives precise information on when to buy and sell the best small cap stocks.

AUDIENCE: Beginning, Individual   RISK LEVEL: Moderate, Aggressive
TOPICS: Stocks

Economy at a Glance, The

Argus Research Corporation
17 Battery Place
New York, NY 10004

PH: (212) 425-7500
Cost: $160.00
Frequency: Monthly

Includes fundamental analysis. Covers economic analysis. Economic analysis portrayed by charts and bar graphs showing various economic trends with commentary for each graph or chart. Also includes a calendar of release dates for important economic indicators.

AUDIENCE: Individual   RISK LEVEL: Moderate, Aggressive
TOPICS: All

Ehrenkrantz Report, The

Ehrenkrantz King Nussbaum, Inc.
635 Madison Avenue
New York, NY 10022

PH: (212) 407-0575
(800) 867-8600
Cost: $120.00
Frequency: Monthly
Date of first issue: approximately
  10 years

Includes fundamental analysis. Covers stocks. Each issue highlights a specific stock as well as giving performance results on the model portfolio.

AUDIENCE: Beginning, Individual   RISK LEVEL:
TOPICS: Stocks

Electric Utility Rankings

Argus Research Corporation
17 Battery Place
New York, NY 10004

PH: (212) 425-7500
Cost: $225.00
Frequency: Monthly
Date of first issue: 1934

Includes fundamental analysis. Covers stocks. "Ranks 50 utility companies according to five 'quality' categories ranging from 'highest' to 'lowest' within the respective quality groups, each company's stock is then rated 'Buy,' 'Hold,' or 'Sell.' Includes a subscription to Electric Utility Spotlight."

AUDIENCE: Beginning, Individual, Professional   RISK LEVEL: Moderate, Aggressive
TOPICS: Stocks

Electric Utility Spotlight

Argus Research Corporation
17 Battery Place
New York, NY 10004

PH: (212) 425-7500
Cost: $225.00
Frequency: Monthly
Date of first issue: 1934

Includes fundamental analysis. Covers stocks. Focuses on subjects of interest to electric utility stock investors. Generally contains extensive tabulations supporting the points made. Includes a subscription to Electric Utility Rankings.

AUDIENCE: Beginning, Individual, Professional   RISK LEVEL: Moderate, Aggressive
TOPICS: Stocks

Elliott Wave Currency and Commodity Forecast, The

Peter Desario, James P. Chorek
Elliott Wave International and
  Robert Kelley
P.O. Box 1618
Gainesville, GA 30503

PH: (404) 536-0309
(800) 336-1618 ORDERS
Cost: $249.00 annually
$270.00 overseas
Frequency: Monthly
Date of first issue: 1987

Technical analysis. Commodities, currencies. For speculator wishing to recognize tradable turning points in the physical commodities and currencies. Charts of over 25 commodities, currencies, and indexes using the Wave principle, Fibonacci calculations and supporting methods to identify the key emerging markets. Hotline with subscription: $299/yr.

AUDIENCE: Individual, Professional   RISK LEVEL: Aggressive
TOPICS: Futures/Commodities

Elliott Wave Theorist, The

Robert R. Prechter, Jr.
Elliott Wave International
P.O. Box 1618
Gainesville, GA 30503

PH: (404) 536-0309
(800) 336-1618 ORDERS
Cost: $233.00 annually
$250.00 overseas
Frequency: Monthly
Date of first issue: 1978

Technical analysis. Stocks, bonds, gold and silver and social and economic trends. Thoroughly analyzes Elliott Wave, Fibonacci relationships, fixed time cycles, momentum, sentiment, and supply-demand factors in a comprehensive approach covering stocks, precious metals, interest rates and the economy. Hotline with subscription additional: $377/yr.

AUDIENCE: Individual, Professional   RISK LEVEL: Moderate, Aggressive
TOPICS: Bonds, Mutual Funds, Stocks, Options, Futures/Commodities

Emerging and Special Situations Standard & Poor's

Emerging and Special Situations
Standard & Poor's
25 Broadway
New York, NY 10004

PH: (800) 777-4858
(212) 208-8768
Cost: $24.00/yr
Date of first issue: 1982

Regular features: stock choices and new issues. Points out lesser known stocks which S&P's analysts deem to be overlooked and undervalued. Alerts investors to the growth situations that have appreciation potential. Also provides all regarded analysis of new issues before they go public.

AUDIENCE: Individual   RISK LEVEL: Moderate, Aggressive
TOPICS: Stocks

Emerging Markets Week

Institutional Investor, Inc.
488 Madison Avenue
New York, NY 10022-5782

PH: (800) 543-4444
FAX: (212) 303-3353
Cost: $1,395.00/yr
Date of first issue: 6/93
Frequency: Weekly
Fundamental Analysis

"Covers the financing plans of corporations and governments in Latin America, Southeast Asia and Eastern Europe. Reports on emerging market investment strategies used by savvy money managers around the globe."

AUDIENCE: Individual, Professional   RISK LEVEL: Moderate, Aggressive
TOPICS: Bonds, Stocks, Futures/Commodities

Emerging Profit Newsletter

Ron Cram
26127 Edgemont Drive
Highland, CA 92346

Cost: $120.00
Frequency: Monthly

Includes fundamental analysis. Covers stocks. Focuses on emerging profit stocks in the high tech and mid tech areas. Has a model portfolio and provides specific recommendations.

AUDIENCE: Beginning, Individual   RISK LEVEL: Moderate, Aggressive
TOPICS: Stocks

Environmental Investing News

Robert Mitchell Associates
2 Cannon Street
Newton, MA 02161-9923

PH: (617) 244-7819
Cost: $108.00
Frequency: Monthly
Date of first issue: 1989

Includes fundamental analysis. Covers stocks. Focuses on environmental industries and provides news and information to assist subscribers in making their own sound investment decisions. Profiles several companies each issue and gives news on the most recent developments in environmental regulations and enforcement.

AUDIENCE: Individual, Professional   RISK LEVEL: Moderate, Aggressive
TOPICS: Stocks

Executive Stock Report

Media General Financial Services
P.O. Box 85333
Richmond, VA 23293

PH: (804) 649-6587
(800) 446-7922
FAX: (804) 649-6097
Cost: $236.00 for 12 monthly reports;
$182.00 for 4 quarterly reports
Frequency: Monthly or quarterly
Date of first issue: 10 - 15 years

Fundamental data and performance analysis on the companies chosen by the subscriber from Media General's database of 7,000 public held companies. Current financial data, comparisons, gains and losses, trends, price performance analysis, price and volume analysis and performance measures relative to peer groups and major market indexes.

AUDIENCE: Individual, Professional   RISK LEVEL: Moderate, Aggressive
TOPICS: Stocks

Executive Wealth Advisory

National Institute of Business
  Management, Inc.
P.O. Box 25338
Alexandria, VA 22313

PH: (800) 543-2054
(212) 971-3300 in VA
Cost: $96.00 annually
Frequency: Twice a month
Date of first issue: 1978

Covers stocks, mutual funds, market timing, municipal bonds, economy, taxes, financial planning. A personal financial guide to increasing wealth.

AUDIENCE: Individual   RISK LEVEL: Conservative, Moderate, Aggressive
TOPICS: Bonds, Mutual Funds, Stocks, Investment Planning

F.X.C. Report

F.X.C. Investors Corporation
62-19 Cooper Avenue
Glendale, NY 11385

PH: (718) 417-1330
Cost: $190.00/yr
Frequency: 2 - 4 times a month
Date of first issue: 1971

Includes fundamental analysis. Covers securities and bonds. Reports on the securities of companies that have the potential for extreme capital appreciation. Offers news of research for investors with risk capital, investment recommendations, and performance reports.

AUDIENCE: Beginning, Individual   RISK LEVEL: Moderate, Aggressive
TOPICS: Stocks

Fabian's Investment Resource

Richard J. Fabian
Fabian Companies
2100 Main Street, Suite 300
Huntington Beach, CA 92648

PH: (800) 950-8765
(714) 536-1931
Cost: $137.00 annually
Frequency: Monthly
Date of first issue: 1977

Includes investment plan that generates buy and sell signals (1 per year, on average) for stock mutual funds, with a goal of 17-20% annualized compounded growth. Monitors 400 U.S., international, gold, and asset allocation funds. Covers a variety of investment news and timely issues. Starting materials teach you how to use the Fabian Compounding Plan.

AUDIENCE: Beginning, Individual   RISK LEVEL: Moderate, Aggressive
TOPICS: Mutual Funds, Asset Allocation

Facts on the Funds

Vickers Stock Research Corp.
226 New York Ave.
Huntington, NY 11743

PH: (516) 423-7710
Cost: $195.00/yr
Frequency: Quarterly
Editor: Jim Van Dyke

Provides a list of investment companies and their assets. Also lists the portfolios of the largest funds.

AUDIENCE: Beginning, Individual   RISK LEVEL: Moderate, Aggressive
TOPICS: Mutual Funds

"Fament" Stock Advisory Service

Gordon D. Mors
9157 Trujillo Way
Sacramento, CA 95826

PH: (916) 363-2138
Cost: $168.00
Frequency: Bimonthly
(even numbered months)
Date of first issue: 10/80

General market commentary with specific buy/sell/hold recommendations.

AUDIENCE: Individual   **RISK LEVEL: Moderate, Aggressive**
TOPICS: Bonds, Stocks

Fed Tracker, The

Seraphim Press
4805 Courageous Lane
Carlsbad, CA 92008

PH: (619) 720-0107
Cost: $96.00/yr
Frequency: Monthly
Date of first issue: 1982
Technical and Fundamental
  Analysis

Spotlights the market and influences that affect it. Covers investments in stocks, banking and finance, bonds, currencies, energy, domestic and international businesses, futures, metals, and treasury bills. Tracks money flow into the economy and investment ventures. Comprehensive market and investment newsletter covering all markets with recommendations.

AUDIENCE: Individual, Professional   **RISK LEVEL: Conservative, Moderate, Aggressive**
TOPICS: Bonds, Stocks

Fidelity Investments Mutual Fund Guide

Fidelity Publishing
82 Devonshire St., R25A
Boston, MA 02109-3614

PH: (617) 726-6027
FAX: (617) 728-6732
Cost: $89.00/yr U.S.
Date of first issue: 1987
Frequency: Monthly
Fundamental Analysis

Includes a digest of newsletters, details of 13 and 39-week moving averages for all Fidelity Funds and performance comparisons to non-Fidelity Mutual funds. Editor: Peggy Malaspina.

AUDIENCE: Beginning, Individual   **RISK LEVEL: Moderate, Aggressive**
TOPICS: Mutual Funds

Fidelity Monitor

Jack Bowers
P.O. Box 1294
Rocklin, CA 95677-7294

PH: (800) 397-3094
Cost: $96.00 annually
Frequency: Monthly
Date of first issue: 1986

Covers Fidelity Mutual Funds. Five model portfolios offer an easy way to invest with options ranging from conservative to aggressive. Free trial issue available on request.

AUDIENCE: Beginning, Individual   **RISK LEVEL: Moderate, Aggressive**
TOPICS: Mutual Funds, Asset Allocation

Fidelity Select Advisor, The

New Wave Publishing
15073 92nd Street
Elk River, MN 55330

PH: (612) 241-0520
Cost: $89.00/yr.
Frequency: Monthly
Editor: Loren H. Smith
Date of first issue: 1993

Covers Fidelity mutual funds. Provides model portfolios and buy/sell/hold recommendations.

AUDIENCE: Beginning, Individual   RISK LEVEL: Moderate, Aggressive
TOPICS: Mutual Funds

Finance Over 50

The Ron Jackson Company
661 Calmar Avenue
Suite 1002
Oakland, CA 94610

PH: (415)
Cost: $79.00
Frequency: Monthly

Includes fundamental analysis. Gives conservative advice on investing over 50. Includes specific, low-risk recommendations, tax and real estate advice and more.

AUDIENCE: Beginning, Individual   RISK LEVEL: Conservative, Moderate, Aggressive
TOPICS: Bonds, Mutual Funds, Stocks, Investment Planning

Financial Flows and the Developing Countries

The World Bank
P.O. Box 8080
Philadelphia, PA 19101-9353

FAX: (201) 476-2197
Cost: $150.00/yr
Frequency: Quarterly
Date of first issue: 11/93

"You will have access to some of the same authoritative intelligence World Bank financial analysts, loan officers, investment officer and economists use to access risk and to make their investment and lending decisions." International lending and capital markets, equity portfolio and foreign direct investments, secondary markets for developing country debt.

AUDIENCE: Individual, Professional   RISK LEVEL: Moderate, Aggressive
TOPICS: Bonds, Stocks

Financial Planning Strategies

Liberty Publishing, Inc.
42 Cherry Hill Drive
Danvers, MA 01923

PH: (800) 722-7270 ext 128
Cost: Minimum100 copies at 45
  cents each bimonthly; and 50
  cents each quarterly
Frequency: Bimonthly
Date of first issue: Nov. 1990

Includes fundamental analysis. Mutual funds, bonds (municipal and government), financial planning. A personally imprinted client and prospect newsletter available exclusively to Certified Financial Planner professionals. Institute of Certified Financial Planners.

AUDIENCE: Professional   RISK LEVEL: Conservative, Moderate, Aggressive
TOPICS: Bonds, Mutual Funds, Stocks, Investment Planning

Fitch Insights

Fitch Investors Service, Inc.
5 Hanover Sq.
New York, NY 10004

PH: (212) 908-0500
(800) 753-4824
FAX: (212) 480-4437
Frequency: Biweekly
Cost: $1,040.00/yr
Date of first issue: April 2, 1990

Provides ratings and extensive reports on corporate bonds and municipal and government bonds.

AUDIENCE: Beginning, Individual, Professional   RISK LEVEL: Conservative, Moderate
TOPICS: Bonds

Fitch Rating Register

Fitch Investors Service, Inc.
5 Hanover Sq.
New York, NY 10004

PH: (212) 908-0500
(800) 753-4824
FAX: (212) 480-4437
Frequency: Monthly
Cost: $225.00

Provides ratings and evaluative information on corporate bonds, preferred stock, government and municipal departments, and health care.

AUDIENCE: Individual, Professional   RISK LEVEL: Conservative, Moderate
TOPICS: Bonds, Stocks

Forbes Special Situation Survey

Forbes Investors Advisory Institute, Inc.
60 Fifth Avenue
New York, NY 10011

PH: (212) 620-2210
Cost: $495.00/yr
Frequency: Monthly
Date of first issue: 1954

Includes fundamental analysis. Covers securities. "For sophisticated investors seeking potential above-average capital gains and able to take a degree of risk. Recommends individual speculative equity securities."

AUDIENCE: Individual   RISK LEVEL: Aggressive
TOPICS: Stocks

Ford Value Report

Ford Investor Services, Inc.
11722 Sorrento Valley Road
Suite 1
San Diego, CA 92121

PH: (619) 755-1327
Cost: $120.00
Frequency: Monthly
Date of first issue: 1970

Includes fundamental analysis. Covers stocks. Provides financial data on 2,000 leading common stocks, investment value analysis to determine if over or undervalued, analysis of current earning trends and stock market commentary on fundamentals and recommendations.

AUDIENCE: Individual, Professional   RISK LEVEL: Moderate, Aggressive
TOPICS: Stocks

Forecaster

Forecaster Publishing Company
19623 Ventura Blvd.
Tarzana, CA 91356

PH: (818) 345-4421
Cost: $120.00 annually
Frequency: Weekly - 40/year
Date of first issue: 1962

Includes fundamental analysis. Covers gold, silver, and wholesale coin market. A weekly money letter for speculators. Provides exclusive information on the gold, silver, and wholesale coin market, business trends, predictions and forecasts.

AUDIENCE: Individual, Professional   RISK LEVEL: Moderate, Aggressive
TOPICS: Futures/Commodities

Forecasts & Strategies

Phillips Publishing, Inc.
7811 Montrose Road
Potomac, MD 20854

PH: (800) 777-5005
(301) 340-2100
Cost: $177.00 annually
Frequency: Monthly
Date of first issue: 1980

Includes fundamental analysis. Covers stocks, mutual funds, bonds (municipal, corporate, government) and currencies. Concentrates on low-risk investments, protection of capital. Gives general investment advice with a few specific recommendations

AUDIENCE: Individual   RISK LEVEL: Moderate, Aggressive
TOPICS: Bonds, Mutual Funds, Stocks

Foreign Activity Report

Security Industry Association
120 Broadway
New York, NY 10271

PH: (212) 608-1500
Cost: US and Canada: $40.00/yr for
  members
$60.00/yr for all others
Frequency: Quarterly
Fundamental analysis
Date of first issue: 1978

Reports on U.S. activity in foreign securities and vice-versa and shows comparisons between the U.S. dollar and other foreign currencies.

AUDIENCE: Individual, Professional   RISK LEVEL: Conservative, Moderate,
TOPICS: Bonds, Stocks, Futures/Commodities   Aggressive

Foreign Markets Advisory

Muller Associates, Inc.
Box 75
Fairfax Station, VA 22039

PH: (703) 425-5961
FAX: (703) 425-6263
Cost: $225.00/yr.
Date of first issue: 1992
Frequency: Monthly
Editor: David G. Muller

Covers stock markets and economies of 40 countries. Designed primarily for American investment managers. Includes a model portfolio and coverage of all U.S. listed closed-end foreign equity funds. Subscription includes an annual edition of The Directory of Foreign Stocks Traded in the United States.

AUDIENCE: Individual, Professional   RISK LEVEL: Moderate, Aggressive
TOPICS: Bonds, Mutual Funds, Stocks

Fortucast Commodity Market Timing

Barry Rosen
P.O. Box 2066
Fairfield, IA 52556

PH: (515) 472-6866
(800) 247-3678
Cost: $289.00
Frequency: Monthly
Date of first issue: 1988

Includes technical analysis. Covers market timing, futures and commodities. A futures market timing newsletter providing precise entry and exit dates, usable 3-, 6-, 18-plus-month forecasts, 5,000 year old ancient Indian trading secrets, and hidden Gann, Timed Elliott Waves and Fibonacci secrets. Several different Hotlines available at a discount.

AUDIENCE: Beginning, Individual, Professional   RISK LEVEL: Aggressive
TOPICS: Futures/Commodities

Fortucast Propicks Hotline

Barry Rosen
P.O. Box 2066
Fairfield, IA 52556

PH: (900) 988-3342
Cost: $2.00 per minute
Frequency of update: Daily,
Sunday–Thursday

Telephone newsletter covering stocks, commodities, municipal bonds, corporate bonds, government bonds, currencies, gold, silver, crude. The call begins with all the new trades, followed by commentary on financials, grains, then metals.

AUDIENCE: Beginning, Individual, Professional   RISK LEVEL: Conservative,
                                                                  Moderate, Aggressive
TOPICS: Bonds, Mutual Funds, Stocks, Options, Futures/Commodities

Fortucast Regular Hotline

Barry Rosen
P.O. Box 2066
Fairfield, IA 52556

PH: (800) 247-3678 to subscribe
Cost: $649.00 includes monthly
Newsletter
Frequency of update: 3 times per
  week
24 Hour Service

Telephone newsletter covering futures and commodities. "Trades, stops and detailed commentary including support and resistance, breakouts, breakdowns, direction and velocity of the markets over the next few days on 16-20 markets covered in the Fortucast Commodity Market Timing Newsletter."

AUDIENCE: Individual, Professional   RISK LEVEL: Aggressive
TOPICS: Options, Futures/Commodities

Fractal Behavior of Markets, The

LJH Investments
18484 Preston Road
Suite 102-LB-160
Dallas, TX 75252-5474

PH: (214) 985-7571
(900) 226-1618 - $2.25 per minute
Cost: $233.00
Frequency: Monthly
Date of first issue: 1991

Covers stocks, market timing, treasury bonds, gold, OEX and DJA. Provides advance notice of market reversals which are precise, accurate and consistent.

AUDIENCE: Individual, Professional   RISK LEVEL: Moderate, Aggressive
TOPICS: Bonds, Stocks, Options, Futures/Commodities

Fractal Behavior of Markets, The

LJH Investments
18484 Preston Road
Suite 102 LB-160
Dallas, TX 75252-5474

PH: (900) 226-1618
(214) 985-7571
Cost: $2.25 per minute
Frequency: Daily

Telephone newsletter covering stocks, Treasury bonds, gold and market timing. Market timing to give advance warning of market reversals.

AUDIENCE: Beginning, Individual, Professional RISK LEVEL: Moderate, Aggressive
TOPICS: Bonds, Stocks, Options, Futures/Commodities

Franklin's Insight

Franklin Research & Development
711 Atlantic Avenue
Boston, MA 02111

PH: (617) 423-6655
Cost: $195.00 annually
Frequency: Monthly
Date of first issue: 1983

Fundamental analysis. Covers stocks. Investment newsletter specializing in socially responsible investing. Model portfolio and recommended list. Monthly letter "Investing for a Better World" for the socially responsible investor, gives recommendations/commentary. "Equity Briefs" - profiles of the social and financial performance of selected companies.

AUDIENCE: Beginning, Individual, Professional RISK LEVEL: Moderate, Aggressive
TOPICS: Mutual Funds, Stocks

Fraser Opinion Letter, The

Fraser Management Associates, Inc.
309 S. Willard Street
Burlington, VT 05402

PH: (802) 658-0322
FAX: (802) 658-0260
Cost: $70.00/yr
Date of first issue: 1975
Frequency: Biweekly
Fundamental Analysis

"Thoughtful contrary comments in a survey of current economic events and trends in business, finance and public thinking....a provoking letter with a human and essentially fundamental approach."

AUDIENCE: Beginning, Individual, Professional   RISK LEVEL: Conservative,
TOPICS: All   Moderate, Aggressive

Friedberg's Commodity & Currency Comments

Friedberg Commodity Management, Inc.
347 Bay Street, 2nd Floor
Toronto, ON, Canada M5H 2R7

PH: (416) 364-1171
(212) 943-5300
Cost: $295.00/yr
Date of first issue: 1971
Technical and Fundamental
   Analysis
ISSN: 0229 4559

Covers precious metals, sugar, cocoa, P & S, stock indices, futures, currencies and other commodities. Provides news of interest and specific buy/sell/hold recommendations. Includes hotline service.

AUDIENCE: Individual, Professional   RISK LEVEL: Aggressive
TOPICS: Futures/Commodities

FSA Market Outlook

G. Jules Csaszi
FSA, Inc.
P.O. Box 6547
Lake Worth, FL 33466

Cost: $195.00/yr
Frequency: 48 times a year
Date of first issue: 1980

Includes technical analysis. Covers commodities, charts. Advisory service features cycles, sesonals, supports and resistances, specific signals and profitable trades. With the exclusive JC System 34, Market Outlook is #1 in profits. Available: JC System 34 Manual for $245, Trading Tips for $55. Weekly FAX.

AUDIENCE: Individual, Professional   **RISK LEVEL: Aggressive**
TOPICS: Futures/Commodities

Fund Exchange, The

Paul A. Merriman and Associates, Inc.
1200 Westlake Avenue N.
Suite 700
Seattle, WA 98109-3530

PH: (800) 423-4893
FAX: (206) 286-2079
Cost: $125.00 annually
Frequency: Monthly

Includes fundamental analysis. Covers mutual funds and market timing. Offers for the do-it-yourself investor timing signals for equity, bond, gold, and international mutual funds. Includes 10 model portfolios, feature articles on investing in no-load funds and tips for the market timing investor.

AUDIENCE: Beginning, Individual   **RISK LEVEL: Moderate, Aggressive**
TOPICS: Mutual Funds

Fund Performance Chartbook

Wellington Financial Corporation
Bert Dohmen
6600 Kalanianole Highway, Suite 114C
Honolulu, HI 96825-1299

PH: (800) 992-9989
FAX: (808) 396-8640
Cost: $25.00 per issue
Frequency: Quarterly
Date of first issue: 1991

Covers mutual funds. Over 100 charts showing relative performance versus S&P 500. The charts cover the last $5^1/_2$ years.

AUDIENCE: Beginning, Individual   **RISK LEVEL: Moderate, Aggressive**
TOPICS: Mutual Funds, Stocks

Fund Watch

The Institute for Economic Research
3471 N. Federal Hwy.
Ft. Lauderdale, FL 33306

PH: (800) 442-9000
Cost: $80.00
Frequency: Monthly
Date of first issue: 1991

"The Official Guide to High Performance Mutual Funds." Every issue of Fund Watch features charts of specially-selected top-performing mutual funds, the ones with the highest profit potential.

AUDIENCE: Beginning, Individual   **RISK LEVEL: Moderate, Aggressive**
TOPICS: Mutual Funds

Fundline

David H. Menashe & Company
P.O. Box 663
Woodland Hills, CA 91365

PH: (818) 346-5637
Cost: $127.00/yr - includes
  telephone hotline
Frequency: Monthly

Includes technical analysis. Covers mutual funds and market timing. Specializes exclusively in the Fidelity Selects funds, including the gold and international funds. Uses a 2-fold system based on theory exclusive "39-week Momentum" formula and proprietary "Trading Oscillator and Long Term Indicator." Includes investment strategies.

AUDIENCE: Beginning, Individual   RISK LEVEL: Aggressive
TOPICS: Mutual Funds

Future Link

Oster Communications
219 Parkade
Cedar Falls, IA 50613-2735

PH: (800) 553-2910
Cost: $99.00/month+satellite
  equipment
Editor: Jim Wyckoff

Quotes and news wire on futures and options chart with 12 years historical data.

AUDIENCE: Individual, Professional   RISK LEVEL: Aggressive
TOPICS: Options, Futures

Futures and Options Factors: The Futures Portfolio Advisor

Published and Edited by Russell
  Wasendorf
802 Main Street
P.O. Box 849
Cedar Falls, IA 50613

PH: (319) 268-0441
Cost: $228.00 per year
Frequency: Weekly
Date of first issue: 1980

Includes fundamental and technical analysis. Covers futures and options on futures. "Analyzes actively traded commodity futures markets in the U.S. based on commodity index analysis in various market groupings, including grains, meats, metals, food/fiber, and financial/currencies." Contains graphs and charts.

AUDIENCE: Individual, Professional   RISK LEVEL: Aggressive
TOPICS: Options, Futures/Commodities

Futures and Options News, The

Montreal Exchange
800 Sq. Victoria, P.O. Box 61
Montreal, PQ, Canada H4Z 1A9

PH: (514) 871-2424
FAX: (514) 871-3559
Frequency: Quarterly
Cost: Free (also available in French)
Date of first issue: April, 1985
Technical and Fundamental Analysis

Derivatives product developments at the Montreal Exchange. Contains an options and futures strategy section and statistical trading summary for all option and futures contracts, including stock, bond, ten-year Canadian Government bond futures, and Canadian Bankers' Acceptance Futures and Options on the ten-year Government of Canada Bond Futures.

AUDIENCE: Individual, Professional   RISK LEVEL: Aggressive
TOPICS: Stocks, Options, Futures/Commodities

Futures Charts

Nick Van Nice
Commodity Trend Service
P.O. Box 32309
Palm Beach Gardens, FL 33410

PH: (800) 331-1069
FAX: (407) 622-7623
Cost: $450.00 annually, $145.00
  quarterly, $250.00 six months
$275.00 1/yr bimonthly, $180.00
  1/yr monthly
Frequency: Weekly
Date of first issue: 1973

Chart service. Includes technical analysis. Covering commodities, financial and agricultural markets. The industry's most comprehensive charts. In addition to covering all key markets, futures charts also provides: daily bar charts with this Friday's close; stochastics on daily, weekly, and monthly charts; stochastics and RSI plotted on every market.

AUDIENCE: Individual, Professional   **RISK LEVEL: Aggressive**
TOPICS: Bonds, Stocks, Options, Futures/Commodities

FX Week

Waters Information Services, Inc.
P.O. Box 2248
Binghamton, NY 13902-2248

PH: (800) 947-7947
FAX: (212) 925-7585
Frequency: Weekly
Cost: $1,295.00/yr.
Date of first issue: May 1990
Fundamental Analysis

Covers trends in foreign exchange market and internal information on individual companies including strategies, products and personnel movement.

AUDIENCE: Individual, Professional   **RISK LEVEL: Conservative, Moderate, Aggressive**
TOPICS: Bonds, Stocks, Options, Futures/Commodities

Garside Forecast, The

Garside and Co.
5200 Irvine Blvd., #370
Irvine, CA 92720

PH: (714) 259-1670
Cost: $125.00 annually
Frequency: Twice a month
Date of first issue: March 1971

Provides technical analysis. Covers stocks and market timing. Market commentary and outlook. Indicator summaries and buy and short recommendations.

AUDIENCE: Beginning, Individual   **RISK LEVEL: Moderate, Aggressive**
TOPICS: Stocks

Global Business Conditions

Published and Edited by Russell
  Wasendorf
802 Main Street
P.O. Box 849
Cedar Falls, IA 50613

PH: (319) 268-0441
Cost: $95.00/yr
Published monthly
Date of first issue: 1994

Includes charts and analysis of world economics. Covers up to 200 charts plus economic information. Provides economic information for individual countries. Includes Gross Domestic Product, currency, and stock market information for numerous countries, plus more detailed U.S. economic information.

AUDIENCE: Beginning, Individual, Professional   **RISK LEVEL: Conservative,**
TOPICS: All   **Moderate, Aggressive**

Global Market Perspective

Elliott Wave International
P.O. Box 1618
Gainesville, GA 30503

PH: (800) 472-9283
(404) 534-6680
Cost: $599.00/yr
Frequency: Monthly
Date of first issue: 1/91

Includes technical analysis. Covers stocks, bonds, currencies, commodities, charts. Each issue gives you over 100 pages (with more than 50 charts) covering: more than 20 world equity markets, over a dozen global fixed-income markets, international currency and cross rate relationships, precious metals, crude oil, social and economic trends.

AUDIENCE: Individual, Professional   RISK LEVEL: Conservative, Moderate, Aggressive
TOPICS: Bonds, Stocks, Options, Futures/Commodities

Global Market Strategist 900 Update, The

Supercycle Research, Inc.
P.O. Box 5309-H
Gainesville, GA 30504

PH: (900) USA-2200
(303) 440-3344 if 900 number is
  blocked.
Cost: per minute $2.00
24 Hour service
Frequency: Daily, 10am & 2pm

Covers stocks, commodities, municipal, corporate, government bonds, and currencies. "The ultimate intraday telephone hotline!"

AUDIENCE: Beginning, Individual, Professional   RISK LEVEL: Conservative,
TOPICS: Bonds, Stocks, Futures/Commodities   Moderate, Aggressive

Global Market Strategist, The

Dan Ascani
Supercycle Research, Inc.
P.O. Box 5309 H
Gainesville, GA 30504

PH: (800) 633-1332
(404) 967-1332
Cost: $297.00/yr
Frequency: Monthly
Date of first issue: 1991

Includes technical analysis and chart services. Covers stocks, commodities, market timing, world stock markets, interest rates, currencies and commodities. Get Mr. Ascani's eye-opening technical and Elliott Wave analysis. COMMENTS: Mr. Ascani built the Elliott Wave Currency and Commodity Forecast into one of the most highly regarded market letters.

AUDIENCE: Individual, Professional   RISK LEVEL: Moderate, Aggressive
TOPICS: Bonds, Stocks, Futures/Commodities

Global Money Management

Institutional Investor, Inc.
488 Madison Ave.
New York, NY 10022-5751

PH: (212) 303-3233
(212) 303-3300
FAX: (212) 421-7038
Frequency: Biweekly
Cost: $1,295.00/yr
Date of first issue: 1990
Editor: Tom Lamont

Features up-to-the-minute news affecting international fund management. This service is based in London and geared towards investment professionals.

AUDIENCE: Professional   RISK LEVEL: Conservative, Moderate, Aggressive
TOPICS: Bonds, Stocks, Options, Futures/Commodities

Global Research

Nelson Publications
1 Gateway Plaza
Port Chester, NY 10573

PH: (800) 333-6357
FAX: (914) 937-8908
Cost: $95.00 annually
Frequency: 10 issues per year
Date of first issue: 1985

Fundamental analysis. Global Research provides investment and financial professionals with a complete catalog of research reports - over 50,000 reports a year. Sections: 1 - Research reports by company -U.S.; 2 - Research reports by company - International; 3 - Research reports by originating firm; 4 - Industry reports.

AUDIENCE: Individual, Professional	RISK LEVEL: Moderate, Aggressive
TOPICS: Stocks	

Goerlich/van Brunt Newsletter

Mr. Goerlich and Bob van Brunt
604 S. Washington Square
Suite 2715
Philadelphia, PA 19106

PH: (215) 923-8870
Cost: $160.00 annually
Frequency: Bimonthly
Date of first issue: 1989

Technical analysis. Covers stocks and market timing. Stock market updates, twice a month bullish list of 50–75 stocks, bearish also.

AUDIENCE: Beginning, Individual	RISK LEVEL: Moderate, Aggressive
TOPICS: Stocks	

Going Public: The IPO Reporter

Investment Dealer's Digest, Inc.
2 World Trade Center, 18th Floor
New York, NY 10048

PH: (212) 227-1200
FAX: (212) 432-1039
Cost: $1,195.00/yr
Date of first issue: Published for
 10+ years
Technical and Fundamental
 Analysis

Editor: Tom Pratt. Publishes information, primarily fundamental information, on initial public offerings pertaining to investments such as securities, municipal funds, restaurants and pharmaceuticals. Accepts display advertising. Includes charts.

AUDIENCE: Individual, Professional	RISK LEVEL: Moderate, Aggressive
TOPICS: Bonds, Stocks	

Gold Mining Stock Report

Target, Inc.
Box 1217
Lafayette, CA 94549-1217

PH: (510) 283-4848
Cost: $119.00/yr
Frequency: Monthly
Date of first issue: 10/83

Fundamental analysis. "Offers analysis and specific recommendations for investors interested in penny mining stocks, particularly shares traded in Spokane and Vancouver."

AUDIENCE: Beginning, Individual	RISK LEVEL: Moderate, Aggressive
TOPICS: Stocks	

Gold News

Gold Institute
1112 16th St., N.W., Suite 240
Washington, DC 20036

PH: (202) 835-0185
Cost: $25.00
Frequency: Bimonthly
Technical and Fundamental Analysis
Date of first issue: 1976

Covers the gold markets and reports on current trends. Also reports on research items and includes gold prices chart for the year.

AUDIENCE: Beginning, Individual   RISK LEVEL: Moderate, Aggressive
TOPICS: Futures/Commodities

Gold Newsletter

James U. Blanchard, III
Jefferson Financial, Inc.
400 Jefferson Highway, Suite 600
Jefferson, LA 70121

PH: (504) 837-3033
(800) 877-8847
Cost: $95.00 annually
Frequency: Monthly
Date of first issue: 1970

Economic commentary on news affecting gold.

AUDIENCE: Beginning, Individual, Professional   RISK LEVEL: Moderate, Aggressive
TOPICS: Futures/Commodities

Gold Stocks Advisory

Paul Sarnoff
Box 1437
Burnsville, MN 55337

Cost: $96.00/yr
Frequency: Monthly
Date of first issue: 1988

Fundamental analysis. Commentary on news affecting gold shares. The editor, Paul Sarnoff, has two goals: in bad markets his goal is to help subscribers preserve their capital; in the good markets to help subscribers be among the beneficiaries. Bonus offer with subscription.

AUDIENCE: Beginning, Individual, Professional   RISK LEVEL: Moderate, Aggressive
TOPICS: Futures/Commodities

Good Money

Ritchie P. Lowry
Good Money Publications
P.O. Box 363
Worcester, VT 05682

PH: (800) 535-3551
FAX: (802) 223-8949
Cost: $75.00 annually
Frequency: Bimonthly
Date of first issue: 1982

Fundamental analysis. Covering stocks, bonds, and mutual funds. The first issue for socially concerned investors. Profiles 13 major socially screened funds, 9 environmental sector funds, 9 funds with limited social screens and includes social funds for institutional investors. Includes performance comparisons, social analysis of fund investment.

AUDIENCE: Beginning, Individual, Professional   RISK LEVEL: Moderate, Aggressive
TOPICS: Bonds, Mutual Funds, Stocks, Investment Planning

Grant's Interest Rate Observer

Patricia Kavanagh
233 Broadway
New York, NY 10279

PH: (212) 608-7994
FAX: (212) 608-5925
Cost: $450.00/yr
Frequency: Every other Friday
Date of first issue: 11/83

Includes fundamental analysis. Covers stocks, bonds, securities. Grant's emphasizes the fundamentals of interest rate movement and the credit markets but includes an extraordinary range of subjects.

AUDIENCE: Individual, Professional   RISK LEVEL: Conservative, Moderate, Aggressive
TOPICS: Bonds, Mutual Funds, Stocks

Granville Market Letter, The

Joseph E. Granville
P.O. Box 413006
Kansas City, MO 64141

PH: (816) 474-5353
(800) 876-LETTER
Cost: $800.00 year for 46 issues
  faxed Thursday morning

Fax service covering stocks and market timing, technical analysis. Market commentary and analysis, review of indicators and 3 extensive model portfolios - common stocks, options and low-priced stock for speculators. Comments: Mr. Granville is available for telephone consultation for $900 per half hour with a minimum of one-half hour.

AUDIENCE: Beginning, Individual   RISK LEVEL: Moderate, Aggressive
TOPICS: Stocks, Options

Granville Market Letters, The

Joseph E. Granville
P.O. Drawer 413006
Kansas City, MO 64141

PH: (816) 474-5353
(800) 876-LETTER
Cost: $250.00 annually
Frequency: 46 issues annually
Date of first issue: 1963

Includes technical analysis. Covers stocks and market timing. Includes market commentary and analysis, review of indicators, and 3 extensive model portfolios one for common stocks and one for options and one for low priced stocks. Mr. Granville is available for telephone consultations for $900 per half hour ($1/2$ hour minimum)

AUDIENCE: Beginning, Individual   RISK LEVEL: Moderate, Aggressive
TOPICS: Stocks, Options

Graphic Fund Forecaster

Fred Hohn
P.O. Box 673
Andover, MA 01810

PH: (508) 470-3511
Cost: $145.00 annually
$30.00 for two-month trial with
  reports
Frequency: 26 issues every other
  week
Date of first issue: 1984
To Order: 1-800-532-2322

Fidelity and Invesco mutual funds newsletter provides charts with which you can track funds. Graphic Fund Forecaster attempts to forecast the market and provide technical analysis of mutual funds. There are approximately 54 charts and a small section which ranks the funds and highlights the best.

AUDIENCE: Beginning, Individual   RISK LEVEL: Moderate, Aggressive
TOPICS: Mutual Funds, Investment Planning

Growth Fund Guide

Growth Fund Research, Inc.
Box 6600
Rapid City, SD 57709

PH: (800) 621-8322
(605) 341-1971
Cost: $89.00
Frequency: Monthly
Date of first issue: 1968

Includes fundamental and technical analysis. "The nation's oldest and most sophisticated no-load fund publication." Several model portfolios and market information included.

AUDIENCE: Beginning, Individual	RISK LEVEL: Moderate, Aggressive
TOPICS: Mutual Funds	

Growth Stock Outlook

Charles Allmon
Growth Stock Outlook, Inc.
P.O. Box 15381
Chevy Chase, MD 20825

PH: (301) 654-5205
Cost: $195.00 annually
Frequency: Twice a month
Date of first issue: 1964

Includes fundamental analysis. Covers stocks. Designed for brokers, institutions, sophisticated private investors who recognize the risks and possible rewards of investing in vigorously growing companies. Includes model portfolio, insider trading information, charts and periodic new company recommendations mailed at anytime. Extensive stock selection.

AUDIENCE: Professional	RISK LEVEL: Moderate
TOPICS: Stocks, Asset Allocation	

Guarantor, The

American Banker - Bond Buyer
1 State St. Plaza
New York, NY 10004

PH: (212) 943-8341
(800) 407-8241
Cost: $995.00
Fundamental Analysis
Frequency: Weekly

Covers the corporate bond, public municipal, private placement and Eurobond markets and reports on legislation and regulation, activities and news in these markets.

AUDIENCE: Individual, Professional	RISK LEVEL: Conservative
TOPICS: Bonds	

Guardian Research Report

Guardian Financial Corporation
2207 Third Street
Livermore, CA 94550

PH: (510) 443-7010
Cost: $180.00
Frequency: Monthly
Date of first issue: 1985

Includes fundamental analysis. Covers stocks. Market perspective and commentary with recommendations and 2 model portfolios (speculative and conservative).

AUDIENCE: Beginning, Individual	RISK LEVEL: Moderate, Aggressive
TOPICS: Stocks	

Guru Revue

Jeff Bower
1740 44th Street SW
Suite 209
Wyoming, MI 49509

Technical analysis. Covers stocks, mutual funds, market timing. Offers Financial News Network commentator Jeff Bower's market and mutual fund timing as well as stock recommendations, "Sentiment Survey" and more.

Cost: $233.00
Frequency: 17 issues per year

AUDIENCE: Beginning, Individual   RISK LEVEL: Moderate, Aggressive
TOPICS: Mutual Funds, Stocks

Halco Trading Strategies

Halco Trading Strategies
P.O. Box 795429
Dallas, TX 75379

PH: (214) 385-2570
Cost: $495.00 annually
Frequency: Monthly
Date of first issue: 1974

Chart service includes technical analysis and chart service with every issue. Covers commodities. Leaders in cyclic and technical analysis of the financial and agricultural markets since 1974. Each issue contains specific recommendation with bull and bear scenarios and trading strategies. Monthly, weekly and daily charts covering 21 markets.

AUDIENCE: Individual, Professional   RISK LEVEL: Aggressive
TOPICS: Futures/Commodities

Harmonic Research

Gregory Beret
Harmonic Research, Inc.
650 Fifth Avenue
New York, NY 10019

PH: (212) 484-2065
Cost: $360.00 annually
or $960.00 including weekly
FAX service with specific
   recommendations
Frequency: Monthly
Date of first issue: 1984

Technical analysis. Covers small companies, high growth stocks and S&P, T-bond and Gold Futures. Ten page letter covering futures and stock markets from a unique cycle and Gann perspectives.

AUDIENCE: Individual, Professional   RISK LEVEL: Moderate, Aggressive
TOPICS: Stocks, Options, Futures/Commodities

Harry Browne's Special Reports

Harry Browne
P.O. Box 5586
Austin, TX 78763

PH: (512) 453-7313
(800) 531-5142
Cost: $225.00 for 10 issues
Frequency: Approx 8-10 issues a
   year
Date of first issue: 1974

Fundamental and technical analysis, including log charts of all major investment categories. Covers stocks; commodities; municipal, corporate, and government bonds; market timing. The "Fundamental" portfolio is the safe, conservative recommendations. The "Variable" portfolio consists of speculative recommendations.

AUDIENCE: Beginning, Individual   RISK LEVEL: Conservative, Moderate, Aggressive
TOPICS: Bonds, Mutual Funds, Stocks, Options, Futures/Commodities

Heim Investment Letter

Lawrence H. Heim
Heim Investment Services, Inc.
P.O. Box 19435
Portland, OR 97219

PH: (503) 228-9553
(503) 624-4816
(503) 244-2223
Cost: $150.00/yr
Frequency: Every 2 weeks

Fundamental and technical analysis. Covers stocks, currencies, gold and silver. The letter is a comprehensive investment service for the professional and private investor. Includes technical and fundamental studies on national and international developments affecting stocks, bonds, gold, silver and coins.

AUDIENCE: Individual, Professional   RISK LEVEL: Moderate, Aggressive
TOPICS: Stocks, Options, Futures/Commodities

Herzfeld Guide to Closed End Funds

Thomas J. Herzfeld Advisors, Inc.
The Herzfeld Bldg.
Box 161465
Miami, FL 33116

PH: (305) 271-1900
Cost: $25.85
Editor: Thomas J. Herzfeld
Frequency: Annual

Closed-end funds: What they are, how they work, and trading strategies. Statistical information on over 400 closed end funds.

AUDIENCE: Beginning, Individual, Professional   RISK LEVEL: Moderate, Aggressive
TOPICS: Mutual Funds, Stocks

Hot Wire

Hot Wire
PH: (900) 468-9473 (hotline)
Cost: $2 first minute + $1 each
additional minute

Telephone newsletter covering buyouts, buybacks, recommendations and rumors. The hottest news on companies experiencing unusual trading, from the Dow Jones Professional Investor.

AUDIENCE: Individual, Professional   RISK LEVEL: Moderate, Aggressive
TOPICS: Stocks, Options

Hotline

TLM, Inc.
420 Westchester Avenue
Port Chester, NY 10573

PH: (800) 451-1392
Cost: $69.00 annually
Updated daily after 6PM EST

Fax service covering index futures and options. TLM's proprietary trading model uses the high, low, and close of the index daily and generates two to four trading signals per month for options and two signals per month for futures trading. The simple manual explains how to make your trade and manage it with stops.

AUDIENCE: Individual, Professional   RISK LEVEL: Aggressive
TOPICS: Options, Futures/Commodities

Hulbert Financial Digest

Mark Hulbert
316 Commerce Street
Alexandria, VA 22314

PH: (703) 683-5905
Cost: $135.00 annually
5 month trial: $37.50
Frequency: Monthly
Date of first issue: 6/80

Tracks the performance of 145 financial newsletters. Gives a percentage rating on each based on following their recommendations. In January and July issues, he rates the performance of each newsletter going back to 1980.

AUDIENCE: Individual, Professional	RISK LEVEL: Conservative, Moderate,
TOPICS: All	Aggressive

Hume MoneyLetter, The

Hume Publishing, Inc.
835 Franklin Ct.
Marietta, GA 30067

PH: (800) 222-4863
(404) 426-1920
Cost: $95.00 annually
Frequency: Monthly
Date of first issue: 1976

Fundamental analysis. Covers securities. The Hume MoneyLetter features several authors who write articles and give recommendations on various investments. Each letter ends with an investment update on previously recommended investments.

AUDIENCE: Beginning, Individual, Professional	RISK LEVEL: Conservative,
TOPICS: All	Moderate, Aggressive

Hummer Market Letter, The

Wayne Hummer & Company
175 West Jackson Blvd.
Chicago, IL 60690

PH: (312) 431-1700
(800) 621-4477
FAX: (312) 431-0704
Cost: Free
Frequency: Monthly
Date of first issue: Jan. 1932

Fundamental analysis. Covers stocks and bonds. Written by experienced professionals of Wayne Hummer & Co., gives timely investment advice and comments on the stock and bond markets. Gives several recommendations per issue.

AUDIENCE: Beginning, Individual, Professional	RISK LEVEL: Conservative,
	Moderate, Aggressive
TOPICS: Bonds, Mutual Funds, Stocks, Asset Allocation, Investment Planning, General Reference	

IBC's Money Market Insight

The Donoghue Organization, Inc.
290 Eliot Street
P.O. Box 9104
Holliston, MA 01721-9104

PH: (800) 343-5413
FAX: (508) 429-2452
Cost: $445.00 annually
Frequency: Monthly
Date of first issue: 1983

Fundamental analysis. Covers money markets. This publication will provide: insight into the money market industry today; expert analysis and commentary on important issues affecting the $2-trillion money market industry; trends in short-term investing, interest rates and yields; developments in the international arena.

AUDIENCE: Beginning, Individual, Professional	RISK LEVEL: Conservative
TOPICS: Bonds, Mutual Fund	

IBC'S Quarterly Report on Money Fund Performance

Donoghue Organization
IBC USA, Inc.
290 Eliot Street
Ashland, MA 01721

PH: (508) 881-2800
FAX: (508) 429-1835
Cost: $425.00 to $825.00/yr
Published: Quarterly
Date of first issue: 1988
Fundamental Analysis

For the institutional investor. Provides commentary on current trends and important fundamental data on over 800 money funds, including quarterly yields and expense ratios.

AUDIENCE: Professional	RISK LEVEL: Conservative
TOPICS: Bonds	

In-Touch

In-Touch
PH: (900) 468-6824 (hotline)
Cost: per minute $2.99
24 hour service
Frequency of update: Daily

Covers stocks. Predicts short-term stock market direction, tops & bottoms.

AUDIENCE: Beginning, Individual	RISK LEVEL: Moderate, Aggressive
TOPICS: Stocks, Options	

Income Fund Outlook - The Consumer's Guide to High Yields

The Institute for Econometric
  Research
3471 N. Federal Highway
Ft. Lauderdale, FL. 33306

PH: (800) 442-9000
Cost: $49.00 annually
Frequency: Monthly
Date of first issue: 1981
ISSN: 0891-1215

Fundamental and technical analysis. Covers mutual funds, government securities, and charts. Every issue contains "Best Buys" Income Investment Directory, interest rate forecasts, recommendations on new funds, "avoid" warnings, tax strategies and continuous follow-ups on all income investments. Income and Safety is devoted to income investments.

AUDIENCE: Beginning, Individual, Professional	RISK LEVEL: Conservative, Moderate
TOPICS: Bonds, Mutual Funds	

Income Stocks

Elton Stephens
4016 S. Michigan St.
South Bend, IN 46614-3823

PH: (800) 553-5866
FAX: (219) 291-3823
Frequency: Annual
Cost: $45.00/yr
Date of first issue: 1972
ISSN: 0892 6018

Recommends income stocks that have good earnings and dividends.

AUDIENCE: Beginning, Individual	RISK LEVEL: Conservative
TOPICS: Stocks	

Individual Investor Special Situations Report

Financial Data Systems, Inc.
38 E. 29th Street, 4th Floor
New York, NY 10016

PH: (800) 995-1695
OTHER: (212) 689-2777
FAX: (212) 689-3296
Cost: $165 annually
Frequency: Monthly
Date of first issue: 12/15/89

Fundamental analysis. Monthly in-depth confidential report on the single most promising stock Individual Investor sees in the market. Their unqualified #1 buy recommendation, updates on already featured stocks included each month. One in five stocks featured has increased over 100%.

AUDIENCE: Beginning, Individual   RISK LEVEL: Aggressive
TOPICS: Stocks

IndustriScope

Media General Financial Services
P.O. Box 85333
Richmond, VA 23293

PH: (804) 649-6587
(800) 446-7922
FAX: (804) 649-6097
Frequency: Monthly
Cost: $324.00/yr

Provides "precision financial data on 7,000 companies by industry group. Company-to-company, company-to-industry, and industry-to-industry comparisons are easily made."

AUDIENCE: Individual, Professional   RISK LEVEL: Moderate, Aggressive
TOPICS: Bonds, Stocks

Industry Forecast

The Jerome Levy Economics
  Institute
P.O. Box 26
Chappaqua, NY 10514

PH: (914) 238-3665
Cost: $295.00 annually worldwide
Frequency: Monthly and quarterly
Date of first issue: 1949

Descriptions, analysis, and forecasts on the economy. Also includes four quarterly reports relating economic conditions to the financial markets.

AUDIENCE: Beginning, Individual, Professional   RISK LEVEL: Conservative,
TOPICS: General Reference   Moderate, Aggressive

Inger Letter, The

Gene Inger
100 E. Thousand Oaks Blvd.
Suite 227
Thousand Oaks, CA 91360

PH: (900) 933-GENE
(800) 966-9965
Cost: $2.00 for the first minute, $.95
  thereafter
24 Hour service
Frequency of update: hourly

Telephone newsletter covering stocks and market timing. Includes specific S&P, stock and option targets, gold, oil and bond calls.

AUDIENCE: Individual, Professional   RISK LEVEL: Aggressive
TOPICS: Stocks, Options, Futures/Commodities

Insider Alert

Soundview Publications
1350 Center Drive, #100
Dunwoody, GA 30338

PH: (404) 668-0432
(800) 728-2288
FAX: (404) 668-0692
Frequency: Monthly
Cost: $87.00/yr
Date of first issue: 1993

An investment newsletter focusing on how political events affect the markets.

AUDIENCE: Beginning, Individual, Professional   RISK LEVEL: Moderate, Aggressive
TOPICS: Stocks

Insider Report

Larry Abraham
P.O. Box 84903
Phoenix, AZ 85071

PH: (602) 252-4477
(800) 528-0559
Cost: $124.00/yr special rate
$199.00 per year regular rate
Frequency: Monthly
Date of first issue: 5/83

Fundamental analysis. Covers stocks. Every issue is based on an understanding of who the key Insiders are and what they are doing now. Each investment recommendation is based on the same question -What are the Insiders up to?

AUDIENCE: Individual, Professional   RISK LEVEL: Moderate, Aggressive
TOPICS: Stocks

Insiders Option Report

Vickers Stock Research Corp.
226 New York Ave.
Huntington, NY 11743

PH: (516) 423-7710
Cost: $85.00/yr
Frequency: Weekly

Reports on corporate officer's exercising of options. Gives the individual's name and title, price per share, number of shares, and shares outstanding.

AUDIENCE: Individual, Professional   RISK LEVEL: Moderate, Aggressive
TOPICS: Stocks

Insiders, The

The Institute for Econometric
  Research
3471 N. Federal Highway
Ft. Lauderdale, Fl. 33306

PH: (305) 563-9000
(800) 442-9000
Cost: $49.00 annually
Frequency: Twice a month
Date of first issue: 1980
ISSN: 0730-2908

Technical analysis. Designed to be a complete stock selection and investment program. Contains insider ratings on thousands of stocks, specific buy and sell recommendations, market timing, advice, the "Nifty Fifty" list of industry rankings and recommendation follow-ups. Includes weekly telephone and FAX hotline free.

AUDIENCE: Beginning, Individual, Professional   RISK LEVEL: Moderate, Aggressive
TOPICS: Stocks

Insightful Investor

Agora, Inc.
824 E. Baltimore Street
Baltimore, MD 21202-4799

PH: (401) 234-0515
(800) 433-1528
FAX: (410) 837-3879
Frequency: Monthly
Cost: $59.00/yr
Editor: Dan Levine

Provides knowledge of investments and what they are doing. Covers fundamental and technical analysis of stocks and bonds.

AUDIENCE: Beginning, Individual   RISK LEVEL: Moderate, Aggressive
TOPICS: Bonds, Stocks

Institutional Portfolio Guide

Vickers Stock Research Corp.
226 New York Ave.
Huntington, NY 11743

PH: (516) 423-7710
Cost: $695.00
Frequency: Quarterly
Editor: Jim Van Dyke

Lists stock positions held in the portfolios of major U.S. and Canadian investment management companies. Listed in alphabetical order.

AUDIENCE: Individual, Professional   RISK LEVEL: Moderate, Aggressive
TOPICS: Mutual Funds, Stocks

Intelligence Report

Phillips Business Information, Inc.
1201 Seven Locks Road
Potomac, MD 20854-3394

PH: (800) 677-5005
FAX: (301) 309-3847
Frequency: Monthly
Cost: $99.95/yr
Date of first issue: 1986
Editor: Richard Young

Tips on how to invest your money wisely. Also provides recommendations and model portfolios.

AUDIENCE: Beginning, Individual   RISK LEVEL: Moderate, Aggressive
TOPICS: Mutual Funds, Stocks

Interactive Multimedia Investor

Paul Kagan Associates, Inc.
126 Clock Tower Place
Carmel, CA 93923-8734

PH: (408) 624-1536
FAX: (408) 625-3225
Cost: $595.00/yr
Frequency: Twice monthly

"Follows the public stocks and private deals that will shape the media future. Analyzes publicly held interactive multimedia companies, tracks key industry subgroups through Kagan stock averages that relate to companies by product lines, project growth of new TV and data networks, programming and technology, economic modeling of new corporate ventures.

AUDIENCE: Individual, Professional   RISK LEVEL: Moderate, Aggressive
TOPICS: Stocks

Interinvest Review and Outlook

Interinvest Corporation
294 Washington Street
Suite 754
Boston, MA 02108

PH: (617) 423-1166
Cost: $125.00/yr
Frequency: Monthly
Date of first issue: 1/77

Fundamental analysis. "Provides a review of domestic and international markets. Includes information on the U.S. stock market and currency exchange rates. Comments on relevant geopolitical issues. Issues a portfolio review."

AUDIENCE: Individual, Professional   RISK LEVEL: Moderate, Aggressive
TOPICS: Stocks

International Financial Comment

Optima Investment Research, Inc.
327 S. LaSalle Street, Suite 1300
Chicago, IL 60604

PH: (312) 427-3616
Cost: $195.00 to $295.00 per month
Published daily via fax, computer
  dial-up, electronic mail, and over
  FutureSource and Track Data's
  MarkeTrack-MX systems

A fundamental analysis of the international financial markets plus a technical analysis of the T-Bonds, T-Notes, Eurodollars, Forex and Stock Indexes. Information is primarily for professional investors and no recommendations are provided.

AUDIENCE: Professional   RISK LEVEL: Aggressive
TOPICS: Bonds, Options, Futures/Commodities

InvesTech Market Analyst

James B. Stack
Investech
2472 Birch Glen
Whitefish, MT 59937

PH: (406) 862-7707
(406) 862-7777
Cost: $175.00 annually
Frequency: Every three weeks (18
  per year)
Date of first issue: 1981
ISSN: 0896-4157

Technical analysis. Covers stocks and market timing, bond market analysis. Technical and monetary investment analysis. Model portfolio and position review in each issue. Includes twice weekly hotline. Subscribe to Investech Mutual Fund Advisor also for only $235 for both letters.

AUDIENCE: Individual, Professional   RISK LEVEL: Conservative, Moderate, Aggressive
TOPICS: Bonds, Mutual Funds, Stocks

InvesTech Mutual Fund Advisor

James B. Stack
Investech
2472 Birch Glen
Whitefish, MT 59937

PH: (800) 955-8500
(406) 862-7777
Cost: $175.00 annually
Frequency: Every 3 weeks
Date of first issue: 1987
ISSN: 0896-4165

Technical analysis. Covers mutual funds and market timing. Model portfolio and recommendations based on an objective, technical approach. Also includes the Top Rated Funds from Lipper Analytical Services, Inc. Includes twice weekly hotline. Subscribe to Investech Market Analyst also for only $235 for both letters.

AUDIENCE: Beginning, Individual   RISK LEVEL: Moderate, Aggressive
TOPICS: Mutual Funds

Investment Counselors Incorporated

Mark J. Deschaine, President
1010 Market Street
Suite 1540
St. Louis, MO 63101

PH: (314) 421-3080
FAX: (314) 421-5287
Cost: Free
Frequency: Quarterly
Date of first issue: 1987

Technical analysis. Newsletter contains topics of interest to their firm, general market information, and a list of their current holdings, economic, political and financial issues.

AUDIENCE: Professional   RISK LEVEL: Conservative, Moderate
TOPICS: Bonds, Stocks, Asset Allocation, Investment Planning

Investment Guide

American Investment Services, Inc.
Division St.
Great Barrington, MA 01230

PH: (413) 528-1216
Cost: $49.00/yr
Frequency: Monthly
Date of first issue: 20 years

Stock market analysis and trading strategies.

AUDIENCE: Beginning, Individual   RISK LEVEL: Moderate, Aggressive
TOPICS: Stocks

Investment Horizons

Investment Information Services, Inc.
680 N. Lake Shore Dr.
Tower Offices, No. 2038
Chicago, IL 60611

PH: (312) 649-6940
Cost: $147.00/yr
Frequency: Semimonthly
Date of first issue: April 1983

Provides research and recommendations on small-cap companies.

AUDIENCE: Individual, Professional   RISK LEVEL: Moderate, Aggressive
TOPICS: Stocks

Investment Quality Trends

Geraldine Weiss
7440 Girard Avenue, #4
La Jolla, California, 92037

PH: (619) 459-3818
FAX: (619) 459-3819
Cost: $275.00
Frequency: Bimonthly
Date of first issue: 4/66

Technical and fundamental analysis. Covers stocks, market timing and charts. Follows 350 blue chips. Recommendations made in each issue as well as investment outlooks and editorial comments on market.

AUDIENCE: Individual, Professional   RISK LEVEL: Moderate, Aggressive
TOPICS: Stocks

Investment Reporter

Patrick McKeough
MPL Communications, Inc.
133 Richmond Street West, Suite 700
Toronto, ON, Canada M5H3M8

PH: (416) 869-1177
FAX: (416) 869-0456
Cost: $257.00 annually
Frequency: Weekly
Date of first issue: 1941

Fundamental analysis. Canadian stock market investment advisory newsletter. You will know "What to Buy," "When to Switch," "When to Sell" and get opinions and recommendations that are clear and specific. Hotline available for $75.00.

AUDIENCE: Individual, Professional   RISK LEVEL: Moderate, Aggressive
TOPICS: Stocks, Investment Planning

Investor Forecasts

Sy Harding
Asset Management Research Corp.
P.O. Box 352016
4440 N. Oceanshore Blvd.
Palm Coast, FL 32135

PH: (904) 446-0823
Cost: $195.00/yr
Frequency: every 3 weeks
Date of first issue: 1987

Technical analysis. Market timing, stocks, bonds, gold, mutual funds. Undervalued, relatively undiscovered stocks, then monitors them until they're ready to move. Each issue has specific recommendations, model portfolios and follow-ups Twice-weekly telephone hotline included.

AUDIENCE: Beginning, Individual   RISK LEVEL: Moderate, Aggressive
TOPICS: Bonds, Mutual Funds, Stocks, Futures/Commodities

Investor's Digest

Norman King Fosback - Editor
The Institute for Econometric
  Research
3471 N. Federal Highway
Ft. Lauderdale, FL. 33306

PH: (800) 442-9000
Cost: $29.00 annually
Frequency: Monthly
Date of first issue: May 1990

Fundamental and technical analysis. Every issue includes stock recommendations and market timing advice, mutual fund selections, stock of the month, market timers index, short sales, portfolio strategies and advisory sentiment index. Includes free daily hotline telephone and fax.

AUDIENCE: Beginning, Individual   RISK LEVEL: Moderate, Aggressive
TOPICS: Bonds, Mutual Funds, Stocks

Investor's Fax Weekly

Investor's Fax Weekly
12335 Santa Monica Blvd.
Suite 128
Los Angeles, CA 90025

PH: (900) 535-9800 ext 627
(213) 479-0645
FAX: (213) 394-0220
Cost: $150.00/yr
Frequency of update: Weekly

Telephone newsletter. Computer based analysis performs a weekly review of all NYSE, AMEX and OTC issues. Criteria used to select stocks include: current and annual earnings, new highs, shares outstanding, industry leaders, institutional sponsorship and market movement.

AUDIENCE: Individual, Professional   RISK LEVEL: Moderate, Aggressive
TOPICS: Stocks

Investor's Fax Weekly (Hotline)

Investor's Fax Weekly
12335 Santa Monica Blvd.
Suite 128
Los Angeles, CA 90025

PH: (213) 479-0645
Cost: $2.00 per minute
Frequency: Weekly
Date of first issue: 06/15/91

Technical and fundamental analysis. Each letter contains 6 - 10 recommended issues and gives a specific buypoint recommendation representing a chart breakout. Newsletter is faxed on Sunday for Monday's opening. Hotline available for $2 per minute - (900) 535-9800 extension 627.

AUDIENCE: Individual   RISK LEVEL: Moderate, Aggressive
TOPICS: Stocks

Investor's Intelligence

Michael L. Burke - Editor
Chartcraft, Inc.
30 Church Street, P.O. Box 2046
New Rochelle, NY 10801

PH: (914) 632-0422
FAX: (914) 632-0335
Cost: $184.00 annually
Frequency: Biweekly
Date of first issue: 35 years

Fundamental and technical analysis. General market newsletter by Contrarians. Have model portfolios on mutual funds and stocks. Also surveys other leading newsletters and analyzes their sentiments on the market. Includes toll-free hotline.

AUDIENCE: Beginning, Individual   RISK LEVEL: Moderate, Aggressive
TOPICS: Bonds, Mutual Funds, Stocks, Options

Investor's Intelligence

Investor's Intelligence
PH: (900) 990-0909 ext 31 (hotline)
Cost: $2.00 per minute
Frequency of update: daily at
  11:00 AM except Monday at 9:30
AM.

Portfolio changes on Monday and Wednesday. Mike Burke's mutual switch fund portfolio.

AUDIENCE: Beginning, Individual   RISK LEVEL: Moderate, Aggressive
TOPICS: Mutual Funds

Investor's Update

Investor's Update
525 W. Manchester Blvd.
Inglewood, CA 90301

PH: (213) 674-3330
Cost: $25.00
Frequency: Bimonthly

Fundamental analysis. "Provides investment information for rare coins and the precious metals market, as well as oil and commodity futures markets. Carries economic statistics and news of world events affecting investors. Reviews previous investment recommendations."

AUDIENCE: Individual, Professional   RISK LEVEL: Aggressive
TOPICS: Options, Futures/Commodities

Investors Hotline

Investors Hotline
PH: (900) 420-8606
Cost: $10 per call - about 30
    seconds
24 Hour service
Frequency: Daily

Buy and sell recommendations from Wall Street's most successful traders. Key call and put option recommendations. Gold and Oil strategy. Includes general information on market and current news and its affect on the market.

AUDIENCE: Individual, Professional   RISK LEVEL: Aggressive
TOPICS: Stocks, Options, Futures/Commodities

IRA-Stocks

Elton Stephens
4016 S. Michigan St.
South Bend, IN 46614-3823

PH: (219) 291-3823
(800) 553-5866
FAX: (219) 291-3823
Frequency: Annual
Cost: $45.00/yr
Date of first issue: February 1986

Recommends stocks that have good earnings and dividends which are suitable for IRA Investments.

AUDIENCE: Individual   RISK LEVEL: Moderate
TOPICS: Stocks

It's Your Money/The Jorgensen Report

Jorgensen & Associates, Inc.
810 Idyllberry Road
San Rafael, CA 94903

PH: (800) 359-6267
(415) 472-6265
Cost: $38.00 annually
Frequency: Monthly
Date of first issue: 1983

Fundamental Analysis. A 12 page letter on financial planning and money management. Covers stocks and bonds trends, tax-free and tax-deferred investments and mutual funds. Shows how to protect your credit, plan for college, what to avoid, etc.

AUDIENCE: Beginning, Individual   RISK LEVEL: Conservative, Moderate, Aggressive
TOPICS: Bonds, Mutual Funds, Stocks, Investment Planning

J & J's Hedged Option Trader

J & J Market Letters
1112 Bering Drive
Suite 65
Houston, TX 77057

PH: (800) 992-6123
Cost: $175.00 plus online charges
Frequency: Daily
Date of first issue: 2/90

Fundamental Analysis. Covers market timing, options. Focuses on short-term, speculative, aggressive capital growth through option trading. Delivered by computer only via IBM-PC or compatible with modem.

AUDIENCE: Individual, Professional   RISK LEVEL: Aggressive
TOPICS: Options

J & J's Undervalued Growth Stocks Letter

J & J Market Letters
1112 Bering Drive
Suite 65
Houston, TX 77057

PH: (800) 992-6123
Cost: $135.00 plus online charges
Frequency: Weekly
Date of first issue: 2/90

Fundamental analysis. Covers stocks, market timing. Seeks aggressive capital growth via growth stocks trading at a discount to their true value. Recommendations and portfolio and performance information. Delivered by computer only via IBM-PC or compatible with modem.

AUDIENCE: Individual   RISK LEVEL: Aggressive
TOPICS: Stocks

Jacobs Report on Asset Protection Strategies

Research Press, Inc.
4500 W. 72nd Terr.
P.O. Box 8137
Prairie Village, KS 66208-2824

PH: (913) 362-9667
FAX: (913) 383-3505
Frequency: Monthly
Cost: $145.00/yr
Date of first issue: 1989
Editor: Vernon Jacobs

Subtitled "Complex Financial Strategies in Plain English." The editor and assorted guest writers analyze and comment on the current strategies for retirement and estate planning and asset protection.

AUDIENCE: Beginning, Individual   RISK LEVEL: Conservative, Moderate, Aggressive
TOPICS: Bonds, Mutual Funds, Stocks, Asset Allocation, Investment Planning

Jag Notes

Jag Notes
125 Half Mile Road
Red Bank, NJ 07701

PH: (908) 747-6938
Cost: $1,850.00/yr or $500.00 per
  quarter
Frequency: Three times daily

Telephone newsletter covering stocks. Have all the latest market information and recommendations on your desk at 9:00 sharp (EST) each morning. Daily summary of over 25 brokerage firms and market timers early each morning. Comments and recommendations.

AUDIENCE: Individual, Professional   RISK LEVEL: Moderate, Aggressive
TOPICS: Bonds, Mutual Funds, Stocks, Options, Futures/Commodities

Japanese Candlestick Charts

Nick Van Nice, Editor
Commodity Trend Service
P.O. Box 32309
Palm Beach Gardens, FL 33420

PH: (800) 331-1069
FAX: (407) 622-7623
Cost: $450.00/yr
Frequency: Weekly
Date of first issue: 10/90

Chart service. Technical analysis. Covering commodity futures. Candlesticks can spot technical strengths and/or weaknesses by highlighting the relationship between the open and close. The candlestick method gives you deeper insight into market conditions by creating a visual aid for each trading period.

AUDIENCE: Individual, Professional   RISK LEVEL: Aggressive
TOPICS: Futures/Commodities

Jay Taylor's Gold and Gold Stocks

Taylor Hard Money Advisors, Inc.
P.O. Box 1065
Jackson Heights, NY 11372

PH: (718) 457-1426
Cost: $89.00 annually
Frequency: Monthly; includes
weekly hotline

Fundamental and technical analysis. Includes gold, stocks, and charts. North American Gold Mining Stocks newsletter covers Junior Gold Stocks, and special situation. Features include: Industry Review, Portfolio and Performance Summary and more.

AUDIENCE: Beginning, Individual   RISK LEVEL: Moderate, Aggressive
TOPICS: Stocks, Options, Futures/Commodities

John Bollinger's Capital Growth Letter

John Bollinger
P.O. Box 3358
Manhattan Beach, CA 90266

PH: (800) 888-8400
(310) 798-8855
Cost: $225.00
Frequency: Monthly

Technical and fundamental analysis. Covers stocks, bonds, gold, the dollar, international markets. Specific recommendations, current trends in gold, the dollar, oil and the foreign markets with charts and technical analysis to support the recommendations. Twice-weekly hotline and daily Bollinger Bands numbers.

AUDIENCE: Individual, Professional   RISK LEVEL: Moderate
TOPICS: Bonds, Stocks, Asset Allocation

John Pugsley's Journal

Marketing and Publishing Assoc.,
  Ltd.
2300 Route 208
Fair Lawn, NJ 07410

PH: (210) 794-1879
FAX: (201) 794-1221
Cost: $125.00/yr
Frequency: Monthly

"An analysis of how current economic and political events will affect people's perceptions and, thereby, investment values." Gives some recommendations and studies on different investments based on principles derived from a scientific analysis of human nature.

AUDIENCE: Beginning, Individual, Professional   RISK LEVEL: Conservative,
TOPICS: All   Moderate, Aggressive

Journal Phone

Dow Jones Information Services
Group
P.O. Box 300
Princeton, NJ 08543

PH: (900) JOURNAL
(800) 800-4WSJ
Cost: 95 cents per minute
24 Hour service
Frequency of update: Continual

Journal Phone offers 24-hour access via touch-tone phone to constantly updated business news, stock quotes, company news and sports. Payment on 1-800-800-4WSJ is by MC or Visa; you can also create a personal ID number and avoid credit-card entry on future calls. For help or a free Journal Phone guide, call 1-800-345-NEWS.

AUDIENCE: Beginning, Individual, Professional   RISK LEVEL: Conservative,
                                                                      Moderate, Aggressive
TOPICS: Bonds, Mutual Funds, Stocks, Options, Futures/Commodities

Junk Bond Reporter

American Banker - Bond Buyer
A Division of The Thomson
  Publishing Corporation
P.O. Box 30240
Bethesda, MD 20824

PH: (800) 733-4371
(301) 654-5580
Cost: $645.00
Frequency: Weekly
Date of first issue: 1990

Fundamental analysis. Covers junk bonds. Gives a brief bond market commentary and highlights specific issues which have been in the news and gives other news relevant to this market. Also includes latest price, yield, ratings, call date and other information on the "Bellwether Group" of actively traded high yield issues.

AUDIENCE: Individual, Professional   RISK LEVEL: Moderate, Aggressive
TOPICS: Bonds

Kelly 900 Hotline

Kelly 900 Hotline
PH: (900) 226-2466
(303) 476-9731
Cost: $2.45 per minute

Telephone newsletter covering S&P futures. An S&P Futures Day Trading System. "Specific, Unambiguous Buy, Sell and Exit Recommendations."

AUDIENCE: Individual, Professional   RISK LEVEL: Aggressive
TOPICS: Options, Futures/Commodities

Ken Gerbino's Smart Investing

Phillips Publishing, Inc.
7811 Montrose Road
Potomac, MD 20854

PH: (301) 424-3700
(800) 777-5005
Cost: $139.00 annually
Frequency: Monthly
Date of first issue: 6/84

The newsletter includes "Your Portfolio"; investment strategy; fundamental analysis; analysis of economic and stock market trends; economic update. Covers: growth and value stocks, both domestic and international; convertible securities; mutual funds; short sales.

AUDIENCE: Beginning, Individual   RISK LEVEL: Moderate, Aggressive
TOPICS: Bonds, Mutual Funds, Stocks, Asset Allocation

Kenneth J. Gerbino Investment Letter

Ken Gerbino and Co.
595 Wilshire Blvd.
9 Suite 200
Beverly Hills, CA 90212

PH: (213) 550-6304
FAX: (213) 550-0814
Cost: $78.00 annually
Frequency: Monthly
Date of first issue: 6/84

Fundamental analysis. Covers stocks and gold. Stock market strategy, stock follow-ups, market updates, the Gold Report, The Economy, and Ken's editorial and analysis.

AUDIENCE: Individual   RISK LEVEL: Moderate, Aggressive
TOPICS: Stocks, Futures/Commodities

Key-Volume Strategies

Key-Volume Strategies, Inc.
P.O. Box 407
White Plains, NY 10602

PH: (800) 334-0411 ext. 12
(914) 997-1276
Cost: $219.00/yr
Frequency: 48 issues/yr
Date of first issue: 1969
Fundamental Analysis

Concentrates of actively traded stocks and options. Columns include Market Window, Short Term Outlook, Trader's Action Report and Delayed Buying Screen.

AUDIENCE: Individual, Professional   RISK LEVEL: Moderate, Aggressive
TOPICS: Stocks, Options

Kimball Letter

Kimball Associates
4640 Rummell Rd.
St. Cloud, FL 34771

PH: (407) 892-8555
Cost: $65.00/yr

Market commentary and statistical information on the futures markets. Also provides charts and information on large trades.

AUDIENCE: Individual, Professional   RISK LEVEL: Aggressive
TOPICS: Futures/Commodities

Kiplinger Washington Letter, The

Austin Kiplinger
1729 H. Street NW
Washington, DC 20077-2733

PH: (202) 887-6400
(800) 544-0155
Cost: $68.00
Frequency: Weekly
Date of first issue: over 70 years old

Covers business and investment news. Provides insightful business and investment forecasts to subscribers before the trends ever hit the news. Consists of four easy to read pages packed with concise, to the point forecasts on the outlook for business and investment growth.

AUDIENCE: Beginning, Individual, Professional   RISK LEVEL: Conservative, Moderate, Aggressive
TOPICS: Bonds, Mutual Funds, Stocks

Kirkpatrick's Market Strategist

Kirkpatrick & Co.
Box 1066
Exeter, NH 03833-1066

PH: (603) 772-5551
FAX: (603) 772-6247
Cost: $495.00/yr. individual
Editor: Charles Kirkpatrick
Frequency: Weekly

Provides a weekly computer generated list of recommended stocks via fax. The monthly newsletter consists of short and intermediate term market commentary

AUDIENCE: Individual, Professional   RISK LEVEL: Moderate, Aggressive
TOPICS: Stocks

Knight-Ridder Commodity Perspective

Knight-Ridder Financial Publishing
P.O. Box 94513
Chicago, IL 60690

PH: (800) 621-5271
(312) 454-1801
FAX: (312) 454-0239
Cost: $455.00
Frequency: Weekly
Date of first issue: 21 years

Chart service with commodity charts showing: daily prices, moving averages, stochastics, weekly ranges, spreads, cash markets, RSI's, volume/open interest, Bullish consensus, technical comments, option volatilities and more.

AUDIENCE: Professional   RISK LEVEL: Aggressive
TOPICS: Options, Futures/Commodities

Kon-Lin Letter, The

Kon-Lin Research and Analysis
Corporation
5 Water Road
Rocky Point, NY 11778

PH: (516) 744-8536
Cost: $95.00
Frequency: Monthly
Date of first issue: about 10 years
  old

Fundamental and technical analysis. Covers stocks and market timing. "Reviews 30-35 different stocks on a monthly basis and monitors a broad range of technical indicators for the best possible Market Timing Device. Low priced stocks under $10 with an emphasis on emerging growth and special situations poised for explosive price appreciation."

AUDIENCE: Individual   RISK LEVEL: Moderate, Aggressive
TOPICS: Stocks

La Loggia's Special Situation Report and Stock Market Forecast

Charles M. LaLoggia
P.O. Box 167
Rochester, NY 14601

PH: (800) 836-4330
Cost: $230.00 annually
Frequency: Every 3 weeks
Date of first issue: 1974

Covers stocks and bonds (municipal, corporate, government). An 8 page newsletter covers takeover candidates, short sell recommendations, stock and bond market analysis, and economic outlook.

AUDIENCE: Individual, Professional   RISK LEVEL: Conservative, Moderate, Aggressive
TOPICS: Bonds, Stocks

Lancz Letter, The

Alan B. Lancz and Associates, Inc.
2400 N. Reynolds Road
Toledo, OH 43615

PH: (419) 536-5200
FAX: (419) 536-5401
Cost: $250.00 annually
Frequency: 15-18 issues annually
Date of first issue: 1981

Fundamental Analysis. Market commentary and opinions. Has specific stock recommendations and several model portfolios to follow depending on objectives, i.e., high income, blue-chip, aggressive growth. Also gives portfolio allocation recommendations.

AUDIENCE: Beginning, Individual   RISK LEVEL: Moderate, Aggressive
TOPICS: Stocks

Lead Contract

Data Lab Publications
7333 N. Oak Park Avenue
Niles, IL 60648

PH: (800) 422-1599
(708) 647-6678
Cost: $295.00/yr
Frequency: Weekly
Date of first issue: 15 years old
  Chart service

Commodity futures charting service which includes: high, low, open, close, RSI and Stochastic Indicators, stacked "Back Contracts" for hedging analysis, intra and inter commodity spreads and more.

AUDIENCE: Individual, Professional   RISK LEVEL: Aggressive
TOPICS: Futures/Commodities

Long Term Values

Daily Graphs
William O'Neil & Co.
P.O. Box 24933
Los Angeles, Ca 90024-0933

PH: (310) 448-6843
Cost: $227.00 annually
Frequency: Every 6 weeks

Chart service. Includes technical analysis. Covers stocks. 15 year graphs on over 4,000 stocks. Information includes description of company, quarterly earnings, EPS, sales performance, percentages, volume, earnings, beta & more.

AUDIENCE: Beginning, Individual, Professional   RISK LEVEL: Aggressive
TOPICS: Stocks

Louis Rukeyser's Wall Street

Louis Rukeyser
P.O. Box 25527
Alexandria, VA 22313

PH: (800) 892-9702
Cost: $49.50 annually
$99.00/ 2 years
Frequency: Monthly
Date of first issue: March 1992

Includes analysis from Wall Street's top analysts, economists, and market experts. Each page features a different analyst with ideas, recommendations, and economic forecasts.

AUDIENCE: Beginning, Individual, Professional RISK LEVEL: Moderate, Aggressive
TOPICS: Bonds, Mutual Funds, Stocks

Low Priced Stock Survey, The

Dow Theory Forecasts, Inc.
7412 Calumet Avenue
Hammond, IN 46324-2692

PH: (219) 931-6480
Cost: $82.00/yr
Frequency: Biweekly
Date of first issue: 1946

Fundamental analysis. Stocks in the survey come from many industry groups and most trade under $25. Each issue includes a 2 page analysis of a new stock and also includes a Recommended List of low-priced stocks with our "Best Value" selections clearly highlighted for you. Nearly 90% of the recommended stocks are under $15 per share.

AUDIENCE: Beginning, Individual   RISK LEVEL: Moderate, Aggressive
TOPICS: Stocks

Low Priced Stocks

Elton Stephens
4016 S. Michigan St.
South Bend, IN 46614-3823

PH: (800) 553-5866
FAX: (219) 291-3823
Frequency: Annual
Cost: $45.00/yr
Date of first issue: 1972
ISSN: 0892 984x

Recommends low priced stocks that have good earnings and dividends.

AUDIENCE: Beginning, Individual	RISK LEVEL: Moderate, Aggressive
TOPICS: Stocks	

Lynch International Investment Survey

Lynch-Bowes, Inc.
301 Main St.
Suite 206
Port Washington, NY 11050-2705

PH: (516) 883-7094
FAX: (516) 883-4338
Cost: $175.00/yr. U.S. & Canada
Date of first issue: 1971
Frequency: Weekly

Specializes in stocks, bonds, precious metals and currencies. Offers a model portfolio and specific recommendations.

AUDIENCE: Individual, Professional	RISK LEVEL: Moderate, Aggressive
TOPICS: Bonds, Stocks	

Major Moves

Bruce Babcock
1731 Howe Avenue
Suite 149
Sacramento, CA 95825

PH: (916) 677-7562
(800) 999-CTCR
Cost: $195.00 annually
Frequency: Bimonthly
Date of first issue: 4/85

Technical analysis and chart service covering commodities. Searches for special situations designed for long-term commodity traders. Gives specific recommendations illustrated with charts. Free with subscription to CTCR.

AUDIENCE: Individual, Professional	RISK LEVEL: Aggressive
TOPICS: Futures/Commodities	

Managed Account Advisor, The

Zin Investment Services
7 Switchbud Place #192-312
The Woodlands, TX 77380

PH: (713) 363-1000
Cost: $144.00
Frequency: Monthly

Technical analysis. A mutual funds advisory letter with specific buy/sell recommendations. Includes a free hotline.

AUDIENCE: Individual	RISK LEVEL: Moderate, Aggressive
TOPICS: Bonds, Mutual Funds, Stocks	

Managed Account Reports

Managed Account Reports, Inc.
220 Fifth Avenue
19th Floor
New York, NY 10001

PH: (212) 213-6202
Cost: $299.00 annually for U.S.,
  Canada, Mexico
$370.00 annually elsewhere
Frequency: Monthly

Technical analysis. Covers mutual funds, options and futures/commodities. The publication provides in-depth reports on trading advisors, monthly performance data on over 100 private pools and all publicly held offered futures funds, as well as important educational research and current development material to help you better understand what to look for in determining the true performance of account managers.

AUDIENCE: Individual, Professional   RISK LEVEL: Aggressive
TOPICS: Mutual Funds, Options, Futures/Commodities

Mansfield Stock Chart Service

Mansfield Investments
2973 Kennedy Blvd.
Jersey City, NJ 07306

PH: (201) 795-0629
Date of first issue: 1971

Chart service. Costs and frequencies: annually. OTC & American - weekly - $688, biweekly -$422, - monthly - $217. NYSE - weekly - $728, biweekly - $447, monthly - $232. Covers: stocks. Weekly plotted charts on all stocks on NYSE, America, and OTC exchanges. Charts updated each Friday after the close and leave printer at 10:30 PM for delivery.

AUDIENCE: Beginning, Individual, Professional RISK LEVEL: Moderate, Aggressive
TOPICS: Stocks

MAR/Hedge

Managed Account Reports, Inc.
220 Fifth Avenue
19th Floor
New York, NY 10001-7781

PH: (212) 213-6202
Cost: $245.00 annually for US,
  Canada, Mexico
$295.00 for rest of world
Frequency: Monthly

Technical Analysis. Covers hedge funds and funds of funds. Supplies a global look at hedge fund advisors, as well as monthly updates on over 100 hedge funds, fund of funds, and similar investment programs. Profiles of hedge fund managers and fund of funds, quantitative research studies, rankings of funds, performance tables and industry developments.

AUDIENCE: Professional   RISK LEVEL: Aggressive
TOPICS: Bonds, Mutual Funds, Stocks, Options, Futures/Commodities

Margo's Market Monitor

Margo Parrish/Minuteman
Publishing Co.
P.O. Box 642
Lexington, MA 02173

PH: (617) 861-0302 (Order Line)
FAX: (617) 861-1489
Cost: 4-issue (2 months) Trial $25.00
24-issue (1 year) Subscription $125.00
Date of first issue: August 1980

The six-page letter includes fundamental and technical analysis. Covers common stocks and Mutual Funds (the 35 Fidelity Select Funds) and includes charts as well as three Model portfolios. Margo's primary aim is long-term capital appreciation.

AUDIENCE: Beginning, Individual   RISK LEVEL: Moderate, Aggressive
TOPICS: Mutual Funds, Stocks

Market Action

New Era Trading Company
6205 S. Mirror Lake Drive
Sebastian, FL 32958

Cost: $69.00/yr
Frequency: Approximately every 2
  weeks
Date of first issue: 11/87

"The letter's objective is to find 'Action Levels' where buying or selling can be done with minimum risk, whether you are trading stocks, futures, options or switching mutual funds."

AUDIENCE: Individual   RISK LEVEL: Aggressive
TOPICS: Mutual Funds, Stocks, Options, Futures/Commodities

Market Advisory

Market Advisory
PH: (900) TEK-MOVE
Cost: $2.25 per minute
24 Hour service
Frequency of update: daily and
  sporadically throughout the day

Telephone newsletter covering stocks, commodities, municipal bonds, corporate bonds, and government bonds. Provides current market trends/actions, entry/exit points, resistance/support levels and target prices for specific issues.

AUDIENCE: Individual, Professional   RISK LEVEL: Conservative, Moderate, Aggressive
TOPICS: Bonds, Stocks, Futures/Commodities

Market Beat

Market Beat, Inc.
1436 Granada
Ann Arbor, MI 48103

PH: (313) 426-2146
Cost: $150.00 annually
Frequency: Monthly
Date of first issue: 1987

Technical analysis. Covers stocks and includes charts. The newsletter offers a mechanical trading signal that has outperformed the Dow; predicted dates of future highs and lows in the stock market given up to one year in advance; interest rate barometers given weekly on the hotline and forecasts for the high and low dates.

AUDIENCE: Individual, Professional   RISK LEVEL: Moderate, Aggressive
TOPICS: Stocks

Market Charts

Market Charts, Inc.
10 Hanover Square, 20th floor
New York, NY 10005-3516

PH: (212) 509-0944, Editorial Office
(800) 431-6082, Subscription Info.
Cost: $555.00 annually twice monthly
$335.00 annually for monthly
$35.00 single issue 1-pt.
$65.00 single issue 3-pt.
Date of first issue: 1971

Chart service covering stocks and market indicators. Market Charts is the only P&F service that publishes both short-term and long-term charts based on intra-day moves. The 1-point reversal (short-term) chartbook is available on a twice monthly or monthly basis and either subscription includes the Long-Term Quarterly, 3-pt. reversal service.

AUDIENCE: Beginning, Individual, Professional   RISK LEVEL: Moderate, Aggressive
TOPICS: Stocks

Market Cycle Investing

Andrews Publications
1544 Via Arroyo
Paso Robles, CA 93466

PH: (408) 778-2925
Cost: $140.00/yr
Frequency: 12/yr
Date of first issue: 1974

Fundamental analysis. R. Earl Andrews, editor. "Advises investors of economic and business trends, including the cycle phase of the investment market, interest rates, stocks, bonds, and real estate." Comment: Looseleaf format; back issues available.

AUDIENCE: Individual, Professional   RISK LEVEL: Moderate, Aggressive
TOPICS: Bonds, Mutual Funds, Stocks, Investment Planning

Market Express

Corporate Relations
1801 Lee Rd.
Suite 301
Winter Park, FL 32789

PH: (407) 290-9600
(800) 333-5697
Cost: $29 annually
Frequency: Not a regular schedule
Date of first issue: 1974

Fundamental analysis. This publication enables the reader to 'jump' on unique opportunities. The purpose of Market Express is to bring you fast, accurate information requiring immediate action so you can maximize your profits, i.e., stock recommendations.

AUDIENCE: Beginning, Individual   RISK LEVEL: Aggressive
TOPICS: Stocks

Market Fax

Glenn Cutler
Market Fax DMC Market Fax
PH: (415) 952-8853
Cost: $99.00 introductory offer / 2 months
Regularly $150.00 a month
Frequency: Nightly

Fax service covering stocks, bonds, gold, and currencies. Market Fax arrives on your fax just hours before the stock market opens. And in just 5 minutes, you'll know what the nation's #1 Stock Market Timer is thinking and which stocks to buy and sell. By Glenn Cutler.

AUDIENCE: Beginning, Individual   RISK LEVEL: Moderate, Aggressive
TOPICS: Bonds, Stocks, Futures/Commodities

Market Logic

The Institute for Econometric Research
3471 N. Federal Highway
Ft. Lauderdale, FL 33306

PH: (800) 442-9000
(305) 563-9000
Cost: $95.00 annually for individual monthly newsletter; rent list $150.00
Frequency: Semiweekly
Date of first issue: 1975

Fundamental and technical analysis. Every issue features stock recommendations, market advice, continuous follow-ups, gold forecast, option portfolio, strongest stocks advisory survey, Dow Theory, chart folio, the economy, and much more.

AUDIENCE: Individual, Professional   RISK LEVEL: Moderate, Aggressive
TOPICS: All

Market Mania

Market Mania, Inc.
P.O. Box 1234
Pacifica, CA 94044

PH: (415) 952-8853
Cost: $119.00 annually
Frequency: Monthly
Date of first issue: 1983

Fundamental analysis. The newsletter generally follows growth stocks and undervalued stocks. Most of the recommendations are OTC and AMEX stocks trading under $20 per share. It looks for insider buying and 13D filings for potential takeovers and special situations. Hotline service is offered 3 days a week.

AUDIENCE: Individual	RISK LEVEL: Moderate, Aggressive
TOPICS: Stocks	

Market Momentum

Thomas D. Kienlen Corporation
P.O. Box 2245
Jasper, OR 97438
PH: (800) 999-3303
(900) 988-1838 ext. 819 - $2.00 per
  minute for updates
Cost: $175.00
Frequency: Monthly
Date of first issue: 1991

Technical analysis. Uses technical analysis to "determine the market's direction, distance and duration." Gives specific buy/sell/hold recommendations and an in-depth report on a technical factor each month.

AUDIENCE: Individual	RISK LEVEL: Moderate, Aggressive
TOPICS: Mutual Funds, Stocks	

Market Momentum

Thomas D. Kienlen Corporation
P.O. Box 2245
Jasper, OR 97438

PH: (800) 999-3303
(900) 884-4878, ext. 49
Cost: $2.25 per minute

Telephone newsletter that uses technical analysis to "determine the markets' direction, distance and duration." Gives specific buy/sell/hold recommendations.

AUDIENCE: Individual	RISK LEVEL: Moderate
TOPICS: Mutual Funds, Asset Allocation	

Market Month

Standard & Poor's Corporation
25 Broadway
New York, NY 10004

PH: (212) 208-8000
Cost: $53.00/yr
Frequency: Monthly
Date of first issue: 1984

Fundamental Analysis. Covers stocks, tables, graphs. "Supplies individual investors with current market information in order to stimulate new business opportunities. Discusses market trends and offers specific stock recommendations and advice on pruning portfolios."

AUDIENCE: Individual	RISK LEVEL: Moderate, Aggressive
TOPICS: Stocks	

Market Trend Analysis

Lowry
631 US HWY 1, Suite 305
N. Palm Beach, FL 33408

PH: (800) 345-0186
FAX: (407) 842-1523
Cost: $260.00 to $420.00
Frequency: Weekly
FAX service also available
Date of first issue: 1960

Technical analysis. "Includes weekly Market Trend Analysis Report plus Special Studies, operating manual updates and quarterly posting graphs."

AUDIENCE: Individual, Professional	**RISK LEVEL: Moderate, Aggressive**
TOPICS: Stocks	

Market Viewpoint

Mike Chalek
PH: (900) 420-4246
Cost: $2.99 per minute

Telephone Newsletter market forecasting in the financials and energies markets.

AUDIENCE: Individual, Professional	**RISK LEVEL: Aggressive**
TOPICS: Bonds, Stocks, Options, Futures/Commodities	

Market-Scan Report

Eric Hamilton
Hamilton Asset Management
303 Congress St.
Boston, MA 02210

PH: (800) 237-8400 ext. 722
Cost: $69.00 annually
Frequency: Monthly
Date of first issue: 1988
6 month trial $39.00

Fundamental and technical analysis. Each month over 6500 stocks are screened to find the best performers. Then the issue tells you why a stock was chosen, gives information about the stock and price graphs for recent past. Portfolio performance is also tracked each issue.

AUDIENCE: Individual, Professional	**RISK LEVEL: Moderate, Aggressive**
TOPICS: Stocks	

Marketarian, Inc.

Marketarian, Inc.
P.O. Box 1283
Grand Island, NE 68802

PH: (900) 226-6699
(800) 279-7751
Cost: $2.00 per minute
Frequency: 10:00 a.m., 3:00 p.m.,
　and 7:00 p.m. EST

Telephone newsletter covering S&P Futures. Message is approximately 1 to 2 minutes in length.

AUDIENCE: Individual, Professional	**RISK LEVEL: Aggressive**
TOPICS: Mutual Funds, Stocks, Futures/Commodities	

Marketarian Letter, The

Marketarian, Inc.
P.O. Box 1283
Grand Island, NE 68802-1283

PH: (800) 658-4325
(308) 381-2121
Cost: $225.00/yr
Frequency: Every 3 weeks

Covers stocks, bonds, options and futures, and market timing. Each issue provides stock recommendations, industry group analysis, bond timing advice, up-to-date analysis of current market activity, mutual fund switching, model portfolio review and model portfolios. Hotline available for $2 per minute: (900) 226-6699.

AUDIENCE: Individual, Professional   RISK LEVEL: Moderate, Aggressive
TOPICS: Mutual Funds, Stocks, Futures/Commodities

Marples Business Newsletter

Marples Business Newsletter
117 W. Mercer St.
Seattle, WA 98119-3960

PH: (206) 622-0155
Cost: $72.00 annually
Frequency: Every other Wednesday
Date of first issue: 1949

Fundamental analysis. Covers stocks and includes company reviews. The letter keeps busy executives and businesspeople up to date in important developments in the Pacific Northwest. In addition to covering important economic trends, companies in the Pacific Northwest are regularly profiled that may be of interest to investors.

AUDIENCE: Individual, Professional   RISK LEVEL: Moderate, Aggressive
TOPICS: Bonds, Stocks

Master Indicator of the Stock Market, The

The Master Indicator of the Stock
  Market
P.O. Box 3024
West Palm Beach, FL 33402

PH: (407) 793-8316
Cost: $79.00
Technical Analysis

A stock market advisory newsletter which utilizes technical indicators to determine the new leaders in industry groups and stocks.

AUDIENCE: Individual, Professional   RISK LEVEL: Moderate, Aggressive
TOPICS: Stocks

MBH Weekly Commodity Letter

MBH Commodity Advisors, Inc.
P.O. Box 353
Winnetka, IL 60093

PH: (708) 291-1870
(800) 678-5253
Cost: $895.00/hour
Date of first issue: 1972
Frequency: Weekly

Provides futures market commentary and technical review of actively traded markets. Also provides specific recommendations.

AUDIENCE: Individual, Professional   RISK LEVEL: Aggressive
TOPICS: Futures/Commodities

McAlvany Intelligence Advisor

Research Publications
P.O. Box 84904
Phoenix, AZ 85071

PH: (800) 528-0559
(800) 525-9556 Colorado
Cost: $95.00 annually
Frequency: Monthly
Date of first issue: 1978

Fundamental and Technical Analysis. Covers precious metals and stocks. Uses charts. Global economic review of in-depth monetary and geopolitical trends that impact the gold and precious metals markets.

AUDIENCE: Individual, Professional   RISK LEVEL: Moderate, Aggressive
TOPICS: Stocks, Options, Futures/Commodities

Medical Technology Stock Letter

Jim McCamant Piedmont Venture
  Group
P.O. Box 40460
Berkeley, CA 94704

PH: (510) 843-1857
FAX: (510) 843-0901
Cost: $320.00 annually
Frequency: Twice a month
Date of first issue: 12/83

Fundamental analysis. Covers stocks and market timing. An 8 page newsletter written in layman's language discussing current developments in medical technology. Gives specific buy price limits on recommended stocks and updated target prices until a sale is advised.

AUDIENCE: Beginning, Individual, Professional   RISK LEVEL: Aggressive
TOPICS: Stocks

Mega-Trades

Taurus Corporation
P.O. Box 767
Winchester, VA 22601

PH: (703) 667-4827
Cost: $425.00/yr
Frequency: Monthly
Date of first issue: 1983

Fundamental analysis. "Provides specific recommendations in the commodities investment field. Feeds and grains; livestock; foodstuffs; metals; cotton; heating oil and wood products; British, Canadian, German, Swiss, and Japanese currencies; Value Line, Standard & Poor's 500; and Treasury bills and bonds."

AUDIENCE: Individual, Professional   RISK LEVEL: Aggressive
TOPICS: Options, Futures/Commodities

Merrill Lynch Market Letter

Merrill Lynch
World Financial Center
North Tower
New York, NY 10281

PH: (212) 236-1000
(212) 449-8076
Cost: $49.00
Frequency: Bimonthly
Date of first issue: 1974

Fundamental analysis. Market and economic commentary, investment ideas, earnings reports on recommended stocks, calendar with news to watch for.

AUDIENCE: Beginning, Individual   RISK LEVEL: Moderate, Aggressive
TOPICS: Mutual Funds, Stocks

Merriman Market Analyst Cycles Report

Merriman Market Analyst Cycles
  Report
P.O. Box 250012
W. Bloomfield, MI 48325

PH: (313) 626-3034
(800) 962-4613
Cost: $249.00 annual
Frequency: Every 3 weeks
Date of first issue: 1985

Fundamental and technical analysis. Covers gold, stocks, commodities, bonds, and includes graphs and charts. The main focus point of the newsletter is gold and other commodities. Features include: Review and Preview, Precious Metals, Trader's Recommendations, Stocks, T-Bonds and Foreign Currencies, Grains and more.

AUDIENCE: Individual, Professional   RISK LEVEL: Aggressive
TOPICS: Stocks, Options, Futures/Commodities

Michael Murphy

Michael Murphy
PH: (900) 321-4321
Cost: $2.00 per minute
Frequency: Daily

Gives market commentary, easy to understand - not technical - for novice/average investor. Different categories accessed by touch-tone phone, longs or shorts.

AUDIENCE: Beginning, Individual   RISK LEVEL: Moderate, Aggressive
TOPICS: Stocks

Middle/Fixed Income Letter

MASTCA Publishing Corp.
P.O. Box 55
Loch Sheldrake, NY 12759

PH: (914) 794-5792
Cost: $45.00 annually
Frequency: Monthly
Date of first issue: 1981

Educational perspective. Covers all types of investment instruments. Uses an educational perspective to teach the functions of various financial instruments.

AUDIENCE: Beginning   RISK LEVEL: Conservative, Moderate
TOPICS: Bonds, Mutual Funds, Stocks, Asset Allocation, Investment Planning, General
        Reference

MMS Weekly Economic Survey

MMS International
1301 Shoreway Rd., Suite 300
Belmont, CA 94002

PH: (415) 595-0610
(800) 227-7304
FAX: (415) 637-4303
Frequency: Weekly
Cost: $600.00/yr.
Date of first issue: May 1977

Provides market sentiment and the effect of market sentiment on key financial variables, interest rates on T-Bonds, Fed Policy (Discount Rate, Feds Funds Rate, Free Reserve), Foreign Exchanges (Euro Dollar, DM, Yen and more), Equity (DJIA and S&P 500), plus market commentary.

AUDIENCE: Professional   RISK LEVEL: Conservative, Moderate, Aggressive
TOPICS: All

Momentum

Momentum
7516 Castlebar Road
P.O. Box 470146
Charlotte, NC 28226

PH: (704) 365-4070
Cost: $88.00
Frequency: Monthly
Date of first issue: 1985

Fundamental analysis. Covers stocks, mutual funds, market timing, convertible bonds. Market commentary. Stock analysis divided into industry groups and including buy/sell/hold advice and stops. Same information provided for mutual funds. Also includes 6 model portfolios.

AUDIENCE: Individual	RISK LEVEL: Moderate, Aggressive
TOPICS: Bonds, Mutual Funds, Stocks	

Monday Morning Market Memo

William M. LeFevre, Editor
Ehrenkrantz King Nussbaum, Inc.
635 Madison Avenue
New York, NY 10022

PH: (212) 407-0576
(800) 867-8600
Cost: $200.00
Frequency: Weekly (48 issues)
Date of first issue: March 1973

A typical issue describes what the market did last week, what it might do in the coming week and why. Focuses on the intermediate term. Uses both fundamental and technical approaches. Frequently recommends stocks.

AUDIENCE: Individual, Professional	RISK LEVEL: Moderate, Aggressive
TOPICS: Bonds, Stocks, Asset Allocation, Investment Planning	

Monetary Digest

Certified Mint
2873 Sky Harbor Blvd.
Phoenix, AZ 85034

PH: (800) 528-1380
Cost: $36.00/yr
Frequency: Quarterly
Date of first issue: 1974

Fundamental analysis. "Published as a service to customers of Certified Mint, a broker of precious metals. Reviews economic, monetary, and political developments affecting the prices of gold and silver. Lists current gold and silver prices and makes recommendations."

AUDIENCE: Individual, Professional	RISK LEVEL: Aggressive
TOPICS: Options, Futures/Commodities	

Monetary & Economic Review

FAMC, Inc.
3500 JFK Parkway
United Bank Building
Fort Collins, CO 80525

PH: (800) 325-0919
(800) 528-0559
FAX: (303) 223-4996
Cost: $150.00
Frequency: Monthly
Date of first issue: 1984

Fundamental analysis. Covers options, stocks, commodities/futures, and precious metals. Table of Contents: Investments at a Glance; Taxes; U.S. & World Update; Inflation Watch; Financial Education; Book Review; Financial Insights; Inside Washington; Opinion of the Month; Letter. Economic and market forecasting.

AUDIENCE: Individual, Professional	RISK LEVEL: Aggressive
TOPICS: Stocks, Options, Futures/Commodities	

Money Management Letter

Institutional Investor Systems
488 Madison Avenue
New York, NY 10022
PH: (212) 303-3300

Cost: $1,150.00 annually
Frequency: Weekly
Fundamental Analysis
Date of first issue: 1975

Covers pension fund investments (domestic stocks, bonds, and international securities). Money Management Letter is a biweekly newsletter which covers the business of U.S. pension fund investment management. MML reports on which pension funds are hiring new money managers and why, what new strategies and products are being utilized.

AUDIENCE: Professional   RISK LEVEL: Conservative, Moderate
TOPICS: Bonds, Mutual Funds, Stocks

Money Reporter

MPL Communications
133 Richmond Street West
Suite 700
Toronto, Ontario M5H3M8

PH: (416) 869-1177
(416) 869-3021 Hotline for updates
Cost: $197 annually
Frequency: Every two weeks
Date of first issue: 1971

Fundamental analysis. Covers Canadian stocks. A Canadian financial advisory newsletter providing recommendations, investment and tax tips, money rates and more.

AUDIENCE: Individual   RISK LEVEL: Moderate, Aggressive
TOPICS: Stocks, Asset Allocation, Investment Planning

Moneyline

USA Today
1000 Wilson Blvd.
Arlington, VA 22229

PH: (900) 555-5555
(800) USA-0001
Cost: $.95 per minute
24 Hour service

Telephone newsletter covering stocks. Use your touch tone phone to access stock quotes, CD rates, interest calculations, updates on your personal investments and used car prices. Quotes are delayed 15 minutes during trading hours.

AUDIENCE: Individual   RISK LEVEL: Conservative, Moderate, Aggressive
TOPICS: Bonds, Mutual Funds, Stocks

Moneypaper, The

Temper of the Times
Communications, Inc.
1010 Mamroneck Avenue
Mamroneck, NY 10543

ISSN: 0745-9858
PH: (914) 381-5400
Cost: $72.00 annually, $108.00 for
  2 years
Frequency: Monthly
Date of first issue: 1981

Fundamental analysis. Covers stocks and bonds. The contents of this newsletter are: Market Outlook, Portfolio Follow-up, Smarts - The ideas and information for this section are those of the editors or as a result of their research, Stocktrack - recommended stocks, Summing Up - Reaction to or restatement of items of interest read elsewhere.

AUDIENCE: Beginning, Individual   RISK LEVEL: Conservative, Moderate, Aggressive
TOPICS: Bonds, Stocks

Monthly Statistics - Closed-End Investment Companies

Investment Company Institute
1401 H Street NW
Suite 1200
Washington, DC 20005

PH: (202) 326-5800
Cost: $75.00/yr
Published monthly

Includes underwritings and new issues for bond and equity categories. Also includes an annual survey of closed-end funds which provides outstanding assets, annual volume of underwritings and other data.

AUDIENCE: Beginning, Individual   RISK LEVEL: Moderate, Aggressive
TOPICS: Mutual Funds

Monthly Statistics - Open-End Investment Companies

Investment Company Institute
1401 H Street NW
Suite 1200
Washington, DC 20005

PH: (202) 326-5800
Cost: $225.00/yr or $425.00/yr by
  fax
Published: Monthly

"News releases with accompanying tables describing mutual fund sales, exchanges, redemptions, assets, cash holdings and portfolio transactions classified by investment objective and method of sales are available monthly. Sales data for long-term funds are provided quarterly on a state-by-state basis."

AUDIENCE: Beginning, Individual, Professional   RISK LEVEL: Moderate, Aggressive
TOPICS: Mutual Funds

Monthly Statistics - Unit Investment Trusts

Investment Company Institute
1401 H Street NW
Suite 1200
Washington, DC 20005

PH: (202) 326-5800
Cost: $75.00/yr
Published: Monthly

Provides value and number of deposits of new trusts by type, maturity and insurance feature.

AUDIENCE: Individual, Professional   RISK LEVEL: Conservative, Moderate, Aggressive
TOPICS: Bonds, Mutual Funds, Stocks

Moody's Bond Survey

Moody's Investors Service
99 Church Street
New York, NY 10007

PH: (212) 553-0383
(212) 553-0437 - subscriptions
Cost: $1,175.00
Frequency: Weekly
Date of first issue: 1909

Technical analysis. "Presents statistical information and analysis of corporate, municipal, government, federal agency, and international bonds, preferred stock, and commercial paper. Ratings changes and withdrawals, calendars of recent bond offerings, and Moody's bond and preferred stock yield averages."

AUDIENCE: Individual, Professional   RISK LEVEL: Conservative, Moderate
TOPICS: Bonds

Mortgage-Backed Securities Letter

Investment Dealers Digest, Inc.
Two World Trade Center
18th Floor
New York, NY 10048-0203

PH: (212) 227-1200
FAX: (212) 321-2336
Cost: $1,595.00/yr.
Date of first issue: 1990
Frequency: Weekly

Covers all commercial mortgage and asset backed securities for professional bond traders and money managers. Editor: Clint Winstead.

AUDIENCE: Professional   RISK LEVEL: Conservative, Moderate
TOPICS: Bonds

Motion Picture Investor

Paul Kagan Associates, Inc.
126 Clock Tower Place
Carmel, CA 93923-8734

PH: (408) 624-1536
Cost: $575.00
Frequency: Monthly
Date of first issue: 1984

Fundamental analysis. Covers stocks, tables, graphs. "Concerned with motion picture investment, financing and limited partnerships. Analyzes trends in motion picture stocks of publicly held companies, makes projections, and reports industry news."

AUDIENCE: Individual, Professional   RISK LEVEL: Moderate, Aggressive
TOPICS: Stocks

MPT Review

Navellier & Associates, Inc.
P.O. Box 10012
Incline Village, NV 89450-1012

PH: (702) 831-1396
FAX: (702) 832-4909
Cost: $225.00
Frequency: Monthly
Date of first issue: 1980

Fundamental analysis. Louis Navellier's MPT Review specializes in modern portfolio theory. Features include: Portfolios from $10,000 to $1,000,000; Buy List; Investment Outlook and Strategy; Stocks to Watch; Q&A; Qualified Collective Trust; and Money Management information.

AUDIENCE: Beginning, Individual   RISK LEVEL: Moderate, Aggressive
TOPICS: Stocks, Asset Allocation, Investment Planning, General Reference

Muni Week

American Banker - Bond Buyer
One State Street
New York, NY

PH: (212) 943-8200
(800) 367-3989
(214) 741-1210 Dallas
Cost: $525.00 annually
Frequency: Weekly
Date of first issue: 1988

Fundamental analysis. Muni Week is news for tax-exempt issuers, lawyers and finance professionals. Contents include: market review, investing, state budgets, public finance, law, issuers, opinion, editor's comments, and Washington Watch.

AUDIENCE: Individual, Professional   RISK LEVEL: Conservative, Moderate
TOPICS: Bonds

Municipal Bond Book

Standard & Poor's Corporation
25 Broadway
New York, NY 10004

PH: (212) 208-8000
Cost: $1,135.00/yr.
Date of first issue: 1987
Editor: Byron Klapper

Debt ratings on municipal issues.

AUDIENCE: Individual, Professional   RISK LEVEL: Conservative, Moderate
TOPICS: Bonds

Mutual Fund Forecaster

The Institute for Econometric
  Research
3471 N. Federal Highway
Ft. Lauderdale, FL. 33306

PH: (800) 442-9000
(305) 563-9000
Cost: $49.00 annually
Frequency: Monthly
Date of first issue: 1979

Fundamental analysis and charts. Each issue is filled with specific recommendations, market advice, money making ideas, performance ratings, follow-ups of prior recommendations, and a mutual fund directory. Includes free telephone and fax hotline updated every Tuesday and Friday evening.

AUDIENCE: Beginning, Individual   RISK LEVEL: Moderate, Aggressive
TOPICS: Mutual Funds

Mutual Fund Investing

Phillips Publishing, Inc.
7811 Montrose Road
Potomac, MD 20854

PH: (800) 722-9000
Cost: $187.00/yr
Frequency: Monthly
Date of first issue: 3/85

Fundamental analysis. "Offers analysis and advice concerning the mutual fund market. Makes specific recommendations and discusses related financial management issues."

AUDIENCE: Beginning, Individual   RISK LEVEL: Moderate
TOPICS: Mutual Funds, Asset Allocation, Investment Planning

Mutual Fund Letter, The

Investment Information Services, Inc.
680 N. Lake Shore Drive
Tower Suite 2038
Chicago, IL 60611

PH: (312) 649-6940
(800) 326-6941
Cost: $135.00/yr
FAX: (312) 649-5537
Date of first issue: 1983

Fundamental analysis. Each issue contains investment outlook and strategy, model portfolios for five different investment objectives, investment ideas and portfolio management strategies, buy/hold/sell advice for specific funds, funds family reports and much more.

AUDIENCE: Beginning, Individual   RISK LEVEL: Moderate, Aggressive
TOPICS: Mutual Funds, Asset Allocation, Investment Planning

Mutual Fund Marketing Newsletter

Investment Company Institute
1600 M Street, N.W.
Suite 600
Washington, D.C. 20036

PH: (202) 293-7700
Cost: $25.00 annually
Frequency: Quarterly
Date of first issue: 1988

Fundamental Analysis. Covers mutual funds. A quarterly newsletter that addresses issues of interest to those involved in mutual funds marketing and communications. It contains articles of interest by member mutual fund organization marketers, outside experts, and Institute staff.

AUDIENCE: Beginning, Individual	RISK LEVEL: Moderate, Aggressive
TOPICS: Mutual Funds	

Mutual Fund Strategist

Charlie Hooper
Mutual Fund Strategist, Ltd.
P.O. Box 446
Burlington, VT 05402

PH: (802) 658-3513
Cost: $149.00/yr
Frequency: Monthly
Date of first issue: 1982

Fundamental and Technical Analysis. Covers mutual funds and market timing. Features short to intermediate and long-term timing indicators for switching between growth and money market funds, buy/sell recommendations and model portfolios. Includes daily free hotline.

AUDIENCE: Beginning, Individual	RISK LEVEL: Moderate, Aggressive
TOPICS: Mutual Funds, Asset Allocation, Investment Planning	

Mutual Fund Trends

Growth Fund Research, Inc.
Growth Fund Research Bldg.
P.O. Box 6600
Rapid City, SD 57709

PH: (605) 341-1971
(800) 621-8322
Cost: $119.00/yr
Technical and Fundamental Analysis
Frequency: Monthly

Monitors and tracks the performance and trends of mutual funds.

AUDIENCE: Individual	RISK LEVEL: Moderate, Aggressive
TOPICS: Mutual Funds	

Mutual Fund Trends Online

Growth Fund Research, Inc.
Growth Fund Research Bldg.
P.O. Box 6600
Rapid City, SD 57709

PH: (605) 341-1971
(800) 621-8322
Cost: Contact vendor
Technical and Fundamental Analysis
Frequency: Monthly

Monitors and tracks the performance and trends of mutual funds.

AUDIENCE: Individual, Professional	RISK LEVEL: Conservative, Moderate, Aggressive
TOPICS: Mutual Funds	

Mutual Funds

American Business Directories, Inc.
5711 S. 86th Circle
Box 27347
Omaha, NE 68127-4146

PH: (402) 593-4600
Cost: $315.00

Provides name, address, phone numbers, key person in charge and number of employees on approximately 4,400 companies who advertise in the yellow pages under the heading "Mutual Funds."

AUDIENCE: Beginning, Individual   RISK LEVEL: Moderate, Aggressive
TOPICS: Mutual Funds

Mutual Funds Guide

Commerce Clearing House, Inc.
4025 West Peterson Avenue
Chicago, IL 60646

PH: (312) 583-8500
Cost: $665.00 annually
Frequency: Every other week
Date of first issue: 1969

Fundamental analysis. Covers mutual funds. The Mutual Fund Guide combines federal and state regulatory requirements. The guide discusses initial planning strategies and formation of funds to the effective day-to-day operational details. Comments: 2 looseleaf volumes updated every other week.

AUDIENCE: Beginning, Individual   RISK LEVEL: Moderate, Aggressive
TOPICS: Mutual Funds

Myers Finance Review

Myers Finance and Energy
P.O. Box 3082
Spokane, WA 99220

PH: (509) 534-7132
Cost: $129.00 annually
$199.00 /2 years
Frequency: Monthly

Fundamental analysis. Covers stocks, precious metals. Overview of worldwide economic situation recommendations on where to safely invest your money.

AUDIENCE: Individual   RISK LEVEL: Moderate, Aggressive
TOPICS: Stocks, Futures/Commodities

National Association of Investors Corporation's Investor Advisory Service

National Association of Investors
  Corp.
1515 East Eleven Mile Road
Royal Oak, MI 48067

PH: (313) 543-0612
Cost: $125.00 - Club; $108.00 -
  Individual
Frequency: Monthly
Date of first issue: 1941

Fundamental analysis. Covers stocks and includes charts. A report on three stocks which are judged to be in the buy range. With the report of the three companies, you will receive a completed stock selection guide on each company so that you can see the record yourself and check the conclusions of the investment advisors.

AUDIENCE: Individual   RISK LEVEL: Moderate, Aggressive
TOPICS: Stocks

Nelson's Earnings Outlook

Nelson Publications
1 Gateway Plaza
Port Chester, NY 10573

PH: (800) 333-6357
FAX: (914) 937-8908
Cost: $240.00 annually
Frequency: Monthly
Date of first issue: 1990

Fundamental Analysis. Covers stocks. Gives investors instant access to Wall Street's latest earnings estimates on 3,000 stocks - NYSE, AMEX, NASDAQ. The most significant changes in earnings estimate from the previous month. "Up" and "Downs." EPS for latest fiscal year, consensus earnings estimate for current and next fiscal year.

AUDIENCE: Individual, Professional   RISK LEVEL: Moderate, Aggressive
TOPICS: Bonds, Stocks

New Issues

The Institute for Econometric
  Research
3471 N. Federal Highway
Ft. Lauderdale, FL 33306

PH: (800) 442-9000
(305) 563-9000
Cost: $95.00/yr
Frequency: Monthly
Date of first issue: 1978

Fundamental analysis. Covers stocks - new issues. An authoritative source of information on the exciting new issues market. Each issue contains comprehensive analysis of the #1 new issue recommendations, other buy recommendations, avoid warnings, IPO calendar, follow-ups and more. Includes free hotline weekly hotline.

AUDIENCE: Individual, Professional   RISK LEVEL: Moderate, Aggressive
TOPICS: Stocks

New Timing Device, The

K.D. Angle & Co. LP
24 East Ave.
Box 1290
New Canaan, CT 06840

PH: (203) 972-1776
FAX: (203) 972-3192
Cost: $450 annually
Frequency: Monthly
Date of first issue: 1985

Analysis on futures and market timing. A 4 page letter concentrating on most active markets. Includes daily hotline, daily FAX service available as well. Can fill trades for subscribers through brokerage division.

AUDIENCE: Individual, Professional   RISK LEVEL: Aggressive
TOPICS: Futures/Commodities

Ney Report

Richard Ney
Associates Asset Management
P.O. Box 92223
Pasadena, CA 91109

PH: (818) 441-2222
(800) 444-2044
Cost: $295.00/yr
Frequency: Twice an month
Date of first issue: 1976

Fundamental and technical analysis. Covers stocks and includes charts. The newsletter tracks stock exchange specialists - buying what they buy and selling what they sell. Mr. Ney starts by tracking the activity of 500 high-quality stocks on the ticker tape every day. Data are programmed to record big block transactions and coordinate data with charts.

AUDIENCE: Beginning, Individual   RISK LEVEL: Moderate, Aggressive
TOPICS: Stocks, Options

Nielsen's International Investment Letter

Thor Nielsen
P.O. Box 7532
Olympia, WA 98507

Cost: Free to Clients
Frequency: As needed
Date of first issue: 1982
Fundamental Analysis

Tracks domestic and international stock markets and economies, precious metals and other commodities, USA and foreign bonds, interest rates, foreign currencies and real estate. Offers specific buy and sell recommendations on domestic and international investments for both traders and investors. Emphasizes capital appreciation.

AUDIENCE: Individual, Professional   RISK LEVEL: Moderate, Aggressive
TOPICS: Bonds, Stocks, Commodities, Asset Allocation

No Load Fund Investor, The

Sheldon Jacobs
P.O. Box 318
Irvington-on-Hudson, NY 10533

PH: (800) 252-2042
(914) 693-7420
Cost: $109.00
Frequency: Monthly
Date of first issue: 15 years old

Fundamental analysis. Covers mutual funds. "Gives concrete practical advice and sound strategies for creating an investment portfolio that will grow steadily and safely." "Each issue tracks 876 no load funds and gives you comparative reports of their performance based on original research." Also provides specific recommendations and model portfolios.

AUDIENCE: Beginning, Individual   RISK LEVEL: Moderate, Aggressive
TOPICS: Mutual Funds, Asset Allocation

No Load Fund X

Burton Berry
DAL Investment Co.
235 Montgomery Street #662
San Francisco, CA 94101

PH: (800) 323-1510
FAX: (415) 986-1595
Cost: $75.00 annually
Frequency: Monthly
Date of first issue: 1976

Chart service includes fundamental analysis covering mutual funds and market timing. Highlights the 5 best funds by risk categories. A unique monitoring system designed to provide fund investors with the key information they need to know which funds to be in and when.

AUDIENCE: Beginning, Individual   RISK LEVEL: Moderate, Aggressive
TOPICS: Mutual Funds

No-Load Fund Analyst

L/G Research, Inc.
4 Orinda Way
Suite 230-D
Orinda, CA 94563

PH: (800) 776-9555 orders
FAX: (510) 254-0335
Cost: $195.00/yr
Frequency: Monthly
Date of first issue: 1988

Each issue contains 4 models portfolios along with market commentary; 1 or 2 feature articles analyzing current developments in various financial markets; a thorough review and analysis of 1 or 2 funds; updates on several funds; "Bits & Pieces," "Closed-End Fund Corner," "Taxable & Tax-Exempt Yield Analysis" and Recent Fund Developments.

AUDIENCE: Beginning, Individual   RISK LEVEL: Moderate, Aggressive
TOPICS: Mutual Funds

NYSE-Weekly Stock Buys

Elton Stephens Investments
Box 476
South Bend, IN 46624-0476

PH: (219) 291-3823
(900) 226-8721
FAX: (219) 291-3823
Frequency: Weekly
Cost: $.95/minute
Date of first issue: 1991

Weekly hotline providing recommendations on Blue Chip, income and growth stocks. Editor: Elton Stephens.

AUDIENCE: Individual, Professional	RISK LEVEL: Moderate, Aggressive
TOPICS: Stocks	

O.I.L.: Oil Income Letter

Securities Investigations, Inc.
Mill Hill Road
P.O. Box 888
Woodstock, NY 12498

PH: (914) 679-2300
Cost: $145.00/yr
Frequency: Monthly
Date of first issue: 11/83

Fundamental analysis. Covers oil and gas investments. "Presents information and analysis of current developments in the oil income industry. Provides advice concerning oil and gas funds as investments and as tax shelters. Also reviews legislation and governmental regulation affecting the industry."

AUDIENCE: Individual, Professional	RISK LEVEL: Moderate, Aggressive
TOPICS: Mutual Funds, Stocks	

Oberweis Report, The

Hamilton Investments, Inc.
One Constitution Drive
Aurora, IL 60506

PH: (800) 323-6166
Cost: $119.00/yr or $249.00 by
  FAX
Frequency: Monthly
Date of first issue: 1976

Fundamental analysis. Covers stocks. Each issue highlights several current stocks of interest, gives extensive data on current portfolio including performance figures, lists closed out positions by year showing gain/loss and number of months held.

AUDIENCE: Individual, Professional	RISK LEVEL: Aggressive
TOPICS: Stocks	

On The Wires

Dow Jones News Services
Dow Jones and Company, Inc.
P.O. Box 300
Princeton, NJ 08543-0300

PH: (800) 223-2274
Cost: Free
Frequency: Monthly

Highlights from the prior broad tape news.

AUDIENCE: Beginning, Individual, Professional	RISK LEVEL: Conservative,
TOPICS: All	Moderate, Aggressive

Opportunities in Options

David L. Caplan
P.O. Box 2126
Malibu, CA 90265

PH: (800) 456-9699
OTHER: (310) 456-9699 CA
Cost: $450.00 annually
Frequency: Monthly
Date of first issue: 1983

Technical analysis and option volatility. Covers commodities and options. Includes actual trades. Professional option strategy - newsletter and "Hands On" trading manual. Includes twice a week hotline, and "Ask a Trader" personalized advice and weekly update on Hotline with recommendations.

AUDIENCE: Individual, Professional   RISK LEVEL: Aggressive
TOPICS: Options, Futures/Commodities

Option Advisor, The

Investment Research Institute
110 Boggs Lane
Suite 365
Cincinnati, OH 45246

PH: (800) 922-4869
Cost: $99.00 annually
Frequency: Monthly
Date of first issue: 1981

Technical analysis. Covers options. Easy to follow advice tells you exactly what to buy and when to sell. Speculative and aggressive portfolios.

AUDIENCE: Individual, Professional   RISK LEVEL: Aggressive
TOPICS: Options

Option Traders Hotline

Option Traders Hotline
Charles M. LaLoggia
PH: (900) 988-8080
INFO: (800) 836-4330
Cost: $2.00 per minute or any
  portion thereof
24 Hour service
Frequency: Daily M-F at noon
  EST

Daily option trading recommendations, U.S. market commentary, and Tokyo market commentary for Nikkeii put traders. Message: market commentary, optionable stocks for call option buyers with specific breakout levels to watch for, optionable stocks for put option buyers with specific breakdown levels to watch for, optionable stocks.

AUDIENCE: Individual, Professional   RISK LEVEL: Aggressive
TOPICS: Stocks, Options, Futures/Commodities

OTC Growth Stock Watch

OTC Research Corp.
1040 Great Plain Ave.
Needham, MA 02192

PH: (617) 327-8420
$299.00 w/unlimited advisory line
Frequency: Monthly
Date of first issue: 1979

Fundamental analysis. Covers stocks. Little-known companies in the five to one hundred million dollar sales range that are growing at a rate consistently higher than most larger corporations. Market Commentary; Our Stock Recommendation of the Month; Corporate News Updates; Update List.

AUDIENCE: Beginning, Individual, Professional   RISK LEVEL: Aggressive
TOPICS: Stocks

Outlook, The

Standard & Poor's
25 Broadway
New York, NY 10004

PH: (800) 777-4858
(212) 208-8768
Cost: $280.00 annually
Frequency: Weekly

Regular features: stock choice and market update. Analyzes and projects business and stock market trends. Brief data on individual securities with buy recommendations. Also includes current S&P market indexes.

AUDIENCE: Individual, Professional   RISK LEVEL: Moderate, Aggressive
TOPICS: Stocks, Options

Outstanding Investor Digest

Outstanding Investor Digest, Inc.
14 East 4th Street
Suite 501
New York, NY 10012

PH: (212) 777-3330
Cost: $495.00 annually (10 issues)
Frequency: Monthly
Date of first issue: 1985

Fundamental analysis. Covers interviews of equity money managers. Outstanding Investor Digest brings you the most important ideas and insights of the money managers with the best long-term records in the business. Each issue provides you with a clear window on their personalities, investment philosophies, strategies, and approaches.

AUDIENCE: Beginning, Individual, Professional   RISK LEVEL: Moderate, Aggressive
TOPICS: Stocks

Overpriced Stock Service

Michael Murphy
P.O. Box 308
Half Moon Bay, CA 94019

PH: (415) 726-8495
FAX: (415) 726-8494
Cost: $495.00 annually
Frequency: Monthly
Date of first issue: 1983

Fundamental Analysis. Covers short-selling overpriced stocks and industries, scams, hypes, etc. Subscription includes in-house Hot Line recording updated twice a week.

AUDIENCE: Individual, Professional   RISK LEVEL: Aggressive
TOPICS: Stocks

P.Q.'s Real Time Market Comments

P.Q. Wall
P.O. Box 480601
Denver, CO 80248-0601

PH: (900) 234-7777 ext 77
(303) 440-3344
Cost: $2.00 per minute
24 Hour service
Frequency: 4 times daily EST 10:10,
  12:30, 3:00, 5:00

Covers commodities, and market timing. Tries to keep recordings under one minute. Market commentary with recommendations to buy/sell based on level of Dow.

AUDIENCE: Individual, Professional   RISK LEVEL: Aggressive
TOPICS: Futures/Commodities

Partnership Watch

Robert Stanger & Co.
1129 Broad Street
Shrewsbury, NJ 07701

PH: (800) 631-2291
(201) 389-3600
Cost: $147.00 annually
Frequency: Monthly
Date of first issue: 1978

Chart service covering partnerships. Tracks all current and open partnerships. Lists and ranks each partnership, gives description, minimum purchase, all other pertinent details including telephone numbers. For $395 total, also receive Stanger Report on all closed partnerships.

AUDIENCE: Individual   RISK LEVEL: Moderate, Aggressive
TOPICS: Mutual Funds, Stocks, Investment Planning, General Reference

Pearson Investment Letter

Pearson Investment Letter
1628 White Arrow
Dover, FL 33527

PH: (813) 659-2560
Cost: $175.00 annually
1-month trial letter, $10
Frequency: Monthly
Date of first issue: 1982

Fundamental analysis. Covers stocks. The newsletter addresses current economic occurrences throughout the country. Each letter lists 10 or more stocks with recommendations on what are good buys. Subscribing to this service will enable you to use a discount broker.

AUDIENCE: Beginning, Individual   RISK LEVEL: Moderate, Aggressive
TOPICS: Stocks

Penny Stock Analyst, The

Joseph K. Cohen
The Penny Stock Analyst
P.O. Box 333
Woodstock, MD 21163-0333

Cost: $45.00/yr
Frequency: Monthly

"An investor's guide to low priced stocks." Provides specific recommendations on several issues each month.

AUDIENCE: Beginning, Individual   RISK LEVEL: Aggressive
TOPICS: Stocks

Pensions and Investments

Crain Communications, Inc.
740 Rush Street
Chicago, IL 60611

PH: (312) 649-5200
FAX: (312) 649-5228
Cost: $180.00 annually
Published: Biweekly
Date of first issue: 1973

Regular specialized issues include company reviews, stock articles, bond articles, pension funds, real estate, money manager interviews, and stock and bond indexes. The newspaper of corporate and institutional investors. Departments include: Frontlines, P&I Indexes, Valuation Index, Commentary, From the Editor, Letters to the Editor, People, Portfolio Management, Money Movers, Classifieds. Also included are articles on financing, international issues, real estate, and special reports.

AUDIENCE: Professional   RISK LEVEL: Conservative, Moderate, Aggressive
TOPICS: Bonds, Mutual Funds, Stocks, Options, Futures/Commodities, Asset Allocation

Personal Advantage/Finance

Boardroom Reports, Inc.
P.O. Box 5371
Boulder, CO 80322

PH: (212) 239-9000
(800) 365-0939
Cost: $49.00 annually
Frequency: Twice a month
Date of first issue: 1988

Covers stocks and bonds. The purpose of this newsletter is to bring businesspeople the most useful and timely advice from knowledgeable experts on all facets of personal finance. Features include: Fresh Thinking, Tax Advantage, Portfolio Strategy, Income Improvement, Recession Advantage, Bargains, Tax Traps, and Capital Preservation.

AUDIENCE: Individual   RISK LEVEL: Conservative, Moderate, Aggressive
TOPICS: All

Personal Finance

Stephen Leeb - Editor
KCI Communications, Inc.
1101 King Street
Suite 400
Alexandria, VA 22314

PH: (800) 832-2330
Cost: $59.00 annually
Frequency: Biweekly
Date of first issue: 1973

Covers stocks, mutual funds, bonds and options. America's most popular full coverage investment advisory. Follows growth stocks, mutual funds, income investments with a model portfolio in each. Money wise column dealing with topics of interest such as: taxes, insurance, divorce, etc. Includes free hotline with daily updates and recommendations. 12 pages.

AUDIENCE: Beginning, Individual   RISK LEVEL: Conservative, Moderate, Aggressive
TOPICS: Bonds, Mutual Funds, Stocks, Investment Planning

Peter Dag Investment Letter, The

Peter Dag & Associates, Inc.
65 Lake Front Drive
Akron, OH 44319

PH: (216) 644-2782
Cost: $250.00/yr
Frequency: 29 times a year
Date of first issue: 10/77

Fundamental analysis. Covers stocks, bonds, precious metals. "Describes how to develop an investment strategy that will allow one to take advantage of emerging opportunities. Offers forecasts of short- and long-term stock market trends, short-term interest rates, bond prices, gold and silver, the economy, and overall business conditions."

AUDIENCE: Beginning, Individual   RISK LEVEL: Moderate
TOPICS: Bonds, Mutual Funds, Stocks, Asset Allocation

Petroleum Outlook

John S. Herold, Inc.
5 Edgewood Ave.
Greenwich, CT 06830

PH: (203) 869-2585
Cost: $520.00/yr
Frequency: Monthly
Technical and Fundamental Analysis
Date of first issue: 1948

Analyses and reports on the latest developments in the petroleum industry. Covers petroleum, exploration drilling and oil industry service companies.

AUDIENCE: Individual, Professional   RISK LEVEL: Moderate, Aggressive
TOPICS: Stocks

Philadelphia Advisor, The

Andrew Cardwell
P.O. Box 1369
Woodstock, GA 30188

PH: (404) 591-7030
FAX: (404) 591-0672
Cost: $595.00 annually
Frequency: Bimonthly
Date of first issue: 1985

Fundamental analysis. Covers stocks, futures, and market timing. A trade service focusing on intermediate and long-term moves in commodity futures, stocks, and Dow timing. It has a totally technical trading program based on the RSI and designed to identify those few low-risk, high-profit opportunities that occur each month. Telephone update issues buy points.

AUDIENCE: Individual, Professional   RISK LEVEL: Moderate, Aggressive
TOPICS: Stocks, Options, Futures/Commodities

PivotPlus Signals

PivotPlus Signals
PH: (900) 329-7001
(312) 989-7151
Cost: $2.00 per minute
24 Hour service
Frequency: 3 to 5 times daily

Telephone newsletter covering S&P Futures, Bonds, OEX, NYFE, Gold, Crude, and Currencies.

AUDIENCE: Individual, Professional   RISK LEVEL: Aggressive
TOPICS: Options, Futures/Commodities

Plain Talk Investor

Fred Gordon, Editor
Plain Talk Investor, Inc.
1500 Skokie Blvd., Suite 203
Northbrook, IL 60062

PH: (708) 564-1955
Cost: $115.00 annually
Frequency: every 3 weeks (17 times
    a year)
Date of first issue: 1983

Covers stocks. Includes fundamental and technical analysis. The newsletter includes: Portfolio Notes - a follow-tip and news on recommended stocks, pro or con; Portfolio Reviews - every issue, every recommended stock is listed: date purchased, cost, current price, percent of gain or loss, and the price at which you should sell.

AUDIENCE: Beginning, Individual   RISK LEVEL: Moderate, Aggressive
TOPICS: Stocks, Asset Allocation

Portfolio Letter

Institutional Investor Systems
488 Madison Avenue
New York, NY 10022

PH: (212) 303-3300
Cost: $1,150.00 annually
Frequency: Weekly
Date of first issue: 1975

Fundamental analysis. Covers stocks. Portfolio Letter covers the equity markets worldwide by breaking down news on issues that affect the broad market and its industry groups, and by covering developments in specific stocks. Portfolio Letter speaks to money managers, analysts, institutional salesmen, traders, and arbitragers.

AUDIENCE: Individual, Professional   RISK LEVEL: Moderate, Aggressive
TOPICS: Bonds, Stocks, Asset Allocation

Portfolio Reports

Outstanding Investor Digest, Inc.
14 East 4th Street
New York, NY 10012

PH: (212) 777-3330
Cost: $575.00 annual (12 reports)
Frequency: Monthly or quarterly
Date of first issue: 1985

Fundamental analysis. Covers common stock purchases. Portfolio Reports brings you the most important and latest common stock purchases of the money managers with the best long-term records in the business. Each report the 10 stocks most purchased recently by more than 80 top managers in well over 100 of their portfolios.

AUDIENCE: Individual, Professional	RISK LEVEL: Moderate, Aggressive
TOPICS: Stocks	

Portfolio Selector

Argus Research Corporation
17 Battery Place
New York, NY 10004

PH: (212) 425-7500
Cost: $390.00
Frequency: Monthly
Date of first issue: 1934

Fundamental analysis. Covers stocks. Represents Argus's best buy ideas. Stocks are arranged by investment objectives such as Capital Gains and Income, Long-Term Growth, Businessman's Risk and Emerging growth. Fundamental data and commentary included on the recommended stocks. Includes subscription to Viewpoint.

AUDIENCE: Individual, Professional	RISK LEVEL: Moderate, Aggressive
TOPICS: Stocks	

Portfolios Investment Advisory

Portfolios Investment Advisory
Box 997
Lynchburg, VA 24505-0997

PH: (804) 384-3261
Cost: $150.00/yr
Frequency: Monthly
Technical and Fundamental Analysis

General investment newsletter focusing primarily on stocks. Provides recommendations.

AUDIENCE: Individual	RISK LEVEL: Moderate, Aggressive
TOPICS: Stocks	

Powell Monetary Analyst

Reserve Research
P.O. Box 4135
Portland, ME 04101

PH: (207) 774-4971
Cost: $285.00 annually
$150 for 6 months
$85.00 3 months
Frequency: Biweekly
Date of first issue: 1971

Fundamental analysis. Covers stocks, gold, silver, platinum. Focuses on fundamental trends in the economy. A large portion of the letter addresses the trends and demands on gold, silver, and platinum. Usually one company is reviewed. There are also sections on foreign currency and gold coin.

AUDIENCE: Individual	RISK LEVEL: Moderate, Aggressive
TOPICS: Stocks, Futures/Commodities	

Power and Velocity Ratings

Lowry
631 US HWY 1, Suite 305
N. Palm Beach, FL 33408

PH: (800) 345-0186
FAX: (407) 842-1523
Cost: $260.00 annually
Frequency: Weekly
FAX service also available
Date of first issue: 1960

Chart service covering stocks. Provides unique relative strength rankings on 700+ institutional quality NYSE issues.

AUDIENCE: Individual, Professional   **RISK LEVEL: Moderate, Aggressive**
TOPICS: Stocks

PQ Wall Forecast, Inc.

P.Q. Wall
P.O. Box 15558
New Orleans, LA 70175

PH: (800) 259-0088
FAX: (504) 895-4852
Cost: $198.00 annually
Frequency: Monthly
Date of first issue: 1981/ 1/1/88 as PQ Wall
Phone updates available @ additional
  cost

Fundamental analysis. Covers stocks and market timing. Stock market letter with specific recommendations, market commentary and his theories. For additional $300/yr - receive daily telephone update. Available one-hour and $1^1/_2$ hour after the market closes.

AUDIENCE: Individual, Professional   **RISK LEVEL: Moderate, Aggressive**
TOPICS: Stocks

Precision Timing

Don Vodopich
P.O. Box 11722
Atlanta, GA 30355

PH: (404) 355-0447
Cost: $205.00/yr
Frequency: Weekly
Date of first issue: 1974

Covers commodities and futures. The letter focuses on the futures market including an overall look at all major markets.

AUDIENCE: Individual, Professional   **RISK LEVEL: Aggressive**
TOPICS: Options, Futures/Commodities

Price Perceptions

Commodity Information Systems
211 N. Robinson Ave., #3000
Oklahoma City, OK 73102-7101

PH: (405) 235-5687
FAX: (713) 890-4938
Frequency: Semimonthly
Cost: $360.00/yr
Date of first issue: 1968
Editor: William Gary

Twice monthly market letter on the commodity markets. Includes a hotline with specific recommendations. The CIS Trade Selection Program, a commodity advisory letter based on fundamental research, provides investors with specific market recommendations and the rationale behind them.

AUDIENCE: Individual, Professional   **RISK LEVEL: Aggressive**
TOPICS: Commodities

Primary Trend, The

James R. Arnold
Arnold Investment Counsel, Inc.
First Financial Center
700 N. Water Street
Milwaukee, WI 53202

PH: (800) 443-6544
Cost: $180.00/yr
Frequency: Monthly
Date of first issue: 4/79

Fundamental analysis. Covers stocks, mutual funds, government bonds, tables, graphs. "Comments on general market conditions and makes recommendations to buy, sell or hold specific stocks based on the investment philosophy of Arnold Investment Counsel." And it is the same advice that is used to guide The Primary Trend Fund.

AUDIENCE: Individual   RISK LEVEL: Conservative, Moderate, Aggressive
TOPICS: Bonds, Mutual Funds, Stocks

Pring Market Review

International Institute for Economic
  Research
P.O. Box 329
Washington Depot, CT 06794

PH: (800) 221-7514
FAX: (203) 868-2683
Cost: $395.00 annually
Frequency: Monthly
Date of first issue: 1984

Technical analysis. Covers stocks, commodities, market timing, chart service, municipal and government bonds. Designed and written for the resourceful and sophisticated investor who is willing to learn the art of cyclical investing through a study of technical analysis.

AUDIENCE: Individual, Professional   RISK LEVEL: Moderate, Aggressive
TOPICS: Stocks, Options, Futures/Commodities

Professional Tape Reader

Stan Weinstein
P.O. Box 2407
Hollywood, FL 33022

PH: (800) 868-7857
Cost: $295.00 annually
Frequency: Bimonthly
Date of first issue: 1976

Technical analysis. Covers stocks, mutual funds, options, and market timing. Technical advisory newsletter.

AUDIENCE: Beginning, Individual, Professional   RISK LEVEL: Moderate, Aggressive
TOPICS: Mutual Funds, Stocks, Options

Professional Tape Reader, The

RADCAP, Inc.
P.O. Box 2407
Hollywood, FL 22033

PH: (900) 872-4787 (Hotline)
Cost: $2.00 per minute
Frequency: daily at 8PM EST

Covers stocks, bonds, gold. It covers the market's short-term outlook, stock index futures, most promising and most vulnerable stocks and trading outlook for bonds and gold.

AUDIENCE: Individual, Professional   RISK LEVEL: Moderate, Aggressive
TOPICS: Bonds, Stocks, Futures/Commodities

Professional Timing Service

Curtis Hesler - Publisher
Professional Timing Service
P.O. Box 7483
Missoula, MT 59807

PH: (800) 348-2729 ext 13
(Orders) (406) 543-4131
Cost: $185.00 for 14 months
Frequency: Monthly
Date of first issue: 1987

Fundamental and technical analysis. Covers stocks, bonds, mutual funds, and market timing. The model is based on monitoring money flow - if money is flowing into the market at sufficient intensity, the model tells us to buy. At that time, we switch managed accounts into equity funds and announce on our hotline that subscribers should do likewise.

AUDIENCE: Individual   RISK LEVEL: Conservative, Moderate, Aggressive
TOPICS: Bonds, Mutual Funds, Stocks

Profit Letter, The

Profit Letter, Inc.
908-4390 Grange Street
Burnaby, BC, Canada V5H1P6

PH: (604) 436-3751
FAX: (604) 436-3751
Cost: $125.00
Frequency: Bimonthly
Date of first issue: 1987

Fundamental analysis. Covers stocks. Concentrates on capital gain stocks and gives specific recommendations and updates on previous recommendations.

AUDIENCE: Beginning, Individual   RISK LEVEL: Moderate, Aggressive
TOPICS: Stocks

Prudent Speculator, The

Al Frank Asset Management, Inc.
P.O. Box 1767
Santa Monica, CA 90406-1767

PH: (310) 587-2410
Cost: $45.00 trial offer 3 issues
$175.00 yearly 12 issues
Frequency: Monthly
Date of first issue: 1977

Fundamental and technical analysis. Covers stocks, charts, market timing. The Prudent Speculator recommends under-valued stock selling at 50% of value which will at a minimum double in 3-5 years. Includes strategies for investing in common stocks using fundamental analysis for stock selection and technical analysis for market timing.

AUDIENCE: Individual   RISK LEVEL: Moderate, Aggressive
TOPICS: Bonds, Stocks, Options

Rapaport Diamond Report

Rapaport Diamond Corp
15 W. 47th St.
Suites 700-702
New York, NY 10036

PH: (212) 354-0575
Cost: $180.00/2nd class mail;
  $220.00/1st class mail
Frequency: Weekly
Technical and Fundamental Analysis

Lists "approximate cash New York asking price indications" for diamonds. Also lists stones for which Rapaport is broker, approximate broker sell indications, and diamond industry news. Recurring features include information on diamond auctions and a column titled Comments From the Trading Desk. Includes tables.

AUDIENCE: Individual, Professional   RISK LEVEL: Moderate, Aggressive
TOPICS: Investment Planning

Rational Investment Outlook

Arie Vilner
Vilner Enterprises, Inc.
Bowling Green Station
P.O. Box 1605
New York, NY 10274-1132

Cost: $139.00
Frequency: Monthly
Date of first issue: 1990

Technical analysis. Covers stocks, mutual funds, market timing, gold. Uses a proprietary method of market trend forecasting - not the typical technical analysis. Provides stock and mutual fund selections, company report, investment strategies, new technologies, world investment environment and more.

AUDIENCE: Beginning, Individual   RISK LEVEL: Moderate, Aggressive
TOPICS: Mutual Funds, Stocks

Reaper, The

A.N., Inc.
P.O. Box 84901
Phoenix, AZ 85071

PH: (800) 528-0559
Cost: $195.00 per year
Frequency: 36 issues a year
Date of first issue: 6/77

Fundamental analysis. Covers commodities. "Provides investors with an analysis of the international and domestic economic, political and financial environment. Offers projections particularly in the area of commodities, specific buy and sell recommendations in the commodity futures markets, and instructions on how to analyze the market."

AUDIENCE: Individual, Professional   RISK LEVEL: Aggressive
TOPICS: Options, Futures/Commodities

Red Book of 5-Trend Security Charts

Securities Research Co.
101 Prescott Street
Wellesley Hills, MA 02181

PH: (617) 235-0900
Cost: $124.00/yr
Frequency: Monthly

21 month chart service covering the weekly performance of over 1,100 leading stocks.

AUDIENCE: Beginning, Individual, Professional   RISK LEVEL: Moderate, Aggressive
TOPICS: Stocks

REIT Watch

National Association of Real Estate
Investment Trusts, Inc.
1129 20th Street, N.W.
Suite 705
Washington, D.C. 20036

PH: (202) 785-8717
Cost: $145.00 annually
Frequency: Quarterly
Date of first issue: Fall 1990

Fundamental analysis. Covers REITs. Investment publication detailing REIT industry performance including a concise review of industry activities, comparative investment return scorecard, total return, dividend yield and other stats for all publicly traded REITs, REIT article reference list and discussion of issues relevant to REITs.

AUDIENCE: Individual, Professional   RISK LEVEL: Moderate, Aggressive
TOPICS: Stocks, Investment Planning

Retirement Letter

Phillips Publishing
7811 Montrose Road
Potomac, MD 20854

PH: (800) 777-5005
Cost: $49.91/yr
Frequency: Monthly
Date of first issue: 1973

Fundamental analysis. Covers stocks, mutual funds. "Provides analysis of the performance of 83 mutual funds and of the economic and market outlook. Also carries stock and gold market forecasts and two model portfolios."

AUDIENCE: Beginning, Individual   RISK LEVEL: Moderate
TOPICS: Mutual Funds, Stocks

Richard Russell's Dow Theory Letters

Richard Russell
P.O. Box 1759
La Jolla, CA 92038

PH: (619) 454-0481
Cost: $225.00/yr
Frequency: Every two weeks
Date of first issue: 1958

Fundamental and technical analysis. Covers stocks, mutual funds, charts, precious metals. Primarily an investment theory/trend letter. Focuses on the Primary Trend Index. Provides some general investment recommendations. Publishes "a wealth of information, ideas and practical suggestions" on the stock and bond markets based on the Dow Theory.

AUDIENCE: Beginning, Individual   RISK LEVEL: Moderate, Aggressive
TOPICS: Mutual Funds, Stocks, Futures/Commodities

Richard Young's Intelligence Report

Phillips Publishing, Inc.
7811 Montrose Rd.
Potomac, MD 20854

PH: (301) 340-2100
(800) 777-5005
Cost: $99.95
Date of first issue: 1985
Frequency: Monthly
Fundamental Analysis

A conservative approach to investing and building wealth without principal. Each issue contains 3 model portfolios with specific recommendations as well as Mr. Young's comments on the state of the economy and how it affects the business cycle.

AUDIENCE: Individual   RISK LEVEL: Conservative
TOPICS: Stocks

Richland Report, The

Kennedy Gammage
P.O. Box 222
La Jolla, California 92038

PH: (619) 459-2611
Cost: $197.00 annually
Frequency: Every 2 weeks
Date of first issue: 1976

Covers stocks, mutual funds, and market timing. General overview of the market, concentrating on market timing, McClellan Oscillator, occasional market recommendations.

AUDIENCE: Individual   RISK LEVEL: Moderate, Aggressive
TOPICS: Mutual Funds, Stocks

Rick Dupuis "Inside Money" Newsletter

Rick Dupuis "Inside Money"
 Newsletter
2061 Boca Raton Blvd.
Suite 103
Boca Raton, FL 33431
PH: (800) 749-6785
Cost: Free/copy

TV show "Inside Money" (PBS). Host: Rick Dupruis (CFD); Producer: Susan Fusari. It's bursting with useful investing ideas to help you get ahead, such as future Topics, Interviews with money managers, Tax tips.

AUDIENCE: Beginning, Individual, Professional   RISK LEVEL: Moderate, Aggressive
TOPICS: Bonds, Mutual Funds, Stocks Asset Allocation, Investment Planning

Risk Factor Method of Investing

Invest/O - Registered Investment
 Advisors
65575 Sisemore Rd., P.O. Box 5996
Bend, OR 97708-5996

PH: (503) 389-3676
FAX: (503) 389-3676
Cost: $100.00/yr, weekly updates
available at $75.00 additional
Technical and Fundamental Analysis
Frequency: Monthly

Provides charts and market commentary as well as a model portfolio, recommendations and quotes from investment advisors.

AUDIENCE: Individual, Professional   RISK LEVEL: Moderate, Aggressive
TOPICS: Stocks

Risk Report, The

Richard Schmidt
3479 N. High Street
Columbus, OH 43214

PH: (800) 466-RISK
Cost: $199.00
Frequency: Every 3 weeks
Date of first issue: 1991

Technical analysis. Covers stocks, mutual funds, municipal bonds, corporate bonds, government bonds. An investment advisory newsletter with a common sense approach. Information is delivered in plain English and includes very specific investment recommendations. Also available via fax for an additional $129.00.

AUDIENCE: Beginning, Individual   RISK LEVEL: Conservative, Moderate, Aggressive
TOPICS: Bonds, Mutual Funds, Stocks

Risk Report Online/Fax, The

Richard Schmidt
3479 N. High Street
Columbus, OH 43214

PH: (800) 466-RISK
Cost: Contact vendor
Frequency of update: Every 3 weeks
Fax service

Telephone newsletter covering stocks, mutual funds and bonds. An investment advisory service with a common sense approach delivered in plain English. Gives very specific recommendations.

AUDIENCE: Beginning, Individual   RISK LEVEL: Conservative, Moderate, Aggressive
TOPICS: Bonds, Mutual Funds, Stocks

Roesch Market Memo, The

Larry Roesch
P.O. Box 4242
Shawnee Mission, KS 66204

PH: (913) 381-0857
Cost: $42.00 annually
Frequency: Every 25 days
Date of first issue: February 1981
Technical and Fundamental
Analysis

Editor: Larry E. Roesch. Takes a "fundamental and technical look at common stocks and their price movements" and makes specific recommendations. Concerned with domestic and international economics and politics and their effect on Wall Street. Recurring features include a model portfolio of common stocks recommended over the past 24 months.

AUDIENCE: Individual, Professional   RISK LEVEL: Moderate, Aggressive
TOPICS: Stocks, Asset Allocation

Ron Paul Survival Report, The

Ron Paul & Associates, Inc.
18333 Egret Bay, Suite 265
Houston, TX 77058

PH: (713) 333-4888
Date of first issue: 1985
Cost: $99.00 annually
Frequency: Monthly
New subscribers can access
financial hotline every Monday

Fundamental analysis. Covers stocks, commodities, mutual funds, and bonds. Each month Ron Paul gives the facts and analysis and specific recommendations that you need to protect yourself, and dramatically increase your wealth, in the spastic economy of the 1990s.

AUDIENCE: Individual   RISK LEVEL: Conservative, Moderate, Aggressive
TOPICS: Bonds, Mutual Funds, Stocks

Rouge Et Noir Securities Watch

Rouge Et Noir, Inc.
Box 1146
Midlothian, VA 23113

PH: (804) 230-0736
FAX: (804) 230-4931
Cost: $520.00/yr
Date of first issue: 1990
Frequency: Weekly

Press releases, insider transactions, 10K and 10-Q summaries and news on publicly traded casinos.

AUDIENCE: Individual, Professional   RISK LEVEL: Moderate, Aggressive
TOPICS: Stocks

Ruff Times, The

The Ruff Times
757 South Main
Springville, UT 84663

PH: (801) 489-0222
ISSN: 0891-5547
Cost: $89.00 annually
Frequency: Every three weeks
Date of first issue: 1976

Fundamental analysis. Covers stocks, mutual funds, and bonds (municipal, corporate, government). Focuses on the general market - strong vs weak areas. Howard Ruff looks closely at long-term trends before making his recommendations. Some of the features include: Ruff Goofs, Ask Howard, Good News/Bad News, Truth in Lending and more.

AUDIENCE: Beginning, Individual   RISK LEVEL: Conservative, Moderate, Aggressive
TOPICS: Bonds, Mutual Funds, Stocks

Ruta Financial Newsletter, The

Phillip Ruta
P.O. Box 952
Bronxville, NY 10708

PH: (914) 779-1983
(800) 832-1891
Cost: $90.00 annually
Frequency: Monthly
Date of first issue: 1984

Offers in-depth comprehensive reports on growth stocks, special situations, income stocks, asset plays, and turnaround stocks. The only newsletter which gives its subscribers "FREE UNLIMITED PERSONALIZED INVESTMENT ADVICE (TOLL FREE)."

AUDIENCE: Beginning, Individual   RISK LEVEL: Moderate, Aggressive
TOPICS: Stocks

S.T.A.R. Futures Daily

John J. Kosar
S.T.A.R. Futures, Inc.
P.O. Box 88510
Carol Stream, IL 60188-8510

PH: (708) 830-0800
Cost: $175.00 to 400.00 per month
(available via fax)
Frequency: Daily
Date of first issue: 1982

Technical analysis. Covers commodities. A daily traders' report on 17 futures markets including grains, stock indices, interest rates, foreign currencies, metals, softs. Their daily support and resistance levels included in each day's report have been used by Chicago floor traders and the arbitrage and trading desks of many major trading firms since 1982.

AUDIENCE: Individual, Professional   RISK LEVEL: Aggressive
TOPICS: Bonds, Futures/Commodities

S&P 500 Directory

Standard & Poor's Corporation
25 Broadway
New York, NY 10004

PH: (212) 208-8000
Cost: $39.95/yr.
Frequency: Annually

Names and addresses of the companies in the S&P 500.

AUDIENCE: Beginning, Individual, Professional RISK LEVEL: Moderate, Aggressive
TOPICS: Stocks

Safe Money Report

Weiss Research, Inc.
2200 N. Florida Mango Road
West Palm Beach, FL 33409

PH: (407) 684-8100
(800) 289-9222
Cost: $145.00
Frequency: Monthly
Date of first issue: 1971

Fundamental analysis. Covers stocks, municipal bonds, corporate bonds, government bonds, foreign bonds, interest rates, insurance. Features articles on important news and developments relating to T-Bills, banks, interest rates, insurance companies and more. Investment advice for the conservative and speculative investor.

AUDIENCE: Beginning, Individual   RISK LEVEL: Conservative, Moderate, Aggressive
TOPICS: Bonds, Mutual Funds, Stocks

Sarcoh Report

Sarcoh Report, Inc.
48 Park Terrace
Spring Valley, NY 10977

PH: (914) 354-0030
(914) 354-2114
Cost: $165.00 annually
Frequency: 20-24 issues per year
Date of first issue: 1991

Fundamental and technical analysis. Covers stocks, bonds, futures, options, market timing, mutual funds. A conservative investment advisory letter focused on risk avoidance. Includes charts and several recommendations. Also includes daily telephone updates.

AUDIENCE: Beginning, Individual   RISK LEVEL: Moderate
TOPICS: All

Scientific Investments

Predictions Agora, Inc.
824 E. Baltimore St.
Baltimore, MD 21202-4799

PH: (410) 234-0691
Cost: $49.00
Frequency: Monthly

Focuses on emerging tech stocks poised for significant growth and provides specific investment recommendations.

AUDIENCE: Beginning, Individual, Professional   RISK LEVEL: Aggressive
TOPICS: Stocks

Scott Letter, The

Cole Publications Inc.
8659 Rio Grande Rd.
Richmond, VA 23229

PH: (804) 741-8707
FAX: (703) 899-6381
Cost: $150.00/yr
Fundamental Analysis
Frequency: Monthly

Information on equity and bond closed-end investment companies for educational reasons.

AUDIENCE: Beginning, Individual   RISK LEVEL: Moderate, Aggressive
TOPICS: Bonds, Mutual Funds, Stocks

Seasonal Trader Report, The

The Seasonal Trader Report
P.O. Box 172143
Memphis, TN 38187-2143

PH: (800) 526-4612
(901) 757-5889 (outside U.S.)
Frequency: Weekly
Cost: $349.00 annually
Date of first issue: 1987

Fundamental Analysis. Covers commodities, precious metals, and financials. A 4-page weekly letter with one specific short-term recommendation based on computer research. Detailed historical performance data on each recommendation is provided, plus a quarterly book containing 10 years of daily price history on 25 commodities.

AUDIENCE: Individual, Professional   RISK LEVEL: Aggressive
TOPICS: Futures/Commodities

SEC Docket

Commerce Clearing House, Inc.
4025 West Peterson Avenue
Chicago, IL 60646

PH: (312) 583-8500
Cost: $230.00 annually
Frequency: Weekly
Date of first issue: November 1981

Fundamental analysis. Covers SEC Dockets. Every week you receive new releases of SEC Dockets. An updated index is included every 20 issues.

AUDIENCE: Professional　　　　RISK LEVEL: Conservative, Moderate, Aggressive
TOPICS: All

SEC Today

Washington Service Bureau
655 15th Street, N.W.
Suite 270
Washington, D.C. 20005

PH: (202) 508-0600
(800) 955-5219
Cost: $640.00 annually
Frequency: Daily
Date of first issue: 1983

The newsletter begins with a letter form the editor addressing a current news item. Daily lists of Williams Act Filings, 8-Ks, no-action letters, and registrations, including initial public offerings. SEC News Digest, which provides daily briefs on administrative/civil proceedings, Commission announcements, Investment Company Act releases, and rulings.

AUDIENCE: Professional
TOPICS: All

Sector Fund Connection

Mannie Webb
8949 La Riviera Drive
Sacramento, CA 95826

PH: (916) 363-2055
Cost: $35.00 annually
Frequency: none
Date of first issue: 1981

Includes technical timing analysis. Covers mutual funds. The newsletter covers a variety of mutual fund trading methods.

AUDIENCE: Individual　　　　RISK LEVEL: Aggressive
TOPICS: Mutual Funds, Asset Allocation

Securities Industry Trends

Securities Industry Association
Research Department
120 Broadway
35th Floor
New York, NY 10271

PH: (212) 608-1500
Cost: $60 for members
$90 for nonmembers
Frequency: 8 per year

Includes fundamental analysis. Covers securities. "Examines economic developments affecting securities firms, including tax policy, the changing composition of the securities industry, and major trends in the industry. Supplies a series of security industry statistics tables and a reading list."

AUDIENCE: Individual, Professional　　　　RISK LEVEL: Conservative, Moderate, Aggressive
TOPICS: All

Securities Regulation & Law Report

Bureau of National Affairs, Inc. (BNA)
1231 25th St, N.W.
Washington, DC 20037

PH: (800) 372-1033
FAX: (202) 822-8096
Cost: $768.00/yr.
TELEX: 285656 BNAI WSH
Frequency: Weekly, indexed every
  6 weeks, cumulative index issued
  semiannually
Date of first issue: May 8, 1969
Fundamental Analysis

Securities and commodities activity at federal and state levels. Congress, the Administration Securities Exchange Commission, Commodities Futures Commission, banking regulations. Financial Accounting Standards Board, professional associations, courts, and industry. Regulations, Legislation, News and Comment, SEC No-Action & Interpretive Letters.

AUDIENCE: Professional   RISK LEVEL: Conservative, Moderate, Aggressive
TOPICS: All

Securities Week

McGraw-Hill Publications
1221 Avenue of the Americas
New York, NY 10020

PH: (212) 512-3144
(800) 445-9786
Cost: $1,310.00 annually
Frequency: Weekly
Date of first issue: 1972

Fundamental analysis. Covers stocks and commodities/futures. A report on the securities industry and financial futures markets. The four areas of security firms covered are: exchange, institutional investment banking firms, futures and options, regulatory and legislative.

AUDIENCE: Professional   RISK LEVEL: Conservative, Moderate, Aggressive
TOPICS: All

Security Dealers of North America

Standard & Poor's Corporation
25 Broadway
New York, NY 10004

PH: (212) 208-8000
Cost: $515.00/yr.
Frequency: Semiannual
Editor: Lily DeAngelis
Date of first issue: 1922

A directory listing of all investment firms and their executives.

AUDIENCE: Professional   RISK LEVEL: Conservative, Moderate, Aggressive
TOPICS: All

Sentinel Investment Letter

Hanover Investment Management Corp.
P.O. Box 189
52 South Main Street
New Hope, PA 18938

PH: (215) 862-5454
Cost: $150.00 annually
Frequency: Monthly
Date of first issue: 1978

Fundamental analysis. Covers stocks and bonds. The newsletter focuses on unique things that affect the stock market, such as interest rates and inflation. The author also discusses opportunities of when to buy and sell.

AUDIENCE: Individual   RISK LEVEL: Conservative, Moderate
TOPICS: Bonds, Mutual Funds, Stocks, Investment Planning

Shelburne Securities Forecast

Robert Shelburne
P.O. Box 5566
Arlington, VA 22205

PH: (703) 532-4416
Cost: $49.00 annually
Frequency: Twice a month
Date of first issue: 1976

Fundamental analysis. Covers utilities stocks. This 6-8 page newsletter covers stocks and utilities.

AUDIENCE: Beginning, Individual   RISK LEVEL: Moderate, Aggressive
TOPICS: Stocks

Short Term Consensus Hotline

Dr. Harry B. Schiller
PH: (900) 860-9990
(415) 956-3766
Cost: $2.00 for the first minute -
  $1.00 thereafter

Telephone newsletter covering market timing. Rating service for short-term timers.

AUDIENCE: Individual   RISK LEVEL: Aggressive
TOPICS: Stocks, Options, Futures/Commodities

Shortex

Shortex
6669 Security Blvd., #201
Dept. S
Baltimore, MD 21207-4024

PH: (800) 877-6555
Cost: $249.00/yr
Frequency: Biweekly

Fundamental and technical analysis. Covers stocks. Chart selected short sales. New trades in each issue with stop loss, profit objective and price to cover. Also includes a special advisory on long positions.

AUDIENCE: Beginning, Individual, Professional   RISK LEVEL: Aggressive
TOPICS: Stocks

Siegel Weekly Market Letter, The

Siegel Trading Company, Inc.
549 W. Randolph, 7th Fl.
Chicago, IL 60606

PH: (800) 422-9903
FAX: Ask for FAX at above #
Frequency: Weekly
Cost: Free to clients, free 4 weeks
  to prospective clients
Date of first issue: 1950
Fundamental Analysis

Analyzes 16 major markets and provides technical and fundamental commentary on each. Each issue highlights the 1 or 2 most promising markets for the week as well as long-term market commentary. Also provides pertinent government news relative to the market.

AUDIENCE: Individual, Professional   RISK LEVEL: Aggressive
TOPICS: Futures/Commodities

Silver and Gold Report

Dan Rosenthal
Weiss Research Publications, Inc.
P.O. Box 2923
West Palm Beach, FL 33402

PH: (800) 289-8100
Cost: $156.00 annually
Frequency: Monthly
Date of first issue: 1981

Fundamental analysis. Covers silver and gold. The author, Dan Rosenthal, surveys 23 leading firms in the bullion industry. He explains where and what to buy is as important as when to buy. He also lists dealers with the best prices.

AUDIENCE: Individual	RISK LEVEL: Moderate, Aggressive
TOPICS: Futures/Commodities	

Small + Tomorrow's Commodities

Robert Jubb
Techno-Fundamental Investments, Inc.
P.O. Box 6216
Scottsdale, AZ 85261

PH: (602) 996-2908
Cost: $295.00 annually
Frequency: Twice monthly
Date of first issue: 1974

Fundamental and technical analysis. Covers commodities. Detailed analysis of only a few recommendations using proprietary technical and fundamental research tools. Includes charts and follow-up discussion of previous recommendations.

AUDIENCE: Individual, Professional	RISK LEVEL: Aggressive
TOPICS: Options, Futures/Commodities	

Smart Money

The Hirsch Organization
6 Deer Trail
Old Tappan, NJ 07675

PH: (201) 664-3400
Cost: $98.00 annually
Frequency: Monthly
Date of first issue: 1972

Fundamental analysis. Covers company reviews and stocks. Smart Money focuses on America's most undiscovered companies.

AUDIENCE: Beginning, Individual	RISK LEVEL: Moderate, Aggressive
TOPICS: Stocks	

SMR Commodity Service

Security Market Research, Inc.
Box 7476
Boulder, CO 80306-7476

PH: (303) 442-4121
FAX: (303) 444-3997
Cost: $15.00/copy; $575.00 annually
Frequency: Weekly
Date of first issue: 1966
Technical Analysis

Editor: Jerry Hodges. Charts commodity and stock charts with timing indices and hotline to update standard bar or Japanese candlestick. Daily/weekly charts. Daily FAX service which includes recommendations is an additional cost.

AUDIENCE: Individual, Professional	RISK LEVEL: Aggressive
TOPICS: Futures/Commodities	

SMR Stock Service

Security Market Research, Inc.
Box 7476
Boulder, CO 80306-7476

PH: (303) 442-4121
FAX: (303) 444-3997
Cost: $15.00/copy; $575.00 annually
Date of first issue: 1966
Technical Analysis

Charts commodity and stock charts with timing indices and hotline to update standard bar or Japanese candlestick. Daily/weekly charts. Daily FAX service which includes recommendations is an additional cost.

AUDIENCE: Individual, Professional   RISK LEVEL: Moderate, Aggressive
TOPICS: Stocks, Futures/Commodities

Sound Advice

Gray Emerson Cardiff
370 Diablo Rd.
Suite 201
Danville, CA 94526

PH: (800) 423-8423
Cost: $150.00 annually
Frequency: Monthly
Date of first issue: 1981

Fundamental and technical analysis. Precious metals, stocks, and includes charts. Sound Advice is the advisory letter for panic-proof investing. Features which may be included: Business Cycle Signals, The Stock Market Risk Indicator, Precious Metals and Portfolio Update.

AUDIENCE: Individual   RISK LEVEL: Moderate, Aggressive
TOPICS: Stocks, Futures/Commodities

Sound Mind Investing

Pryor & Associates
2337 Glen Eagle Dr.
Louisville, KY 40222

PH: (502) 426-7420
Cost: $59.00/yr
Frequency: Monthly

Highlights no load mutual funds and provides global and domestic news. Provides general personal finance news and advice from a biblical perspective. Specific recommendations are provided.

AUDIENCE: Beginning, Individual   RISK LEVEL: Moderate, Aggressive
TOPICS: Mutual Funds

Southeast Business Alert

Word Merchants, Inc.
2000 Riveredge Parkway
Atlanta, GA 30328

PH: (404) 577-9194
Cost: $198.00
Frequency: Monthly
Date of first issue: 1989

Fundamental analysis. Covers Southeast businesses stocks, and provides some charts. This 8 page newsletter focuses on businesses in the Southeast. A few regular features are: Insider Trading Report, Six month Activity Summary and Business Brief.

AUDIENCE: Beginning, Individual, Professional RISK LEVEL: Moderate, Aggressive
TOPICS: Bonds, Stocks

Special Investment Situations

George W. Southerland
P.O. Box 4254
Chattanooga, TN 37405

PH: (615) 886-1628
Cost: $160.00/yr.
Frequency: Monthly
Fundamental Analysis
Date of first issue: June 1979

Provides stock market investment recommendations. Focuses on companies that "offer the prospect of a substantial capital gain in a relatively short time with comparatively small risk." Includes a description of the company, pertinent financial data, and factors influencing the recommendation. Also updates previous recommendations.

AUDIENCE: Individual, Professional	RISK LEVEL: Moderate, Aggressive
TOPICS: Stocks	

Special Situation Report

Charles LaLoggia
P.O. Box 167
Rochester, NY 14601

PH: (716) 232-1240
Cost: $230.00 annually
Frequency: Every 3 weeks
Date of first issue: 1974

Fundamental and technical analysis. Covers stocks and provides some charts. The report gives a general market commentary and what to look for in regards to takeover targets. The author also recommends other stocks with an emphasis on insider buying or selling.

AUDIENCE: Individual	RISK LEVEL: Moderate, Aggressive
TOPICS: Stocks	

Special Situation Report

Individual Investor
P.O. Box 2484
Secaucus, NJ 07094-2484

PH: (800) 995-1695
Cost: $195.00 annually
Frequency: Monthly
Date of first issue: 1974

Concentrates on small-cap stocks. Every month you'll receive a comprehensive new research report, plus updates on stocks previously featured, with on-going buy, sell and hold.

AUDIENCE: Individual, Professional	RISK LEVEL: Moderate, Aggressive
TOPICS: Stocks	

Special Situations

Argus Research Corporation
17 Battery Place
New York, NY 10004

PH: (212) 425-7500
Cost: $390.00
Frequency: Monthly
Date of first issue: 1934
Editor: Rick Foote

Fundamental analysis. Covers stocks. A new stock pick is introduced every other issue and updates on previous recommendations are included. Each issue contains EPS, price/earnings ratio, return on equity and performance record on all recommendations.

AUDIENCE: Individual, Professional	RISK LEVEL: Moderate, Aggressive
TOPICS: Stocks	

Special Situations Newsletter

Charles H. Kaplan
26 Broadway
Room 200
New York, NY 10004

PH: (212) 908-4168
Cost: $100.00/yr
Frequency: Monthly

Fundamental analysis. Covers stocks. "Examines companies by providing a corporate profile and analysis of investment rating, financial condition, earnings per share growth for the year, and takeover potential, then suggests an investment strategy."

AUDIENCE: Beginning, Individual	RISK LEVEL: Moderate, Aggressive
TOPICS: Stocks	

Speculator, The

Growth In Funds, Inc.
77 South Palm Avenue
Sarasota, FL 34236

PH: (813) 954-0330
Cost: $95.00 for six months,
   $175.00 annually
Frequency: Every 3 weeks
Date of first issue: 1968

Fundamental and technical analysis. Covers stocks and uses charts. The Speculator includes: buying ideas, including low-prices OTC choices; trading suggestions; insider buying details; "What to Do About" the most active low-priced stocks; "Stock of the Week" feature and follow-ups.

AUDIENCE: Individual	RISK LEVEL: Aggressive
TOPICS: Stocks	

Spread Scope Commodity Charts

Spread Scope, Inc.
P.O. Box 950841
Mission Hills, CA 91345

PH: (800) 232-7285
FAX: (818) 782-6640
Cost: $205.00 to $325.00
Frequency: Weekly, biweekly, or
   monthly.
Date of first issue: 1976

Technical analysis. Covers commodities. Spread Scope Commodity Spread Charts offers both agricultural and financial charts.

AUDIENCE: Individual, Professional	RISK LEVEL: Aggressive
TOPICS: Options, Futures/Commodities	

Spread Scope Commodity Spread Letter

Spread Scope, Inc.
P.O. Box 950841
Mission Hills, CA 91345

PH: (800) 232-7285
(818) 782-0774
FAX: (818) 782-6640
Cost: $195.00 annually
Frequency: Weekly
Date of first issue: 1974

Technical analysis. Covers commodities. The Spread Letter includes current open positions, recommendations, and comments. Provides specific spread trading advice on the commodity market. Recommends only trades that are placed for the corporation's own model account, and follows them until they are closed out.

AUDIENCE: Individual, Professional	RISK LEVEL: Aggressive
TOPICS: Options, Futures/Commodities	

Spread Scope Long Term Charts

Spread Scope, Inc.
P.O. Box 950841
Mission Hills, CA 91345

PH: (800) 232-7285
FAX: (818) 782-6640
Cost: $35.00 for 80 charts
$20.00 for 40 bar charts, $20.00 for
  40 spread charts
Frequency: Monthly
Date of first issue: 1976

Technical analysis. Covers commodities, chart service. Spread Scope Long Term Charts offers both agricultural and financial charts. Weekly high-low close published monthly.

AUDIENCE: Individual, Professional   RISK LEVEL: Aggressive
TOPICS: Options, Futures/Commodities

Springfield Report, The

Vincent Cosentino
1131 W. B St.
Suite 4
Ontario, CA 91762

PH: (909) 984-7423
Cost: $95.00/yr
Frequency: Monthly
Technical and Fundamental Analysis
Date of first issue: 1984

Market commentary and evaluations primarily based on economic conditions and indicators. Recommendations are offered based on insider buying information.

AUDIENCE: Individual   RISK LEVEL: Moderate, Aggressive
TOPICS: Stocks

SRC Blue Book of 5 Trend Cyclic - Graph

Babson-United Investment
  Advisors, Inc.
101 Prescott Street
Wellesley Hills, MA 02181

PH: (617) 235-0900
FAX: (617) 235-9450
Cost: $30.00 ea or $104.00 annually
Frequency: Quarterly
Date of first issue: 1935

Fundamental analysis. Stock chart service. 12 year coverage of 1,108 listed stocks. Set each stock's extended history of monthly price ranges, relative market action, volume, earnings, and dividends. Semilogarithmic grids present information in a clear, visually accurate format suited to easy measurement and immediate comparisons.

AUDIENCE: Beginning, Individual, Professional   RISK LEVEL: Moderate, Aggressive
TOPICS: Stocks

SRC Orange Book of 1012 Active OTC Stocks

Babson-United Investment
  Advisors, Inc.
101 Prescott Street
Wellesley Hills, MA 02181

PH: (617) 235-0900
FAX: (617) 235-9450
Cost: $33.00 each or $114.00
  annually
Frequency: Quarterly
Date of first issue: 1991

Fundamental analysis. Stock chart service. 256 pages chart the 12-year trends in earnings and dividends of 1,012 active OTC stocks. Prices, volume, and relative performance are charted monthly, plus 48 month moving averages.

AUDIENCE: Beginning, Individual, Professional   RISK LEVEL: Moderate, Aggressive
TOPICS: Stocks

SRC Red Book of 1108 Security Charts (Securities Research Co.)

Babson-United Investment
  Advisors, Inc.
101 Prescott Street
Wellesley Hills, MA 02181

PH: (617) 235-0900
FAX: (617) 235-9450
Cost: $17.00 each or $124.00
  annually
Frequency: Monthly
Date of first issue: 1935
Technical Analysis

Covers stocks, chart service. 288 pages of charted data, fully adjusted for stock dividends and splits. Unabridged 21 months of graphics of 1,108 listed stocks feature weekly price ranges, volumes, relative performance, 13 & 39 week moving averages and quarterly earnings and dividends.

AUDIENCE: Beginning, Individual, Professional   RISK LEVEL: Moderate, Aggressive
TOPICS: Stocks

Standard & Poor's The Edge

Standard & Poor's
25 Broadway
New York, NY 10004

PH: (800) 777-4858
Cost: $360.00 per year
Frequency: Twice monthly
Date of first issue: Late 1990

Fundamental analysis. Covers stocks. Considers input from 2,500 security analysts at 140 brokerage firms. Combines proven stock selection strategies that focus on capital appreciation with price and earnings data resulting in winning ideas. Portfolio and economic overview, industry and company reviews, model portfolio and recommendations.

AUDIENCE: Individual, Professional   RISK LEVEL: Moderate, Aggressive
TOPICS: Stocks

Standard & Poor's Trendline Chart Guide

Standard & Poor's
25 Broadway
New York, NY 10004

PH: (800) 777-4858
Cost: $108.00/yr
Frequency: Monthly
Date of first issue: 1991

Fundamental analysis. Covers stocks, chart service. Details on over 4,400 NYSE, AMEX, and NASDAQ issues in a format similar to Standard & Poor's Stock Guide. Price performance data for past 52 weeks including high, low, close and volume, 30 week moving average, exclusive relative strength values, industry group, number of shares, etc.

AUDIENCE: Beginning, Individual, Professional   RISK LEVEL: Moderate, Aggressive
TOPICS: Stocks

Standard & Poor's Credit Week

Standard & Poor's
25 Broadway
New York, NY 10004

PH: (800) 777-4858
(212) 208-8768
Cost: $1,695.00/yr

Focuses on trends and outlooks for fixed income securities including corporate and government bonds and money market instruments. Offers the latest info on S&P's new and changed ratings for corporate, municipal and structured issuers.

AUDIENCE: Individual, Professional   RISK LEVEL: Conservative, Moderate
TOPICS: Bonds

Standard & Poor's Industry Surveys

Standard & Poor's Corp.
25 Broadway
New York, NY 10004

PH: (212) 208-8786
Cost: $1,475.00/yr
Frequency: Irregular (indexed monthly)

Covers 21 different industry groups. Each *Survey* provides a broad picture of the industry it covers, examines its operating environment and reviews key issues facing the industry. More detailed info. is discussed in 'Current Surveys', monthly 'Trends and Projections', and Monthly 'Earnings Supplements.' All data are supported with extensive charts and graphs.

AUDIENCE: Individual, Professional   RISK LEVEL: Moderate, Aggressive
TOPICS: Bonds, Stocks

Stanger Report

Robert Stanger & Co.
1129 Broad Street
Shrewsbury, NJ 07701

PH: (800) 631-2291
(201) 389-3600
Cost: from $350.00 annually
Frequency: Monthly
Date of first issue: 1978

Chart service covering partnerships. A guide to partnership investing. Follows closed partnership and the secondary market. Tracks all closed partnerships and gives evaluations, total performance, distributions, tax benefits, and other pertinent information. For an additional $45 subscribe to Partnership Watch — a newsletter on current partnerships.

AUDIENCE: Beginning, Individual   RISK LEVEL: Moderate, Aggressive
TOPICS: Mutual Funds, Stocks, Investment Planning, General Reference

Stark Research CTA Report

Stark Research, Inc.
7777 Fay Ave, Suite E
LaJolla, CA 92037

PH: (619) 459-0818
Cost: $495.00
Frequency: Quarterly
Also available: Norwood Index
  Report, public futures funds and
  private placements; $245/monthly
Technical analysis

Provides statistics and comprehensive performance charts on over 250 commodity trading advisors. Also includes an extensive ranking section.

AUDIENCE: Individual, Professional   RISK LEVEL: Aggressive
TOPICS: Mutual Funds, Options, Futures/Commodities

Stark Research CTA Report Online/Fax

Stark Research, Inc.
7777 Fay Ave., Suite E
LaJolla, CA 92037

PH: (619) 459-0818
Cost: Contact vendor
Frequency: Quarterly
Also available: Norwood Index
Report, public futures funds and
private placements; $245/monthly
Technical Analysis

Provides statistics and comprehensive performance charts on over 250 commodity trading advisors. Also includes an extensive ranking section.

AUDIENCE: Individual, Professional   RISK LEVEL: Aggressive
TOPICS: Mutual Funds, Options, Futures/Commodities

Steve Puetz Letter, The

Puetz
1105 Sunset Ct
W. Lafayette, TN 47906

PH: (317) 884-0600
Cost: $90.00/6 months
Technical and Fundamental Analysis
Frequency: Weekly

Provides commentary on the stock, bond, gold and silver and foreign markets as well as the economic outlook. No specific recommendations.

AUDIENCE: Individual, Professional   RISK LEVEL: Moderate, Aggressive
TOPICS: Bonds, Stocks, Futures/Commodities

Stock and Bond Brokers

American Business Directories
5711 S. 86th Circle
Box 27347
Omaha, NE 68127-4146

PH: (402) 593-4600
Cost: $833.00 includes 6 months
update

Provides name, address, phone number, contact name, number of employees, years in business and credit rating on 13,598 companies who advertise under "Stock and Bond Brokers" in the yellow pages.

AUDIENCE: Individual, Professional   RISK LEVEL: Conservative, Moderate, Aggressive
TOPICS: Bonds, Mutual Funds, Stocks

Stock Market Cycles

Stock Market Cycles
P.O. Box 6873
Santa Rosa, CA 95406-0873

PH: (707) 579-8444
Cost: $480.00 annually w/hotline
$252.00 annually w/periodic mutual
  fund update line
Frequency: Every 3 weeks
Date of first issue: 1975

Covers stock index futures, bills, bonds, gold, and market timing. This newsletter is a stock market timing advisory service covering stock index futures, bills, bonds, and gold.

AUDIENCE: Individual, Professional   RISK LEVEL: Aggressive
TOPICS: Options, Futures/Commodities

Stock of the Month Club, The

Erie Hamilton
8 Park Plaza
Suite 417
Boston, MA 02117

PH: (800) 237-8400 ext. 722
Cost: $119.00 annually
Frequency: Monthly
Date of first issue: 1988

Fundamental and technical analysis. Covers stocks. Each month screens over 6,500 stocks to find the best performers. Then tells you why a stock was chosen, gives information about the stock and price graphs for recent past. Portfolio performance is also tracked each issue.

AUDIENCE: Beginning, Individual   RISK LEVEL: Moderate, Aggressive
TOPICS: Stocks

Stock Tips @ Your Fingertips

UniBridge - The Anytime,
  Anyplace, Investment Advisor
PH: (900) 820-STOCK
Cost: $1.50 per first minute,
75 cents each additional;
24 Hour service
Frequency of update: Continual

Covers stocks and market timing. Comprehensive reference library covering real time quotes on over 50,000 securities, market alerts, insider trading tips, ratings on over 3,000 stocks, expert buy-sell recommendations. Obtained by using touchtone phone and extensive menu choices.

AUDIENCE: Beginning, Individual, Professional   RISK LEVEL: Conservative,
TOPICS: All   Moderate, Aggressive

Stocks, Bonds, Bills and Inflation

James Davidson & Lord William
  Rees-Mogg
Strategic Investment
Agora, Inc.
824 E. Baltimore Street
Baltimore, MD 21202

PH: (800) 787-0138
(301) 234-0515
Cost: $109.00 annually
Frequency: Monthly
Date of first issue: 1980

Technical analysis. Covers stocks, currencies, treasuries, options, and futures. An 8-page monthly letter covering the entire political and investment universe. Emphasis on inside information and anticipating trends. Various investment portfolios are handled by individual experts.

AUDIENCE: Individual, Professional   RISK LEVEL: Conservative, Moderate, Aggressive
TOPICS: Bonds, Stocks, Options, Futures/Commodities

Straight Talk on Your Money

Ken & Daria Dolan
7811 Montrose Rd
Potomac, MD 20854

PH: (800) 777-5005
FAX: (301) 340-2647
Cost: $39.50
Fundamental Analysis
Frequency: Monthly

A general financial newsletter giving tips and advice on how to earn money, save money, spend money, and invest better.

AUDIENCE: Beginning, Individual   RISK LEVEL: Conservative, Moderate, Aggressive
TOPICS: Bonds, Mutual Funds, Stocks, Investment Planning

Strategies

Strategies
245 East 93rd Street, Box 9E
New York, NY 10028

PH: (900) 446-6555 Strategies
  Marketline
Cost: $1.00 per minute
OTHER: (900) 226-7952 Strategies
  Market Commentary
Cost: $2.00 per minute
24 Hour service

Telephone newsletter which gives the latest stock market data and business news. Also available is a monthly newsletter for sophisticated investors. Call (900) 246-3200 to order - $9.95 per issue.

AUDIENCE: Individual, Professional   RISK LEVEL: Aggressive
TOPICS: Stocks, Options

Successful Investing and Money Management

Hume Publishing
835 Franklin Ct.
Atlanta, GA 30067

PH: (800) 222-4863
(404) 426-1920
Cost: $23.90/shipment
Date of first issue: 10 years
Frequency: 2 lessons every 21 days

A home-study course designed to make people rich. This "is a specific, detailed roadmap for building wealth systematically—not through get-rich-quick schemes, but by taking advantage of today's great opportunities and smartest strategies to amass wealth through smart investing."

AUDIENCE: Beginning, Individual   RISK LEVEL: Moderate, Aggressive
TOPICS: Mutual Funds, Stocks, Investment Planning

Switch Fund Advisor

Physiconomis, Inc.
P.O. Box 368
Norwalk, CA 90651

PH: (800) 676-5424
FAX: (310) 866-0972
Cost: $195.00/yr
Date of first issue: 1990
Frequency: Bimonthly
Technical Analysis

"Employs reformulated Dow theory (using interest rates) and investor psychology to determine the market primary trend and provides switching signals between growth stock funds and money market funds based on them."

AUDIENCE: Beginning, Individual   RISK LEVEL: Moderate, Aggressive
TOPICS: Mutual Funds, Asset Allocation

Switch Fund Timing

Dave Davis (editor and publisher)
P.O. Box 25430
Rochester, NY 14625

PH: (716) 385-3122
Cost: $89.00 annually
Frequency: Monthly
Date of first issue: 1983

Covers stocks, mutual funds, market timing. This newsletter is directed towards long-term investors offering strategies on market timing.

AUDIENCE: Beginning, Individual, Professional   RISK LEVEL: Conservative,
TOPICS: All   Moderate, Aggressive

Sy Harding

Sy Harding Investor Forecasts
Palm Coast, FL 32135

PH: (900) 776-7427 (hotline)
Cost: $2.00 per minute
Frequency: 9 AM, 1 PM and 7 PM
  every trading day

Covers options, stocks, gold and market timing. Daily message includes: latest market timing, plus "best stocks, options and short sales of the week."

AUDIENCE: Beginning, Individual, Professional   RISK LEVEL: Conservative, Moderate,
                                                                      Aggressive
TOPICS: Gold, Bonds, Mutual Funds, Stocks, Options, Asset Allocation

Systems and Forecasts

Gerald Appel
Signalert Corporation
150 Great Neck Road
Great Neck, NY 11021

PH: (516) 829-6444
Cost: $195.00
Frequency: Biweekly
Date of first issue: 17 years old

Technical analysis. Covers stocks, mutual funds, market timing. A stock and bond market timing service. Includes rankings of top 60 of more than 200 mutual funds tracked for relative strength with 3 model portfolios. Also includes book reviews and advisory service information and a free hotline.

AUDIENCE: Beginning, Individual, Professional	RISK LEVEL: Conservative, Moderate, Aggressive
TOPICS: All	

Taipan

Agora, Inc.
824 E. Baltimore Street
Baltimore, MD 21202-4799

PH: (301) 234-0515
(800) 787-0138
FAX: (301) 837-3879
Cost: $87.00 annually
Frequency: Monthly
Date of first issue: 1981

Covers foreign stocks and bonds. Foreign market commentary, recommendations, forecasts, and analysis. Based on foreign technologies.

AUDIENCE: Beginning, Individual, Professional	RISK LEVEL: Conservative, Moderate, Aggressive
TOPICS: All	

Taurus-Z

Taurus Corporation
P.O. Box 767
Winchester, VA 22601

PH: (703) 667-4827
Cost: $660.00/yr; w/FAX updates
$910.00/yr; includes hotline
Frequency: Weekly
Date of first issue: 1/76

Fundamental analysis and technical analysis. Covers commodities. "Makes specific recommendations on 30 commodities including buy-sell points and stop-loss points. Includes news items, book reviews, editorials, and seminar notices."

AUDIENCE: Beginning, Individual, Professional	RISK LEVEL: Conservative, Moderate, Aggressive
TOPICS: All	

Technical Alert Letter

Howard V. Prenzel Research
Association
P.O. Box 893
Floral City, FL 32636

PH: (904) 726-1339
Cost: $75.00
Frequency: Monthly

Technical analysis. Covers stocks. Includes two model portfolios: the aggressive account and the investment management account. Also gives market commentary and general investment advice.

AUDIENCE: Beginning, Individual, Professional	RISK LEVEL: Conservative, Moderate, Aggressive
TOPICS: All	

Technical Traders Bulletin

Rahseldt and Associates
P.O. Box 7115
Jupiter, FL 33468

PH: (407) 746-1605
Cost: $144.00 annually
Frequency: Monthly
Date of first issue: 7/89

Technical analysis. Covers commodities. The newsletter for technical analysts. Includes valuable tips and advice, readers idea exchange, informative interviews, day trading tactics, stochastics (parabolic), moving averages (interest rates), momentum (ADX/DMI, MACD), relative strength.

AUDIENCE: Beginning, Individual, Professional   RISK LEVEL: Conservative,
TOPICS: All   Moderate, Aggressive

Technical Trends-The Indicator Accuracy Service

Technical Trends
P.O. Box 792
Wilton, CT 06897

PH: (203) 762-0229
(800) 736-0229
Cost: $147.00 annually, US/Canada
$180.00 foreign; $25.00/6 week trial
Frequency: Weekly
Date of first issue: 1959

Provides charts and data of the most accurate, publicly available stock market indicators. Also commentary and education on the indicators and the market. Indicators tested and weighed frequently.

AUDIENCE: Beginning, Individual, Professional   RISK LEVEL: Conservative,
TOPICS: Stocks   Moderate, Aggressive

TeloFund Investment Funds

David C. Joel
1355 Peachtree Street N.E.
Suite 1280
Atlanta, GA 30309

PH: (404) 881-6221
(800) 828-2219
Cost: $250.00
Frequency: Monthly
Date of first issue: 10/22/90

Includes fundamental analysis and technical analysis. Covers mutual funds. A telephone switch advisory based on an extensively researched computer model. Currently offers three hotline systems: The Vanguard family of funds and two involving the Fidelity Family of Funds.

AUDIENCE: Beginning, Individual, Professional   RISK LEVEL: Conservative,
TOPICS: All   Moderate, Aggressive

Tiger on Spreads

Phillip E. Tiger
P.O. Box 1414
McLean, VA 22101

PH: (202) 463-8608
Cost: $240.00/yr
Frequency: Semi-monthly
Date of first issue: 8/81

Includes fundamental, cyclic, and technical analysis. Covers commodities. "Discusses spread relationships in commodity futures, including agricultural commodities, metals, financial futures and currencies, and international commodities. Surveys the market with attention to overall price movement and the state of the economy."

AUDIENCE: Individual, Professional   RISK LEVEL: Aggressive
TOPICS: Bonds, Futures/Commodities

Timer Digest

Jim Schmidt
P.O. Box 1688
Greenwich, CT 06836

PH: (800) 356-2527
Cost: $225.00 annually
Frequency: Every 3 weeks
Date of first issue: 1982

Top rated mutual fund program. Fundamental and technical analysis. Covers stocks and market timing. Monitors 90-100 market timers and rates their performance against the S&P 500. Each issue publishes the top 10 timers, a model portfolio plan with strategy and stock recommendations. Free hotline - updated Wed and Sat evenings.

AUDIENCE: Beginning, Individual   RISK LEVEL: Moderate, Aggressive
TOPICS: Stocks, Mutual Funds

Timing

Timing Financial Services, Ltd.
3219 W. Mescal St
Phoenix, AZ 85029

PH: (602) 942-3111
FAX: (602) 789-7883
Cost: $144.00/yr; $6.00/copy
Technical and Fundamental Analysis
Frequency: Biweekly

Provides worldwide weather information, support, resistance and trend data and covers 30 commodities on an individual basis.

AUDIENCE: Individual, Professional   RISK LEVEL: Aggressive
TOPICS: Commodities

Timing Market Letter

Timing Financial Services, Ltd.
3219 West Mescal Street
Phoenix, AZ 85029

PH: (602) 942-3111
Cost: $144.00 annually
Frequency: Twice a month
Date of first issue: 1980

Fundamental and technical analysis. Covers commodities, futures, market timing and uses charts. Contains a lead article as well as a weather article by Timing Climatologist Cliff Harris. This letter attempts to be medium to long-term oriented in its views and recommendations. Also, the letter gives projected turn dates, support and resistance points.

AUDIENCE: Individual, Professional   RISK LEVEL: Aggressive
TOPICS: Futures/Commodities

Today's Options

Robert Jubb
Techno-Fundamental Investments, Inc.
P.O. Box 6216
Scottsdale, AZ 85261

PH: (602) 996-2908
Cost: $195.00 annually
Frequency: Twice monthly

Fundamental and technical analysis. Covers options. Detailed analysis of a few recommendations using proprietary technical and fundamental research tools. Includes charts and updates on previous recommendations.

AUDIENCE: Individual, Professional   RISK LEVEL: Aggressive
TOPICS: Options

Trade Plans

Futures and Options Daily Trading
  Group, Inc.
1220 S.W. Morrison, Suite 815
Portland, OR 97205

PH: (800) 444-3684
FAX: (503) 241-1015
Cost: $180.00 annually
Frequency: Weekly (42 issues)
Date of first issue: 1/90

Technical analysis. Covers commodities, options. A weekly market analysis newsletter designed to give speculators possible futures trades to concentrate on during the following trade week. Features a "Trade of the Week" and "Trades to consider this Week" and a "Weekly Strength and Trend Analysis." Also available via FAX for additional $40.

AUDIENCE: Individual, Professional   RISK LEVEL: Aggressive
TOPICS: Options, Futures/Commodities

Tradecenter Market Letter

Knight - Ridder Financial
  Information
55 Broadway
New York, NY 10006

PH: (212) 269-1110
Cost: $400.00 annually
Frequency: Weekly
Date of first issue: 1988

Technical analysis. Covers stocks commodities/futures, bonds, dollar, cross currencies, and precious metals. Makes recommendation on actively traded futures markets and stocks based exclusively on technical analysis. Views of futures markets are typically for one week while the investment horizon for stocks is usually no longer than three months.

AUDIENCE: Individual, Professional   RISK LEVEL: Moderate, Aggressive
TOPICS: Bonds, Stocks, Options, Futures/Commodities

Trader Vic's Market Views

Victor Sperandeo
Rand Management Corporation
1 Chapel Hill Road
Short Hills, NJ 07078

PH: (900) 933-0933
Cost: $1.65 per minute
24 Hour Service
Frequency: Daily

Telephone newsletter covering stocks and commodities. Different topics scheduled throughout the day such as: Today's Trading Views, Stock and Commodity Picks, Closing Out the Day, Reasons for the Future, The "Why's" of the past week and the "How's" of the coming week.

AUDIENCE: Individual, Professional   RISK LEVEL: Aggressive
TOPICS: Options, Futures/Commodities

Trader's and Timers Hotline, The

Teleshare, Inc.
6684 Gunpark Drive East
Boulder, CO 80301

PH: (800) 777-4273
(303) 292-3362
Cost: $1.50 per minute
24 Hour service
Frequency: Daily except Sunday

Covers mutual funds. Mutual fund switch instructions for two different programs: long-term investors and aggressive investors.

AUDIENCE: Beginning, Individual   RISK LEVEL: Moderate, Aggressive
TOPICS: Mutual Funds

Trader's Hotline

Commodity Information Systems, Inc.
P.O. Box 690652
Houston, TX 77269-0652
PH: (900) 990-0909
(713) 890-2700
Cost: $2.00 per minute or
$120.00 for FAX service
Frequency: Daily

Covers commodities. Daily recording providing "short-term" recommendations based on a technical trading system. This service is free to subscribers of Trade Selection Program (see Newsletter section).

AUDIENCE: Individual, Professional   **RISK LEVEL: Aggressive**
TOPICS: Options, Futures/Commodities

Trading Advisor

Richard Luna
1737 Central Street
Denver, CO 80211
PH: (303) 433-3202

(800) 950-9339
FAX: (303) 433-2731
Cost: $295.00/yr
Date of first issue: 1986

Fundamental analysis. The leading source of Commodity Trading Advisor information in the nation with both an extensive data base and a large number of accounts traded with Commodity Trading Advisors. Profiles specific Trading Advisors and includes their performance. Rates the top Commodity Trading Advisors.

AUDIENCE: Individual, Professional   **RISK LEVEL: Aggressive**
TOPICS: Options, Futures/Commodities

Trading Cycles

Andrews Publications
1544 Via Arroyo
Paso Roblee, CA 93466

PH: (408) 778-2925
Cost: $140.00 annually
Frequency: 12 times per year
Date of first issue: 1973

Technical analysis. Covers market timing, S&P Futures, T-Bonds, currencies, gold, indices. A technical timing newsletter which "interprets technical price volume, momentum data and evaluates the extremes of investor reactions to the market.... It then projects the next minor and major lows or highs."

AUDIENCE: Individual   **RISK LEVEL: Aggressive**
TOPICS: Mutual Funds, Stocks, Options

Trading Trends

Minneapolis Grain Exchange
150 Grain Exchange Building
400 S. Fourth Street
Minneapolis, MN 55415

PH: (612) 338-6212
Frequency: Weekly

Technical analysis. Covers commodities. "Monitors grain and oil seed trading. Compiles analysis and statistics on specific commodities."

AUDIENCE: Individual, Professional   **RISK LEVEL: Aggressive**
TOPICS: Options, Futures/Commodities

Trend-Setter

Nick Van Nice
Commodity Trend Service
P.O. Box 32309
Palm Beach Gardens, FL 33420

PH: (800) 331-1069
FAX: (407) 622-7623
Cost: $595.00/yr
$995.00 a year for FAX
$995.00 a year for IBM with Modem
Frequency: Daily

Covers futures. Provides a comprehensive daily coverage of over 40 top futures markets. A complete trading program incorporating five different trading rules: Trade with the Trend, Have a Plan, Limit Losses and Allow Profits to Grow, Use Stops, and Do Not Overtrade. You get daily entry and exit signals and stops for each position, summary of all trades in progress.

AUDIENCE: Individual, Professional   RISK LEVEL: Aggressive
TOPICS: Futures/Commodities

Trendline Chart Guide

Standard & Poor's
25 Broadway
New York, NY 10004

PH: (212) 208-8792
(800) 221-5277
Cost: $155.00 annually
Frequency: Monthly
Date of first issue: 1962

Covers stocks and chart service. Includes over 4,400 stock charts from NYSE, AMEX and OTC exchanges. Each chart covers one year of market activity and shows the weekly high/low, close and volume, and 30 week moving averages. Also shows industry grouping, exchange traded on, 12 month earnings data, dividend rate, and more.

AUDIENCE: Beginning, Individual, Professional   RISK LEVEL: Moderate, Aggressive
TOPICS: Mutual Funds, Stocks

Trendline Current Market Prospectives

Standard & Poor's
25 Broadway
New York, NY 10004

PH: (800) 777-4858
(212) 208-8792
Cost: $215.00 annually + 24.60
  postage
Frequency: Monthly
Date of first issue: 1970

Technical analysis. Chart service for stocks. Gives weekly price volume charts on over 1,400 widely traded stocks for a period of up to 4 years. Alternate issues include an Industry Group Relative Strength Line to provide comparisons of stocks vs industry group performance and vs S&P 500. Also includes 3 year data on sales, earnings, dividends and yields.

AUDIENCE: Beginning, Individual, Professional   RISK LEVEL: Moderate, Aggressive
TOPICS: Stocks

Trendline Daily Action Stock Charts

Standard & Poor's
25 Broadway
New York, NY 10004

PH: (800) 777-4858
(212) 208-8792
Cost: $572.00 annually + $75.40
  postage
Frequency: Weekly
Date of first issue: 1970

Fundamental and technical analysis. Chart service showing daily trends for the past 12 months on 728 active NYSE and ASE stocks. Charts are plotted daily and issued every Friday after the markets close. Also includes most actively traded options.

AUDIENCE: Beginning, Individual, Professional RISK LEVEL: Moderate, Aggressive
TOPICS: Stocks

Trendline OTC Chart Manual

Standard & Poor's
25 Broadway
New York, NY 10004

PH: (800) 777-4858
(212) 208-8768
Cost: $160.00 annually + $14.40
  postage
Frequency: Bimonthly
Date of first issue: 1970

Fundamental and technical analysis. Covers stocks. Charts on over 800 actively traded OTC Stocks. Each chart presents the weekly bid price range, closing bid and volume for a period up to 4 years. Also includes sales data, dividends, yields, profit margins, cash flow and more.

AUDIENCE: Beginning, Individual, Professional   RISK LEVEL: Moderate, Aggressive
TOPICS: Stocks

Trends in Futures

Glen Ring - Editor
Oster Communications, Inc.
219 Parkade
Cedar Falls, IA 50613

PH: (800) 221-4352 ext. 434
(319) 277-1271
Cost: $199 annually
Frequency: 44 times per year
Date of first issue: 1978

Technical analysis. Covers commodities. Provides you with complete technical data, educational market information, and analysis of intermediate to long-term trends in 34 of the most popular and widely traded markets. Includes free hotline updated three times daily.

AUDIENCE: Individual, Professional   RISK LEVEL: Aggressive
TOPICS: Futures/Commodities

Trends in Mutual Fund Activity

Investment Company Institute
1600 M St., N.W., Suite 600
Washington, DC 20036

PH: (202) 326-5800
FAX: (202) 326-5985
Cost: $225.00/yr.
Date of first issue: 1980
Frequency: 12 per year
Fundamental Analysis

Monthly statistical report. Broken down by sales and inventory, objective, information provided by YTD and current month.

AUDIENCE: Individual, Professional   RISK LEVEL: Moderate, Aggressive
TOPICS: Mutual Funds

Turnaround Letter, The

New Generations, Inc.
225 Friend Street
Suite 801
Boston, MA 02114

PH: (617) 573-9550
Cost: $195.00 annually
Frequency: Monthly
Date of first issue: 1987

Fundamental analysis. Covers stocks. The newsletter tracks bankrupt companies and gives recommendations on associated stocks.

AUDIENCE: Individual, Professional   RISK LEVEL: Moderate, Aggressive
TOPICS: Stocks

Turning Point

C.E.R. Institute, Inc.
P.O. Box 12176
Scottsdale, AZ 85267

PH: (900) 234-7777 ext 50
Cost: $2.00 per minute
Frequency: Several times a day

Fax service. Can receive free sample Fibonacci/Gann projections. Specific recommendations by Walter Studnicki, Editor of Turning Point.

AUDIENCE: Individual, Professional   RISK LEVEL: Aggressive
TOPICS: Stocks, Options, Futures/Commodities

Turning Point

C.E.R. Institute, Inc.
P.O. Box 12176
Scottsdale, AZ 85267

PH: (602) 991-3410
Cost: $144.00 annually
Frequency: Monthly
Date of first issue: Jan. 1985

Covers stocks, commodities, government bonds, gold, Eurodollars, Swiss Franc. The newsletter pinpoints, well in advance, the most probable tops and bottoms. Projects turning points well in advance, teaches Fibonacci/Gann technique, Elliott Wave Theory, Dow Theory, cyclic concepts, and other technical tools.

AUDIENCE: Individual, Professional   RISK LEVEL: Aggressive
TOPICS: Stocks, Options, Futures/Commodities

Turtle Talk

Russell Sands
1800 Northeast 114th St., Suite 401
Miami, FL 33181

PH: (305) 895-2951
(800) 532-1563
FAX: (305) 895-1366
Cost: $295.00/yr
Frequency: Monthly
Date of first issue: September 1993

Each issue shows "thorough a combination of historical lessons and real-time current positions, the exact trades and techniques that the Turtles still use to consistently extract profits from the Futures Markets."

AUDIENCE: Individual, Professional   RISK LEVEL: Aggressive
TOPICS: Futures/Commodities

Tuxworth Stock Advisory

Robert Buffington, Ph.D.
P.O. Box 33794
Decatur, GA 30033-0794

PH: (404) 325-8348
Cost: $60.00 annually for non-
   clients
Frequency: Monthly
Date of first issue: 1988

Fundamental and technical analysis. Covers stocks and market timing. Market commentary and forecasting, performance tracking of proprietary Market Direction Indicator, current portfolio and performance data.

AUDIENCE: Beginning, Individual   RISK LEVEL: Moderate, Aggressive
TOPICS: Stocks

TV Program Investor

Paul Kagan Associates, Inc.
126 Clock Tower Place
Carmel, CA 93923-8734

PH: (408) 624-1536
FAX: (408) 625-3225
Cost: $495.00/yr
Frequency: Monthly;
   indexed: semiannually
Date of first issue: September 1985
Fundamental Analysis

Editor: Paul Kagan. Monitors trends in television program syndication. Reports market data on the monetary value of television programs and networks, as well as the value of public and private companies engaged in the television program business. Also analyzes the impact of industry mergers and acquisitions. Tables and graphs tracking Kagan. ISSN: 0885-2340.

AUDIENCE: Individual, Professional	RISK LEVEL: Moderate, Aggressive
TOPICS: Stocks	

U.S. Investment Report

U.S. Investment Report
25 Fifth Avenue 4-C
New York, NY 10003

PH: (212) 995-2963
FAX: (212) 477-6070
Cost: $228.00
Frequency: Every 2 weeks
Date of first issue: 1985

Fundamental analysis. Provides stock recommendations based on newsletter with both a conservative and aggressive model portfolio. Emphasizes established stocks leaders and emerging leaders in growth industries. Provides price targets loss limits and updated buy/sell ratings.

AUDIENCE: Individual	RISK LEVEL: Aggressive
TOPICS: Stocks	

Unit Investment Trusts Service

Moody's Financial Information
Services
99 Church Street
New York, NY 10007

PH: (212) 553-0435
FAX: (212) 553-4700
Cost: $1,025.00/ year
Published: Weekly
Fundamental Analysis

A combination of "Moody's Weekly Reports, UIT Manual and Annual Payment Record - providing updates and details on over 31,000 payment options." Amount paid, record date, payment date, current year total, previous year total, cusip #, distribution history, description, annual report information, state of condition, original offering info and background.

AUDIENCE: Beginning, Individual, Professional	RISK LEVEL: Moderate, Aggressive
TOPICS: Bonds, Mutual Funds, Stocks, General Reference	

United and Babson Investment Report

Babson-United Investment Advisors,
   Inc.
101 Prescott Street
Wellesley Hills, MA 02181

PH: (617) 235-0900
FAX: (617) 235-9450
Cost: $238.00
Frequency: Weekly
Date of first issue: 1916

Fundamental analysis. Covers stocks, municipal and corporate bonds, and market timing. 12 page report including market commentary, forecasts of business, financial and economic conditions, and stock recommendations. ISSN: 0845-5689.

AUDIENCE: Beginning, Individual, Professional	RISK LEVEL: Moderate, Aggressive
TOPICS: Bonds, Mutual Funds, Stocks	

United Mutual Fund Selector

Babson United Investment Advisors, Inc.
101 Prescott Street
Wellesley Hills, MA 02181

PH: (617) 235-0900
FAX: (617) 235-9450
Cost: $130.00 annually - 1st class
$125.00 annually 2nd class
Frequency: Biweekly

Fundamental analysis. Covers mutual funds. 12-page newsletter giving performance comparisons and other information including data on specific recommended funds.

AUDIENCE: Beginning, Individual   RISK LEVEL: Moderate, Aggressive
TOPICS: Mutual Funds

Value Investing Letters

Charlie Davis
41 Sutter Street #1355
San Francisco, CA 94104

PH: (415) 776-5622
Cost: $55.00
Frequency: 8 times per year
Date of first issue: 1990

Covers stocks. Market commentary strategy for stock picking and specific recommendations and lists the editor's current portfolio with a summary.

AUDIENCE: Individual   RISK LEVEL: Moderate, Aggressive
TOPICS: Stocks

Value Line Convertibles

Value Line, Inc.
711 Third Avenue
New York, NY 10017

PH: (212) 687-3965
(800) 633-2252 (subscriptions)
Cost: $475.00/yr
Frequency: Weekly

Fundamental analysis. Covers stocks. "Shows the investor how to build and maintain a convertible portfolio, how to decide upon the appropriate amount of risk, and how to select issues that fall within those risk limitations. Provides weekly evaluations of 585 convertibles, investment strategies, and market news."

AUDIENCE: Individual, Professional   RISK LEVEL: Moderate, Aggressive
TOPICS: Bonds, Stocks

Value Line Investment Survey, The

Value Line, Inc.
711 Third Avenue
New York, NY 10017-4064

PH: (800) 833-0046 ext. 2964 -
credit card orders only
(212) 687-3965
Cost: $525.00 annually
Frequency: Weekly
Date of first issue: 1943

Fundamental and technical analysis. Covers stocks. "Presents specific investment advice, including year-ahead and 3-5 year performance evaluations, projections of key financial measures, and concise, objective commentary on current operations and future prospects for over 1,700 stocks. Also offers analysis of the economy.

AUDIENCE: Beginning, Individual, Professional   RISK LEVEL: Moderate, Aggressive
TOPICS: Stocks

Value Line Mutual Fund Survey, The

Value Line Publishing
711 Third Avenue
New York, NY 10017-4064

PH: (800) 284-7607
Cost: $295.00
Frequency: Biweekly
Date of first issue: 1993

"Analyzes rates & reports on 2,000 stock & bond funds." Two information packed binders provide full page analyses of 1,500 established funds. Each fund is updated 3 times a year.

AUDIENCE: Beginning, Individual   **RISK LEVEL: Moderate, Aggressive**
TOPICS: Mutual Funds

Value Line Options

Value Line, Inc.
711 Third Avenue
New York, NY 10017

PH: (212) 687-3965
(800) 633-2252 (subscriptions)
Cost: $445.00/yr
Frequency: Weekly
Date of first issue: 5/75

Fundamental analysis. Designed to show the investor how to build and maintain an option portfolio, how to decide on the appropriate amount of risk, and how to select issues that fall within those risk limitations. Provides weekly evaluations of over 8,000 options, investment strategies, and market news.

AUDIENCE: Individual, Professional   **RISK LEVEL: Aggressive**
TOPICS: Stocks, Options

Vancouver Stockwatch

Canjex Publishing, Ltd.
700 W. Georgia Street, Box 10371
Pacific Centre
Vancouver, British Columbia, Canada
  V7Y 136

PH: (800) 267-7400
Cost: $395.00/yr, U.S. and Canada
Frequency: Available daily, weekly
  or quarterly, all at same price
Date of first issue: 1984

Weekly magazine covering stock choices. An information service which provides valuable information on every company (over 1,500) listed on the Vancouver Stock Exchange.

AUDIENCE: Individual, Professional   **RISK LEVEL: Moderate, Aggressive**
TOPICS: Stocks

Venture Capital Portfolio, The

Zin Investment Services
7 Switchbud Place #192-312
The Woodlands, TX 77380

PH: (713) 363-1000
Cost: $195.00 - includes a free hotline
Frequency: Monthly

Technical analysis. Covers stocks. "A stock advisory service which specializes in analyses of the publicly traded companies that have been financed by professional venture capitalists." Recommendations and a model portfolio. Hotline is also available for $2 per minute - (900) 226-5463.

AUDIENCE: Beginning, Individual, Professional   **RISK LEVEL: Moderate, Aggressive**
TOPICS: Stocks

Venture Returns

Karl Drobnic, Publisher
1855 N.W. Tyler Avenue
Corvallis, OR 97330

PH: (503) 758-4706
Cost: $75.00/yr
Frequency: 24 issues per year
Date of first issue: June, 1990

Covers stocks and convertible bonds. Each issue recommends one stock or cv bond, provides economic and market commentary, and follows up on previous recommendations. Companies are selected either for above-average yield or for outstanding growth potential. Venture Returns strives for a balance between income and growth in readers' portfolios.

AUDIENCE: Individual, Professional	RISK LEVEL: Moderate, Aggressive
TOPICS: Bonds, Stocks, Options	

Vickers Weekly Insider Report

Vickers Stock Research Corp.
226 New York Ave.
Huntington, NY 11743

PH: (516) 423-7710
(800) 645-5043
Frequency: Weekly
Cost: $97.00/yr + $15.00 shipping
Fundamental Analysis

Lists all form 4 filings and provides 1 week and 8 week sell/buy ratios of insider trading on the OTC, NYSE, ASE markets. Insiders index, commentary, risk portfolio, company indexes.

AUDIENCE: Individual, Professional	RISK LEVEL: Moderate, Aggressive
TOPICS: Stocks	

Volume Reversal Survey, The

Mark Leibovit
Almarco Trading Corp., P.O. Box 1451
Sedonia, AZ 86336

PH: (800) 554-5551
Date of first issue: 1979
Cost: $19.00/yr., $360.00/yr
includes telephone hotline
Frequency: every 3 weeks - 17
   issues a year

Technical analysis. Covers stock, treasuries, currencies, precious metals and futures. Every issue contains: volume analysis of all major markets; clear and specific instructions on whether to buy, sell, or hold stocks, bonds, precious metals and select futures markets; proprietary Volume Reversal technique. ISSN: 8755-3406.

AUDIENCE: Professional	RISK LEVEL: Aggressive
TOPICS: Stocks, Options	

Vomund Investment Services FAX Advisory

Vomund Investment Services
P.O. Box 6253
Incline Village, NV 89450

PH: (702) 831-1544
FAX: (702) 831-6784
Cost: Stock Alert - $298.00/yr; Fund
   Alert - $238.00/yr
Frequency: Weekly

Stock Alert covers market timing, industry group timing, and stock selection with an emphasis on small company growth stocks. Fund Alert covers market timing and mutual fund timing with an emphasis on sector funds. In the analysis, uses AIQ TradingExpert software, an expert system software package.

AUDIENCE: Individual	RISK LEVEL: Aggressive
TOPICS: Mutual Funds, Stocks	

Wall Street Bargains

KCI Communications, Inc.
1101 King Street
Suite 400
Alexandria, VA 22314

PH: (800) 832-2330
Cost: $39.00 for 12 issues
Frequency: Monthly

Wall Street Bargains is a monthly newsletter featuring high-growth stocks and mutual funds selling between $5 and $25. "Buy more with less in WALL STREET BARGAINS. . . . Invest only $5,000 and you'll easily get into 5 different investments!"

AUDIENCE: Beginning   RISK LEVEL: Moderate, Aggressive
TOPICS: Mutual Funds, Stocks

Wall Street Digest, The

Donald H. Rowe
1 Sarasota Tower, #602
2 N. Tamiami Trail, Suite 602
Sarasota, FL 34236

PH: (813) 954-5500
Cost: $150.00/yr.
Date of first issue: February 1977
Frequency: Monthly
Technical and Fundamental Analysis

Subtitled: A Digest of the Best Investment Advice from the Leading Advisors. Covers stocks, bonds, precious metals, foreign currencies, tax shelters, real estate and estate planning.

AUDIENCE: Individual   RISK LEVEL: Conservative, Moderate, Aggressive
TOPICS: Bonds, Stocks, Investment Planning

Wall Street Generalist, The

The Wall Street Generalist
800 Sarasota Quay
Sarasota, FL 34236

PH: (813) 366-5645
Cost: $160.00
Frequency: Every three weeks
Technical and Fundamental Analysis

Provides recommendations on a wide range of investments, primarily long-term, which are relayed through professional computer-generated models and graphs. Also provides Mutual Fund timing advice and industry reports model stock portfolio and twice weekly telephone update.

AUDIENCE: Individual   RISK LEVEL: Moderate, Aggressive
TOPICS: Mutual Funds, Stocks

Wall Street Letter

Institutional Investor Systems
488 Madison Avenue
New York, NY 10022

PH: (212) 303-3300
Cost: $1,450.00 annually
Frequency: Weekly
Fundamental Analysis
Date of first issue: 1975

Focuses on institutional and retail brokerage news and trends by covering the big firms and the small regional brokerages, mutual funds and service companies. You'll also get coverage of Washington and the exchanges.

AUDIENCE: Professional   RISK LEVEL: Conservative, Moderate, Aggressive
TOPICS: Mutual Funds, Stocks, Options, Futures/Commodities

Wall Street Micro Investor

Howard Young
P.O. Box 6
Riverdale, NY 10471

PH: (212) 884-5408
Cost: $30.00 annually
Frequency: Bimonthly
Date of first issue: Jan. 1982

Technical analysis. Covers stocks and computer investing. Wall Street Micro Investor: key indicators; creates an expert system to generate buy-sell signals; provides options and technical indicators; new indicators - directional index, point and figure charting, Elliott Wave Theory, anatomy of a stock; identifying trading patterns.

AUDIENCE: Individual, Professional   RISK LEVEL: Moderate, Aggressive
TOPICS: Mutual Funds, Stocks, Options, Futures/Commodities

Wall Street S.O.S.

Securities Objective Services
17175 N. Lake Dr.
Bay Minette, AL 36507

PH: (205) 937-6308
Cost: $2.50 per access
Genie, Delphi and CompuServe
Technical Analysis
Frequency: Daily
Date of first issue: 1991

Provides technical analysis and specific recommendations of New York Stock Exchange and American Stock Exchange common stocks. Includes daily analysis of trends and recommendations and forecasts for the next three to five days, based on the S.O.S. Bull/Bear Index. Market timing and stock selection service.

AUDIENCE: Individual   RISK LEVEL: Moderate, Aggressive
TOPICS: Stocks

Wall Street S.O.S. Options Alert

Securities Objective Services
17175 N. Lake Dr.
Bay Minette, AL 36507

PH: (205) 937-6308
Cost: $2.50 per access
Genie, Delphi, and CompuServe
Frequency: Daily
Fundamental Analysis
Date of first issue: 1991

Covers index options trading, including specific recommendations and trading strategy for the four most popular options. Also covers stock options from selected stocks from SOS's proprietary Bull/Bear Index.

AUDIENCE: Individual   RISK LEVEL: Aggressive
TOPICS: Options

Washington Bond & Money Market Report

David A. Alecock
1545 New York Avenue, N.E.
Washington, D.C. 20002

PH: (800) 345-2611
(202) 526-9664
FAX: (202) 636-3992
Cost: $325.00 annually
Frequency: Biweekly
Date of first issue: 1946

Fundamental analysis. Covers municipal and government bonds, and treasuries. Sound, on-the-money analyses of the thinking in official Washington and in the market in New York. Subjects include the interest rate outlook, where the economy and the money supply are heading, how the Federal Reserve is reacting to current trends, and the impact of developments abroad.

AUDIENCE: Beginning, Individual, Professional   RISK LEVEL: Conservative
TOPICS: Bonds

Washington International Business Report

IBC, Inc.
818 Connecticut Avenue, N.W.
Suite 1200
Washington, D.C. 20006

ISSN 0049-691X
PH: (202) 872-8181
Cost: $288.00 annually
Frequency: Monthly
Date of first issue: 1972

Fundamental analysis. The report is an analytical review and outlook on major government developments impacting international trade and investment.

AUDIENCE: Beginning, Individual, Professional	RISK LEVEL: Conservative, Moderate, Aggressive
TOPICS: All	

Water Investment Newsletter

U.S. Water News, Inc.
230 Main Street
Halstead, KS 67056

PH: (800) 251-0046
Cost: $140.00
Frequency: Monthly
Date of first issue: 1987

Fundamental analysis. Covers publicly held companies in the water industry. "A newsletter on Water Stocks and Investments." Provides a stock profile, model portfolio with performance data and news relevant to investments in the water industry each month.

AUDIENCE: Beginning, Individual, Professional	RISK LEVEL: Moderate, Aggressive
TOPICS: Stocks	

Weber's Fund Advisor

Ken Weber
P.O. Box 3490
New Hyde Park, NY 11040

PH: (516) 466-1252
Cost: $135.00 annually
Frequency: Monthly
Date of first issue: 1983

Fundamental and technical analysis. Covers mutual funds. Each month you'll see Ken Weber's analysis of the stock market in general and commentary about developments affecting the mutual fund investor. Uses a "Go-with-the-winner" strategy which finds the hottest mutual funds and stays with them till they cool off. Over 115 funds are tracked.

AUDIENCE: Beginning, Individual	RISK LEVEL: Moderate, Aggressive
TOPICS: Mutual Funds	

Weekly Report of the Market

Coffee, Sugar and Cocoa
  Exchange, Inc.
Four World Trade Center
New York, NY 10048

PH: (212) 938-2800
Cost: $20
Frequency: Weekly

Technical analysis. Covers commodities. Synopsis of market activity in each commodity traded on the CSCE.

AUDIENCE: Individual, Professional	RISK LEVEL: Aggressive
TOPICS: Options, Futures/Commodities	

Weekly Stock Charts. Canadian and U.S. Industrial Companies

Independent Survey Co.
P.O. Box 6000
Vancouver, BC, Canada V6B 4B9

PH: (604) 731-5777
Cost: $25.60 Canadian
Frequency: Annual
Editor: Michael den Hertog

Two quarterly price and volume charts for 1,000 Canadian and U.S. industrial companies.

AUDIENCE: Individual, Professional   RISK LEVEL: Moderate, Aggressive
TOPICS: Stocks

Weekly Stock Charts. Canadian Resource Companies

Independent Survey Co.
P.O. Box 6000
Vancouver, BC, Canada V6B 4B9

PH: (604) 731-5777
Cost: $25.60 Canadian
Frequency: Annual
Editor: Michael den Hertog

Two quarterly price and volume charts for 1,200 Canadian mining and oil stocks.

AUDIENCE: Individual, Professional   RISK LEVEL: Moderate, Aggressive
TOPICS: Stocks

Weekly Technical Letter

W. D. Gann Research, Inc.
P.O. Box 8508
St. Louis, MO 63126

PH: (314) 843-1810
Cost: $210.00/yr
Frequency: Weekly
Date of first issue: 1919

Technical analysis. Covers stocks, commodities and options. Strictly a technical trading newsletter based on proven chart principles with preservation of capital as a prime concern. Gives specific recommendations with stops.

AUDIENCE: Individual, Professional   RISK LEVEL: Aggressive
TOPICS: Stocks, Options, Futures/Commodities

Wellington Letter

Wellington Financial Corp.
733 Bishop St., Suite 1800
Honolulu, HI 96813

PH: (808) 524-8063
(800) 992-9989
FAX: (808) 528-5016
Frequency: Monthly
Cost: $450.00
Technical and Fundamental Analysis

Provides in-depth analysis of all the markets, concentrating on the economy and the Federal Reserve. There is a Fund Investors page for mutual fund investors and specific stock recommendations.

AUDIENCE: Individual, Professional   RISK LEVEL: Conservative, Moderate, Aggressive
TOPICS: Bonds, Mutual Funds, Stocks, Futures/Commodities

Whitfield's Utility Letter

J. Charles Whitfield
2472 Bolsover
Suite 240
Houston, TX 77005

PH: (713) 521-2536
Cost: $99.00/yr; $59.00/6 months
Frequency: Monthly, usually sent by
   the third or fourth of the month
Date of first issue: 1984

Fundamental analysis. Covers stocks. Market commentary and specific buy/sell recommendations on utility stocks.

AUDIENCE: Individual   RISK LEVEL: Moderate
TOPICS: Stocks

Wolanchuk Report, The

Don Wolanchuk
28037 Gratiot
Roseville, MI 48066

PH: (900) 288-6663
Cost: $2.75 first minute
Frequency: Consistently updated
24 Hour service

Telephone newsletter covering market timing, treasury bond futures, gold futures, and financial futures. Market commentary and analysis with recommendations. Timer Digests 1990 Timer of the Year.

AUDIENCE: Individual, Professional   RISK LEVEL: Aggressive
TOPICS: Stocks, Options, Futures/Commodities

World Investment Strategic Edge

Courtney D. Smith
Pinnacle Capital Management
P.O. Box 3295
Chicago, IL 60690-3292

PH: (312) 587-7051
FAX: (312) 587-7052
Cost: $395.00/yr
Frequency: 20 times per year
Date of first issue: 1991

Covers stocks, bonds, currencies, gold. Searches the globe for investments with the potential for superior returns and limited risk. Includes specific recommendations and market commentary.

AUDIENCE: Individual, Professional   RISK LEVEL: Moderate, Aggressive
TOPICS: Bonds, Stocks, Futures/Commodities, Asset Allocation

World Market Perspective

WMP Enterprises, Inc.
P.O. Box 2289
2211 Lee Road
Suite 103
Winter Park, FL 32790

PH: (407) 290-9600
Cost: $49.00 annually
Frequency: Monthly
Date of first issue: 1959

Technical and fundamental analysis. Covers gold and currencies, includes charts. Research in economic science and world markets aimed at discovery and dissemination of significant ideas and information.

AUDIENCE: Individual, Professional   RISK LEVEL: Moderate, Aggressive
TOPICS: Bonds, Stocks, Futures/Commodities

World Money Analyst

Newstar Orient, Ltd.
45 Lyndhurst Terrace
Hong Kong

PH: 541-6110
FAX: (852) 854-1695
Cost: $189.00
Frequency: 10 times per year plus 2
special reports

Fundamental and technical analysis. International news relevant to investing, currency and interest rate trend charts, broad investment recommendations. Includes hotline updated weekly.

AUDIENCE: Individual, Professional   RISK LEVEL: Conservative, Moderate, Aggressive
TOPICS: Bonds, Options, Futures/Commodities

Worldwide Investment News

Offshore Banking News Service
301 Plymouth Drive, N.E.
Dalton, GA 30721-9983

PH: (404) 259-6035
Cost: $90.00
Frequency: Monthly
Date of first issue: 1983

Fundamental analysis. Covers mutual funds, international investments. "The world's first and foremost sentinel of offshore banking and investment opportunities." Covers a wide array of international investments and gives an international resource directory as well as a brief opportunities classified section.

AUDIENCE: Beginning, Individual, Professional   RISK LEVEL: Moderate, Aggressive
TOPICS: Bonds, Mutual Funds, Stocks

Zweig Forecast, The

Dr. Martin E. Zweig
P.O. Box 360
Bellmore, NY 11710

PH: 800-633-2252 ext 9000
FAX: (516) 785-0537
Cost: $265.00 annually
Frequency: Every 3 weeks
Date of first issue: 1971

Technical analysis. Covers stocks. Model portfolio, gives specific stock recommendations, when to buy and when to sell. 24 hour hotline access free with subscription. 3 times per week gives latest readings of his key indicators and specific strategy recommendations.

AUDIENCE: Individual, Professional   RISK LEVEL: Moderate, Aggressive
TOPICS: Bonds, Mutual Funds, Stocks, Asset Allocation

COMPUTER AND QUOTE SERVICES

Any investor with a computer can benefit from today's rapidly expanding market in financial software and on-line data services. As we approach the turn of the century, the computer industry has responded to investors' needs with a powerful and innovative array of choices.

Finding the right type of software or data service can drastically improve confidence and performance, but the number of choices available has literally tripled since the 1980s.

Studying this chapter before testing or selecting software and on-line services can save any investor a good deal of time and money. Most all available programs from stand-alone financial planning software to news and quote services are listed with descriptions and pricing. If a company offers several different services, they are listed separately. Tax and accounting software has been included only if it is investment-focused.

News and quote services can improve the performance of any stock investor, from beginner to advanced. Chart services for the computer have the added advantage of providing instantly available updates. Interest rate updates on money market funds, CDs and bonds are available from many of the entries listed.

Institutional investors will be interested in the services available from giants such as Moody's, Standard & Poor's, and Reuters. Research buyers will want to check into services such as INVESTEXT and Mead Data's LEXIS/NEXIS. Traders will be able to find FUTURESOURCE, CQG, AIQ and other technical analysis services listed with their on-line compatibilities.

Mutual fund buyers will find unique services. In historical databases such as CDA TECHNOLOGIES, almost any fund can be run with hypothetical investment amounts over past periods up to 10 years. This allows investors to test drive historic account values in net performance dollars, free of promotions and "hot fund rankings."

For stock, bond, and mutual fund investors, the developments within the computer industry can be both empowering and overwhelming. This chapter is designed to put the spectrum of choices and capabilities at your fingertips.

20/20

Radix Research Limited
P.O. Box 91181
West Vancouver, BC,
   Canada V7V 3N6

PH: (604) 926-5308
FAX: (604) 925-2607
SOFTWARE
Cost: $199.00 (Canadian)
Technical Analysis
Technical Support: Phone, M-F
Newsletter

Program contains all of the popular indicators plus SmartCursor and big-system features such as AutoScale and graph compression of data from 1 to 12 years. Contains Datalink. Comes with 6 years of data for the indexes.

AUDIENCE: Beginning, Individual   RISK LEVEL: Moderate, Aggressive
TOPICS: Stocks, Options, Futures/Commodities

3D

Mesa
P.O. Box 1801
Goleta, CA 93116

PH: (800) 633-6375
(805) 969-6478
FAX: (805) 969-1358
SOFTWARE
Cost: $199.00
Technical Analysis
Technical Support: Phone, M-F
BBS

User can plot the profitability of 5 indicators and choose the best indicator due to market conditions. The 5 indicators are stochastics, RSI, MACD, double moving average, and parabolic stop reverse. Trade resulting can be viewed on the chart display.

AUDIENCE: Individual, Professional   RISK LEVEL: Moderate, Aggressive
TOPICS: Stocks, Futures/Commodities

AB-Data Disks

AB-DATA, Inc.
194 Rock Road
Glen Rock, NJ 07452

PH: (201) 612-0870
FAX: (201) 612-9082
Transmission: Diskette
ON-LINE DATABASE
Access Fees: $50
AAII Discount: 15%

Gives financial information from corporate annual and quarterly reports. Is compatible with many spreadsheet programs including Lotus 1-2-3 and Excel. It does not provide historical price data.

AUDIENCE: Individual   RISK LEVEL: Moderate, Aggressive
TOPICS: Stocks

Access Custom Financial System

Prophet Software Corp.
3350 West Bayshore, #106
Palo Alto, CA 94303

PH: (800) 772-8040
FAX: (415) 856-1143
Transmission: Modem, Diskette
No. of Users: 3,400
Start-Up Fee: $49.95
ON-LINE DATABASE

Gives historical financial data and daily updates customized to individual specifications. Stock and index databases on all U.S. equity markets for over a decade. Futures database contains all futures going back as far as a quarter century. Daily updates.

AUDIENCE: Individual, Professional   RISK LEVEL: Aggressive
TOPICS: Stocks, Options, Futures/Commodities

Accuron

National Computer Network
1929 N. Harlem Ave.
Chicago, IL 60635

PH: (800) 942-6262
FAX: (312) 622-6889
ON-LINE DATABASE
Transmission: Modem
No. of Users: 300
Start-Up Fee: $129.95

Combines software and database system that gives access to securities, stock, corporate and government bonds, mutual funds, financial and commodity futures, and indexes on all U.S. listed stocks, futures options, and index.

AUDIENCE: Beginning, Individual   RISK LEVEL: Moderate, Aggressive
TOPICS: All

Advanced Business Valuation

Essential Software, Corp.
1126 South 70th Street
West Allis, WI 53214

PH: (414) 775-3450
FAX: (414) 475-3578
SOFTWARE
Cost: $295.00
Technical Support: Phone, M-F

Uses fundamental analysis for determining the value of a business for buy/sell purposes, stock offerings, etc. Performs financial statement analysis and forecasting with three dimensional graphics and a variety of valuation techniques.

AUDIENCE: Individual, Professional   RISK LEVEL: Moderate
TOPICS: Bonds, Stocks

Advanced Channel Entry (ACE)

Essex Trading Company, Ltd.
24 W. 500 Maple Avenue
Suite 108
Naperville, IL 60540

PH: (800) 726-2140
FAX: (708) 416-3558
SOFTWARE
Cost: $995.00-$1,995.00

Contains seven programs on futures trading markets (Treasury bonds, stock index-futures, foreign currency futures, grains, energies, metals, and international stock indexes). 14 years of historical data, historical testing routine, and graphics.

AUDIENCE: Individual, Professional   RISK LEVEL: Aggressive
TOPICS: Bonds, Options, Futures/Commodities

Advanced G.E.T.

Trading Techniques, Inc.
677 W. Turkey Foot Lake Road
Akron, OH 44319

PH: (216) 645-0077
FAX: (216) 645-1230
SOFTWARE
Cost: $2,750.00
Technical Analysis
Technical Support: Phone, M-F
BBS

Use Gann and Elliot techniques specially designed for the futures market. Price projections for each market swing and other indicators. 3 degree automatic Elliot wave counts, Gann angles, potential change in trend dates, auto price calculations and Fibonacci.

AUDIENCE: Individual, Professional   RISK LEVEL: Aggressive
TOPICS: Futures/Commodities

Advanced Total Investor (ATI)

Hughes Financial Services
P.O. Box 1244
Nashua, NH 03061-1244

PH: (603) 598-4676
FAX: (603) 598-4676
SOFTWARE
Cost: $129.00
Technical Analysis
Technical Support: Phone, M-F
BBS, Newsletter

Graphically display trendlines, text, analysis graphs, security's price history, and portfolio allocation. Basic features of Total Investor Plus; candlestick, equivolume, P&F, linear/log, open/open interest, spreads, line/bar charts, Chaiken oscillator, stochastics.

AUDIENCE: Individual, Professional   RISK LEVEL: Moderate, Aggressive
TOPICS: All

Agrivisor

Ohio Farm Bureau Federation
Two Nationwide Plaza, 6th Floor
Columbus, OH 43215

PH: (614) 249-2427
FAX: (614) 249-2200
Former Name: AgriQuote
Transmission: Modem, Satellite, FM
Start-Up Fee: $149.00
Access Fees: $239.00 per year

Gives real-time market information service for commodity futures and options markets. It uses FM sidebands to deliver quotes in OH, MI and IL, C-band home satellite and KU band satellite in areas not covered by the FM sideband signal. It has a standard delayed quotes.

AUDIENCE: Individual, Professional   RISK LEVEL: Moderate, Aggressive
TOPICS: Stocks, Options, Futures/Commodities

AIQ Market Expert

AIQ Systems, Inc.
916 Southwood Blvd.
Suite 2C
P.O. Drawer 7530
Incline Village, NV 89450

PH: (800) 332-2999
SOFTWARE
Cost: $249.00

Market timing and charts. Signals near-term changes in the direction of the market. Signaled both the 1987 and 1989 October crashes. This technical analysis system does not forecast, it generates signals for market timing based on a knowledge base.

AUDIENCE: Individual, Professional   RISK LEVEL: Moderate, Aggressive
TOPICS: Mutual Funds, Stocks, Options

AIQ Option Extension

AIQ Systems, Inc.
916 Southwood Blvd.
Suite 2C
P.O. Drawer 7530
Incline Village, NV 89450

PH: (800) 332-2999
FAX: (702) 831-6784
SOFTWARE
Cost: $249.00

Options, market timing, and charts. Expert equity option system with capability to signal short-term stock moves. Analyzes daily price and volume data and recommends the best strategy or positions to take and when to clear positions. Both equity and index option.

AUDIENCE: Individual, Professional   RISK LEVEL: Aggressive
TOPICS: Mutual Funds, Stocks, Options

AIQ Stock Expert

AIQ Systems, Inc.
916 Southwood Blvd.
Suite 2C
P.O. Drawer 7530
Incline Village, NV 89450

PH: (800) 332-2999
FAX: (702) 831-6784
SOFTWARE
Cost: $498.00

Covers stocks, market timing, and charts. An expert system that does technical analysis for you. It is capable of sorting through huge amounts of data and signaling buy and sell recommendations. Through connecting with communications networks, it analyzes daily price and volume movements and computes an Expert Rating for every stock you follow. The system then prints a daily Expert Analysis Report and an Action List that select which stocks you should consider for trading. Once you take a position, the Stock Expert Profit Management function takes over to protect your principle and your profits, advising you to hold, sell or cover based on your own risk parameters.

AUDIENCE: Individual, Professional   RISK LEVEL: Moderate, Aggressive
TOPICS: Stocks, Options

AIQ Trading Expert

AIQ Systems, Inc.
916 Southwood Blvd.
P.O. Drawer 7530
Incline Village, NE 89450

PH: (800) 332-2999
FAX: (702) 831-6784
Cost: $996.00
SOFTWARE

Trading Expert is the most powerful and comprehensive stock selection and market timing system anywhere, at any price. Trading Expert integrates a state of the art, end of day, expert system with sophisticated quantitative method.

AUDIENCE: Individual, Professional   RISK LEVEL: Aggressive
TOPICS: Mutual Funds, Stocks, Options

Alexander Steele's Mutual Fund Expert

Alexander Steele Systems
Technologies, Inc.
12021 Wilshire Blvd., Suite 407
Los Angeles, CA 90025

PH: (800) 678-3863
FAX: (310) 479-4131
SOFTWARE
Cost: $95.00/yr

Screens 4,000 mutual funds by providing 81 market indexes. All the reports can be applied to a filtered group of funds or the whole universe. Reports show current fund ranking, averages, short-term performance, long-term performance, annual performance, and more. Money market edition available.

AUDIENCE: Beginning, Individual   RISK LEVEL: Moderate
TOPICS: Mutual Funds

All-Quotes

All-Quotes, Inc.
40 Exchange Plc., Suite 1500
New York, NY 10005

PH: (800) 888-7559
FAX: (212) 425-6895
ON-LINE DATABASE
Transmission: Modem
No. of users: 2,000
Start-Up fee: $150 to $250
Access Fees: 39 cents/min.
or $150/mo. Current Quote Fees:
39 cents/min. or $175/mo.

Provides real-time and delayed stock, option and commodity trading from exchanges. Financial business information database and markets on-line financial information service, as well as the financial and business news. Interbank foreign exchange quotes up to the second.

AUDIENCE: Individual, Professional   RISK LEVEL: Moderate, Aggressive
TOPICS: Bonds, Mutual Funds, Stocks, Options, Futures/Commodities

Alliance 5.0

New High Co.
RD #2
Riverhead, NY 11901

PH: (800) 643-8950
FAX: (516) 722-5409
SOFTWARE
Cost: $69.95
Technical Analysis
Technical Support: Phone, M-F

A charting program that uses numerous technical analysis models. Daily charting program combines as many issues as desired. Various groups can be charted against each other or against the market as a whole.

AUDIENCE: Individual, Professional   RISK LEVEL: Moderate, Aggressive
TOPICS: Stocks

America Online

America Online
8619 Westwood Center Dr.
Vienna, VA 22182

PH: (800) 827-6364
FAX: (703) 883-1509
ON-LINE DATABASE
Transmission: Modem
Access Fees: $9.95 mo. & $3.50/hour
Free 30-day trial (10 free hours)

NewsGrid; market news; NYSE, AMEX, NASDAQ, advances, declines, volume, Dow Jones indexes, price change high-low; S&P Index; option index put and call volume; most active issues; gains and losses percentage; news on bonds, commodities, and OTC currency.

AUDIENCE: Individual, Professional   RISK LEVEL: Moderate, Aggressive
TOPICS: Stocks, Options, Futures/Commodities

An Option Valuator/Option Writer

Revenge Software
P.O. Box 1073
Huntington, NY 11743

PH: (516) 271-9556
SOFTWARE
Cost: $99.95
Technical Support: Phone, M-F

Program has 2 interactive modules, an Option Valuator and an Option Writer, which enable user to analyze and implement an option strategy. Black-Sholes equation to predict the future market value of securities. Put option, volatility and hedge ratios.

AUDIENCE: Individual, Professional   RISK LEVEL: Aggressive
TOPICS: Options

Analyst

Tech Hackers, Inc.
50 Broad Street
New York, NY 10004

PH: (212) 344-9500
SOFTWARE
Cost: Financial Analysts $195.00,
Stats Analysts $195.00, Bond
Analysts $495.00, Options Analysts
$495.00, MBS Analysts $495.00
$50.00 discount for each additional
library when purchasing more than
one library.

Covers options, bonds (municipal, agency, corporate, and government). Analyst is a series of four mathematical and financial function add-in libraries for Lotus 1-2-3, Excel, QPW and Symphony. Each library is comprehensive and offers sophisticated analytics.

AUDIENCE: Individual, Professional   RISK LEVEL: Conservative, Moderate, Aggressive
TOPICS: Bonds, Stocks, Options, Futures/Commodities

Analyst Tool

AB-DATA, Inc.
194 Rock Road
Glen Rock, NJ 07452

PH: (201) 612-0870
FAX: (201) 612-9082
Transmission: Diskette
ON-LINE DATABASE
Access Fees: $5/company
Minimum Usage: $500
AAII Discount: 15%

Annual and quarterly financial statements for utility, gas, telephone, financial, and industrial companies. Automated applications to determine the creditworthiness, ranking of companies, allows search and compare, creates unlimited ratios.

AUDIENCE: Individual, Professional   RISK LEVEL: Moderate, Aggressive
TOPICS: Bonds, Stocks

Andrew Tobias' Managing Your Money

Meca Software, Inc.
55 Walls Drive
Fairfield, CT 06430-5139

PH: (203) 255-1441
FAX: (203) 255-6300
SOFTWARE
Cost: $79.95
Technical Support: Phone, M-F & Sat.
BBS
Newsletter

Access nine integrated programs in one. Check-free electronic bill paying, investment counselor, tax estimator, financial calculator, budget and checkbook manager, and payable/receivables with aging. Analysis of tax shelters, portfolios, and insurance.

AUDIENCE: Beginning   RISK LEVEL: Moderate
TOPICS: Bonds, Mutual Funds, Stocks, Asset Allocation, Investment Planning

APEX-BCI

N North Systems
4443 Nalani Court SE
Salem, OR 97302

PH: (503) 364-3829
FAX: (503) 391-5929
SOFTWARE
Cost: $390.00

Graphic time series analysis software. APEX-BCI stands for Access, Plot, & Export - Business Cycle Indicators. The BCI database provides you with over 225 Economic and Business Cycle Indicators. Update indicators at release, produce charts, identify turnarounds.

AUDIENCE: Individual, Professional
TOPICS: Investment Planning, General Reference

Argus On-Line

Argus Research Corporation
17 Battery Place, 18th Floor
New York, NY 10004

PH: (212) 425-7500
FAX: (212) 509-5408
ON-LINE DATABASE
Type: Full-text; numeric

Accessibility to current economic, market, industry and individual stock analysis. 400 companies and 40 industries. Availability to review Market comments, Investment Policy & Economic Outlook, Industry Comments, Stock Analysis Rating by Symbol, Stock Screens. Contact: Richard Cunero, Production Manager.

AUDIENCE: Individual, Professional   RISK LEVEL: Moderate, Aggressive
TOPICS: Bonds, Mutual Funds, Stocks

Asset Allocator

Portfolio SOFTWARE
14 Lincoln Avenue
Quincy, MA 02170

PH: (617) 328-8248
SOFTWARE
Cost: $39.00
Technical Analysis
Technical Support: Phone, M-F

Applies Markowitz algorithm to asset portfolio management to reduce risk and maximize returns. Shows how to allocate assets in portfolio to accomplish higher returns. Can incorporate data from CompuServe files.

AUDIENCE: Individual, Professional   RISK LEVEL: Moderate, Aggressive
TOPICS: Bonds, Stocks, Asset Allocation

Atlas (R)

Technical Data
11 Farnsworth St.
Boston, MA 02210

PH: (617) 345-2526
Type: Numeric; full-text
ON-LINE DATABASE
On-line Availability: Telerate
  Systems, Inc.

Gives financial data and analysis of 7 major government bond markets of: Australia, Canada, European Currency Units (ECUs), Germany, France, Japan, and The Netherlands. Provides trading recommendations and strategies on investments in those countries. Contact: Leslie Keefe, Product Manager, E-mail: 9650 (DIALMAIL).

AUDIENCE: Individual, Professional   RISK LEVEL: Conservative, Moderate
TOPICS: Bonds

Auto-Candle

Trader's Insight, Inc.
8 Renwick Avenue
Huntington, NY 11743-3052

PH: (516) 423-2413
SOFTWARE
Cost: $195.00
Technical Analysis
Technical Support: Phone, M-F

User can create candlestick charts with automatic pattern recognition. Program has a tutorial aid and historical research tool. Outline and label each pattern which assists even beginners in recognizing patterns in the market.

AUDIENCE: Individual   RISK LEVEL: Moderate, Aggressive
TOPICS: Stocks, Futures/Commodities

Autoportfolio

Automated Investments, Inc.
201 Consumers Road, Suite 105
Willowdale, ON, Canada
OM M25 468

PH: (416) 491-8242
(416) 498-1562
SOFTWARE
Cost: $95.00
Technical Support: Phone, M-F

Portfolio management for stocks, mutual funds, and options using Lotus 1-2-3. Automatic portfolio valuation updating, total portfolio variance from cost, gains/losses/annual yields against the market, and report printing. Signal-Link and ProQuote.

AUDIENCE: Individual   RISK LEVEL: Moderate, Aggressive
TOPICS: Bonds, Mutual Funds, Stocks, Options

AXYS

Advent Software, Inc.
301 Brannan Street
San Francisco, CA 94107

PH: (800) 648-7005
(415) 543-7696
FAX: (415) 543-5070
SOFTWARE
Cost: Starts at $15,000.00
Technical Support: Phone, M-F
Newsletter

Portfolio accounting and performance measure for stocks, bonds indexes, futures, options, and real estate. Automates access to information with brokerage firms, pricing and data vendors, and other informational sources. Advent Software.

AUDIENCE: Professional
TOPICS: Bonds, Mutual Funds, Stocks, Options, Futures/Commodities

Banxquote On-Line

Masterfund Inc.
2001 Fairfield Dr.
Wilmington, DE 19810-4309

PH: (302) 529-2200
Type: Numeric
Knight-Ridder Money Center
On-line Availability: Masterfund
 Inc., $200.00 + $90 quarterly

Gives the yields and interest rates for certificates of deposits along with money market investment accounts offered by Federally Insured institutions. Contact: Norbert Mehl, President.

AUDIENCE: Beginning, Individual   RISK LEVEL: Conservative
TOPICS: Bonds

Basic Cycle Analysis

Foundation for the Study of Cycles
900 West Valley Road, Suite 502
Wayne, PA 19087

PH: (800) 477-0741
FAX: (714) 261-1708
Cost: $450.00 for members
$500.00 for non-members
SOFTWARE
Technical Analysis
Technical Support: Phone, M-F

Program performs a complete cycle analysis of a time series. User can access routines and statistically test cycles. Requires no special skill or expertise. Internal parameters can be customized by user. Additional Investment Topic: Real Estate.

AUDIENCE: Beginning, Individual, Professional
TOPICS: Bonds, Mutual Funds, Stocks

Behold!

NTEC
P.O. Box 164075
Austin, TX 78716

PH: (512) 328-8000
SOFTWARE
Cost: Call for price
Technical Analysis

Program allows user defined studies to be incorporated with numerous technical analysis calculations. Other features include back testing, optimization, portfolio testing, regression channels, day-end auto run, real-time link and free upgrades.

AUDIENCE: Individual, Professional   RISK LEVEL: Aggressive
TOPICS: Stocks, Options, Futures/Commodities

Biotechnology Investment Opportunities

High Tech Publishing Company
P.O. Box 1923
Brattleboro, VT 05301

PH: (802) 254-3539
Type: Full-text
ON-LINE DATABASE
On-line Availability: NewsNet, Inc.
 (IV06)
Access Fees: Call for Costs

Newsletter concerning investment opportunities in genetic engineering. Public stock offerings, company profiles and activities, current research, market and commercial applications, industry trends, government policies, and activities in this field.

AUDIENCE: Individual, Professional	RISK LEVEL: Moderate, Aggressive
TOPICS: Bonds, Stocks	

Blakjak

Trion Systems
1417 Davis Road
Hillsborough, NC 27278

PH: (800) 229-4517
SOFTWARE
Cost: $99.00
Technical Support: Phone, M-F
Technical Analysis

Track and analyze market data for 15,000 + items; stocks, optionable stocks, bonds, mutual funds, money market futures, indexes and options. Four tables with user-selected alarm limits displayed for each market; percent change in price, volume and momentum.

AUDIENCE: Individual, Professional	RISK LEVEL: Moderate, Aggressive
TOPICS: Bonds, Mutual Funds, Stocks, Options, Futures/Commodities	

Blue List Bond Ticker

Kenny S&P Information Services
Blue List Division
65 Broadway
New York, NY 10006

PH: (212) 770-4600
Type: Numeric
ON-LINE DATABASE
Coverage: United States
Access Fees: Call for Costs

Provides real-time corporate and municipal bond advertisers' listings, including changes and updates. Offerings are sorted by maturity range, state, and blocksize. Includes Standard & Poor's ratings, municipal and corporate indicators. On-line Availability: Kenny S&P Information Services, Blue List Division.

AUDIENCE: Individual, Professional	RISK LEVEL: Conservative
TOPICS: Bonds	

Blue List Corporate Bond Service

Kenny S & P Information Services
Blue List Division
65 Broadway
New York, NY 10006

PH: (212) 770-4600
Type: Numeric
ON-LINE DATABASE
Access Fees: Call for Costs

Provides real-time data on corporate bond offerings and price information. Comprises the following information: corporate bond offerings, corporate bond evaluations, and bond commentary. On-line Availability: Kenny S&P Information Services, Blue List Division.

AUDIENCE: Professional	RISK LEVEL: Conservative, Moderate
TOPICS: Bonds	

Blue List Retrieval

Kenny S & P Information Services
Blue List Division
65 Broadway
New York, NY 10006

PH: (212) 770-4340
Type: Directory; numeric
ON-LINE DATABASE
Access Fees: Call for Costs

Contains data on the municipal and corporate bond offerings. Includes state, par amount, maturity, yield, price, CUSIP number, insurance, advertiser, and rating by S&P. On-line Availability: Kenny S&P Information Services, Blue List Division (available on a usage basis).

AUDIENCE: Individual, Professional   RISK LEVEL: Conservative, Moderate
TOPICS: Bonds

Blue Sky Practice For Public And Private Limited Offerings

Clark Boardman Callaghan
375 Hudson St., 2nd Floor
New York, NY 10014

PH: (212) 929-7500
Type: Full-text
ON-LINE DATABASE
On-line Availability: WESTLAW
  (CB-CSP)
Access Fees: Call for Costs

Detailed information on state regulation covering all security officers of direct participation programs. Also provides references to the federal and uniform regulations.

AUDIENCE: Professional
TOPICS: Bonds, Mutual Funds, Stocks, Options, Futures/Commodities

BMW

Portside Market
10926 Adare Drive
Arlington, VA 22032

PH: (703) 425-2275
SOFTWARE
Cost: $99.00
Analysis: Bond, Spreadsheets
Technical Support: Phone

Use Lotus 1-2-3 and Symphony macros to form a bond analysis system. Calculates settlement date, maturity date, coupon, price, yield, and call price.

AUDIENCE: Beginning, Individual   RISK LEVEL: Conservative
TOPICS: Bonds

BNA International Finance Daily

The Bureau of National Affairs, Inc.
  (BNA)
1231 25th St., N.W.
Washington, DC 20037
PH: (202) 452-4132
(800) 452-7773
FAX: (202) 822-8092
ON-LINE DATABASE
Type: Full-text
On-line Availability: NEXIS, HRIN,
  WESTLAW
Access Fees: Call for Costs

Information on international banking, finance, and investments. From the Federal Reserve Board, SEC, U.S. Export-Import Bank, the Organization of Economic Cooperation and Development, the European Commission, and the Overseas Private Investment Corporation.

AUDIENCE: Individual, Professional   RISK LEVEL: Conservative, Moderate, Aggressive
TOPICS: All

BNA Securities Law Daily

The Bureau of National Affairs, Inc.
  (BNA)
1231 25th St., N.W.
Washington, DC 20037

PH: (800) 452-7773
FAX: (202) 822-8092
ON-LINE DATABASE
Type: Full-text
On-line Availability: HRIN, LEXIS,
  WESTLAW
Access Fees: Call for Costs

State and federal legislation regulatory, and judicial actions affecting securities, commodities, and corporate activities. Taken from U.S. Congress, state and federal courts, the Securities and Exchange Commission, and the Financial Accounting Standards Board.

AUDIENCE: Professional
TOPICS: All

Bollinger Bands

Koltys, Inc.
P.O. Box 862215
Marietta, GA 30062

PH: (404) 594-7860
SOFTWARE
Cost: $185.00
Technical Analysis
Technical Support: Phone, M-F

Program calculates a 20-day moving average of the S&P 500 and S&P 100 along with an upper and lower volatility band. Adjust program to within 2 standard deviations from the moving average using the last 100 days of data. Performs numerous technical functions.

AUDIENCE: Individual, Professional   RISK LEVEL: Conservative, Moderate,
TOPICS: Stocks   Aggressive

Bond Accountant

Intex Solutions, Inc.
35 Highland Circle
Needham, MA 02194

PH: (617) 449-6222
FAX: (617) 444-2318
SOFTWARE
Cost: $5,000.00
Technical Support: Phone, M-F
Newsletter

Interfaces with Lotus 1-2-3 spreadsheet and generates accounting entries for any bond in currency. Program can accommodate CMOs, IOs, POs, and Z-tranches according to FASB 91 and EITF 89-4. Input of cash flow dates in any sequence, support for variable or fixed.

AUDIENCE: Professional   RISK LEVEL: Conservative, Moderate, Aggressive
TOPICS: Bonds

Bond Buyer Full Text

Dialog Information Services, Inc.
3460 Hillview Avenue
Palo Alto, CA 94304

PH: (800) 334-2564
(415) 858-3785
FAX: (415) 858-7069
ON-LINE DATABASE
Cost: Std Service Plan - $45.00
Annual Service Fee - $35.00
On-line charges $2.50/min. or
  $150.00/hr.

Covers corporate bonds, government bonds. On-line database containing daily coverage of government and Treasury securities, financial futures, corporate bonds, and mortgage securities. Corresponds to publications The Bond Buyer and Credit Markets.

AUDIENCE: Individual, Professional   RISK LEVEL: Conservative, Moderate
TOPICS: Bonds

Bond Buyer Full Text, The

American Banker-Bond Buyer
One State Street Plaza, 30th Floor
New York, NY 10004

PH: (800) 356-4763
FAX: (212) 943-2222
Type: Directory; full-text
ON-LINE DATABASE
Access Fees: Call for Costs

News and information on fixed-income securities market. Municipal bond issues available in each state, bond sales by state, bond elections and issues, and federal laws and regulations about taxable and tax-exempt bonds, U.S. Treasury bonds and securities. Contact: Peter T. Leach, Vice President, Financial Information Services. E-mail: 14015 (DIALMAIL).

AUDIENCE: Professional	RISK LEVEL: Conservative
TOPICS: Bonds	

Bond Data Base

ADP Data Services
42 Broadway, 17th Floor
Suite 1730
New York, NY 10004

PH: (212) 908-5400
Type: Numeric
ON-LINE DATABASE
Access Fees: Call for Costs

Contains historical prices and trading volumes for more than 33,000 corporate, government, and agency bonds. Includes yield-to-maturity rates, interest rates, coupon rates, maturity date, and S&P rating.

AUDIENCE: Professional	RISK LEVEL: Conservative, Moderate
TOPICS: Bonds	

Bond Data Fundamental Service

Technical Data
11 Farnsworth St.
Boston, MA 02210

PH: (617) 345-2526
Type: Numeric; full-text
ON-LINE DATABASE
On-line Availability: Knight-Ridder
  MoneyCenter, Telerate Systems, Inc.
Access Fees: Call for Costs

Real-time data including graphs and analysis on U.S. government bonds, bills, and notes. Short-term forecasts, evaluation of financial futures, and yield-to-maturity rates updated throughout the day. Contact: Leslie Keefe, Product Manager, E-mail: 9650 (DIALMAIL).

AUDIENCE: Individual, Professional	RISK LEVEL: Conservative
TOPICS: Bonds	

Bond$Mart

Portside Market
10926 Adare Drive
Arlington, VA 22032

PH: (703) 425-2275
SOFTWARE
Cost: $395.00
Analysis: Bond, Spreadsheets
Technical Support: Phone

Program can be used for all types of bonds and notes. Calculates yield to maturity, CD equivalent yield, Macauley duration, horizon duration, price volatility reinvested rate-to-yield, etc. Includes a spreadsheet interface for data transfer to Lotus 1-2-3.

AUDIENCE: Individual, Professional	RISK LEVEL: Conservative, Moderate, Aggressive
TOPICS: Bonds	

Bond Portfolio

Heizer Software
P.O. Box 232019
Pleasant Hill, CA 94523

PH: (800) 888-7667
FAX: (510) 943-6882
Cost: $25.00
SOFTWARE
Analysis: Bond, Spreadsheets
Technical Support: Phone, M-F

User can calculate duration, modified duration, duration based on periods, volatility, current yield, yield to maturity, and yield to first call. Bond portfolio can be tracked. Summary of totals and averages on whole portfolio capability.

AUDIENCE: Beginning, Individual	RISK LEVEL: Conservative, Moderate
TOPICS: Bonds	

Bond Portfolio Manager

Larry Rosen Co.
7008 Springdale Road
Louisville, KY 40241

PH: (502) 228-4343
FAX: (502) 228-4782
SOFTWARE
Cost: $89.00
Technical Support: Phone, M-F

Program calculates duration, convexity, and many other functions for bonds and portfolios. Keeps track of value, evaluates the credit of the issuer of each bond, housekeeping information of bond location, serial number call, put, etc.

AUDIENCE: Individual, Professional	RISK LEVEL: Conservative, Moderate
TOPICS: Bonds	

Bond Pricing

Heizer Software
P.O. Box 232019
Pleasant Hill, CA 94523

PH: (800) 888-7667
FAX: (510) 943-6882
Cost: $15.00
SOFTWARE
Analysis: Bond, spreadsheets
Technical Support: Phone, M-F

Program calculates bond price, current yield, yield to maturity, and coupon and maturity data. Calculates from parameters set by users.

AUDIENCE: Individual, Professional	RISK LEVEL: Conservative, Moderate
TOPICS: Bonds	

Bond Sheet

Emerging Market Technologies, Inc.
1230 Johnson Ferry Road, Suite F-1
Marietta, GA 30068

PH: (404) 973-2300
FAX: (404) 973-3003
SOFTWARE
Cost: $149.00

Bond calculator including bond swap module.

AUDIENCE: Individual, Professional	RISK LEVEL: Conservative
TOPICS: Bonds	

Bond Smart

Wall Street Consulting Group
89 Millburn Avenue
Millburn, NJ 07041

PH: (201) 762-4300
SOFTWARE
Cost: Basic monthly charge $175.00

Covers: municipal bonds, corporate bonds, government bonds, foreign bonds. System for managing, accounting, reporting and tracking bonds in single or multiportfolios. General ledger accounting, bond calculator, mortgage calculator, over 70 standard reports.

AUDIENCE: Individual, Professional   RISK LEVEL: Conservative, Moderate
TOPICS: Bonds

Bond Value

Resource Software International, Inc.
330 New Brunswick Avenue
Fords, NJ 08863

PH: (201) 738-8500
SOFTWARE
Cost: Hook-up charges $65.00

Municipals, corporates, governments, foreign bonds. Calculates the present value of available bonds. By comparing the calculated value of the bond to a preestablished minimum return on investments, determines if the bond can be purchased at a value price.

AUDIENCE: Individual, Professional   RISK LEVEL: Conservative, Moderate
TOPICS: Bonds

Bond-Tech's Bond Calculator

Bond-Tech, Inc.
P.O. Box 192
Englewood, OH 45322

PH: (513) 836-3991
FAX: (513) 836-1497
SOFTWARE
Cost: $49.00
Technical Support: Phone, M-F

Bond analysis comparing the relative value (e.g., notes, bonds, money market instruments). Program computes various values of the security: dollar price, discount rate, yield, discount basis equivalent, bond equivalent, CD equivalent yield duration, etc.

AUDIENCE: Individual, Professional   RISK LEVEL: Conservative, Moderate
TOPICS: Bonds

Bondcalc

Bondcalc, Corp.
295 Greenwich Street
Apt. 3B
New York, NY 10007-1050

PH: (212) 587-0097
FAX: (212) 587-9141
SOFTWARE
Cost: $2,900.00
Technical Support: Phone

Cash flows for fixed income securities: after tax, leveraging, and multicurrency capabilities. Portfolio management and bond analysis program for private placements, bank loans, high-yield securities, municipals, emerging market debt, convertibles, corporate.

AUDIENCE: Individual, Professional   RISK LEVEL: Conservative, Moderate
TOPICS: Bonds

BondData Fundamental Service

Technical Data
11 Farnsworth Street
Boston, MA 02210

PH: (617) 345-2526
Type: Numeric; full-text
On-line Availability: Knight-Ridder
  MoneyCenter
ON-LINE DATABASE
Access Fees: Call for Costs

Contains news and fundamental analysis of U.S. securities market. Covers government bonds, bills, and more. Includes a "Squawk Box" feature covering interviews with market traders, and analysis of major portfolios.

AUDIENCE: Individual, Professional   RISK LEVEL: Conservative, Moderate
TOPICS: Bonds

Bonds

Emerging Market Technologies, Inc.
1230 Johnson Ferry Road
Suite F-1
Marietta, GA 30068

PH: (404) 973-2300
FAX: (404) 973-3003
SOFTWARE
Cost: $395.00

Bond portfolio system that includes duration calculations.

AUDIENCE: Individual, Professional   RISK LEVEL: Conservative, Moderate
TOPICS: Bonds

Bonds and Interest Rates

Programmed Press
599 Arnold Road
W. Hempstead, NY 11552

PH: (516) 599-6527
SOFTWARE
Cost: Contact vendor

Bonds and interest rates evaluation package. Evaluates price, risk and return on fixed income securities and annuities.

AUDIENCE: Beginning, Individual   RISK LEVEL: Conservative
TOPICS: Bonds

Bonds Pro Series And Premium Series

Montgomery Investment Group
P.O. Box 508
Wayne, PA 19087-0508

PH: (215) 688-2508
FAX: (215) 688-5084
SOFTWARE
Cost: Pro Series $395.00
Premium Series $695.00
Technical Support: Phone, M-F

A Lotus 1-2-3 add-in which allows custom templates for quantitative techniques. Yield, prices, duration, modified duration horizon, market timing, rolling yield curve, portfolio optimization, for U.S. treasuries, notes, munis corporates, zeros.

AUDIENCE: Individual, Professional   RISK LEVEL: Conservative, Moderate
TOPICS: Bonds

Bonds Xl Pro And Premium Series

Montgomery Investment Group
P.O. Box 508
Wayne, PA 19087-0508

PH: (215) 688-2508
FAX: (215) 688-5084
SOFTWARE
Cost: Pro Series $395.00
Premium Series $695.00
Technical Support: Phone, M-F

Excel add-in calculates bond yields, prices, duration, modified duration, etc. Treasuries, munis, corporate, and more. Templates can be customized for quantitative techniques live horizon, rolling yield curve, market timing, and portfolio optimization.

AUDIENCE: Individual, Professional	RISK LEVEL: Conservative, Moderate
TOPICS: Bonds	

Bondseye

Ergo, Inc.
1419 Wyant Road
Santa Barbara, CA 93108

PH: (800) 772-6637
(805) 969-9366
SOFTWARE
Cost: $65.00
Technical Support: Phone, M-F

Calculator. Yield-to-maturity, call, price from yield, swap analysis, duration, accrued interest, equivalent bond yield, future value, sum of coupons, interest on interest, crossover yield, and convertible bond analysis. Corporate, municipal, and T-bonds.

AUDIENCE: Beginning, Individual	RISK LEVEL: Conservative, Moderate
TOPICS: Bonds	

Bondsheet

Ones & Zeros
708 W. Mt. Airy Avenue
Philadelphia, PA 19119

PH: (800) 882-2764
(215) 248-1010
FAX: (215) 248-1010
SOFTWARE
Cost: $95.00
Analysis: Bonds
Technical Support: Phone, M-F

A bond calculator that computes yield to maturity, yield to call, current yield, before or after tax. Performs a swap analysis between bonds. Supports Monroe-compatible standard yields and true yields. Price can be computed from yields or analysis programs.

AUDIENCE: Individual, Professional	RISK LEVEL: Conservative
TOPICS: Bonds	

Bondspec

BondSpec Financial Information, Ltd.
4 London Wall Bldgs.
Bloomfield Street
London, EC2M 5NT, England

PH: (071) 920-0522
Contact: Edward B. Chaplin, Director
ON-LINE DATABASE
Access Fees: Call for Costs

Provides detailed information on more than 3,500 bonds issued worldwide. Includes historical price, yield comparisons, calculations, graphs, and management groups.

AUDIENCE: Individual, Professional	RISK LEVEL: Conservative, Moderate
TOPICS: Bonds	

BondWare

Davidge Data Systems Corp.
20 Exchange Place
New York, NY 10005

PH: (212) 269-0901
Cost: Complete BondWare $450.00
Pop-up Yield Calculator $89.95
Up-grade new version $35.00

Covers municipal, government, and corporate bonds and agencies. The integrated solution to Fixed Income Security Yield Calculation, Portfolio Analysis and Swap Analysis including the Revolutionary Bond Swap Modeler.

AUDIENCE: Individual, Professional	RISK LEVEL: Conservative, Moderate
TOPICS: Bonds	

Bonneville Market Information

BMI
3 Triad Center
Salt Lake City, UT 84180

PH: (800) 255-7374
FAX: (801) 532-3202
QUOTE SERVICE
Cost: Satellite $597.00
Installation: $150.00 to $395.00

Covers stocks, futures, also chart service. BMI delivers stock, commodities, futures, index, bond, option and mutual funds quotes - with news, weather and private mail via satellite and FM radio stations throughout the United States.

AUDIENCE: Individual, Professional	RISK LEVEL: Conservative, Moderate,
TOPICS: All	Aggressive

Boras

First Data Services, Inc.
38 Park Avenue
Rutherford, NJ 07070

PH: (201) 507-5910
SOFTWARE
Cost: Quarterly - $750.00 per year
Monthly - $1,500.00 per year
Weekly - $3,500.00 per year

Covers corporate, government, and convertible bonds. A bond research and analysis system that provides a complete database of over 8,000 corporate, convertible and government bonds, fully footnoted with cash call and sinking fund schedules.

AUDIENCE: Individual, Professional	RISK LEVEL: Conservative, Moderate
TOPICS: Bonds	

Brainmaker

California Scientific Software
10024 Newton Road
Nevada City, CA 95959

PH: (800) 284-8112
(916) 478-9041
FAX: (916) 478-9042
SOFTWARE
Cost: $195.00
Technical Support: Phone, M-F
BBS

Neural Network for stocks, bonds, mutual funds, indexes, options, futures, and real estate. Software system is designed for building, testing, and analyzing data quickly and accurately. Performs complex arithmetic calculations on user's data.

AUDIENCE: Individual, Professional	RISK LEVEL: Aggressive
TOPICS: Stocks, Options, Futures/Commodities	

Brainmaker Professional

California Scientific Software
10024 Newton Road
Nevada City, CA 95959

PH: (800) 284-8112
FAX: (916) 478-9042
SOFTWARE
Cost: $795.00
Technical Support: Phone, M-F
BBS

Professional version of BrainMaker neural network. Supports 25,000 independent variables, graphics output, high-speed Binary and Hypersonic training. System includes automatic and semi-automatic development tools for network optimization.

AUDIENCE: Professional   RISK LEVEL: Moderate, Aggressive
TOPICS: Stocks, Options, Futures/Commodities

Broker's Notebook

Quotron Systems, Inc.
17 Haverford Station Road
Haverford, PA 19041

PH: (215) 896-8780
Cost: from $895.00
$210.00 per year maintenance
$300.00 - per additional user
Windows version available soon

Custom report capabilities, predesigned reports such as holdings summary, annual income statements, realized gains/losses, and more, automatically posts dividends, interest and reinvestment, tickler lists, mail/merge data and much, much more.

AUDIENCE: Professional   RISK LEVEL: Conservative, Moderate, Aggressive
TOPICS: All

BTC-64

BMI
3 Triad Center
Temple, UT 84180

PH: (800) 255-7374
FAX: (801) 532-3202
QUOTE SERVICE
Cost: $597.00 + $197.00 per mo.
Hardware provided

Futures: 64 pages of tick-by-tick information, three news pages, specialty news, opening calls, financial update, two programmable pages, options, spread page, crawl line, high, low, last, net, volume, bid/ask, opening range, closing range, open interest.

AUDIENCE: Professional   RISK LEVEL: Aggressive
TOPICS: Futures/Commodities

Business Conditions Digest Historical Data

Public Brand Software
P.O. Box 51315
Indianapolis, IN 46251

PH: (800) 426-3475
FAX: (317) 856-2086
ON-LINE DATABASE
Transmission: Diskette
Start-Up Fee: $10.00

Gives the same information as the Business Cycle Indicators from present back to 1945.

AUDIENCE: Individual, Professional
TOPICS: Investment Planning, General Reference

Business Connection

Dialog Information Services, Inc.
3460 Hillview Ave.
Palo Alto, CA 94304

PH: (800) 334-2564
FAX: (415) 858-7069
ON-LINE DATABASE
Transmission: Modem
Start-Up Fee: $295.00
Access Fees: Varies

On-line access to data on public and private companies worldwide. Some of the databases on the service include: Dun & Bradstreet, Standard & Poor's, Moody's and Disclosure. Corporate intelligence, financial screening, product and markets.

AUDIENCE: Individual, Professional   RISK LEVEL: Moderate
TOPICS: Bonds, Stocks

Business Cycle Indicators

Public Brand Software
P.O. Box 51315
Indianapolis, IN 46251

PH: (800) 426-3475
FAX: (317) 856-2086
ON-LINE DATABASE
Transmission: Diskette
Access Fees: $100/year

Official data on 250 economic indicators, indexes and composite indexes from the Department Commerce, and Bureau of Economic Analysis. It contains information for the last four years in a flat ASCII format.

AUDIENCE: Individual, Professional   RISK LEVEL: Conservative, Moderate,
TOPICS: All   Aggressive

Business Week Mutual Fund Scoreboard

Business Week Mutual Fund
  Scoreboard
P.O. Box 1597
Fort Lee, NJ 07024

PH: (800) 553-3575
FAX: (201) 461-9808
ON-LINE DATABASE
Transmission: Diskette
Cost: $399/year for monthly or
  $299/year for quarterly updates
AAII Discount: 25%

Screening and database tool for equity and fixed-income mutual funds. Fund name, ticker, telephone, size, fees, objective, performance figures, portfolio data, risk level, weighted maturity in years, Business Week ratings, search and rank.

AUDIENCE: Beginning, Individual   RISK LEVEL: Moderate, Aggressive
TOPICS: Mutual Funds

Business Wire

Dialog Information Services, Inc.
3460 Hillview Avenue
Palo Alto, CA 94304

PH: (800) 334-2564
FAX: (415) 858-7069
ON LINE-DATABASE
Cost: Standard Service Plan - $45.00,
  $35.00 annual fee
Online charges $1.60/min. or
  $96.00/hour

On-line database containing unedited text of news releases from over 10,000 sources including companies, public relations firms, government agencies, political organizations, colleges and universities, and research institutes. Updated continuously.

AUDIENCE: Individual, Professional
TOPICS: All

Buy-Write Model

Niche Software Products
P.O. Box 3574
Manassas, VA 22110

PH: (703) 368-8372
SOFTWARE
Cost: $50.00
Analysis: Options
Technical Support: Phone, M-F

Exercise probabilities/return potentials for simultaneous equity buy/sell call. Calculate the fair value of options to discern overpriced/underpriced securities, break-even/loss protection buying holding scenarios, option yields, lowest rate of risk.

AUDIENCE: Individual, Professional   RISK LEVEL: Moderate, Aggressive
TOPICS: Options

Buyouts

Venture Economics, Inc.
1180 Raymond Blvd.
Newark, NJ 07102

PH: (201) 622-4500
FAX: (201) 662-1421
Type: Full-text
ON-LINE DATABASE

A newsletter of recent management buyout and leveraged acquisition industries on a biweekly basis. Also contains profiles of LBO groups and lenders, emerging trends, and aggregate industry statistics. On-line availability; as part of PTS Newsletter Database and PTS PROMT (each database is described in a separate entry).

AUDIENCE: Individual, Professional   RISK LEVEL: Moderate, Aggressive
TOPICS: Bonds, Stocks, Options

Buysel

Dynacomp, Inc.
178 Phillips Road
Webster, NY 14580

PH: (800) 828-6772
SOFTWARE
Cost: $99.95
Technical Support: Phone, M-F

Analysis stocks, options, and futures using technical analysis, options analysis, and statistics. 4 distinct trading methods and money management systems, explicit buy/sell transaction signals; Black-Sholes call option model, and statistical correlation.

AUDIENCE: Individual, Professional   RISK LEVEL: Moderate, Aggressive
TOPICS: Stocks, Options, Futures/Commodities

C-Port

Interactive Data Services, Inc. (IDSI)
14 Wall St.
12th Floor
New York, NY 10005

PH: (212) 285-0700
Type: Directory
On-line Availability: Interactive
  Data Services, Inc. (IDSI)
ON-LINE DATABASE
Access Fees: Call for Costs

Price and market evaluations data on municipal bonds. Also gives disclosure information required under Rules G-12 and G-15 of the Municipal Securities Rulemaking Board. Contact: Jim Perry, Production Manager.

AUDIENCE: Individual, Professional   RISK LEVEL: Conservative
TOPICS: Bonds

Cadence Universe Online

CDA Investment Technologies, Inc.
1355 Piccard Dr.
Rockville, MD 20850

PH: (301) 975-9600
(800) 833-1394
FAX: (301) 590-1350
Transmission: Modem, Diskette
Start-Up Fee: $100
Access Fees: $55/hour (from $25 to $60/report)

Instant on-line access to CDA's library of bank, insurance company, mutual fund, and investment advisors data for comparison and analysis. It also gets the returns and compares over 80 market and specialized indexes.

AUDIENCE: Beginning, Individual, Professional   RISK LEVEL: Conservative,
TOPICS: Bonds, Mutual Funds, Stocks   Moderate, Aggressive

Calcugram Stock Options System

Dynacomp, Inc.
178 Phillips Road
Webster, NY 14580

PH: (800) 828-6772
SOFTWARE
Cost: $99.95
Compatibility: DOS
Technical Support: Phone, M-F

Focuses on options analysis and fundamental analysis for options and futures. The daily follow-up program lets the user know when to close out at best advantage. The pricing model used is based on modern portfolio theory. A 3rd program follows progress daily.

AUDIENCE: Individual, Professional   RISK LEVEL: Aggressive
TOPICS: Options, Futures/Commodities

California Public Finance

American Banker-Bond Buyer
One State Street Plaza, 30th Floor
New York, NY 10004

PH: (800) 356-4763
FAX: (212) 943-2222
Type: Full-text
ON-LINE DATABASE
On-line Availability: NewsNet, Inc.
(F165).

A weekly guide of the California municipal bond market which includes ratings and revenue bond yields. Contact: Peter T. Leach, Vice President, Financial Information Services. E-mail 14015 (DIALMAIL).

AUDIENCE: Individual, Professional   RISK LEVEL: Conservative
TOPICS: Bonds

Called Bonds Service

Interactive Data Services, Inc. (IDIS)
14 Wall St.
12th Floor
New York, NY 10005

PH: (212) 285-0700
Former Database Name: IDSI
Corporate Call Features
ON-LINE DATABASE
Type: Numeric
On-line Availability: as part of IDSI
   Pricing and Evaluation Service
Access Fees: Call for Costs

Announces the redemption of corporate and municipal bonds on weekly basis. Contact: Jim Perry, Product Manager.

AUDIENCE: Individual, Professional   RISK LEVEL: Conservative
TOPICS: Bonds

Candle Power 2.1

N-Squared Computing
5318 Forest Ridge Road
Silverton, OR 97381

PH: (503) 873-4420
(214) 680-1445
FAX: (214) 680-1435
SOFTWARE
Cost: $295.00 includes chart service

Japanese Candlestick charting, ARMs equivolume charting, standard bar charting and the new CandlePower charting - all in one software program. A new and upcoming analysis technique that combines the best of Japanese candlesticks with the equivolume principles.

AUDIENCE: Individual, Professional   RISK LEVEL: Aggressive
TOPICS: Options, Futures/Commodities

CandlePower 4.0

N. North Systems
4443 Nalani Court, SE
Salem, OR 97302

PH: (503) 364-3829
FAX: (503) 391-5929
SOFTWARE
Compatibility with IBM/DOS
Cost: $395.00

Japanese Candlestick Charting, ARMs equivolume charting, standard bar charting and the new CandlePower charting - all in one software program. A new and upcoming analysis technique that combines the best of Japanese candlesticks with the equivolume principals.

AUDIENCE: Individual, Professional   RISK LEVEL: Aggressive
TOPICS: Stocks, Options, Futures/Commodities

Candlestick Forecaster

International Pacific Trading Co.
1050 Calle Cordillera, 3 105
San Clemente, CA 92672-6240

PH: (800) 347-5311
(714) 498-4009
FAX: (714) 498-5263
SOFTWARE
Cost: $249.00
Technical Analysis
Technical Support: Phone, M-F

Graphically displays candlestick charts, interprets 700 patterns, issues buy/sell signals, and gives information about candlestick patterns using proprietary artificial intelligence, neural networking structures, and pattern recognition systems.

AUDIENCE: Individual, Professional   RISK LEVEL: Aggressive
TOPICS: Stocks, Options, Futures/Commodities

Candlestick Forecaster Master Edition

International Pacific Trading Co.
1050 Calle Cordillera, 3 105
San Clemente, CA 92672-6240

PH: (800) 347-5311
(714) 498-4009
FAX: (714) 498-5263
SOFTWARE
Cost: $249.00
Technical Analysis
Technical Support: Phone, M-F

Recognizing over 1,000 patterns. Uses western technical studies and neural network to send market-sensitive messages for investment. Calculate buy/sell signals, continuation. Features include candle watch, candle vision, and trendlines.

AUDIENCE: Individual, Professional   RISK LEVEL: Aggressive
TOPICS: Stocks, Options, Futures/Commodities

Candlestick Forecaster Real Time

International Pacific Trading Co.
1050 Calle Cordillera, 3 105
San Clemente, CA 92672-6240

PH: (800) 347-5311
(714) 498-4009
FAX: (714) 498-5263
SOFTWARE
Cost: $1,700.00
Technical Analysis
Technical Support: Phone, M-F

Real-time candlestick trading program recognizes over 1,000 patterns and uses western technical studies and neural networking to issue market-sensitive messages. Program issues buy/sell signal, continuation, confluence, and combination patterns.

AUDIENCE: Individual, Professional   RISK LEVEL: Aggressive
TOPICS: Stocks, Options, Futures/Commodities

Capital Investment System

Portfolio Dynamics
53 West Jackson, Suite 562
Chicago, IL 60604

PH: (312) 461-9760
FAX: (312) 461-0380
SOFTWARE
Cost: Contact Vendor

Capabilities include option writing (puts, calls, expirations, exercises and assignments.) Satisfies total Schedule D reporting requirement. Cash report ties in with either general ledger and/or bank statements. Interfaces with Lotus 1-2-3, dBase III, Chartmaster.

AUDIENCE: Individual, Professional   RISK LEVEL: Aggressive
TOPICS: Stocks, Options, Futures/Commodities

Capital Markets Report (CMR)

Dow Jones & Company, Inc.
200 Liberty St.
New York, NY 10281

PH: (212) 416-2758
Type: Full-text; numeric
On-line Availability: Dow Jones
  News/Retrieval
ON-LINE DATABASE
Access Fees: Call for Costs

Gives news, commentaries and quotations on the capital futures markets worldwide. Also includes currency, interest rate, and stock index futures and options. Contact: Robert Prinsky, Managing Editor, Capital Markets Report; or Dow Jones News/Retrieval Customer Service Hotline.

AUDIENCE: Individual, Professional
TOPICS: All

Captool

Techserve, Inc.
Box 9
Issaquah, WA 98027

PH: (206) 747-5598
(800) 826-8082
SOFTWARE
Cost: $129.00

Covers stocks, commodities, mutual funds, options, and bonds (municipal, corporate, and government). Portfolio management security evaluation, data acquisition, and client management for individual investors and investment professionals.

AUDIENCE: Individual, Professional   RISK LEVEL: Conservative, Moderate, Aggressive
TOPICS: Bonds, Mutual Funds, Stocks, Options, Futures/Commodities

CCH Blue Sky Law Reporter

Commerce Clearing House, Inc. (CCH)
4025 W. Peterson Ave.
Chicago, IL 60646

PH: (312) 583-8500
(800) 835-0105
Type: Full-text
On-line Availability: LEXIS,
Westlaw
ON-LINE DATABASE
Access Fees: Call for Costs

Complete "Blue Sky" laws and related regulatory and legislative material on the registrations and sale of securities in the U.S., the District of Columbia, Puerto Rico, and Guam. It also includes information concerning takeovers, and insurance securities laws.

AUDIENCE: Individual, Professional   RISK LEVEL: Moderate, Aggressive
TOPICS: Bonds, Stocks

CDA HySales for Mutual Funds

CDA Investment Technologies
1355 Piccard Drive
Rockville, MD 20850

PH: (800) 232-2285
SOFTWARE
Cost: $695.00 - includes FREE
   unlimited technical support

Hypothetical software — quarterly updates. Covers open-end mutual funds. This powerful hypothetical software package puts 15 years of performance information on 4,000 mutual funds and 62 market indexes at your fingertips. Customized reports can compare up to ten funds.

AUDIENCE: Professional   RISK LEVEL: Moderate, Aggressive
TOPICS: Mutual Funds, Asset Allocation

CDA/Wiesenberger Mutual Fund Performance

CDA Investment Technologies, Inc.
1355 Piccard Dr.
Rockville, MD 20850

PH: (301) 975-9600
FAX: (301) 590-1350
Former Database Name: CDA
   Mutual Fund Report
ON-LINE DATABASE
Alternate Electronic Formats: Diskette

Gives mutual fund identification and financial information which includes the rate of return, net asset value, load, and risk factors. Hypothetical analysis of fund performance under certain conditions are examined. On-line Availability: CDA Investment Technologies, Inc.

AUDIENCE: Beginning, Individual, Professional   RISK LEVEL: Moderate, Aggressive
TOPICS: Mutual Funds

CDA/Investnet

CDA/Investnet
3265 Meridian Parkway, Suite 130
Ft. Lauderdale, FL 33331

PH: (800) 243-2324
FAX: (305) 384-1540
Transmission: Modem, Diskette
Start-Up Fee: $50.00
ON-LINE DATABASE
Access Fees: $1/minute ($35/month
   minimum)
AAII Discount: $50; applies to start-up

Database of all securities transactions of directors, officers, and major shareholders of all publicly held corporations. It also tracks securities by watch list and provides ranking and summary reports by list or portfolio.

AUDIENCE: Individual, Professional   RISK LEVEL: Moderate, Aggressive
TOPICS: Bonds, Stocks, Options

CDA/Spectrum Institutional Ownership

CDA Investment Technologies, Inc.
1355 Piccard Dr.
Rockville, MD 20850

PH: (301) 975-9600
FAX: (301) 590-1350
Farmer Database Name: Spectrum
Universe On-line
ON-LINE DATABASE
On-line Availability: CDA
Investment Technologies, Inc.
Access Fees: Call for Costs

Information on stocks held by 13(f) institutions. Selections are by industry group, capitalization ranges, or stock exchange. This allows a user to study the price performance against competitors for a time up to ten years.

AUDIENCE: Individual, Professional   RISK LEVEL: Moderate, Aggressive
TOPICS: Stocks

Centerpiece

Performance Technologies, Inc.
4814 Old Wake Forest Road
Raleigh, NC 27609

PH: (800) 528-9595
FAX: (919) 876-2187
SOFTWARE
Cost: $895.00 professional system
$150.00 FNN signal interface;
Technical Support: Phone, M-F
Newsletter

Bond analysis calculates current yield, unrealized gain or loss, yield to maturity, yield to call, duration, etc. Portfolio management position, performance, unrealized gains or losses by trade lot, realized gains and losses, projection of monthly income.

AUDIENCE: Individual, Professional   RISK LEVEL: Conservative, Moderate
TOPICS: Bonds, Mutual Funds, Stocks, Options

Channel Trend Analysis

Channel Trend Associates
3232 McKinney Ave.
Suite 865
Dallas, TX 75204

PH: (800) 527-7736
(214) 855-0660
Cost: $8,000/yr
SOFTWARE
Analysis Capability: Technical
Analysis

A database of over 2,000 stocks published and updated weekly to assist investment decisions based on quantitative risk-reward equity model. Pricing discipline to discover stocks that are overpriced and underpriced.

AUDIENCE: Individual, Professional   RISK LEVEL: Moderate
TOPICS: Stocks

Chartcraft by FAX

Chartcraft, Inc.
30 Church St.
New Rochelle, NY 10801

PHONE: (914) 632-0422
FAX: (914) 632-0335
Frequency: weekly
Costs: $260 annually; $5 per week
minimum 3 months-$70

"FIRST CRACK" at Sentiment Index Figures, NYSE and ASE Moving Averages, Bullish %s and other market indicators. "You don't have to call Hotline, we fax the data to you first!"

AUDIENCE: Individual, Professional   RISK LEVEL: Moderate, Aggressive
TOPICS: Stocks, Options, Futures/Commodities

Chartistalert

Roberts-Slade, Inc.
619 N. 500 West
Provo, UT 84601

PH: (800) 433-4276
FAX: (801) 373-2775
SOFTWARE
Cost: $195.00-$280.00/month
Technical & Fundamental Analysis
Technical Support: Phone, M-F
BBS
Newsletter

User can create formulas and customize program through the use of numerous modules. Completely automate trading system. Analysis of stocks, bonds, indexes, etc. Other features include quotes, news, portfolio management advanced charting, and technical analysis.

AUDIENCE: Individual   RISK LEVEL: Moderate, Aggressive
TOPICS: Bonds, Stocks, Options, Futures/Commodities

Chartpro

Ret-Tech Software, Inc.
151 Deer Lane
Barrington, IL 60010

PH: (708) 382-3903
FAX: (708) 382-3906
SOFTWARE
Cost: $54.00
Technical Analysis
Technical Support: Phone, M-F

Relative strength, Fibonacci, line oscillators, all moving averages, support/resistance studies, Williams percentage-R, directional movement, commodity cycle index, MACD CCI, accumulation distribution index, stochastics, Gann, and much more. Charts.

AUDIENCE: Individual, Professional   RISK LEVEL: Aggressive
TOPICS: Stocks, Options, Futures/Commodities

Citibase

Fame Software Corp.
88 Pine St., 16th Floor
New York, NY 10005

PH: (212) 898-7200
FAX: (212) 742-8956
Transmission: Modem, Diskette, Tape
ON-LINE DATABASE
Start-Up Fee: $200
Access Fees: $95/hour.

Unites States macroeconomic database with monthly, quarterly, and annual times series from public and private sources, national income and product, manufacturing and trade, prices, labor, construction, interest rates, energy, and credit.

AUDIENCE: Individual, Professional   RISK LEVEL: Conservative, Moderate, Aggressive
TOPICS: All

Citibase Daily

Fame Software Corp.
88 Pine St., 16th Floor
New York, NY 10005

PH: (212) 898-7200
FAX: (212) 742-8956
Start-Up Fee: $200
Transmission: Modem, Tape
Access Fees: $95/hour
Minimum Usage: $30

Provides daily financial indicators. Includes international and domestic stock market statistics, futures, commodities, interest rates and exchange rates.

AUDIENCE: Individual, Professional   RISK LEVEL: Conservative, Moderate, Aggressive
TOPICS: All

Citibase-Estima

Estima
1800 Sherman Ave., Suite 612
Evanston, IL 60201

PH: (708) 864-8772
(800) 822-8038
FAX: (708) 864-6221
ON-LINE DATABASE
Transmission: Diskette
Access Fees: $400-$2,800/year
depending on update schedule

Is U.S. macroeconomics database of Citicorp Database Services. The full version of the database has almost 6,000 data series. A mini version includes 600 of the most frequently used data series. The series are annual, monthly or quarterly.

AUDIENCE: Individual, Professional   RISK LEVEL: Conservative, Moderate, Aggressive
TOPICS: All

Citibase Weekly

Fame Software Corp.
88 Pine St., 16th Floor
New York, NY 10005

PH: (212) 898-7200
FAX: (212) 742-8956
Compatibility: DOS, Unix
Transmission: Modem, Diskette,
Tape, 8mm, 1/4", 1/2"
ON-LINE DATABASE
Start-Up Fee: $200
Access Fees: $95/hour

It has macroeconomic and financial indicators of weekly frequency. Included topics are: banking industry, interest rates, money supply, commodity prices, futures, and production and Standard & Poor's indexes. Most of the series date back to 1980.

AUDIENCE: Individual, Professional   RISK LEVEL: Conservative, Moderate, Aggressive
TOPICS: All

Client Asset Management System (dbCAMS)

Financial Computer Support, Inc.
145 Commerce Drive
Oakland, MD 21550

PH: (301) 334-1800
SOFTWARE
Cost: Contact Vendor

Covers data management system for tracking insurance, assets, portfolios, gain/loss, mutual funds and money market funds for either consolidated family or individual reporting.

AUDIENCE: Beginning, Individual   RISK LEVEL: Conservative, Moderate, Aggressive
TOPICS: Bonds, Mutual Funds, Stocks

Comex Comcalc

Commodity Exchange, Inc.
4 World Trade Center, Room 6404
New York, NY 10048

PH: (800) 333-2900
(212) 938-7921
FAX: (212) 938-2660
SOFTWARE
Cost: $49.95
Compatibility: DOS
Technical Support: Phone, 9 am - 5
pm, M-F

Program helps determine the fair value, implied volatility, and delta of futures options.

AUDIENCE: Professional   RISK LEVEL: Aggressive
TOPICS: Futures/Commodities

Comex, The Game

Commodity Exchange, Inc.
4 World Trade Center, Room 6404
New York, NY 10048

PH: (800) 333-2900
(212) 938-7921
FAX: (212) 938-2660
SOFTWARE
Cost: $69.95
Technical Support: Phone, 9 am - 5
    pm, M-F

Program that uses the gold and silver marketplace to instruct about futures and options trading. Extensive options and futures price data; price history charts automatic calculation of the margin, profit/loss graphs, and a ticker relating next-day movements.

AUDIENCE: Beginning, Individual, Professional   RISK LEVEL: Aggressive
TOPICS: Options, Futures/Commodities

Commodex Signals

Equidex, Inc.
7000 Blvd East
Guttenberg, NJ 07093-4808

PH: (800) 336-1818
(201) 868-2600
Cost: $1,695.00 per year; must have
    a built in or external modem

Covers futures. Receive instant 24 hour access through computer telephone network to commodex signals. New signals processed twice daily. Intra-day bulletin available at approximately 12:30 PM EST. Service now available by FAX.

AUDIENCE: Professional   RISK LEVEL: Aggressive
TOPICS: Futures/Commodities

Commodities 2000

Reuters Ltd.
85 Fleet St.
London EC4P 4AJ, England

PH: 071-250 1122
0800 010701
FAX: 071-696 8761
Type: Numeric, full-text
Contact: Michael Cooling, Manager,
    Corporate Relations
ON-LINE DATABASE
On-line Availability: Reuters Ltd.

Contains commodities futures contracts and option series, as well as news affecting the market. Financial Futures; Metals; Soft Commodities; Grains and Oilseeds; and Livestock. There are also analysis and commentaries from Agra Europe and Metal Bulletin.

AUDIENCE: Professional   RISK LEVEL: Aggressive
TOPICS: Options, Futures/Commodities

Commodities and Futures Software

Programmed Press
599 Arnold Road
W. Hempstead, NY 11552

PH: (516) 599-6527
SOFTWARE
Cost: Hook-up charge $144.00

Covers commodities. Package provides forecasting capabilities concerning the evaluation of price, risk and return on commodities and futures.

AUDIENCE: Individual   RISK LEVEL: Aggressive
TOPICS: Options, Futures/Commodities

Commodities Database

Interactive Data Corporation
95 Hayden Ave.
Lexington, MA 02173-9144

PH: (617) 863-8100
Type: Numeric
ON-LINE DATABASE
On-line Availability: Westlaw (CB
-SEC 13)
Access Fees: Call for Costs

Descriptive information, cash and contract settlement prices, open
interest, and volumes on agricultural and metal commodities for
major U.S., Canadian, and U.K. commodity exchanges. Also
includes financial, currency, stock index, and interest rate futures.
Contact: Beth VanderVleet, Sales Analysis.

AUDIENCE: Professional   **RISK LEVEL: Aggressive**
TOPICS: Options, Futures/Commodities

Commodity Data Plus Software

Micro Futures
3338 Jennings Rd.
Whitmore Lake, MI 48189

PH: (313) 449-0609
Compatibility: DOS
ON-LINE DATABASE
Current Quote Fees: contact vendor
Transmission: Diskette

Gives commodity information on floppy disk or via telephone
access on MJK. Historical data for some dates back to 1969.
Companion software for data success to MJK.

AUDIENCE: Individual, Professional   **RISK LEVEL: Aggressive**
TOPICS: Options, Futures/Commodities

Common Stock Decision Aide

V.A. Denslow & Associates
4151 Woodland Avenue
Western Springs, IL 60558

PH: (708) 246-3365
FAX: (708) 246-3365
SOFTWARE
Cost: $49.00
Fundamental Analysis
Technical Support: Phone, M-F

Basis for investment decisions is the compounded after tax returns
of common stocks for the past 12 years up to the present. Calculates
earnings, growth rates, dividend yields, price/earnings ratio ranges,
projected current high and low price share.

AUDIENCE: Individual, Professional   **RISK LEVEL: Moderate, Aggressive**
TOPICS: Stocks

Common Stock Selector

Village Software
186 Lincoln Street
Boston, MA 02111

PH: (800) 724-9332
(617) 695-9332
FAX: (617) 695-1935
Cost: $59.00
SOFTWARE
Fundamental Analysis
Technical Support: Phone, M-F

Shows earnings growth rates, price/earnings ratio ranges, projected
high/low prices per share and compounded returns. Compares stock
performance with DJIA and the S&P 500. Make buy/sell/hold
decisions based on comparative data.

AUDIENCE: Beginning, Individual   **RISK LEVEL: Moderate, Aggressive**
TOPICS: Stocks

Compact D/'33

Disclosure, Inc.
5161 River Road
Bethesda, MD 20816

PH: (301) 951-1300
FAX: (301) 657-1962
Transmission: Modem, CD-ROM
ON-LINE DATABASE
Access Fees: $5,800/monthly,
 $4,800/quarterly, $2,300/annual

Access to the 1993 Act Registrations and Prospectuses data for
SEC reporting companies. 1933 Act Registrations Statements filed
on Forms S-1, S-2, S-3, S-4, S-9, S-18, F-1, F-2, F-3, F-4, pre and
post-effective amendments, final prospectus and supplements.

AUDIENCE: Professional   **RISK LEVEL: Moderate, Aggressive**
TOPICS: Bonds, Stocks

Compact D/Canada

Disclosure, Inc.
5161 River Rd.
Bethesda, MD 20816

PH: (301) 951-1300
FAX: (301) 657-1962
Transmission: CD-ROM
ON-LINE DATABASE
Access Fees: $4,500/year,
 Commercial; $3,600/year
Non-profit

Gives unlimited access on CD-ROM to facts and figures on private,
public and crown companies in all 10 Canadian provinces. It is
organized into 3 main sections: Resume section, Financial section,
and Summary section. There are over 100 search variables
available.

AUDIENCE: Individual, Professional   **RISK LEVEL: Moderate, Aggressive**
TOPICS: Bonds, Stocks

Compact D/Sec

Disclosure, Inc.
5161 River Rd.
Bethesda, MD 20816

PH: (301) 951-1300
FAX: (301) 657-1962
Transmission: Modem, CD-ROM
ON-LINE DATABASE
Access Fees: $5,800/year
 Commercial; $4,500/year
Non-profit

Provides instant accessible corporate information on public
companies whose securities are traded on the AMEX, NYSE,
NASDAQ, and OTC. The information is obtained from documents
filed with the SEC. Zacks Investment Database of Wall Street
Estimates.

AUDIENCE: Professional   **RISK LEVEL: Moderate, Aggressive**
TOPICS: Bonds, Stocks

Company and Industry Reports

Mead Data Central, Inc. (MDC)
9443 Springboro Pike
P.O. Box 933
Dayton, OH 45401

PH: (800) 227-4908
Type: Full-text
FAX: (513) 865-6909
ON-LINE DATABASE
On-line Availability: LEXIS (COIND)
Access Fees: Call for Costs

Research reports of U.S. multinational companies and industries
complied by analysts, investment banking, brokerage and research
firms. Provides descriptions and analysis of the company's plans
and forecast of the major corporations in each industry.

AUDIENCE: Individual, Professional   **RISK LEVEL: Moderate, Aggressive**
TOPICS: Bonds, Stocks

Company Intelligence

Dialog Information Services, Inc.
3460 Hillview Avenue
Palo Alto, CA 94304

PH: (800) 334-2564
FAX: (415) 858-7069
ON-LINE DATABASE
Cost: $45.00 , On-line charges $1.75
    per min. or $105.00 per hr.

On-line database containing a combined directory and company news file published by Information Access Company. Contains current address, financial and marketing information on approximately 10,000 U.S. private and public companies. Updated daily.

AUDIENCE: Individual, Professional   RISK LEVEL: Moderate, Aggressive
TOPICS: Bonds, Stocks

Complete Bond Analyzer

Larry Rosen Co.
7008 Springdale Road
Louisville, KY 40241

PH: (502) 228-4343
FAX: (502) 228-4782
SOFTWARE: Cost: $89.00
Technical Support: Phone, M-F

Program functions include yield to maturity, price, given yield to maturity, call, accrued interest at sale, duration and revised duration, theoretical spots, etc. Can be used for government, agency, conventional, or zero-coupon bonds.

AUDIENCE: Beginning, Individual   RISK LEVEL: Conservative, Moderate
TOPICS: Bonds

Compu Trac

Compu Trac Software, Inc.
1017 Pleasant Street
New Orleans, LA 70115

PH: (800) 535-7990
FAX: (504) 895-3416
SOFTWARE
Cost: $900.00 - $1,990.00
Macintosh $695.00
Technical Support: Phone, M-F
Newsletter

Program provides user with technical analysis, technical screening, options analysis, and spreadsheets. Features include bar charts, moving averages to oscillators, and stochastics. Programming allows for precision charts, trendlines, and user programming.

AUDIENCE: Individual, Professional   RISK LEVEL: Aggressive
TOPICS: Stocks, Options, Futures/Commodities

Compu/Chart EGA

New Tek Industries
P.O. Box 46116
Los Angeles, CA 90046

PH: (213) 874-6669
SOFTWARE
Cost: $239.95 - $329.95 with 1200
baud modem

Chart service. Automatic data retrieval and technical analysis program using high-resolution color graphics. Chart screens include Moving Averages/Bar Chart, The Portfolio Scanner, Oscillator-Scan, Comparisons, Point and Figure Chart. "The Retriever."

AUDIENCE: Individual, Professional   RISK LEVEL: Aggressive
TOPICS: Mutual Funds, Stocks, Futures/Commodities

Compusec Portfolio Manager

Dynacomp, Inc.
178 Phillips Road
Webster, NY 14580

PH: (800) 828-6772
SOFTWARE
Cost: $99.95
Technical Support: Phone, M-F

Ranks each stock in any portfolio, showing which stocks should be reduced or eliminated and which should be increased. Calculates the compound growth rate and earnings per share. Shows daily volume, unrealized gains and losses, and realized capital gains and losses.

AUDIENCE: Beginning, Individual   RISK LEVEL: Moderate, Aggressive
TOPICS: Stocks

CompuServe Data Engine for Microsoft Excel

CompuServe, Inc.
120 Broadway, Suite 3330
New York, NY 10271

PH: (800) 543-4616
(212) 227-3881
FAX: (212) 227-7194
SOFTWARE
Cost: $2,500.00/month and up
Technical Support: Phone, M-F
Newsletter

Program performs technical screening and analysis, fundamental screening and analysis, portfolio management, bond and options analysis, and spreadsheets. Allows user to implement standard templates or to customize templates.

AUDIENCE: Individual, Professional   RISK LEVEL: Conservative, Moderate, Aggressive
TOPICS: All

CompuServe Information Service

An H&R Block Company
CompuServe Information Service
5000 Arlington Centre Blvd.
Columbus, OH 43220

PH: (800) 848-8199
(614) 457-0802
Cost: Membership Fee - $49.95
Monthly Fee - $8.95
Online charges - from $4.80 per hour

Stocks, commodities, charts, mutual funds, options, and currencies. Personal investing. Services include Quote, Snapshot (quotes relative to market), historical trading, range-review, up to 12 years of daily, weekly, and monthly pricing statistics.

AUDIENCE: Beginning, Individual   RISK LEVEL: Moderate, Aggressive
TOPICS: All

CompuServe Research Manager

CompuServe, Inc.
120 Broadway
Suite 3330
New York, NY 10271

PH: (800) 543-4616
(212) 227-3881
FAX: (212) 227-7194
SOFTWARE
Cost: $250.00 - 1,300.00/month and up
Technical Support: Phone, M-F
Newsletter

Collection of databases, 190,000 North American securities; 90,000 international securities, Zacks, Compustat, and I/B/E/S. Portfolio management, fundamental analysis, technical analysis, fundamental and technical screening, bond and options analysis.

AUDIENCE: Beginning, Individual, Professional   RISK LEVEL: Moderate, Aggressive
TOPICS: Bonds, Mutual Funds, Stocks, Options, Futures/Commodities

CompuTrac

Telerate, Inc.
1017 Pleasant Street
New Orleans, LA 70115

PH: (800) 535-7990;
(504) 895-1474
(800) 274-4028
FAX: (504) 895-3416
SOFTWARE
Hook-up charges $1,900.00 includes
chart services. Optional maintenance
program for $300.00 per year.

Covers stocks, commodities, chart service, market timing, options. Superior technical analysis software can take the gray out of your trading decisions and give you more time to judge the buy and sell signals. Complete library of price forecasting techniques.

AUDIENCE: Beginning, Individual   RISK LEVEL: Moderate, Aggressive
TOPICS: Mutual Funds, Stocks, Options, Futures/Commodities

Comstock

Standard & Poor's Information
Group
670 White Plains Road
Scarsdale, NY 10583

PH: (800) 431-5019
(914) 725-3477 (NY & Canada)
FAX: (914) 725-4271
Cost: Hook-up charges $750.00
Basic monthly charge $420.00
Online chgs per min n/a, Security
    deposit $500.00

Immediate stock quote service. Chart Service available. Stocks, bonds (municipal, government, corporate, foreign), commodities, mutual funds, market timing, and charts. Provides global market data coverage and extensive news service.

AUDIENCE: Beginning, Individual, Professional   RISK LEVEL: Conservative,
TOPICS: All   Moderate, Aggressive

Connect Business Information Network

Connect, Inc.
10161 Bubb Road
Cupertino, CA 95014

PH: (408) 973-0110
(800) 262-2638
FAX: (408) 973-0493
ON-LINE DATABASE
Start-Up Fee: $150
Access Fees: $14 for 1 hour connect
    and 100,000 characters

Gives global computer communications. It includes Standard & Poor's Ticker III, and has a 15 minute delay feed from North American Stock Exchanges. It also has a screen or tone alarm activated by price or volume levels.

AUDIENCE: Beginning, Individual, Professional RISK LEVEL: Moderate, Aggressive
TOPICS: Bonds, Mutual Funds, Stocks, Options, Futures/Commodities

Continuous Contractor

Technical Tools
334 State Street, Suite 201
Los Altos, CA 94022

PH: (415) 948-6124
SOFTWARE
Cost: $150.00

Software which synthesizes long, continuous contracts from the individual contract data. Allows you to set up data files into a number of different popular formats such as CSI, CompuTrac, Lotus, Symphony, MetaStock, etc.

AUDIENCE: Individual, Professional   RISK LEVEL: Aggressive
TOPICS: Futures/Commodities

Convertible Bond Analyst

Analytical Service Association
21 Hollis Road
Lynn, MA 01904

PH: (617) 593-2404
SOFTWARE
Cost: Hook-up charges $99.95

Convertible bonds. Premium over investment value in points and percent, conversion parity price, premium over conversion in percent, current yield, pay back in years, break-even time in years, yield to maturity, undervaluation factor.

AUDIENCE: Individual, Professional   **RISK LEVEL: Moderate, Aggressive**
TOPICS: Bonds

Corporate Data Exchange

LAFOUNTAIN Research Corp.
128 Conway Ave.
Narberth, PA 19072

PH: (215) 668-9970
Compatibility: Any computer,
   modem, communications software
ON-LINE DATABASE
Access Fees: Call for Costs

Is a shareholder communications electronic bulletin that communicates information from companies to their shareholders and other interested parties. It is a distributions channel and serves as an electronic archive with a minimum one year file retention.

AUDIENCE: Individual, Professional   **RISK LEVEL: Moderate, Aggressive**
TOPICS: Bonds, Stocks

Corporate Ownership Watch

Invest/Net, Inc.
3265 Meridian Pkwy.
Suite 130
Ft Lauderdale, FL 33331

PH: (305) 384-1500
FAX: (305) 384-1540
Contact: John H. Wright, Director of
   Marketing
ON-LINE DATABASE
On-line Availability: Dow Jones
   News/Retrieval
Access Fees: Call for Costs

Stock market transactions by corporate insiders. Also shows the 25 most active issues for the most recent 3 months.

AUDIENCE: Individual, Professional   **RISK LEVEL: Moderate, Aggressive**
TOPICS: Stocks

Corporate Watch

McCarthy, Crisanti & Maffei, Inc.
   (MCM)
Electronic Information Services
71 Broadway
New York, NY 10006

PH: (212) 509-5800
FAX: (212) 509-7389
ON-LINE DATABASE
On-line Availability: Quotron
   Systems, Inc.; Telerate Systems,
   Inc.
Access Fees: Call for Costs

News and analysis of new issue U.S. corporate bond market. Contains files about these subjects: Company Comments, New Issues, Rating Changes, RATING WATCH, Street Talk.

AUDIENCE: Individual, Professional   **RISK LEVEL: Conservative, Moderate**
TOPICS: Bonds

Covered Options

Dynacomp, Inc.
178 Phillips Road
Webster, NY 14580

PH: (800) 828-6772
SOFTWARE
Cost: $99.95
Compatibility: DOS
Technical Support: Phone, M-F

Option analysis for options and futures. Emphasizes options "covered" by owned securities as well as uncovered positions. Allows user to evaluate the options on a stock so they can select the highest value for sale or the cheapest value for purchase.

AUDIENCE: Individual, Professional   RISK LEVEL: Moderate, Aggressive
TOPICS: Stocks, Options

CQG System One

CQG, Inc.
P.O. Box 758
Glenwood Springs, CO 81602-0758

PH: (800) 525-7082
(303) 945-8686
Cost: $390.00 + exchange fees
Chart services: $50.00/mo. and up
Compatibility: CQG hardware

Covers commodities, chart service, news - Futures World News. Turn-key system - hardware and data link, comprehensive market quotation service that is ready when you need it for quotes, charts, news, market and technical information.

AUDIENCE: Individual, Professional   RISK LEVEL: Aggressive
TOPICS: Options, Futures/Commodities

Crystal Ball

Decisioneering, Inc.
1380 Lawrence Street
Suite 520
Denver, CO 80204

PH: (800) 289-2550
FAX: (303) 534-2118
SOFTWARE
Cost: $295.00
Technical Support: Phone, M-F
Newsletter

A forecasting and risk analysis program using fundamental analysis. Uses Monte Carlo simulation to forecast all statistically possible results for a given situation along with a confidence level for each situation. Also has graphic reporting format.

AUDIENCE: Individual, Professional   RISK LEVEL: Moderate, Aggressive
TOPICS: Stocks, Options, Futures/Commodities

CSI Data Retrieval Service

Commodity Systems, Inc. (CSI)
200 W. Palmetto Park Road
Boca Raton, FL 33432

PH: (407) 392-8663
(800) 274-4727
FAX: (407) 392-1379
ON-LINE DATABASE
Transmission: Modem, Diskette
Start-Up Fee: $39
Current Quote Fees: $11/mo. and up

Daily updates and historical data on all United States stocks, mutual funds, futures, foreign futures, futures options, stock index options, and cash markets. Programs to download so they can manage graphically, review and analyze the market information.

AUDIENCE: Individual, Professional   RISK LEVEL: Moderate, Aggressive
TOPICS: Mutual Funds, Stocks, Options, Futures/Commodities

Currencycast

Ultravision\USA
1095 Market Street, Suite 709
San Francisco, CA 94103-1630

PH: (800) 998-3540
FAX: (415) 255-9392
Cost: $69.95/year
SOFTWARE
Technical Analysis
Technical Support: Phone, M-F

Designed to forecast European Economic Community exchange rates for 1 day, 1 week, 1 month in advance. Includes analysis for closing values for gold, British Pound, Canadian dollar, Swiss franc, Japanese yen, German mark and E.C.U. in terms of U.S. dollars.

AUDIENCE: Individual, Professional	RISK LEVEL: Moderate, Aggressive
TOPICS: Bonds, Options, Futures/Commodities	

D&B-Dun's Financial Records Plus

Dialog Information Services, Inc.
3460 Hillview Avenue
Palo Alto, CA 94304

PH: (800) 334-2564
(415) 858-3810
FAX: (415) 858-7069
ON-LINE DATABASE
Cost: $45.00
Online charges: $2.45/min. or
   $147.00/hr.

Provides up to three years of financial statements for over 650,000 private and public companies. Information provided by Dun & Bradstreet Credit Services. Updated quarterly.

AUDIENCE: Individual, Professional	RISK LEVEL: Moderate, Aggressive
TOPICS: Bonds, Stocks	

Daily Comment

MMS International
1301 Shoreway Rd.
Suite 300
Belmont, CA 94002

PH: (415) 595-0610
Type: Full-text; numeric
ON-LINE DATABASE
On-line Availability: CompuServe
Information Service
Access Fees: Call for Costs

Data, analysis, and commentary on debt market activity, including the cash and futures market for notes, bonds, bills, certificates of deposit, Euro-dollars, and Government National Mortgage Association (GNMA) mortgages.

AUDIENCE: Professional	RISK LEVEL: Conservative, Moderate
TOPICS: Bonds, Options, Futures/Commodities	

Daily Financial Market Research

Optima Investment Research
327 S. LaSalle St.
Suite 1300
Chicago, IL 60604

PH: (312) 427-3616
(800) 344-4403
FAX: (312) 427-9840
ON-LINE DATABASE
Current Quote Fees: $195/month

Provides daily fundamental and technical research on financial cash and futures markets. It includes the International Morningstar Report. The fundamental analysis has economic analysis of events in the U.S. and international financial markets.

AUDIENCE: Professional	RISK LEVEL: Conservative, Moderate, Aggressive
TOPICS: Bonds, Options, Futures/Commodities	

Daily Summary

Commodity Information Services
327 S. LaSalle, Suite 1133
Chicago, IL 60604

PH: (800) 800-7227
FAX: (312) 341-1494
ON-LINE DATABASE
No. of Users: 150
Start-Up Fee: $45
Access Fees: $0.25/1,000 characters
AAII Discount: None

Daily summary services on futures and their related cash instruments for those who maintain their own database files and analysis programs. The users can use strength index, stochastics and trading models for detailed research.

AUDIENCE: Individual, Professional   RISK LEVEL: Moderate, Aggressive
TOPICS: Options, Futures/Commodities

Dallas Morning News Stock/Business Hotline, The

PH: (900) 990-9900 (then enter 195)
(214) 977-8809
Cost: $.95 per minute
Frequency of update: every 15 minutes
QUOTE SERVICE

Includes stocks. Covers business news. Use your touch-tone phone to get timely stock quotes (15 minute delayed) on more than 9,000 publicly traded issues and concise hourly business news updates prepared by business experts from Associated Press.

AUDIENCE: Beginning, Individual   RISK LEVEL: Moderate, Aggressive
TOPICS: Bonds, Mutual Funds, Stocks

Data Connections

Genesis Financial Data Services
411 Woodman Ct.
Colorado Springs, CO 80919

PH: (719) 260-6111
(800) 808-3282
FAX: (719) 260-6113
ON-LINE DATABASE
Transmission: Modem, Diskette
Start-Up Fee: $85
Current Quote Fees: $65/month

Daily and historical price data on stocks, mutual funds, futures and options. 8 years of continuous and cash contracts for 21 commodities and stock history for the Dow 30 Industrial stocks. Also gives an 8 year history for the DJIA, SPX and OEX stock index.

AUDIENCE: Individual   RISK LEVEL: Moderate, Aggressive
TOPICS: Mutual Funds, Stocks, Options, Futures/Commodities

Data Mover (CompuTrac)

Automated Data Collection
Winning Strategies, Inc.
761 Covington Road
Los Altos, CA 94022-4906

PH: (415) 969-8576
Cost: $79.00 for Data Mover and users manual

Covers options, stocks, commodities, and indexes. Features: update CompuTrac daily files from Telemet, Signal, PC-Quote files; up to 600 files may be updated at once; program automatically selects appropriate stock or commodity data files for file updating.

AUDIENCE: Individual, Professional   RISK LEVEL: Moderate, Aggressive
TOPICS: Mutual Funds, Stocks, Options, Futures/Commodities

Data Retriever

Time Trend Software
337 Boston Road
Billerica, MA 01821

PH: (508) 663-3330
FAX: (508) 667-1269
SOFTWARE
Cost: $45.00
Data collection
Technical Support: Phone, 9 am - 5
   pm, M-F

Downloads current and historical data from Dial/Data on mutual funds, stocks, market indexes and commodities. Automatic dividend adjustment. Designed to be used with Fund Master TC, can also write DIF and ASCII files for importing and exporting data.

AUDIENCE: Individual   RISK LEVEL: Moderate, Aggressive
TOPICS: Mutual Funds, Stocks, Options, Futures/Commodities

Data Smoother Semi-Spline/Polynomial Data

Dynacomp, Inc.
178 Phillips Road
Webster, NY 14580

PH: (800) 828-6772
SOFTWARE
Cost: $39.95 - $49.95
Compatibility: DOS
Technical Support: Phone, 9 am -
   5 pm, M-F

Uses fundamental analysis, technical analysis, and statistics to smooth out day-to-day stock market fluctuations to see the overall market behavior.

AUDIENCE: Individual, Professional   RISK LEVEL: Moderate, Aggressive
TOPICS: Stocks, Options, Futures/Commodities

Data-Star

Data-Star
1 Commerce Square, Suite 1010
Philadelphia, PA 19103

PH: (800) 211-7754
FAX: (215) 687-0984
ON-LINE DATABASE
Transmission: Modem
Access Fees: Varies
Historical Quote Fees: From $2.72
AAII Discount: 12/hours

Over 250 international business databases allowing access to company brokerage and intelligence reports. Frost & Sullivan market research, disclosure of public companies trading on the U.S. exchanges, Investext, Extel Card, Canadian Financial Database.

AUDIENCE: Individual, Professional   RISK LEVEL: Moderate, Aggressive
TOPICS: Bonds, Mutual Funds, Stocks

Datadisk Information Services

Cambridge Planning & Analytics, Inc.
55 Wheeler Street, P.O. Box 276
Cambridge, MA 02138

PH: (800) 328-3475
FAX: (617) 354-7295
ON-LINE DATABASE
No. of Users: 300
Start-Up Fee: $200.00
Access Fees: $395.00 to $695.00
AAII Discount: No start-up fee

It provides for economic, financial and business databases for analysis and presentation. Monthly updated databases that have general economic, financial, equities, production, consumer and retail information.

AUDIENCE: Individual, Professional   RISK LEVEL: Conservative, Moderate, Aggressive
TOPICS: All

Datafeed for AIQ Systems Trading Expert

Interactive Data Corp.
Mail Location LI-AI
95 Hayden Ave.
Lexington, MA 02173-9144

PH: (617) 863-8100
FAX: (617) 860-8289
ON-LINE DATABASE
Transmission: Modem, Diskette
Start-Up Fee: $25.00

Links database to AIQ Systems Trading Expert. Daily, weekly and monthly high/low/close or bid/ask prices and volume for North American stocks, market indicators back to 1981, market indexes and market indicators, historical stock and market index back to 1968.

AUDIENCE: Beginning, Individual, Professional   RISK LEVEL: Moderate, Aggressive
TOPICS: Stocks

Datalink

Integrated Financial Solutions, Inc.
(formerly RJT Systems)
1049 S.W. Baseline, Suite B-200
Hillsboro, OR 97123

PH: (800) 729-5037
FAX: (503) 648-9528
SOFTWARE
Cost: $89.00
Analysis Capabilities: Downloading
Technical Support: Phone, M-F

Program downloads prices on stocks, indexes, and futures by end-of-day analysis from DTN screen. Compatibility between DTN Wall Street and Lotus, MetaStock, CompuTrac, OptionVue and 20 other technical, portfolio management, and forecasting systems.

AUDIENCE: Individual, Professional   RISK LEVEL: Moderate, Aggressive
TOPICS: Bonds, Mutual Funds, Stocks, Futures/Commodities

Datanet

Cablesoft, Inc.
1807 2nd Street, Suite 26
Santa Fe, NM 87501

PH: (505) 986-8052
FAX: (505) 986-8240
No. of Users: 500
ON-LINE DATABASE
Start-Up Fees: $100 for unlimited use
AAII Discount: 10%

Historical information for 2.5 years of weekly data and 7 months of daily data on 14,000 symbols.

AUDIENCE: Individual, Professional   RISK LEVEL: Moderate, Aggressive
TOPICS: Bonds, Mutual Funds, Stocks

DataTimes

DataTimes
14000 Quail Springs Parkway, Suite 450
Oklahoma City, OK 73134

PH: (800) 642-2525
(405) 751-6400
Cost: Pay-as-you-go or flat fee pricing options available

Provider of information business services, with an on-line network providing access to more than 2,500 publications, newswires, and financial database. Compliment fundamental research with regional and industry news and analysis of companies and industries.

AUDIENCE: Beginning, Individual, Professional RISK LEVEL: Moderate, Aggressive
TOPICS: Bonds, Mutual Funds, Stocks

DBC/Link2

Computer Investing Consultants
9002 Swinburne Ct.
San Antonio, TX 78240

PH: (512) 681-0491
Cost: $98.00

Covers stocks. For use with CompuTrac. DBC/LINK2, a program for interfacing FNN/Marketwatch data to MetaStock, CompuTrac or N2 (stocks and indexes). Can save up to 255 stocks to your database in about 2 minutes, identify major price and volume moves.

AUDIENCE: Individual, Professional   RISK LEVEL: Moderate, Aggressive
TOPICS: Stocks

DCA

Emerging Market Technologies, Inc.
1230 Johnson Ferry Road, Suite F-1
Marietta, GA 30068

PH: (404) 973-2300
FAX: (404) 973-3003
SOFTWARE
Cost: $95.00

Modeling software for dollar cost averaging for bond and stock investments.

AUDIENCE: Individual, Professional   RISK LEVEL: Moderate, Aggressive
TOPICS: Bonds, Mutual Funds, Stocks

Decision Analysis

Dynacomp, Inc.
178 Phillips Road
Webster, NY 14580

PH: (800) 828-6772
SOFTWARE
Cost: $39.95
Compatibility: DOS
Technical Support: Phone, 9am - 5
  pm, M-F

Organizes choices and factors involved to assist the investor with decision analysis. User defines choices, criteria, and supply ratings to show how each choice compares with others in present analysis tables.

AUDIENCE: Individual, Professional   RISK LEVEL: Moderate, Aggressive
TOPICS: Bonds, Mutual Funds, Stocks

Delphi

Delphi
1030 Massachusetts Ave.
Cambridge, MA 02138

PH: (617) 491-3393
(800) 695-4005
FAX: (617) 491-6642
ON-LINE DATABASE
Access Fees: 10/4 plan - $10/month
includes 4 hours, $4/hour thereafter

Provides quotes and market analysis, futures information, stock and market analysis, CD rates, portfolio analysis, press release wires, and software shopping.

AUDIENCE: Individual, Professional   RISK LEVEL: Conservative, Moderate, Aggressive
TOPICS: Bonds, Mutual Funds, Stocks, Options, Futures/Commodities

Dial Data

Track Data Corp.
Dial/Data Division
95 Rockwell Place
Brooklyn, NY 11217

PH: (800) 275-5544
FAX: (718) 522-6847
Cost: Hook-tip charges $35.00
Monthly flat fee
Services range $35.00 - $125.00

Covers stocks, commodities, mutual funds, options, and bonds (municipal, corporate and government). You can track daily, weekly, and monthly prices for securities. Intra-day prices are available for securities, options, commodity futures and commodity future options. Provides historical information also.

AUDIENCE: Individual, Professional   RISK LEVEL: Conservative, Moderate, Aggressive
TOPICS: Bonds, Mutual Funds, Stocks, Options, Futures/Commodities

Dialog

Dialog Information Services, Inc.
3460 Hillview Avenue
Palo Alto, CA 94304

PH: (800) 334-2564
Costs: $45.00 start-up fee (separate)
Starter packages $125.00 to $230.00

The DIALOG service lets you search through thousands - even millions - of documents in seconds. DIALOG draws from more sources than any other on-line service in the world. Locate financial data on over 2.5 million public and private companies.

AUDIENCE: Individual, Professional   RISK LEVEL: Moderate, Aggressive
TOPICS: Bonds, Stocks

Dialog Quotes and Trading

Dialog Information Services, Inc.
3460 Hillview Avenue
Palo Alto, CA 94304

PH: (800) 334-2564
(415) 858-3810
FAX: (415) 858-7069
ON-LINE DATABASE
$45.00 for the first password
On-line charges $.60 per minute

Covers stocks. Stocks and options quotes delayed at least 20 minutes from the New York and American Stock Exchanges, NASDAQ, and the four major options exchanges. Order entry allows purchase or sale of any stock or option listed in The Wall Street Journal.

AUDIENCE: Individual, Professional   RISK LEVEL: Moderate, Aggressive
TOPICS: Mutual Funds, Stocks, Options, Futures/Commodities

Director Utilities For AIQ Systems-Auto-Q

Nirvana Systems
3415 Greystone Drive
Suite 205
Austin, TX

PH: (800) 880-0338
(512) 345-2545
FAX: (512) 345-2592
SOFTWARE
Cost $249
Technical Analysis
Technical Support: Phone, M-F

(1) Auto-Q director utilities program for AIQ systems that automates the daily screening of stocks using any trading strategy. Director automation shell allows the utility to run unattended at a sequence or certain time period. (2) Back-Tester. (3) Profit Tester.

AUDIENCE: Individual, Professional   RISK LEVEL: Conservative, Moderate, Aggressive
TOPICS: Stocks

Director Utilities For Metastock Pro-Autostock

Nirvana Systems
3415 Greystone Drive, Suite 205
Austin, TX

PH: (800) 880-0338
(512) 345-2545
FAX: (512) 345-2592
SOFTWARE
Cost: $69.00
Technical Analysis
Technical Support: Phone, M-F

(1) AutoStock produces a ranked list of buy sell signals for securities from MetaStock (2) What Works A utility for MetaStock that test a list of systems and finds the most profitable (3) Systems! 40 pre-defined trading systems for MetaStock.

AUDIENCE: Individual, Professional   RISK LEVEL: Conservative, Moderate, Aggressive
TOPICS: Mutual Funds, Stocks

Directory of East European Businesses

The Reference Press, Inc.
6448 Highway 290 E.
Suite E-104
Austin, TX 78723

PH: (512) 454-7778
FAX: (512) 454-9401
Cost: $74.95
First Published: 1992

Features information on the leading 2,000 manufacturing and engineering companies in Albania, Bulgaria, Czechoslovakia, the former East Germany, Hungary, Poland, Romania, and Commonwealth of Independent States and regions of the former Yugoslavia.

AUDIENCE: Individual, Professional   RISK LEVEL: Moderate, Aggressive
TOPICS: Stocks

Disclosure Database

Disclosure Incorporated
5161 River Rd.
Bethesda, MD 20816

PH: (301) 951-1300
(800) 843-7747
FAX: (301) 657-1962
ON-LINE DATABASE
On-line Availability: ADP Network
Services, Inc., BRS Online
Access Fees: Call for Costs

Publicly held companies with a minimum of 500 shareholders of one class stock, at least five million dollars in assets, and have filed a 10K or 20F report with the U.S. SEC in the last 18 months, or new companies must have filed appropriate registrations.

AUDIENCE: Individual, Professional   RISK LEVEL: Moderate, Aggressive
TOPICS: Bonds, Stocks

Disclosure/Worldscope

Disclosure, Inc.
5161 River Rd.
Bethesda, MD 20816

PH: (301) 951-1300
FAX: (301) 657-1962
Transmission: Modem, CD-ROM
ON-LINE DATABASE
Access Fees: $8,000/year with
  monthly updates, Commercial;
  $5,200/year with monthly updates,
Non-profit.

Provides unlimited access to information on companies from 32 countries worldwide. It is updated quarterly and has a database that includes general corporate information, financial information, country and industry averages, and financials.

AUDIENCE: Individual, Professional   RISK LEVEL: Moderate, Aggressive
TOPICS: Bonds, Stocks

Discovery

Cyber-Scan, Inc.
3601 Pulaski Road N.E.
Buffalo, NY 55313

PH: (612) 682-4150
SOFTWARE
Cost: $350.00
Technical Support: Phone, 9 am - 5
pm, M-F

Performs more than 60 technical functions in analyzing futures, stocks, and options, including bar charts, moving averages, stochastics, RSI, MACD, CCI spreads, and stops using DTN Monitor.

AUDIENCE: Individual, Professional   RISK LEVEL: Moderate, Aggressive
TOPICS: Stocks, Options

Dividend Announcements Services

Interactive Data Services, Inc. (IDSI)
14 Wall St.
12th Floor
New York, NY 10005

PH: (212) 285-0700
On-line: Interactive Data Services,
 Inc. (IDSI)
Access Fees: Call for Costs

Information on dividend-paying securities in the United States and Canada. Contact: Jim Perry, Product Manager.

AUDIENCE: Individual, Professional   RISK LEVEL: Moderate, Aggressive
TOPICS: Stocks

Dividend Reinvestment Plan Stocks

Heizer Software
P.O. Box 232019
Pleasant Hill, CA 94523

PH: (510) 943-7667
(800) 888-7667
FAX: (510) 943-6882
ON-LINE DATABASE
Transmission: Diskette
Start-Up Fee: $40 full address

Is a database of companies with dividend reinvestment plans for stocks. Investing guidelines for DRPs are in text format.

AUDIENCE: Beginning, Individual   RISK LEVEL: Moderate
TOPICS: Stocks

Dollarlink

Dollarlink Software
1407 Douglass Street
San Francisco, CA 94131

PH: (415) 641-0721
FAX: (415) 282-8486
SOFTWARE
Cost: $1,300.00 or $100.00/mo. rental
Technical Support: Phone M-F

Real-time technical analysis program for stock, indexes, and commodities. Tracks up to 1,000 symbols. Can chart 80 80 intraday and historical studies in up to 496 windows on any portfolio symbol. Uses Signal, Bonneville, or PC Quote.

AUDIENCE: Individual, Professional   RISK LEVEL: Aggressive
TOPICS: Stocks, Options, Futures/Commodities

Dow Daily Close 1960-1991

Heizer Software
P.O. Box 232019
Pleasant Hill, CA 94523

PH: (800) 888-7667
FAX: (510) 943-6882
ON-LINE DATABASE
Transmission: Diskette
Start-Up Fee: Program $59.00;
   updates $12.00

Is for analysis of market movements or historical prices or to backtest trading systems. Daily closing averages for the Dow Jones industrials, utilities and transportation averages for the last 32 years.

AUDIENCE: Beginning, Individual   RISK LEVEL: Moderate, Aggressive
TOPICS: Stocks

Dow Industrials

Heizer Software
P.O. Box 232019
Pleasant Hill, CA 94523

PH: (800) 888-7667
FAX: (510) 943-6882
ON-LINE DATABASE
Transmission: Diskette
Start-Up Fee: $12

Provides monthly stock price averages for the Dow Jones industrials. Provides monthly averages from 1951 through 1990. Information is supplied in a database format.

AUDIENCE: Individual   RISK LEVEL: Moderate, Aggressive
TOPICS: Stocks

Dow Jones Business and Financial Report

Dow Jones & Company, Inc.
P.O. Box 300
Princeton, NJ 08543-0300

PH: (609) 520-4000
Type: Full-text; numeric
ON-LINE DATABASE
On-line Availability: Dow Jones
  News/Retrieval
Access Fees: Call for Costs

Provides news and information on the business and financial scene worldwide.

AUDIENCE: Individual, Professional   RISK LEVEL: Conservative, Moderate, Aggressive
TOPICS: All

Dow Jones Enhanced Current Quotes

Dow Jones & Company, Inc.
P.O. Box 300
Princeton, NJ 08543-0300

PH: (609) 520-4000
Type: Numeric; full-text
ON-LINE DATABASE
PRODIGY
On-line Availability: Dow Jones
  News/Retrieval (CQE: prime-time
  rates: $2.16/connect minutes (2400
  baud)

Current quotes for common and preferred stocks and NASDAQ prices (15 minute delay during market hours). Also has up to date news alerts.

AUDIENCE: Individual, Professional   RISK LEVEL: Moderate, Aggressive
TOPICS: Bonds, Mutual Funds, Stocks, Options

Dow Jones Futures and Index Quotes

Dow Jones & Company, Inc.
P.O. Box 300
Princeton, NJ 08543-0300

PH: (609) 520-4000
Type: Numeric
ON-LINE DATABASE
On-line Availability: Dow Jones
  News/Retrieval - $2.16/connect
  minutes (2400 baud)

Gives historical and current quotes for contracts on North American stock exchanges. There is a 10-30 minute delay during market hours.

AUDIENCE: Individual, Professional   RISK LEVEL: Aggressive
TOPICS: Stocks, Options, Futures/Commodities

Dow Jones International News

Dow Jones & Company, Inc.
P.O. Box 300
Princeton, NJ 08543-0300

PH: (609) 520-4000
Type: Full-text
ON-LINE DATABASE
On-line Availability: Dow Jones
  News/Retrieval - $2.16/connect
  minute (2400 baud)

Provides the general and business financial and economic news which affects the markets, corporations, and industries around the world. It updates 2,000 items a day.

AUDIENCE: Individual, Professional   RISK LEVEL: Conservative, Moderate,
TOPICS: All   Aggressive

Dow Jones News/Retrieval

Dow Jones News/Retrieval
P.O. Box 300
Princeton, NJ 08540

PH: (800) 522-3567 x 2251
FAX: (609) 520-4660
ON-LINE DATABASE
Transmission: Modem
Start-Up Fee: $29.95
Access Fees: $1.20-$1.95/min. +
  $1.14-$1.89/information unit.

Provides a broad selection of business and financial information composed of more than 60 on-line services. Users can receive real-time or delayed quotes from all major exchanges. It provides historical quotes on stocks, indexes, mutual funds and futures.

AUDIENCE: Individual, Professional   RISK LEVEL: Conservative, Moderate,
TOPICS: All   Aggressive

Dow Jones Real-Time Quotes (RTQ)

Dow Jones & Company, Inc.
P.O. Box 300
Princeton, NJ 08543-0300

PH: (609) 520-4000
ON-LINE DATABASE
On-line Availability: Dow Jones
News/Retrieval $2.16/connect min.

Provides the real-time stock quotations.

AUDIENCE: Individual, Professional   RISK LEVEL: Moderate, Aggressive
TOPICS: Bonds, Mutual Funds, Stocks, Options

Dow Jones Text Library

Dow Jones & Company, Inc.
P.O. Box 300
Princeton, NJ 08543-0300

PH: (609) 520-4000
Type: Full-text
ON-LINE DATABASE
On-line Availability: Dow Jones
  News/Retrieval $2.01-$1.41/connect
  minute, 90 cents/Information Unit

Contains the national and international business and financial news. It contains the following files: Barron's, The Business Library, Dow Jones News, McGraw-Hill Library, The Wall Street Journal, and The Washington Post.

AUDIENCE: Beginning, Individual, Professional	RISK LEVEL: Conservative, Moderate, Aggressive
TOPICS: All	

Dow Month-By-Month Set

Heizer Software
P.O. Box 232019
Pleasant Hill, CA 94523

PH: (800) 888-7667
FAX: (510) 943-6882
Transmission: Diskette
Start-Up Fee: $25

It gives monthly averages of Dow Jones industrials, transportation, utility and composite averages for the last 35 years. Supplied in database format.

AUDIENCE: Beginning, Individual, Professional	RISK LEVEL: Conservative, Moderate, Aggressive
TOPICS: All	

Dowcast

Ultravision\USA
1095 Market Street, Suite 709
San Francisco, CA 94103-1630

PH: (800) 998-3540
FAX: (415) 255-9392
Cost: $199.95
SOFTWARE
Technical Analysis
Technical Support: Phone, M-F

An expert system designed to forecast the closing of DJIA, S&P 500, T-bills, silver and the Japanese yen. Has on-line manual, charting inference engine, data input, forecasting and knowledge base. Forecasts values for 1-, 5-, 22-day and 1 year closings.

AUDIENCE: Beginning, Individual, Professional	RISK LEVEL: Conservative, Moderate, Aggressive
TOPICS: All	

Downloader

Equis International
3950 South 700 E.
Suite 100
Salt Lake City, UT 84107

PH: (800) 882-3040
FAX: (801) 265-3999
SOFTWARE
Cost: $195.00; Dial/Data $69.00;
Signal $69.00; CompuServe $69.00
Technical Support: Phone, M-F

Stock market data collection program for stocks, bonds, indexes, mutual funds, options, and futures. Uses historical and end-of-day price quotes to be used with MetaStock or compatible programs. Access to five vendors: CompuServe, Dial/Data, DJN/R, Market Scan, or Signal.

AUDIENCE: Beginning, Individual, Professional	RISK LEVEL: Conservative, Moderate, Aggressive
TOPICS: All	

Dowquest

Dow Jones & Company, Inc.
P.O. Box 300
Princeton, NJ 08543-0300

PH: (609) 520-4000
Type: Full-text
ON-LINE DATABASE
On-line Availability: Dow Jones
  News/Retrieval, 60 – 90 cents;
  Information Unit, 90 cents

Provides the general and business news from about 400 national, regional, local, and industry-wide business journals. It also allows searches by single words, English-language queries, and performs "relevance feedback" searches using all the words in up to three selected articles as search words.

AUDIENCE: Beginning, Individual, Professional	RISK LEVEL: Conservative,
TOPICS: All	Moderate, Aggressive

DRI Business Fixed Investment Forecast

DRI/McGraw-Hill
Data Products Division
24 Hartwell Ave.
Lexington, MA 02173

PH: (617) 863-5100
ON-LINE DATABASE
Type: Time series
On-line Availability: DRI/McGraw-Hill
Access Fees: Call for Costs

Historical and forecast series of expenditures for durable equipment and construction. For equipment it covers nominal and real spending, price deflators, real and net capital stocks, cost of capital, investment tax credit rates, present value depreciation allowances, and tax lifetimes. In the area of nonresidential structures it covers nominal and real spending, price deflators, capital stock for major categories, cost of capital for major categories. Contact: Linda Ansil, Marketing Coordinator.

AUDIENCE: Beginning, Individual, Professional	RISK LEVEL: Conservative,
TOPICS: All	Moderate, Aggressive

DRI Financial and Credit Statistics (DRIFACS)

DRI/McGraw-Hill
Data Products Division
24 Hartwell Ave.
Lexington, MA 02173

PH: (617) 863-5100
ON-LINE DATABASE
Type: Time series
On-line Availability: DRI/McGraw-Hill
Access Fees: Call for Costs

Lists over 20,500 financial time series which include the releases of the Federal Reserve and the U.S. Treasury Department. It covers domestic and international money market rates on a daily, weekly, and monthly basis; fixed income markets, foreign exchange and Eurocurrency markets, performance measurement statistics, and U.S financial operating statistics. It includes information from 1973 to date and is updated depending on the series. Contact: Linda Ansil, Marketing Coordinator.

AUDIENCE: Beginning, Individual, Professional	RISK LEVEL: Conservative,
TOPICS: All	Moderate, Aggressive

DRI Financial Market Indexes

DRI/McGraw-Hill
Data Products Division
24 Hartwell Ave.
Lexington, MA 02173

PH: (617) 863-5100
ON-LINE DATABASE
Type: Numeric
On-line Availability: DRI/
  McGraw-Hill (@ INDEX/DATA)
Access Fees: Call for Costs

Shows the performance of financial markets worldwide which include domestic and international opinions and futures, fixed income, equity, exchange, and other financial statistics. Contact: Linda Ansill, Marketing Coordinator.

AUDIENCE: Beginning, Individual, Professional	RISK LEVEL: Conservative,
TOPICS: All	Moderate, Aggressive

DRI ITIS Trade Series C

DRI/McGraw-Hill
Data Products Division
24 Hartwell Ave.
Lexington, MA 02173

PH: (617) 863-5100
ON-LINE DATABASE
Type: Time Series
On-line Availability: DRI/
  McGraw-Hill (@ITIS/ACCESS).
Access Fees: Call for Costs

Annual series on import and export trade flows for 24 OECD member countries with more than 190 trading partners. Commodity coverage of more than 2,100 products and can be accessed at the 5-digit SITC leve, with 1-, 2-, and 3-digit aggregations. Contact: Linda Ansill, Marketing Coordinator.

AUDIENCE: Beginning, Individual, Professional   RISK LEVEL: Conservative,
TOPICS: All   Moderate, Aggressive

DRI U.S. Annual Model Forecast

DRI/McGraw-Hill
Data Products Division
24 Hartwell Ave.
Lexington, MA 02173

PH: (617) 863-5100
Type: Time Series
On-line Availability: DRI/
  McGraw-Hill (@USANNSIM).
Access Fees: Call for Costs

It covers business fixed investment, employment, capital stock, consumption, energy, financial sector, industrial production, inventories, population, labor force, and participation rates, prices, wages, and productivity, residential fixed investment, federal government, state and local government, and trade.

AUDIENCE: Beginning, Individual, Professional RISK LEVEL: Conservative,
TOPICS: All   Moderate, Aggressive

DRPDisk

DRPSOFT
P.O. Box 169
Oxford, MA 01540

PH: (508) 987-1962
ON-LINE DATABASE
No. of Users: 250
Transmission: Diskette
Start-Up Fee: $36
AAII Discount: 11%

Gives a complete listing of available dividend reinvestment plans. It lists common stocks by name, industry, symbol, state, address, cash limits, discounts, price, dividend and yield. It notes stocks which have split or paid a stock dividend.

AUDIENCE: Beginning, Individual   RISK LEVEL: Moderate, Aggressive
TOPICS: Stocks

DTN Wall Street

Data Transmission Network, Corp.
9110 W. Dodge Rd., Suite 200
Omaha, NE 68114

PH: (800) 485-4000
FAX: (402) 390-9690
ON-LINE DATABASE Satellite
  with proprietary equipment
Start-Up Fee: $295
Current Quote Fees: $37.95/month

It is an electronic video service that gives quotes for stocks, bonds, mutual funds, and futures. It also provides financial news and information. There is a 15 minute delay on stock, bond, and fund quotes, with futures having a 10-30 minute delay.

AUDIENCE: Individual, Professional   RISK LEVEL: Moderate, Aggressive
TOPICS: Bonds, Mutual Funds, Stocks, Options, Futures/Commodities

Duff & Phelps Fixed Income Ratings

Duff & Phelps, Inc.
55 E. Monroe St.
Suite 4000
Chicago, IL 60603

PH: (312) 263-2610
Type: Full-text; numeric
ON-LINE DATABASE
On-line Availability: Duff & Phelps,
  Inc.
Access Fees: Call for Costs

Gives the financial investment information on about 500 major
U.S. corporations. Also includes rating changes in past 3 months,
and individual company ratings with commentaries.

AUDIENCE: Individual, Professional   RISK LEVEL: Conservative, Moderate
TOPICS: Bonds

Dun's Business Update

Dun & Bradstreet Information
Services
Three Sylvan Way
Parsippany, NJ 07054-3896

PH: (800) 223-1026
FAX: (201) 605-6921
ON-LINE DATABASE

Gives up-to-date information on over 600,000 business
establishments and professionals in the United States. On-line
Availability: DIALOG Information Services, Inc. (514, D&B -
Dun's Business Update: $108/connect hour + $2.50/full record)

AUDIENCE: Individual, Professional   RISK LEVEL: Moderate, Aggressive
TOPICS: Bonds, Stocks

Dun's Million Dollar Directory (MDD)

Dun & Bradstreet Information
Services
Three Sylvan Way
Parsippany, NJ 07054-3896

PH: (201) 605-6000
(800) 223-1026
FAX: (201) 605-6921
ON-LINE DATABASE

Information on 160,000 private and public U.S. companies with a
new worth of $500,000 or more which can be either company
headquarters or single-locations establishments. Manufacturers,
wholesalers and retailers, industrial companies. On-line
Availability: DIALOG Information Services, Inc. (517, D&B -
Dun's Directory: $105/connect hour + $2.20/full record)

AUDIENCE: Individual, Professional   RISK LEVEL: Moderate, Aggressive
TOPICS: Bonds, Stocks

Dynamic Analysis Volume Charts

Volume Dynamics, Inc.
3536 Swallow Drive
Suite 11
Melbourne, FL 32935

PH: (407) 259-5751
SOFTWARE
Cost: $99.50
Technical Analysis
Technical Support: Phone, M-F

Investment decisions based on technical analysis program for
stocks, commodities and indexes. Analysis program summarizes 6
technical factors and flags stock that has a rise in the volume on any
day exceeding 2 times the average daily volume.

AUDIENCE: Individual   RISK LEVEL: Aggressive
TOPICS: Stocks, Options, Futures/Commodities

E*Trade System

E*Trade Securities
480 California Ave., 3rd Floor
Palo, Alto, CA 94306

PH: (800) 786-2575
FAX: (415) 324-3578
Transmission: Modem
ON-LINE DATABASE
Access Fees: $0.22/minute
Current Quote Fees: $30.00 month

Trading systems featuring touch-tone or PC trading 24 hours a day, real time news alters and quotes, updating of portfolios, portfolio and tax record management, place and review orders, Black-Schole option analysis, and free use in choice of Money Market Fund.

AUDIENCE: Individual   RISK LEVEL: Moderate, Aggressive
TOPICS: Stocks, Options, Futures/Commodities

Earnings Estimates

Securities Data Company, Inc.
1180 Raymond Blvd.
5th Floor
Newark, NJ 07102

PH: (201) 622-3100
Type: Numeric
ON-LINE DATABASE
Access Fees: Call for Costs

Contains data on mean, median, and standard deviation of estimates; revision momentum; and stock beta information provided over the first call network. The data are produced by stock brokers in North America.

AUDIENCE: Individual, Professional   RISK LEVEL: Moderate, Aggressive
TOPICS: Stocks

Easy Money Plus

Money Tree Software
1753 Wooded Knolls Drive
Philomath, OR 97370

PH: (503) 929-2140
FAX: (503) 929-2787
SOFTWARE
Cost: $500.00
Analysis Capability: Financial
  Planning, Spreadsheets
Technical Support: Phone, M-F

Comprehensive financial planning made easy. Data entry features include graphs, charts, diagrams, and reports. Reports include information on asset allocation, retirement, insurance planning, income tax, tax estate, education funding, and more.

AUDIENCE: Beginning   RISK LEVEL: Conservative, Moderate, Aggressive
TOPICS: Bonds, Mutual Funds, Stocks

Econ

DC Econometrics
2920 Mount Royal Court
Fort Collins, CO 80526

PH: NA
SOFTWARE
Cost: $39.99

Fundamental and technical analysis allow for econometric stock market forecasting models on the S&P 500, T-bond, and T-bill interest rates. User can get statistically optimized forecasts for 3, 6, and 12 months into the future. Asset allocation.

AUDIENCE: Beginning, Individual   RISK LEVEL: Moderate, Aggressive
TOPICS: Bonds, Mutual Funds, Stocks

Econplot

Marasys, Inc.
2615 N. 4th Street, #755
Coeur d'Alene, ID 83814

PH: (408) 448-0648
SOFTWARE
Cost: $49.95
Fundamental Analysis
Technical Support: Phone, M-F

Plots the 4 year business cycle with over 250 indicators. User can plot up to 15 indicators per window with one or two windows per screen. Separate or common scales can be used per window.

AUDIENCE: Beginning, Individual   **RISK LEVEL: Moderate, Aggressive**
TOPICS: Mutual Funds, Stocks

Electronic Futures Trend Analyzer

Knight-Ridder Financial Publishing
30 S. Wacker Dr.
Suite 18820
Chicago, IL 60606

PH: (312) 454-1801
(800) 526-3282
FAX: (312) 454-0239
Transmission: Diskette, CD-ROM
Start-Up Fee: $50.00/month

A medium- to long-term trading system.

AUDIENCE: Individual, Professional   **RISK LEVEL: Aggressive**
TOPICS: Options, Futures/Commodities

Electronic Money Fund Report

IBC/Donoghue, Inc.
290 Eliot St.
P.O. Box 9104
Ashland, MA 01721-9104

PH: (508) 881-2800
(800) 343-5413
FAX: (508) 811-0982
Transmission: Modem
No. of Users: 60
Start-Up Fee: $2,695/year

Gives access to money fund data via modem the same day the data is compiled. The weekly data is available on Thursday (4 days earlier than on paper), the monthly data is available on or before the 20th of each month (8 days earlier than in print).

AUDIENCE: Professional   **RISK LEVEL: Conservative**
TOPICS: Bonds

Electronic Symbol Index

Integrated Financial Solutions, Inc.
(formerly RJT Systems)
1049 S.W. Baseline, Suite B-200
Hillsboro, OR 97123

PH: (800) 729-5037
(503) 640-5303
FAX: (503) 648-9528
SOFTWARE
Cost: $49.00
Analysis Capabilities: Ticker Utility
Technical Support: Phone, M-F

Electronically update issues as they become available on the market using DATALINK and DTN Wall Street. Cross-reference database contains 15,000 stocks, bonds, and mutual funds.

AUDIENCE: Individual, Professional   **RISK LEVEL: Conservative, Moderate, Aggressive**
TOPICS: Bonds, Mutual Funds, Stocks

Encore

Telemet America, Inc.
325 First Street
Alexandria, VA 22314

PH: (800) 368-2078
(703) 548-2042
Cost: $169.00 + $12.00-$80.00/mo.

Covers stocks, commodities, chart service. News -McGraw Hill. A sophisticated market quotation and news system which gives you instant stock, option, futures quotes, and business news 24 hours a day.

AUDIENCE: Individual, Professional   RISK LEVEL: Moderate, Aggressive
TOPICS: Mutual Funds, Stocks, Options, Futures/Commodities

Enhanced Chartist

Roberts-Slade, Inc.
619 N. 500 West
Provo, UT 84601

PH: (800) 433-4276
(801) 375-6850
FAX: (801) 373-2775
SOFTWARE
Cost: $1,895.00
Technical Analysis

A program which tracks and charts stocks, mutual funds, indexes, options with more than 50 technical indicators. Multiple windows and multiple monitors. Displays 1,024 live quotes and can store 22 years of daily history. Charts 168 items intraday and tick-by-tick.

AUDIENCE: Individual, Professional   RISK LEVEL: Moderate, Aggressive
TOPICS: Stocks, Options, Futures/Commodities

Enhanced Communications

Savant Software, Inc.
 (Formerly Savant Corp.)
120 Bedford Center Road
Bedford, NH 03110

PH: (800) 231-9900
FAX: (603) 472-5981
QUOTE UTILITY
Cost: $245.00
Technical Support: Phone, M-F

Communication program for Savant's Fundamental Investor, Technical Investor, and Fundamental Investor. Retrieves prices from Signal, TrackData, and DJN/R.

AUDIENCE: Individual, Professional   RISK LEVEL: Moderate, Aggressive
TOPICS: Stocks, Options, Futures/Commodities

Enhanced Fund Master Optimizer

Time Trend Software
337 Boston Road
Billerica, MA 01821

PH: (508) 663-3330
FAX: (508) 667-1269
SOFTWARE
Cost: $150.00
Technical Analysis
Technical Support: Phone, M-F

Simulation model that runs in conjunction with Fund Master TC or Fund Pro. Analyzes results and gives parameters for best performance of various trading strategies. Can use moving averages or exponential average crossover, overbought/oversold simulations.

AUDIENCE: Individual   RISK LEVEL: Moderate, Aggressive
TOPICS: Mutual Funds, Stocks, Futures/Commodities

Ensign 5

BMI
19 W. South Temple, Suite 200
Salt Lake City, UT 84101-1503

PH: (800) 255-7374
FAX: (801) 532-3202
Former Database Name: Ensign IV
ON-LINE DATABASE
Start-Up Fee: $697.00 - $1,295.00
Current Quote Fees: $227/month

Real-time technical analysis program that allows the investor to follow stocks, commodities, options, mutual funds, and indexes. Equity table follows portfolio profits and losses; a top 20 lists of stocks and commodities by volume, best yield percentage for day.

AUDIENCE: Individual, Professional　　　RISK LEVEL: Moderate, Aggressive
TOPICS: Bonds, Mutual Funds, Stocks, Options, Futures/Commodities

EPIC

Ford Investor Services, Inc.
11722 Sorrento Valley Road, Suite 1
San Diego, CA 92121

PH: (619) 755-1327
FAX: (619) 455-6316
ON-LINE AND SOFTWARE
Cost: $3,600.00/mo. to $7,200.00
On-line service add $24.00 per hour

Covers stocks. Equity Portfolio and Investment Computing (EPIC) Screen and rank stocks, perform sector and industry analysis, compute portfolio data averages, and S&P 500 averages, maintain a portfolio of companies, add, delete, or modify database records.

AUDIENCE: Individual, Professional　　　RISK LEVEL: Moderate, Aggressive
TOPICS: Stocks, Options

Epoch Pro

Mesa
P.O. Box 1801
Goleta, CA 93116

PH: (800) 633-6375
FAX: (805) 969-1358
SOFTWARE
Cost: $99.00
Technical Analysis
Technical Support: Phone, M-F
BBS

Program for mechanical trading based on short term cycles. Profitability chart versus a trading parameter allows parameters to be placed in the most active region with minimum sensitivity to market variations. Buy/sell indicators, stop/loss values.

AUDIENCE: Individual, Professional　　　RISK LEVEL: Aggressive
TOPICS: Bonds, Stocks, Futures/Commodities

Equalizer

Charles Schwab & Company, Inc.
101 Montgomery Street
Department S
San Francisco, CA 94104

PH: (800) 334-4455
FAX: (415) 403-5503
ON-LINE DATABASE
Transmission: Modem
No. of Users: 55,000
Start-Up Fee: $69
Current Quote Fees: Up to $1.45/min.

It combines information access and portfolio management, and on-line trading. Schwab account members will have access to Schwab Brokerage Services on GEnie. Also allows access to Dow Jones News/Retrieval, and Standard & Poor MarketScope.

AUDIENCE: Individual　　　RISK LEVEL: Moderate, Aggressive
TOPICS: Mutual Funds, Stocks, Options, Futures/Commodities

Equities

Bridge Information Systems, Inc.
717 Office Parkway
St. Louis, MO 63141

PH: (800) 325-3282
(314) 567-8100
FAX: (314) 432-5391
Cost: Basic monthly charge
$2,000.00 minimum + exchange fees

Covers stocks, commodities, money market instruments, listed bonds, currencies, options, futures, indexes, and includes charts. Provides market professionals with a wide range of investment information on more than 150,000 financial instruments.

AUDIENCE: Individual, Professional   RISK LEVEL: Conservative, Moderate, Aggressive
TOPICS: All

Equivolume Charting Software

Arms Equivolume, Corp.
6201 Upton Boulevard N.E.
Suite 203
Albuquerque, NM 87110

PH: (800) 223-2767
(505) 883-8856
FAX: (505) 883-8876
SOFTWARE
Cost: $365.00 - $565.00

Program uses charting methods and search methods for performance of stocks, bonds, futures, options, and mutual funds. Equivolume charts on the computer screen and allows user to vary time frames and moving averages.

AUDIENCE: Individual   RISK LEVEL: Moderate, Aggressive
TOPICS: Bonds, Mutual Funds, Stocks, Options, Futures/Commodities

Euro Equities

Detroyat & Associates, Inc.
535 Madison Avenue, 37th floor
New York, NY 10022

PH: (212) 759-0160
FAX: (212) 759-0109
SOFTWARE
Cost: $12,000.00 updated twice
  monthly.

Covers European equities. European listed companies designed for investment professional, research analysts and traders. Includes 1,500 companies in 15 European countries, 8 years of historical data, 2 years of estimates, 12 months of price charts and profiles.

AUDIENCE: Individual, Professional   RISK LEVEL: Moderate, Aggressive
TOPICS: Bonds, Stocks

Eurotrader

Essex Trading Company, Ltd.
24 W. 500 Maple Avenue
Suite 108
Naperville, IL 60540

PH: (800) 726-2140
(708) 416-3530
FAX: (708) 416-3558
SOFTWARE: Cost: $995

Futures securities markets with functions in technical analysis, bond analysis, and futures analysis. It is designed to capture profits from longer-term moves in the futures market. Fourteen years of historical data and a historical testing routine.

AUDIENCE: Individual, Professional   RISK LEVEL: Aggressive
TOPICS: Options, Futures/Commodities

Excalibur

Futures Truth, Co.
815 Hillside Road
Hendersonville, NC 28739

PH: (704) 696-0273
FAX: (704) 692-7375
SOFTWARE
Cost: $3,400.00 to $3,900.00
Technical Analysis
Technical Support: Phone, M-F

Test the stock or commodity trading system in three ways: (1) modify FORTRAN code; (2) compile and execute code using the FORTRAN/020 compiler by Absoft; (3) scan reports and analysis of the completed run using color charts to verify buy and sell points.

AUDIENCE: Professional   **RISK LEVEL: Aggressive**
TOPICS: Stocks, Futures/Commodities

Exchange Access

Warner Computer Systems, Inc.
17-01 Pollitt Drive
Fair Lawn, NJ 07410

PH: (201) 797-4633
(800) 336-5376;
Cost: $60.00 plus 8 cents/min. and
up

Covers stocks, mutual funds, market indices and indicators, options futures, and bonds (municipal and corporate). A data service designed to meet the needs of the serious investor. Exchange Access is your gateway to a single comprehensive source of investment information created and maintained by Warner's staff of professionals. Gives you both end of the day and historical securities information.

AUDIENCE: Individual, Professional   **RISK LEVEL: Conservative, Moderate, Aggressive**
TOPICS: All

Exotics Xl and Exotics

Montgomery Investment Group
P.O. Box 508
Wayne, PA 19087-0508

PH: (215) 688-2508
FAX: (215) 688-5084
SOFTWARE
Cost: Pro Series $395.00
Premium Series $695.00
Technical Support: Phone, M-F

Evaluate exotic options with Exotics XL for Excel or Exotics for Lotus 1-2-3. Calculate average price, lookback, knockout, average strike, and spreads. Contracts evaluated include foreign exchange, commodities, energy, agriculture, metals, and more. Analysis Capability: Financial Planning, Bond Analysis, Simulation Games, Spreadsheets.

AUDIENCE: Professional   **RISK LEVEL: Aggressive**
TOPICS: Stocks, Options, Futures/Commodities

Expert Trading System

Applied Artificial Intelligence
Corporation
1446 S. Highway 327
Box 25
Florence, SC 29506

PH: (803) 667-1986
SOFTWARE
Cost: Varies

Uses artificial intelligence techniques to attempt to pick the direction of the market. Trades in securities, futures, and options.

AUDIENCE: Individual, Professional   **RISK LEVEL: Moderate, Aggressive**
TOPICS: Stocks, Options, Futures/Commodities

F&S Index Plus Text

Information Access Company
362 Lakeside Dr.
Foster City, CA 94404

PH: (415) 378-5000
(800) 277-8431
FAX: (415) 378-5369
ON-LINE DATABASE
Transmission: CD-ROM
Access Fees: $3,500.00 to $6,000/year

Is a digest of worldwide trade and business journals, periodicals, and business press and government publications. It includes market share, financial reporting, expenditures and revenues, joint ventures, merger and acquisition, and government regulation.

AUDIENCE: Individual, Professional   RISK LEVEL: Conservative, Moderate, Aggressive
TOPICS: All

Fast Track

Investors Fast Track
11754 F.S. Harrell's Ferry
Baton Rouge, LA 70812

PH: (800) 749-1348
Cost: $39.95 one month access to database; introductory offer complete product then pay $69.00 for manual and software.

Over 1,000 mutual funds, and provides a chart service, plus 30 market indexes. Fast Track helps you take advantage of "telephone switching" offered by the fund companies. Fast Track shows how your current fund compares to the market and other funds in its family.

AUDIENCE: Beginning, Individual   RISK LEVEL: Moderate
TOPICS: Mutual Funds

Faxtel

Faxtel Information Systems, Ltd.
133 Richmond St., W.
Toronto, ON, Canada M5H 2L3

PH: (416) 365-1899
FAX: (416) 364-6599
Former Database Name: MARKETFAX.
ON-LINE DATABASE
On-line Availability: Faxtel
  Information Systems, Ltd
Access Fees: Call for Costs

Securities and investment information and analysis for the New York, American, Toronto, Montreal, and Vancouver Stock Exchanges. It also provides currency data which can be used in graphic analysis. Contact: Karl Wagner, Vice President, Marketing.

AUDIENCE: Individual, Professional   RISK LEVEL: Moderate, Aggressive
TOPICS: Stocks, Options, Futures/Commodities

Federal Reserve Bulletin

U.S. Federal Reserve System
Board of Governors
20th St. & Constitution Ave., N.W.
Room MS-138
Washington, DC 20551

PH: (202) 452-3244
ON-LINE DATABASE
Type: Full text
On-line Availability: LEXIS
  (FEDRB: $6-$91 per search)

Is a monthly publication of the Board of Governors of the Federal Reserve. It covers U.S. monetary policy issues, proposed regulations and rules, proposed changes and final regulations. Also quarterly reports on foreign currency operations and interventions.

AUDIENCE: Professional   RISK LEVEL: Conservative, Moderate, Aggressive
TOPICS: Bonds, Futures/Commodities

Fedwatch

MMS International
1301 Shoreway Rd.
Suite 300
Blemont, CA 94002

PH: (415) 595-0610
Type: Full-text
On-line Availability: LEXIS
CompuServe Information Service
Access Fees: Call for Costs

A weekly newsletter specializing in Federal Reserve, debt market, and foreign exchange analysis. It focuses on relevant federal reserve data, interest rate trends, indicators of economic strength and weaknesses, and money supply/funds rate outlook.

AUDIENCE: Professional	RISK LEVEL: Conservative, Moderate, Aggressive
TOPICS: Bonds, Futures/Commodities	

Fibnodes

Coast Investment Software
358 Avenida Milano
Sarasota, FL 34242-1517

PH: (813) 346-3801
FAX: (813) 346-3901
SOFTWARE
Cost: $595.00
Technical Support: Phone, M-F

All securities can be analyzed, using technical analysis and screening, bond analysis, futures analysis, options analysis, real estate analysis, and statistics. Fibonacci retracement and objective calculator are designed for high-pressure intraday trading.

AUDIENCE: Individual, Professional	RISK LEVEL: Moderate, Aggressive
TOPICS: All	

Fidelity On-Line Express

Fidelity Investments
82 Devonshire Street, R20A
Boston, MA 02190

PH: (800) 544-0246
FAX: (617) 728-7257
SOFTWARE
Cost: $49.95
Analysis: Financial
Technical Support: Phone M-Sat.

Program allows user to send orders directly on-line to the exchange for execution. Confirmation can also be received on-line. Real-time quotes on stocks, bonds, mutual funds, and options. Program compatible with DJN/R, Telescan, MarketScope, and S&P.

AUDIENCE: Beginning, Individual	RISK LEVEL: Moderate, Aggressive
TOPICS: Mutual Funds, Stocks, Options, Futures/Commodities	

Final Markets End-of-Day Price Service

Knight-Ridder Financial Publishing
30 S. Wacker Dr., Suite 1820
Chicago, IL 60606

PH: (312) 454-1801
(800) 526-3282
FAX: (312) 454-0239
ON-LINE DATABASE
Transmission: Diskette, CD-ROM
Start-Up Fee: Free 5 day trial
Historical Quote Fees: 1-50,000/day
    order-$0.01/day

Gives access to end-of-day prices for over 360 futures markets that includes open/high/low/settle prices and total volume/open interest. Packages start at $20/month.

AUDIENCE: Beginning, Individual	RISK LEVEL: Moderate, Aggressive
TOPICS: Bonds, Mutual Funds, Stocks, Options, Futures/Commodities	

Finance and Commerce Daily Newspaper

615 S. 7th St.
Minneapolis, MN 55415
Mailing: P.O. Box 15047
Minneapolis, MN 55415

PH: (612) 333-3243
FAX: (612) 333-3243
Costs: $119/yr
ON-LINE SERVICE
Fundamental Analysis

On-line service available Tuesday-Saturday, includes: General Business, Finance, Banking, Real Estate. Available on AP, PR newswire, and Businesswire.

AUDIENCE: Individual   RISK LEVEL: Conservative, Moderate, Aggressive
TOPICS: All

Financial

The WEFA Group
401 City Line Ave.
Suite 300
Bala Cynwyd, PA 19004-1780

PH: (215) 660-6300
FAX: (215) 660-6477
ON-LINE DATABASE
Alternate Electronic Formats:
  Diskette magnetic tape
Access Fees: Call for Costs

Over 4,000 weekly, monthly, quarter, and annual financial time series on all key financial indicators for the U.S. Market. From the Federal Reserve Board, and the U.S. Department of Energy. Daily coverage on interest rates, bond and stock activities. Contact: Robert Davies, Senior Financial Database Specialist.

AUDIENCE: Individual, Professional   RISK LEVEL: Conservative, Moderate, Aggressive
TOPICS: Bonds, Stocks, Options, Futures/Commodities

Financial Access II

Financial Navigator International
254 Polaris Avenue
Mountainview, CA 94043

PH: (800) 468-3636
(415) 962-0300
FAX: (415) 962-0703
Cost: $249.00 to $1,149.00
SOFTWARE
Technical Support: Phone, M-F
BBS, Newsletter

Obtain current and historical data from Dial/Data, DJN/R, CompuServe, Interactive Data, and Prodigy. Capable of downloading 60,000 common and preferred stocks, bonds, warrants, mutual funds, traded options, corporate bonds, or municipal bonds.

AUDIENCE: Individual, Professional   RISK LEVEL: Conservative, Moderate, Aggressive
TOPICS: Bonds, Mutual Funds, Stocks, Options

Financial Forecast

The WEFA Group
401 City Line Ave.
Suite 300
Bala Cynwyd, PA 19004-1780

PH: (215) 660-6300
FAX: (215) 660-6477
ON-LINE DATABASE
Access Fees: Call for Costs

Monthly time series of historical and forecast on key financial market indicators for the economy. The forecasts provide a standard forecast and three alternatives. The sources are government agencies and central banks. Contact: Joe Ford, Senior Financial Analyst.

AUDIENCE: Individual, Professional   RISK LEVEL: Conservative, Moderate, Aggressive
TOPICS: All

Financial Management System

Dynacomp, Inc.
178 Phillips Road
Webster, NY 14580

PH: (800) 828-6772
SOFTWARE
Cost: $149.95/IBM; CP/M $154.95
Technical Support: Phone, M-F

Financial planning, fundamental analysis, and bond analysis to compute stocks, bonds, indexes, mutual funds, options and futures. Financial ratios (liquidity, leverage, profitability), Dupont analysis, break-even analysis, net present value, rates of return.

AUDIENCE: Beginning, Individual   RISK LEVEL: Conservative, Moderate
TOPICS: Bonds, Mutual Funds, Stocks, Options, Futures/Commodities, Investment Planning

Financial Navigator

Financial Navigator International
254 Polaris Avenue
Mountainview, CA 94043

PH: (800) 468-3636
(415) 962-0300
FAX: (415) 962-0703
Cost: $495.00
SOFTWARE
Technical Support: Phone, M-F
BBS, Newsletter

Financial management for investors with marketable securities, owners of real estate or oil and gas interests, trusts, and non-profits. Double-entry bookkeeping with simple data entry. Produces over 60 different reports, including balance sheets, income statements, and tax summaries.

AUDIENCE: Individual   RISK LEVEL: Conservative, Moderate, Aggressive
TOPICS: Bonds, Mutual Funds, Stocks, Options

Financial Pak

G.C.P.I.
P.O. Box 790, Dept. #50-E
Marquette, MI 49855

PH: (906) 226-7600
SOFTWARE
Cost: $149.95
Analysis Capabilities: Financial
Planning, Portfolio Management
Technical Support: Phone, M-F

Aids the investor by reporting stock and mutual fund buy/sell information based on an average-cost basis with an emphasis on obtaining consistent returns. (1) stock market investment aid; (2) loan program; (3) lump sum and annuity information.

AUDIENCE: Beginning, Individual   RISK LEVEL: Conservative, Moderate
TOPICS: Mutual Funds, Stocks

Financial Planning Toolkit

Financial Data, Corp.
P.O. Box 1332
Bryn Mawr, PA 19010

PH: (215) 525-6957
FAX: (215) 520-0492
SOFTWARE
Cost: $249.00
Analysis Capabilities: Bond
Analysis, Financial Planning,
Portfolio Management, Real Estate
Technical Support: Phone, M-F

Program for use with Lotus 1-2-3 or compatible spreadsheets. Performs calculations in 7 major areas. Determines the performance of stocks, bonds, T-bills, and stock rights while accounting for inflation on capital, assets, income, IRAs, and college savings.

AUDIENCE: Beginning, Individual   RISK LEVEL: Conservative, Moderate
TOPICS: Bonds, Mutual Funds, Stocks

Financial Post Securities

The Financial Post Datagroup
333 King St. E.
Toronto, ON, Canada M5A 4N2

PH: (416) 350-6440
FAX: (416) 350-6501
ON-LINE DATABASE
On-line Availability: Reuters
  Information Services (Canada) Ltd.
Access Fees: Call for Costs

Provides information on Canadian stocks traded on the Montreal, Toronto, Vancouver, and Calgary exchanges. It also provides the daily volume, closing prices, and the high, low prices for the past 260 trading days. Contact: Cuyler Bowness, General Manager.

AUDIENCE: Individual, Professional	RISK LEVEL: Moderate, Aggressive
TOPICS: Stocks	

Financial Ratios Database

U.S. Department of Commerce
Economics and Statistics Administration
Office of Business Analysis (OBA)
Herbert C. Hoover Bldg., Room 4885
Washington, DC 20230

PH: (202) 482-1431
Type: Time series
FAX: (202) 482-2164
ON-LINE DATABASE
Available On-line As Part Of: The
Economic Bulletin Board
Access Fees: Call for Costs

Financial and operating ratios for the two-digit and several three-digit ESIC groups such as chemicals, textiles, iron and steel, primary metals, and motor vehicles. Data on 23 industry groups taken from the U.S. Bureau of the Census Annual Survey.

AUDIENCE: Professional	RISK LEVEL: Moderate, Aggressive
TOPICS: Bonds, Stocks	

Financial Services Report

Phillips Business Information, Inc.
(PBI)
7811 Montrose Rd.
Potomac, MD 20854-3363

PH: (301) 340-2100
FAX: (301) 424-7261
Former Database Name: Financial
Services Week
ON-LINE DATABASE

Biweekly newsletter of the financial services industry that includes cross-selling, networking, regulation, deregulation, market segmenting, new technology, and consumer trends. On-line Availability: NewsNet, Inc. NEXIS $6-$91 per search.

AUDIENCE: Professional	RISK LEVEL: Conservative, Moderate, Aggressive
TOPICS: All	

Financial Statement Analyzer

Essential Software, Corp.
1126 South 70th Street
West Allis, WI 53214

PH: (414) 775-3450
FAX: (414) 475-3578
SOFTWARE
Cost: $165.00
Technical Support: Phone, M-F

Uses fundamental analysis to produce 79 business/financial ratios. Evaluates liquidity, profitability, efficiency, solvency, and investment potential. Results can be graphically illustrated.

AUDIENCE: Individual, Professional	RISK LEVEL: Moderate, Aggressive
TOPICS: Bonds, Stocks	

Financial Statement Cash Flow Forecaster

Essential Software, Corp.
1126 South 70th Street
West Allis, WI 53214

PH: (414) 775-3450
FAX: (414) 475-3578
SOFTWARE
Cost: $165.00
Technical Support: Phone, M-F

Creates financial statements by using fundamental analysis to assist in financial planning and investing. Creates financial statements, provides 60 financial ratios, and provides user-defined graphs.

AUDIENCE: Individual, Professional   RISK LEVEL: Moderate, Aggressive
TOPICS: Bonds, Stocks

Financial System One

Automatic Data Processing
2 Journal Square Plaza
Jersey City, NJ 07306-0817

PH: (201) 714-3000
ON-LINE DATABASE
Cost: $650.00, $85.00 per desk unit.

Covers stocks, commodities, option, and bonds (municipal, corporate, and government). A dedicated on-line stock market information system that delivers up to the second quotes on over 35,000 stocks, bonds, commodities, and options.

AUDIENCE: Individual, Professional   RISK LEVEL: Conservative, Moderate, Aggressive
TOPICS: All

FINIS: Financial Industry Information Service

Dialog Information Services, Inc.
3460 Hillview Avenue
Palo Alto, CA 94304

PH: (800) 334-2564
(415) 858-3810
FAX: (415) 858-7069
ON-LINE DATABASE
Cost: $45.00
Online charges $1.30 minute
  or $78.00 hour

Marketing information on organizations that comprise the financial services industry and on products and services offered to corporate and retail customers. Information provided by Bank Marketing Association (BMA), Chicago, IL. Updated every two weeks.

AUDIENCE: Individual, Professional   RISK LEVEL: Conservative, Moderate,
TOPICS: All   Aggressive

First Release

Dialog Information Services, Inc.
3460 Hillview Ave.
Palo Alto, CA 94304

PH: (800) 334-2564
FAX: (415) 858-7069
ON-LINE DATABASE
Transmission: Modem
Start-Up Fee: $295 for access to
  entire DIALOG service.
Access Fees: $1.60/minute.

Gives the latest news from four major news wire databases within 15 minutes of transmission. Provides the business news, financial coverage, commodity coverage. Accessed from the PR Newswire, Reuter's Business Report, and Reuter's Library Service.

AUDIENCE: Individual, Professional   RISK LEVEL: Conservative, Moderate,
TOPICS: All   Aggressive

FISTS

Bond-Tech, Inc.
P.O. Box 192
Englewood, OH 45322

PH: (513) 836-3991
FAX: (513) 836-1497
SOFTWARE
Cost: $1,250.00
Compatibility: DOS
Technical Support: Phone, M-F

Bonds, options, and futures are the securities targeted for this program which is for the fixed income securities market. Bond analysis, futures analysis, and options analysis. Features a range of computations. Includes Black-Sholes and Cox-Ross-Rubenstein.

AUDIENCE: Professional   RISK LEVEL: Conservative, Moderate
TOPICS: Bonds, Options, Futures/Commodities

Fixed Income Pricing Services

Street Software Technology
230 Park Avenue, Suite 857
New York, NY 10169

PH: (212) 922-0500
FAX: (212) 922-0588
SOFTWARE
Cost: Hookup charges $300.00,
  $450.00 monthly, on-line charges
  from $25.00

A fixed-income pricing service that has been supplying prices to Wall Street Banking Community since 1975. Daily prices are ready at 4:30 EST and include CUSIP # for easy identification. Intraday prices are updated every 15 minutes between 9AM and 3PM - EST.

AUDIENCE: Professional   RISK LEVEL: Conservative, Moderate
TOPICS: Bonds

Folioman

E-sential Software
P.O. Box 41705
Los Angeles, CA 90041

PH: (213) 257-2524
SOFTWARE
Cost: $89.00
Technical Support: Phone, 12 pm - 8
  pm, M-F

Financial planning and portfolio planning for stocks, bonds, indexes, mutual funds, options, futures, real estate, CDs, and collectibles. Can track an unlimited number of portfolios and view, rate, and compare investments in 40 different ways.

AUDIENCE: Beginning, Individual   RISK LEVEL: Conservative, Moderate, Aggressive
TOPICS: Bonds, Mutual Funds, Stocks, Options

Folioman+

E-sential Software
P.O. Box 41705
Los Angeles, CA 90041

PH: (213) 257-2524
SOFTWARE
Cost: $129.00
Technical Support: Phone, M-F

Performs all of Folioman's functions but includes full support for futures trading. Can directly update from ChartPro and Megatech charting programs.

AUDIENCE: Beginning, Individual   RISK LEVEL: Conservative, Moderate, Aggressive
TOPICS: Bonds, Mutual Funds, Stocks, Options, Futures/Commodities

Forbes Annual Directory

Forbes, Inc.
60 Fifth Ave.
New York, NY 10011

PH: (212) 620-2368
Type: Directory; numeric
ON-LINE DATABASE

A yearly publication of the 500 highest ranked publicly owned U.S. companies. Provides complete information and financial data on the companies. Contact: Steve Kichen, Senior Editor. On-line Availability: LEXIS—FORBAD: $6-$91 per search depending on the database selected; $48/connect hour.

AUDIENCE: Individual, Professional   RISK LEVEL: Moderate, Aggressive
TOPICS: Bonds, Stocks

Ford Database

Ford Investor Services, Inc.
11722 Sorrento Valley Rd., Suite 1
San Diego, CA 92121

PH: (619) 755-1327
Type: Numeric
ON-LINE DATABASE
Alternate Electronic Formats:
  Diskette, Magnetic Tape, Batch
  Access (Ford Database)
Access Fees: Call for Costs

Financial data on 2,000 leading common stock investments. Analysis performed by Ford Investor Services. Updated weekly.

AUDIENCE: Individual   RISK LEVEL: Moderate, Aggressive
TOPICS: Stocks

Forecast

Engineering Management
Consultants
P.O. Box 12518
Tallahassee, FL 32317-2518

PH: (904) 668-0635
SOFTWARE
Cost: $300.00
Technical Support: Phone, M-F

Uses fundamental analysis, technical analysis, and statistics in the analysis of multiple time series for stocks, bonds, indexes, mutual funds, options, and futures. Analyzes cycles and then combines and forecasts them to provide an indicator.

AUDIENCE: Individual, Professional   RISK LEVEL: Moderate, Aggressive
TOPICS: Bonds, Mutual Funds, Stocks, Options, Futures/Commodities

Forecasting Edge, The

Dynacomp, Inc.
178 Phillips Road
Webster, NY 14580

PH: (800) 828-6772
SOFTWARE
Cost: $99.95
Technical Support: Phone, M-F

Menu-driven economic analysis program that uses multiple regression techniques for statistical analysis and forecasting. Uses VisiCalc and Lotus data files. Features data management, seasonal adjustments, and plotting in high resolution graphics.

AUDIENCE: Individual, Professional   RISK LEVEL: Moderate, Aggressive
TOPICS: Bonds, Mutual Funds, Stocks, Options, Futures/Commodities

Foreign Exchange

ADP Network Services, Inc.
175 Jackson Plaza
Ann Arbor, MI 48106

PH: (313) 769-6800
Type: Time series
ON-LINE DATABASE
On-line Availability: ADP Network
  Services, Inc.

Daily exchange rates of 35 currencies worldwide. Domestic currency, Eurocurrency, interest rates, gold and silver prices, economic and financial indicators for the US, European countries, key Middle East and Asian countries, taken from the Telerate Systems, Inc.

AUDIENCE: Individual, Professional   RISK LEVEL: Moderate, Aggressive
TOPICS: Bonds, Options, Futures/Commodities

Fourier Analysis Forecaster

Dynacomp, Inc.
178 Phillips Road
Webster, NY 14580

PH: (800) 828-6772
SOFTWARE
Cost: $99.95 to $169.95
Technical Support: Phone, M-F

A software package for studying data containing cyclical components. Fourier technical analysis for determining cycles without understanding the math. Types of trends are polynomial in time or inverse in time trends. Includes stock and commodity cycles.

AUDIENCE: Beginning, Individual, Professional   RISK LEVEL: Moderate, Aggressive
TOPICS: Bonds, Stocks, Options, Futures/Commodities

Free Financial Network (FFN)

Micro Code Technologies
220 E. 54th St., #12-J
New York, NY 10022

PH: (212) 838-6324
FAX: (212) 966-8231
Former Name: Financial Software
Exchange
ON-LINE DATABASE
Transmission: Modem
No. of Users: 10,000
Current Quote Fees: $49.95/year

The on-line information has closing stock quotes, financial magazines, professional associations, investment newsletters investment and financial computing roundtables and forums, and recommendations. Start-Up Fee: Free to end-users, Access Fees: Free to end-users.

AUDIENCE: Beginning, Individual   RISK LEVEL: Moderate, Aggressive
TOPICS: Mutual Funds, Stocks, Options, Futures/Commodities

FTI Banc Investor: Securities Accounting System

Financial Technology, Inc.
70 East Lake Street
Suite 1200
Chicago, IL 60601

PH: (800) 541-9537
(312) 606-1500
SOFTWARE
Cost: $3,300.00 to $8,500.00

Bond Accounting System, Portfolio Analysis, Multi-Bond Swapper and Bond Calculator. Permits in-house securities analysis, accounting and pricing on a PC. Bond Swapper Module, Bond Calculator Module, Graphics/Spreadsheet Interface and Telecommunications Pricing.

AUDIENCE: Individual, Professional   RISK LEVEL: Conservative, Moderate
TOPICS: Bonds

Fund Master TC

Time Trend Software
337 Boston Road
Billerica, MA 01821

PH: (508) 663-3330
FAX: (508) 667-1269
SOFTWARE
Cost: $289.00
Technical Analysis
Technical Support: Phone, M-F

Program is oriented toward mutual funds but has the flexible capability to run in-depth analysis on stocks. Charting includes moving averages, exponential averages, trendlines, trading bands, trend channels, graphics, and overlay capabilities.

AUDIENCE: Beginning, Individual   RISK LEVEL: Moderate, Aggressive
TOPICS: Mutual Funds, Stocks

Fund Pro

Time Trend Software
337 Boston Road
Billerica, MA 01821

PH: (508) 663-3330
FAX: (508) 667-1269
SOFTWARE
Cost: $789.00
Technical Analysis
Technical Support: Phone, M-F

Includes all Fund Master TC functions but can handle up to 1,000 portfolios. Features include client billing, global purchases and sales and global adjustments for distributions. Calculates total funds and composite annual rate of return for all managed funds.

AUDIENCE: Professional   RISK LEVEL: Moderate, Aggressive
TOPICS: Mutual Funds

Fundamental Investor

Savant Software, Inc.
(Formerly Savant Corp.)
120 Bedford Center Road
Bedford, NH 03110

PH: (800) 231-9900
FAX: (603) 472-5981
SOFTWARE
Cost: $395.00
Fundamental Analysis
Technical Support: Phone, M-F

Store over 300 data items on more than 10,000 with this program. Data can be entered automatically by modem or manually. Customize parameters for a single stock or stocks. Calculate financial ratios from basic financial information and sort stocks.

AUDIENCE: Beginning, Individual   RISK LEVEL: Moderate, Aggressive
TOPICS: Stocks

Fundgraf

Parsons Software
1230 W. 6th Street
Loveland, CO 80537

PH: (303) 669-3744
SOFTWARE
Cost: $100.00 for program and data
   for 32 funds
Additional data disks, $20.00
Technical Analysis
Technical Support: Phone, M-F

Finds and graphs the best performing mutual funds for up to 260 weeks. Dividends, capital gains distributions, splits for any time period. Relative strengths for all funds, buy/sell signals generated, and trend change are some of the added functions.

AUDIENCE: Beginning   RISK LEVEL: Moderate, Aggressive
TOPICS: Mutual Funds

Fundgraf Supplemental Programs, Disk 1

Parsons Software
1230 W. 6th Street
Loveland, CO 80537

PH: (303) 669-3744
SOFTWARE
Cost: $20.00
Technical Analysis
Technical Support: Phone, M-F

Make-PRN and ADD-PRN allows movement of data between Fundgraf files. Calculates initial investment and uses a moving average signal for effectiveness of fund. Computes tax advantages and spreadsheets for use in investment decisions.

AUDIENCE: Beginning, Individual	RISK LEVEL: Moderate, Aggressive
TOPICS: Mutual Funds	

Funds-On-Line

Mutual Fund On-Line Data, Inc.
405 El Camino Real
Suite 418
Menlo Park, CA 94025

PH: (415) 329-1842
(800) 831-7777
FAX: (415) 326-9705
Start-Up Fee: $75
Access Fees: $20/month
AAII Discount: 20%.

Focusing on comparing mutual funds and analyzing the optimal time to buy and sell. The systems contains 308 funds. Color graphs allow the choice of the NAV plus any 2 EMAs or a market index or a 2nd fund for viewing comparative performance.

AUDIENCE: Beginning, Individual	RISK LEVEL: Moderate, Aggressive
TOPICS: Mutual Funds	

Fundscope

American River Software
1523 Kingsford Dr.
Carmichael, CA 95608

PH: (916) 483-1600
ON-LINE DATABASE
Access Fees: $65/single update,
  $200/year for quarterly updates,
  $480/year for monthly updates.
Transmission: Diskette

Screening and ranking program on equity and bond funds, market indexes, transportations, utilities, bonds, and the S&P 500. Fund contact information, inception date, investment minimums, telephone exchange availability fund objective, assets, asset growth, loads.

AUDIENCE: Beginning, Individual	RISK LEVEL: Moderate, Aggressive
TOPICS: Mutual Funds	

Fundscope

The Planner's Edge
1412 112th Avenue, NE
Bellevue, WA 98004

PH: (800) 859-8039
(206) 451-8462
FAX: (206) 454-2165
Software Cost: $1,295.00/yr
Technical/Fundamental Analysis
Technical Support: Phone, toll free

Select, rank, graph, and print mutual fund data. Features include load/no-load indexes, 10 years of data history, buy/sell signals from moving averages, compounded yields, weighted momentum scores and more. Risk free subscription and 1st month's data free.

AUDIENCE: Beginning, Individual	RISK LEVEL: Moderate, Aggressive
TOPICS: Mutual Funds	

Fundwatch

Dynacomp, Inc.
178 Phillips Road
Webster, NY 14580

PH: (800) 828-6772
SOFTWARE
Cost: $39.95
Technical Support: Phone, M-F

Evaluation and comparison of various investments, including stocks, bonds, mutual funds, and commodities. Programs calculate yields, evaluate trends with moving averages, and provide direct comparisons with other investments.

AUDIENCE: Beginning, Individual   RISK LEVEL: Conservative, Moderate, Aggressive
TOPICS: Bonds, Mutual Funds, Stocks, Options, Futures/Commodities

Fundwatch Plus

Hamilton Software, Inc.
6432 East Mineral Place
Englewood, CO 80112

PH: (800) 733-9607
SOFTWARE
Cost: Hook-up charges $29.00

Covers mutual funds. Evaluates and compares common investments including mutual funds, stocks, many commodities and market averages such as the Dow Jones. Allows home investors to evaluate investments inexpensively without a modem or on-line data.

AUDIENCE: Beginning, Individual   RISK LEVEL: Moderate, Aggressive
TOPICS: Mutual Funds, Stocks

Future Source

Future Source
955 Parkview Blvd.
Lombard, IL 60148

PH: (800) 621-2628
(708) 620-8444
FAX: (708) 620-4315

Covers real-time futures, options and cash market prices, news, charting and technical analysis. Futures and options quotes on all major worldwide exchanges, as well as cash market pricing and information on the FX, metals, and energy markets. Chart database.

AUDIENCE: Individual, Professional   RISK LEVEL: Aggressive
TOPICS: Bonds, Options, Futures/Commodities

FutureLink

Oster Communications
219 Parkade
Cedar Falls, IA 50613

PH: (800) 553-2910 ext 224
Cost: Hook-up charges $45.00,
Basic monthly charge $99.00
On-line charges per minute n/a
Need Satellite Dish $640.00

Covers futures and options on futures. 10 minute snap-shot price quotes, worldwide on-line market news, complete futures and options prices, floor commentary, technical commentary and studies, bar charts, automatic position and spread tracking, and more.

AUDIENCE: Individual, Professional   RISK LEVEL: Aggressive
TOPICS: Futures/Commodities

Futures Market Analyzer

Investment Tools, Inc.
P.O. Box 98916
Reno, NV 89507

PH: NA
SOFTWARE
Cost: $795.00/yr.
Analysis Capability: Technical
  Analysis, Futures Analysis

Program accepts daily quote information and monitors 39 futures contracts including stock index futures, currencies, meats, grains, crude oil, heating oil, coffee, etc. User inputs information to generate a report giving buy/sell signal, entry price, and exit.

AUDIENCE: Individual, Professional   **RISK LEVEL: Aggressive**
TOPICS: Futures/Commodities

Futures Pro

Essex Trading Co., Ltd
24 W. 500 Maple Ave.
Suite 108
Naperville, IL 60540

PH: (800) 726-2140
(708) 416-3530
SOFTWARE
Cost: $295.00 - 3 markets,
  additional markets - $200.00 each

Advanced trading system for Treasury Bond futures featuring a fully researched ready to trade program along with comprehensive back-testing routines. Charts - graphics at no additional cost. Automatic updates through CSI and FNN.

AUDIENCE: Individual, Professional   **RISK LEVEL: Aggressive**
TOPICS: Bonds, Futures/Commodities

Futuresoft

Commodity Information Services
327 S. LaSalle
Suite 1133
Chicago, IL 60604

PH: (800) 800-7227
(312) 922-3661
FAX: (312) 341-1494
SOFTWARE
Cost $295
Technical Support: Phone, M-F

Uses technical and futures analysis for options and futures. Analyzes daily and historical prices on foreign currency, metal, and other futures. Calculates technical indicators: moving averages, oscillators, spreads, and trading models.

AUDIENCE: Individual, Professional   **RISK LEVEL: Aggressive**
TOPICS: Options, Futures/Commodities

Futuresource Homework

Futuresource
955 Parkview Blvd.
Lombard, IL 60148

PH: (708) 620-8444
(800) 621-2628
FAX: (708) 620-4315
ON-LINE DATABASE
Transmission: Modem, Satellite
Access Fees: $150/month plus fees

Combines real-time futures and options quotes with technical analysis. Flexible pages, mixing of charts, technical studies, prices or news. Theoretical option calculator and strategy, Market Profile and OptionSource, charting intraday and daily price data.

AUDIENCE: Individual, Professional   **RISK LEVEL: Aggressive**
TOPICS: Options, Futures/Commodities

Fxbase

Fame Software, Corp.
88 Pine St.
16th Floor
New York, NY 10005

PH: (212) 898-7200
FAX: (212) 742-8956
Transmission: Modem, Diskette, Tape
ON-LINE DATABASE
Start-Up Fee: $200

Provides daily foreign exchange and Eurocurrency interest rates for 20 countries. Series dates back to 1985. The database from the IMF, OECD, and Statistics Canada are available.

AUDIENCE: Professional   RISK LEVEL: Moderate, Aggressive
TOPICS: Bonds, Options, Futures/Commodities

Ganntrader

Gannfost Publishing Co.
11670 Riverbend Drive
Leavenworth, WA 98826-9305

PH: (509) 548-5990
FAX: (509) 548-4679
SOFTWARE
Cost: $1,295.00
Technical Analysis
Technical Support: Phone, M-F

Plot charts with angles, plot angles from highs, lows, 360 degree angles, squares and planets. Analyzes up to 5 Gann squares. Calculates MOF, CE Average, aspects, plot planets, averages, support and resistance, Square of 9, Hexagon chart positions.

AUDIENCE: Professional   RISK LEVEL: Aggressive
TOPICS: Bonds, Stocks, Options, Futures/Commodities

General Business File

Information Access Company
362 Lakeside Dr.
Foster City, CA 94404

PH: (415) 378-5000
(800) 277-8431
FAX: (415) 378-5369
ON-LINE DATABASE
Transmission: CD-ROM
Access Fees: $10,500 annual

Business reference database. Business Index which indexes and abstracts articles each year from over 700 business related periodicals. Updates records from Ward's Business directory on public and private U.S. companies.

AUDIENCE: Individual, Professional   RISK LEVEL: Conservative, Moderate, Aggressive
TOPICS: All

Genesis Data Service

Genesis Data Service
P.O. Box 49578
Colorado Springs, CO 80949

PH: (719) 260-6111
(800) 808-DATA
Cost: prices are too variable to list

Covers stocks, commodities, and mutual funds. Historical data software to update your Metastock, CompuTrac, AIQ and CSI format files for all your favorite stocks, options and commodities. Dow Jones, Lotus, Symphony ASCII have been added in V 3.0.

AUDIENCE: Individual, Professional   RISK LEVEL: Moderate, Aggressive
TOPICS: Mutual Funds, Stocks, Options, Futures/Commodities

Genie Quotes Securities Database

GE Information Services (GEIS)
GEnie (General Electric Network
  for Information Exchange)
401 N. Washington Blvd.
Rockville, MD 20850

PH: (301) 340-4000
(800) 638-9636
ON-LINE DATABASE
Type: Numeric

Information on securities, common and preferred stocks, and mutual funds from the New York Stock Exchange, American Stock Exchange, and NASDAQ. On-line Availability: GEnie (General Electric Network for Information Exchange), prime-time rates: $18/connect hour

AUDIENCE: Individual, Professional   RISK LEVEL: Moderate, Aggressive
TOPICS: Mutual Funds, Stocks, Options

Glendale

Cyber-Scan, Inc.
3601 Pulaski Road N.E.
Buffalo, NY 55313

PH: (612) 682-4150
SOFTWARE
Cost: $100.00
Technical Support: Phone, M-F

A quote utility: transfers information from DTN to perform such functions as: update historical files; bar, point, and charting files; and maintaining historical files.

AUDIENCE: Individual, Professional   RISK LEVEL: Moderate, Aggressive
TOPICS: Mutual Funds, Stocks, Options, Futures/Commodities

Global Guaranty

American Banker - Bond Buyer
1 State Street Plaza
New York, NY 10004

PH: (212) 943-6700
(215) 527-8030
Predicasts, 11001 Cedar Ave.
Cleveland, OH 44106
(216) 795-3000
Cost: Varies with vendor
Fundamental Analysis

News of the financial credit enhancement industry. Reports on activities in the public municipal, corporate bond, private placement, and Eurobond markets; regulations and legislation. Online through: NewsNet, Inc., 945 Haverford Rd., Bryn Mawr, PA 19010.

AUDIENCE: Professional   RISK LEVEL: Conservative, Moderate
TOPICS: Bonds

Global Information for Executive Decisions

DRI/McGraw-Hill
24 Hartwell Avenue
Lexington, MA 02173

PH: (617) 863-5100
(800) 541-9914
FAX: (617) 860-6332
Minimum Cost: $2,500.00 annually
Online charges - $1.00/min.

Provides comprehensive coverage of key financial markets, industry trends, and economic conditions, along with in-depth analysis of events as they affect your organization. World markets, United States, Regional U.S. markets, Europe, Canada, Energy and Chemical.

AUDIENCE: Individual, Professional   RISK LEVEL: Conservative, Moderate, Aggressive
TOPICS: All

Global Information Services' Report on Business

Globe Information Services
444 Front Street West
Toronto, Ontario, Canada M5V 2S9

PH: (800) 268-9128
Cost: Varies

Global Information Services Report on Business database is a comprehensive fundamental database featuring over 2,200 Canadian companies. It includes 1,700 public companies trading on Canadian and other North American exchanges; 575 private corporations.

AUDIENCE: Individual, Professional   RISK LEVEL: Moderate, Aggressive
TOPICS: Stocks, General Reference

Global Report

Citicorp
77 Water St., 2nd Floor
New York, NY 10043

PH: (800) 842-8405
FAX: (212) 742-8769
Type: Full-text; numeric
ON-LINE DATABASE
On-line Availability: Citicorp
  Database Services
Access Fees: Call for Costs

Provides information of worldwide business and finance in the following areas: Foreign Exchange, Country Reports, Money Markets, Bonds, Companies, Industries, and News, and other business affairs. It is updated continuously throughout the day. Contact: Jeff Davis, Director, National Sales.

AUDIENCE: Individual, Professional   RISK LEVEL: Moderate, Aggressive
TOPICS: All

Global Trader Calculator

ADS Associates, Inc.
23586 Calabasas Road
Suite 200
Calabasas, CA 91302

PH: (800) 323-4666
FAX: (818) 591-2372
SOFTWARE
Cost: $195.00
Technical Service: Phone, M-F

A software calculator that specializes in bond analysis for fixed income securities. Calculates yield-to-maturity, yield-to-call, yield-to-average life, duration, accrued interest, principal amount, and discount margin in a single key stroke.

AUDIENCE: Individual, Professional   RISK LEVEL: Conservative, Moderate
TOPICS: Bonds

Grand Master

Enertex Engineering
P.O. Box 744
Waterloo, ON, Canada N2J 4C2

PH: (519) 886-2672
FAX: (519) 885-2738
SOFTWARE
Cost: $3,000.00
Technical Support: Phone, 9 am - 5
  pm, M-F

A commodity trading system that provides preprogrammed buy and sell indicators plus back-testing to verify performance. 4 years of data is provided on 9 commodities. Data can be entered manually. Supports CSI and Future Source data formats.

AUDIENCE: Individual, Professional   RISK LEVEL: Aggressive
TOPICS: Options, Futures/Commodities

Hedgemaster

Commodity Exchange, Inc.
4 World Trade Center
Room 6404
New York, NY 10048

PH: (800) 333-2900
FAX: (212) 938-2660
SOFTWARE
Cost: $99.95
Technical Support: Phone, M-F

The trading environment of a program trader is simulated using physical, forward, futures, and options markets. Enter positions and trades of metal owned, and through use of historical data, simulate different strategies.

AUDIENCE: Individual, Professional   RISK LEVEL: Moderate, Aggressive
TOPICS: Bonds, Options, Futures/Commodities

Hi-Portfolio

CCF Group, PLC., Eldon House
203 Eldon Street
London, England EC2M7LS

PH: 01-377-9755
SOFTWARE
Cost: Contact Vendor

World markets. Provides comprehensive coverage of key financial markets, industry trends, and economic conditions, along with in-depth analysis of events. United States, Regional U.S. markets, Europe, Canada, Energy and Chemical, Cost and Inflation Information.

AUDIENCE: Individual, Professional   RISK LEVEL: Conservative, Moderate, Aggressive
TOPICS: All

Historical ADL

Tools For Timing
11345 Highway 7, #499
Minnetonka, MN 55305

PH: (800) 325-1344
FAX: (612) 938-1275
Cost: $175.00
SOFTWARE
Technical Analysis
Technical Support: Phone M-F

Use DJIA, S&P 500, advance-decline line, new high indicator, new low indicator and a selection of momentum indicators to direct investing strategy. Graphs can track 5 trades and more. Includes historical data from 1928 till the day before shipping.

AUDIENCE: Individual, Professional   RISK LEVEL: Aggressive
TOPICS: Stocks, Futures/Commodities

Historical Commodity Data

Cost Investment Software
358 Avenida Milano
Sarasota, FL 34242-1517

PH: (813) 346-3801
FAX: (813) 346-3901
ON-LINE DATABASE
Current Quote Fees: $35.00 per 1.2Mg
Access Fees: Call for Costs

Gives a variety of current and historical commodity data as far back as 10 years. The disk formats range from CP/M to MS-DOS, binary to ASCII.

AUDIENCE: Individual, Professional   RISK LEVEL: Aggressive
TOPICS: Options, Futures/Commodities

Historical Data

Knight-Ridder Financial Publishing
30 S. Wacker Dr., Suite 1820
Chicago, IL 60606

PH: (800) 526-3282
FAX: (312) 454-0239
ON-LINE DATABASE
Transmission: Diskette, CD-ROM

Gives historical price information on futures, options and cash markets. Daily prices date back 50 years in some markets. Historical Quote Fees: 1-50,00/day order-$0.01/day; over 50,000/day order-$0.005/day.

AUDIENCE: Individual, Professional	RISK LEVEL: Aggressive
TOPICS: Options, Futures/Commodities	

Historical Data Services

Historical Data Services
205 S. M-291 Highway
Suite 195
Lee's Summit, MO 64063

PH: (800) 873-8861
(816) 633-7593
ONLINE OR DISKETTE
Cost: Consult company for pricing

Covers stocks, commodities, mutual funds. Responsive efficient and highly accurate reporting of historical financial information including historical data on more than 15,000 stocks; 1,500 mutual funds; 100 commodities/futures, all major markets.

AUDIENCE: Individual, Professional	RISK LEVEL: Moderate, Aggressive
TOPICS: All	

Historical Dow Jones Averages

Dow Jones & Company, Inc.
P.O. Box 300
Princeton, NJ 08543-0300

PH: (609) 520-4000
Type: Numeric
ON-LINE DATABASE
On-line Availability: Dow Jones
News/Retrieval $2.16/connect
  minute (2400 baud), 90
  cents/Information Unit

Historical stock quotations, and high and lows for industrial, transportation, utilities, and 65 stock composite indexes.

AUDIENCE: Individual, Professional	RISK LEVEL: Moderate, Aggressive
TOPICS: Stocks	

Historical Futures Contracts

Commodity Information Services
327 S. LaSalle, Suite 1133
Chicago, IL 60604

PH: (312) 992-3661
(800) 880-7227
FAX: (312) 341-1494
ON-LINE DATABASE
No. of Users: 150

Gives historical futures price and volume data from 1969 to the present. Historical Quote Fees: $4/life of contract; $3/month commodity (tick data).

AUDIENCE: Individual, Professional	RISK LEVEL: Aggressive
TOPICS: Options, Futures/Commodities	

Holt Advisory, The

Weiss Research, Inc.
2200 N. Florida Mango Rd.
West Palm Beach, FL 33409

PH: (407) 684-8100
Type: Full-text
ON-LINE DATABASE
On-line Availability: NewsNet, Inc.
  (FI51: $60/connect hour)

A newsletter covering investing and finance, stock market updates, placing an emphasis on gold shares. Updated twice a month.

AUDIENCE: Beginning, Individual   RISK LEVEL: Moderate, Aggressive
TOPICS: Stocks, Options, Futures/Commodities

Hourly DJIA

Tools For Timing
11345 Highway 7, #499
Minnetonka, MN 55305

PH: (800) 325-1344
FAX: (612) 938-1275
Cost: $50.00
SOFTWARE
Technical Analysis
Technical Support: Phone M-F

The DJIA on an hourly basis, along with the last hour indicator, can be used with several momentum indicators calculated from hourly parameters. Last hour indicator, trading bands, Bollinger bands, relative strength index, stochastics and MACD.

AUDIENCE: Individual, Professional   RISK LEVEL: Moderate, Aggressive
TOPICS: Stocks, Futures/Commodities

I/B/E/S Canadian Database

I/B/E/S, Inc.
345 Hudson St.
New York, NY 10014

PH: (800) 438-IBES
FAX: (212) 727-1386
ON-LINE DATABASE
Type: Time series
On-line Availability: Interactive
Data Corporation.
CompuServe Information Service.
Access Fees: Call for Costs

Wall Street earnings forecasts and consensus for more than 400 Canadian corporations. It provides current and historical data of interest and stock quotes.

AUDIENCE: Individual, Professional   RISK LEVEL: Moderate, Aggressive
TOPICS: Stocks

I/B/E/S International Database

I/B/E/S, Inc.
345 Hudson St.
New York, NY 10014

PH: (212) 243-3335
(800) 438-IBES
FAX: (212) 727-1386
ON-LINE DATABASE
Access Fees: Call for Costs

Wall Street earnings forecasts and consensus for over 7,734 publicly traded companies in 31 nations, excluding the U.S. and Canada. It provides current and historical data of interest to investors and stock quotes.

AUDIENCE: Individual, Professional   RISK LEVEL: Moderate, Aggressive
TOPICS: Stocks

I/B/E/S United States Database

I/B/E/S, Inc.
345 Hudson St.
New York, NY 10014

PH: (800) 438-IBES
FAX: (212) 727-1386
ON-LINE DATABASE
Type: Time series
Access Fees: Call for Costs

Wall Street earnings forecasts and consensus for U.S. publicly traded companies. It provides the current and historical data of interest to investors, and stock quotes. Updated daily. On-line Availability: CompuServe Information Service. Interactive Data Corporation., Quotron Systems, Inc.

AUDIENCE: Individual, Professional   RISK LEVEL: Moderate, Aggressive
TOPICS: Stocks

IBC/Donoghue's Money Fund Report/Electronic

IBC/Donoghue, Inc.
290 Eliot St., P.O. Box 9104
Ashland, MA 01721-9104

PH: (508) 881-3982
(800) 343-5413
FAX: (508) 429-2452
ON-LINE DATABASE
On-line Availability:
IBC/Donoghue, Inc.
Access Fees: Call for Costs

Money market mutual fund information and analysis, including taxable and tax-free money funds, Institutions-Only, Stockbroker and General Purposes, U.S. Treasury.

AUDIENCE: Beginning, Individual, Professional   RISK LEVEL: Conservative
TOPICS: Bonds

ICC British Company Financial Datasheets

Dialog Information Services, Inc.
3460 Hillview Avenue
Palo Alto, CA 94304

PH: (800) 334-2564
FAX: (415) 858-7069
ON-LINE DATABASE
Cost: $45.00 for the first password
    On-line charges $1.60 per minute or
    $96.00 per hour

Financial information for over 100,000 British companies including up to 100 leading companies in 140 selected industry sectors. Information provided by ICC Information Group Ltd., London, England. Updated weekly.

AUDIENCE: Individual, Professional   RISK LEVEL: Moderate, Aggressive
TOPICS: Bonds, Stocks

ICC Stockbroker Research Reports

ICC Information Group Ltd./ICC
Online Services Division
Field House
72 Oldfield Rd.
Hampton, Middlesex TW12 2HQ, England

PH: 081 (783) -1122
FAX: 081 (783) - 0049
ON-LINE DATABASE
Type: Full-text
Also On-line As Part Of: ICC
    International Business Research

Provides U.K. and European Stockbroker investment reports of companies and trends in the securities industry, regional and economic reports, projected performance analysis and recommendations. On-line Availability: Data-Star (ICBR, ICC Stockbroker Research: $107/connect hour, $4 per text paragraph printed online), FT.

AUDIENCE: Individual, Professional   RISK LEVEL: Moderate, Aggressive
TOPICS: Bonds, Stocks

ICDI Mutual Fund Database

Investment Company Data, Inc.
2600 72nd Street, #A
Des Moines, IA 50322-4724

PH: (515) 270-8600
FAX: (515) 270-9022
ON-LINE DATABASE
Start-Up Fee: $50.
Cost: $0.35/fund; $0.02/NAV (daily
and monthly)

Mutual fund database and analysis software. Statistics, total returns, total net assets, net asset values, asset compositions, distributions, cash flow analysis for mutual funds and index. Daily database begins in 1971 for 200 funds, 1985 for the remainder.

AUDIENCE: Beginning, Individual   RISK LEVEL: Moderate, Aggressive
TOPICS: Mutual Funds

IDCPrice

Interactive Data
95 Hayden Avenue
Lexington, MA 02173-9144

PH: (617) 863-8100
Cost: initial set up fee $25.00

Options, stocks, and commodities. For use with CompuTrac. Retrieve and store data.

AUDIENCE: Individual, Professional   RISK LEVEL: Moderate, Aggressive
TOPICS: Stocks, Options, Futures/Commodities

IDSI Municipal Descriptive Data Service

Interactive Data Services, Inc. (IDSI)
14 Wall St.
12th Floor
New York, NY 10005

PH: (212) 285-0700
Access Fees: Call for Costs

International and North American securities market data, including bond quotes. It consists of three files: EXSHARE, Historical data, and Summary data.

AUDIENCE: Individual, Professional   RISK LEVEL: Conservative, Moderate,
TOPICS: All   Aggressive

IDSIport

Interactive Data Services, Inc. (IDSI)
14 Wall St.
12th Floor
New York, NY 10005

PH: (212) 285-0700
Access Fees: Call for Costs

Price data for all government, municipal and corporate securities traded on the American Stock Exchange, New York Stock Exchange, and NASDAQ Over-The-Counter market. It also gives dividends and interest, and securities information from exchanges worldwide.

AUDIENCE: Individual, Professional   RISK LEVEL: Conservative, Moderate,
TOPICS: All   Aggressive

IFS Securities History Data

Iverson Financial Systems, Inc.
111 W. Evelyn Ave.
Suite 206
Sunnyvale, CA 94086-6140

PH: (408) 522-9900
FAX: (408) 522-9900
Access Fees: Call for Costs

Data service on stocks, futures, mutual funds and indices. Buy only needed data, closing prices, any periodicity; special formats and processing request welcomed; weekly highest high; ad hoc requests, daily closing prices.

AUDIENCE: Professional   RISK LEVEL: Conservative, Moderate, Aggressive
TOPICS: Mutual Funds, Stocks, Options, Futures/Commodities

Individual Stock Investor

Design Creations
15387 Camino Del Parque
Sonora, CA 95370

PH: (800) 933-5910
(209) 532-8413
FAX: (209) 532-1545
SOFTWARE
Cost: $59.95

10 directories and 58 databases are designed to perform portfolio management, fundamental analysis, and fundamental screening. Performs research and analysis on the decision making process. Tutorial for interaction with CompuServe, Prodigy, and Signal.

AUDIENCE: Individual, Professional   RISK LEVEL: Conservative, Moderate, Aggressive
TOPICS: All

Infomart Online

Southam Business Information and Communications
1450 Don Mills Road
Don Mills, ON, Canada M3B2X7

PH: (800) 668-9215
(416) 445-6641
FAX: (416) 445-3508
Cost: $175.00 hook-up charges

Canadian stocks, news. Six hundred news and business sources (including Dow Jones News/Retrieval). Access to Canadian stock quotes, current and historical; more than 7,000 Canadian companies; daily newspapers from across the country.

AUDIENCE: Individual, Professional   RISK LEVEL: Moderate, Aggressive
TOPICS: Bonds, Stocks

Innovest

Innovest Financial Information Systems, Inc.
4299 First Ave.
Suite G
Tucker, GA 30084

PH: (404) 368-0910
Cost: $2.16/connect minute

Provides listing of near-term forecasts of price changes for stocks traded on the U.S. exchanges for at least 150 of the past 200 trading days.

AUDIENCE: Individual, Professional   RISK LEVEL: Moderate, Aggressive
TOPICS: Stocks

Inside Market Data

Waters Information Services, Inc.
P.O. Box 2248
Binghamton, NY 13902

PH: (607) 772-8086
FAX: (607) 798-1692
ON-LINE DATABASE
Access Fees: Call for Costs

A monthly newsletter on real-time financial information services, announcements of new hardware, software, and data products for service; provides analyses of industry trends.

AUDIENCE: Individual, Professional   RISK LEVEL: Conservative, Moderate, Aggressive
TOPICS: All

Insider, The

New High Co.
RD #2
Riverhead, NY 11901

PH: (800) 643-8950
(516) 722-5407
FAX: (516) 722-5409
SOFTWARE
Cost: $179
Technical Analysis

Real-time program that evaluates Signal's trade volume of a security to reveal stock's trading. Analyses include OBV, NVI, PVI, TRIN, open TRIN, equivolume, and more.

AUDIENCE: Individual, Professional   RISK LEVEL: Aggressive
TOPICS: Stocks

Insider Trading Monitor

Dialog Information Services, Inc.
3460 Hillview Avenue
Palo Alto, CA 94304

PH: (800) 334-2564
(415) 858-3810
FAX: (415) 858-7069
ON-LINE DATABASE
On-line charges $1.40 per minute or
$84.00 per hour

The transaction details of all insider trader filings (ownership changes) received by the U.S. Securities and Exchange Commission since January 1984. Updated daily. Information provided by Invest/Net, Inc., North Miami, FL.

AUDIENCE: Individual, Professional   RISK LEVEL: Moderate, Aggressive
TOPICS: Stocks

Insiderline

Disclosure Incorporated
5161 River Rd.
Bethesda, MD 20816

PH: (301) 951-1300
(800) 843-7747
FAX: (301) 657-1962
ON-LINE DATABASE

Information of stocks traded by company officials and 100 shares plus trades of the companies reporting to the Securities and Exchange Commission. On-line Availability: Disclosure Incorporated ($110/connect hour ($110 monthly minimum)).

AUDIENCE: Individual, Professional   RISK LEVEL: Moderate, Aggressive
TOPICS: Stocks

International Interest Rate Database

Multinational Computer Models,
  Inc. (MCM)
333 Fairfield Rd.
Fairfield, NJ 07004

PH: (201) 575-8333
FAX: (201) 575-8474
ON-LINE DATABASE
On-line Availability: Multinational
Computer Models, Inc., (MCM)
Access Fees: Call for Costs

Daily Euro interest rates of 9 key currencies. End of the month interest rates for foreign (local) and U.S. money markets and long-term interest rates are derived from the wire services, banks, and the Federal Reserve Bank of New York.

AUDIENCE: Professional   RISK LEVEL: Moderate, Aggressive
TOPICS: Bonds, Options, Futures/Commodities

International Stocks Database

Vision Information, Inc.
295 Greenwich St., 10th Floor
New York, NY 10007

PH: (212) 840-6557
FAX: (212) 619-2724
ON-LINE DATABASE
On-Line Availability: NewsNet, Inc.
Access Fees: Call for Costs

Business and financial information on companies traded on stock exchanges worldwide.

AUDIENCE: Individual, Professional	RISK LEVEL: Moderate, Aggressive
TOPICS: Bonds, Stocks	

Intex Bond Amortization Program

Intex Solutions, Inc.
161 Highland Avenue
Needham, MA 02194

PH: (617) 449-6222
FAX: (617) 444-2318
SOFTWARE
Cost: $295.00

Produces a bond amortization schedule and calculates bond yield for tax and accounting purposes. Supports the straight-line method and the scientific method.

AUDIENCE: Individual, Professional	RISK LEVEL: Conservative
TOPICS: Bonds	

Intex Bond Calculations

Intex Solutions, Inc.
35 Highland Circle
Needham, MA 02194

PH: (617) 449-6222
FAX: (617) 444-2318
SOFTWARE
Cost: $495 basic, $795 advanced,
$995 int'l version

An add-in program that allows the user to compute yield, price, duration, and more within Lotus 1-2-3 or Excel. Functions can be added to spreadsheet or database with a single keystroke.

AUDIENCE: Individual, Professional	RISK LEVEL: Conservative
TOPICS: Bonds	

Intex CMO Analyst (formerly Intex CMO/Remic Model)

Intex Solutions, Inc.
35 Highland Circle
Needham, MA 02194

PH: (617) 449-6222
FAX: (617) 444-2318
SOFTWARE
Cost: $1,200.00

Add-in to Microsoft Excel designed to analyze and manage CMOs. Key CMO calculations: price, yield, analyzes deals, generates a cash flow for the entire life of the bond, and WAL. Vector analysis and forwarding settlement. Intex's database of over 20,000 bonds.

AUDIENCE: Professional	RISK LEVEL: Conservative
TOPICS: Bonds	

Intex Fixed Income Subroutines For Bonds, MBSs, CMOs

Intex Solutions, Inc.
35 Highland Circle
Needham, MA 02194

PH: (617) 449-6222
FAX: (617) 444-2318
SOFTWARE
Cost: $2,400.00

Program includes calculations for more than 36 functions for bonds, MBSs, and CMOs. Functions include yield, duration, convexity, accrued interest, bond equivalent, discount yield, and discount rate.

AUDIENCE: Individual, Professional RISK LEVEL: Conservative
TOPICS: Bonds

Intex Mortgage Backed Calculations

Intex Solutions, Inc.
35 Highland Circle
Needham, MA 02194

PH: (617) 449-6222
FAX: (617) 444-2318
SOFTWARE
Cost: $495 and up

An MBS analysis program designed to interface with spreadsheet or database. Calculations: prepayment rates, delay days, and service costs are calculated. Basic is a CPR prepayment model; advanced provides CPR, PSA, and FHA models and support for ARMs.

AUDIENCE: Professional RISK LEVEL: Conservative, Moderate
TOPICS: Bonds

Intex Option Adjusted Spread

Intex Solutions, Inc.
161 Highland Avenue
Needham, MA 02194

PH: (617) 449-6222
FAX: (617) 444-2318
SOFTWARE
Cost: $8,000.00 for a single user

Mortgage-backed securities. Values callable bonds and MB securities including pools and whole loans. Several prepayment models to take into account effects of future interest rate volatility. Projects cash flows, stable yield and bond equivalent yield.

AUDIENCE: Individual, Professional RISK LEVEL: Conservative, Moderate
TOPICS: Bonds

Intex Option Price Calculations

Intex Solutions, Inc.
35 Highland Circle
Needham, MA 02194

PH: (617) 449-6222
FAX: (617) 444-2318
SOFTWARE
Cost: $495
Options Analysis, Spreadsheets

Three pricing models, Black-Scholes, binomial, and "down and out" provide option analysis on bonds, stocks, commodities, futures, and currencies. "Greek" sensitivity ratios (delta, gamma, theta, rho, vega, and psi). Implied and essential volatility functions.

AUDIENCE: Professional RISK LEVEL: Conservative, Moderate, Aggressive
TOPICS: Bonds

Intex Solutions

Intex Solutions
161 Highland Avenue
Needham, MA 02194

PH: (617) 449-6222
FAX: (617) 444-2318
SOFTWARE
Cost: $395.00 basic; $695.00
advanced; $895.00 international

Options and bonds, municipal, corporate, government and agencies. Expand the analytical capabilities of Lotus 1-2-3 and Symphony. Intex functions: Intex Bond Calculations, Intex Mortgage Backed Calculations, Intex Option Price Calculations, etc.

AUDIENCE: Individual, Professional   RISK LEVEL: Conservative, Moderate
TOPICS: Bonds

Invest Now! Personal

Emerging Market Technologies, Inc.
1230 Johnson Ferry Road
Suite F-1
Marietta, GA 30068

PH: (404) 973-2300
FAX: (404) 973-3003
SOFTWARE
Cost: $79.00

Personal version of stock/option calculator.

AUDIENCE: Beginning, Individual   RISK LEVEL: Aggressive
TOPICS: Stocks, Options

Invest Now! Professional Version 2.0

Emerging Market Technologies, Inc.
1230 Johnson Ferry Road
Suite F-1
Marietta, GA 30068

PH: (404) 973-2300
FAX: (404) 973-3003
SOFTWARE
Cost: $129.00

Covers equity investment scenarios: buy calls, buy puts, combinations, stock yield, dividend roll, short sales, spreads, covered calls, naked calls and naked puts. Many calculations for stock and option investments. "What-if " capability.

AUDIENCE: Individual, Professional   RISK LEVEL: Moderate, Aggressive
TOPICS: Stocks, Options

Investability Mutual Fund Database

Investability Corp.
P.O. Box 43307
Louisville, KY 40253

PH: (502) 722-5700
ON-LINE DATABASE
Access Fees: $29/quarter; $99/year
for quarterly updates.

Gives information on over 4,400 mutual funds. The funds can be sorted and ranked by return as a whole or by investment objective. Find individual funds or distribution companies. The newest feature provides hypothetical and side-by-side comparisons.

AUDIENCE: Beginning, Individual   RISK LEVEL: Moderate, Aggressive
TOPICS: Mutual Funds

Investdata Systems

Telekurs AG
Hardturmstr. 201
CH-8021 Zurich, Switzerland

PH: 01 2792111
FAX: 01 2718010
Telekurs AG
ON-LINE DATABASE
Access Fees: Call for Costs

Provides information on worldwide stocks, commodities, money market, and bonds. Information continuously updated.

AUDIENCE: Individual, Professional   RISK LEVEL: Moderate, Aggressive
TOPICS: Bonds, Stocks, Options, Futures/Commodities

Investext

The Investext Group/Thomson
  Financial Services
II Farnsworth Street
Boston, MA 02210

PH: (617) 345-2000
(800) 662-7878
FAX: (617) 330-1986
ON-LINE DATABASE
Cost: Starter kit $95.00
On-line charges per hour $99.00

A full-text online database comprised of company and industry reports from 300 of the world's leading investment banks and research firms. Contains over 600,000 research reports on more than 14,000 domestic and international public companies, 53 industries.

AUDIENCE: Professional   RISK LEVEL: Moderate, Aggressive
TOPICS: Bonds, Stocks

INVESTigator +

Investment Technology
5104 Utah
Greenville, TX 75401

PH: (800) 833-0269
(903) 455-3255
Cost: $199.00

Covers stocks, commodities, mutual funds, indices, and options. Provides chart service. Charting, technical analysis, and data management program for stocks, options, indices, mutual funds, or commodities. Up to 300 data files, with up to 900 days or weeks.

AUDIENCE: Individual, Professional   RISK LEVEL: Moderate, Aggressive
TOPICS: Mutual Funds, Stocks, Options, Futures/Commodities

Investigator

Investment Technology
5104 Utah Street
Greenville, TX 75402

PH: (903) 455-3255
SOFTWARE
Cost: $99

A charting, technical analysis, and data management program that can maintain up to 1,000 days or weeks of data for 1,000 different issues. Dial/Data. Program calculates numerous technical indicators developed by contributors in technical analysis field.

AUDIENCE: Individual, Professional   RISK LEVEL: Moderate, Aggressive
TOPICS: Mutual Funds, Stocks, Options, Futures/Commodities

Investing Advisor

Dynacomp, Inc.
178 Phillips Road
Webster, NY 14580

PH: (800) 828-6772
SOFTWARE
Cost: $49.95

Uses technical analysis to assist the investor in buying and selling investments. Includes short-term and long-term trends choosing a strategy. User can initialize database, add or delete investments, improve transaction decisions, and adjust for splits.

AUDIENCE: Professional   RISK LEVEL: Moderate, Aggressive
TOPICS: Bonds, Mutual Funds, Stocks

Investment Analy$T

Telebase Systems, Inc. (TSI)
435 Devon Park Dr.
Wayne, PA 19087

PH: (215) 293-4700
(800) 220-9553
FAX: (215) 341-9660
ON-LINE DATABASE
On-line Availability: GEnie
Access Fees: Call for Costs

Provides current and historical stock price data for stocks traded on the New York Stock Exchange, American Stock Exchange, and NASDAQ stocks and mutual funds. Track portfolios, identify market trends, monitor competitors and check insider movement.

AUDIENCE: Individual   RISK LEVEL: Moderate, Aggressive
TOPICS: Bonds, Mutual Funds, Stocks

Investment Analysis For Stocks, Bonds, and Real Estate

Larry Rosen Company
7008 Springdale Road
Louisville, KY 40241

PH: (502) 228-4343
SOFTWARE
Cost: $89.00 for a single user

Evaluates existing and proposed real estate, stock and bond investments by internal rate of return analysis after taxes. Cashflow analysis. Both with and without reinvestment.

AUDIENCE: Individual   RISK LEVEL: Moderate, Aggressive
TOPICS: Bonds, Stocks, Real Estate

Investment Analyst

Omni Software Systems, Inc.
702 N Ernest
Griffith, IN 46319

PH: (219) 924-3522
SOFTWARE
Cost: $95.00

Analyze investments or potential investments with adjustments for inflation, deflation, depreciation methods, cash flow, tax rates, financing, and future sale. Gain/loss after taxes, internal rate of return, expense items, cash flow analysis, and depreciation.

AUDIENCE: Beginning, Individual   RISK LEVEL: Conservative, Moderate, Aggressive
TOPICS: Bonds, Stocks

Investment IRR Analysis for Stocks, Bonds, and Real Estate

Larry Rosen Co.
7008 Springdale Road
Louisville, KY 40241

PH: (502) 228-4343
FAX: (502) 228-4782
SOFTWARE
Cost: $89.00

Internal rate of return for stocks, bonds, and real estate. Analyzes current investments or proposed investments at desired rate of reinvestment of cash flows and performs a cash flow analysis. Annual income, interest, expenses, principal, pretax and after-tax cash flows.

AUDIENCE: Beginning, Individual   RISK LEVEL: Conservative, Moderate
TOPICS: Bonds, Stocks

Investment Manager I

Integrated Decision Systems, Inc.
1950 Sawtelle
Suite 255
Los Angeles, CA 90025

PH: (310) 478-4015
SOFTWARE
Cost: $4,000.00 for complete
  package

A comprehensive single-user portfolio management system for small to mid-size investment firms. Tracks positions in all investment vehicles, continually updates entire portfolios as new information is entered and produces over 40 internal and client reports.

AUDIENCE: Professional	RISK LEVEL: Conservative, Moderate, Aggressive
TOPICS: All	

Investment Master

G.C.P.I.
P.O. Box 790, Dept. #50-E
Marquette, MI 49855

PH: (906) 226-7600
SOFTWARE
Cost: $49.95
Financial Planning

Analyzes your investment summaries. Solves for unknown investment parameters. Useful in obtaining answers about periodic savings deposit plans, mutual funds, IRAs, and lump-sum investments. Information can be displayed on screen, output to disk, or printed.

AUDIENCE: Beginning	RISK LEVEL: Conservative, Moderate, Aggressive
TOPICS: Mutual Funds	

Investment Performance Chart

Heizer Software
P.O. Box 232019
Pleasant Hill, CA 94523

PH: (800) 888-7667
(510) 943-7667
FAX: (510) 943-6882
Cost: $15.00
SOFTWARE
Financial Planning, Spreadsheets

Evaluates performance of IRAs, investment plans, stocks, bonds, mutual funds, or company investment plans. Plots amount invested, value of investment, and annual interest rates at the time of investment. Has "what if" capabilities for analysis.

AUDIENCE: Beginning	RISK LEVEL: Conservative, Moderate
TOPICS: Bonds, Mutual Funds, Stocks	

Investment Software

SCIX Corp.
P.O. Box 3244
Williamsport, PA 17701-0244

PH: (717) 323-3276
ON-LINE DATABASE
Access Fees: Call for Costs

Provides a description of IBM PC investment software programs. It gives the name, features, functions, price and product review. The user can order software on-line.

AUDIENCE: Beginning, Individual, Professional	RISK LEVEL: Conservative, Moderate, Aggressive
TOPICS: All	

Investment Wizard

Investa, Inc.
1400 Post Oak Blvd., Suite 800
Houston, TX 77056

PH: (713) 877-1206
(800) 359-9359
FAX: (713) 877-1650
ON-LINE DATABASE
Start-Up Fee: $49., Access
    Fees : $15/hour.

Is a daily updated on-line database of current Wall Street opinions and predictions on U.S. and foreign stocks, industry groups, mutual funds, stocks and bond markets, U.S. and world economy, and interest rates.

AUDIENCE: Individual, Professional   RISK LEVEL: Moderate, Aggressive
TOPICS: Bonds, Mutual Funds, Stocks

Investnow!-Personal

Emerging Market Technologies, Inc.
1230 Johnson Ferry Road
Suite F1
Marietta, GA 30068

PH: (404) 973-2300
FAX: (404) 973-3003
SOFTWARE
Cost: $99.00

Provides futures and options analysis. Simulation games. Input actual brokerage fees or have the program provide "typical" fees for buy/sell transactions. Computes simple and annual returns on investments and performs necessary margin requirements.

AUDIENCE: Beginning, Individual   RISK LEVEL: Aggressive
TOPICS: Options, Futures/Commodities

Investnow!-Professional

Emerging Market Technologies, Inc.
1230 Johnson Ferry Road
Suite F1
Marietta, GA 30068

PH: (404) 973-2300
FAX: (404) 973-3003
SOFTWARE
Cost: $129.00

Performs same functions as the Investnow!-Personal but with added capabilities: the buying of calls and puts, writing naked and covered calls, and writing naked puts. Determines a stocks simple and annual returns and applies all necessary margin requirements.

AUDIENCE: Individual   RISK LEVEL: Aggressive
TOPICS: Options, Futures/Commodities

Investograph Plus, Optimizer

Liberty Research Corporation
Bldg. 2, Suite 304, 1250 Capital of
   Texas Hwy
Austin, TX 78746

PH: (800) 827-0090
(512) 329-2762
FAX: (512) 329-2588
SOFTWARE
Cost: $399.00

Technical analysis. Calculates over 20 technical functions and provides many proprietary tools. RSI, stochastics, moving averages, relative strength charts, MACD. Proprietary calculations include oscillations, Formula X, Formula Y, Formula H oscillators.

AUDIENCE: Individual, Professional   RISK LEVEL: Aggressive
TOPICS: Stocks, Options, Futures/Commodities

Investor, The

Village Software
186 Lincoln Street
Boston, MA 02111

PH: (800) 724-9332
(617) 695-9332
FAX: (617) 695-1935
Cost: $129.00
SOFTWARE

Tracks securities, charts stocks and allows user to make buy/sell/hold decisions based on 40 key indicators, trend charts, and true technical analysis. Stock information can be retrieved on Prodigy, CompuServe and GEnie. More advanced data links also available.

AUDIENCE: Beginning, Individual   RISK LEVEL: Moderate, Aggressive
TOPICS: Stocks

Investor's Accountant

Hamilton Software, Inc.
6432 East Mineral Place
Englewood, CO 80112

PH: (800) 733-9607
SOFTWARE
Cost: $395.00

Investment portfolio accounting and analysis system. Tracks performance of investments individually and by type. Includes fully integrated version of Fundwatch Plus for tracking, evaluating and graphing securities.

AUDIENCE: Beginning, Individual   RISK LEVEL: Conservative, Moderate, Aggressive
TOPICS: All

Investor's Guide And Mutual Fund Directory

The Association of No-Load Funds
Mutual Fund Education Alliance
1900 Erie St.
Suite 120
Kansas City, MO 64116

PH: (816) 471-1454
SOFTWARE
Cost: $99.00

Information on some mutual funds that do not charge sales commission, as well as investment information. Annual update.

AUDIENCE: Beginning, Individual   RISK LEVEL: Moderate, Aggressive
TOPICS: Mutual Funds

Investor's Portfolio

Savant Software, Inc.
  (Formerly Savant Corp.)
120 Bedford Center Road
Bedford, NH 03110

PH: (800) 231-9900
FAX: (603) 472-5981
SOFTWARE
Cost: $795 standard version; $995
  international version
Portfolio Management

Program tracks stocks and bonds, indexes stock dividends, short positions, and open orders. Calculates commissions, fees, taxes, and establishes warnings when positions exceed limits. Prints IRS schedules and more.

AUDIENCE: Individual, Professional   RISK LEVEL: Conservative, Moderate, Aggressive
TOPICS: Bonds, Mutual Funds, Stocks

Investor's Tool Kit

Niche Software Products
P.O. Box 3574
Manassas, VA 22110

PH: (703) 368-8372
SOFTWARE
Cost: $50

Program designed for option traders and the stock investor. Symbol finds OTC option symbols and calculates theta, expiration date, delta, implied volatility, and calculates taxable vs. non-taxable returns. Many other functions accessible.

AUDIENCE: Individual, Professional   RISK LEVEL: Aggressive
TOPICS: Stocks, Options

Investors Forum

CompuServe Information Service
5000 Arlington Centre Blvd.
P.O. Box 20212
Columbus, OH 43220

PH: (614) 457-8600
(800) 848-8199
FAX: (614) 457-0348
ON-LINE DATABASE
Access Fees: Call for Costs

Gives party line investment advice. It features a number of public domain software and information text files.

AUDIENCE: Beginning, Individual   RISK LEVEL: Moderate, Aggressive
TOPICS: All

IRMA

Dynacomp, Inc.
178 Phillips Road
Webster, NY 14580

PH: (800) 828-6772
SOFTWARE
Cost: $49.95

Assists in the financial planning and portfolio management of bonds, stocks, indexes, mutual funds, options, and real estate. Portfolio can contain up to 90 investments including preferred stocks, bonds, deposit accounts, options, partnerships.

AUDIENCE: Beginning, Individual   RISK LEVEL: Conservative, Moderate, Aggressive
TOPICS: Bonds, Mutual Funds, Stocks, Options, Investment Planning

It's Alive

New High Co.
RD #2
Riverhead, NY 11901

PH: (800) 643-8950
(516) 722-5407
FAX: (516) 722-5409
SOFTWARE
Cost: $195.00

Daily based charting for real-time, on-line, intraday charting and analysis. Stores data on securities from Signal portfolio in 5-, 15-, 30-, and 60 minute files. Runs technical analysis: CompuServe, Byte's Professional Breakout System, and Metastock.

AUDIENCE: Individual, Professional   RISK LEVEL: Moderate, Aggressive
TOPICS: Stocks, Options, Futures/Commodities

Klatu Software

Nirvana Systems, Inc.
3415 Greystone Drive
Suite 205
Austin, TX 78731

PH: (512) 345-2545
Cost: $595.00 for software package

Stocks and mutual funds. Combination batch file and macro programs work inside your favorite programs. Collect data late at night when it is less expensive, convert and transport data between programs. Named 1989 "Product of the Year" by Commodity Trader's Almanac.

AUDIENCE: Beginning, Individual   RISK LEVEL: Moderate, Aggressive
TOPICS: Mutual Funds, Stocks

Knight-Ridder End-of-Day News Reports

Knight-Ridder Financial Publishing
30 S. Wacker Dr., Suite 1820
Chicago, IL 60606

PH: (312) 454-1801
(800) 526-3282
FAX: (312) 454-0239
ON-LINE DATABASE
Access Fees: Call for Costs

Reports cover major events of the day affecting the futures markets.

AUDIENCE: Individual, Professional   RISK LEVEL: Aggressive
TOPICS: Options, Futures/Commodities

Knight-Ridder Financial News

Dialog Information Services, Inc.
3460 Hillview Avenue
Palo Alto, CA 94304

PH: (800) 334-2564
FAX: (415) 858-7069
ON-LINE DATABASE
Cost: $1.60 per minute or $96.00
  per hour

Has complete text of news stories on worldwide financial and commodity markets and the events that move them. Information provided by Knight-Ridder Financial Information, Inc., New York, NY. Updated continuously.

AUDIENCE: Individual, Professional   RISK LEVEL: Moderate, Aggressive
TOPICS: All

LaPorte Asset Allocation System

Burlington Hall Asset Management,
  Inc.
126 Petersburg Road
Hackettstown, NJ 07840

PH: (201) 852-1694
SOFTWARE
Cost: $1,975/yr with all updates.

Commodities, mutual funds, and charts. Optimize combinations of investments or investment managers, storing performance data on an unlimited number of investments, performance graphs, pie charts of asset allocations, and project a range of future performance.

AUDIENCE: Individual, Professional   RISK LEVEL: Moderate, Aggressive
TOPICS: Mutual Funds, Futures/Commodities, Asset Allocation, Investment Planning

Lexis Financial Information Service

Mead Data Central, Inc.
9443 Springboro Pike, P.O. Box 933
Dayton, OH 45401-9964

PH: (800) 277-4809
FAX: (513) 865-1666
ON-LINE DATABASE
Start-Up Fee: $50.00
Access Fees: $50.00/month

Stock quotes, international news and country analysis reports by country, region and topic. Offers ALERT library which is updated every 3 hours. Part of the NEXIS service of Mead Data Central. Search international files by region, individually or all at once. Current Quote Fees: $1.00/quote plus connect time.

AUDIENCE: Individual, Professional	RISK LEVEL: Moderate, Aggressive
TOPICS: Bonds, Mutual Funds, Stocks	

Lexis/Nexis

Mead Data
P.O. Box 933-NR
Dayton, OH 45401

PH: (800) 543-6862
(800) 227-4908
Basic monthly charge from
  $1,000.00

Covers stocks, news. Comprehensive electronic information source: real time quotes, two major newswires updated every fifteen minutes from 8 am - 8 pm each business day, wire services from more than 650 worldwide news bureaus updated four times daily.

AUDIENCE: Individual, Professional	RISK LEVEL: Moderate, Aggressive
TOPICS: Bonds, Mutual Funds, Stocks	

Linear Programmer Minimax

Dynacomp, Inc.
178 Phillips Road
Webster, NY 14580

PH: (800) 828-6772
SOFTWARE
Cost: $69.95

Functions as an asset/investment optimization program. Treats over-constrained and under-constrained problems, maximizes an objective function, and solves simultaneous linear equations.

AUDIENCE: Individual, Professional RISK LEVEL: Moderate, Aggressive
TOPICS: Bonds, Mutual Funds, Stocks, Asset Allocation

Link/Screen

Computer Investing Consultants
9002 Swineburne Court
San Antonio, TX 78240

PH: (210) 681-0491
FAX: (210) 349-0978
SOFTWARE
Cost: $95

Technical analysis and screening are used with MetaStock/Compu Trac databases. Comparative relative strength calculations to individual stocks and against a market index, technical screening for buy/sell opportunities, calculation variables, and technical indicators.

AUDIENCE: Individual, Professional	RISK LEVEL: Moderate, Aggressive
TOPICS: Bonds, Stocks, Options	

Live Wire

CableSoft, Inc.
8207 Melrose Drive
Suite 111
Lenexa, KS 66214

PH: (913) 888-4449
Cost: $595.00; tracks
   1,000-plus issues

Includes charts. Automates every step of the investment process. In real-time Live Wire lets you monitor quotes, graph and analyze price movements, compare investments, set alarms, enter transaction, measure profit and loss. Provides technical analysis.

AUDIENCE: Individual	RISK LEVEL: Moderate, Aggressive
TOPICS: Stocks	

Live-Line

National Computer Network
1929 N. Harlem Ave.
Chicago, IL 60635

PH: (312) 622-6666
(800) 942-6262
FAX: (312) 622-6889
ON-LINE DATABASE
Cost: $6-$10/hour; $25/monthly
   minimum charge

Is a menu-driven real-time quote display system that monitors all U.S. equities, options, indexes, futures and options on futures. It can constantly monitor 66 issues. Provides theoretical values for stock, index and future options.

AUDIENCE: Individual	RISK LEVEL: Aggressive
TOPICS: Stocks, Options, Futures/Commodities	

Livewire Personal Investor

Cablesoft, Inc.
1807 2nd Street, Suite 26
Santa Fe, NM 87501

PH: (505) 986-8052
(505) 484-9219
SOFTWARE
Cost: $295.00

Portfolio management, technical analysis, and simulation games for stocks, bonds, indexes, mutual funds, options, and futures. Operates both real-time and delayed data services. Integrates price and volume alarms, historical graphs, updates positions.

AUDIENCE: Individual, Professional	RISK LEVEL: Conservative, Moderate, Aggressive
TOPICS: All	

Livewire Professional

Cablesoft, Inc.
1807 2nd Street
Suite 26
Santa Fe, NM 87501

PH: (505) 986-8052
(505) 484-9219
SOFTWARE
Cost: $595

Historical data on up to 1,000 symbols for stocks, bonds, indexes, mutual funds, options, and futures. Provides multiple portfolio management with cash accounting. Users can view dollar gain, percentage gain, and rate of return for symbols and portfolios.

AUDIENCE: Professional	RISK LEVEL: Conservative, Moderate, Aggressive
TOPICS: All	

Log Scale Comparison

Tools for Timing
11345 Highway 7, #499
Minnetonka, MN 55305

PH: (800) 325-1344
(612) 939-0076
FAX: (612) 938-1275
Cost: $50.00
SOFTWARE

Each index is placed on its own log scale for comparisons to other indexes for at least a nine day period. Indexes include DJIA, S&P 500, DJT, DJU - 1968, NYSE Composite, ASE and OSE Composites and OEX. Includes data from the first of 1978 to day prior to shipping.

AUDIENCE: Individual, Professional	RISK LEVEL: Moderate, Aggressive
TOPICS: Stocks, Futures/Commodities	

Lotus 1-2-3 for Macintosh

Lotus Development Corporation
55 Cambridge Parkway
Cambridge, MA 02142

PH: (800) 343-5414
(617) 577-8500
SOFTWARE
Cost: $495.00

Program allows direct manipulation of worksheet elements and desktop customization. Numerous calculations provided in program. Fully compatible with Apple's System 7 operating system. Will also read and write Microsoft Excel files and translate Excel macros.

AUDIENCE: Individual, Professional	RISK LEVEL: Conservative, Moderate,
TOPICS: All	Aggressive

Lotus 1-2-3 for OS/2

Lotus Development Corporation
55 Cambridge Parkway
Cambridge, MA 02142

PH: (800) 343-5414
(617) 577-8500
SOFTWARE
Cost: $495 standard edition, $595
for network server edition

Graphical version of Lotus 1-2-3 designed for OS/2. Presentation manager provides full interface. Same functions as Lotus 1-2-3 for Macintosh calculated.

AUDIENCE: Individual, Professional	RISK LEVEL: Conservative, Moderate,
TOPICS: All	Aggressive

Lotus Realtime

Lotus Development Corp
55 Cambridge Parkway
Cambridge, MA 02142

PH: (800) 343-5414
Lotus Realtime Engine $350.00 -
$1,000.00

Covers securities. Lotus 1-2-3 Release 3 is an ideal analysis, display, and modeling environment for securities traders and analysts. Lotus Realtime enables you to perform realtime analytics on data from any digital data source, directly within Lotus 1-2-3.

AUDIENCE: Individual, Professional	RISK LEVEL: Conservative, Moderate,
TOPICS: All	Aggressive

Lowry's Market Trend Analysis Database On Diskette

Lowry's Reports, Inc.
631 U.S. Highway 1, Suite 305
North Palm Beach, FL 33408

PH: (407) 842-3514
FAX: (407) 842-1523
ON-LINE DATABASE
Cost: $25.00/year

Daily information from 1/1/40 for DJIA high/low and close; Lowry's Buying Power Index, Selling Pressure index and Short-Term Index; NYSE issues, volume, and points; NYSE new highs and lows and Lowry's average power rating. ASCII, MetaStock or Compu Trac.

AUDIENCE: Individual, Professional   RISK LEVEL: Moderate, Aggressive
TOPICS: Stocks, Options, Futures/Commodities

M-Search

Emerging Market Technologies, Inc.
1230 Johnson Ferry Road
Suite F-1
Marietta, GA 30068

PH: (404) 973-2300
FAX: (404) 973-3003
SOFTWARE
Cost: $3,000 annually

Search through hundreds of money managers located all over the U.S.

AUDIENCE: Individual, Professional   RISK LEVEL: Moderate, Aggressive
TOPICS: Bonds, Stocks, Asset Allocation

Macquotes

War Machine
1700 Taylor N.
#301
Seattle, WA 98109

PH: (206) 283-3708
SOFTWARE
Cost: $295

Allows investor to use Lotus Signal on a Macintosh or IBM. Tracks up to 250 symbols and allows up to 150 alerts. Up to 16 windows allow user to customize pages to be displayed immediately.

AUDIENCE: Beginning, Individual   RISK LEVEL: Moderate, Aggressive
TOPICS: All

MacRats

Estima (formerly VAR
Econometrics)
1800 Sherman Ave., Suite 612
Evanston, IL 60201

PH: (800) 822-8038
(708) 864-8772
FAX: (708) 864-6221
SOFTWARE
Cost: $300.00

Program performs analysis of time series data. Forecasting techniques: Box-Jenkins, exponential smoothing, vector autoregressions, spectral analysis, and time series. Also capable of full econometrics and regression. Has support for daily, weekly, and data with multiple entries per day.

AUDIENCE: Professional   RISK LEVEL: Moderate, Aggressive
TOPICS: Stocks

Macro*World Investor

Macro*World Research, Corp.
4265 Brownsboro Road, Suite 170
Winston-Salem, NC 27106-3429

PH: (800) 841-5398
(919) 759-0600
FAX: (919) 759-0636
SOFTWARE
Cost: $699.95

Analysis and forecasting models use the best indicators to forecast performance of securities and the markets. Rates of return, degrees of risk, buy/hold/sell signals, optimal risk/return mix, fundamental forecasts of earnings, book values, and earnings.

AUDIENCE: Individual, Professional   RISK LEVEL: Moderate, Aggressive
TOPICS: All

Market Action Timer

Tempo Investment Products, Inc.
4102 Elm Court
Midland, MI 48642

PH: (517) 832-3148
SOFTWARE
Cost: $99.00

Adds 8 weekly data points: DJIA, S&P 500 Composite, number of advancing stocks, number of declining stocks, weekly price, NASDAQ Composite, and others to calculate moving averages, trend analysis and advice on the market situation. Buy/sell or hedge signal.

AUDIENCE: Individual   RISK LEVEL: Moderate, Aggressive
TOPICS: Mutual Funds, Stocks, Futures/Commodities

Market Analyzer

N-Squared Computing
5318 Forest Ridge Road
Silverton, OR 97381

PH: (503) 873-4420
(214) 680-1445
FAX: (214) 680-1435
SOFTWARE
Cost: $395.00

Sophisticated data manipulation and charting. Manipulate any type of data, create spreads, chart interest rates, overlay any 2 data items. General market breadth indicators and mutual funds. Complete database management and downloading of data from Warner.

AUDIENCE: Individual   RISK LEVEL: Moderate, Aggressive
TOPICS: Bonds, Mutual Funds, Stocks

Market Analyzer 2.0

Dow Jones & Co., Inc
P.O. Box 300
Princeton, NJ 08543-0300

PH: (609) 520-4641
(609) 520-4000
FAX: (609) 520-4660
SOFTWARE
Cost: $349

Stocks, mutual funds, bonds (corporate, government, and foreign), options, and stock indexes. Spot issues that are driving the market and identify underlying market trends. Charting power creates technical analysis charts. Automatically collects prices.

AUDIENCE: Individual   RISK LEVEL: Moderate, Aggressive
TOPICS: Bonds, Mutual Funds, Stocks

Market Analyzer Plus

Dow Jones & Co., Inc
P.O. Box 300
Princeton, NJ 08543-0300

PH: (609) 520-4641
(609) 520-4000
FAX: (609) 520-4660
SOFTWARE
Cost: $499.00

Covers stocks, commodities, mutual funds, bonds (corporate, government, and foreign), options and treasuries. A complete investment program with sophisticated charting, flexible technical screening and detailed portfolio management.

AUDIENCE: Individual, Professional   RISK LEVEL: Conservative, Moderate,
TOPICS: Bonds, Mutual Funds, Stocks   Aggressive

Market Base

Marketbase, Inc.
P.O. Box 37
Needham Heights, MA 02194

PH: (617) 449-8460
(800) 735-0700
FAX: (617) 449-3978
ON-LINE DATABASE
Cost: $2,300.00/year

Fundamental analysis system. Covers companies whose common stock trades on AMEX, NYSE, NASDAQ National Market System exchanges. Screening capabilities using over 100 fields. It has a custom report generator, 52-week and 60-month closing price trend graphs, creations and analysis of ticker portfolios.

AUDIENCE: Individual, Professional   RISK LEVEL: Moderate, Aggressive
TOPICS: Stocks

Market Briefings

MMS International
1301 Shoreway Rd.
Suite 300
Belmont, CA 94002

PH: (415) 595-0610
ON-LINE DATABASE
Access Fee: Call for Costs

Six reports on U.S. financial and economic indicators: Foreign Exchange Report, Futures Market Overview, GNP Outlook, Monetary Outlook, Real Sector Briefing, and Treasury Auction Analysis. Key issues affecting the debt, stock, futures, and foreign exchange.

AUDIENCE: Individual, Professional   RISK LEVEL: Conservative, Moderate,
TOPICS: Bonds, Stocks, Options, Futures/Commodities   Aggressive

Market Center

BMI
19 W. South Temple, Suite 200
Salt Lake City, UT 84101-1503

PH: (801) 532-3400
(800) 255-7374
FAX: (801) 532-3202
ON-LINE DATABASE
Cost: $397 for software; $597 for
   satellite hardware

Superquote page to view all symbol information transmitted by BMI; Graphs; display of last eight ticks; volume, price and news alerts; transfer data to other programs; built-in portfolio manager. Technical analysis charts are available for minute/daily/weekly.

AUDIENCE: Individual, Professional   RISK LEVEL: Moderate, Aggressive
TOPICS: All

Market Center 5

BMI
3 Trade Center, Suite 100
Salt Lake City, UT 84180

PH: (800) 255-7374
FAX: (801) 532-3202
QUOTE SERVICE
Cost: $397.00 plus monthly $232.00

Options, stocks, commodities. Realtime or delayed quotes on commodities, real-time quotes on stocks and options, follow up to 6,000 quotes with added memory, automatic option chaining, trend for last eight ticks, spread quotes, snap quotes, indices.

AUDIENCE: Individual, Professional   RISK LEVEL: Moderate, Aggressive
TOPICS: Stocks, Options, Futures/Commodities

Market Decision System 7

ADP Brokerage Information
  Services Group (ADP/BISG)
2 Journal Square Plaza
Jersey City, NJ 07306

PH: (201) 714-3000
ON-LINE DATABASE
Access Fee: Call for Costs

Provides real-time financial and economic information involving investments in stocks, bonds, currencies, commodities, and options.

AUDIENCE: Individual, Professional   RISK LEVEL: Conservative, Moderate,
TOPICS: Bonds, Stocks, Options, Futures/Commodities   Aggressive

Market Expert

AIQ Systems, Inc.
916 Southwood Boulevard
Incline Village, NV 89450

PH: (800) 332-2999
(702) 831-2999
FAX: (702) 831-6784
SOFTWARE
Cost: $249

Uses technical analysis and technical screening to help determine the direction of the market. Combines 17 pieces of daily market data and 32 technical analysis indicators to form a fact base from which to make a decision. 24 technical indicators. Graphic Display.

AUDIENCE: Individual, Professional   RISK LEVEL: Moderate, Aggressive
TOPICS: Stocks, Options

Market Forecaster

Dynacomp, Inc.
178 Phillips Road
Webster, NY 14580

PH: (800) 828-6772
SOFTWARE
Cost: $69.95

Uses technical analysis and statistics to predict the magnitude and direction of stock market movements over the next 2 to 4 months. Gives indicators when it is best to buy stocks, mutual funds, or options and when to reduce your position. What if capability.

AUDIENCE: Individual, Professional   RISK LEVEL: Moderate, Aggressive
TOPICS: Mutual Funds, Stocks, Options

Market Guide Data Base: Market Screen

Market Guide, Inc.
49 Glen Head Rd.
Glen Head, NY 11545

PH: (800) 642-3840
ON-LINE DATABASE
Type: Full-text; numeric

Provides stock and financial information on companies that are unreported or undervalued on the American, New York, and over-the-counter exchanges. Contact: John D. Case, President.

AUDIENCE: Individual, Professional   RISK LEVEL: Moderate, Aggressive
TOPICS: Bonds, Stocks

Market Intelligence Swing Cather Trading System

Trend Index Company
Box 5
Altoona, WI 54720

PH: (715) 833-1234
FAX: (715) 833-8040
SOFTWARE
Cost: $995.00

60 price indicators based on recent price relationships. Buy/sell indicators triggered based on total point value of the indicators combined with pattern recognition and cycle techniques. The entire trade can be sent to the broker, including stop/loss price.

AUDIENCE: Professional	RISK LEVEL: Aggressive
TOPICS: Futures/Commodities	

Market Maker

Inmark Associates
139 Fulton Street
Suite 810
New York, NY 10038

PH: (212) 785-1300
SOFTWARE
Cost: $1,295.00

Charting package to create classical and customized technical studies for stocks, commodities and options. Includes the Inmark Strength Indicator which tracks the movement of money. Has communications package.

AUDIENCE: Individual, Professional	RISK LEVEL: Moderate, Aggressive
TOPICS: Stocks, Options, Futures/Commodities	

Market Manager Plus (Version 2.0)

Dow Jones and Co., Inc.
P.O. Box 300
Princeton, NJ 08543-0300

PH: (609) 520-4641
(609) 520-4000
FAX: (609) 520-4660
SOFTWARE
Cost: $299.00

Tracks buy, sell, short sell and buy to cover transactions; collects automatically from News/Retrieval prices for stocks, bonds, options, mutual funds, and treasury notes and bonds. Update your portfolio, saves collected security prices in SYLK format.

AUDIENCE: Individual, Professional	RISK LEVEL: Conservative, Moderate,
TOPICS: Bonds, Mutual Funds, Stocks, Options	Aggressive

Market Master

Ingenious Technologies Corp./RMC
P.O. Box 60842
Sunnyvale, CA 94088-0842

PH: (408) 773-8715
Cost: $395 - two indicator version,
to $1,595 - six indicator version

Forecast the direction, magnitude, and target of future price movements for any stock, future contract, market index, foreign stock, or futures exchange with this forecasting software. Quantitative pattern analysis, error detection and learning.

AUDIENCE: Individual, Professional	RISK LEVEL: Moderate, Aggressive
TOPICS: Stocks, Options, Futures/Commodities	

Market Master

Dancotec
2835 Sierra Rd.
San Jose, CA 951132

PH: (800) 344-2545
FAX: (408) 923-7061
SOFTWARE
Cost: $399.00 to $699.00; File
    converter, $50.00.

Covers stocks and provides chart service. New algorithm technology. The spreadsheet employs a spreadsheet-like command menu. Only high, low, close, and possibly volume are required for input. Both end-of-day and intraday analysis are supported.

AUDIENCE: Individual, Professional	RISK LEVEL: Moderate, Aggressive
TOPICS: Stocks, Options	

Market Max

TriStar Market Data, Inc.
600 Montgomery Street
San Francisco, CA 94111

PH: (415) 627-2345
SOFTWARE
Cost: Call Vendor

Covers futures options, stocks, commodities. Market Max is a Macintosh-based dynamic trader workstation. Quotes, analysis, fundamental and historical data on U.S. stocks, options, futures, futures options and listed corporate bonds, Canadian and London.

AUDIENCE: Individual, Professional	RISK LEVEL: Moderate, Aggressive
TOPICS: Stocks, Options, Futures/Commodities	

Market Monitor

BMI
3 Triad Center
Salt Lake City, UT 84180

PH: (800) 255-7374
FAX: (801) 532-3202
QUOTE SERVICE
Cost: $597.00 plus monthly
    $197.00
Hardware provided

Commodities. 46 pages of real-time tick-by-tick information, one page of financial and industrial averages, three news pages, two fully programmable pages, price alerts, high, low, net, last trade, volume, opening range, bid/ask, open interest, options.

AUDIENCE: Individual, Professional	RISK LEVEL: Aggressive
TOPICS: Futures/Commodities	

Market Monitor 5

BMI
19 W. South Temple, Suite 200
Salt Lake City, UT 84101-1503

PH: (801) 532-3400
(800) 225-7374
FAX: (801) 532-3202
ON-LINE DATABASE
Start-Up Fee: $1,797.00
Cost: $227/month plus exchange fees

Complete turn-key trading system. Super quote page that allows the trader to view all symbol information transmitted by BMI; volume, price and news alerts; detailed weather maps and business and financial graphs; display of last eight ticks, portfolio manager.

AUDIENCE: Individual, Professional	RISK LEVEL: Aggressive
TOPICS: Futures/Commodities	

Market Newsalert

Comtex Scientific Corporation
911 Hope Street
Stamford, CT 06907

PH: (203) 358-0007
(800) 624-5089
FAX: (203) 358-0236
Access Fees: Call for Costs

Gives background and news information on the AMEX, NYSE, NASDAQ, SEC filings, pink sheet companies, stock offerings, and press releases. The news is given by industry, company, and business activity.

AUDIENCE: Individual, Professional   RISK LEVEL: Moderate, Aggressive
TOPICS: Stocks

Market Newsalert Online/Fax

Comtex Scientific Corporation
911 Hope St.
P.O. Box 4838
Stamford, CT 06907

PH: (203) 358-0007
(800) 624-5089
FAX: (203) 358-0236
ON-LINE DATABASE
Access Fees: Call for Cost

Provides business information and news on companies traded on the American, New York, and NASDAQ over-the-counter exchanges and some Pink Sheet Companies which is continuously updated throughout the day.

AUDIENCE: Individual, Professional   RISK LEVEL: Moderate, Aggressive
TOPICS: Stocks

Market Plus (Level 2)/Market Plus (Level 3)

F2S Enterprises
P.O. Box 1011
LaPorte, TX 77572-1011

PH: (713) 471-7998
FAX: (713) 471-7220
SOFTWARE
Cost: $115, $145 extended version

There are three dozen technical charting tools that include: Wilders RSI, Williams %R, moving averages, exponential moving averages, Bollinger bands, Fibonacci studies, Andrews method, and trading bands. Calculate stock splits/dividend adjustments.

AUDIENCE: Professional   RISK LEVEL: Aggressive
TOPICS: Stocks, Futures/Commodities

Market Pro 1.3

Reinhart Investment Management
1250 Oakmead Parkway
Suite 210
Sunnyvale, CA 94087

PH: (408) 738-2311
SOFTWARE
Cost: $4,875

Sophisticated program calculates RSI, MACD, automated Fibonacci, trendlines, envelopes, and Babson and Andrews indicators. User can develop and implement automated trading system using Babson and Andrews lines. Intraday and daily trading.

AUDIENCE: Individual, Professional   RISK LEVEL: Aggressive
TOPICS: Stocks, Options, Futures/Commodities

Market Profile® Liquidity DataBank®

Chicago Board of Trade
(CBOT)/Information Systems &
Telecommunications Group
141 W. Jackson Blvd.
Chicago, IL 60604

PH: (312) 435-3732
ON-LINE DATABASE
Access Fees: Call for Costs

Information of price, time, and value of all commodities, securities, and currency futures traded in the United States and selected futures traded on foreign exchanges. It also provides highest and lowest prices, open and close prices.

AUDIENCE: Individual, Professional   RISK LEVEL: Aggressive
TOPICS: Stocks, Options, Futures/Commodities

Market Scan Plus - Investors Package

Globe Information Services
444 Front Street West
Toronto, Ontario, Canada M5V 259

PH: (416) 585-5250
(800) 456-9190
FAX: (416) 585-5249
ON-LINE DATABASE
Cost: $99.00

5 year listing of price, volume, dividend, and earnings data for most North American exchanges. Index, commodity, futures, options, stock and bond data. Financial statements, news articles, performance data and profile for 2,500 Canadian companies.

AUDIENCE: Individual, Professional   RISK LEVEL: Moderate, Aggressive
TOPICS: Bonds, Stocks, Options, Futures/Commodities

Market Screen

Market Guide, Inc.
49 Glen Head Road
Glen Head, NY 11545

PH: (516) 759-1253
SOFTWARE
Cost: $3,599.00 a year updated on a
  weekly basis diskette

Market Guide's analytic software can be used to search the database of 6,700 U.S. and foreign public companies for companies that fit a given profile. Design the screening criteria for stock selection, then create reports for printing or downloading.

AUDIENCE: Individual, Professional   RISK LEVEL: Moderate, Aggressive
TOPICS: Stocks

Market Statistics Data Base (MARSTAT)

CSI Data Retrieval Service
200 W. Palmetto Park Road
Boca Raton, FL 33432

PH: (800) 274-4727
(407) 392-8663
FAX: (407) 392-1379
SOFTWARE
Compatibility: IBM or compatibles
Cost: $490.00

Covers stocks, commodities, and mutual funds. Historical data base. Holds a multitude of financial data which supports the specific interests of commodity and stock traders. Includes Perpetual Contracts and Perpetual Indices.

AUDIENCE: Individual, Professional   RISK LEVEL: Aggressive
TOPICS: Stocks, Options, Futures/Commodities

Market Strategist

Hamilton Software, Inc.
6432 E. Mineral Place
Englewood, CO 80112

PH: (800) 733-9607
(303) 795-5572
SOFTWARE
Cost: $295.00

Design allows user to use 7 years of S&P 100 index historical stock market data to develop and test rules or system for actual stock trading. Trading system performance can be graphed beside the S&P 500 index. Technical analysis and fundamental trading criteria.

AUDIENCE: Individual	RISK LEVEL: Moderate, Aggressive
TOPICS: Stocks, Investment Planning	

Market Strategist 100, The

Hamilton Software, Inc.
6432 East Mineral Place
Englewood, CO 80112

PH: (800) 733-9607
(303) 770-9607
SOFTWARE
Cost: $79.00

A 7-year historical database of S&P 100 stocks and industry sectors with full charting and export features.

AUDIENCE: Individual, Professional	RISK LEVEL: Moderate, Aggressive
TOPICS: Stocks	

Market Timer

Dynacomp, Inc.
178 Phillips Road
Webster, NY 14580

PH: (800) 828-6772
SOFTWARE
Cost: $119.95

Technical analysis and statistics provide the investor with the necessary buy/sell signals based on trend analysis of Value Line composite index. Performance testing of market trends, including a daily 10 year history of the Value Line Composite Index.

AUDIENCE: Individual, Professional	RISK LEVEL: Moderate, Aggressive
TOPICS: Stocks	

Market Timing Utility

Hughes Financial Services
P.O. Box 1244
Nashua, NH 03061-1244

PH: (603) 598-4676
FAX: (603) 598-4676
SOFTWARE
Cost: $59.00

A spreadsheet template that works with Advanced Total Investor to calculate and display market indexes. Thirteen indicators: McClellan Oscillator, Summation Index, A/D Ratio, A/D Line, A/D Differential, STIX, breadth thrust, A/D volume ratio, and more.

AUDIENCE: Professional	RISK LEVEL: Moderate, Aggressive
TOPICS: Stocks, Options	

Market Watch

FNN Data Broadcasting Corp.
1900 S. Norfolk Street
San Mateo, CA 94403

PH: (800) 367-4670
ON-LINE DATABASE
Cost: $99.00. Basic monthly charge
  $30.00, $180.00 real time

Covers stocks, commodities, and options. Works off existing TV cable giving a choice of real-time or 15 minute delayed quotes that are second to none in accuracy and reliability. 25,000 stocks, options, futures and commodities from all the major exchanges.

AUDIENCE: Individual, Professional   RISK LEVEL: Moderate, Aggressive
TOPICS: Stocks, Options, Futures/Commodities

Market Watch

Hamilton Software, Inc.
6432 E. Mineral Place
Englewood, CO 80112

PH: (800) 733-9607
(303) 795-5572
SOFTWARE
Cost: $99.00

Compare and evaluate stocks, options, commodities, money market funds, and indexes. Calculate annualized yields, price movement, price trends, hi/lo close volumes, candlesticks, moving averages, and evaluates performance of securities or portfolios.

AUDIENCE: Individual   RISK LEVEL: Moderate, Aggressive
TOPICS: Stocks, Options, Futures/Commodities

Market Window

F.B.S. Systems
P.O. Drawer 248
Aledo, IL 61231

PH: (309) 582-5628
SOFTWARE
Cost: Contact Vendor

Features include automatic file update and chart generation, chart file and directory, price interrogation, 200M, frame, trendlines, channels, percentage mode, moving averages, volume open interest and cycle finder.

AUDIENCE: Individual, Professional   RISK LEVEL: Moderate, Aggressive
TOPICS: Stocks, Options, Futures/Commodities

Market-By-Price

The Toronto Stock Exchange
The Exchange Tower, Z
1st Canadian Place
Toronto, Canada M5X1J2

PH: (800) 387-1010
(416) 941-0843
FAX: (416) 947-4727
Monthly charge from $750.00

Covers Canadian stocks. Real time transmission of the central orderbook of the TSE. Delivers all committed, tradeable limit orders at the market and up to four price levels away for all stocks traded on the TSE (Toronto Stock Exchange).

AUDIENCE: Individual, Professional   RISK LEVEL: Moderate, Aggressive
TOPICS: Stocks

MarketBase

MarketBase, Inc.
P.O. Box 37, 388 Hillside Avenue
Needham Heights, MA 02194

PH: (800) 735-0700
(617) 449-8460
SOFTWARE
Cost: $2,300 with weekly updates

Covers stocks. Analysis and database system that finds stocks you believe offer the best investment opportunity. Provides data of unsurpassed accuracy directly from annual reports and the latest company SEC filings on about 5,800 stocks.

AUDIENCE: Individual, Professional   RISK LEVEL: Moderate, Aggressive
TOPICS: Stocks

Marketedge

SASI Software Corp.
P.O. Box 457
Sherwood, OR 97140

PH: (503) 625-5384
SOFTWARE
Cost: $39.00

Focus on the timing of the overall market to identify major tops and bottoms. Market Breadth data (advances, declines, volume) is integrated into a Master Breadth Index. Stochastics, relative strength index, and Bollinger Bands. Menus and full color graphs.

AUDIENCE: Conservative   RISK LEVEL: Moderate, Aggressive
TOPICS: Bonds, Mutual Funds, Stocks, Options, Futures/Commodities

MarketFax Charting Stock Selection System

Faxtel Information Systems, Ltd.
133 Richmond Street West, Suite 405
Toronto, ON, Canada M5H 2L3

PH: (416) 365-1728
FAX: (416) 364-6599
ON-LINE DATABASE
Cost: $125/month plus
   communications

An electronic stock picking systems that filters out investment candidates by user specific multiple criteria. The results are delivered in chart or ASCII format. It delivers 150 charts per hour to user's hard disk or personal computer.

AUDIENCE: Individual, Professional   RISK LEVEL: Moderate, Aggressive
TOPICS: Stocks

Marketview - Realtick III for Windows

Marketview Software, Inc.
14 East Jackson Blvd.
Suite 1220
Chicago, IL 60604

PH: (312) 786-0110
FAX: (312) 939-8289
ON-LINE DATABASE
Cost: $495/month plus exchange
   fees.

Combines real-time data with software which gives a graphic real-time market monitoring system. High resolutions color graphics. Interfaces with most major data feeds such as S&P, Reuters, PC Quote, Knight-Ridder and Bonneville.

AUDIENCE: Individual, Professional   RISK LEVEL: Moderate, Aggressive
TOPICS: Stocks

Marstat - CSI Data Retrieval Service

Commodity Systems, Inc. (CSI)
200 W. Palmetto Park Road
Boca Raton, FL 33432

PH: (407) 392-8663
(800) 274-4727
FAX: (407) 392-1379
ON-LINE DATABASE
Access Fees: Call for Costs

End-of-day and historical information on all United States and most overseas futures and cash markets. AMEX, NYSE, NASDAQ, mutual funds, options, indices and money markets. Perpetual contract data arrange futures price history into a continuous time series.

AUDIENCE: Individual, Professional   RISK LEVEL: Aggressive
TOPICS: Stocks, Options, Futures/Commodities

Master Brain Pop Up, The

Decision Programming Corporation
807 Georgia Avenue
Suite 401
Silver Spring, MD 20910

PH: (301) 585-7121
SOFTWARE
Cost: $149.00

A Bond Calculator. Covers municipal bonds, government bonds. Handles live major types of fixed-income investments: Munis, Treasuries, Notes, Certificates and Discounts. Zero coupon securities including Accretion Schedules or Amortization Schedules.

AUDIENCE: Beginning, Individual, Professional   RISK LEVEL: Conservative
TOPICS: Bonds

Master Chartist

Robert Slade, Inc.
750 N. Freedom Blvd.
Suite 301-B
Provo, UT 84601

PH: (800) 433-4276 ext. 250
(801) 375-6847 ext. 250 (UT)
FAX: (801) 375-6847
Cost: $295.00 per year

Covers stocks, bonds (municipal, government, corporate, and foreign), mutual funds, commodities, and charts. A technical analysis service. Tracks stocks, commodities, options, cash and news.

AUDIENCE: Professional   RISK LEVEL: Aggressive
TOPICS: Stocks, Futures/Commodities

Matfund

Tempo Investment Products, Inc.
4102 Elm Court
Midland, MI 48642

PH: (517) 832-3148
SOFTWARE
Cost: $99, $50 with Market Action
   Timer

Menu-driven spreadsheet which provides data for the 20th Century Stock Mutual Funds: Balanced Investors, Gift Trust, Growth, Heritage, Ultra and Vision. Compares the relative performance of the mutual funds to the S&P indicating current relative strength.

AUDIENCE: Individual   RISK LEVEL: Moderate, Aggressive
TOPICS: Mutual Funds, Stocks, Futures/Commodities

MBS Analysis System

Financial Publishing Company
82 Brookline Avenue
Boston, MA 02215

PH: (617) 262-4040
SOFTWARE
Cost: $845.00 per month

Analyzes yields, prices and cash flows of agency mortgage-backed securities. Includes a database of all agency pools and is updated monthly. Available in three versions, GNMA-only, FNMA/FHLMC data and a complete version.

AUDIENCE: Individual, Professional   RISK LEVEL: Conservative, Moderate
TOPICS: Bonds

MBS/ABS Calculator

Bond-Tech, Inc.
P.O. Box 192
Englewood, OH 45322

PH: (513) 836-3991
FAX: (513) 836-1497
SOFTWARE
Cost: $75.00

Analytical tool for comparing the different MBS/ABS securities. Program evaluates dollar price, MBS/ABS yield, duration, modified duration semiannual equivalent yield, extension interest, and extension total. Help system, tutorial, and mouse support provided.

AUDIENCE: Individual, Professional   RISK LEVEL: Conservative, Moderate
TOPICS: Bonds

McClellan Oscillator Program

Foundation for the Study of Cycles
900 West Valley Road, Suite 502
Wayne, PA 19087

PH: (800) 477-0741
(714) 261-7261
FAX: (714) 261-1708
Cost: $450
SOFTWARE

Developed to use timing tools for the stock market. Graphically presents oscillator and summation index in issues and volume. Data can be viewed on screen from months to four years. Include 30 years of stock market data and nearly 20 years of volume data.

AUDIENCE: Individual, Professional   RISK LEVEL: Conservative, Moderate, Aggressive
TOPICS: Stocks

Media General Database Service

Medial General Financial Services
301 E. Grace St.
Richmond, VA 23219

PH: (804) 649-6587
(800) 446-7922
FAX: (804) 649-6097
ON-LINE DATABASE
Access Fees: Call for Costs

Statistical information on common stocks listed on AMEX, NYSE and NASDAQ National Market issues. Databases that track mutual funds, industries and the financial markets. Detailed income statement and balance sheet data, historical price and volume statistics.

AUDIENCE: Individual, Professional   RISK LEVEL: Moderate, Aggressive
TOPICS: Mutual Funds, Stocks

Media General Plus

Dialog Information Services, Inc.
3460 Hillview Avenue
Palo Alto, CA 94304

PH: (800) 334-2564
(415) 858-3810
FAX: (415) 858-7069
ON-LINE DATABASE
Cost: $45.00, $1.40 per minute or
$84.00 per hour

Provides detailed financial and stock price information on approximately 5,100 public companies. Covers all New York Stock Exchange and American Stock Exchange companies, plus all NASDAQ National Market System companies and selected OTC companies.

AUDIENCE: Individual, Professional	RISK LEVEL: Moderate, Aggressive
TOPICS: Stocks	

Media General Price And Volume History

Media General Financial Services
301 E. Grace St.
Richmond, VA 23219

PH: (804) 649-6587
(800) 446-7922
FAX: (804) 649-6097
ON-LINE DATABASE
Access Fees: Call for Costs

Fully adjusted price history available on 7,000 stocks, 60 industry groups and 32 major market indexes. Data available on a daily, weekly, monthly or quarterly basis.

AUDIENCE: Individual, Professional	RISK LEVEL: Moderate, Aggressive
TOPICS: Stocks	

Media General Screen & Select

Medial General Financial Services
301 E. Grace St.
Richmond, VA 23219

PH: (804) 649-6587
(800) 446-7922
FAX: (804) 649-6097
ON-LINE DATABASE
Access Fees: Call for Costs

Allows the user to customize data service by selecting desired data, desired population of companies, and any data-screening criteria.

AUDIENCE: Individual, Professional	RISK LEVEL: Moderate, Aggressive
TOPICS: Stocks	

Media General Standard Data Diskette

Medial General Financial Services
301 E. Grace St.
Richmond, VA 23219

PH: (804) 649-6587
(800) 446-7922
FAX: (804) 649-6097
ON-LINE DATABASE
Required @ $65/month; diskette
updated monthly.

A standard monthly diskette of vital financial data and performance statistics on publicly held companies. It contains basic data and broad company coverage for different kinds of quantitative analyses. It has a current file of 35 key data items.

AUDIENCE: Individual, Professional	RISK LEVEL: Moderate, Aggressive
TOPICS: Stocks	

Megatech Chart System

Knight-Ridder Financial Publishing
30 S. Wacker Drive, Suite 1820
Chicago, IL 60606

PH: (800) 526-3282
(312) 454-1801
FAX: (312) 454-0239
SOFTWARE
Cost: $170 plus $5 shipping &
    handling

Over 50 high-resolution technical studies can be customer charted on bar and line charts. Use daily, weekly, or monthly trends for charting purposes.

AUDIENCE: Individual   RISK LEVEL: Moderate, Aggressive
TOPICS: Stocks, Futures/Commodities

Megatech Chart System

Ret-Tech Software, Inc.
151 Deer Lane
Barrington, IL 60010

PH: (708) 382-3903
FAX: (708) 382-3906
SOFTWARE
Cost: $175.00

Program includes all of the ChartPro calculations plus user has unlimited banks of 30 preprogrammable 1 key screens. Up to 16 charts per screen. Prodigy support is included.

AUDIENCE: Individual, Professional   RISK LEVEL: Moderate, Aggressive
TOPICS: Stocks, Options, Futures/Commodities

MESA

Mesa
P.O. Box 1801
Goleta, CA 93116

PH: (800) 633-6375
(805) 969-6478
FAX: (805) 969-1358
SOFTWARE
Cost: $350.00

Program measures short-term cycles with a maximum entropy technique. Cycles are combines to form a prediction based on their continuation. Measured cycles can be displayed. Trend and cycle modes are identified by price action in relation to a trendline.

AUDIENCE: Individual, Professional   RISK LEVEL: Moderate, Aggressive
TOPICS: Bonds, Stocks, Futures/Commodities

MetaStock

Equis International
3950 South 700 E.
Suite 100
Salt Lake City, UT 84107

PH: (800) 882-3040
(801) 265-8886
FAX: (801) 265-3999
Cost: $349.00

Looks at stocks, bonds, mutual funds, options, and futures and studies the relationships between securities' price movements, past price, and volume. More than 75 preprogrammed technical indicators to analyze securities. Can display up to 50 charts simultaneously.

AUDIENCE: Individual, Professional   RISK LEVEL: Moderate, Aggressive
TOPICS: Bonds, Mutual Funds, Stocks, Options, Futures/Commodities

MetaStock RT Update

Equis International
3950 South 700 E.
Suite 100
Salt Lake City, UT 84107

PH: (800) 882-3040
(801) 265-8886
FAX: (801) 265-3999
SOFTWARE
Cost: $495.00

Provides all of MetaStock features and capabilities in real-time. User can track securities using tick charts, 1, 2, and 5 minute bars and more. Automatically updates and recalculates charts, formulas, and indicators in realtime as price information is received.

AUDIENCE: Beginning, Individual, Professional   RISK LEVEL: Moderate, Aggressive
TOPICS: Bonds, Mutual Funds, Stocks, Options, Futures/Commodities

MF Analysis

Spreadware
P.O. Box 4552
Palm Desert, CA 92261-4552

PH: (619) 347-2365
SOFTWARE
Cost: $14.95 for software

Mutual funds. Analyze mutual funds to determine the return on investment (ROI) and gain/loss you would experience if the position were to be liquidated. Keep a running analysis on a mutual fund investment, including tax basis cost, funds withdrawn, etc.

AUDIENCE: Beginning, Individual   RISK LEVEL: Moderate, Aggressive
TOPICS: Mutual Funds

Micro Box-Jenkins Forecasting

Dynacomp, Inc.
178 Phillips Road
Webster, NY 14580

PH: (800) 828-6772
SOFTWARE
Cost: $149.95

A time series forecasting system based on the Box-Jenkins methodology. User can proceed through data manipulation, analysis, graphics, and forecasting models for investment decisions.

AUDIENCE: Individual, Professional   RISK LEVEL: Moderate, Aggressive
TOPICS: Stocks, Options, Futures/Commodities

Microcomputer Bond Program

Dynacomp, Inc.
178 Phillips Road
Webster, NY 14580

PH: (800) 828-6772
SOFTWARE
Cost: $59.95

Uses bond analysis to estimate prices and yields of fixed-income securities and makes estimates about future direction.

AUDIENCE: Individual, Professional   RISK LEVEL: Conservative, Moderate
TOPICS: Bonds

Microcomputer Chart Program

Dynacomp, Inc.
178 Phillips Road
Webster, NY 14580

PH: (800) 828-6772
SOFTWARE
Cost: $59.95

Uses price charts, volume charts, smoothed volume lines, smoothed velocity line to perform technical analysis on stocks, indexes, and mutual funds.

AUDIENCE: Individual, Professional   RISK LEVEL: Moderate, Aggressive
TOPICS: Mutual Funds, Stocks

Microcomputer Stock Program

Dynacomp, Inc.
178 Phillips Road
Webster, NY 14580

PH: (800) 828-6772
SOFTWARE
Cost: $55.95

Autoregression price trend analysis establishes buy and sell timing signals for stocks. The only data required are weekly high, low and closing prices, and volume.

AUDIENCE: Individual, Professional   RISK LEVEL: Moderate, Aggressive
TOPICS: Stocks

Microsoft Excel

Microsoft Corporation
One Microsoft Way
Redmond, WA 98052

PH: (800) 426-9400
(206) 882-8080
FAX: (206) 936-7329
SOFTWARE
Cost: $495.00

Integrated spreadsheet, charting, and database program with multiple spreadsheet capability. Program can create new functions or use 131 built-in functions for bond evaluation. Includes 6 basic chart types which can be combined to produce over 50 charts.

AUDIENCE: Individual, Professional   RISK LEVEL: Conservative, Moderate
TOPICS: Bonds

MIRAT (formerly Moron)

Tools For Timing
11345 Highway 7, #499
Minnetonka, MN 55305

PH: (800) 325-1344
(612) 939-0076
FAX: (612) 938-1275
Cost: $250
SOFTWARE

A mechanical trading system based on the theory that the market moves in cycles defined by peaks in the number of new lows. Use only two indicators to determine investment strategy. Includes data from 1/1/1978 to day prior to shipping.

AUDIENCE: Beginning   RISK LEVEL: Moderate, Aggressive
TOPICS: Stocks, Futures/Commodities

MJK

MJK Associates
1885 Lundy Ave., #207B
San Jose, CA 95131-1835

PH: (408) 456-5000
FAX: (418) 456-0302
ON-LINE DATABASE
Cost: $35.00-$50.00

Is a time-sharing commodity data information service with daily futures and cash data for all major commodities. The system is available 24 hours a day, with local phone access in most U.S. cities and world capitals. Simulation, evaluation, optimization.

AUDIENCE: Individual	RISK LEVEL: Aggressive
TOPICS: Options, Futures/Commodities	

MMS Muni Market Analysis

MMS International
1301 Shoreway Rd.
Suite 300
Belmont, CA 94002

PH: (415) 595-0610
ON-LINE DATABASE
Access Fees: Call for Costs

A technical analysis of the municipal bond market. It updates information on how variables affect the bond market. Includes federal, economic, and Treasury calendars, with information to chart new issue bonds in the market from the most recent 30 days.

AUDIENCE: Individual, Professional	RISK LEVEL: Conservative, Moderate
TOPICS: Bonds	

Modelware

Teranet IA Incorporated
Suite 1106
700 West Pender St.
Vancouver, BC, Canada V6C 7G8

PH: (800) 667-2722
(604) 684-4226
FAX: (604) 684-2099
Cost: $495
SOFTWARE

Models any financial market or individual financial security, including the bond market and commodities. Predictive models. Select fundamental indicators, technical indicators or a mixture of the two. Recognizes complex non-linear patterns into tradeable information.

AUDIENCE: Individual, Professional	RISK LEVEL: Moderate, Aggressive
TOPICS: Mutual Funds, Stocks, Futures/Commodities	

Money Center

Knight-Ridder Financial (KRF)
75 Wall Street, 23rd floor
New York, NY 10005

PH: (800) 433-8930
(212) 269-1110
QUOTE SERVICE
Cost: $880.00, Basic monthly charge
$475.00

Covers stocks, commodities, and bonds (municipal and corporate). PC based service gives real time quotes plus financial news on all the securities you buy, sell or hedge. Create your own dynamic yield or price charts and spreads, download to Lotus spreadsheets and more.

AUDIENCE: Individual, Professional	RISK LEVEL: Moderate, Aggressive
TOPICS: Bonds, Stocks, Options, Futures/Commodities	

Money Data

Technical Data
11 Farnsworth St.
Boston, MA 02210

PH: (617) 345-2526
ON-LINE DATABASE
Access Fees: Call for Costs

Provides real-time information of the U.S. and Eurodollar money markets.

AUDIENCE: Individual, Professional	RISK LEVEL: Conservative, Moderate
TOPICS: Bonds	

Money Decisions

Dynacomp, Inc.
178 Phillips Road
Webster, NY 14580

PH: (800) 828-6772
SOFTWARE
Cost: $149.95

The interactive problem solving programs allow 70 investments, loans, business management, forecasting, and graphics to be used in investment decisions. A communications interface is provided along with 1 free hour of connect time to CompuServe.

AUDIENCE: Individual, Professional	RISK LEVEL: Moderate, Aggressive
TOPICS: All	

Money Machine

Bruce Gould
P.O. Box 16
Seattle, WA 98111

PH: NA
Textbook
Cost: $2,500
Technical Analysis, Fundamental
  Analysis

Manual of Bruce Gould, experienced futures and commodities trader, detailing a method of investing. Mr. Gould has authored 15 books including the Dow Jones-Irwin Guide to Commodities Trading. Calculations require 5 minutes per day for commodity followed.

AUDIENCE: Individual, Professional	RISK LEVEL: Aggressive
TOPICS: Stocks, Futures/Commodities	

Money Magazine Financial Information Center

Time, Inc.
Time-Life Bldg.
New York, NY 10020

PH: (212) 522-1212
ON-LINE DATABASE
On-line Availability: CompuServe
  Information Service
(MONEYMAG: $12.80/connect
  hour 1200 and 2400 baud);
  $22.80/connect hour (9600 baud)

Extensive information on mutual fund performance.

AUDIENCE: Individual	RISK LEVEL: Moderate, Aggressive
TOPICS: Mutual Funds	

Money Maker for Windows

Q-West Associates
13233 Black Mountain Road, #1-410
San Diego, CA 92129

PH: (800) 618-6618
FAX: (619) 484-8606
SOFTWARE
Cost: $499.00
Analysis Capability: Fundamental,
Bond, Futures, Options, Real Estate,
Portfolio Management, Financial
Planning

Two programs, Money Maker Analyzer & Money Maker Portfolio.
Money Market Analyzer does in-depth analysis on stocks, bonds,
options, real estate, mutual funds, and stocks. The portfolio section
is a bookkeeping tool that tracks the investments. Tables and charts.

AUDIENCE: Individual	RISK LEVEL: Conservative, Moderate, Aggressive
TOPICS: Bonds, Mutual Funds, Stocks	

Money Market Database

Interactive Data Corporation
95 Hayden Ave.
Lexington, MA 02173-9144

PH: (617) 863-8100
ON-LINE DATABASE
Access Fees: Call for Costs

Gives the daily market rates for money market instruments, along
with the direct government obligations, federal agency instruments,
and municipal instruments. Bank and interbank rates are given.
Contact: Beth VanderVleet, sales analyst.

AUDIENCE: Individual, Professional	RISK LEVEL: Conservative
TOPICS: Bonds	

Money Market Rates (MRATE)

Reuters Information Services
  (Canada) Ltd./Data Services Division
Exchange Tower, Suite 1900
2 First Canadial Place
Toronto, ON, Canada M5X 1E3

PH: (416) 364-5361
(800) 387-1588
FAX: (416) 364-0646
ON-LINE DATABASE
Access Fees: Call for Costs

Provides the money market rates for several countries around the
world. It includes treasury bills, certificates of deposit, banker's
acceptance, commercial paper, prime rates, dollar swaps, special
drawing rights, finance company paper, and trust company paper.

AUDIENCE: Individual, Professional	RISK LEVEL: Conservative
TOPICS: Bonds	

Money Markets Database

Interactive Data Corporation
95 Hayden Ave.
Lexington, MA 02173-9144

PH: (617) 863-8100

On-line Availability: Interactive
Data Corporation.
ON-LINE DATABASE
Access Fees: Call for Costs

Daily market rates that include certificates of deposit, banker's
acceptances, commercial paper, government obligations, federal
agency instruments, and municipal notes. Contact: Beth
VanderVleet, sales analyst.

AUDIENCE: Beginning, Individual, Professional	RISK LEVEL: Conservative
TOPICS: Bonds	

Money Watch

McCarthy, Crisanti & Maffei, Inc. (MCM)
Electronic Information Services
71 Broadway
New York, NY 10006

PH: (212) 509-5800
FAX: (214) 509-7389
ON-LINE DATABASE

Gives commentaries and analyses factors and developments affecting the U.S. money market. Provides current information, economic indicators as well as daily, weekly, monthly, and quarterly forecasts.

AUDIENCE: Individual, Professional	RISK LEVEL: Moderate, Aggressive
TOPICS: All	

Moneycenter

Dialog Information Services, Inc.
3460 Hillview Ave.
Palo Alto, CA 94304

PH: (415) 858-3785
(800) 334-2564
FAX: (415) 858-7069
ON-LINE DATABASE
Cost: $295 with $2.00/minute

News, quotes, and fixed pages. Domestic and international events affecting the markets. The quotes are real- time. The fixed pages are screens of information items such as mortgage-backed securities, economic indicators, credit markets, and energy prices.

AUDIENCE: Individual, Professional	RISK LEVEL: Moderate, Aggressive
TOPICS: All	

Moneyline

USA Today
1000 Wilson Blvd.
Arlington, VA 22229

PH: (900) 555-5555
(800) USA-0001
Cost: $.95 per minute
24 Hour service

Touchtone phone to access stock quotes, CD rates, interest calculations, updates on your personal investments and used car prices. Quotes are delayed 15 minutes during trading hours.

AUDIENCE: Beginning, Individual	RISK LEVEL: Conservative, Moderate, Aggressive
TOPICS: Bonds, Mutual Funds, Stocks	

Moody's Bond Information Database Service (BIDS)

Moody's Investor Service
99 Church Street
New York, NY 10007

PH: (800) 342-5647 ext 0435
(212) 553-0435
FAX: (212) 553-4700
Cost: $5,000.00/year

Covers corporate bonds. Accurate and authoritative information on over 10,000 U.S. corporate bond issues updated monthly. Includes bond ratings, coupon rates, maturity dates and more. Gives you immediate access to a world of comprehensive up-to-date information in a way that lets you sort, screen, and analyze debt issues by CUSIP, company name, issue name, Moody's ratings, coupon rate, maturity, interest dates or bond issue features. A vital source for any financial professional who needs immediate access to information about the corporate bond market.

AUDIENCE: Professional	RISK LEVEL: Conservative, Moderate
TOPICS: Bonds	

Moody's Corporate News - U. S.

Moody's Investors Service, Inc.
99 Church St.
New York, NY 10007

PH: (212) 553-0546
(800) 342-5647
FAX: (212) 553-4700
ON-LINE DATABASE
Access Fees: Call for Costs

Business and financial news on public and private U.S. corporations on topics of acquisitions, mergers, new products, labor relations, corporate financing actions, bankruptcy proceedings, and contracts.

AUDIENCE: Individual, Professional   RISK LEVEL: Moderate, Aggressive
TOPICS: All

Moody's Corporate Profiles

Moody's Investors Service, Inc.
99 Church St.
New York, NY 10007

PH: (212) 553-0546
(800) 342-5647
FAX: (212) 553-4700
ON-LINE DATABASE
Access Fees: Call for Costs

Financial information on publicly held U.S. companies. It also shows the most recent developments and corporate outlook for companies of high interest to investors.

AUDIENCE: Individual, Professional   RISK LEVEL: Conservative, Moderate,
TOPICS: Bonds, Stocks   Aggressive

Moody's Municipal Network

Moody's Investors Service, Inc.
99 Church St.
New York, NY 10007

PH: (212) 553-0546
(800) 342-5647
FAX: (212) 553-4700
ON-LINE DATABASE
Access Fees: Call for Costs

Municipal bond and note ratings and debt issues.

AUDIENCE: Individual, Professional   RISK LEVEL: Conservative
TOPICS: Bonds

Morgan Stanley Capital International Indices

DRI/McGraw-Hill
Data Products Division
24 Hartwell Ave.
Lexington, MA 02173

PH: (617) 863-5100
ON-LINE DATABASE

Equity indexes for industries in energy, materials, capital equipment, consumer goods, services and finance sectors in major industrialized countries worldwide. Price indexes in local currency and U.S. dollars which includes return and total return net with dividends.

AUDIENCE: Individual, Professional   RISK LEVEL: Moderate, Aggressive
TOPICS: All

Morningstar Mutual Funds On Floppy

Morningstar
53 West Jackson Blvd.
Chicago, IL 60604

PH: (312) 427-1985
(800) 876-5005
FAX: (312) 427-9215
Cost: $45/one-time diskette,
  $95/year for quarterly updates,
  $185/year for monthly updates

Gives fundamental data on mutual funds. It allows you to screen and rank more than 90 fields of information. OnFloppy also allows users to produce customized mutual-fund reports and performance graphs. On-line help is available and technical support is free.

AUDIENCE: Beginning, Individual   RISK LEVEL: Moderate, Aggressive
TOPICS: Mutual Funds

Morningstar Mutual Funds Ondisc

Morningstar
53 West Jackson Blvd.
Chicago, IL 60604

PH: (800) 876-5005
FAX: (312) 427-9215
ON-LINE DATABASE
Cost: $295/year for annual update,
$495/year for quarterly updates,
$795/year for monthly updates

CD-ROM based software program/information service to compare, analyze and track mutual funds and produce customized reports and graphs. Over 160 fields of information for each mutual fund and dates back 1976. Search, rank, average, graph and print.

AUDIENCE: Beginning, Individual   RISK LEVEL: Moderate, Aggressive
TOPICS: Mutual Funds

Mortgage-Backed Securities

Interactive Data Corporation
95 Hayden Ave.
Lexington, MA 02173-9144

PH: (617) 863-8100
ON-LINE DATABASE
Access Fees: Call for Costs

Information on government mortgages.

AUDIENCE: Individual, Professional   RISK LEVEL: Conservative, Moderate
TOPICS: Bonds

Mortgage Data

Technical Data
11 Farnsworth St.
Boston, MA 02210

PH: (617) 345-2526
ON-LINE DATABASE
Access Fees: Call for Costs

Provides real-time financial data, analyses, and trading recommendations for U.S. mortgage-backed securities.

AUDIENCE: Individual, Professional   RISK LEVEL: Conservative, Moderate
TOPICS: Bonds

Mortgage-Backed Securities

Interactive Data Corporation
95 Hayden Ave.
Lexington, MA 02173-9144

PH: (617) 863-8100
Contact: Beth VanderVleet, Sales Analyst
ON-LINE DATABASE
Access Fees: Call for Costs

Monthly time series of government mortgages from pools provided by the Government National Mortgage Association, Fannie Mae, and Freddie Mac. Also gives detailed information on each pool.

AUDIENCE: Individual, Professional   RISK LEVEL: Conservative, Moderate
TOPICS: Bonds

MSS Equity Market Analysis (EMA)

MMS International
1301 Shoreway Rd.
Suite 300
Belmont, CA 94002

PH: (415) 595-0610
ON-LINE DATABASE
Cost: $195 per month
On-line Availability: Bloomberg Financial Markets

On-line analysis of fundamental factors that directly affect the equity market. Also provides monthly financial indicators and a schedule of events and data releases.

AUDIENCE: Individual, Professional   RISK LEVEL: Moderate, Aggressive
TOPICS: Stocks, Options, Futures/Commodities

Multbj Multivariable Box-Jenkins

Lincoln Systems Corp.
P.O. Box 391
Wesford, MA 01886

PH: (508) 692-3910
SOFTWARE
Cost: $250

Fundamental analysis provides computations and graphics based upon the MARMA model forecasts. Identifying types of terms with a 95% confidence level are calculated for dependent variables based on past values or the ARMA model.

AUDIENCE: Professional   RISK LEVEL: Moderate, Aggressive
TOPICS: All

Mutual Fund Composite Worksheet

Village Software
186 Lincoln Street
Boston, MA 02111

PH: (800) 724-9332
(617) 695-9332
FAX: (617) 695-1935
Cost: $90
SOFTWARE

Lotus 1-2-3 template designed to calculate switch signals for growth mutual funds. Signals are based on 39 week moving averages of DJIA, DJTA and a composite of 5 mutual funds. Graphs of price and moving averages and relative strengths are displayed.

AUDIENCE: Individual   RISK LEVEL: Moderate, Aggressive
TOPICS: Mutual Funds

Mutual Fund Decision Aide

V.A. Denslow & Associates
4151 Woodland Avenue
Western Springs, IL 60558

PH: (708) 246-3365
FAX: (708) 246-3365
SOFTWARE
Cost: $49.00
Analysis Capability: Portfolio
Management, Fundamental Analysis,
Spreadsheets

Evaluates fund performance using available data. Calculates up to 12 past years to current date. Gives total return and distribution yield for each year on the same bases. Growth volatility and trends in performance for recent years can be calculated. Ranks funds.

AUDIENCE: Beginning, Individual	RISK LEVEL: Moderate, Aggressive
TOPICS: Mutual Funds	

Mutual Fund Edge

Emerging Market Technologies, Inc.
1230 Johnson Ferry Road, Suite F-1
Marietta, GA 30068

PH: (404) 973-2300
FAX: (404) 973-3003
SOFTWARE
Cost: $265

Add on product to Telescan Analyzer/Edge from Emerging Market Technologies. Allows searches on mutual funds.

AUDIENCE: Beginning, Individual	RISK LEVEL: Moderate, Aggressive
TOPICS: Mutual Funds	

Mutual Fund Investor

American River Software
1523 Kingsford Drive
Carmichael, CA 95608

PH: (916) 483-1600
SOFTWARE
Cost: $295

Closely monitor performance of up to 104 funds and other securities as well as client portfolio tracking. Several thousand client portfolios can be monitored with reporting of current portfolio value, share balance, internal rate of return, cross referencing.

AUDIENCE: Professional	RISK LEVEL: Moderate, Aggressive
TOPICS: Mutual Funds	

Mutual Fund Manager

Denver Data, Inc.
9785 Maroon Drive, Meridian One
Suite G-126
Englewood, CO 80112

PH: (303) 790-7327
SOFTWARE
Cost: $49

Portfolio management and technical analysis to monitor and track any size mutual fund or money market portfolio. Tracks all purchases, redemptions and distributions, profit/loss, percentage change for each fund, beta, and moving averages. Generates bar and graph line performance charts.

AUDIENCE: Individual, Professional	RISK LEVEL: Conservative, Moderate, Aggressive
TOPICS: Mutual Funds	

Mutual Fund Reinvestment

Heizer Software
P.O. Box 232019
Pleasant Hill, CA 94523

PH: (800) 888-7667
(510) 943-7667
FAX: (510) 943-6882
Cost: $15.00
SOFTWARE

Provides mutual fund record keeping when earnings are reinvested. Calculates numbers of shares, capital gains, total investment, average share price, growth rate, and more. Excel or Works required.

AUDIENCE: Beginning	RISK LEVEL: Moderate, Aggressive
TOPICS: Mutual Funds	

Mutual Fund Selector

Village Software
186 Lincoln Street
Boston, MA 02111

PH: (800) 724-9332
(617) 695-9332
FAX: (617) 695-1935
Cost: $59
SOFTWARE

Calculates after-tax, after-load fee and other compounded returns. Allows user to compare investment with DJIA and S&P 500. Compare growth, volatility, trends, etc. with program features.

AUDIENCE: Beginning, Individual	RISK LEVEL: Moderate, Aggressive
TOPICS: Mutual Funds	

Mutual Fund/Corporate/Government/Agency Board

Interactive Data Corporation
95 Hayden Ave.
Lexington, MA 02173-9144

PH: (617) 863-8100
ON-LINE DATABASE
Access Fees: Call for Costs

Provides daily prices, evaluation and matrix prices on government, agency, and corporate bonds.

AUDIENCE: Individual, Professional	RISK LEVEL: Conservative, Moderate
TOPICS: Bonds, Mutual Funds	

Mutual Funds

Glove Information Services
444 Front St. W.
Toronto, ON, Canada M5V 2S9

PH: (416) 585-5250
(800) 268-9128
FAX: (416) 585-5249
ON-LINE DATABASE
Fundamental Analysis
Access Fees: Call for Costs

Information concerning Canadian mutual fund prices.

AUDIENCE: Beginning, Individual	RISK LEVEL: Moderate, Aggressive
TOPICS: Mutual Funds	

Mutual Funds Performance Report

Media General Financial Services, Inc. (MGFS)
301 E. Grace St.
Richmond, VA 23219

PH: (804) 649-6736
FAX: (804) 649-6097
ON-LINE DATABASE
Access Fees: Call for Costs

Performance rankings on mutual funds.

AUDIENCE: Beginning, Individual   **RISK LEVEL: Moderate, Aggressive**
TOPICS: Mutual Funds

N-Train

Scientific Consultant Services
20 Stagecoach Road
Selden, NY 11784

PH: (516) 696-3333
FAX: (516) 696-3333
SOFTWARE
Cost: $747
Technical Support: Phone, M-F

A neural network system that can be used to calculate fundamental or technical indicators of any security. Double precision math and user has full control over transfer functions, learning rules, etc. For user who plans to develop neural trading system.

AUDIENCE: Individual, Professional   **RISK LEVEL: Moderate, Aggressive**
TOPICS: Mutual Funds, Stocks, Options, Futures/Commodities

NAIC Stock Selection Guide

Heizer Software
P.O. Box 232019
Pleasant Hill, CA 94523

PH: (800) 888-7667
(510) 943-7667
FAX: (510) 943-6882
Cost: $30
SOFTWARE

Duplicates NAIC's Stock Selection guide and evaluates data for buy/sell/hold recommendations.

AUDIENCE: Beginning   **RISK LEVEL: Moderate, Aggressive**
TOPICS: Stocks

National Bond Summary

National Quotation Bureau, Inc.
150 Commerce Rd.
Cedar Grove, NJ 07009-1208

PH: (201) 239-6100
FAX: (201) 239-0080
Cost: $420/year

Covers the U.S. and Non U.S. bond markets. Information on over 56,000 securities that include both actively traded and inactive securities. Dividends (cash and stock), current prices, mergers, bankruptcies, defaults, calls par values, exchanges.

AUDIENCE: Individual, Professional   **RISK LEVEL: Conservative, Moderate**
TOPICS: Bonds

Nature's Pulse

Kasanjian Research
P.O. Box 4608
Blue Jay, CA 92317

PH: (909) 337-0816
SOFTWARE
Cost: $495.00

Program reads AIQ, CSI, TC 2000, DJ, MetaStock, Computrac, ASCII, MegaTech and other ASCII files without data conversion. Portfolio automatically scanned and future trend change dates displayed. Trendlines, MACD, charting and standard technical features.

AUDIENCE: Individual, Professional   RISK LEVEL: Moderate, Aggressive
TOPICS: Mutual Funds, Stocks, Options, Futures/Commodities

Navapatterns

Nava Development Corporation
251-A Portage Road
Lewiston, NY 14092-1710

PH: (716) 754-9254
FAX: (716) 754-1410
SOFTWARE
Cost: Contact Vendor

A trading pattern environment based on statistical patterns. User can establish buy/sell signals, project the high/low/close for the next 1-30 days on a chart.

AUDIENCE: Individual, Professional   RISK LEVEL: Aggressive
TOPICS: Stocks, Options, Futures/Commodities

Navigator

Genesis Financial Data Services
411 Woodman Court
Colorado Springs, CO 80919

PH: (800) 808-3282
(719) 260-6111
FAX: (719) 260-6113
SOFTWARE
Cost: $195.00
Technical Analysis

User can daily update and convert files from CSI, Compu Trac, MetaStock, ASCII, and Lotus 1-2-3 for stocks, commodity futures, and options. Cataloging, creating, deleting, printing, and viewing contracts for daily, weekly, monthly, or quarterly files.

AUDIENCE: Individual, Professional   RISK LEVEL: Moderate, Aggressive
TOPICS: Mutual Funds, Stocks, Options, Futures/Commodities

Neuraledge

Teranet IA Incorporated
Suite 1106
700 West Pender St.
Vancouver, BC, Canada V6C 7G8

PH: (800) 667-2722
(604) 684-4226
FAX: (604) 684-2099
Cost: $1,795.00
SOFTWARE

A neural network for recognizing patterns and an expert system for filtering trades and managing risk. A short-term position trading model designed to trade the S&P 500 and the NYSE index futures markets, as well as S&P 500 and OEX 100. Back testing capabilities.

AUDIENCE: Individual, Professional   RISK LEVEL: Moderate, Aggressive
TOPICS: Mutual Funds, Stocks, Futures/Commodities

Neuralyst for Excel

Epic Systems, Corp.
P.O. Box 277
Sierra Madre, CA 91025-0277

PH: (818) 355-2988
FAX: (818) 355-6162
SOFTWARE
Cost: $195.00

Uses technical analysis, spreadsheets, statistics, and neural network for stock, bonds, indexes, mutual funds, options, and futures. Will learn from historical examples and identify patterns and relationships that may lead to successful predictions.

AUDIENCE: Individual, Professional   RISK LEVEL: Moderate, Aggressive
TOPICS: All

News Real

Data Broadcasting Corporation
1900 S. Norfolk Street
San Mateo, CA 94403

PH: (800) 367-4670
FAX: (415) 571-8507
ON-LINE DATABASE
Cost: $49.00
Access Fees: $11.95/month database
fee plus on-line DJN/R charges.

It is an electronic news manager that gives customized business and financial news. Stories are obtained from The Wall Street Journal, Barron's, and Dow Jones News/Retrieval as well as some other financial news sources, inclusive of the last 90 days.

AUDIENCE: Individual, Professional   RISK LEVEL: Conservative, Moderate,
TOPICS: All   Aggressive

News-A-Tron Market Reports

News-a-tron Corp.
70 Washington St.
Suite 110
Salem, MA 01970

PH: (617) 744-4744
Cost: Contact Vendor

Market analyses and price quotations for commodities traded on the U.S. and foreign exchanges. It includes grains, livestock, precious metals, and petroleum products.

AUDIENCE: Individual, Professional   RISK LEVEL: Aggressive
TOPICS: Options, Futures/Commodities

Newsnet

Newsnet
945 Haverford Rd.
Bryn Mawr, PA 19010

PH: (215) 527-8030
(800) 952-0122
FAX: (215) 527-0338
ON-LINE DATABASE
Starter kit for $79.95
Current Quote Fees: $84/hour
($1.40/minute)

Specializes in the quick delivery of news and time-critical information. Provides finance related newsletters involving security and industry analysis, federally insured instruments yields, technical market studies and mutual fund investing.

AUDIENCE: Individual, Professional   RISK LEVEL: Conservative, Moderate, Aggressive
TOPICS: Bonds, Mutual Funds, Stocks, Futures/Commodities

Nexturn: Advanced

Scientific Consultant Services
20 Stagecoach Road
Selden, NY 11784

PH: (516) 696-3333
FAX: (516) 696-3333
SOFTWARE
Cost: $679.00

Artificial intelligence to forecast turning points in stock indexes and index futures. Displays candlestick chart format complete with Bollinger Bands, neural network, and other indicators. Menu-driven architecture, text-mode, and graphics reports.

AUDIENCE: Individual, Professional   RISK LEVEL: Aggressive
TOPICS: Mutual Funds, Stocks, Options, Futures/Commodities

Nightly Computer Hotline

Wall Street On-Line Publishing
P.O. Box 6
Riverdale, NY 10471-0006

PH: (212) 884-5408
ON-LINE DATABASE
Cost: $125.00 annual fee

Stocks, market timing, options and futures and commodities. Market predictions and recommendations. Updated daily - Sunday through Thursday.

AUDIENCE: Individual, Professional   RISK LEVEL: Aggressive
TOPICS: Stocks, Options, Futures/Commodities

NIS Fixed Income Research Environment

Northfield Information Services, Inc.
184 High Street, 5th Floor
Boston, MA 02110-3001

PH: (800) 262-6085
(617) 451-2222
FAX: (617) 451-2122
SOFTWARE
Cost: $23,000

Portfolio analytical and reporting tools to evaluate strategic investment decisions that conform to portfolio objectives. 3 integrated models: a "what-if" capability to model alternative yield environments, a data integrator that links users accounting system, and a reporting system for fixed-income portfolios.

AUDIENCE: Professional   RISK LEVEL: Conservative, Moderate
TOPICS: Bonds

NIS Macroeconomic Equity System

Northfield, Information Services, Inc.
184 High Street, 5th Floor
Boston, MA 02110-3001

PH: (800) 262-6085
(617) 451-2222
FAX: (617) 451-2122
SOFTWARE
Cost: $12,000

Stock portfolio management from a macroeconomic standpoint. Over 4,500 stocks analyzed to establish relationships between changes in the economy and individual stock performances. Inputs such as inflation, interest rates, and industrial production.

AUDIENCE: Professional   RISK LEVEL: Moderate, Aggressive
TOPICS: Stocks

NIS Performance Analysis System

Northfield, Information Services, Inc.
184 High Street, 5th Floor
Boston, MA 02110-3001

PH: (800) 262-6085
(617) 451-2222
FAX: (617) 451-2122
SOFTWARE
Cost: $16,000.00

11 fundamental factors provide evaluation of equity portfolio. Benchmark index of beta and 55 industry groups assist factors in identifying the impact of market timing, style, characteristics, industry, and stock selection.

AUDIENCE: Professional	RISK LEVEL: Moderate, Aggressive
TOPICS: Stocks	

Nite-Line

National Computer Network
1929 N. Harlem Ave.
Chicago, IL 60635

PH: (312) 622-6666
(800) 942-6262
FAX: (312) 622-6889
ON-LINE DATABASE
Cost: $30.00
Current Quote Fees: $9-$34/hour.

Financial database that provides closing market data and has 12 years of historical data on all U.S. and some Canadian exchanges on commodity futures, futures options, stock options, stocks, bonds and mutual funds.

AUDIENCE: Individual, Professional	RISK LEVEL: Moderate, Aggressive
TOPICS: Options, Futures/Commodities	

OECD Main Economic Indicators

Estima
1800 Sherman Ave.
Suite 612
Evanston, IL 60201

PH: (708) 864-8772
(800) 822-8038
FAX: (708) 864-6221
ON-LINE DATABASE
Cost: $600-$2,100/year

Provides a compilation of macroeconomic data on major Western economies. GNP, industrial production, money, stock, price indexes, principal interest rates, unemployment, exchange rate. Most of the data go back to 1960. A full set has data on 25 countries.

AUDIENCE: Individual, Professional	RISK LEVEL: Moderate, Aggressive
TOPICS: All	

OEX/SPX/DJIA Expert System

Wall Street On-Line Publishing
P.O. Box 6
Riverdale, NY 10471-0006

PH: (718) 884-5408
FAX: (718) 543-2117
SOFTWARE
Cost: $100.00

Disk has formulas for technical indicators built-in with the disk data that provides user with the historical data for the index. User enters high/low close of the index and use one key to bring up indicators. Buy/sell signals to determine when buy/sell is present.

AUDIENCE: Individual, Professional	RISK LEVEL: Aggressive
TOPICS: Stocks, Options, Futures/Commodities	

Omninews

Comtex Scientific Corp.
911 Hope Street
Stamford, CT 06907

PH: (203) 358-0007
(800) 624-5089
FAX: (203) 358-0236
ON-LINE DATABASE
Access Fees: Call for Costs

Information from over 12 major international news wires, the SEC, NASD, and other specialized sources. It gives real-time coverage of corporate, political, economic and market developments along with SEC filings by publicly traded companies.

AUDIENCE: Individual, Professional   RISK LEVEL: Moderate, Aggressive
TOPICS: All

On-Line Database

Duff & Phelps Equity Ideas
Duff & Phelps, Inc.
55 E. Monroe St.
Suite 4000
Chicago, IL 60603

PH: (312) 263-2610
ON-LINE DATABASE
Access Fees: Call for Costs

Gives descriptive and financial information on 700 companies and 60 industry sectors which include financial data, stocks, price ranges, debt-to-equity ratio, current and projected earnings, dividends, and quarterly earnings-per-share (EPS) data.

AUDIENCE: Individual, Professional   RISK LEVEL: Moderate, Aggressive
TOPICS: Bonds, Stocks

One Day At A Time

Trend Research, Ltd.
5615 McLeansville Road
McLeansville, NC 27301

PH: (919) 292-1402
FAX: (919) 292-0914
SOFTWARE
Cost: $395.00

Technical analysis features RSI, DMI, trading volatility index, commodity selection index, ADXR, ADX and the parabolic system, MACD, Fibonacci retracement lines, Bollinger bands, commodity channel index, 3 simple and 3 exponential moving averages and more.

AUDIENCE: Individual, Professional   RISK LEVEL: Moderate, Aggressive
TOPICS: Stocks, Options, Futures/Commodities

One Source

One Source Information Services, Inc.
150 Cambridge Parkway
Cambridge, MA 02140

PH: (617) 441-7000
(800) 554-5501
FAX: (617) 441-7058
ON-LINE DATABASE
Access Fees: Call for Costs

Business and financial information products delivered on CD-ROM. Allows the user to organize, analyze and disseminate information. The CD/Investment product line provides U.S. and international financial information on companies, stocks and financial issues.

AUDIENCE: Individual, Professional   RISK LEVEL: Conservative, Moderate,
TOPICS: All   Aggressive

Option Evaluator

Pumpkin Software
P.O. Box 4417
Chicago, IL 60680

PH: (312) 685-6677
FAX: (312) 685-6677
SOFTWARE
Cost: $129.00

Program calculates fair market value, volatility, delta, theta, vega for all futures and stock options. Produces 2 option matrixes for predicting future value over underlying strike prices. Optional graphics module can predict the implied volatility levels.

AUDIENCE: Individual, Professional   RISK LEVEL: Aggressive
TOPICS: Stocks, Futures/Commodities

Option Master

Institute for Options Research, Inc.
P.O. Box 6586
Lake Tahoe, NV 89449

PH: (800) 334-0854 x 840
(702) 588-3590
FAX: (702) 588-8481
SOFTWARE
Cost: $89.00

User can measure the theoretical value of options and the profitability when buying, writing or entering an option strategy. Program can determine the fair value of any stock, index, or commodity. Does not require access to database.

AUDIENCE: Beginning, Individual   RISK LEVEL: Aggressive
TOPICS: Options

Option Pricing Model

Spreadware
P.O. Box 4552
Palm Desert, CA 92261-4552

PH: (619) 347-2365
SOFTWARE
Cost: $21.95

Spreadware Option Pricing Model is designed to estimate a call option's theoretical price based on the price that has been determined. Up to five comparative analyses of the option can be simultaneously conducted to determine the effects of a change.

AUDIENCE: Individual, Professional   RISK LEVEL: Aggressive
TOPICS: Options

Option Pro

Essex Trading Company, Ltd.
24 W. 500 Maple Avenue, Suite 108
Naperville, IL 60540

PH: (800) 726-2140
(708) 416-3530
FAX: (708) 416-3558
SOFTWARE
Cost: $495.00 - $990.00

Specializes in Technical Analysis and Options Analysis for traders of stock and stock index options. Gives signals on OEX options. User can test different option trading models and also modify strategies to fit personal trading style.

AUDIENCE: Individual, Professional   RISK LEVEL: Aggressive
TOPICS: Options

Option Risk Management

Townsend Analytics, Ltd.
100 S. Wacker Drive, Suite 1506
Chicago, IL 60606

PH: (800) 827-0141
(312) 621-0141
FAX: (312) 621-0487
SOFTWARE
Cost: $189.00

Compute risk/return for option positions and spreads. Control parameters for interest rates, volatilities, volatility skew, vega range and market movement range. Analyzes all types of spreads, calculates profit/loss, premium value and technical risk measure.

AUDIENCE: Individual, Professional   RISK LEVEL: Aggressive
TOPICS: Stocks, Options, Futures/Commodities

Option Tools Deluxe

RK Microsystems
17365 Alvin Lane
Brookfield, WI 53045

PH: (414) 786-7333
SOFTWARE
Cost: $50.00

Uses Black-Sholes and Cox-Ross-Rubenstein binomial models to evaluate long/short positions, covered calls, option values, future fair market value, dollar gains/losses, hedge ratios, annualized investment yield and more.

AUDIENCE: Individual, Professional   RISK LEVEL: Aggressive
TOPICS: Options

Option Values and Arbitrage Software

Programmed Press
599 Arnold Road
W. Hempstead, NY 11552

PH: (516) 599-6527
SOFTWARE
Cost: $144.00

Options and futures valuation package. Evaluate price, risk, arbitrage and return on options and futures. Includes Black-Scholes, Bookbinder, Empirical P Models and Arbitrage.

AUDIENCE: Individual, Professional   RISK LEVEL: Aggressive
TOPICS: Options, Futures/Commodities

Option Vue IV

Option Vue Systems International,
Inc.
175 E. Hawthorne Parkway
Suite 180
Vernon Hills, Illinois 60061

PH: (800)733-6610
(708) 816-6610
Cost: $895.00 and $500.00/month

Covers options. On-line options analysis program. Fully equips you to trade every type of option and perform every type of options analysis ever conceived. Use it to test option strategies, find money making opportunities and avoid costly mistakes.

AUDIENCE: Individual, Professional   RISK LEVEL: Aggressive
TOPICS: Options, Futures/Commodities

Option-Warrant Combo

Heizer Software
P.O. Box 232019
Pleasant Hill, CA 94523

PH: (800) 888-7667
(510) 943-7667
FAX: (510) 943-6882
Cost: $49.00
SOFTWARE

Calculates theoretical value for up to 6 warrants and options. Black-Sholes model calculations help find most undervalued and overvalued option of any stock. Requires Excel.

AUDIENCE: Individual   RISK LEVEL: Aggressive
TOPICS: Options, Futures/Commodities

Optioncalc

Montgomery Investment Group
P.O. Box 508
Wayne, PA 19087-0508

PH: (215) 688-2508
FAX: (215) 688-5084
SOFTWARE
Black-Sholes Series $79.95,
Binomial Series $99.95

Option prices evaluated using binomial and Black-Sholes pricing methods. Calculate foreign exchange, commodities, European style options, and options with smooth cash flows or dividends. Binomial series calculates LEAPS, American style options.

AUDIENCE: Individual, Professional   RISK LEVEL: Aggressive
TOPICS: Options

Optionfind

Investor Services, Inc.
3367 S. Oneida Way, Suite 4B
Denver, CO 80224

PH: (303) 758-1696
FAX: (303) 753-8842
ON-LINE DATABASE
Cost: $300/month individual
contract: $450/month corporate
  contract

Search and find system using a live database to locate options trades that satisfy strategy/criteria. Employs the Black-Scholes mode, delta for options, theoretical and implied volatilities, random walk statistical model, last sale, open interest on options.

AUDIENCE: Individual, Professional   RISK LEVEL: Aggressive
TOPICS: Options

Optionomic Systems

Optionomics Corporation
2835 E. 3300 South, Suite 200
Salt Lake City, UT 84109

PH: (800) 255-3374
(801) 466-2111
FAX: (801) 466-7320
SOFTWARE
Cost: $4,200/yr

Real-time analyzing option strategies and a risk management tool on commodity futures and stock indexes. Quote systems with Signal, real-time option analysis that shows gamma, rho, vega, theta, implied volatility, etc. Strategy simulation. Plot volatility.

AUDIENCE: Professional   RISK LEVEL: Aggressive
TOPICS: Options, Futures/Commodities

Options - 80 Advanced Stock Option Analyzer

Patrick N. Everett Ph.D.
P.O. Box 471
Concord, MA 01742

PH: (508) 369-1589
Cost: $150.00 for program

Covers stocks with charts. Analyzes calls, puts, and spreads, does Black-Scholes modeling, and calculates market implied volatility. It plots annualized return on investment against expiration price of underlying stock, guiding the user to optimum investment.

AUDIENCE: Individual, Professional   RISK LEVEL: Aggressive
TOPICS: Options

Options Analysis ***

Dynacomp, Inc.
178 Phillips Road
Webster, NY 14580

PH: (800) 828-6772
SOFTWARE
Cost: $99.95

Uses the Black-Sholes formula in determining the value of the put and call options as a function of both stock price and time to expiration.

AUDIENCE: Individual, Professional   RISK LEVEL: Aggressive
TOPICS: Stocks, Options

Options And Arbitrage Software Package

Programmed Press
599 Arnold Road
West Hempstead, NY 11552

PH: (516) 599-6527
SOFTWARE
Cost: $144.00, plus shipping

Six option valuation models include: Black-Sholes, Stoll-Parkinson, bookbinder, empirical put and call models, stock index futures and arbitrage analysis.

AUDIENCE: Individual, Professional   RISK LEVEL: Aggressive
TOPICS: Stocks, Options, Futures/Commodities

Options Laboratory

Mantic Software Corporation
1523 Country Club Road
Fort Collins, CO 80524

PH: (800) 730-2919
(303) 224-1615
SOFTWARE
Cost: $129.95

Real or simulated prices to explore option strategies. Textbook accompanies interactive graphic learning software package. Options basics and strategies, conservative and speculative techniques help in analysis techniques for risk management.

AUDIENCE: Beginning, Individual   RISK LEVEL: Aggressive
TOPICS: Stocks, Options

Options Pro, Premium, And Extended Binomial Series

Montgomery Investment Group
P.O. Box 508
Wayne, PA 19087-0508

PH: (215) 688-2508
FAX: (215) 688-5084
SOFTWARE
Cost: Pro Series $395.00; Premium
Series $695.00

Allows theoretical calculations directly within Lotus 1-2-3 on implied volatilities, option prices, and sensitivity values, delta and gamma. 10 option models including Binomial, Eurodollar, Indexes, Leaps, Black, Garmon-Lohlhagen, Black-Scholes, and Adesi-Whaley.

AUDIENCE: Individual, Professional   RISK LEVEL: Aggressive
TOPICS: Stocks, Options, Futures/Commodities

Options Strategy Projections

Compu-Vest Software
545 Fairview Avenue
Glen Ellyn, IL 60137

PH: (708) 469-4437
SOFTWARE
Cost: $30.00

Project profit or loss from an option strategy at a closeout date. Options are calculated using the Black-Scholes method. 90 different option strategies and can calculate puts/calls, profit/loss at closeout, closeout a date with different strategies.

AUDIENCE: Individual, Professional   RISK LEVEL: Aggressive
TOPICS: Options

Options Valuation

Larry Rosen Co.
7008 Springdale Rd.
Louisville, KY 40241

PH: (502) 228-4343
FAX: (502) 228-4782
Cost: $89.00

Option values for (1) stocks and (2)futures (3) time spread or elapsed time; (4) average weighted life; (5) Macaulay duration; (6) modified duration; (7) spot rates and forward rates; (8) historic or future volatility and (9) implied volatility.

AUDIENCE: Individual, Professional   RISK LEVEL: Aggressive
TOPICS: Stocks, Options, Futures/Commodities

OTC Newsalert

Comtex Scientific Corp.
911 Hope Street
Stamford, CT 06907

PH: (203) 358-0007
(800) 624-5089
FAX: (203) 358-0236
ON-LINE DATABASE
Access Fees: Call for Costs

Gives up-to-the-minute news service on NASDAQ and Pink Sheet companies. It also has late breaking news about new products, joint ventures, SEC filings, IPOs, and earnings.

AUDIENCE: Individual, Professional   RISK LEVEL: Moderate, Aggressive
TOPICS: Stocks

OVM/Focus

Radix Research Limited
P.O. Box 91181
West Vancouver, BC, Canada
  V7V 3N6

PH: (604) 926-5308
FAX: (604) 925-2607
SOFTWARE
Cost: $399.00 (Canadian)

All the features of 20/20 Plus with option trading package and analysis updates. Valuation models, volatility screening, charting package, and universal option position worksheet, and Parkinson extreme volatility methods. Valuation matrix screen.

AUDIENCE: Individual, Professional   RISK LEVEL: Aggressive
TOPICS: Stocks, Options

Owl Personal Portfolio Manager

Otto-Williams, Ltd.
P.O. Box 794
Lanham, MD 20703-0794

PH: (301) 306-0409
SOFTWARE
Cost: $45, $55 with programmed
  disk

Fully integrated investment recordkeeping program for stock charting and technical analysis. Can keep up to 5,000 stocks, bonds, mutual funds, and savings accounts in up to 500 portfolios. "What-if " analysis capability. Customize 15 reports to include.

AUDIENCE: Beginning, Individual   RISK LEVEL: Moderate, Aggressive
TOPICS: Bonds, Mutual Funds, Stocks

Own-Write Model

Niche Software Products
P.O. Box 3574
Manassas, VA 22110

PH: (703) 368-8372
SOFTWARE
Cost: $50.00

Calculates exercise probabilities/return potentials for stock covered call writing. Determines options yield best for return at lowest risk, fair option price, expected returns, and graphs that show profit of stock. Graphs created by running B&S model.

AUDIENCE: Individual, Professional   RISK LEVEL: Moderate, Aggressive
TOPICS: Stocks, Options

Paradigm Options Database

Paradigm Trading Systems
985 University Ave., Suite 36
Los Gatos, CA 95030

PH: (415) 399-4385
ON-LINE DATABASE
Cost: $100/month

Gives delayed and historical data on stocks, indexes, options and futures with the information dating back 10 years. The data may be accessed by any computer, or Paradigm produces programs which access and analyze the data.

AUDIENCE: Individual, Professional   RISK LEVEL: Moderate, Aggressive
TOPICS: Stocks, Options, Futures/Commodities

Parity Plus

Partech Software Systems
2 Bryant Street
Suite 200
San Francisco, CA 94105

PH: (415) 546-9316
FAX: (415) 546-9319
SOFTWARE
Cost: $179

A stock charting and technical analysis program for Windows with more than 50 indicators. Chart types include high/low/close/bar chart, Japanese candlesticks, 12 types of points and figure charts, line charts, and histograms.

AUDIENCE: Individual, Professional   RISK LEVEL: Moderate, Aggressive
TOPICS: Mutual Funds, Stocks, Futures/Commodities

PC Chart Plus

Guru Systems, Ltd.
3873 Airport Way, Box 9754
Bellingham, WA 98227

PH: (604) 299-1010
FAX: (604) 299-1099
SOFTWARE
Cost: $160.00

Technical analysis program that combines charting, database, and telecommunications capabilities. Stock charts, graphing, moving averages, relative strength, RSI, candlesticks, Fibonacci, relative strength, alpha/beta, trendlines, volume, and more.

AUDIENCE: Individual, Professional   RISK LEVEL: Moderate, Aggressive
TOPICS: Mutual Funds, Stocks, Options, Futures/Commodities

PC Market Analyst

Computerized Investment Strategies
5252 Allstone Drive
Huntington Beach, CA 92649

PH: (800) 733-5565
(714) 846-9594
SOFTWARE
Cost: $95.00

Contains 12 technical analyses methods to analyze stock and commodity market investments. Program capabilities include: simple moving averages, weighted moving averages, exponential moving averages, stochastic, oscillator/momentum, lag-lead analysis, etc.

AUDIENCE: Individual, Professional   RISK LEVEL: Moderate, Aggressive
TOPICS: Stocks, Options, Futures/Commodities

PC Quote

PC Quote, Inc.
401 S. LaSalle St., Suite 1600
Chicago, IL 60605

PH: (312) 786-5400
(800) 225-5657
FAX: (312) 427-8607
ON-LINE DATABASE
Cost: $250.00 for self installation
Cost: $195.00/month

Delivers open, high, low, volume, last-sale, bid/ask quotations via satellite and modem from U.S. stock, option and commodity exchanges and Canadian stock exchanges. It also provides alerts, and financial news.

AUDIENCE: Beginning, Individual   RISK LEVEL: Moderate, Aggressive
TOPICS: Bonds, Mutual Funds, Stocks, Options, Futures/Commodities

PC Software

TLM, Inc.
420 Westchester Avenue
Port Chester, NY 10573

PH: (800) 451-1392
SOFTWARE
Cost: $89.00 plus $5.00 postage and handling

Investments covered include options and index futures. TLM's proprietary trading model uses the high, low, and close of the index daily and generates 2-4 trading signals per month for options and 2 signals per month for futures trading.

AUDIENCE: Individual, Professional   RISK LEVEL: Aggressive
TOPICS: Options, Futures/Commodities

Peerless Intermediate-Term Market Timing Package

Tiger Investment Software
P.O. Box 9491
San Diego, CA 92169

PH: (619) 459-8577
SOFTWARE
Cost: $275.00

A 200 page manual tracks and explains buy/sell signals between 1969-1992. Both major and minor signals appear automatically. Five years of back data provided. Daily manual updating can be performed.

AUDIENCE: Individual, Professional   RISK LEVEL: Moderate, Aggressive
TOPICS: Mutual Funds, Stocks, Futures/Commodities

Peerless Short-Term Market Timing Package

Tiger Investment Software
P.O. Box 9491
San Diego, CA 92169

PH: (619) 459-8577
SOFTWARE
Cost: $620.00

A 200 page manual shows how the best technical tools reliably call short-term (one week to one month) DJIA, OPX, S&P and NASDAQ market tops and bottoms. Back tested to 1972 gives historical reliability for intraday trading techniques.

AUDIENCE: Individual, Professional   RISK LEVEL: Moderate, Aggressive
TOPICS: Mutual Funds, Stocks, Futures/Commodities

Per % Sense

Ones & Zeros
708 W. Mt. Airy Avenue
Philadelphia, PA 19119

PH: (800) 882-2764
(215) 248-1010
FAX: (215) 248-1010
SOFTWARE
Cost: $99.95

Models for loan analysis, passbook savings, mortgage comparisons provided with this program. A calculation tool that analyzes IRRs for complex investments. Includes COLA-stepped payments and calculates the present value of a cash flow stream.

AUDIENCE: Beginning, Individual   RISK LEVEL: Conservative, Moderate,
TOPICS: Bonds, Mutual Funds, Stocks   Aggressive

Personal Analyst

Trendsetter Software
P.O. Box 6481
Santa Ana, CA 92706

PH: (800) 825-1852
(714) 547-5005
FAX: (714) 547-5063
Cost: $395
SOFTWARE

Market analysis program that features charting system for bar, Japanese candle, point and figure and line on demand. Daily, weekly, or monthly charts created with customer layouts with up to 9 charts per channel and 16 indicators per chart. Rank and sort.

AUDIENCE: Individual   RISK LEVEL: Aggressive
TOPICS: Mutual Funds, Stocks, Options, Futures/Commodities

Personal Computer Automatic Investment Management

Dynacomp, Inc.
178 Phillips Road
Webster, NY 14580

PH: (800) 828-6772
SOFTWARE
Cost: $149.95

Based on the Robert Lichello book, "How to Make $1,000,000 Automatically," the program calculates stock value, portfolio value, buy/sell, market orders and return on investment. Maintains current and historical records of transactions for evaluation.

AUDIENCE: Beginning, Individual	RISK LEVEL: Moderate, Aggressive
TOPICS: Stocks	

Personal Hotline

Trendsetter Software
P.O. Box 6481
Santa Ana, CA 92706

PH: (800) 825-1852
(714) 547-5005
FAX: (714) 547-5063
Cost: $595.00
SOFTWARE

Expert model lets user discern parameters for charts and when is the best time for buy/sell actions. Personal analyst features but has added investment signal sensitivity based on channel identification and chart pattern recognition. Tracks results.

AUDIENCE: Individual, Professional	RISK LEVEL: Moderate, Aggressive
TOPICS: Mutual Funds, Stocks, Options, Futures/Commodities	

Personal Market Analysis

Investment Software
543 CR 312
Ignacio, CO 81137

PH: (303) 884-4130
SOFTWARE
Cost: $149.00

Predefined indicators and user indicators can be set to calculate moving average convergence/divergence, relative strength index, stochastic oscillators. Several volume indicators, parabolic time/price system, and directional moving indicators. Charting.

AUDIENCE: Individual, Professional	RISK LEVEL: Moderate, Aggressive
TOPICS: Bonds, Mutual Funds, Stocks, Futures/Commodities	

Personal Portfolio Analyzer

Charles L. Pack
25303 La Loma Drive
Los Altos, CA 94022-4542

PH: (415) 949-0887
SOFTWARE
Cost: $44.95

Portfolio management, numerical analysis, and reporting on existing portfolio of stocks, bonds, mutual funds, and other types of securities. Realized and unrealized gains/losses, holding periods, yields, ROI, portfolio beta, and relative comparisons.

AUDIENCE: Beginning, Individual	RISK LEVEL: Moderate, Aggressive
TOPICS: Bonds, Mutual Funds, Stocks	

Personal Portfolio Manager

Abacus Software
5370 52nd Street S.E.
Grand Rapids, MI 49512

PH: (800) 451-4319
(616) 698-0330
FAX: (616) 698-0325
SOFTWARE
Cost: $150.00

Keeps track of stocks, bonds, options, futures, and mutual funds. Data input can be manual or automatic through DJN/R on-line service. Customize reports, use analysis requirements, and fix reports for gains/losses, tax liabilities, buy/sell alarms.

AUDIENCE: Beginning, Individual   RISK LEVEL: Moderate, Aggressive
TOPICS: Bonds, Mutual Funds, Stocks, Options, Futures/Commodities

Personal Portfolio Manager

Prodata, Inc.
12101 Menaul Boulevard, Northeast
Albuquerque, NM 87112

PH: (505) 294-1530
SOFTWARE
Cost: $49.95

Maintain multiple portfolios of stocks, bonds, options and money market funds. Performance reports include portfolio, individual stock, dividend, and performance versus set targets.

AUDIENCE: Beginning, Individual   RISK LEVEL: Conservative, Moderate,
TOPICS: Bonds, Mutual Funds, Stocks   Aggressive

Personal Stock Technician

RazorLogic Systems
P.O. Box 335
Morgan Hill, CA 95038

PH: (408) 778-0889
SOFTWARE
Cost: $99.50

Covers stocks, mutual funds. Technical analysis and stock market tracking system. Generates buy and sell signals based on established criteria.

AUDIENCE: Beginning, Individual   RISK LEVEL: Moderate, Aggressive
TOPICS: Bonds, Mutual Funds, Stocks

Personal Ticker Tape

Flexsoft
7172 Regional Street, #276
Dublin, CA 94568

PH: (510) 829-9733
FAX: (510) 829-9733
ON-LINE SERVICE
Cost: $75.00

Downloads daily closing quotes from CompuServe, DJN/R, and GEnie. Directly updates stock from MetaStock or MegaTech. Contains a historical data maintenance facility to modify files and color coded daily update screens.

AUDIENCE: Individual, Professional   RISK LEVEL: Moderate, Aggressive
TOPICS: Bonds, Mutual Funds, Stocks

Phase 3

Phase 3 Systems, Inc.
504 Totten Pond Road
Waltham, MA 02154

PH: (617) 466-9800
Access Fees: Call for Cost.

Tandem Non-stop Systems. Securities processing, stocks, and bonds (municipal, corporate, and government), mortgage backs, treasuries, zeroes. Phase 3 is a real-time, integrated securities processing system for the brokerage and banking community.

AUDIENCE: Professional   RISK LEVEL: Conservative, Moderate, Aggressive
TOPICS: Bonds, Stocks

PIMS Portfolio Information Management System

Atlantic Portfolio Analytics and
  Management, Inc.
201 E. Pine Street, Suite 600
Orlando, FL 32801

PH: (407) 843-7110 ext 333
FAX: (407) 843-7399
SOFTWARE
Cost: $25,000 multi-users $99,500

Covers asset-backed securities, stocks, futures/commodities, municipal and government bonds. A multi-user software system that documents and controls transactions and positions in actively managed portfolios of assets, liabilities, and hedges. PIMS.

AUDIENCE: Individual, Professional   RISK LEVEL: Conservative, Moderate, Aggressive
TOPICS: Bonds, Mutual Funds, Stocks, Futures/Commodities

Pisces MetaStock Export Utility

Pisces Software
P.O. Box 579-9171
Chicago, IL 60613

PH: (312) 281-7916
FAX: (312) 281-7916
ON-LINE DATABASE
Cost: $75.00

Export data to chart programs, spreadsheets or to other MetaStock directories. All export formats are under user's control and include volume conversion. Delimits fields with commas, spaces, or columns of text. Exports from daily, weekly, or monthly.

AUDIENCE: Individual, Professional   RISK LEVEL: Moderate, Aggressive
TOPICS: All

Platform Alert

Roberts-Slade, Inc.
619 N. 500 West
Provo, UT 84601

PH: (800) 433-4276
(801) 375-6850
FAX: (801) 373-2775
SOFTWARE
Cost: $125/month
Compatibility: DOS, Macintosh

Track stocks, commodities, and options. Includes numerous technical indicators, option analysis, and statistics. Includes 125 customized quote fields, baskets, news, and various alerts.

AUDIENCE: Individual, Professional   RISK LEVEL: Moderate, Aggressive
TOPICS: Mutual Funds, Stocks, Options, Futures/Commodities

Pocket Quote Pro

Telemet America, Inc.
325 First St.
Alexandria, VA 22314

PH: (703) 548-2042
(800) 368-2078
Cost: $395.00
Transmission: FM
Current Quote Fees: $27.50/month

It is a hand-held calculator size quote monitor. Gives direct access to real-time stock, index, options, and futures prices within 50 miles of almost 24 major metropolitan areas in the United States. It monitors 160 issues.

AUDIENCE: Individual, Professional   RISK LEVEL: Moderate, Aggressive
TOPICS: Mutual Funds, Stocks, Options, Futures/Commodities

Portfolio Accounting Management System (PAMS)

Information Resource Management,
  Inc.
1800 East Denison Road
Suite 100
Naperville, IL 60565

PH: (312) 369-5757
SOFTWARE
Cost: $5,000.00

Realtime information and reporting on security portfolios. Has many retrieval displays and parameter driven reporting. Provides reports and tax schedules.

AUDIENCE: Professional   RISK LEVEL: Conservative, Moderate, Aggressive
TOPICS: All

Portfolio Analyzer

Hamilton Software, Inc.
6432 East Mineral Place
Englewood, CO 80112

PH: (800) 733-9607
(303) 770-9607
SOFTWARE
Cost: $169.00

Provides maintenance and analysis of investment portfolios containing stocks, bonds, options, savings accounts, annuities, collectibles and others. Tracks performance of investments. Provides year-to-date tax liability and schedules B and D.

AUDIENCE: Beginning, Individual   RISK LEVEL: Conservative, Moderate, Aggressive
TOPICS: All

Portfolio Data Manager

Dynacomp, Inc.
178 Phillips Road
Webster, NY 14580

PH: (800) 828-6772
SOFTWARE
Cost: $149.95

Portfolio performance on stocks, bonds, and mutual funds can be recorded and monitored. Technical analysis includes trendlines, moving averages, momentum rate of change, acceleration curves, and relative strength graphs. Up to 10 years for any security.

AUDIENCE: Individual, Professional   RISK LEVEL: Moderate, Aggressive
TOPICS: Bonds, Mutual Funds, Stocks

Portfolio Decisions

Dynacomp, Inc.
178 Phillips Road
Webster, NY 14580

PH: (800) 828-6772
SOFTWARE
Cost: $149.95

Makes portfolio management easier by organizing, recording, and evaluating investments. Communicate through DJN/R or CompuServe facilities and automatic updating. Evaluates tax return interest, dividends, capital gains and losses, and monthly income forecasts.

AUDIENCE: Individual   **RISK LEVEL: Conservative, Moderate, Aggressive**
TOPICS: Bonds, Mutual Funds, Stocks

Portfolio Management

Dynacomp, Inc.
178 Phillips Road
Webster, NY 14580

PH: (800) 828-6772
SOFTWARE
Cost: $69.95

User defines investment categories for portfolio management. Program has sorting and plotting capabilities.

AUDIENCE: Beginning, Individual   **RISK LEVEL: Conservative, Moderate, Aggressive**
TOPICS: All

Portfolio Management

Spreadware
P.O. Box 4552
Palm Desert, CA 92261-4552

PH: (619) 347-2365
SOFTWARE
Cost: $24.95

Stocks, options and bonds. Designed to manage and analyze a personal portfolio. Record routine investment transactions, as well as analyze the position of the portfolio. Individual investments can be analyzed to determine the break-even price.

AUDIENCE: Beginning, Individual   **RISK LEVEL: Conservative, Moderate, Aggressive**
TOPICS: Bonds, Mutual Funds, Stocks

Portfolio Management System

Omni Software Systems, Inc.
702 N Ernest
Griffith, IN 46319

PH: (219) 924-3522
SOFTWARE
Cost: $150

User can manage up to 100 stocks in portfolio. Program provides reports and schedules, tracks due dates, dividends received and reinvested, and calculates long- and short-term gains/losses.

AUDIENCE: Beginning, Individual   **RISK LEVEL: Moderate, Aggressive**
TOPICS: Mutual Funds, Stocks

Portfolio Management System

SunGard Financial Systems, Inc.
1 Corporate Drive
Andover Corporate Center
Andover, MA 01810

PH: (508) 691-6000
SOFTWARE
Cost: $10,000.00- $200,000.00

On-line investment securities accounting package. Automates accounting functions and provides reporting for stocks, U.S. Treasury, municipal securities, variable rate, callable, mortgage backed securities, zero coupon bonds, repurchase agreements.

AUDIENCE: Professional   RISK LEVEL: Conservative, Moderate, Aggressive
TOPICS: All

Portfolio Manager Plus

DIS Software
1751 W. Country Road B
Suite 105
Roseville, MN 55113

PH: (800) 333-8776
(612) 633-2300
FAX: (612) 633-8678
SOFTWARE
Cost: $49.95

Allows user to track stocks, bonds, and other securities. Functions include buying and selling of securities, stock splits, short sales, dividends, and interest payments. Updates user's securities through modem using DJN/R, CompuServe, DTN, and Prodigy.

AUDIENCE: Individual, Professional   RISK LEVEL: Conservative, Moderate,
TOPICS: Bonds, Mutual Funds, Stocks, Options   Aggressive

Portfolio Selection

IBC/Donoghue
290 Eliot Street, P.O. Box 9104
Ashland, MA 01721-9104

PH: (800) 343-5413
FAX: (508) 881-0982
SOFTWARE
Cost: $7,975.00
Analysis Capabilities: Technical,
  Composition, Financial Planning,
  Fundamental Screening, Technical
  Screening, Spreadsheets, Statistics

Monitors and compares one, or several, portfolios to specified money markets. Creates money fund data. Graphs and charts can display market trends vs. portfolio performance. Fund type, portfolio composition, compound yields, expense ratios, asset size.

AUDIENCE: Professional   RISK LEVEL: Conservative
TOPICS: Bonds

Portfolio Spreadsheets

Donald H. Kraft & Associates
9325 Kenneth Avenue
Skokie, IL 60076

PH: (708) 673-0597
FAX: (708) 673-0597
SOFTWARE
Cost: $195.00

Lotus 1-2-3 spreadsheets enable the user to manage an unlimited number of portfolios of stocks, bonds, mutual funds, and options. calculates net worth, bond yield to maturity, annualized ROI, etc. Specific menus; can select printed reports and charts.

AUDIENCE: Individual, Professional   RISK LEVEL: Conservative, Moderate,
TOPICS: Bonds, Mutual Funds, Stocks, Options   Aggressive

Portfolio Spreadsheets - Bonds

Donald H. Kraft & Associates
9325 Kenneth Avenue
Skokie, IL 60076

PH: (708) 673-0597
FAX: (708) 673-0597
SOFTWARE
Cost: $100.00

Lotus 1-2-3 enables portfolio management, bond analysis, and spreadsheets. Recordkeeping, arranging bond portfolios, unrealized gain/loss, maturity date, early call, current yield, plan bond purchases with a ladder of maturities report, and summary reports.

AUDIENCE: Individual, Professional   RISK LEVEL: Conservative
TOPICS: Bonds

Portfolio Spreadsheets - Stocks

Donald H. Kraft & Associates
9325 Kenneth Avenue
Skokie, IL 60076

PH: (708) 673-0597
FAX: (708) 673-0597
SOFTWARE
Cost: $100

Automated Lotus 1-2-3 for stock and mutual fund management. Track unlimited number of stocks and mutual funds and perform functions as calculating portfolio diversification by stock and industry, scheduling and posting dividends, performance, EPS, P/E, and beta.

AUDIENCE: Individual, Professional   RISK LEVEL: Moderate, Aggressive
TOPICS: Mutual Funds, Stocks

Portfolio Status

Dynacomp, Inc.
178 Phillips Road
Webster, NY 14580

PH: (800) 828-6772
SOFTWARE
Cost: $69.95

Program generates an analysis of the portfolio indicating the current market value, profit/loss, percent profit, and days since purchase of each security.

AUDIENCE: Individual   RISK LEVEL: Moderate, Aggressive
TOPICS: Bonds, Mutual Funds, Stocks

Portfolio Tracker

Ram Technologies, Inc.
371 Bronte Street, Unit 53
Milton, ON, Canada L9T 3K5

PH: (416) 876-4246
FAX: (416) 876-4246
SOFTWARE
Professional version
Cost: $74.95
  personal use version, $49.95
Analysis Capability: Portfolio
  Management

Program produces various reports on current value and performance of investments. Data history, commissions, total assets under management, and transfers of all accounts can be maintained. Handles multi-currency accounts.

AUDIENCE: Professional   RISK LEVEL: Conservative, Moderate, Aggressive
TOPICS: Bonds, Mutual Funds, Stocks

Portfolio Tracking System

SCIX Corporation
2010 Laconic Street
Williamsport, PA 17701

PH: (717) 323-3276
SOFTWARE
Cost: $765

Portfolio tracking system that can handle stocks, bonds, options, mutual funds and futures. Can select quotes from seven data vendors. Also supports money market funds, T-bills and commercial paper investments.

AUDIENCE: Individual, Professional	RISK LEVEL: Conservative, Moderate,
TOPICS: All	Aggressive

Portfolio Watcher

Portfolio Watcher
Box 175
Wilton, CT 06897

PH: (203) 762-7820
SOFTWARE
Cost: $149.95
Analysis Capability: Portfolio
  Management

Program records stocks, bonds, mutual funds and cash transactions for complete recordkeeping of investment portfolio. Unlimited portfolios can be analyzed for portfolio valuation, open position, and dividends received. Interfaces with Wall Street Watcher.

AUDIENCE: Individual, Professional	RISK LEVEL: Conservative, Moderate,
TOPICS: Bonds, Mutual Funds, Stocks	Aggressive

PORTIA® for Portfolio Reporting, Trading, and Investment Analysis

Thomson Investment
22 Pittsburge St.
Boston, MA 02210

PH: (617) 345-2700
FAX: (617) 951-2520
SOFTWARE
Base system starts at $18,500

Covers futures, stocks and options, all types of bonds, and agencies. PORTIA runs a local area network of personal computers, which allows multiple users to simultaneously enter, access, and analyze up-to-the-second investment information.

AUDIENCE: Individual, Professional	RISK LEVEL: Conservative, Moderate,
TOPICS: All	Aggressive

Portview 2020

Dynacomp, Inc.
178 Phillips Road
Webster, NY 14580

PH: (800) 828-6772
SOFTWARE
Cost: $79.95

A portfolio management system for stocks, bonds, options, mutual funds, indexes, and futures. Combines record keeping, tax planning, and investment analysis. Computes ROI, price history, net worth, and the performance between any two dates.

AUDIENCE: Individual	RISK LEVEL: Conservative, Moderate, Aggressive
TOPICS: All	

Power Center

Wilson Associates International
7535 E. Hampden Ave., Ste. 101
Denver, CO 80231

PH: (303) 750-5535
SOFTWARE
Fundamental Analysis, Portfolio
  Management
Cost: $349.00 per month

Asset allocation program which provides monthly data on 300+ mutual funds, 215 asset classes and 6,000 stocks. Graphic displays of portfolio growth, correlation analysis, historical performance plots, current rate of return, expected rate of return.

AUDIENCE: Individual, Professional	RISK LEVEL: Conservative, Moderate,
TOPICS: All	Aggressive

Practice First

New High Co.
RD #2
Riverhead, NY 11901

PH: (800) 643-8950
(516) 722-5407
FAX: (516) 722-5409
SOFTWARE
Cost: $139.00
Technical Analysis, Simulation
  Games

User can train and test skills by replaying actual data exactly as it happened on a given day. Beginner and experienced investors hone skills using technical analysis for exiting and entering markets. System calculates the value of the trader's portfolio in real time.

AUDIENCE: Beginning, Individual	RISK LEVEL: Moderate, Aggressive
TOPICS: Stocks, Options, Futures/Commodities	

Precision Trader - 3.4

Reinhart Investment Management
1250 Oakmead Parkway, Suite 210
Sunnyvale, CA 94087

PH: (408) 738-2311
SOFTWARE
Cost: $395.00
Analysis Capability: Technical
  Analysis, Futures Analysis,
  Options Analysis

"Software Supports the Babson and Andrews indicators, RSI, MACD, automated Fibonacci, trendlines and envelopes. Supports 5 data formats."

AUDIENCE: Individual, Professional	RISK LEVEL: Aggressive
TOPICS: Stocks, Options, Futures/Commodities	

Price Data

Technical Data
11 Farnsworth St.
Boston, MA 02210

PH: (617) 345-2526
Contact: Leslie Keefe, Product
Manager. E-mail: 9650
(DIALMAIL).
ON-LINE DATABASE

Price estimates on the U.S. Treasury bond market.

AUDIENCE: Individual, Professional	RISK LEVEL: Conservative
TOPICS: Bonds	

Price/Stress

Chronometrics, Inc.
1901 Raymond Dr.
Northbrook, IL 60062-6714

PH: (708) 272-0949
ON-LINE DATABASE
On-line Availability: Telerate
  Systems, Inc.
Access Fees: Call for Costs

Trading advice for financial markets as well as technical market alerts.

AUDIENCE: Individual, Professional   RISK LEVEL: Aggressive
TOPICS: All

Prodigy

Prodigy Services Company
445 Hamilton Ave.
White Plains, NY 10601

PH: (914) 993-8000
ON-LINE DATABASE
Access Fees: Call for Costs

Personal computer-based services covering a broad range of information that includes reviews of movies and videocassettes, national and local news, a 15 minute delay of stock quotes, credit reports, credit cards, and financial planning.

AUDIENCE: Beginning, Individual   RISK LEVEL: Moderate, Aggressive
TOPICS: Mutual Funds, Stocks, Options, Futures/Commodities

Professional Analyst

Trendsetter Software
P.O. Box 6481
Santa Ana, CA 92706

PH: (800) 825-1852
(714) 547-5005
FAX: (714) 547-5063
Cost: $595
SOFTWARE
Analysis Capability: Technical
  Analysis

Has a "custom layout" feature that allows switching from one series of charts to another quickly. Studies overlay directly on charts for ease of comparison with up to 14 studies per chart and 9 charts per screen.

AUDIENCE: Individual, Professional   RISK LEVEL: Moderate, Aggressive
TOPICS: Bonds, Mutual Funds, Stocks, Options, Futures/Commodities

Professional Breakout System

New High Co.
RD #2
Riverhead, NY 11901

PH: (800) 643-8950
(516) 722-5407
FAX: (516) 722-5409
SOFTWARE
Cost: $385
Analysis Capability: Technical
  Analysis, Simulation Games

17 technical indicators give entry and exit signals for user. Program uses volatility breakout system with charting and technical analysis features to filter and confirm trades. Reads CSI, CompuTrac, MetaStock, or ASCII formats.

AUDIENCE: Individual, Professional   RISK LEVEL: Aggressive
TOPICS: Stocks, Options, Futures/Commodities

Professional Investor Report (PIR)

Dow Jones & Company, Inc.
P.O. Box 300
Princeton, NJ 08543-0300

PH: (609) 520-4000
Type: Numeric; full-text
ON-LINE DATABASE
Access Fees: $2.16 per minute
(2400 baud)

Provides information on stocks showing unusual trading activity on the New York and American stock exchanges, and National Market System of the NASDAQ Over-the-Counter market. Includes analyses by Dow Jones staff of reasons for unusual trading activity.

AUDIENCE: Professional   RISK LEVEL: Moderate, Aggressive
TOPICS: Stocks, Options

Professional Portfolio

Advent Software, Inc.
301 Brannan Street
San Francisco, CA 94107

PH: (800) 648-7005
(415) 543-7696
FAX: (415) 543-5070
SOFTWARE
Approx $7,700.00

Portfolio management system that tracks all trades, splits, interest, dividends, and gains/losses for stocks, bonds, mutual funds, CMOs CDs, and cash equivalents. Enter transactions through individual transaction file or through the Trade Blotter.

AUDIENCE: Professional   RISK LEVEL: Conservative, Moderate, Aggressive
TOPICS: All

Professional Trader's Daily

CISCO
327 S. LaSalle Street
Suite 1133
Chicago, IL 60604

PH: (312) 922-3661
(800) 666-1223
ONLINE
Cost: $75.00 plus monthly charge
  $200.00

Bonds, S&P, yen, gold, crude oil, soybean futures. Designed for experienced traders, it blends the interactive thought processes of seasoned traders with the quantitative powers of a computer. For the 1st time, a computer has been taught how to understand markets.

AUDIENCE: Individual, Professional   RISK LEVEL: Aggressive
TOPICS: Options, Futures/Commodities

Profit Planner Plus

Village Software
186 Lincoln Street
Boston, MA 02111

PH: (800) 724-9332
FAX: (617) 695-1935
Cost: $99.00
SOFTWARE
Analysis Capability: Fundamental
  Analysis, Financial Planning, Real
  Estate, Business Forecasting,
  Spreadsheets

Build sets of financial statements for business plan, operations forecast or business acquisition. Analyzes 12 years of historical information and creates projections. Generates all standard pro forma financial tables in detail, summary, or percentage.

AUDIENCE: Beginning, Individual   RISK LEVEL: Moderate, Aggressive
TOPICS: Bonds, Stocks

Profit Taker

Emerging Market Technologies, Inc. Technical and fundamental analysis of commodities.
1230 Johnson Ferry Road
Suite F-1
Marietta, GA 30068

PH: (404) 973-2300
FAX: (404) 973-3003
SOFTWARE
Cost: Call Vendor

AUDIENCE: Individual, Professional	RISK LEVEL: Aggressive
TOPICS: Futures/Commodities	

Program Writer II

Technicom, Inc.
736 NE 20th Avenue
Ft. Lauderdale, FL 33304

PH: (305) 523-5394
FAX: (305) 523-3245
SOFTWARE
Cost: $995.00 for package

Covers commodities and futures. Provides you with a complete and powerful shell that contains all the features of historical testing, automatic optimization, graphics, data management, and automatic daily trading recommendations.

AUDIENCE: Individual, Professional	RISK LEVEL: Aggressive
TOPICS: Futures/Commodities	

Proquote

Automated Investments, Inc.
201 Consumers Rd., Suite 105
Willowdale, ON, Canada M25 468

PH: (416) 491-8242
FAX: (416) 498-1562
ON-LINE DATABASE
Access Fees: Call for Costs

Gives real-time quotes, charting and technical analysis. It features access to quotes and daily/weekly charts, intraday charting, technical analysis, price and volume filters and alarms, mouse or keyboard access, and ASCII import/export.

AUDIENCE: Individual, Professional	RISK LEVEL: Moderate, Aggressive
TOPICS: All	

Prosper-II Mkt

Advanced Analysis, Inc.
48408 Red Run Drive
Canton, MI 48187

PH: (804) 745-8008
FAX: (313) 981-4680
SOFTWARE
Cost: $189

Technical analysis and technical screening functions, stock, bonds, indexes, mutual funds, options, and futures. Analyze quote data for 4,620 issues. 40 indicators and tools for signals of price reversals, trends, volume traded, and distribution.

AUDIENCE: Individual, Professional	RISK LEVEL: Moderate, Aggressive
TOPICS: All	

Prosper-II Poweronline

Advanced Analysis, Inc.
48408 Red Run Drive
Canton, MI 48187

PH: (804) 745-8008
FAX: (313) 981-4680
SOFTWARE
Cost: $199.00

Intraday technical analysis program with signal analyzing quote data at cycles less than 20 seconds. Quote Listing Mode lists quotes as they are gathered; Value Mode; Analysis Mode. Price, volume, RSI, K%D, m-K%D, MACD, etc.

AUDIENCE: Individual, Professional   RISK LEVEL: Aggressive
TOPICS: Stocks, Options, Futures/Commodities

Prosper-II Professional

Advanced Analysis, Inc.
48408 Red Run Drive
Canton, MI 48187

PH: (804) 745-8008
FAX: (313) 981-4680
SOFTWARE + Online
Access Fees: Call for Costs

Real-time technical analysis for stocks, indexes, options, and futures. On-line parameter optimization for optimal trading profits. Includes automatic alert system for all indicators of Poweronline for all the issues.

AUDIENCE: Professional   RISK LEVEL: Aggressive
TOPICS: Stocks, Options, Futures/Commodities

Pulse Portfolio Management System

Equis International
3950 South 700 E.
Suite 100
Salt Lake City, UT 84107

PH: (800) 882-3040
(801) 265-8886
FAX: (801) 265-3999
SOFTWARE
Cost: $195.00

Provides portfolio management, simulation games, and statistics for stocks, bonds, mutual funds, options, futures, and real estate. 80 preprogrammed calculations including annualized return, beta, yield, yield-to-call, yield-to-maturity, cost tax basis, and more.

AUDIENCE: Individual, Professional   RISK LEVEL: Moderate, Aggressive
TOPICS: All

Put/Call

Tools For Timing
11345 Highway 7, #499
Minnetonka, MN 55305

PH: (800) 325-1344
(612) 939-0076
FAX: (612) 938-1275
Cost: $50.00
SOFTWARE
Analysis Capability: Technical
  Analysis

Graphically expresses 7 different relationships of OEX, put/call, volume and open interest. Put/call ratio, Hines ratio, put/call volume with put/call open interest, put/call volume as a percentage of put/call interest, and other variations.

AUDIENCE: Individual, Professional   RISK LEVEL: Aggressive
TOPICS: Options

Q-Trax For Windows

EDMS
5859 New Peachtree Road
Suite 119
Atlanta, GA 30340

PH: (800) 395-7670
(404) 998-4088
SOFTWARE
Cost: $69.95

Financial planning, portfolio management, fundamental analysis, technical analysis, bond analysis, simulation games, spreadsheets, and statistics. Designed to analyze and track the performance of stocks, bonds, and mutual funds.

AUDIENCE: Beginning, Individual   RISK LEVEL: Conservative, Moderate, Aggressive
TOPICS: Bonds, Mutual Funds, Stocks

QOS-30

Financiometrics, Inc.
P.O. Box 1788
Lafayette, CA 94549

PH: (510) 254-9338
FAX: (510) 254-2932
SOFTWARE
Cost: $2,500 first year, $1,250 every
    year after
Analysis Capabilities: Financial
    Planning, Statistics

Optimization system for optimal asset allocation. Uses fast algorithm that helps structure portfolio optimization. Portfolio attributes, portfolio beta, upper/lower bounds, transaction cost and size, turnover constraint, and quadratic and linear equations.

AUDIENCE: Professional   RISK LEVEL: Conservative, Moderate, Aggressive
TOPICS: Bonds, Mutual Funds, Stocks

Quant IX Portfolio Evaluator

Quant IX Software
5900 N. Port Washington Road
Suite 142
Milwaukee, WI 53217

PH: (800) 247-6354
SOFTWARE
Cost: $169.00
Analysis Capability: Fundamental
Analysis, Fundamental Screening,
Portfolio Management, Financial
Planning

A security analysis program and a portfolio manager combine to provide easy use. Portfolio manager: single or multiple portfolio management for stocks, mutual funds, government issues, cash items, etc. The security analysis calculates 6 security valuation models.

AUDIENCE: Individual, Professional   RISK LEVEL: Moderate, Aggressive
TOPICS: Bonds, Mutual Funds, Stocks, Options

Quarterly No-Load Mutual Fund Update On Disk

American Association of Individual
Investors
625 N. Michigan Ave., Suite 1900
Chicago, IL 60611

PH: (312) 280-0170
FAX: (312) 280-1625
ON-LINE DATABASE
Cost: $50/year for quarterly updates

Quarterly updated program and newsletter with 70 variables on no-load and low-load mutual funds that allows the ranking and screening of funds. Expense ratio, portfolio turnover, portfolio manager and tenure, portfolio composition summary, and information.

AUDIENCE: Beginning, Individual   RISK LEVEL: Moderate, Aggressive
TOPICS: Mutual Funds

Quarterly Report On Money Fund Performance

IBC/Donoghue, Inc.
290 Eliot Street
P.O. Box 9104
Ashland, MA 01721-9104

PH: (508) 881-2800
(800) 343-5413
FAX: (508) 881-0982
ON-LINE DATABASE
Cost: $775.00/year

Gives charges and incurred expense ratios of taxable and tax-free funds, broken into the same categories as Money Fund Report for 3 months and for quarter. It includes top performing funds by new yield and gross in six categories.

AUDIENCE: Beginning, Individual, Professional   RISK LEVEL: Conservative
TOPICS: Bonds, Mutual Funds

Quicken

Intuit
P.O. Box 3014
Menlo Park, CA 94026

PH: (800) 624-8742
SOFTWARE
Cost: $59.95
Analysis Capability: Portfolio
    Management, Financial Planning

Financial calculator for a small business, financial counselor, or investor. Program allows for analysis of investment portfolios, taxes, and accounts payable/receiving with aging. Check-free electronic bill paying option is a built in feature.

AUDIENCE: Individual   RISK LEVEL: Conservative, Moderate, Aggressive
TOPICS: Bonds, Mutual Funds, Stocks, Investment Planning

Quickplot/Quick Study

CSI Data Retrieval Service
200 W. Palmetto Park Road
Boca Raton, FL 33432

PH: (800) 274-4727
(407) 392-8663
FAX: (407) 392-1379
SOFTWARE
Cost: $99.00

Covers stocks, futures. Used for graphically analyzing and manipulating data bank information. Lets you choose among calculations for moving averages, RSI, CCI, Detrend, On-Balance Volume, MACD, Stochastics, and others. Quicktreive/QuickManager.

AUDIENCE: Individual, Professional   RISK LEVEL: Aggressive
TOPICS: Stocks, Options, Futures/Commodities

Quicktrieve/Quick Manager

CSI Data Retrieval Service
200 W. Palmetto Park Road
Boca Raton, FL 33432

PH: (800) 274-4727
(407) 392-8663
FAX: (407) 392-1379
SOFTWARE
Cost: $59.00 hookup and monthly
charge from $12.00

Covers stocks, commodity futures and options, cash, and mutual funds. The software interacts with the CSI Data Retrieval Service and captures historical data as well as daily data that are tailored to each individual portfolio.

AUDIENCE: Individual, Professional   RISK LEVEL: Aggressive
TOPICS: Stocks, Options, Futures/Commodities

Quicktrieve/Trade Data Manager

Commodity Systems, Inc. (CSI)
200 W. Palmetto Park Road
Boca Raton, FL 33432

PH: (800) 274-4727
(407) 392-8663
FAX: (407) 392-1379
SOFTWARE
Cost: $39.00

Downloading system that retrieves daily prices for current date and up to previous 9 weeks. Works together with QUICKPLOT/QUICKSTUDY.

AUDIENCE: Individual, Professional   RISK LEVEL: Aggressive
TOPICS: Stocks, Options, Futures/Commodities

Quickway

Quick & Reilly, Inc.
460 California Ave., Suite 302
Palo Alto, CA 94306

PH: (415) 326-4200
(800) 634-6214
FAX: (415) 326-2432
ON-LINE DATABASE
Current Quote Fees: $30/month

Buy and sell securities 24 hours a day and receive real-time, delayed or historical security prices. Automatically maintains tax records and manages a portfolio on-line. It allows the users to specify their price ranges.

AUDIENCE: Individual, Professional   RISK LEVEL: Moderate, Aggressive
TOPICS: Mutual Funds, Stocks, Options

QUOTDIAL

Quotron Systems, Inc.
5300 McConnell
Los Angeles, CA 90066

PH: (310) 302-4720
(800) 427-4770
FAX: (212) 747-8752
ON-LINE DATABASE
Cost: $10 monthly minimum;
 $30/hour prime time

Accesses Quotron's price and market database. Real-time, 15 minute delay and after market data on stocks, bonds, mutual funds, commodities, market index, and options. Also offers earnings forecasts, dividends, statistics, intraday graphs, and studies.

AUDIENCE: Individual, Professional   RISK LEVEL: Conservative, Moderate,
TOPICS: All   Aggressive

Quote Collector

Serenson Consulting Service
P.O. Box 266
Thomaston, CT 06787

PH: (203) 283-8111
QUOTE UTILITY

Uses X*press Information to collect data on stock quotes for a historical database. Outputs data compatible with technical programs: MetaStock, CompuTrac, NSQ, Prosper II plus, FundMaster, AIQ Stock Expert, Option Expert, Viking, and MarketMaster.

AUDIENCE: Individual, Professional   RISK LEVEL: Moderate, Aggressive
TOPICS: Stocks, Options

Quote Commander

Cyber-Scan, Inc.
3601 Pulaski Road N.E.
Buffalo, NY 55313

PH: (612) 682-4150
SOFTWARE
Cost: $99.95

Collects and lists up to 2,500 quote symbols and 36 lists. Alarms for trades at specific levels for up to 20 issues, automatic export of data in ASCII, MetaStock, or CSI formats. Program uses all quotes on DTN.

AUDIENCE: Individual	RISK LEVEL: Moderate, Aggressive
TOPICS: Stocks, Options	

Quote Exporter, The

Fossware
1000 Campbell Road
Suite 208-626
Houston, TX 77055

PH: (713) 467-3195
Cost: $99.00

Covers options, stocks, and commodities. For use with CompuTrac. The Quote Exporter is a companion program to The Quote Monitor. It provides a bridge between quote retrieval and analysis. It transfers data saved by TQM.

AUDIENCE: Individual, Professional	RISK LEVEL: Aggressive
TOPICS: Stocks, Options, Futures/Commodities	

Quote Line

Technical Tools
334 State Street
Suite 201
Los Altos, CA 94022

PH: (415) 948-6124
SOFTWARE
Cost: $50.00 on-line charges per
  minute

A dial-up electronic data service which provides daily end-of-day price information for futures contracts traded on U.S. and Canadian exchanges. Data available by 4:00 PM Pacific time and operational 23 hours a day.

AUDIENCE: Individual	RISK LEVEL: Aggressive
TOPICS: Futures/Commodities	

Quote Master

Strategic Planning Systems, Inc.
21021 Soledad Canyon Road
Suite 504
Santa Clara, CA 91351

PH: (800) 488-5898
(805) 254-5897
Cost: $395.00; Quote Master
Professional $495.00

Covers stocks, commodities, mutual funds, options, futures, indexes, and provides chart service. FNN signal and Telemet America broadcast market information directly.

AUDIENCE: Individual, Professional	RISK LEVEL: Moderate, Aggressive
TOPICS: Mutual Funds, Stocks, Options, Futures/Commodities	

Quote Reporter

Fossware
1000 Campbell Road
Suite 208-626
Houston, TX 77055

PH: (713) 467-3195
ON-LINE SERVICE
Cost: $99.00

Program downloads daily closing or intraday prices from Quote Monitor to formats of technical analysis programs. Formats include AIQ, CompuTrac, Investograph Plus, MetaStock, OptionView, Savant, SCTA, FCTA, FCTA and the Right Time.

AUDIENCE: Individual, Professional   RISK LEVEL: Aggressive
TOPICS: Mutual Funds, Stocks, Options, Futures/Commodities

Quote Translator

Guru Systems, Ltd.
3873 Airport Way
Box 9754
Bellingham, WA 98227

PH: (604) 299-1010
FAX: (604) 299-1099
SOFTWARE
Cost: $99

Access and convert data from Apex, ASCII, CSI, MetaStock, PC Chart, Prodigy, and TeleChart. User can append and split files by time periods for continuous commodities futures contracts. Program can be customized for user.

AUDIENCE: Individual, Professional   RISK LEVEL: Aggressive
TOPICS: Options, Futures/Commodities

QuoteExpress

Integrated Financial Solutions, Inc.
  (formerly RJT Systems)
1049 S.W. Baseline, Suite B-200
Hillsboro, OR 97123

PH: (800) 729-5037
(503) 640-5303
FAX: (503) 648-9528
SOFTWARE
Cost: $195.00, + optimal modules

Program interfaces with DTN Wall Street allowing investor to perform analysis on stocks, bonds, mutual funds, indexes, and market indicators. Access to last price on DTN and update analysis base. Creates charts and technical analysis.

AUDIENCE: Individual, Professional   RISK LEVEL: Moderate, Aggressive
TOPICS: Bonds, Mutual Funds, Stocks, Options

Quotes And Trading

Dialog Information Services, Inc.
3460 Hillview Ave.
Palo Alto, CA 94304

PH: (415) 858-3785
(800) 334-2564
FAX: (415) 858-7069
ON-LINE DATABASE
Cost: $295.00
Access Fees: $0.60/minute.

It gives stock and options quotes with a 20 minute delay from AMEX, NYSE, NASDAQ, and four major options exchanges. Purchase or sell any stocks or options listed in The Wall Street Journal, track portfolio gains and losses, and project dividend income.

AUDIENCE: Individual   RISK LEVEL: Moderate, Aggressive
TOPICS: Stocks, Options

Quotrek

Data Broadcasting Corp.
1900 S. Norfolk
San Mateo, CA 94403

PH: (800) 367-4670
Cost: $495.00 for unit, $351.00
    basic monthly

Covers stocks, commodities, mutual funds, market timing, municipal, corporate, government, and foreign bonds, with news via Dow Jones News Alert. Hand held portable unit giving real-time quotes from all major U.S. futures, options, and equities exchanges.

AUDIENCE: Individual, Professional   RISK LEVEL: Moderate, Aggressive
TOPICS: All

Radio Exchange

Telemet America
325 First Street
Alexandria, VA 22314

PH: (800) 368-2078
(703) 548-2042
Cost: $349.00; basic monthly charge
    of $33.25

Covers stocks, commodities, mutual funds, market timing, chart service. Links your PC to all major securities exchanges and McGraw-Hill Headlines news. Hailed by leading computer magazines and investor services as the "best value" in quotes today.

AUDIENCE: Individual, Professional   RISK LEVEL: Moderate, Aggressive
TOPICS: Mutual Funds, Stocks, Options, Futures/Commodities

Rapid

Greenstone Software, Inc.
20 Roehampton
Brampton, ON, Canada L6Y 2R4

PH: (905) 459-8242
SOFTWARE
Cost: $277
Analysis Capabilities: Portfolio
    Management, Technical Analysis,
    Bond Analysis, Futures Analysis,
    Option Analysis, Statistics

Program uses dozens of technical tools to assist investor in buy and sell decisions for stocks and commodities. Tools include: RSI, stochastics, MACD, candlesticks, Bollinger bands, and moving averages.

AUDIENCE: Individual, Professional   RISK LEVEL: Aggressive
TOPICS: Stocks, Options, Futures/Commodities

Rategram

Bradshaw Financial Network
P.O. Box 3517
San Rafael, CA 94912-3517

PH: (415) 479-3815
FAX: (415) 479-2730
ON-LINE DATABASE

Locate the country's highest yields on federally insured liquid money market accounts, taxable or tax-exempt money market funds, CDs, and jumbo CDs. Weekly updates on interest rates, annual percentage yields and moving averages.

AUDIENCE: Beginning, Individual, Professional   RISK LEVEL: Conservative
TOPICS: Bonds

Rational Indicators

Trader's Insight, Inc.
8 Renwick Avenue
Huntington, NY 11743-3052

PH: (516) 423-2413
SOFTWARE
Cost: $345.00; $445.00 with
  candlestick charting
Technical Analysis

Chart prices according to the "Random Walk" Index. Decides if index is trending or moving randomly. Candle charts include automatic recognition patterns to reduce arbitrary choices in investing.

AUDIENCE: Individual   RISK LEVEL: Aggressive
TOPICS: Stocks, Futures/Commodities

RDB Chart

RDB Computing, Inc.
8910 N. Kenton Ave.
Skokie, IL 60076

PH: (708) 982-1910
SOFTWARE
Cost: $295.00
Technical Analysis, Futures
  Analysis, Spreadsheets

Develop technical analysis tools or trading systems with a spreadsheet or programming language such as Basic or C. High/low close indicators, indicator values, buy/sell signals, daily equity, and volume are entered into an ASCII file. Charts with buy/sell.

AUDIENCE: Individual, Professional   RISK LEVEL: Aggressive
TOPICS: Stocks, Options, Futures/Commodities

RDB Computing Custom Trader

RDB Computing, Inc.
8910 N. Kenton Ave.
Skokie, IL 60076

PH: (708) 982-1910
SOFTWARE
Analysis Capability: Technical
  Analysis, Bond Analysis, Futures
  Analysis, Options Analysis,
  Statistics
Cost: Contact Vendor

Provides a foundation from which to build technical analysis programs. Setup screens, charts, and system performance statistics can be included while supporting various data formats. New technical analysis indicators, charts.

AUDIENCE: Individual   RISK LEVEL: Aggressive
TOPICS: Bonds, Mutual Funds, Stocks, Options, Futures/Commodities

RDB Programmer Libraries

RDB Computing, Inc.
8910 N. Kenton Ave.
Skokie, IL 60076

PH: (708) 982-1910
SOFTWARE
Cost: $295.00 C-language data
  access; $895.00 C-language
  charting; $495.00 compiled
  libraries (data access plus charting)

Libraries for adding data file access and technical charting to your technical analysis program. Charting library supports up to 5 charts per screen, bar charts, indicator charts overlaying bar charts, and buy/sell arrows.

AUDIENCE: Individual, Professional   RISK LEVEL: Aggressive
TOPICS: Bonds, Mutual Funds, Stocks, Options, Futures/Commodities

RDB System Tester

RDB Computing, Inc.
8910 N. Kenton Ave.
Skokie, IL 60076

PH: (708) 982-1910
SOFTWARE
Cost: $495.00 C-language data
   access; $895.00 C-language
   charting; $495.00 compiled
   libraries (data access plus charting)

"Shell program for historical testing and daily trade signal generation of technical analysis tools and trading systems." Analysis of stocks, bonds, options, futures, indexes, and mutual funds can be interfaced with graphics program.

AUDIENCE: Individual, Professional   RISK LEVEL: Aggressive
TOPICS: Stocks, Options, Futures/Commodities

Real-Time Stock Quotes

Mead Data Central, Inc. (MDC)
9443 Springboro Pike
P.O. Box 933
Dayton, OH 45401

PH: (513) 865-6800
(800) 227-4908
FAX: (513) 865-6909
ON-LINE DATABASE
Access Fees: Call for Costs

Real-time data on stocks, bonds, equities, mutual funds, and money market on the New York, American, U.S. Regional, and Canadian stock exchanges, NASDAQ Over-The-Counter market, and NASDAQ National Market System.

AUDIENCE: Individual, Professional   RISK LEVEL: Moderate, Aggressive
TOPICS: Stocks, Options

Realtick III

Townsend Analytics, Ltd.
100 S. Wacker Drive, Suite 1506
Chicago, IL 60606

PH: (800) 827-0141
FAX: (312) 621-0487
SOFTWARE
Analysis Capability: Futures
   Analysis, Options Analysis,
   Fundamental Analysis, Technical
   Analysis, Bond Analysis,
   Spreadsheets, Statistics

Real-time graphics for stocks, indexes, options and more. Displays intraday and daily charts, technical studies, market profiles, tables and quote screens in windows or multiple programmable pages. Technical studies can be overlaid on bar charts and parameters.

AUDIENCE: Individual, Professional   RISK LEVEL: Aggressive
TOPICS: Stocks, Options, Futures/Commodities

Recurrence III

Avco Financial Corp.
8 Grigg Street
Greenwich, CT 06830

PH: (203) 661-7381
(203) 869-0253
SOFTWARE
Cost: $2,500.00

Program uses technical analysis, technical screening, and futures analysis for tracking the futures market. A real-time trading system designed as an add-on product for traders who use only the current markets, with overnight exposure.

AUDIENCE: Individual, Professional   RISK LEVEL: Aggressive
TOPICS: Futures/Commodities

Relevance III-Advanced Market Analysis

Relevance III, Inc.
4741 Trousdale Drive
Suite One
Nashville, TN 37220

PH: (615) 333-2005
FAX: (615) 834-5688
SOFTWARE
Cost: $795.00

Professional trading methods can filter Gann, Andrews, Elliot, Fibonacci, Wyckoff, and others. Calculates MACD, Williams %R accumulation, distribution index, ultimate oscillator, day-by-day simulation mode, risk/reward analysis, candlesticks.

AUDIENCE: Individual, Professional   RISK LEVEL: Aggressive
TOPICS: Stocks, Options, Futures/Commodities

Return On Investment

Essential Software Corp.
1126 South 70th Street
West Allis, WI 53214

PH: (414) 775-3450
FAX: (414) 475-3578
SOFTWARE
Cost: $195.00

Concentrates on using real estate in investment analysis returns. Includes internal rate of return, discounted cash flow, loan amortization, and payback. Performs monthly, quarterly, and yearly analysis.

AUDIENCE: Individual, Professional   RISK LEVEL: Moderate, Aggressive
TOPICS: All

Reuter Money Report

Reuters Ltd.
85 Fleet St.
London EC4P 4AJ, England

PH: 071-250 1122
FAX: 071-696 8761
ON-LINE DATABASE
On-line Availability: NEXIS
Access Fees: Call for Costs

Financial markets worldwide and currency exchange rates news.

AUDIENCE: Individual, Professional   RISK LEVEL: Conservative, Moderate,
TOPICS: Bonds, Options, Futures/Commodities   Aggressive

Reuter Monitor Capital Markets Service

Reuters Ltd.
85 Fleet St.
London EC4P 4AJ, England

PH: 071-250 1122
FAX: 071-696 8761
ON-LINE DATABASE
On-line Availability: Reuters Ltd.
Access Fees: Call for Costs

Contains prices and commentary of interest to international capital markets. Some of the files are: Money/Financial Futures, Money Markets, Grain/Livestock, Metals, Softs (coffee, coca, sugar, orange juice market, etc.), Energy, Securities, Optional News.

AUDIENCE: Individual, Professional   RISK LEVEL: Conservative, Moderate,
TOPICS: All   Aggressive

Reuter Monitor Money News Service

Reuters Ltd.
85 Fleet St.
London EC4P 4AJ, England

PH: 071-250 1122
FAX: 071-696 8761
ON-LINE DATABASE
On-line Availability: Reuters Ltd.
Access Fees: Call for Costs

Worldwide news which affects foreign exchange and the money market.

AUDIENCE: Individual, Professional   RISK LEVEL: Conservative, Moderate,
TOPICS: Bonds, Options, Futures/Commodities   Aggressive

Reuter Monitor Money Rates Service

Reuters Ltd.
85 Fleet St.
London EC4P 4AJ, England

PH: 071-251 1122
FAX: 071-696 8761
ON-LINE DATABASE
On-line Availability: Reuters Ltd.
Access Fees: Call for Costs

Real-time information on worldwide money markets, and foreign exchange data.

AUDIENCE: Individual, Professional   RISK LEVEL: Conservative, Moderate,
TOPICS: Bonds, Options, Futures/Commodities   Aggressive

Reuters

Dialog Information Services, Inc.
3460 Hillview Avenue
Palo Alto, CA 94304

PH: (800) 334-2564
(415) 858-3810
FAX: (415) 858-7069
ONLINE
Online charges: $1.60 per minute or
$96.00 per hour

Complete text of news releases from the Reuter Business Report and the Reuter Library Service newswires. Updated continuously. Provided by Reuters U.S., New York, NY.

AUDIENCE: Individual, Professional   RISK LEVEL: Conservative, Moderate,
TOPICS: All   Aggressive

Right Time

T.B.S.P. Inc. (The Better Software People)
610 Newport Center Drive, Suite 830
Newport Beach, CA 92660

PH: (714) 721-8603
FAX: (714) 721-8635
SOFTWARE
Cost: $499.00 each for Stock
program, $899.00 for Day Trading
Programs on Stock, Futures, and
Indexes (Combined program).

Include stocks, mutual funds, indexes, futures. A computerized trading system which was developed by an expert portfolio manager for his own personal use. Analyzes volume/price, support/demand, and global market trends and all at the same time.

AUDIENCE: Individual, Professional   RISK LEVEL: Moderate, Aggressive
TOPICS: Mutual Funds, Stocks, Options, Futures/Commodities

@Risk

Palisade Corp.
31 Decker Road
Newfield, NY 14867

PH: (800) 432-7475
FAX: (607) 277-8001
SOFTWARE
Cost: $395.00
Analysis Capability: Fundamental,
  Technical, Financial Planning,
  Simulation Games, Spreadsheets,
  Statistics

Monte Carlo simulation is used for risk analysis and to evaluate the uncertainty. Probability distributions are added to cells in the worksheet using 30 probability distribution built in functions. Over 32,000 iterations can be run per simulation.

AUDIENCE: Individual, Professional	RISK LEVEL: Moderate, Aggressive
TOPICS: Bonds, Mutual Funds, Stocks	

Riskalert

Roberts-Slade, Inc.
619 N. 500 West
Provo, UT 84601

PH: (800) 433-4276
FAX: (801) 373-2775
SOFTWARE
Cost: $390.00/month
Analysis Capability: Technical,
  Options, Technical Screening,
  Statistics

"What if " analysis capabilities and option trading section of the program are for the advanced trader. Price, volatility, historical and implied volatility charts, matrix reports, strategy testing, and much more.

AUDIENCE: Individual, Professional	RISK LEVEL: Aggressive
TOPICS: Options	

Roll Model

Niche Software Products
P.O. Box 3574
Manassas, VA 22110

PH: (703) 368-8372
SOFTWARE
Cost: $45.00
Options Analysis
Technical Support: Phone, M-F

Analyze possible action when short call options are near expiration and are in-the-money. Enter current position and selected prospective positions. Calculations to determine the best course of action.

AUDIENCE: Individual, Professional	RISK LEVEL: Aggressive
TOPICS: Options	

Rory Tycoon Options Trader

Coherent Software Systems
1012 Elk Grove Avenue
Venice, CA 90291

PH: (319) 452-1175
SOFTWARE
Cost: $49.95

Spreadsheet template retrieves quotations and analyzes over 50 possible option trades. System automatically retrieves the current stock price from an electronic quote service and presents a variety of strategies suited to the current stock price.

AUDIENCE: Individual, Professional	RISK LEVEL: Aggressive
TOPICS: Options	

Rory Tycoon Portfolio Analyst

Coherent Software Systems
1012 Elk Grove Avenue
Venice, CA 90291

PH: (319) 452-1175
SOFTWARE
Cost: $150.00

Real-time and historical charting assist the portfolio manager along with other program features: technical analysis, bond analysis, futures analysis, and options analysis. Program computes price, volume momentum, and moving averages of any duration.

AUDIENCE: Individual, Professional   RISK LEVEL: Moderate, Aggressive
TOPICS: Bonds, Mutual Funds, Stocks, Options, Futures/Commodities

S & P 1957-1994 Monthly

Heizer Software
P.O. Box 232019
Pleasant Hill, CA 94523

PH: (510) 943-7667
(800) 888-7667
FAX: (510) 943-6882
ON-LINE DATABASE
Access Fees: Call for Costs

Provides monthly averages of the Standard & Poor's stock price index dating back to 1957. Supplied in database format.

AUDIENCE: Individual, Professional   RISK LEVEL: Moderate, Aggressive
TOPICS: Stocks, Options

S & P Daily 1953-1994

Heizer Software
P.O. Box 232019
Pleasant Hill, CA 94523

PH: (510) 943-7667
(800) 888-7667
FAX: (510) 943-6882
ON-LINE DATABASE
Access Fees: Call for Costs

Provides daily prices from the Standard & Poor's 500 stock price index dating back to 1953. Supplies in database format.

AUDIENCE: Individual, Professional   RISK LEVEL: Moderate, Aggressive
TOPICS: Stocks, Options

S & P Daily 1980-1990

Heizer Software
P.O. Box 232019
Pleasant Hill, CA 94523

PH: (510) 943-7667
(800) 888-7667
FAX: (510) 943-6882
ON-LINE DATABASE
Access Fees: Call for Costs

Gives daily closing prices from the Standard & Poor's composite. Includes prices for every trading day from 1/1/80 to 12/31/90. Including monthly Standard & Poor's dividend yields and monthly T-bill rates. Supplied in database format.

AUDIENCE: Individual, Professional   RISK LEVEL: Moderate, Aggressive
TOPICS: Stocks, Options

S & P Marketscope

Standard & Poor's Corporation
25 Broadway
New York, NY 10004

PH: (212) 208-8300
FAX: (212) 412-0498
ON-LINE DATABASE
Access Fees: Call for Costs

Financial and descriptive, business and investment information on companies. Files available for search: Reference section, Action section, Daily updated data, and Weekly updated data.

AUDIENCE: Individual, Professional	RISK LEVEL: Moderate, Aggressive
TOPICS: Bonds, Stocks	

Sata-Scan

Wright Investor's Service (WIS)
1000 Lafayette Blvd.
Bridgeport, CT 06604

PH: (800) 232-0013
FAX: (203) 330-5090
On-line Availability: Quotron
    Systems, Inc. (Wright Investor's
    Service)
ON-LINE DATABASE
Access Fees: Call for Costs

Investment information on companies listed on the New York Stock Exchange, and selected other publicly owned companies. Worldscope assigned quality ratings and percentile rankings based on quality, current value, growth, projected earnings and dividends.

AUDIENCE: Individual, Professional	RISK LEVEL: Moderate, Aggressive
TOPICS: Bonds, Stocks	

SBBI/PC Now Core

Ibbotson Associates, Inc.
225 N. Michigan Avenue, Suite 700
Chicago, IL 60601

PH: (312) 616-1620
(800) 758-3557
FAX: (312) 263-1398
SOFTWARE
Cost: Monthly - $1,395.00 1st yr.,
    $1,295.00 each yr. thereafter

Includes stocks and bonds (corporate and government). Specially designed software to quickly and easily compute summary statistics, prepare graphs and perform statistical analysis over any sub-period. Can create sample portfolios.

AUDIENCE: Individual, Professional	RISK LEVEL: Conservative, Moderate, Aggressive
TOPICS: Bonds, Stocks	

Schwab's Investment Roundtable

GE Information Services (GEIS)
GEnie (General Electric Network
for Information Exchange)
401 N. Washington Blvd.
Rockville, MD 20850

PH: (301) 340-4000
(800) 638-9636
On-line Availability: GEnie
ON-LINE DATABASE
Access Fees: Call for Costs

An exchange of information and tips on playing the stock market from other participants.

AUDIENCE: Beginning, Individual	RISK LEVEL: Moderate, Aggressive
TOPICS: Mutual Funds, Stocks, Options, Futures/Commodities	

SDC Risk, SDC Risk/OTC, SDC Sentry, SDC Gards

Systems Development Corporation
141 West Jackson Blvd.
Suite 1240 A
Chicago, IL 60604

PH: (312) 408-1111
FAX: (312) 739-1111
ON-LINE DATABASE
Access Fees: Call for Costs

Options, stocks, commodities/futures. Full spectrum of hedging and options support as well as attendant risk management functions across equities, futures, listed options, cash, and OTC instruments, whether fixed income or foreign exchange.

AUDIENCE: Individual, Professional   RISK LEVEL: Moderate, Aggressive
TOPICS: Stocks, Options, Futures/Commodities

SDS2 Money Service

Reuters Information Services
15303 Dallas Parkway
Suite 510, LB53
Dallas, TX 75248

PH: (800) 441-2645
(214) 661-2645
FAX: (214) 991-3267
Access Fees: Monthly charge
  $550.00 + exchange fees, and up.
On-Line Service

Covers stocks, commodities, bonds (municipal, corporate, government and foreign), and options. A comprehensive investment service. Quotes, complete news coverage, technical charting, color graphics with advanced analytics, and market reports.

AUDIENCE: Individual, Professional   RISK LEVEL: Conservative, Moderate,
TOPICS: All   Aggressive

SEC Online

Dialog Information Services, Inc.
3460 Hillview Ave.
Palo Alto, CA 94304

PH: (800) 334-2564
FAX: (415) 858-7069
ON-LINE DATABASE
Cost: $295.00 for access to entire
  DIALOG service.
Access Fees: $1.40/minute.

Provides a database of reports and documents filed by public companies with the SEC which include those on the New York and American Stock Exchanges, and NASDAQ National Market companies.

AUDIENCE: Individual, Professional   RISK LEVEL: Moderate, Aggressive
TOPICS: Stocks, Options

Securities Accounting

Synon Corporation
5 The Mountain Road
Framingham, MA 01701

PH: (508) 620-8800
SOFTWARE
Cost: Contact Vendor

Provides functions to manage and control an institution's investment portfolio. Computes and posts all accounting transactions. Debt and equity instruments are supported. Interfaces to Lotus 1-2-3 and in-house systems.

AUDIENCE: Professional   RISK LEVEL: Conservative, Moderate, Aggressive
TOPICS: All

Securities History Data

Iverson Financial Systems, Inc.
111 W. Evelyn Ave.
Suite 205
Sunnyvale, CA 94086-6140

PH: (408) 522-9900
FAX: (408) 522-9911
ON-LINE DATABASE
Access Fees: Call for Costs

Gives end-of-day data for all equity issues and indicators for the AMEX, NYSE, NASDAQ, Toronto and Montreal exchanges from 1980 to present. Also gives end-of-day data for mutual funds and money markets from 1986 to present.

AUDIENCE: Individual, Professional   RISK LEVEL: Moderate, Aggressive
TOPICS: Stocks

Securities Pricing

Muller Data Corporation (MDC)
90 5th Ave.
New York, NY 10011

PH: (212) 807-3800
Type: Numeric
ON-LINE DATABASE
Access Fees: Call for Costs

Contains a current price listing on corporate, municipal, government bonds, and securities traded on the domestic and international stock and bond exchanges.

AUDIENCE: Individual, Professional   RISK LEVEL: Conservative, Moderate
TOPICS: Bonds

Sibyl/Runner Interactive Forecasting

Lincoln Systems, Corp.
P.O. Box 391
Wesford, MA 01886

PH: (508) 692-3910
SOFTWARE
Cost: $495.00

Sibyl provides 19 recognized time-series methods for user's data. Runner summarizes statistics for each selection. Complete statistics include 10 aggregate error measures displayed, actual/forecast graphics, and ex-ante forecasts. Lotus 1-2-3.

AUDIENCE: Professional   RISK LEVEL: Moderate, Aggressive
TOPICS: Stocks, Options, Futures/Commodities

Signal

Data Broadcasting Corp.
1900 S. Norfolk Street
San Mateo, CA 94403

PH: (800) 367-4670
FAX: (415) 574-4621
Cost: $495.00 for receiver or
  $295.00 w/annual prepaid
  subscription

Stocks, commodities, mutual funds, and news (Dow Jones: $30.00 per month extra). Real-time data for over 65,000 stocks, commodities, options, indexes, mutual funds, and money market funds. Instant compatibility with over 100 analytical software packages.

AUDIENCE: Individual, Professional   RISK LEVEL: Moderate, Aggressive
TOPICS: Mutual Funds, Stocks, Options, Futures/Commodities

SmartBox III

Research Department, Inc.
200 W. Adams
Chicago, IL 60606

PH: (800) 231-9723
(312) 407-5703
Cost: $95.00
Monthly charge $99.00

Includes research, quote and news. Covers stocks, commodities, mutual funds, government bonds, research, domestic and international news. Expert analysis on financial and agricultural markets, both fundamental and technical.

AUDIENCE: Individual, Professional	RISK LEVEL: Conservative, Moderate, Aggressive
TOPICS: All	

Smartbroker

Charlton Woolard
17280 Anna
Southfield, MI 48075

PH: (313) 557-3766
SOFTWARE
Cost $295.00

Portfolio management, fundamental analysis, technical analysis, technical screening, fundamental screening, and options analysis can be performed with this program on stocks and options. Tracks stocks and options and uses advanced calculus and statistics.

AUDIENCE: Individual, Professional	RISK LEVEL: Moderate, Aggressive
TOPICS: Stocks, Options, Futures/Commodities	

Solve It!

Pine Grove Software
875 Avenue of the Americas
Suite 2101
New York, NY 10001

PH: (800) 242-9192
FAX: (212) 279-5570
SOFTWARE
Cost: $90.00
Analysis Capability: Bond Analysis,
  Real Estate Analysis, Financial
  Planning

Future value of a deposit, future value of a series, present value of a series, uneven cash flow, interest due, present value and time to double, and more. Calculates tax schedules, depreciation routines, rental income property analysis, and bond yields.

AUDIENCE: Individual, Professional	RISK LEVEL: Conservative, Moderate, Aggressive
TOPICS: Bonds, Mutual Funds, Stocks	

Sophisticated Investor

Miller Associates
P.O. Box 4361
Incline Village, NV 89450

PH: (702) 831-0429
SOFTWARE
Cost: $195.00
Analysis Capability: Financial
  Planning, Portfolio Management,
  Technical Analysis, Technical
  Screening, Simulation Games,
  Statistics, Expert System

Optimizes stock portfolios for maximum returns. Risk/return analysis based on Markowitz's Modern Portfolio Analysis. Includes correlation with S&P 500, complete beta and alpha calculations, standard error, and correlation coefficient determinations.

AUDIENCE: Individual, Professional	RISK LEVEL: Moderate, Aggressive
TOPICS: Mutual Funds, Stocks	

Spectrum Gateway

CDA Investment Technologies, Inc.
1355 Piccard Drive
Rockville, MD 20850

PH: (301) 975-9600
FAX: (301) 590-1350
Monthly charge $300.00 plus
  Quotron vendor fee

Covers stocks and convertibles. Easy access to find the exact information you need on 7,500 listed and unlisted common stocks and convertible issues held in the portfolios of over 2,300 institutions. Coverage includes 13(F) filers, U.S. & European.

AUDIENCE: Individual, Professional   RISK LEVEL: Moderate, Aggressive
TOPICS: Bonds, Stocks

Spectrum Ownership Profile

Spectrum Ownership Profile
1355 Piccard Drive
Rockville, MD 20850

PH: (301) 975-9600
FAX: (301) 590-1350
Cost: $53.00 per hour, monthly
  charge $1,800.00

Covers stocks. A comprehensive review of a company's ownership based on 13F Institutional Common Stock Holdings, U.S. Institutional Convertible Holdings, U.S. Investment Company Holdings, Europlan Investment Company Holdings, 13D & 13G .

AUDIENCE: Individual, Professional   RISK LEVEL: Moderate, Aggressive
TOPICS: Stocks

Splot!

Data Base Associates
P.O. Box 1838
Honolulu, HI 96805

PH: (808) 926-5854
FAX: (808) 926-5851
SOFTWARE
Cost: $125.00

Stock and portfolio plotting program for independent investors. Imports data from Dow Jones News Retrieval, CompuServe, Lotus Signal, X-press Executive, and X-press X-change. Printing compatibility for all Hewlett-Packard or Epson compatible printers.

AUDIENCE: Individual, Professional   RISK LEVEL: Moderate, Aggressive
TOPICS: Mutual Funds, Stocks

Spread Maker

Niche Software Products
P.O. Box 3574
Manassas, VA 22110

PH: (703) 368-8372
SOFTWARE
Cost: $50.00
Options Analysis

"Evaluates vertical, horizontal, and diagonal call spread investment candidates." Calculates the potential spread position and shows possible outcomes based on stock price at expiration dates. User can analyze potential outcomes.

AUDIENCE: Individual, Professional   RISK LEVEL: Aggressive
TOPICS: Options

Spreadware Option Pricing Model

Spreadware
P.O. Box 4574
Hayward, CA 94540

PH: (415) 794-4388
SOFTWARE
Cost: $18.95

Estimates a call option's theoretical price based on Black-Scholes Option Pricing Model. Supports 5 comparative analyses of the option.

AUDIENCE: Beginning, Individual, Professional   RISK LEVEL: Aggressive
TOPICS: Options

Spreadware Portfolio Management

Spreadware
P.O. Box 4574
Hayward, CA 94540

PH: (415) 794-4388
SOFTWARE
Cost: $24.95

Package manages security transactions for a portfolio. Individual securities can be analyzed to determine the break-even price and required rate of return price, taking transaction fees, taxes and other expenses into account.

AUDIENCE: Individual, Professional   RISK LEVEL: Moderate, Aggressive
TOPICS: Bonds, Mutual Funds, Stocks, Options

Stable-Technical Graphics

Winterra Software Group
P.O. Box 4106
Highlands Ranch, CO 80126

PH: (303) 470-6323
FAX: (303) 470-6323
SOFTWARE
Cost: $49.95

A stock market technical analysis program. Popular technical analysis techniques with graphics program. As many as 64 security charts can be created for individual or comparison analysis for study. Additional feature is the desktop chart management system.

AUDIENCE: Individual, Professional   RISK LEVEL: Moderate, Aggressive
TOPICS: Stocks

Standard & Poor's Corporate Descriptions

Standard & Poor's Corporation
25 Broadway
New York, NY 10004

PH: (212) 208-8300
FAX: (212) 412-0498
ON-LINE DATABASE
Access Fees: Call for Costs

Provides descriptive information on publicly held U.S. corporations trading securities on the New York, American, regional, selected Canadian and international stock exchanges, the NASDAQ system, and the over-the-counter in the United States.

AUDIENCE: Individual, Professional   RISK LEVEL: Moderate, Aggressive
TOPICS: Bonds, Stocks

Standard & Poor's Corporate Descriptions Plus News

Standard & Poor's Corporation
25 Broadway
New York, NY 10004

PH: (212) 208-8300
FAX: (212) 412-0498
ON-LINE DATABASE
Alternate Electronic Formats: CD-
  ROM
Access Fees: Call for Costs

Financial information on publicly held U.S. corporations trading securities on the New York, American, regional, selected Canadian and international stock exchanges, the NASDAQ system, and the Over-the-Counter. Recent news in Standard & Poor's Daily News.

AUDIENCE: Individual, Professional	RISK LEVEL: Moderate, Aggressive
TOPICS: Bonds, Stocks	

Standard & Poor's Daily News

Standard & Poor's Corporation
25 Broadway
New York, NY 10004

PH: (212) 208-8300
FAX: (212) 412-0498
ON-LINE DATABASE
Access Fees: Call for Costs

Provides financial news stories related to the leading public corporations.

AUDIENCE: Individual, Professional	RISK LEVEL: Conservative, Moderate, Aggressive
TOPICS: All	

Standard & Poor's Divided Record

Standard & Poor's Corporation
25 Broadway
New York, NY 10004

PH: (212) 208-8300
FAX: (212) 412-0498
Alternate Electronic Formats:
Magnetic Tape (Dividend Record)
ON-LINE DATABASE
Access Fees: Call for Costs

Stock dividends disbursements for stock listed on the New York and American stock exchanges, most active traded issues on the NASDAQ over-the-counter exchange, and dividend-paying companies in the Toronto and Montreal Stock exchange.

AUDIENCE: Individual, Professional	RISK LEVEL: Moderate, Aggressive
TOPICS: Stocks	

Standard & Poor's Industry Financial Data Bank

Standard & Poor's Corporation
25 Broadway
New York, NY 10004

PH: (212) 208-8300
FAX: (212) 412-0498
Type: Time series
ON-LINE DATABASE
Access Fees: Call for Costs

Financial data on industry groups and provides disaggregations of manufacturing, transportation sectors, and utilities.

AUDIENCE: Individual, Professional	RISK LEVEL: Moderate, Aggressive
TOPICS: Stocks	

Starquote

Star Data Systems, Inc.
330 Bay St.
Suite 402
Toronto, ON, Canada M5H 2S8

PH: (416) 363-7827
Type: Numeric
ON-LINE DATABASE
Access Fees: Call for Costs

Provides real-time stock and commodities quotes from North America stock exchanges and Marketwatch services. The service monitors trading instruments such as stock options, commodities futures, indices volumes and statistics.

AUDIENCE: Individual, Professional   RISK LEVEL: Aggressive
TOPICS: Options, Futures/Commodities

Startext (R)

Fort Worth Star-Telegram
400 W. 7th St.
P.O. Box 1870
Fort Worth, TX 76102

PH: (817) 390-7400
ON-LINE DATABASE
Access Fees: Call for Costs

Business information of daily closing prices for stocks traded on the American, New York and the NASDAQ Over-the-Counter markets.

AUDIENCE: Individual   RISK LEVEL: Moderate, Aggressive
TOPICS: Bonds, Mutual Funds, Stocks

Stat-Scan

Wright Investor's Service (WIS)
1000 Lafayette Blvd.
Bridgeport, CT 06604

PH: (203) 330-5000
(800) 232-0013
FAX: (203) 330-5090
ON-LINE DATABASE
Access Fees: Call for Costs

NYSE and other stocks. Investment acceptance, Worldscope assigned quality ratings and percentile rankings based on quality, current value, growth, projected earnings and dividends for the next 2 years and a 5 year projected growth rate for earnings.

AUDIENCE: Individual, Professional   RISK LEVEL: Moderate, Aggressive
TOPICS: Stocks

Statistical Analysis Forecasting Software Package

Programmed Press
599 Arnold Road
West Hempstead, NY 11552

PH: (516) 599-6527
SOFTWARE
Cost: $144.00, plus shipping
Analysis Capability: Fundamental
   Analysis, Technical Analysis,
   Statistics

Program has 20 interactive modules that calculate moving averages, variation, seasonal variation, trends, growth rates, time series decomposition, multiple correlation, and regression.

AUDIENCE: Individual, Professional   RISK LEVEL: Conservative, Moderate,
TOPICS: All   Aggressive

STO Quest

Integrated Financial Solutions, Inc.
1049 S.W. Baseline, Suite B-200
Hillsboro, OR 97123

PH: (800) 729-5037
(503) 640-5303
FAX: (503) 648-9528
SOFTWARE
Cost: $249.00
Analysis Capabilities: Fundamental
 Analysis, Fundamental Screening

Collect data on 3,000 stocks, separated by industry, from MetaStock and QuoteExpress Elite. Rank the companies in the industry by performance for future trading decisions.

AUDIENCE: Individual, Professional   RISK LEVEL: Moderate, Aggressive
TOPICS: Stocks

Stock Analyzer

Scientific Consultant Services
20 Stagecoach Road
Selden, NY 11784

PH: (516) 696-3333
FAX: (516) 696-3333
SOFTWARE
Cost: $599
Analysis Capability: Technical
 Analysis

User can determine best timed entry into positions in stocks or stock options. Calculates numerous indicators including MACD, MFI, OBV, RSI, stochastics, and much more. Allows for text-mode and graphics reports.

AUDIENCE: Individual, Professional   RISK LEVEL: Moderate, Aggressive
TOPICS: Stocks, Options

Stock and Futures Analyzer/Optimizer

N-Squared Computing
5318 Forest Ridge Road
Silverton, OR 97381

PH: (503) 873-4420
(214) 680-1445
FAX: (214) 680-1435
SOFTWARE
Cost: $595

A complete technical analysis graphics package designed for use by the advanced technician. Create, optimize, back-test, and visually verify any indicator that you can create using simple easy to follow prompts from N-Squared's powerful Create Indicator module.

AUDIENCE: Individual, Professional   RISK LEVEL: Moderate, Aggressive
TOPICS: Stocks, Options, Futures/Commodities

Stock Charting

Charles L. Pack
25303 La Loma Drive
Los Altos, CA 94022-4542

PH: (415) 949-0887
SOFTWARE
Cost: $49.95

Technical analysis and portfolio management for stocks, bonds, indexes, mutual funds, and other securities. Realized and unrealized gains/losses beta, annual appreciation, total return, asset allocation, ROI, and comparison of any security.

AUDIENCE: Individual, Professional   RISK LEVEL: Moderate, Aggressive
TOPICS: Bonds, Mutual Funds, Stocks, Options

Stock Data Corp

Stock Data Corp
905 Bywater Road
Annapolis, MD 21401

PH: (410) 280-5533
SOFTWARE
Basic monthly charge of $50.00.

Covers stocks. Download the entire 3 U.S. markets (9,000) issues in 2 minutes by modem or mailed weekly. Gives open, high, low, close and volume and will also create data for your favorite spreadsheets or charting programs, historical data available on CD/ROM.

AUDIENCE: Individual, Professional   RISK LEVEL: Moderate, Aggressive
TOPICS: Stocks

Stock Graph Maker

Niche Software Products
P.O. Box 3574
Manassas, VA 22110

PH: (703) 368-8372
SOFTWARE
Cost: $50.00

Database of stock volumes and prices can be tracked. Spreadsheet compatibility allows for data update and further technical analysis. Graphs closing prices, high/low/close, and volume. Automatically updates database through Prodigy through QuoteTrack.

AUDIENCE: Individual, Professional   RISK LEVEL: Moderate, Aggressive
TOPICS: Stocks, Options

Stock Investor

American Association of Individual
  Investors
625 N. Michigan Ave.
Suite 1900
Chicago, IL 60611

PH: (312) 280-0170
FAX: (312) 280-1625
ON-LINE DATABASE
Cost: $150.00

Quarterly updated fundamental financial information on publicly traded companies listed on the American and New York Stock Exchanges, NASDAQ national market, and NASDAQ small cap market. Information on 200 industry groups.

AUDIENCE: Individual, Professional   RISK LEVEL: Moderate, Aggressive
TOPICS: Bonds, Stocks

Stock Investor

Media General Financial Services
301 East Grace Street
Richmond, VA 23219

PH: (804) 649-6587
(800) 446-7922
FAX: (804) 649-6097
Cost: $99.00 for annual subscription
SOFTWARE

Provides easy and convenient way to screen stocks. Screen and analyze over 7,000 stocks. Research stocks by using over 200 predetermined financial variables or create your own financial variables. Custom design reporting capabilities.

AUDIENCE: Individual, Professional   RISK LEVEL: Moderate, Aggressive
TOPICS: Stocks

Stock Manager

Omni Software Systems, Inc.
702 N. Ernest
Griffith, IN 46319

PH: (219) 924-3522
SOFTWARE
Cost: $200.00
Analysis Capability: Financial
  Planning, Portfolio Management

Accounting and reporting capabilities, Stock Manager produces over 10 separate reports from 25 different items of information on each stock. Calculates the long- and short-term gains automatically, stocks sold, dividends reinvested, etc.

AUDIENCE: Individual	RISK LEVEL: Moderate, Aggressive
TOPICS: Mutual Funds, Stocks	

Stock Market Analyzer

Investment Tools, Inc.
P.O. Box 98916
Reno, NV 89507

PH: NA
SOFTWARE
Cost: $395/yr.
Analysis Capability: Technical
  Analysis, Futures Analysis

Inputs daily closing on NYSE composite index, DJ industrial average, volume, number of advancing issues, number of declining issues, and unchanged issues to analyze the internal health of the NYSE. Calculates market entry and exit signals and more.

AUDIENCE: Individual, Professional	RISK LEVEL: Moderate, Aggressive
TOPICS: Stocks	

Stock Market Bargains

Dynacomp, Inc.
178 Phillips Road
Webster, NY 14580

PH: (800) 828-6772
SOFTWARE
Cost: $69.95

Provides several tests for finding undervalued stocks: the Graham approach and a parameter test of price/earnings ratio, ratio of assets to liabilities, changes in earnings per share, number of institutional investors, and current earnings per share.

AUDIENCE: Individual	RISK LEVEL: Moderate, Aggressive
TOPICS: Stocks	

Stock Market Securities Program

Compu-Cast Corporation
1015 Gayley Avenues
Los Angeles, CA 90024

PH: (310) 476-4682
FAX: (310) 476-4682
SOFTWARE
Cost: $190.00

Performs technical analysis which produces accumulation/distribution charts that include closing prices. Charts indicate change of direction ahead of moving averages. Announces approaching top/bottom in securities and the market, buy/sell alert.

AUDIENCE: Individual, Professional	RISK LEVEL: Moderate, Aggressive
TOPICS: Stocks, Options	

Stock Market Software

Programmed Press
599 Arnold Road
W. Hempstead, NY 11552

PH: (516) 599-6527
SOFTWARE
Cost: $120.00

Covers stocks. Evaluates price, risk and return on investment in common stock.

| AUDIENCE: Individual | RISK LEVEL: Moderate, Aggressive |
| TOPICS: Stocks | |

Stock Master

G.C.P.I.
P.O. Box 790, Dept. #50-E
Marquette, MI 49855

PH: (906) 226-7600
SOFTWARE
Cost: $49.95
Analysis Capabilities: Financial
Planning, Portfolio Management

Program provides timely buy/sell information to investor with an emphasis on consistent returns. Menu-driven with options for adding a transaction, listing the transaction log, and evaluating current account status.

| AUDIENCE: Individual | RISK LEVEL: Moderate, Aggressive |
| TOPICS: Bonds, Stocks | |

Stock Master/Stock Plot

Dynacomp, Inc.
178 Phillips Road
Webster, NY 14580

PH: (800) 828-6772
SOFTWARE
Cost: $59.95

Technical analysis and fundamental analysis to assist in portfolio management. Records record stock transactions and tracks price action on selected securities. User may maintain 8 portfolios comprised of up to 30 stocks.

| AUDIENCE: Individual | RISK LEVEL: Moderate, Aggressive |
| TOPICS: Stocks | |

Stock Option Analysis Program

H & H Scientific
13507 Pendleton Street
Fort Washington, MD 20744

PH: (301) 292-2958
SOFTWARE
Cost: $150.00
Options Analysis

The Black-Sholes model is the basis for establishing a calculated fair price. Expected profit/loss transactions, commission schedules, and option volatility can be calculated. Program includes "what if " scenario.

| AUDIENCE: Individual, Professional | RISK LEVEL: Moderate, Aggressive |
| TOPICS: Options | |

Stock Option Calculations And Strategies

Compu-Vest Software
545 Fairview Avenue
Glen Ellyn, IL 60137

PH: (708) 469-4437
SOFTWARE
Cost: $40.00

Options analysis provided with 9 menu-driven programs. Identify over 90 put/call strategies, with or without stock positions and project profit/loss and break-even points. Black-Scholes model. Calculates risk/reward, option expiration, volatility, and more.

AUDIENCE: Individual, Professional	RISK LEVEL: Moderate, Aggressive
TOPICS: Stocks, Options	

Stock Option Scanner

H & H Scientific
13507 Pendleton Street
Fort Washington, MD 20744

PH: (301) 292-2958
SOFTWARE
Cost: $150.00
Options Analysis

Scans a list of 3,000 stock options and ranks the top 50 options according to 5 selected criteria based on annual rate of return and current option price. Data automatically downloaded from DJN/R or Signal.

AUDIENCE: Individual, Professional	RISK LEVEL: Moderate, Aggressive
TOPICS: Options	

Stock Portfolio

Heizer Software
P.O. Box 232019
Pleasant Hill, CA 94523

PH: (800) 888-7667
(510) 943-7667
FAX: (510) 943-6882
Cost: $15.00
SOFTWARE

Program records and evaluates buy/sell transactions and dates, commissions, dividends, portfolio performance, and portfolio statistics. Capable of handling short sales and partial sales for long- and short-term holding periods.

AUDIENCE: Beginning	RISK LEVEL: Moderate, Aggressive
TOPICS: Stocks	

Stock Portfolio Reporter

Micro Investment Systems, Inc.
P.O. Box 8599
Atlanta, GA 30306

PH: (404) 378-7535
SOFTWARE
Cost: $279.00

Maintains up to 200 stocks in a portfolio. Updates market prices using Dow Jones News Retrieval. Adjusts for stock splits and dividends.

AUDIENCE: Beginning, Individual	RISK LEVEL: Moderate, Aggressive
TOPICS: Stocks	

Stock Price Data Base

ADP Data Services
42 Broadway
17th Floor
Suite 1730
New York, NY 10004

PH: (212) 908-5400
ON-LINE DATABASE
Access Fees: Call for Costs

Provides the price of common and preferred stocks traded on the U.S. exchanges.

AUDIENCE: Individual, Professional   RISK LEVEL: Moderate, Aggressive
TOPICS: Stocks

Stock Prophet

Future Wave Software
1330 S. Gertuda Avenue
Redondo Beach, CA 90277

PH: (310) 540-5373
SOFTWARE
Analysis Capability: Fundamental,
Technical, Neural Network
Access Fees: Call for Costs

Stocks, commodities and mutual funds can be traded with artificial intelligence neural network trading system. Clear signals given days and weeks before execution dates. System can be designed, trained and tested to trade within a fraction of an hour.

AUDIENCE: Individual, Professional   RISK LEVEL: Moderate, Aggressive
TOPICS: Stocks, Options, Futures/Commodities

Stock This Week

Toyo Keizai Shinposha Co., Ltd.
1-2-1 Nihonbashi Hongokucho
Chuo-ku
Tokyo 103, Japan

PH: 03 32465580
FAX: 03 32424067
ON-LINE DATABASE

Provides the current week's most traded stock data.

AUDIENCE: Individual   RISK LEVEL: Moderate, Aggressive
TOPICS: Stocks

Stock Valuation

Heizer Software
P.O. Box 232019
Pleasant Hill, CA 94523

PH: (800) 888-7667
(510) 943-7667
FAX: (510) 943-6882
Cost: $25.00
SOFTWARE

Program can evaluate stocks using 5 methods to compute whether stock is undervalued or overvalued. Allows for stock splits and dividends. Growth rate and expected return are also calculated.

AUDIENCE: Beginning, Individual   RISK LEVEL: Moderate, Aggressive
TOPICS: Stocks

Stock Watcher

Micro Trading Software, Inc.
P.O. Box 175
Wilton, CT 06897-0175

PH: (203) 762-7820
SOFTWARE
Cost: $195.00

For investments including futures, stocks, commodities, mutual funds, and chart service. Stock Watcher provides clear, concise charts to aide the decision making process and to track investment returns.

AUDIENCE: Individual, Professional   RISK LEVEL: Moderate, Aggressive
TOPICS: Mutual Funds, Stocks, Options, Futures/Commodities

Stock Watcher

Stock Watcher
Box 175
Wilton, CT 06897

PH: (203) 762-7820
SOFTWARE
Cost: $195.00

Technical analysis performed on stocks, bonds, mutual funds, and market indexes. Functions include stochastics, MACD, moving averages, oscillators, on-balance volume, relative strength, TRIN, and cycle and trendline analysis.

AUDIENCE: Individual   RISK LEVEL: Moderate, Aggressive
TOPICS: Mutual Funds, Stocks, Options

Stock/Expert

Hawkeye Grafix
Box 1400
Oldsmar, FL 34677

PH: (813) 855-8687
SOFTWARE
Cost: $988.00
Cost: $50.00 - 30 day demo

Covers stocks. Recommends what stocks to purchase and when based on "expert" rules in the package. Provides portfolio support to group multiple accounts. Fetches stock closing data daily with online hookup using a modem.

AUDIENCE: Individual   RISK LEVEL: Moderate, Aggressive
TOPICS: Stocks

StockCraft Version 2.0

Decision Economics, Inc.
103 Washington St., Suite 172
Morristown, NJ 07960

PH: (201) 539-6889
SOFTWARE
Cost: $48.00

Covers stocks, mutual funds. Stock market system with portfolio management, technical analysis and optimized trading strategy. Includes a VisiCalc interface.

AUDIENCE: Beginning, Individual   RISK LEVEL: Moderate, Aggressive
TOPICS: Mutual Funds, Stocks

Stockdata

FRI Information Services, Ltd.
1081 McGill College Ave.
Suite 600
Montreal, PQ, Canada H3A 2N4

PH: (514) 842-5091
Contact: David Mallette, Sales
  Executive
ON-LINE DATABASE
Access Fees: Call for Costs

Information on stocks traded on the Toronto, Montreal, Calgary, Vancouver, New York, and American stock exchanges.

AUDIENCE: Individual, Professional   RISK LEVEL: Moderate, Aggressive
TOPICS: Stocks

Stockexpert

AIQ Systems, Inc.
916 Southwood Boulevard
Incline Village, NV 89450

PH: (800) 332-2999
(702) 831-2999
FAX: (702) 831-6784
SOFTWARE
Cost: $249.00

Uses technical indicators and analyzes rating for every stock in the database. Prints reports listing those stocks with the day's highest expert ratings both upside and downside. Profit Manager can also help protect principal and profit by using stop/loss.

AUDIENCE: Individual   RISK LEVEL: Moderate, Aggressive
TOPICS: Stocks

Stockfolio

Zephyr Services
1900 Murray Avenue
Pittsburgh, PA 15217

PH: (412) 422-6600
SOFTWARE
Cost: $29.95

Covers stocks. Maintains a portfolio for up to 40 stocks and will retrieve the latest price for all stocks. Provides portfolio summary and averages.

AUDIENCE: Individual   RISK LEVEL: Moderate, Aggressive
TOPICS: Stocks

StockMate

StockMate Financial Systems, Inc.
17981 Skypark Circle
Suite M
Irvine, CA 92714

PH: (714) 553-8814
4 screens = $117 month/screen
8 screens = $100 month/screen
16 screens = $92 month/screen

StockMate is a complete quotation and information solution for the brokerage industry. Combining S&P Ticker 111, the world's most powerful real-time digital feed.

AUDIENCE: Individual, Professional   RISK LEVEL: Moderate, Aggressive
TOPICS: Stocks

Stockpak II

Standard & Poor's Corporation
25 Broadway
New York, NY 10004

PH: (212) 208-8581
SOFTWARE
Cost: Contact Vendor

Covers stocks. Fundamental analysis that provides monthly, bi-monthly and quarterly updated financial facts on over 4,700 companies that trade on the three major stock exchanges. Downloads data from S&P's Stock Guide Database.

AUDIENCE: Individual, Professional	RISK LEVEL: Moderate, Aggressive
TOPICS: Stocks	

Stocks Trend Analyzer

Investment Tools, Inc.
P.O. Box 98916
Reno, NV 89507

PH: NA
SOFTWARE
Cost: $395.00/yr.
Technical Analysis, Futures
  Analysis

User inputs high, low, close, and volume to gain insight when to buy or sell a stock. Accepts manual input or quote file from DJN/R, DTN, Genesis, Technical Tools, Telemet, Signal, and CompuServe. Monitors up to 500 stocks.

AUDIENCE: Individual, Professional	RISK LEVEL: Moderate, Aggressive
TOPICS: Stocks	

Stokplot

Clarks Ridge Associates
R.D. Box 134
Leesburg, VA 22075

PH: (703) 882-3476
SOFTWARE
Cost: $40.00

Uses technical analysis and price history as the vehicle for investing in stocks, bonds, indexes, and mutual funds. User may select the intervals for the moving averages, buy/sell indicators, and percentage values. Auto-correlation function can be used.

AUDIENCE: Individual	RISK LEVEL: Moderate, Aggressive
TOPICS: Bonds, Mutual Funds, Stocks	

Strategist

Optionomics Corporation
2835 E. 3300 South, Suite 200
Salt Lake City, UT 84109

PH: (800) 255-3374
FAX: (801) 466-7320
SOFTWARE
Cost: $8,700.00/yr.
Analysis Capability: Fundamental
  Analysis, Futures Analysis,
  Options Analysis, Simulation
  Games, Statistics

"Real-time risk analysis software lets the user consolidate portfolios that include over-the-counter options and forwards along with listed futures and options." Theta, gamma, etc. for any portfolio or trades. Unlimited "what-if" capability.

AUDIENCE: Professional	RISK LEVEL: Moderate, Aggressive
TOPICS: Options, Futures/Commodities	

Streetsmart

Charles Schwab & Company, Inc.
101 Montgomery Street
Department S
San Francisco, CA 94104

PH: (415) 627-7000
(800) 334-4455
FAX: (415) 403-5503
ON-LINE DATABASE
Cost: $59.00

Gives real-time market data access to quotes, as well as analysis and news on a wide range of financial instruments. Monitors securities as well as provides a one year database on the AMEX, NYSE, NASDAQ, NMS stocks and on U.S. futures.

AUDIENCE: Beginning, Individual, Professional   RISK LEVEL: Moderate, Aggressive
TOPICS: All

Structured Financing Workstation, The

Wall Street Analytics, Inc.
33-41 85th Street
Jackson Heights, NY 11372

PH: (718) 446-5268
Costs: royalty-free permanent
  license $250,000; non-issuer
  permanent license $49,500 + 4
  basic points on the market price of
  all mortgage-backed securities
  issued.
Special thrift license $39,500.00

Mortgage-backed securities. System for structuring or analyzing MBS including complex derivative products such as CMO/REMICs and residuals. Structures including floating coupon bonds, IO-strips, PO-strips, accrual ("Z") bonds, PACs TACs and companions.

AUDIENCE: Professional   RISK LEVEL: Conservative, Moderate, Aggressive
TOPICS: Bonds

Super Charts

Omega Research, Inc.
9200 Sunset Drive
Miami, Fl 33173-3266

PH: (305) 270-1095
(800) 556-2022
FAX: (305) 270-9650
Cost: $195.00
SOFTWARE

"The first technical analysis program designed to take full advantage of Microsoft Windows. Combines graphical ease and stunning charting features with a powerful system tester that can actually help you discover and improve trading systems."

AUDIENCE: Beginning, Individual   RISK LEVEL: Moderate, Aggressive
TOPICS: Stocks, Options, Futures/Commodities

Super Tic

Cyber-Scan, Inc.
3601 Pulaski Road N.E.
Buffalo, NY 55313

PH: (612) 682-4150
SOFTWARE
Cost: $99.95

User has technical analysis tools for stocks, bonds, indexes, and futures; network as source. Integrates with Discovery for charting capability.

AUDIENCE: Individual   RISK LEVEL: Moderate, Aggressive
TOPICS: Bonds, Stocks, Options, Futures/Commodities

Super/Quote

Pisces SOFTWARE
P.O. Box 579-9171
Chicago, IL 60613

PH: (312) 281-7916
FAX: (312) 281-7916
On-line
Cost: $140.00

Utility function with data collection and data export. Exports data in any text format with limitations by user. The Radio Memory of 320 tickers can be used as a buffer to collect more than 320 prices automatically under batch file control.

AUDIENCE: Individual, Professional   RISK LEVEL: Moderate, Aggressive
TOPICS: Bonds, Mutual Funds, Stocks

Supercharts **

Omega Research, Inc.
Omega Research Building/9200
Sunset Drive
Miami, FL 33173-3266

PH: (800) 556-2022
(305) 270-1095
FAX: (305) 270-9650
SOFTWARE
Cost: $195.00

A Windows program with several unique features: unlimited number of technical indicators can be overlaid on any chart; 43 years of daily data can be displayed on a single chart; multidata chart windows contain up to 50 different data files simultaneously. Program includes prewritten technical indicators and over 150 built-in functions for use in formula creating.

AUDIENCE: Individual   RISK LEVEL: Moderate, Aggressive
TOPICS: Mutual Funds, Stocks, Options, Futures/Commodities

Superdex

Technicom, Inc.
736 NE 20th Avenue
Ft. Lauderdale, Florida 33304

PH: (305) 523-5394
FAX: (305) 523-3245
SOFTWARE

Futures trading system capable of automatically optimizing on any or all of four moving averages. Trade intraday or closing features. Automatic daily trading recommendations print-out. Correct roll-over testing for simulated actual trading, "backtrak" feature.

AUDIENCE: Individual, Professional   RISK LEVEL: Aggressive
TOPICS: Futures/Commodities

Swing Catcher

Trend Index Trading Company
Box 5
Altoona, WI 54720-0005

PH: (715) 833-1234
Cost: $995.00

Covers stocks, commodities, and has chart service. The major features: catches almost every price swing, be it minor, medium, or major trend; you can have very low drawdowns - "Drawdown Minimizer Logic"; AutoRun or Manual.

AUDIENCE: Individual, Professional   RISK LEVEL: Aggressive
TOPICS: Stocks, Options, Futures/Commodities

System Writer Plus for DOS

Omega Research Building
9200 Sunset Drive
Miami, FL 33173-3266

PH: (800) 556-2022
FAX: (305) 270-9650
SOFTWARE
Cost: $1,975.00
Technical Analysis, Technical
  Screening, Bond Analysis, Futures
  Analysis, Options Analysis

User can optimize and historically test any trading system without programming knowledge. Historical simulation using any desired data on any security for the last 5, 10, or 20 years. Charting features: graphing any security's historical performance.

AUDIENCE: Individual, Professional   RISK LEVEL: Moderate, Aggressive
TOPICS: Bonds, Stocks, Options, Futures/Commodities

TA-SRV

Townsend Analytics, Ltd.
100 S. Wacker Drive
Suite 1506
Chicago, IL 60606

PH: (800) 827-0141
(312) 621-0141
FAX: (312) 621-0487
SOFTWARE
Analysis Capability: Quote Utility
Cost: Contact Vendor

A real-time data server implemented under Microsoft Windows for multitasking. The server is the basis for Townsend Analytics trading station. TA-SRV is included with RealTick III and Option Risk Management or a stand-alone program. Builds database.

AUDIENCE: Individual, Professional   RISK LEVEL: Moderate, Aggressive
TOPICS: Bonds, Mutual Funds, Stocks, Options, Futures/Commodities

Take Stock

Triple-I
19221 E. Oakmont Drive
Miami, FL 33015

PH: (305) 829-2892
FAX: (305) 289-5121
SOFTWARE
Cost: $175.00
Analysis Capability: Fundamental
  Analysis, Technical Analysis,
  Fundamental Screening

Provides a number of criteria for analyzing a company's balance sheet and operating dynamics. Historical values and multiples to determine if the stock is a good value and at what price. Provides summary of items to check before buying. Comparison features.

AUDIENCE: Individual   RISK LEVEL: Moderate, Aggressive
TOPICS: Stocks

Technical Analysis Scanner

Flexsoft
7172 Regional Street, #276
Dublin, CA 94568

PH: (510) 829-9733
FAX: (510) 829-9733
ONLINE SERVICE
Cost: $249.00
Analysis Capabilities: Technical
  Analysis, Technical Screening

Analyzes securities using 60 built in technical functions. User can compare values against other indicators or values, make investment decisions from these values, and create specialized reports. Can calculate on a daily basis the performance of the program.

AUDIENCE: Individual, Professional   RISK LEVEL: Moderate, Aggressive
TOPICS: Stocks, Options, Futures/Commodities

Technical Databridge, The

Savant Software, Inc.
11211 Bedford Center Rd.
Suite 301
Bedford, NH 03110

PH: (800) 231-9900
(603) 471-0400
SOFTWARE
Cost: $145.00

For users of the Technical Investor. Provides data transfer between The Technical Investor and Lotus 1-2-3 and other spreadsheet programs.

AUDIENCE: Individual, Professional   RISK LEVEL: Moderate, Aggressive
TOPICS: Mutual Funds, Stocks, Options, Futures/Commodities

Technical Investor

Savant Software, Inc
120 Bedford Center Road
Bedford, NH 03110

PH: (800) 231-9900
(603) 471-0400
FAX: (603) 472-5981
SOFTWARE
Cost: $245

Program has extensive database that can store information on up to 2,500 securities with up to 40 years of daily data for a security. Charting capability for price and volume bars; high, low, close price lines; point and figure charts. Volume indicators and others.

AUDIENCE: Individual, Professional   RISK LEVEL: Moderate, Aggressive
TOPICS: Stocks, Options, Futures/Commodities

Technical Selector, The

Savant Software, Inc.
11211 Bedford Center Rd.
Suite 301
Bedford, NH 03110

PH: (800) 231-9900
(603) 471-0400
SOFTWARE
Cost: $145.00

Covers stocks, market timing. Optional security filter for Savant's The Technical Investor. Uses certain technical analysis studies to select stocks, mutual funds, options, etc. Creates lists of securities that pass each filter.

AUDIENCE: Individual, Professional   RISK LEVEL: Moderate, Aggressive
TOPICS: Stocks

Technician

Equis International
3950 South 700 E.
Suite 100
Salt Lake City, UT 84107

PH: (800) 882-3040
(801) 265-8886
FAX: (801) 265-3999
SOFTWARE
Cost: $249.00; modem updating
   service $120.00/year

Uses technical analysis and statistics to analyze the stock market to anticipate price changes. Offers more than 100 specialized indicators and studies that chart momentum, sentiment, monetary, and relative strength conditions of the market.

AUDIENCE: Individual, Professional   RISK LEVEL: Moderate, Aggressive
TOPICS: Stocks

Technifilter Plus

RTR Software, Inc.
19 W. Hargett Street, Suite 204
Raleigh, NC 27601

PH: (919) 829-0789
FAX: (919) 829-0891
SOFTWARE
Cost: $399.00
Technical Analysis, Technical
  Screening, Futures Analysis

Use historical analysis to test buy/sell strategies on real data. Produce 35 sample reports from over 185 formulas and 20 ready to use strategy "tests." Testing features include the ability to vary 7 groups of different parameters to discover the most profitable.

AUDIENCE: Individual, Professional   RISK LEVEL: Moderate, Aggressive
TOPICS: Stocks, Options, Futures/Commodities

Techniq

Zentas Software
8401 South Long Avenue
Burbank, CA 60459

PH: (708) 425-3573
SOFTWARE
Cost: $179.00
Technical Analysis, Options
  Analysis, Spreadsheets

Technical analysis program that combines graphics, data communications, a mathematics engine, database functions and several other utilities into a single integrated package. Program has 27 preprogrammed studies with over 60 functions.

AUDIENCE: Individual, Professional   RISK LEVEL: Moderate, Aggressive
TOPICS: Stocks, Options, Futures/Commodities

Technova

Technova Research, Inc.
8600 W. 110th St.
Overland Park, KS 66210-1805

PH: (913) 338-2121
(800) 228-2933
Cost: $225.00/month

Provides on-line trading system for futures and options on futures. It has technical analysis studies and permits the use of self-designed or preprogrammed technical indicators. Options analytics and real-time calculation of implied volatility.

AUDIENCE: Individual, Professional   RISK LEVEL: Aggressive
TOPICS: Options, Futures/Commodities

Telemet Encore

Telemet America, Inc.
325 First St.
Alexandria, VA 22314

PH: (703) 548-2042
(800) 368-2078
ON-LINE DATABASE
Cost: $600.00 deposit
Cost: $139.00/month

Offers up to the second market prices and tracks almost 10,000 issues that can be exported to other PC applications with a file export utility. Prices are available within about 50 miles of about 24 metropolitan areas by FM.

AUDIENCE: Individual, Professional   RISK LEVEL: Moderate, Aggressive
TOPICS: Mutual Funds, Stocks, Options

Telerate Financial Information Network

Telerate Systems, Inc.
Harborside Financial Center
600 Plaza Two
Jersey City, NJ 07311

PH: (201) 860-4000
ON-LINE DATABASE
Access Fees: Call for Costs

Money market instruments; government securities; mortgage-backed securities; commercial banking statistics; and international money market rates. Futures in financial, metals, currency, and interest rate options on the New York and American stock exchanges.

AUDIENCE: Professional   RISK LEVEL: Conservative, Moderate
TOPICS: Bonds, Options, Futures/Commodities

Telerate II Historical Database

Telerate Systems, Inc.
Harborside Financial Center
600 Plaza Two
Jersey City, NJ 07311

PH: (201) 860-4000
ON-LINE DATABASE
Access Fees: Call for Costs

Provides U.S. money market rates, certificates of deposit, repurchase agreements, government bond yields, as well as domestic and international money market instruments.

AUDIENCE: Professional   RISK LEVEL: Conservative, Moderate
TOPICS: Bonds

Telerate International Quotations

Telerate Systems, Inc.
Harborside Financial Center
600 Plaza Two
Jersey City, NJ 07311

PH: (201) 860-4000
ON-LINE DATABASE
Access Fees: Call for Costs

Real-time coverage of stock options and futures from North American, London, and Tokyo stock exchanges.

AUDIENCE: Professional   RISK LEVEL: Aggressive
TOPICS: Stocks, Options, Futures/Commodities

Telescan

Telescan, Inc.
10550 Richmond Ave.
Suite 250
Houston, TX 77042-5019

PH: (713) 952-1060
ON-LINE DATABASE
Access Fees: Call for Costs

Gives current and historical and market analyses as well as the prices on stocks that are traded on the New York, American, and NASDAQ over-the-counter markets.

AUDIENCE: Individual, Professional   RISK LEVEL: Moderate, Aggressive
TOPICS: Stocks

Telescan Analyzer 3.0

Telescan, Inc.
10550 Richmond Avenue
Suite 250
Houston, TX 77042

PH: (800) 324-8353
(713) 952-1060
SOFTWARE
Cost: $212.75, On-line charge:
 .94/min prime time

Includes stock quote service (delayed with 20 minute updates), chart services, stocks, options, mutual funds, industry groups, indexes and charts. A critically acclaimed stock analysis program. Retrieves graphs. 100 technical and fundamental indicators.

AUDIENCE: Individual, Professional   RISK LEVEL: Moderate, Aggressive
TOPICS: Mutual Funds, Stocks, Options, Futures/Commodities

Tickerscreen

Max Ule & Company Inc.
26 Broadway
Suite 200
New York, NY 10004

PH: (212) 766-2610
ON-LINE DATABASE

Closing price quotes for stocks traded on the New York Stock Exchange and other market information.

AUDIENCE: Individual   RISK LEVEL: Moderate, Aggressive
TOPICS: Stocks

Tickerwatcher

Linn Software, Inc.
3199 Hammock Creek Court
Lithonia, GA 30058

PH: (404) 929-8802
FAX: (404) 929-8802
SOFTWARE
Cost: $295.00
Portfolio Management, Technical
 Analysis, Spreadsheets

Provides real-time or delayed quote monitoring, portfolio management, and daily charts on ticker symbols. Unlimited number of quote pages can be organized in any sequence. Program provides historical monitoring and charting of portfolio values.

AUDIENCE: Individual, Professional   RISK LEVEL: Moderate, Aggressive
TOPICS: Stocks

Tiger Multiple Stock Screening & Timing System

Tiger Investment Software
P.O. Box 9491
San Diego, CA 92169

PH: (619) 459-8577
SOFTWARE
Cost: $895
Technical Analysis, Technical
Screening, Expert System

Five hundred individual stocks are updated nightly from Worden Brothers and ranked for relative strength, price versus volume divergences, and consistent long-term accumulation measured from intraday volume formula. Back-testing function.

AUDIENCE: Individual, Professional   RISK LEVEL: Moderate, Aggressive
TOPICS: Mutual Funds, Stocks

Timer

Tools For Timing
11345 Highway 7, #499
Minnetonka, MN 55305

PH: (800) 325-1344
FAX: (612) 938-1275
Cost: $350.00
SOFTWARE
Technical Analysis, Simulation
  Games, Expert System

Market activity is defined by 7 primary indicators designed to recognize tops and bottoms of complete cycles in the market. Shows indicators and demonstrates when they are the most effective to aid in investment strategy.

AUDIENCE: Individual   RISK LEVEL: Moderate, Aggressive
TOPICS: Stocks, Futures/Commodities

Timer Professional

Tools For Timing
11345 Highway 7, #499
Minnetonka, MN 55305

PH: (800) 325-1344
(612) 939-0076
FAX: (612) 938-1275
Cost: $450
SOFTWARE
Technical Analysis, Simulation
  Games

Includes Timer and Mirat with added features of a log scale comparison of all three U.S. markets. Program breaks market activity into cycles defined by peaks in the number of new lows.

AUDIENCE: Professional   RISK LEVEL: Moderate, Aggressive
TOPICS: Stocks, Futures/Commodities

Timing Report, The

Timing Financial Services, Ltd.
10410 North 31st Avenue
Suite 404
Phoenix, AZ 85051

PH: (602) 942-3111
(800) 779-5000 (DTN phone)
Cost: $300.00 and $35.00 per
  month.

The Timing Report is transmitted daily via DTN and is 5 (quote machine size) pages long. Blends the technical analysis of Timing editor, William Jaeger and Elliott wave expert, Brent Harris with the fundamental (weather) analysis of Cliff Harris.

AUDIENCE: Individual, Professional   RISK LEVEL: Aggressive
TOPICS: Options, Futures/Commodities

Top Vest

Savant Software, Inc.
11211 Bedford Center Rd.
Suite 301
Bedford, NH 03110

PH: (800) 231-9900
(603) 471-0400
SOFTWARE
Costs: $3,500.00
Technical and Fundamental Analysis

A comprehensive package covering stocks, commodities, mutual funds, options, bonds, and indices. Allows both technical and fundamental analysis and includes communications to retrieve prices and data from Warner, Dow Jones and Ford Investor Services.

AUDIENCE: Professional   RISK LEVEL: Moderate, Aggressive
TOPICS: Mutual Funds, Stocks, Options, Futures/Commodities

Track Online

Track Data Corp.
61 Broadway
New York, NY 10006

PH: (718) 522-6886
(800) 935-7788
Cost: $95.00/mo

Includes options, stocks, commodities/futures, and indices. Access via nationwide networks. Offers a broad range of third party financial databases to keep you on top of your investments, research market trends, and spot investment opportunities.

AUDIENCE: Individual	RISK LEVEL: Moderate, Aggressive
TOPICS: Stocks, Options, Futures/Commodities	

Tracker For Investors Business Daily

New High Co.
RD #2
Riverhead, NY 11901

PH: (800) 643-8950
(516) 722-5407
FAX: (516) 722-5409
SOFTWARE
Cost: $79.00
Technical Analysis

User can build a database to evaluate individual securities or securities by different categories in Investor's Business Daily.

AUDIENCE: Individual, Professional	RISK LEVEL: Moderate, Aggressive
TOPICS: Stocks	

Trade Net

Scientific Consultant Services
20 Stagecoach Road
Selden, NY 11784

PH: (516) 696-3333
FAX: (516) 696-3333
SOFTWARE
Cost: $159.00

Allows N-Train neural network programs to be used with Trade Station.

AUDIENCE: Individual, Professional	RISK LEVEL: Aggressive
TOPICS: Stocks, Options, Futures/Commodities	

Trade*Plus

Trade*Plus, Inc.
480 California Ave.
Suite 301
Palo Alto, CA 94306

PH: (415) 324-4554
(800) 952-9900
ON-LINE DATABASE

Current and historical price information on securities traded on the American and New York Stock Exchanges, as well as NASDAQ National Market System and over-the-counter stocks. It also gives prices for options traded on the Chicago Board of Exchange.

AUDIENCE: Individual, Professional	RISK LEVEL: Moderate, Aggressive
TOPICS: Stocks, Options, Futures/Commodities	

Trade Station

Omega Research, Inc.
9200 Sunset Dr.
Miami, FL 33173

PH: (800) 556-2022
(305) 594-7664
FAX: (305) 477-7808
Cost: $1,895.00 plus data charges

The first only real-time analysis program ever developed that lets your computer automate and track your own custom trading strategies without programming knowledge. (1) Scan dozens of markets simultaneously, (2) Instantly chart, (3) Automate intraday systems.

AUDIENCE: Individual, Professional   RISK LEVEL: Aggressive
TOPICS: Stocks, Options, Futures/Commodities

Tradeline Electronic Stock Guide

IDD Information Services
2 World Trade Center
18th Floor
New York, NY 10048

PH: (212) 432-0045
FAX: (212) 432-2817
Transmission: Diskette, CD-ROM
ON-LINE DATABASE
Cost: $119.00/year

Gives security performance "snapshot" for each publicly traded stocks on the AMEX, NY, NASDAQ exchanges. Each printable snapshot includes average daily stock price/volume, yield, payout ratio, P/E ratio, annual dividend, 52 week high/low price, and total returns.

AUDIENCE: Individual, Professional   RISK LEVEL: Moderate, Aggressive
TOPICS: Stocks

Tradeline International

IDD Information Services
2 World Trade Center
18th Floor
New York, NY 10048

PH: (212) 432-0045
FAX: (212) 432-2817
ON-LINE DATABASE

Price/performance analysis, technical analysis, company analysis, industry evaluation, market indexes, international exchanges, call and put options coverage, dividend and stock split back to 1968, equity, corporate bond, government debt and mutual fund pricing.

AUDIENCE: Individual, Professional   RISK LEVEL: Moderate, Aggressive
TOPICS: Bonds, Mutual Funds, Stocks, Options

Tradeline North America

IDD Information Services
2 World Trade Center, 18th Floor
New York, NY 10048

PH: (212) 432-0045
FAX: (212) 432-2817
ON-LINE DATABASE

Company analysis, technical analysis, price/performance analysis, industry/geographic evaluation, and client reporting. United States and Canadian securities. Market indexes, equity, corporate bond, current earnings, government debt and mutual fund pricing.

AUDIENCE: Individual, Professional   RISK LEVEL: Conservative, Moderate,
TOPICS: Bonds, Mutual Funds, Stocks, Options   Aggressive

Tradeline Pocket Stock Guide

IDD Information Services
Two World Trade Center
18th Floor
New York, NY 10048

PH: (212) 432-0045
FAX: (212) 432-2817
Cost: $199.95
ON-LINE DATABASE
Cost: $69.96/update

Pocket-sized, electronic source for historical information on stocks traded on the AMEX, NYSE, NASDAQ, including market indexes. It charts stock and market performance, screens for stocks based on personal investment criteria, reviews fundamental and pricing.

AUDIENCE: Individual, Professional   RISK LEVEL: Conservative, Moderate,
TOPICS: Bonds, Mutual Funds, Stocks, Options   Aggressive

Tradeline Securities Pricing

IDD Information Services
Two World Trade Center
New York, NY 10048

PH: (212) 432-0045
FAX: (212) 912-1457
Cost: $15,000.00 annually for
    unlimited usage

Covers stocks, all bonds except foreign, options, and mutual funds. Provides as much as 15 years of daily price and dividend information on over 110,000 securities traded on all major North American exchanges and over the counter.

AUDIENCE: Individual, Professional   RISK LEVEL: Conservative, Moderate, Aggressive
TOPICS: Bonds, Mutual Funds, Stocks, Options, Futures/Commodities

Trader

Bechelli, Harris & Asociados
Tte. Gral. J.D. Peron 729, Piso 9
1038 Buenos Aires, Argentina

PH: 468976
ON-LINE DATABASE

Information on import and export opportunities, notices of special merchandise sales and international tenders, and requests for agents and distributors. Also has international trade fair calendar.

AUDIENCE: Individual, Professional   RISK LEVEL: Aggressive
TOPICS: Stocks, Options, Futures/Commodities

Trader Control Package

Commodity Information Services
327 S. LaSalle, Suite 1133
Chicago, IL 60604

PH: (312) 922-3661
(800) 800-7227
FAX: (312) 341-1494
ON-LINE DATABASE

"System contained" and evaluates the futures market on value, resulting in reference points required for trading. Daily market screen, overlay demand cures, and the fundamental value of the future.

AUDIENCE: Individual, Professional   RISK LEVEL: Aggressive
TOPICS: Options, Futures/Commodities

Trader's Profit Motive System

Trader's Software, Inc.
P.O. Box 2690
Edmond, OK 73083

PH: (405) 348-0544
FAX: (405) 341-3361
SOFTWARE
Cost: $2,995.00
Futures

A fully disclosed trading model for commodity futures. User can evaluate the stability of equity growth and adjust trading strategy for the smoothest performance. Includes historical data for 15 commodities.

AUDIENCE: Professional　　　　　**RISK LEVEL: Conservative, Moderate, Aggressive**
TOPICS: Futures/Commodities

Tradestation

Omega Research, Inc./ Omega
Research Building
9200 Sunset Drive
Miami, FL 33173-3266

PH: (800) 556-2022
FAX: (305) 270-9650
SOFTWARE
Cost: $1,895
Technical Analysis, Technical
　Screening, Bond Analysis, Futures
　Analysis, Options Analysis

Technical analysis program that allows user to automate, track, and back-test any trading system in real-time or historical, on dozens of markets simultaneously, without programming knowledge. Exact market orders to be placed or canceled, tracks open positions.

AUDIENCE: Individual, Professional　　　**RISK LEVEL: Aggressive**
TOPICS: Options, Futures/Commodities

Tradex 21

Essex Trading Company, Ltd.
24 W. 500 Maple Avenue
Suite 108
Naperville, IL 60540

PH: (800) 726-2140
(708) 416-3530
FAX: (708) 416-3558
SOFTWARE
Cost: $3,000.00

Provides technical analysis, bond analysis, and futures analysis for markets in currencies, grains, meats, foods, stock-index, and energies.

AUDIENCE: Individual, Professional　　　**RISK LEVEL: Aggressive**
TOPICS: Stocks, Options, Futures/Commodities

Trading Package

Coast Investment Software
358 Avenida Milano
Sarasota, FL 34242-1517

PH: (813) 346-3801
FAX: (813) 346-3901
SOFTWARE
Cost: $295.00

Technical analysis and screening, bond analysis, futures analysis, and options analysis. Provides intraday and end-of-the-day signals. Includes bar chart capability, RSI, a variety of moving averages, trendlines, and Hurst cycle projection capability.

AUDIENCE: Individual, Professional　　　**RISK LEVEL: Aggressive**
TOPICS: Options, Futures/Commodities

Trading Systems Technology

Waters Information Services, Inc.
285 West Broadway
Rm. 350
New York, NY 10013

PH: (212) 925-6990
Cost: $495.00/yr U.S. and Canada,
  $525.00/yr elsewhere
Frequency: 24/yr; indexes annually
Date of first issue: July 1989

Covey E. Bock, editor. Covers technology applications in the financial markets, including trader workstations, trading room data processing and communications technology, analytical software and expert systems, and automation of global market infrastructure.

AUDIENCE: Individual, Professional   RISK LEVEL: Aggressive
TOPICS: Stocks, Options, Futures/Commodities

Tradingexpert

AIQ Systems, Inc.
916 Southwood Boulevard
Incline Village, NV 89450

PH: (800) 332-2999
(702) 831-2999
FAX: (702) 831-6784
SOFTWARE
Cost: $249.00

A wide variety of functions with this program: portfolio management, fundamental analysis, technical analysis, technical screening, options analysis, simulation games, and expert systems. A stock market timing indicator.

AUDIENCE: Individual, Professional   RISK LEVEL: Moderate, Aggressive
TOPICS: Stocks, Options, Futures/Commodities

Trendline Securities Pricing

IDD Information Services
Two World Trade Center
New York, NY 10048

PH: (212) 432-0045
FAX: (212) 912-1457
Cost: Contact Vendor

Covers stocks, all bonds except foreign, options, and mutual funds. Provides as much as 20 years of daily price and dividend information on over 220,000 securities traded on all major North American exchanges and over the counter.

AUDIENCE: Professional   RISK LEVEL: Conservative, Moderate, Aggressive
TOPICS: Bonds, Mutual Funds, Stocks, Options

Trendpoint

Trendpoint Software
9709 Elrod Road
Kensington, MD 20895

PH: (301) 949-8131
SOFTWARE
Cost: $35.00

User helps time important buy/sell decisions from numerous technical indicators. Features include simple, exponential and weighted moving averages; Wilder's relative strength, standard deviation and more. Input data from ASCII files or manually.

AUDIENCE: Individual   RISK LEVEL: Moderate, Aggressive
TOPICS: Stocks, Options, Futures/Commodities

Trendvest Ratings

Trendvest Corporation
P.O. Box 44115
Pittsburgh, PA 15205

PH: (412) 921-6900
ON-LINE DATABASE
Access Fees: Call for Costs

Investment ratings for stock mutual funds and aggregate indicators for the stock, bond, and gold markets.

AUDIENCE: Beginning, Individual	RISK LEVEL: Moderate, Aggressive
TOPICS: Mutual Funds	

TRW Business Credit Profiles

Dialog Information Services, Inc.
3460 Hillview Ave.
Palo Alto, CA 94304

PH: (800) 334-2564
FAX: (415) 858-7069
ON-LINE DATABASE
Cost: $295 for access to entire
DIALOG service
Cost: $1.80/minute

Provides the following information on 2,500,000 companies: payment history, bankruptcy, tax and legal history, UCC filings, bank relationships, Standard Industrial Classification codes, sales ranges, and company records that have financial information.

AUDIENCE: Individual, Professional	RISK LEVEL: Moderate, Aggressive
TOPICS: Bonds, Stocks	

TT Chart Book Systems

Technical Tools
334 State St.
Suite 201
Los Altos, CA 94022

PH: (415) 948-6124
(800) 231-8005
FAX: (415) 948-5697
Cost: $750/month for unlimited
  access

Technical analysis program with data included. It creates daily, weekly, and monthly charts. The program includes scripts to locate and correct "bad" data. End of the day quotes and a full history are included.

AUDIENCE: Individual, Professional	RISK LEVEL: Moderate, Aggressive
TOPICS: Mutual Funds, Stocks	

TValue

Emerging Market Technologies, Inc.
1230 Johnson Ferry Road
Suite F-1
Marietta, GA 30068

PH: (404) 973-2300
FAX: (404) 973-3003
SOFTWARE
Cost: $129.00

Program for IRR, compound interest and loan amortization calculations.

AUDIENCE: Beginning, Individual	RISK LEVEL: Conservative, Moderate
TOPICS: Bonds	

Ultra II SCTA

Wall Street On-Line Publishing
P.O. Box 6
Riverdale, NY 10471-0006

PH: (718) 884-5408
FAX: (718) 543-2117
SOFTWARE
Cost: $25.00
Technical Analysis, Expert System

Stock charting package with communications module to link with Dial/Data, DJN/R or CompuServe. Enables user to draw charts on screen and perform technical analysis using 12 indicators. Features include moving averages, MACD, rate-of-change, Wilder's relative strength, momentum, stochastics and others.

AUDIENCE: Beginning, Individual   RISK LEVEL: Moderate, Aggressive
TOPICS: Stocks

Ultra Market Advisor

Ultra Financial Systems
1633 Arrowhead Drive
Flower Mound, TX 75028

PH: (800) 364-4883
FAX: (214) 539-3803
Cost: $195.00
SOFTWARE
Fundamental Analysis, Technical Analysis, Expert System

Generates buy/sell signal for stock market indexes. Uses fundamental and technical indicators to identify long and medium term market turning points. Indicators include advance/decline line, breadth, volume, stochastics, CCI, RSI, OBV, MACD.

AUDIENCE: Individual, Professional   RISK LEVEL: Aggressive
TOPICS: Stocks, Futures/Commodities

Unistox

United Press International (UPI)
5 Penn Plaza
461 Eighth Ave.
New York, NY 10001

PH: (212) 560-1100
ON-LINE DATABASE

Current and historical information on commodities and stock market prices.

AUDIENCE: Individual, Professional   RISK LEVEL: Moderate, Aggressive
TOPICS: Stocks, Options, Futures/Commodities

United States Bonds

Reuters Information Services (Canada) Ltd./Data Services Division
Exchange Tower, Suite 1900
2 First Canadian Place
Toronto, ON, Canada M5X 1E3

PH: (416) 364-5361
(800) 387-1588
FAX: (416) 364-0646
ON-LINE DATABASE

Provides price and yield data for bond issues listed on the New York and American Stock Exchanges, and U.S. Government and Agency bond issues.

AUDIENCE: Individual, Professional   RISK LEVEL: Conservative, Moderate
TOPICS: Bonds

United States Options

Reuters Information Services (Canada)
Ltd./Data Services Division
Exchange Tower, Suite 1900
2 First Canadian Place
Toronto, ON, Canada M5X 1E3

PH: (416) 364-5361
(800) 387-1588
FAX: (416) 364-0646
ON-LINE DATABASE

Provides interest rate options, stock options, index options, and foreign currency options on major U.S. exchanges; the Chicago Board Options Exchange; American Stock Exchange; Pacific Stock Exchange; and Philadelphia, Baltimore, and Washington Stock Exchanges

AUDIENCE: Individual, Professional   RISK LEVEL: Aggressive
TOPICS: Options

United States Stock Market

Reuters Information Services (Canada)
Ltd./Data Services Division
Exchange Tower, Suite 1900
2 First Canadian Place
Toronto, ON, Canada M5X 1E3

PH: (416) 364-5361
(800) 387-1588
FAX: (416) 364-0646
ON-LINE DATABASE

Information on securities traded on North American exchanges, and includes preferred and common stocks, rights, warrants, and units traded on the New York, American, Montreal, Midwest, Boston, Pacific, Toronto, Philadelphia, Baltimore, and Washington.

AUDIENCE: Individual, Professional   RISK LEVEL: Moderate, Aggressive
TOPICS: Stocks

Universal Exotics Add-in

Financial Systems Software (UK), Ltd.
2 London Wall Bldgs.
London Wall
London, EC2M-5PP, UK

PH: (44-71) 628-4200
SOFTWARE
Cost: $223.50 - $477.00
Bond Analysis, Futures Analysis,
Options Analysis, Financial
Planning, Simulation Games,
Spreadsheets, Statistics

Uses flexible proprietary Monte Carlo simulation to calculate option prices and sensitivities. Handles all options (commodities, currencies, futures) and exotic options such as average price (Asian) barrier (knock-out and knock-ins).

AUDIENCE: Individual, Professional   RISK LEVEL: Moderate, Aggressive
TOPICS: Bonds, Options, Futures/Commodities

Universal Swap Add-in

Financial Systems Software (UK), Ltd.
2 London Wall Bldgs.
London Wall
London, EC2M-5PP, UK

PH: (44-71) 628-4200
SOFTWARE
Cost: $749.25 - $1,498.50
Bond Analysis, Futures Analysis,
Options Analysis, Financial
Planning, Simulation Games,
Spreadsheets, Statistics

Multicurrency interest rate swaps. Track and build a structure of interest rates and a volatility curve for each currency being monitored. Functions include swap, cap, collar, floor, zero curve, discount factor function, FRA, and IRG.

AUDIENCE: Professional   RISK LEVEL: Conservative, Moderate, Aggressive
TOPICS: Bonds, Options, Futures/Commodities

Universal Yield Add-in

Financial Systems Software (UK), Ltd.
2 London Wall Bldgs.
London Wall
London, EC2M-5PP, UK

PH: (44-71) 628-4200
SOFTWARE
Cost: $223.50 - $477.00
Bond Analysis, Futures Analysis,
  Options Analysis, Financial
  Planning, Simulation Games,
  Spreadsheets, Statistics

Program calculates the yield on international fixed-income securities including MTNs, deferred, long or short first coupon bonds, AIBD yields, hedges, repos, and money market yields on all instruments. Calculates risk/return profiles on arbitrage trades.

AUDIENCE: Professional   RISK LEVEL: Conservative, Moderate, Aggressive
TOPICS: Bonds, Options, Futures/Commodities

Universal Zero-Curve Add-in

Financial Systems Software (UK), Ltd.
2 London Wall Bldgs.
London Wall
London, EC2M-5PP, UK

PH: (44-71) 628-4200
SOFTWARE
Cost: $223.50 - $477.00
Bond Analysis, Futures Analysis,
  Options Analysis, Financial
  Planning, Simulation Games,
  Spreadsheets, Statistics

Variety of uses: calculating forward FX rates, swap rates, commodity rates, and zero-curves. Co-exists with Universal Exotics, Options, Swap, and Yield Add-ins, providing the ability to create complex models combining bonds, bond futures, options, and swaps.

AUDIENCE: Professional   RISK LEVEL: Conservative, Moderate, Aggressive
TOPICS: Bonds, Options, Futures/Commodities

Update

Automated Data Collection,
Micron, Inc.
10045 Waterford Drive
Ellicott City, MD 21043

PH: (301) 461-2721
Cost: $298.00

Covers stocks and commodities. For use with CompuTrac. Micron's product update uses the Signal receiver to gather daily data and update CompuTrac's data files. Final data are available from Signal approximately one hour after the market closes.

AUDIENCE: Individual, Professional   RISK LEVEL: Moderate, Aggressive
TOPICS: Stocks, Options, Futures/Commodities

Valuation Pricing Service (VPS)

Telekurs (North America), Inc.
One State Street Plaza
23rd Floor
New York, NY 10004

PH: (212) 487-2700
FAX: (212) 487-2808
ON-LINE DATABASE
Access Fees: Call for Costs

Gives the prices for securities and commodity exchanges, and key market makers worldwide. It has two services: End-of-Day Valuation Pricing Service, and Intraday Valuation Pricing Service.

AUDIENCE: Individual, Professional   RISK LEVEL: Moderate, Aggressive
TOPICS: Bonds, Stocks, Options, Futures/Commodities

Value Line Annual Reports

Value Line Publishing, Inc.
711 Third Ave.
New York, NY 10017

PH: (212) 687-3965
FAX: (212) 986-3243
ON-LINE DATABASE
Access Fees: Call for Costs

Annual financial information on companies traded on major U.S. stock exchanges.

AUDIENCE: Beginning, Individual, Professional   RISK LEVEL: Moderate, Aggressive
TOPICS: Stocks

Value Line Convertible Database

Value Line Publishing, Inc.
711 Third Ave.
New York, NY 10017

PH: (212) 687-3965
FAX: (212) 986-3243
ON-LINE DATABASE
Access Fees: Call for Costs

Information on convertible securities which includes price, yield, premium, issue size, liquidity, and maturity.

AUDIENCE: Individual, Professional   RISK LEVEL: Moderate, Aggressive
TOPICS: Bonds, Stocks

Value Line Datafile

Value Line Publishing, Inc.
711 Third Ave.
New York, NY 10017

PH: (212) 687-3965
FAX: (212) 986-3243
ON-LINE DATABASE
Alternate Electronic Formats: CD-ROM, Diskette
Access Fees: Call for Costs

Provides history and projections for companies and industry composites. Gives related financial data for major industrial retail, utility companies, and transportation; major banks, finance companies, savings and loan associates, and insurance companies.

AUDIENCE: Beginning, Individual, Professional   RISK LEVEL: Moderate, Aggressive
TOPICS: Stocks

Value Line Estimates And Projections File

Value Line Publishing, Inc.
711 Third Ave.
New York, NY 10017

PH: (212) 687-3965
FAX: (212) 986-3243
ON-LINE DATABASE
Alternate Electronic Formats: CD-ROM, Diskette
Access Fees: Call for Costs

Gives projected performance ratings and estimates of earnings-per-share, dividends-per-share, sales/revenue ratios, growth in dividends per share for common stocks that appear in the Value Line Investment Survey.

AUDIENCE: Individual, Professional   RISK LEVEL: Moderate, Aggressive
TOPICS: Bonds, Stocks

Value Line Quarterly Reports

Value Line Publishing, Inc.
711 Third Ave.
New York, NY 10017

PH: (212) 687-3965
FAX: (212) 986-3243
ON-LINE DATABASE
Access Fees: Call for Costs

Gives quarterly financial information on companies that are traded on major U.S. stock exchanges.

AUDIENCE: Individual, Professional **RISK LEVEL: Moderate, Aggressive**
TOPICS: Bonds, Stocks

Value Line Software

Value Line Software
711 Third Avenue
New York, NY 10017

PH: (800) 654-0508
(212) 687-3965
SOFTWARE
Cost: $396.00 a year with monthly
updates; $1,500 a year with weekly

Powerful, easy to use. For selecting stocks and analyzing investment performance over time. Contains information on approximately 1,600 widely traded companies. Value/Screen II is a massive compilation of annual and quarterly financial records.

AUDIENCE: Beginning, Individual, Professional **RISK LEVEL: Moderate, Aggressive**
TOPICS: Bonds, Stocks

Vantagepoint Neural Trading System

Predictive Technologies Group
25941 Apple Blossom
Wesley Chapel, FL 33544

PH: (813) 973-0496
FAX: (813) 973-2700
SOFTWARE
Cost: $2,450.00 for 1st market;
$1,450.00 for 2nd
Technical Analysis, Bond Analysis,
Futures Analysis, Neural Network

Utilizes extensive intermarket analysis with neural network to maximize trading returns. Includes 1 market module (6 modules available) for S&P, yen, Deutchmarc, British pound, Eurodollars, French franc, and T-bonds. Creates strategy by forecasting.

AUDIENCE: Individual, Professional **RISK LEVEL: Aggressive**
TOPICS: Bonds, Stocks, Futures/Commodities

Vencap Data Quest/Portfolio Companies 1.0

AI Research Corporation
2003 St. Julien Court
Mountain View, CA 94043

PH: (415) 852-9140
FAX: (415) 852-9522
ON-LINE DATABASE
Cost: $39.95

A computerized database directory of private companies financed by venture capital firms. Most of the companies are recent IPOs or are potential IPO candidates.

AUDIENCE: Individual, Professional **RISK LEVEL: Moderate, Aggressive**
TOPICS: Stocks

Vertical Spread Model

Niche Software Products
P.O. Box 3574
Manassas, VA 22110

PH: (703) 368-8372
SOFTWARE
Cost: $55.00
Options Analysis

"Shows theoretical curves for option prices as stock prices vary." Probable position of value, net probable value of position, and hedge ratio based on probable movement as a functioning of the changing value of the stock. Profitability Graph.

AUDIENCE: Individual, Professional	RISK LEVEL: Aggressive
TOPICS: Options	

Vestek Portfolio Management System

Vestek Systems, Inc.
388 Market St.
Suite 700
San Francisco, CA 94111

PH: (415) 398-6340
FAX: (415) 392-6831
ON-LINE DATABASE
Access Fees: Call for Costs

Investment and financial information on U.S. securities, bonds, common stocks, options, mortgage-backed securities and derivatives, and global securities.

AUDIENCE: Individual, Professional	RISK LEVEL: Conservative, Moderate,
TOPICS: Bonds, Stocks, Options, Futures/Commodities	Aggressive

Vickers Bond Data

Vickers Stock Research Corporation
226 New York Ave.
Huntington, NY 11743

PH: (516) 423-7710
(800) 645-5043
FAX: (516) 423-7715
ON-LINE DATABASE
Access Fees: Call for Costs

Provides financial and descriptive information on institutional bond holdings.

AUDIENCE: Professional	RISK LEVEL: Conservative, Moderate
TOPICS: Bonds	

Vickers Institutional Stock System

Vickers Stock Research Corporation
226 New York Ave.
Huntington, NY 11743

PH: (516) 423-7710
(800) 645-5043
FAX: (516) 423-7715
ON-LINE DATABASE
Access Fees: Call for Costs

Provides institutional bond holdings, common and preferred stocks, and corporate and financial insider information. Recent purchases and sales by banks, colleges, insurance companies, investment companies, money managers, and portfolio holdings.

AUDIENCE: Professional	RISK LEVEL: Conservative, Moderate, Aggressive
TOPICS: Bonds, Stocks	

Vickers Stock Research

Vickers Online
226 New York Avenue
Huntington, NY 11743

PH: (800) 832-5280 (in NY)
(800) 645-5043
ONLINE
Cost: annual $50.00, online charges
   per minute $1.00.
Compatibility: any PC with modem.

Covers stocks. A menu-driven online dial-up service. Consists of institutional portfolio information. It lists the institutions alphabetically and shows all stocks owned, trading activity, four years of history, insider information (who's buying and selling and how much). Also gives 144 & 13D listings.

AUDIENCE: Beginning, Individual, Professional   RISK LEVEL: Conservative,
TOPICS: All   Moderate, Aggressive

Viking

Delphi Economics, Inc.
8 Bonn Place
Weehawken, NJ 07087

PH: (800) 873-3574
(201) 867-4303
FAX: (201) 867-4666
SOFTWARE
Cost: $495.00

Has mechanical analysis section that includes 40 technical models. Special quick feature for analysis. Fundamental analysis provides balance sheet profit/loss data, ratios, buy/sell signals, and proprietary indexes. Can be equipped with Signal.

AUDIENCE: Individual, Professional   RISK LEVEL: Aggressive
TOPICS: Stocks, Options, Futures/Commodities

Vu/Text

Knight Ridder
325 Chestnut Street
Suite 1300
Philadelphia, PA 19106

PH: (800) 323-2940
(215) 574-4400
Cost: $50.00 hook-up charge.
   Online charges from $1.90 per
   minute.

Covers stocks and news. "The world's largest U.S. Newspaper Databank." Provides full text on over 70 newspapers, 9 magazines, 5 news and business wires and over 200 regional publications. Also offers over 300 Canadian databases and Maritime information.

AUDIENCE: Individual, Professional   RISK LEVEL: Moderate, Aggressive
TOPICS: All

VWD-Videoticker

VWD
Niederurseler Allee 8-10
P.O. Box 6105
D-6236 Eschborn 1, Germany

PH: 6196 405206
FAX: 6196 482007
ON-LINE DATABASE
Access Fees: Call for Costs

Provides current rates for German stocks, options, pension and investments funds, option certificates, international stocks, bonds, currencies, and gold market instruments.

AUDIENCE: Individual, Professional   RISK LEVEL: Moderate, Aggressive
TOPICS: All

Wall Street S.O.S. Options Alert

Securities Objective Service
17175 N. Lake Dr.
Bay Minette, AL 36507

PH: (205) 937-6308
Contact: Jeremy Richard Gentry
ON-LINE DATABASE
Access Fees: Call for Costs

Provides recommendations on the purchase and sale of index option contracts. It also gives trend analyses, updates of performances, market forecasts, and strategy advice.

AUDIENCE: Individual, Professional   RISK LEVEL: Aggressive
TOPICS: Options, Futures/Commodities

Wall Street Trainer

Dynacomp, Inc.
178 Phillips Road
Webster, NY 14580

PH: (800) 828-6772
SOFTWARE
Cost: $29.95

Simulates long or short trading in the stock and futures market. Eight different types of put and call options may be traded on low margins. Teaches how to use optional real-world, automatic stop-loss orders to preclude substantial losses, and how to use optional automatic take-profit orders.

AUDIENCE: Individual
TOPICS: Options, Futures/Commodities

Wall Street Watcher

Wall Street Watcher
Box 175
Wilton, CT 06897

PH: (203) 762-7820
SOFTWARE
Cost: $495.00
Technical Analysis

Increased technical analysis capabilities with over 20 indicators. Functions include Wilder's relative strength index, stochastics, MACD, rate of change momentum, advance/decline lines, Williams %R moving averages, McClellan summation index, oscillators, and more.

AUDIENCE: Individual, Professional   RISK LEVEL: Aggressive
TOPICS: Stocks, Options, Futures/Commodities

War Machine

War Machine
1700 Taylor N.
#301
Seattle, WA 98109

PH: (206) 283-3708
SOFTWARE
Cost: $595.00
Technical Analysis

Combines real-time or delayed data from Signal and software into technical analysis program. Moving averages, standard and exponential oscillators, ratios, spreads, rate-of-change, stochastics, volatility, relative strength, trendlines and more.

AUDIENCE: Individual, Professional   RISK LEVEL: Aggressive
TOPICS: Stocks, Options, Futures/Commodities

Wave Wise Spreadsheet For Windows

Jerome Technology, Inc.
P.O. Box 403
Raritan, NJ 08869

PH: (908) 369-7503
FAX: (908) 369-5993
SOFTWARE
Cost: $150.00
Technical Analysis, Bond Analysis,
  Spreadsheets, Statistics

Program combines traditional spreadsheets with stock market charting. Analysis calculated includes: Elliot Wave analysis, cycle analysis, Fibonacci retracements, "what-if" analysis, and other charting tools.

AUDIENCE: Individual, Professional   RISK LEVEL: Moderate, Aggressive
TOPICS: Bonds, Mutual Funds, Stocks, Options, Futures/Commodities

WealthBuilder

Money Magazine and Reality
  Technologies
3624 Market Street
Philadelphia, PA 19104

PH: (800) 346-2024
(215) 387-6055
FAX: (215) 387-2179
SOFTWARE
Cost: $208.50

Covers stocks, mutual funds and bonds (municipal, corporate, and government). The complete personal planning and investment system. Comprehensive financial plan based on your own personal goals plus a strategy to achieve them based on your optional asset allocation.

AUDIENCE: Beginning, Individual   RISK LEVEL: Conservative, Moderate, Aggressive
TOPICS: Bonds, Mutual Funds, Stocks, Investment Planning

World Equities Report

Dow Jones & Co., Inc.
One S. Wacker Drive
Chicago, IL 60606

PH: (800) 223-2274
(212) 416-2420 ext 937 (NY)
(312) 750-4000
ON-LINE DATABASE
Basic monthly charge - $677

Covers news. An international version of the Dow Jones "broadtape." Operates through Quotron - 24 hours a day Mon-Fri until 1600 Greenwich Mean Time on Saturday. Tightly focused on news that helps equities traders and investors.

AUDIENCE: Individual, Professional   RISK LEVEL: Moderate, Aggressive
TOPICS: Stocks

YEN

Emerging Market Technologies, Inc.
1230 Johnson Ferry Road
Suite F-1
Marietta, GA 30068

PH: (404) 973-2300
FAX: (404) 973-3003
SOFTWARE
Cost: $195.00

Computes theoretical value of new NIKKEI options (warrants).

AUDIENCE: Individual, Professional   RISK LEVEL: Aggressive
TOPICS: Options

Zacks Earnings Estimates

Zacks Investment Research, Inc.
155 N. Wacker Dr.
Chicago, IL 60606

PH: (312) 630-9880
Alternate Electronic Formats: CD-
  ROM
ON-LINE DATABASE
Access Fees: Call for Costs

Provides information compiled from a consensus of brokerage firms and gives projected earnings for major U.S. corporations.

AUDIENCE: Individual, Professional   RISK LEVEL: Moderate, Aggressive
TOPICS: Stocks

Zacks Fundamentals (R)

Zacks Investment Research, Inc.
155 N. Wacker Dr.
Chicago, IL 60606

PH: (312) 630-9880
(800) 767-3771
ON-LINE DATABASE
Access Fees: Call for Costs

Provides earnings information on companies listed on the American, New York Stock Exchanges, or Over-the-Counter.

AUDIENCE: Individual, Professional   RISK LEVEL: Moderate, Aggressive
TOPICS: Bonds, Stocks

PERFORMANCE RANKING SERVICES

A few publications specialize in ranking the performance of stocks, mutual funds, money managers, and even newsletters. This chapter presents a list of these unique publications. The criteria for including publications in this section is that they must actually rank investment products or services.

For selecting stocks, mutual funds, money managers, and newsletters, the opinions of these services can be invaluable because rankings require quantitative analysis based on a set of criteria. The highest quality companies, mutual funds, money managers and newsletters tend to remain good performers. Avoiding poor performers in stocks, funds, and newsletters can save time and, of course, money. By using a performance ranking service, you can begin your research with a clear picture of where to find historically strong management and advice.

The publications listed here present a wide range of choices to the investor, in terms of what is being ranked, how often the rankings are updated, and the cost of each service.

Best 100 Stocks Update, The

Gene Walden
Walden Communications
5805 Dale Avenue, Suite 1000
P.O. Box 39373
Minneapolis, MN 55439-9780

PH: (800) 736-2970
Cost: $12.95
Frequency: Twice/yr
Date of first issue: 1990

Fundamental analysis. Covers stocks and mutual funds. Reports on the fastest growing foreign markets, the changing U.S. Market, the best global mutual funds and the top performing stocks.

AUDIENCE: Beginning, Individual, Professional	RISK LEVEL: Conservative,
TOPICS: All	Moderate, Aggressive

CTCR Commodity Traders Consumer Report

Bruce Babcock
1731 Howe Avenue
Suite 149
Sacramento, CA 95825

PH: (800) 999-CTCR
FAX: (916) 672-0425
Cost: $168.00 annually
Frequency: Every two weeks
Date of first issue: 4/83

Covers commodities. Monitors major commodity trading advisory services - both their letters and hotline and summarizes the results of their recommendation. Designed to make you a smarter consumer and better trader in the exciting world of commodity trading.

AUDIENCE: Individual, Professional	RISK LEVEL: Aggressive
TOPICS: Options, Futures/Commodities	

Fund Performance Chartbook

Bert Dohmen
Wellington Financial Corporation
6600 Kalanianole Highway
Suite 114C
Honolulu, HI 96825-1299

PH: (808) 396-2220
(800) 992-9989
FAX: (808) 396-8640
Cost: $25.00

Covers mutual funds. Over 100 charts showing relative performance versus S&P 500. The charts cover the last 5-1/2 years.

AUDIENCE: Beginning, Individual	RISK LEVEL: Moderate, Aggressive
TOPICS: Mutual Funds	

Hulbert Financial Digest

Mark Hulbert
316 Commerce Street
Alexandria, VA 22314

PH: (703) 683-5905
Cost: $135.00 year
Frequency: monthly
Date of first issue: 6/80

Tracks the performance of 125 financial newsletters. Gives a percentage rating on each based on following their recommendations. In January issue, he rates the performance of each newsletter going back to 1980.

AUDIENCE: Beginning, Individual, Professional	RISK LEVEL: Moderate, Aggressive
TOPICS: All	

Lipper Analytical Service

Mutual Fund Profile
Standard & Poor's
25 Broadway
New York, NY 10004

PH: (800) 221-5277
(212) 208-8812
Frequency: Quarterly
Costs: $145.00/yr

Lists over 1,500 mutual funds categorized by 30 investment objectives and provides performance rankings, portfolio managers, telephone numbers. Gives top performers for 1, 5, & 10 years and other statistics.

AUDIENCE: Beginning, Individual, Professional   RISK LEVEL: Moderate, Aggressive
TOPICS: Mutual Funds

Money Manager Previews

Wall Street Transcript
Richard Holman
99 Wall Street
New York, NY 10005

PH: (212) 747-9500
FAX: (212) 668-9842
Cost: $2,600.00
Frequency: Weekly
Date of first issue: 1987

Weekly magazine covering money manager interviews. Features interviews and discussions with leading money managers and portfolio strategists throughout the world.

AUDIENCE: Individual, Professional   RISK LEVEL: Moderate, Aggressive
TOPICS: Bonds, Mutual Funds, Stocks

Money Manager Verified Ratings

Norman Zadeh
P.O. Box 7634
Beverly Hills, CA 90212

PH: (310) 305-9300
FAX: (310) 273-7941
Cost: $200.00/yr
Frequency: Monthly
Date of first issue: 1990

Covers Money Manager Ratings. Requires money managers to specify a $1,000,000+ account at the beginning of each year and then send copies of brokerage statements to verify performance. Rates the best managers in several different categories: traditional buy and hold, mutual fund timers, small accounts, short selling and more.

AUDIENCE: Individual, Professional   RISK LEVEL: Moderate, Aggressive
TOPICS: Stocks, Futures/Commodities, Asset Allocation, Investment Planning

Morningstar Mutual Fund Values

Morningstar, Inc.
53 W. Jackson Blvd.
Chicago, IL 60604

PH: (800) 876-5005
FAX: (312) 427-9215
Cost: $395.00
Frequency: Every 2 weeks - new
  issue on rotation basis, takes about
  20 weeks to get back to a
  particular mutual fund.

Evaluates over 1,000 funds by performance and risk data, portfolios, operations information, investment criteria, analyst commentary and Morningstar's investment recommendations.

AUDIENCE: Beginning, Individual   RISK LEVEL: Moderate, Aggressive
TOPICS: Mutual Funds

Mutual Fund Directory, The

Investment Company Institute
Probus Publishing Company
118 N. Clinton Street
Chicago, IL

Date of first issue: 1990
Cost: $18.95

Identifies, describes, and categorizes over 2,500 mutual funds.

AUDIENCE: Beginning, Individual	RISK LEVEL: Moderate, Aggressive
TOPICS: Mutual Funds	

Mutual Fund Encyclopedia, The

Gerald W. Perritt
Dearborn Financial Publishing, Inc.
520 N. Dearborn Street
Chicago, IL 60610

Date of first issue: 1990
Cost: $27.95

Profiles 1,100 mutual funds detailing objectives and strategies, financial statistics, current yields, portfolio turnover rate, year by year and 5 year average returns and more.

AUDIENCE: Beginning, Individual	RISK LEVEL: Moderate, Aggressive
TOPICS: Mutual Funds	

Mutual Fund Fact Book

Investment Company Institute
1600 M Street
Washington, D.C. 20036

PH: (202) 293-7700
(202) 955-3536
Published: Every May for the
  previous year.
Cost: $9.95

Includes facts and figures on mutual fund investing, information on the assets of mutual funds, the sales redemption value, a historical background on mutual funds and recent trends affecting various funds.

AUDIENCE: Beginning, Individual	RISK LEVEL: Moderate, Aggressive
TOPICS: Mutual Funds	

Mutual Fund Forecaster

The Institute for Econometric
Research
3471 N. Federal Highway
Ft. Lauderdale, FL 33306

PH: (800) 327-6720
(305) 503-9000
Cost: $100.00/yr
Frequency of update: Monthly

Provides data on over 450 mutual funds including performance projections, risk rating, buy/sell records, loads/no load yield data and phone data, ranks funds in categories such as best buy, buy, hold, sell, etc.

AUDIENCE: Beginning, Individual	RISK LEVEL: Moderate, Aggressive
TOPICS: Mutual Funds	

QPR (Quarterly Performance Report)

Managed Account Reports, Inc.
220 Fifth Avenue
19th Floor
New York, NY 10001-7781

PH: (212) 213-6202
Cost: $299/yr for US, Canada,
    Mexico
$395.00 for rest of world
Frequency: Quarterly

Technical analysis. Covers options and futures and commodities. Delivers in-depth analysis on the performance of over 400 trading advisors in MAR's trading advisor database; these advisors represent $14 billion under management worldwide. Uses over 35 different performance indicators, including graphic displays, to give a five year performance history.

AUDIENCE: Individual, Professional   RISK LEVEL: Aggressive
TOPICS: Options, Futures/Commodities

Trading Advisor

Richard Luna
1737 Central Street
Denver, CO 80211

PH: (303) 433-3202
(800) 950-9339
FAX: (303) 433-2731
Cost: $295.00/yr
Frequency: Monthly
Date of first issue: 1986

Fundamental analysis. The leading source of Commodity Trading Advisor information in the nation with both an extensive data base and a large number of accounts traded with Commodity Trading Advisors. Newsletter profiles specific Trading Advisors and includes their performance. Rates the top Commodity Trading Advisors for the past three years and gives pertinent data.

AUDIENCE: Individual, Professional   RISK LEVEL: Aggressive
TOPICS: Options, Futures/Commodities

Variable Annuity Performance Report/Morningstar

Added/Corp. Morningstar, Inc.
53 West Jackson
Suite 460
Chicago, IL 60604

PH: (312) 696-6000
(800) 876-5005
Frequency: Quarter or monthly
Cost: $55.00/quarterly
$125.00/monthly

Provides accumulated unit values over 12 different time periods, operational information, contact charges, surrender charges and more. Also ranks the top and bottom performers.

AUDIENCE: Beginning, Individual, Professional   RISK LEVEL: Conservative,
TOPICS: All   Moderate, Aggressive

Weisenberger Management Results

Warren, Gorham, & Lamont, Inc.
One Penn Plaza
New York, NY 10119

PH: (800) 950-1209
(617) 423-2020
Cost: $150.00/yr
Frequency: Monthly

Rates mutual funds. Performance reviews of open and closed-end funds. Gives total return and rank by objective as well as asset breakdown and top 20 performers for current year, five-year, and ten-year periods.

AUDIENCE: Beginning, Individual   RISK LEVEL: Moderate, Aggressive
TOPICS: Mutual Funds

Zweig Performance Ratings Report, The

Dr. Martin E. Zweig
P.O. Box 360
Bellmore, NY 11710

PH: (800) 633-2252 ext 9000
FAX: (516) 785-0537
Cost: $205.00/yr
Frequency: Bimonthly

Rates 3,400 stocks from 1 (the top 5%) down to 9 (the worst 5%) for expected price performance over the next 6-12 months.

AUDIENCE: Beginning, Individual   RISK LEVEL: Moderate, Aggressive
TOPICS: Stocks

STOCK AND BOND RESEARCH PUBLICATIONS

Services that provide information on a broad range of companies are listed in this section. Many of these services are now available on the computer and are listed in both this chapter and the Computer and Quote Services chapter.

When selecting stocks and corporate bonds, it is wise to remember that a particular company stands behind the fate of those securities. The services in this chapter are designed to provide you with in-depth research on the management, industries, finances, ratios, and price performance of specific companies. By using one or more of these services, ideas can be screened with a consistent discipline.

The services can also help you put your current knowledge to better use. If you are confident with a particular company and its management, discovering a lesser known bond, preferred stock or debt instrument offered by the same company can raise your cash flow and quite possibly your overall returns.

These services are generally not affiliated with a brokerage firm and must cover a broad list of companies. Consequently, they present an unbiased overview of a wide variety of companies.

Access Nippon 1994 - How to Succeed in Japan

The Reference Press, Inc.
6448 Highway 290 E.
Suite E-104
Austin, TX 78723

PH: (512) 454-7778
FAX: (512) 454-9401
Cost: $34.95; published annually
Date of First Issue: 1988
Fundamental Analysis

Profiles of over 200 of the giants of Japanese industry. Each company profile includes an overview of operations, addresses of major offices, sales broken down by products and exports, product names, list of foreign partners, basic financial information, and much more.

AUDIENCE: Individual, Professional   RISK LEVEL: Moderate, Aggressive
TOPICS: Stocks, General Reference

Asia Pacific Securities Handbook

The Reference Press, Inc.
6448 Highway 290 E
Suite E-104
Austin, TX 78723

PH: (512) 454-7778
FAX: (512) 454-9401
Cost: $99.95; published annually

Covers the stock markets in Australia, Bangladesh, China, Hong Kong, India, Indonesia, Japan, Malaysia, Nepal, New Zealand, Pakistan, the Philippines, Singapore, South Korea, Sri Lanka, Taiwan and Thailand. Profiles include stock exchange addresses and phone numbers, description of stock market practices, market overview, lists of the top stocks and names, addresses and phone numbers for stock brokerage firms.

AUDIENCE: Individual, Professional   RISK LEVEL: Moderate, Aggressive
TOPICS: Stocks, General Reference

Blue Book of CBS Stock Reports, The

MPL Communications, Inc.
133 Richmond Street West
Suite 700
Toronto, ON, Canada M5H3M8

PH: (416) 869-1177
Cost: $279.00 annually
Frequency: Every two weeks
Date of first issue: 1941

Fundamental analysis and technical analysis. Covers Canadian stocks, charts. Statistical financial analysis on Canadian stocks. Provides buy, sell, hold recommendations as well as five year performance data and company description.

AUDIENCE: Individual, Professional   RISK LEVEL: Moderate, Aggressive
TOPICS: Stocks

Canada Company Handbook 1994

The Reference Press, Inc.
6448 Highway 290 E.
Suite E-104
Austin, TX 78723

PH: (512) 454-7778
FAX: (512) 454-9401
Cost: $39.95
Date of first issue: 1994
ISBN: 0-921925-45-X
Fundamental Analysis

A reference book providing information on over 1,300 Canadian companies. Profiles over 400 companies on the Toronto Stock Exchange 300, both current and prior companies. Profiles include a description of the company, performance analysis, stock price performance charts, 5 years of financial data, 2 years of quarterly financial data, stock symbols, and rankings on profit, revenues and assets.

AUDIENCE: Individual, Professional   RISK LEVEL: Moderate, Aggressive
TOPICS: Stocks, General Reference

Company Handbook Spain-The Maxwell Espinosa Shareholders Directory

The Reference Press, Inc.
6448 Highway 290 E.
Suite E-104
Austin, TX 78723

PH: (512) 454-7778
FAX: (512) 454-9401
Cost: $84.95
ISBN: 8-472092-57-7
Fundamental Analysis

Profiles almost 2,000 Spanish corporations. Information includes headquarters, industry, phone and fax numbers, major shareholders, recent year's sales, number of employees as well as advertising agency, attorneys, banks, auditors and other communications contacts.

AUDIENCE: Individual, Professional   **RISK LEVEL: Moderate, Aggressive**
TOPICS: Stocks, General Reference

Company Handbook-Hong Kong

The Reference Press, Inc.
6448 Highway 290 E.
Suite E-104
Austin, TX 78723

PH: (512) 454-7778
FAX: (512) 454-9401
Cost: $44.95
Published twice/yr
Fundamental Analysis

Profiles the 416 companies listed on the Hong Kong Stock Exchange. Includes description of company, major office address and phone number, major stockholders and officers, financial statements, key ratios and profit breakdowns.

AUDIENCE: Individual, Professional   **RISK LEVEL: Moderate, Aggressive**
TOPICS: Stocks, General Reference

Daily Graphs

William O'Neill & Co., Inc
P.O. Box 66919
Los Angeles, CA 90066

PH: (310) 448-6843
Costs and frequencies: NYSE $429
(weekly)
$305 (biweekly), $203 (monthly)
AMEX/OTC $719 (weekly)
$549 (biweekly), $345 (monthly)
Date of first issue: 1974

Chart service. Fundamental and technical analysis covering 2,500 NYSE, AMEX & OTC Companies arranged by industry groups. Includes 41 fundamental and 26 technical factors in every chart.

AUDIENCE: Beginning, Individual, Professional   **RISK LEVEL: Moderate, Aggressive**
TOPICS: Stocks, Options

Daily Graphs Option Guide

William O'Neill and Company, Inc.
P.O. Box 24933
Los Angeles, CA 90024

PH: (213) 820-2583
Cost: $229.00/yr
Frequency: Weekly

Graphic and statistical data on active CBOE, AMEX, PSE, PHIL, NYSE options and underlying issues. It also includes a weekly listing of quarterly earnings due, stocks going x-dividend, short-term technical indicators, computer selected call writes, yearly graphs of market averages with 50 and 200-day moving averages.

AUDIENCE: Individual, Professional   **RISK LEVEL: Aggressive**
TOPICS: Options

European Companies- A Guide to Sources of Information

The Reference Press, Inc.
6448 Highway 290 E.
Suite E-104
Austin, TX 78723

PH: (512) 454-7778
FAX: (512) 454-9401
COST: $89.95
Date of first issue: 1994
ISBN: 0-900246-44-8
Updated Annually

"An invaluable guide to information sources for European companies and for doing business in Europe." Covers 35 countries and over 1,500 entries.

AUDIENCE: Individual, Professional   RISK LEVEL: Moderate, Aggressive
TOPICS: Bonds, Stocks, General Reference

French Company Handbook 1994

The Reference Press, Inc.
6448 Highway 290 E.
Suite E-104
Austin, TX 78723

PH: (512) 454-7778
FAX: (512) 454-9401
Cost: $49.95
Date of first issue: 1994
ISBN: 1-878753-34-7
Fundamental Analysis

A reference book profiling major French companies. Includes operations and company history overview, address and phone number, number of employees, names and titles of top management, dates by product line and geographic area, international activities, exports, and much more. Also provides a wealth of information on the French economy.

AUDIENCE: Individual, Professional   RISK LEVEL: Moderate, Aggressive
TOPICS: Bonds, Stocks, General Reference

Fundamental Story, The

Investor's Daily
P.O. Box 240058
Los Angeles, CA 90024-0058

PH: (800) 235-2888
Cost: $15.00/story
Frequency: Every 2 weeks
(Price decreases with volume -
    example 5 stories at $10 each)
Date of first issue: October 1990

Fundamental analysis, Earnings Analysis, Charts. Covers all markets. Number of stocks covered: 550 when complete. Clear, comprehensive 2 page reviews of companies with a high ranking in earnings per share growth. You'll get basic facts plus color pictures of company's products presented in an objective way with no recommendations. Comments: Next day delivery available for $7.00 extra.

AUDIENCE: Individual, Professional   RISK LEVEL: Moderate, Aggressive
TOPICS: Bonds, Stocks

Handbook of Common Stocks

Moody's Financial Information Services
99 Church Street
New York, NY 10007

PH: (212) 553-0435
FAX: (212) 553-4700
Cost: $235 annually
Frequency: Quarterly
Fundamental Analysis

Includes company overviews, recent developments, prospects, performance statistics, stock movement charts, institutional holdings, price performance statistics, background and financial performance indicators on 950 NYSE and AMEX companies, and financial summaries on 750 additional companies.

AUDIENCE: Beginning, Individual, Professional   RISK LEVEL: Moderate, Aggressive
TOPICS: Stocks

Handbook of NASDAQ Stocks

Moody's Financial Information Services
99 Church Street
New York, NY 10007

PH: (212) 553-0435
FAX: (212) 553-4700
Cost: $175.00
Fundamental Analysis

Provides company overviews, recent developments, performance statistics, stock movement charts, institutional holdings, price performance statistics, background and financial health indicators on over 600 NASDAQ companies.

AUDIENCE: Beginning, Individual, Professional   RISK LEVEL: Moderate, Aggressive
TOPICS: Stocks

Market Guide Select OTC Stock Edition, The

Market Guide, Inc.
49 Glen Head Road
Glen Head, NY 11545

PH: (516) 759-1253
FAX: (516) 676-9240
Cost: $345.00 (quarterly)
Frequency: Weekly
Date of first issue: 1983

Provides both financial and textual information on 800 of the most promising over-the-counter (OTC) stocks selected from the Market Guide Database of over 6,700 stocks. It includes many companies not followed by other sources.

AUDIENCE: Individual, Professional   RISK LEVEL: Moderate, Aggressive
TOPICS: Stocks

Moody's Bond Record

Moody's Investor Service
99 Church Street
New York, NY 10007

PH: (800) 342-5647 ext 0435
FAX: (212) 553-4700
Frequency: Monthly
Cost: $70.00 per monthly issue or
$249.00 year
Date of first issue: 1969

Regular features: bond analysis. The most comprehensive and authoritative source of statistical data on 56,000 corporate, convertible, government, municipal, environmental control revenue, and international bonds, plus preferred stocks and commercial paper.

AUDIENCE: Individual, Professional   RISK LEVEL: Conservative, Moderate
TOPICS: Bonds

Moody's Bond Survey

Moody's Investor Service
99 Church Street
New York, NY 10007

PH: (800) 342-5647
(212) 553-0300
FAX: (212) 553-4700
Frequency: Weekly
Cost: $1,350.00/yr
Date of first issue: 1981

Bond analysis and market update. Gives trends and prospects for the market and for individual bonds. Economic and market condition commentary and opinions, information on factors and issues which influence values of bonds, commercial paper and other debt instruments.

AUDIENCE: Individual, Professional   RISK LEVEL: Conservative, Moderate
TOPICS: Bonds

Moody's Dividend Record

Moody's Investor Service
99 Church Street
New York, NY 10007

PH: (800) 342-5647
(212) 553-0300
FAX: (212) 553-4700
Frequency: Quarterly
Cost: $460.00/yr

Outstanding feature issues are tax status supplements (Jan-Feb-March); annual dividend record—a compilation of full year's dividend information. Detailed reports of current dividend data covering over 18,300 stocks and unit investment trusts.

AUDIENCE: Individual, Professional RISK LEVEL: Moderate, Aggressive
TOPICS: Stocks

Moody's Industrial Manual and News Report

Moody's Investor Service
99 Church Street
New York, NY 10007

PH: (800) 342-5647 ext 0435
FAX: (212) 553-4700
Cost: $1,475.00/year in print;
$1,895.00 on CD-ROM
Frequency: Annual with twice
 weekly updates
Date of first issue: 1900

In addition to fundamental analysis, P/E ratios, and earnings analysis, covers the NYSE and AMEX markets. The most comprehensive resource for full financial and operating data of every industrial corporation in the New York and American stock exchanges. Over 500 on regional exchanges. Provides in-depth analyses, detailed financial and stock performance data, history and background on the country's top corporations.

AUDIENCE: Individual, Professional RISK LEVEL: Moderate, Aggressive
TOPICS: Bonds, Stocks

Moody's Industry Review

Moody's Investor Services
99 Church Street
New York, NY 10007

PH: (800) 342-5647
(212) 553-0300
FAX: (212) 553-4700
Frequency: Every two weeks
Cost: $525 annually

Features company reviews. Comparative statistics and rankings of 4,000 leading corporations in 145 industry groups. Every two weeks receive approximately 10 industry reviews. Each is a profile on an industry including company's trading symbol and exchange, 52 week stock price range, earnings per share, book value, stockholder's equity, long-term debt, and much more.

AUDIENCE: Individual, Professional RISK LEVEL: Moderate, Aggressive
TOPICS: Bonds, Stocks

Moody's International Manual and News Reports

Moody's Investor Service
99 Church Street
New York, NY 10007

PH: (800) 342-5647 ext 0435
FAX: (212) 553-4700
Cost: $2,495.00 annually in print;
$7,000 on CD-ROM
Frequency: annually; updated twice
 a week
First published: 1900

Fundamental analysis. International chart services covering over 5,000 international corporations, incorporated outside of the U.S. and their global units. Includes full company history; up to 7 years of income accounts and balance sheets, descriptions of principal business activities, subsidiaries and properties, capital structure, including long-term debt.

AUDIENCE: Individual, Professional RISK LEVEL: Moderate, Aggressive
TOPICS: Bonds, Stocks

Moody's Municipal and Government Manual and News Reports

Moody's Investor Service
99 Church Street
New York, NY 10007

PH: (800) 342-5647 ext 0435
FAX: (212) 553-4700
Cost: $2,095 annually
Frequency: annually; updated twice
 a week
Date of first issue: 1900

Bonds analysis. Complete coverage of over 15,000 bond issuing
municipalities and government agencies. Full descriptions and
Moody's ratings on bond issues of state agencies such as housing
authorities, colleges and universities, counties, cities, federal
agencies and of the U.S. government itself. In depth information
includes three year growth of tax collections, assessed value and tax
rates, schedule of bonded debt, including bond amounts, interest
rates, redemption features, and due dates, etc.

AUDIENCE: Individual, Professional   RISK LEVEL: Conservative, Moderate
TOPICS: Bonds

Moody's OTC Industrial Manual and News Reports

Moody's Investor Service
99 Church Street
New York, NY 10007

PH: (800) 342-5647 ext 0435
FAX: (212) 553-4700
Cost: $1,350 in print; $1,795.00 on
CD-ROM
Frequency: annually; updated twice
 a week
First published: 1900

The biggest single resource today for full financial and operating
data of over 3,200 OTC industrial companies. Company history; up
to 7 years of income accounts and balance sheets; 7 year
comparisons of statistical records, financial and operating ratios &
analysis of operations for many companies, dividend history,
officers, etc.

AUDIENCE: Individual, Professional   RISK LEVEL: Moderate, Aggressive
TOPICS: Stocks

Moody's OTC Unlisted Manual and News Reports

Moody's Investor Service
99 Church Street
New York, NY 10007

PH: (800) 342-5647 ext 0435
FAX: (212) 553-4700
Cost: $1,225.00/yr; $1,495 on CD-
ROM
Frequency: annually; updated twice
 a week
First published: 1900

Fundamental analysis. A unique reference for dozens of hard to get
financial facts and corporate data on 2,000 unlisted OTC
companies. Gives you verified facts such as 2 year's worth of
income accounts and balance sheets, place and date of
incorporation, company history, mergers and acquisitions, long-
term debts, capital stock, subsidiaries, transfer agent and more.

AUDIENCE: Individual, Professional   RISK LEVEL: Moderate, Aggressive
TOPICS: Stocks

Moody's Public Utility Manual and News Reports

Moody's Investor Service
99 Church Street
New York, NY 10007

PH: (800) 342-5647 ext 0435
(212) 553-0300
FAX: (212) 553-4700
Cost: $1,325 annually in print;
 $1,795.00/yr on CD-ROM
Frequency: annually; updated twice
 a week

Fundamental analysis; industry analysis. A comprehensive
resource of full financial and operating data of all U.S. public
utilities. You get company history and detailed chronology of
mergers and acquisitions up to 7 years of income accounts and
balance sheets, 7 years of comparisons of statistical records,
financial and operating ratios, complete details of all debt and
capital stock, Moody's rating, etc.

AUDIENCE: Individual, Professional   RISK LEVEL: Moderate, Aggressive
TOPICS: Bonds, Stocks

Moody's Transportation Manual and News Reports

Moody's Investor Service
99 Church Street
New York, NY 10007

PH: (800) 342-5647 ext 0435
FAX: (212) 553-4700
Cost: $1,225 annually in print;
$1,495 on CD-ROM
Frequency: Annual Reports/weekly
  updates

Fundamental and industry analysis. A comprehensive resource of full financial and operating data of all U.S. companies in every phase of transportation. Includes up to 7 years of income accounts and balance sheets, description of business, subsidiaries, complete details of all debt and capital stock, Moody's ratings, dividend history, officers, directors, and more.

AUDIENCE: Individual, Professional   RISK LEVEL: Moderate, Aggressive
TOPICS: Bonds, Stocks

National Quotation Service

National Quotation Bureau, Inc.
The Harborside Financial Center
600 Plaza Three
Jersey City, NJ 07311

PH: (201) 435-9000
FAX: (201) 435-9000
Not available online, No software
  available, Printed daily hardcopy
Cost: $744.00 annually
Frequency: Daily

The most complete quotation service of non-exchange traded stocks and bonds available. For daily information and pricing, bonds are printed on "yellow sheets" and stocks are printed on "pink sheets." Quotation service contains indicated Bid, Ask, Market Maker with phone numbers, Symbol, and Security Description. Contains over 10,000 stocks and 3,000 bonds.

AUDIENCE: Individual, Professional   RISK LEVEL: Moderate, Aggressive
TOPICS: Bonds, Stocks

National Stock Summary

National Quotation Bureau, Inc.
150 Commerce Rd.
Cedar Grove, NJ 07009-1208

PH: (201) 239-6100
FAX: (201) 239-0080
Cost: $420.00/yr
Semi annual - $200.00/yr.
1st published in 1913
Fundamental Analysis

Covers the U.S. and Non-U.S. bond markets and deliver information on over 56,000 securities including both actively traded and inactive securities. Dividends, current prices, mergers, bankruptcies, defaults, exchanges, corporate mailing addresses, transfer agents and active market makers are some of the fields of information to be found.

AUDIENCE: Individual, Professional   RISK LEVEL: Moderate, Aggressive
TOPICS: Stocks

Nelson's Directory of Investment Research

Nelson Publications
1 Gateway Plaza
Port Chester, NY 10573

PH: (800) 333-6357
FAX: (914) 937-8908
Date of first issue: 1991
Cost: $450.00/yr

Stock analysis. Published in two volumes. Volume #1 contains expanded research and financial information on over 5,000 U.S. public companies. Volume #2 contains comprehensive information on over 4,000 foreign-based public companies. And, there is analyst coverage of all 9,000 companies, important stock data and research reports on each company.

AUDIENCE: Individual, Professional   RISK LEVEL: Moderate, Aggressive
TOPICS: Bonds, Stocks

Nelson's Directory of "Neglected Stock" Opportunities

Nelson Publications
One Gateway Plaza
Port Chester, NY 10573

PH: (800) 333-6357
FAX: (914) 937-0727
Cost: $225 or $375.00 w/electronic
  diskette database
Published: Annually
Date of first issue: 1988

"A detailed description of over 3,000 company stocks traded on the NYSE, AMEX or NASDAQ which have research coverage by two or fewer firms." Ranks companies by: highest market cap, most profitable, highest rate of sales growth and more.

AUDIENCE: Individual, Professional   **RISK LEVEL: Aggressive**
TOPICS: Stocks

Nelson's Earnings Outlook

Nelson Publications
One Gateway Plaza
Port Chester, NY 10573

PH: (800) 333-6357
FAX: (914) 937-0727
Cost: $240.00/yr
Published: Monthly
Date of first issue: 1990
Fundamental Analysis

Provides estimated earnings per share for more than 3,000 companies on the NYSE, AMEX and NASDAQ. The estimates are compiled by a consensus of over 3,000 security analysts from over 200 research firms. Buy, sell, hold recommendations are also included.

AUDIENCE: Individual, Professional   **RISK LEVEL: Moderate, Aggressive**
TOPICS: Stocks

OTC Market Report

National Quotation Bureau, Inc.
150 Commerce Rd.
Cedar Grove, NJ 07009-1208

PH: (201) 239-6100
FAX: (201) 239-0080
Cost: $240/yr including delivery
Date of first issue: 1965
Frequency: Prepared weekly, each
  Friday, or the prior trading day.

The OTC Market Report is a fundamental analysis service that covers U.S. equity securities. This service includes: Current week and 52 week high and low bid, last bid and ask, quarterly ranges for the past 12 month period, daily high bid and low offer for the current week, names of active market makers.

AUDIENCE: Individual, Professional   **RISK LEVEL: Moderate, Aggressive**
TOPICS: Stocks

Pink Sheets

National Quotation Bureau, Inc.
150 Commerce Rd.
Cedar Grove, NJ 07009-1208

PH: (201) 239-6100
FAX: (201) 239-0080
Cost: $818.00/yr inc. delivery
Frequency: Daily
Date of first issue: 1913

Covers foreign and domestic equity OTC Markets. The most complete quotation service of non-exchange traded stocks available. Information provided is as follows: bid, ask, market makers/trading desk phone numbers, symbol, margin status and more. Covers over 10,000 issues.

AUDIENCE: Individual, Professional   **RISK LEVEL: Moderate, Aggressive**
TOPICS: Stocks

SBBI Quarterly Forecast Reports

Ibbotson Associates
225 N Michigan Ave.
Suite 700
Chicago, IL 60601-7676

PH: (312) 616-1620
FAX: (312) 616-0404
Frequency: Quarterly
Date of First Issue: 1993
Cost: $295.00

Quarterly market consensus forecasts of 12 month returns and long-term forecasts of median assets. At year-end you will receive a 28 page Forecast Edition with comprehensive data, graphs, and statistics.

AUDIENCE: Individual, Professional   RISK LEVEL: Moderate, Aggressive
TOPICS: Bonds, Stocks

Special Situations Report

Individual Investor
Financial Data Systems, Inc.
P.O. Box 92000
Collingswood, NJ 08108

PH: (212) 689-2777
FAX: (609) 858-2007
Cost: $150.00
Frequency: Monthly

In-depth confidential reports on the "single most promising stock Individual Investor sees in the market." Follow-ups and updates are also provided on all previously recommended stocks along with buy/sell/hold advice.

AUDIENCE: Individual   RISK LEVEL: Moderate, Aggressive
TOPICS: Stocks

Standard & Poor's Blue List of Current Municipal and Corporate Offerings

Standard & Poor's
25 Broadway
New York, NY 10004

PH: (212) 208-8471
FAX: (212) 412-0498
Cost: $935.00/yr.
Frequency: Daily publication
Date of first issue: 1935

Reports municipal and corporate bond offerings in the secondary market.

AUDIENCE: Individual, Professional   RISK LEVEL: Conservative, Moderate
TOPICS: Bonds

Standard & Poor's Bond Guide

Standard & Poor's
25 Broadway
New York, NY 10004

PH: (212) 208-8000
(212) 208-8769
Cost: $211.00/yr
Frequency: Monthly
Date of first issue: 1942

Financial summaries on over 6,000 bonds, over 500 convertibles, and over 300 Canadian and international issues. Includes Standard and Poor's ratings - both current and prior, balance sheet data, high-low price range YTD, current price, yield and YTM, and interest payment dates.

AUDIENCE: Individual, Professional   RISK LEVEL: Conservative, Moderate
TOPICS: Bonds

Standard & Poor's Corporation Records

Standard & Poor's
25 Broadway
New York, NY 10004

PH: (212) 208-8363
FAX: (212) 412-1459
Cost: $3,070.00/yr or $1,815.00/yr
Frequency: Updated twice a month
Published: Quarterly
Date of first issue: 1915

Financial data on almost 12,000 companies. Information includes: long-term debt, outstanding shares, corporate background, incorporation date and merger and acquisition data, stock data, earnings and finance information and annual report. Also available on CD-ROM.

AUDIENCE: Individual, Professional **RISK LEVEL: Conservative, Moderate**
TOPICS: Bonds

Standard & Poor's Dividend Record

Standard & Poor's
25 Broadway
New York, NY 10004

PH: (212) 208-8369
Cost: Daily - $735.00/yr, Weekly -
  $370.00/yr, Quarterly - $145.00/yr
Frequency: Daily, Weekly, or
  Quarterly
Date of first issue: 1931

Reports information on corporate dividends.

AUDIENCE: Individual, Professional **RISK LEVEL: Moderate, Aggressive**
TOPICS: Stocks

Standard & Poor's Credit Week

Standard & Poor's
25 Broadway
New York, NY 10004

PH: (800) 777-4858
(212) 208-8768
Cost: $1,695.00/yr
Frequency: Weekly

Bond analysis. Focuses on trends and outlooks for fixed income securities including corporate and government bonds and money market instruments. Offers the latest info on S&P's new and changed ratings for corporate, municipal and structured issuers.

AUDIENCE: Individual, Professional **RISK LEVEL: Conservative, Moderate**
TOPICS: Bonds

Standard & Poor's Industry Reports

Standard & Poor's
1221 Avenue of the Americas
New York, NY 10020

PH: (212) 512-4900
(212) 208-8768
(800) 525-8640
Cost: $255.00 annually
Frequency: Annual with updates
  every two weeks
Date of first issue: 1935

Fundamental analysis. Helps you gauge the investment merits of entire industry groups. They cover 900 companies in 80 industries from Aerospace to Utilities. Every report contains a comparison of industry performance vs. the S&P 500, a side-by-side look at representative companies, stock performance and more.

AUDIENCE: Individual, Professional **RISK LEVEL: Moderate, Aggressive**
TOPICS: Bonds, Stocks

Standard & Poor's Stock Guide

Standard & Poor's
25 Broadway
New York, NY 10004

PH: (212) 208-8786
Cost: $128.00 annually

Monthly stock investment data and mutual fund review. Unique 260 page guide to investment data on over 5,300 common and preferred stocks, listed and OTC, providing rapid reviews of all issues with 48 items of data on each. S&P earnings and dividend rankings, S&P earnings estimates, monthly high/low prices and volume, stock symbol, historical price ranges, summaries of financial positions and more.

AUDIENCE: Beginning, Individual, Professional   RISK LEVEL: Moderate, Aggressive
TOPICS: Stocks

Standard & Poor's Stock Reports

Standard & Poor's
1221 Avenue of the Americas
New York, NY 10020

PH: (212) 512-4900
(800) 525-8640
Cost: $1,185.00/yr NY exch
$ 955.00/yr AMEX exch, $
955.00/yr
  OTC exch
Frequency: Annual/weekly updates

Earnings analysis, P/E ratio, charts, and fundamental analysis. Covers over 4,300 companies listed on the NYSE and AMEX and more than 1,500 of the most active companies traded O-T-C and regionally. Each 2 page report is a succinct profile of the companies' activities and financial position supported by extensive statistics that facilitate - quick year to year comparisons.

AUDIENCE: Individual, Professional   RISK LEVEL: Moderate, Aggressive
TOPICS: Stocks

The NQB Monthly Price Report

National Quotation Bureau, Inc.
150 Commerce Rd.
Cedar Grove, NJ 07009-1208

PH: (201) 239-6100
FAX: (201) 239-0080
Cost: $300.00/yr or $25.00 one
  month
Fundamental Analysis

This fundamental analysis service is composed of a monthly extract from the Pink Sheets of all over-the-counter traded equities. Included are about nine thousand NASDAQ Stock Market and non-NASDAQ securities. Shown are the monthly and annual high bid and low bid, notations for capital changes, marginability, bankruptcy or receivership.

AUDIENCE: Individual, Professional   RISK LEVEL: Moderate, Aggressive
TOPICS: Stocks

The NQB Price List

National Quotation Bureau, Inc.
150 Commerce Rd.
Cedar Grove, NJ 07009-1208

PH: (201) 239-6100
FAX: (201) 239-0080
Cost: $480.00/yr or $40.00 one
  month
Fundamental Analysis

This weekly list is a fundamental analysis service. It is composed of a weekly extract from the Pink Sheets of all over-the-counter traded equities. Included are about nine thousand NASDAQ Stock Market and non-NASDAQ securities. Weekly and annual high bid and low bid, last bid and ask for the current week's period, historic high or low bid, and notations for capital changes, marginability, bankruptcy, etc.

AUDIENCE: Individual, Professional   RISK LEVEL: Moderate, Aggressive
TOPICS: Stocks

Value Line Convertibles

Value Line Publishing
711 Third Avenue
New York, NY 10017-4064

PH: (800) 633-2252
(800) 634-3583
(212) 687-3965
Cost: $475.00 annual
Frequency: Weekly

Rates Investments/services convertible stock and warrants. Each week this service evaluates 585 convertibles, 95 warrants and their underlying common stocks, issues that trade on the Big Board, the AMEX and Over the Counter. You'll clearly see which convertibles and options Value Line feels are undervalued, which are overvalued, and by how much.

AUDIENCE: Individual, Professional   RISK LEVEL: Moderate, Aggressive
TOPICS: Bonds, Stocks

Value Line Investment Survey

Value Line Publishing
711 Third Avenue
New York, NY 10017

PH: (800) 633-2252 ext 2683
FAX: (212) 661-2807
Cost: $525.00 annually; $65.00 for a
   10 week trial
Frequency: Weekly
Date of first issue: 1931

Fundamental and technical analysis, P/E ratio, and charts, and covers the NY and AMEX markets. 2,000 page reference library included. Ranks 1,700 stocks from best to worst for relative year ahead performance. 15 years past performance and 3-5 year future projection. Comments: No risk money back guarantee.

AUDIENCE: Beginning, Individual, Professional   RISK LEVEL: Moderate, Aggressive
TOPICS: Bonds, Stocks

Value Line OTC Special Situations Service

Value Line Publishing
711 Third Avenue
New York, NY 10017

PH: (800) 654-0508
(212) 687-3965
Cost: $390.00 annually; $55.00 for a
   10 week trial
Frequency: Twice monthly
Date of first issue: 1951

Editor: Peter A. Shraga. Covers stocks. A detailed 4 page report on a "Special Situation" chosen for its chance to rise sharply in price. Also includes updates and reviews on previous recommendations. Designed for those willing to take above-average risks on over-the-counter stocks and equities.

AUDIENCE: Individual, Professional   RISK LEVEL: Moderate, Aggressive
TOPICS: Stocks

Vancouver Stock Exchange Review

Vancouver Stock Exchange
P.O. Box 10333
609 Granville Street
Vancouver, BC, Canada V7Y 1H1

PH: (604) 689-3334
Frequency: Monthly
Editor: David Morton
Cost: $117.00 Canadian

"A complete and official summary on the month's transactions on equities and options, recaps listing details, market commentaries and other topical articles."

AUDIENCE: Individual, Professional   RISK LEVEL: Moderate, Aggressive
TOPICS: Stocks

Vector Vest Stock Advisory

Vector Vest
3604 North Fork
P.O. Box 577
Bath, OH 44210-9910

PH: (800) 533-3923
(800) 237-8400
Cost: $395.00 annually
Frequency: Weekly
Date of first issue: 1978

Technical and fundamental analysis. A complete guide to safer, more profitable stock investing which gives specific buy, sell and hold recommendations. Also ranks stocks (best - worst) in several different categories from Relative Value and Relative Safety to stocks under $20.

AUDIENCE: Individual, Professional   **RISK LEVEL: Moderate, Aggressive**
TOPICS: Stocks

Yellow Sheets

National Quotation Bureau, Inc.
150 Commerce Rd.
Cedar Grove, NJ 07009-1208

PH: (201) 239-6100
FAX: (201) 239-0080
Cost: $816.00/yr including delivery
Frequency: Daily
Date of first issue: 1913

Covers foreign and domestic taxable bond markets. Provides the following information: names of market makers, their trading desk phone numbers, margin status of the security, security symbol, bid and ask quotations and more. Yellow sheets are delivered daily to the trading desk by the opening of the trading day.

AUDIENCE: Individual, Professional   **RISK LEVEL: Conservative, Moderate**
TOPICS: Bonds

BROKERAGE RESEARCH PUBLICATIONS

Every day top portfolio managers and investors rely on the comprehensive stock and bond research of major brokerage firms. The information and opinions derived by analysts who have devoted their careers to following a particular industry can be a powerful source of insight. This systematic presentation of well documented stock and bond ideas creates a real advantage to both individual and institutional investors.

Unfortunately, in a recent survey of investors at major brokerage firms, only 3 out of 10 individuals were aware that their firm published extensive stock and bond research reports. This chapter brings to your fingertips access to the major research pieces by listing most of the regularly published reports from selected leading investment firms.

Each entry contains a description of the particular areas covered. Many brokerage firms also publish a list of their favorite stock choices on a weekly or monthly basis.

Even interest rates and economic changes are covered by certain publications. While most investors are interested in a prediction of interest rate movement, few investors bother to check where interest rates are relative to different bonds and maturities. Monthly or weekly access to market and interest changes can substantially improve the performance of a portfolio.

Most firms will publish a "research universe" or similar piece which covers all of the companies followed by that firm. These "research universe" pieces generally list earnings and estimates along with the firm's opinion on the current attractiveness of a stock. Keep in mind that firms are reluctant to issue a negative opinion on a company. A neutral rating on a company's stock can sometimes be interpreted as a negative opinion due to the fact that most firm's research usually lists a wide range of companies as "attractive" or "buy."

Professional investors who are already familiar with these sources of information will benefit from this chapter's listing of available studies and descriptions. For most investment professionals and advanced investors, the INVESTEXT on-line computer service listed in the Computer and Quote Services chapter can be a fast and convenient way to access the reports issued by almost all brokerage firms on specific companies or topics.

The firms whose research is listed are under no obligation to provide investors with free information. Potential clients can request research from a local office or by calling the number listed here. We have made special arrangements with several of the major national brokerage firms to fulfill requests by Sourcebook readers. The Dallas branch offices listed have agreed to send sample research upon request. If you are already a client of a particular firm, this chapter can help you get more from the brokerage firm you are using. If a research piece has been discontinued, be sure to ask what research is available in its place.

Asset Allocation/Equity Valuation

Paine Webber
5151 Beltline Rd.
Suite 101
Dallas, TX 75248

PH: (800) 288-1515
(214) 450-4324
FAX: (214) 450-4350
Monthly publication approximately
   10 pages

Covers bonds and interest rates, economic analysis, and asset allocation. Includes expected rates of return on T-bills, 10 year bonds and stocks. Asset Allocation analysis: vs. bonds, stocks vs. cash, bonds vs. cash. Quantitative analysis: Equity Valuation model.

AUDIENCE: Individual, Professional   RISK LEVEL: Conservative, Moderate,
TOPICS: Bonds, Stocks, Asset Allocation   Aggressive

Bond Market Comments

Dean Witter
5001 Spring Valley Road
530 Providence Towers East
Dallas, TX 75244

PH: (800) 827-2211
(214) 770-9724
Monthly publication approximately
   2 pages

Covers bonds and interest rates. Includes commentary on the tax-free municipal bond market and interest rates. Also contains highlights of attractive municipal issues.

AUDIENCE: Beginning, Individual   RISK LEVEL: Conservative, Moderate
TOPICS: Bonds

Closed-End Country Funds

Smith Barney
13355 Noel Road
1660 One Galleria Tower
Dallas, TX 75240

PH: (800) 442-1357 TX
(800) 527-4175 US
(214) 450-6632
Monthly Approximately 45 pages

Covers economic analysis, and foreign stocks. Includes net asset values, premiums and discounts, holdings of funds and allocations.

AUDIENCE: Individual, Professional   RISK LEVEL: Moderate, Aggressive
TOPICS: Mutual Funds

Convertibles

Smith Barney
13355 Noel Road
1660 One Galleria Tower
Dallas, TX 75240

PH: (800) 442-1357 TX
(800) 527-4175 US
(214) 450-6632
Quarterly Approximately 50 pages

Covers convertible bonds and economic analysis. Includes a comprehensive listing of convertible bonds and preferred stocks; conversion prices, prices, symbols, issue size ratings, yield, pay dates, breakeven, call price, and industry. Also gives market comment and warrant listings.

AUDIENCE: Individual, Professional   RISK LEVEL: Moderate, Aggressive
TOPICS: Bonds, Stocks

Credit Market Comment

Smith Barney
13355 Noel Road
1660 One Galleria Tower
Dallas, TX 75240

PH: (800) 442-1357 TX
(800) 527-4175 US
(214) 450-6632
Monthly Approximately 10 pages

Includes bonds and interest rates, and economic analysis. Includes costs on yield changes for bond types, foreign spreads, corporate yields, economic data, industry and credit market comments, and upcoming economic numbers.

AUDIENCE: Individual, Professional   RISK LEVEL: Conservative, Moderate
TOPICS: Bonds

Diversified Equity Portfolios

Rauscher Pierce Refsnes
5420 LBJ Suite 200
Dallas, TX 75240

PH: (800) 374-3966
FAX (214) 788-3995
Monthly Publication approximately
  3 pages

3 different portfolios: income, conservative growth, and aggressive growth. 10 stocks each. Selected with a 12 month price target with stop orders. Includes earnings per share, 5 year growth rates, dividends, and PE ratios.

AUDIENCE: Individual, Professional   RISK LEVEL: Moderate, Aggressive
TOPICS: Stocks

Environmental Quarterly

Rauscher Pierce Refsnes
5420 LBJ Suite 200
Dallas, TX 75240

PH: (800) 374-3966
FAX (214) 788-3995
Quarterly publication approximately
  20 pages

Covers material handling, waste, and environmental stocks. Includes list of top ten choices for price appreciation in the environmental industry, average monthly trading volume, 52 week range, shares outstanding, overall market value, debt/capital.

AUDIENCE: Individual, Professional   RISK LEVEL: Moderate, Aggressive
TOPICS: Stocks

Focus List

Paine Webber
5151 Beltline Rd.
Suite 101
Dallas, TX 75248

PH: (800) 288-1515
(214) 450-4324
FAX: (214) 450-4350
Monthly publication approximately
  6 pages

Covers stocks (blue chip and small capital stocks). Lists the top recommendations by Paine Webber for value and timeliness. Decisions for recommendations are made by Paine Webber's research policy committee. Also includes technical recommendations.

AUDIENCE: Individual, Professional   RISK LEVEL: Moderate, Aggressive
TOPICS: Stocks

Futures - Agricultural Report

Prudential Securities, Inc.
10440 North Central Expressway
Suite 1600
Dallas, TX 75231

PH: (800) 527-1320
FAX: (214) 373-2788
Cost: Free
Frequency: monthly
Date of first issue: 1988

Covers futures spreads. Gives current positions, closed out positions, market commentary and forecasting, details on current spread opportunities and an extensive review of technical data on the major futures.

AUDIENCE: Individual, Professional   RISK LEVEL: Aggressive
TOPICS: Futures/Commodities

Futures Market Analysis/A Technical Overview

Smith Barney
13355 Noel Road
1660 One Galleria Tower
Dallas, TX 75240

PH: (800) 442-1357 TX
(800) 527-4175 US
(214) 450-6632
Weekly publication approximately
    4 pages

Includes charts, comments, and momentum of currencies, energy, metals, and bonds.

AUDIENCE: Individual, Professional   RISK LEVEL: Aggressive
TOPICS: Futures/Commodities

Futures Monthly Report

Prudential Securities, Inc.
10440 North Central Expressway
Suite 1600
Dallas, TX 75231

PH: (214) 373-2700
Monthly publication approximately
    20 pages

Covers bonds and interest rates, economic analysis, and commodities. Fundamental and technical analysis including global yield comparisons, currency analysis, interest rate analysis, and yield spreads. Also covers oil and metals.

AUDIENCE: Individual, Professional   RISK LEVEL: Aggressive
TOPICS: Futures/Commodities

Futures - Option Strategist

Prudential Securities, Inc.
10440 North Central Expressway
Suite 1600
Dallas, TX 75231

PH: (214) 373-2700
(800) 527-1320
FAX: (214) 373-2788
Cost: Free
Frequency: monthly
Date of first issue: 1989

Covers options on futures. Includes charts and analysis of oil, bonds, Eurodollars, S&P 500, yen, mark, Swiss franc, British pound, Canadian dollar, gold, silver, gasoline, soybean, corn, wheat, sugar, coffee, and cotton.

AUDIENCE: Individual, Professional   RISK LEVEL: Aggressive
TOPICS: Options, Futures/Commodities

Futures - The Technical Analyst

Prudential Securities, Inc.
10440 North Central Expressway
Suite 1600
Dallas, TX 75231

PH: (214) 373-2700
(800) 527-1320
FAX: (214) 373-2788
Frequency: Bimonthly
Date of first issue: 1989

Covers futures and commodities. Includes charts, spreads, and analysis for T-bills, Eurodollar, S&P 500, British pound, yen, Swiss franc, Canadian dollar, Deutsche mark, gold, silver, platinum, oil, heating oil, wheat, corn, oats, soybean, cotton, cattle, feeders, hogs bellies.

AUDIENCE: Individual, Professional   **RISK LEVEL: Aggressive**
TOPICS: Futures/Commodities

Independent Oil and Gas Quarterly

Rauscher Pierce Refsnes
5420 LBJ Suite 200
Dallas, TX 75240

PH: (800) 374-3966
FAX (214) 788-3995
Quarterly publication approximately
  15 pages

Covers independent oil and gas producers and earnings factors within the oil and gas industry. Recent financing transactions, cash flow, and prices are covered. Includes valuation matrix., extensive reserve estimates, stock symbols, 52 week range, shares outstanding, overall market value, and average monthly trading volume.

AUDIENCE: Individual, Professional   **RISK LEVEL: Moderate, Aggressive**
TOPICS: Stocks

International Interest Rate Weekly, The

Prudential Securities, Inc.
10440 North Central Expressway
Suite 1600
Dallas, TX 75231

PH: (214) 373-2700
(800) 527-1320
FAX: (214) 373-2788
Cost: Free
Frequency: weekly

Covers bonds and interest rates. Commentary and forecast on interest rates - domestic and international written by Prudential's staff analysts.

AUDIENCE: Individual, Professional   **RISK LEVEL: Conservative, Moderate**
TOPICS: Bonds

Investext

The Investext Services Group
11 Farnsworth Street
Boston, MA 02210

PH: (800) 662-7878
FAX: (61) 330-1986
U.K. 071-815-3860, FAX 071-815-3850
Hong Kong 852-845-7163
FAX 852-845-0142
$6.25 per page for off-line delivery
  plus $5.00 handling charge

Complete text of company and industry reports written by analysts at more than 300 of the world's leading investment banks and research firms. Currently includes 600,000 reports covering 30,000 companies in 53 industries.   The reports provide competitor profiles, market share data, forecasts, new product and technology data, recent operating results, sales/earnings analysis, critical assessments of industry trends, and bond research.

AUDIENCE: Individual, Professional   **RISK LEVEL: Conservative, Moderate, Aggressive**
TOPICS: Bonds, Stocks, Options, Futures/Commodities, Asset Allocation

Investment Strategy Pyramid

Paine Webber
5151 Beltline Rd.
Suite 101
Dallas, TX 75248

PH: (800) 288-1515
(214) 450-4324
FAX: (214) 450-4350
Monthly publication approximately
    6 pages

Covers stocks (blue chip and small capital stocks). Contains rankings of approximately 330 stocks based on value and price momentum. This publication also ranks 40 industries based on value and price momentum.

AUDIENCE: Individual, Professional   RISK LEVEL: Moderate, Aggressive
TOPICS: Stocks

Market View

Dean Witter
5001 Spring Valley Road
530 Providence Towers East
Dallas, TX 75244

PH: (800) 827-2211
(214) 770-9724
Monthly publication approximately
    7 pages

Covers stocks (blue chip, small capital stocks and foreign), economic analysis asset allocation. Includes economic commentary, top technical and fundamental stock recommendations, asset allocation, economic numbers to be released, and closed and fund updates.

AUDIENCE: Individual, Professional   RISK LEVEL: Moderate, Aggressive
TOPICS: Stocks, Asset Allocation

Merrill Lynch Market Letter

Merrill Lynch
5910 N. Central Expressway
2000 Premier Place
Dallas, TX 75206

PH: (800) 999-3056
(214) 750-2034
Cost: $35.00 a year
A biweekly publication approximately
    6 pages

Covers bonds and interest rates, stocks (blue chip and small capital stocks), and economic analysis. A brief update on economic developments and interest rates. Focuses on Merrill Lynch's top stock recommendations and special industry stock recommendations. Includes highlight of upcoming economic numbers.

AUDIENCE: Individual, Professional   RISK LEVEL: Moderate, Aggressive
TOPICS: Bonds, Stocks

Monthly Investment Strategy

Dean Witter
5001 Spring Valley Road
530 Providence Towers East
Dallas, TX 75244

PH: (800) 827-2211
(214) 770-9724
Monthly publication approximately
    50 pages

Covers bonds and interest rates, economic analysis, stocks (blue chip and small capital stock), and asset allocation. Contains economic analysis; asset allocation; sector and industry analysis; model portfolio charts on stocks, bonds, the dollar, global equity markets, inflation, monetary numbers, economic numbers and corporate profits; and market valuation.

AUDIENCE: Individual, Professional   RISK LEVEL: Moderate, Aggressive
TOPICS: Bonds, Stocks

Monthly Research Review

Merrill Lynch
5910 N. Central Expressway
2000 Premier Place
Dallas, TX 75206

PH: (800) 999-3056
(214) 750-2034
A monthly publication approximately
   125 pages

Covers bonds and interest rates, stocks (blue chip, small capital stocks, and foreign stocks), economic analysis, and asset allocation. Includes economic statistics and forecasts; interest rate analysis; foreign country economic statistics; market data; industry analysis and rankings; stock rankings; stock statistics; pricing, earnings P/E multiples, dividends, forecasts and return on equity, organized by industry; closed-end funds statistics; convertible securities statistics, and international company statistics.

AUDIENCE: Individual, Professional   RISK LEVEL: Conservative, Moderate, Aggressive
TOPICS: Bonds, Stocks

Monthly Statistical Review

Dean Witter
5001 Spring Valley Road
530 Providence Towers East
Dallas, TX 75244

PH: (800) 827-2211
(214) 770-9724
Monthly publication approximately
   60 pages

Covers stocks (blue chip and small capital stocks). Contains statistics on all stocks followed by Dean Witter's research department.

AUDIENCE: Individual, Professional   RISK LEVEL: Moderate, Aggressive
TOPICS: Stocks

Nelson's Directory of Investment Research

Nelson Publications
One Gateway Plaza
Port Chester, NY 10573

PH: (914) 937-8400
(800) 333-6357
FAX: (914) 937-8908
Cost: $435.00
Frequency: annually
Date of first issue: 1975

Covers U.S. and foreign stocks. A 2 volume directory of research on over 9,000 stocks (5,000 U.S. companies and 4,000 foreign companies). Includes 5 year historical sales data, net income, EPS and 5 year growth rate, description, address, phone and fax numbers of each business. The directory also provides extensive analyst coverage information and geographical and industry groupings.

AUDIENCE: Individual, Professional   RISK LEVEL: Moderate, Aggressive
TOPICS: Stocks

Oilfield Services Quarterly

Rauscher Pierce Refsnes
5420 LBJ Suite 200
Dallas, TX 75240

PH: (800) 374-3966
FAX (214) 788-3995
Quarterly publication approximately
   45 pages

Covers companies involved in servicing oil and gas production and exploration. Includes rig counts, sector rankings, top ten list, day rates, international rig counts, oil and gas prices, stock symbols, 52 week ranges, earnings per share, earnings estimates, PE ratios, cash flow per share, and P-CF ratios.

AUDIENCE: Individual, Professional   RISK LEVEL: Moderate, Aggressive
TOPICS: Stocks

Portfolio Manager's Spotlight

Paine Webber
5151 Beltline Rd.
Suite 101
Dallas, TX 75248

PH: (800) 288-1515
(214) 450-4324
FAX: (214) 450-4350
Monthly publication approximately
  30 pages

Covers bonds and interest rates, stocks (blue chip and small capital stocks), economic analysis and asset allocation. This is a narrative piece that includes Paine Webber's asset allocation model and in-depth explanations of current industrial and economic trends. Includes explanations of ranking changes on stocks.

AUDIENCE: Individual, Professional   **RISK LEVEL: Moderate, Aggressive**
TOPICS: Bonds, Stocks

Portfolio Strategist

Smith Barney
13355 Noel Road
1660 One Galleria Tower
Dallas, TX 75240

PH: (800) 442-1357 TX
(800) 527-4175 US
(214) 450-6632
Weekly publication approximately
  30 pages

Includes bonds and interest rates, stocks (blue chip, small capital stocks, and foreign), economic analysis and asset allocation. Includes top stock recommendations, asset allocation model, company comments; global markets report, technical reports on currencies, gold, and bonds; quantitative analysis, earnings estimate changes, closed-end country funds comments, and economic data.

AUDIENCE: Individual, Professional   **RISK LEVEL: Conservative, Moderate,**
TOPICS: Bonds, Stocks   **Aggressive**

Quantitative Monthly

Prudential Securities, Inc.
10440 North Central Expressway
Suite 1600
Dallas, TX 75231

PH: (214) 373-2700
Monthly publication approximately
  65 pages

Covers economic analysis and stocks (blue chip and small capital stocks). Includes Prudential's view of the market and economy along with industry rankings and Model Portfolio Section. Blue chip and small capital stocks are ranked and listed by industry. New buy and sell recommendations are listed. Earnings, dividends, value, and correlations are graphed in the final section.

AUDIENCE: Individual, Professional   **RISK LEVEL: Moderate, Aggressive**
TOPICS: Bonds, Stocks

Recommended List, The

Smith Barney
12222 Merit Drive
Suite 1250
Dallas, TX 75251

PH: (800) 766-1088
(214) 387-8989
Monthly publication approximately
  4 pages

Covers stocks - blue chip and small capital stocks. Includes Shearson's top stock recommendations organized by industry with price performance, earnings, price 52 week range and dividend yield.

AUDIENCE: Individual, Professional   **RISK LEVEL: Moderate, Aggressive**
TOPICS: Stocks

Research Highlights

Merrill Lynch
5910 N. Central Expressway
2000 Premier Place
Dallas, TX 75206

PH: (800) 999-3056
(214) 750-2034
A weekly publication approximately
20 pages

Covers bonds and interest rates, stocks (blue chip, small capital stocks, and foreign stocks), economic analysis, and asset allocation. A condensed piece with economic and interest rate analysis, industry comments, technical comments, top recommendations in stocks, and global comments.

AUDIENCE: Individual, Professional   RISK LEVEL: Conservative, Moderate,
TOPICS: Bonds, Stocks   Aggressive

Research Universe

Smith Barney
12222 Merit Drive
Suite 1250
Dallas, TX 75251

PH: (800) 766-1088
(214) 387-8989
Monthly publication approximately
90 pages
Annual publication approximately
8 pages

Covers stocks - blue chip, small capital stocks, and foreign stocks; economic analysis; mutual funds (closed end). Includes Shearson's top stock recommendations, guided portfolios, listings of all stocks followed by Shearson, projected growth, P/E analysis, return models, beta coefficients, closed-end fund analysis, and economic analysis.

AUDIENCE: Individual, Professional   RISK LEVEL: Moderate, Aggressive
TOPICS: Stocks

Research Week

Smith Barney
13355 Noel Road
1660 One Galleria Tower
Dallas, TX 75240

PH: (800) 442-1357 TX
(800) 527-4175 US
(214) 450-6632
Weekly publication approximately
80 pages

Includes stocks (blue chip) and economic analysis. Includes top stock recommendations, changes in recommendation, industry analysis, comments on specific industries and companies, and a listing of other available research reports.

AUDIENCE: Individual, Professional   RISK LEVEL: Moderate, Aggressive
TOPICS: Stocks

Research Weekly

Prudential Securities, Inc.
10440 North Central Expressway
Suite 1600
Dallas, TX 75231

PH: (214) 373-2700
Weekly publication approximately
25 pages

Covers stocks (blue chip and small capital stocks, and economic analysis). Includes explanations of economic trends, industrial changes and a detailed explanation of changes in stock recommendations.

AUDIENCE: Individual, Professional   RISK LEVEL: Moderate, Aggressive
TOPICS: Stocks

Restaurant Review

Rauscher Pierce Refsnes
5420 LBJ Suite 200
Dallas, TX 75240

PH: (800) 374-3966
FAX (214) 788-3995
Monthly publication approximately
  5 pages

Covers small to large publicly traded restaurant stocks. Includes top ten, bottom ten, returns after cost, industry and theme comments.

AUDIENCE: Individual, Professional   RISK LEVEL: Moderate, Aggressive
TOPICS: Stocks

Statistical Summary

Paine Webber
5151 Beltline Rd.
Suite 101
Dallas, TX 75248

PH: (800) 288-1515
(214) 450-4324
FAX: (214) 450-4350
Monthly publication approximately
  40 pages

Covers stocks (blue chip and small capital stocks). Contains statistics on 638 stocks followed by Paine Webber including earnings, dividends, 52 week range, performance, price to earnings, beta, book value, shares, market value, institutional ownership, trading volume, and debt to equity. Also includes Paine Webber's ranking of each stock. Organized by the industry.

AUDIENCE: Individual, Professional   RISK LEVEL: Moderate, Aggressive
TOPICS: Stocks

Statistical Summary

Smith Barney
13355 Noel Road
1660 One Galleria Tower
Dallas, TX 75240

PH: (800) 442-1357 TX
(800) 527-4175 US
Monthly publication approximately
  50 pages
Includes stocks (blue chip, small
  capital stocks and foreign).

Includes top stock recommendations statistics on approximately 700 blue-chip, small-capitalization, and foriegn stocks followed by Smith Barney; 52 week range, earnings, growth, estimates, dividend, and current opinion. Also includes listings of closed-end country funds and international companies.

AUDIENCE: Individual, Professional   RISK LEVEL: Moderate, Aggressive
TOPICS: Stocks

Strategy Weekly

Prudential Securities, Inc.
10440 North Central Expressway
Suite 1600
Dallas, TX 75231

PH: (214) 373-2700
Weekly publication approximately
  40 pages

Covers bonds and interest rates, stocks (blue chip and small capital stocks), economic analysis, and asset allocation. Contains economic and industrial analysis with asset allocation structure. Also includes economic charts and Prudential's top recommendations put into model portfolios.

AUDIENCE: Individual, Professional   RISK LEVEL: Conservative, Moderate,
TOPICS: Bonds, Stocks   Aggressive

Ten Uncommon Values

Smith Barney
12222 Merit Drive
Suite 1250
Dallas, TX 75251

PH: (800) 766-1088
(214) 387-8989
Annually

Covers blue chip stocks. Includes an annual listing of Shearson's top ten stock recommendations updated each mid-year.

AUDIENCE: Individual, Professional   RISK LEVEL: Moderate, Aggressive
TOPICS: Stocks

The Equity Edge

Rauscher Pierce Refsnes and Dain
 Bosworth
5420 LBJ Suite 200
Dallas, TX 75240

PH: (800) 374-3966
FAX: (214) 788-3995
Monthly publication approximately
 7 pages

Includes the top stock recommendations of both regional brokerages owned by Interregional Financial Group. Top choices of approximately 35 stocks range from mid cap to large cap choices with earnings per share, 52 week range, earnings estimates, dividends and price targets.

AUDIENCE: Individual, Professional   RISK LEVEL: Moderate, Aggressive
TOPICS: Stocks

Universe, The

Rauscher Pierce Refsnes
5420 LBJ Suite 200
Dallas, TX 75240

PH: (800) 374-3966
FAX (214) 788-3995
Monthly publication approximately
 25 pages

Covers small to large cap companies followed by analysts in consumer products, financial services, restaurants, banks, health care services, pipelines, natural gas, oil and gas exploration, pollution control, and technology. Includes top twenty, statistical summary, 52 week range, earnings per share, earnings estimates, PE, dividend, shares outstanding, market capitalization, and rating.

AUDIENCE: Individual, Professional   RISK LEVEL: Moderate, Aggressive
TOPICS: Stocks

Weekly Portfolio Summary

Smith Barney
12222 Merit Drive
Suite 1250
Dallas, TX 75251

PH: (800) 766-1088
Weekly publication
Regular version is approximately
 60 pages
Condensed approximately 4 pages

Covers bonds and interest rates; stocks - blue chip and small capital stocks, economic analysis, and asset allocation. Divided into sections that include Strategy (asset allocation), Sector Analysis (industry groups), Technical Analysis, Global Strategy, Political Analysis, Economics, and comments on individual stocks.

AUDIENCE: Individual, Professional   RISK LEVEL: Moderate, Aggressive
TOPICS: Bonds, Stocks

Weekly Technical Perspective

Dean Witter
5001 Spring Valley Road
530 Providence Towers East
Dallas, TX 75244

PH: (800) 827-2211
(214) 770-9724
Weekly publication approximately
  10 pages

Covers stocks, economic analysis, commodities. Includes technical indicators for the market; put/call ration; investor sentiment; uptick/downtick ratio; index futures; institutional liquidity; CRB, indexes; and top stock recommendations.

AUDIENCE: Individual, Professional   RISK LEVEL: Aggressive
TOPICS: Stocks

Yield Curve

Smith Barney
12222 Merit Drive
Suite 1250
Dallas, TX 75251

PH: (800) 766-1088
(214) 387-8989
Weekly publication approximately
  13 pages

Covers bonds and interest rates, corporate, municipals, government, annuities, preferred stock, money market. Economic analysis. Includes a comprehensive bond market analysis, with an economic outlook, historical charts, yield curve charts, value matrix and analysis, and comments on specific bonds.

AUDIENCE: Beginning, Individual, Professional   RISK LEVEL: Conservative, Moderate
TOPICS: Bonds

FREE BROCHURES AND PAMPHLETS ON INVESTING

This chapter offers one of the best methods for gathering information without spending principal to do so. Brokerage firms and mutual funds publish a wealth of information about tax and investment planning, asset allocation, stocks, bonds, mutual funds, and even options and futures. Most of the time, these publications are available for the asking.

When gathering information on a specific type of investment, a brokerage firm's own descriptive brochure or pamphlet for that type of investment can be invaluable. Remember that the positive points may be overly emphasized.

Several of the publications listed in this chapter concern retirement plans, which is an area of increasing complexity for firms and individuals. For individuals, retirement plan distributions can create opportunities as well as an unexpected tax burden if not handled correctly. Most large investment firms publish brochures to guide investors through the process of correctly handling the IRA "rollover" of a distribution. Employers, meanwhile, will find available brochures that clarify the choices of potential company sponsored retirement plans with the tax and contribution features of each plan type.

Bonds are another area where brokerage firm brochures can be a great educational tool and pave the way for comparison shopping. From municipal bonds to zero coupon Treasury bonds, brochures are published to explain the advantages and pitfalls of each bond type. Ironically, these publications reveal that full service brokerage firms with large bond underwriting capabilities often carry the best bargains in bonds, in many cases undercutting the prices of typically smaller inventories at discount brokerages.

Mutual fund brochures and pamphlets tend to steer an investor towards that particular company's mutual fund program especially when the company only offers one family or group of funds. Therefore, for a mutual fund education, you are probably better off using the Books and Tapes on Investing chapter or the Computer and Quote Services chapter.

Investment and Brokerage firms are constantly updating their inventories of instructional brochures and pamphlets on investing. Therefore a comprehensive list is not possible. Most firms will gladly send an updated list of their available brochures and instructional pamphlets.

The firms listed in this inventory are under no obligation to send material free of charge. However, in an effort to cultivate clients, most will be more than happy to send you any of the items listed in this chapter.

Collateralized Mortgage Obligations - Taxable Fixed Income

Dean Witter
530 Providence Towers East
5001 Spring Valley Road
Dallas, TX 75244

PH: (800) 827-2211
(214) 770-9724
Date of publication: 1994

Covers mortgage backed securities. Includes an explanation of collateralized mortgage obligations, average life, maturity factors and prepayment assumptions.

AUDIENCE: Beginning, Individual   RISK LEVEL: Conservative
TOPICS: Bonds

Consumer Guide to Mutual Funds

Paine Webber
5151 Beltline Rd.
Suite 101
Dallas, TX 75248

PH: (800) 288-1515
(214) 934-3434
FAX: (214) 450-4350
Date of publication: 1993

Covers mutual funds and financial planning. Includes a discussion of mutual fund yield and total return, and explanations of selection criteria.

AUDIENCE: Beginning   RISK LEVEL: Moderate
TOPICS: Mutual Funds

Federally Insured CDs

Smith Barney
12222 Merit Drive
Suite 1250
Dallas, TX 75251

PH: (800) 766-1088
(214) 387-8989
Date of publication: 1990

Covers certificates of deposit. A brief explanation of CDs, federal insurance, and investment considerations.

AUDIENCE: Beginning   RISK LEVEL: Conservative
TOPICS: Bonds

Guide to Option Writing, A

Smith Barney
12222 Merit Drive
Suite 1250
Dallas, TX 75251

PH: (800) 766-1088
(214) 387-8989
Date of publication: 1994

Covers stocks. Includes a brief discussion of option writing to increase returns on current stock holdings, call premium calculations, and a short glossary of relevant terms.

AUDIENCE: Individual   RISK LEVEL: Moderate, Aggressive
TOPICS: Stocks, Options

Guide to Successful Investment Management, A

Smith Barney
12222 Merit Drive
Suite 1250
Dallas, TX 75251

PH: (800) 766-1088
(214) 387-8989
Date of publication: 1993

Covers stocks and bonds. A brief discussion of money managers, selection criteria, and investment styles.

AUDIENCE: Individual, Professional   RISK LEVEL: Moderate, Aggressive
TOPICS: Bonds, Stocks, Asset Allocation

How Municipal Bonds Can Help You Reach Financial Goals

Merrill Lynch
2000 Premier Place
5910 N. Central Expressway
Dallas, TX 75206

PH: (800) 999-3056
(214) 750-2034
Date of publication: 1991

Covers municipal bonds. Includes a brief introduction to the municipal market, explanations of terms, types of municipal bonds, tax-exempt status, and factors that determine a bond's price and yield.

AUDIENCE: Beginning, Individual   RISK LEVEL: Conservative
TOPICS: Bonds

How to Make the Most of Your Retirement Plan Distribution

Merrill Lynch
2000 Premier Place
5910 N. Central Expressway
Dallas, TX 75206

PH: (800) 999-3056
(214) 750-2034
Date of publication: 1988

Covers financial planning. Includes an explanation of retirement distribution, alternatives, tax considerations and calculations, and rollover alternatives.

AUDIENCE: Beginning, Individual   RISK LEVEL: Conservative, Moderate, Aggressive
TOPICS: Bonds, Mutual Funds, Stocks

How to Read a Financial Report

Merrill Lynch
2000 Premier Place
5910 N. Central Expressway
Dallas, TX 75206

PH: (800) 999-3056
(214) 750-2034
Date of publication: 1990

Covers corporate bonds and stocks. Includes an explanation of corporate financial statements: consolidated balance sheets, income statements, cash flow statements and changes in shareholder's equity.

AUDIENCE: Beginning, Individual   RISK LEVEL: Moderate, Aggressive
TOPICS: Bonds, Stocks

How to Take Control of Your Financial Future - Choosing an Annuity That's Right for You

Merrill Lynch
2000 Premier Place
5910 N. Central Expressway
Dallas, TX 75206

PH: (800) 999-3056
(214) 750-2034
Date of publication: 1994

Covers annuities. Includes types of annuities, tax-deferred explanations and advantages, and factors to consider when investigating an annuity.

AUDIENCE: Beginning	RISK LEVEL: Conservative, Moderate
TOPICS: Bonds, Mutual Funds	

Investing for Safety & High Return

Charles Schwab
101 Montgomery Street
San Francisco, CA 94104

PH: (800) 435-4000
Cost: Free
Date of publication: 1990

Fundamental analysis. Covers municipal bonds, corporate bonds, government bonds, zero-coupon bonds, Treasury bonds, CDs. Gives basic investment rules when dealing with fixed income investments as well as descriptions and helpful advice about each instrument.

AUDIENCE: Beginning, Individual	RISK LEVEL: Conservative
TOPICS: Bonds,	

Investing Your Lump Sum Distribution

Smith Barney
12222 Merit Drive
Suite 1250
Dallas, TX 75251

PH: (800) 766-1088
(214) 387-8989
Date of publication: 1992

Covers mortgage-backed securities, bonds (corporate, government, zero-coupon), general investing and financial planning. Includes financial planning advice, rates of return comparisons, analysis of bond yields, discussions of common investing questions, portfolio suggestions, conservative, moderate, and aggressive investments with risk level discussions.

AUDIENCE: Beginning, Individual	RISK LEVEL: Conservative, Moderate
TOPICS: Bonds, Mutual Funds, Stocks	

Investor's Guide to Certificates of Deposit, The

Paine Webber
5151 Beltline Rd.
Suite 101
Dallas, TX 75248

PH: (800) 288-1515
(214) 450-4324
FAX: (214) 450-4350
Date of publication: 1990

Covers financial planning and certificates of deposit. Includes a discussion of CDs, their features, FDIC insurance, insurance limits, and investing information.

AUDIENCE: Beginning	RISK LEVEL: Conservative
TOPICS: Bonds	

Investor's Guide to Ginnie Maes, The

Paine Webber
5151 Beltline Rd.
Suite 101
Dallas, TX 75248

PH: (800) 288-1515
(214) 450-4324
FAX: (214) 450-4350
Date of publication: 1990

Covers mortgage-backed securities. Includes an explanation of the terms associate with Government National Mortgage Association (GNMA) bonds, explanation of common questions, and a list of features of GNMA bonds.

AUDIENCE: Beginning, Individual   RISK LEVEL: Conservative
TOPICS: Bonds

Investor's Guide to Government Securities, The

Paine Webber
5151 Beltline Rd.
Suite 101
Dallas, TX 75248

PH: (800) 288-1515
(214) 450-4324
FAX: (214) 450-4350
Date of publication: 1989

Covers government bonds. Includes a brief explanation of most types of government bonds and a table showing the features of the different types of bonds.

AUDIENCE: Beginning, Individual   RISK LEVEL: Conservative
TOPICS: Bonds

Investor's Guide to Tax-Exempt Securities, An

Paine Webber
5151 Beltline Rd.
Suite 101
Dallas, TX 75248

PH: (800) 288-1515
(214) 450-4324
FAX: (214) 450-4350
Date of publication: 1990/91

Covers municipal bonds. Includes an introduction and definition of tax exempt municipal bonds, explanation of safety, special features, taxable equivalent yield calculations, and a comprehensive glossary of terms used in municipal investing.

AUDIENCE: Beginning, Individual   RISK LEVEL: Conservative
TOPICS: Bonds

Investor's Guide to Tax-Free Zero Coupon Municipal Bonds, The

Paine Webber
5151 Beltline Rd.
Suite 101
Dallas, TX 75248

PH: (800) 288-1515
(214) 450-4324
FAX: (214) 450-4350
Date of publication: 1988

Covers municipal bonds and zero coupon. Includes a brief discussion of zero coupon municipal (tax-free) bonds and an explanation of their features.

AUDIENCE: Beginning, Individual   RISK LEVEL: Conservative
TOPICS: Bonds

Investor's Guide to Treasury Zeros, The

Paine Webber
5151 Beltline Rd.
Suite 101
Dallas, TX 75248

PH: (800) 288-1515
(214) 450-4324
FAX: (214) 450-4350
Date of publication: 1992

Covers government and zero-coupon bonds. Includes a brief discussion of U.S. government zero coupon bonds, their yields and pricing calculations.

AUDIENCE: Beginning, Individual   RISK LEVEL: Conservative
TOPICS: Bonds

IRA Rollover - Making Sense Out of Your Lump Sum Distribution

Dean Witter
530 Providence Towers East
5001 Spring Valley Road
Dallas, TX 75244

PH: (800) 827-2211
(214) 770-9724
Date of publication: 1993

Areas covered by brochure: financial planning. Includes a discussion of options relating to retirement distributions and explains factors to be considered in rolling over a distribution.

AUDIENCE: Beginning, Individual   RISK LEVEL: Conservative, Moderate
TOPICS: Bonds, Mutual Funds, Stocks, Investment Planning

IRA Sourcebook (1994 update)

Merrill Lynch
2000 Premier Place
5910 N. Central Expressway
Dallas, TX 75206

PH: (800) 999-3056
(214) 750-2034
Date of publication: 1988/1994

Includes an explanation of Individual Retirement Accounts, deductibility, tax deferral, Form 8606 non-deductible contributions, and withdrawal requirements.

AUDIENCE: Beginning, Individual   RISK LEVEL: Conservative, Moderate
TOPICS: Bonds, Mutual Funds, Stocks, Investment Planning

Lifetime Strategy for Investing in Common Stocks, A

American Association for Individual Investors
625 N. Michigan Avenue
Chicago, IL 60611

PH: (312) 280-0170
Cost: Free
Date of publication: 1981

Attempts to explain stock market risk and its relationship to returns.

AUDIENCE: Beginning, Individual   RISK LEVEL: Moderate, Aggressive
TOPICS: Stocks

Louis Rukeyser's Investment Strategies Guide

Louis Rukeyser's Investment
Strategies Guide
P.O. Box 25527
Alexandria, VA 22313

Cost: Free with membership in
Louis Rukeyser's Wall Street Club

Provides strategies for building wealth and preserving capital.
Some topics include: The "Rule of 72"; IPOS - Why they're lousy
long-term investments; The single biggest mistake stock-market
investors make; The seven criteria for choosing utility stocks.

AUDIENCE: Beginning, Individual   RISK LEVEL: Moderate, Aggressive
TOPICS: Bonds, Mutual Funds, Stocks

Lump Sum Distribution - How to Make the Most of Them

Smith Barney
12222 Merit Drive
Suite 1250
Dallas, TX 75251

PH: (800) 766-1088
(214) 387-8989
Date of publication: 1989

Covers financial planning. Includes explanations of retirement
distribution alternatives, tax considerations and explanations, and
financial planning considerations.

AUDIENCE: Beginning, Individual   RISK LEVEL: Conservative, Moderate
TOPICS: Bonds, Mutual Funds, Stocks, Asset Allocation, Investment Planning

Managing Your IRA

Smith Barney
12222 Merit Drive
Suite 1250
Dallas, TX 75251

PH: (800)766-1088
(214) 387-8989
Date of publication: 1990

Covers mortgage backed securities, bonds (corporate, government,
zero-coupon), stocks, general investing, and financial planning.
Includes a discussion of investments suited for individual
retirement accounts, including stocks, bonds, mutual funds, CD's,
covered options, and financial planning considerations.

AUDIENCE: Beginning, Individual   RISK LEVEL: Conservative, Moderate
TOPICS: Bonds, Mutual Funds, Stocks Asset Allocation, Investment Planning

Managing Your Retirement Plan Distribution: Tax Alternatives

Paine Webber
5151 Beltline Rd.
Suite 101
Dallas, TX 75248

PH: (800) 288-1515
(214) 450-4324
FAX: (214) 450-4350
Date of publication: 1994

Covers financial planning. Includes an explanation of distribution
tax alternatives, rollover options, penalties, and stock rollovers.

AUDIENCE: Beginning, Individual   RISK LEVEL: Conservative, Moderate
TOPICS: Investment Planning

Maximizing Your Retirement Plan Distribution

Charles Schwab
101 Montgomery Street
San Francisco, CA 94104

PH: (800) 435-4000
Date of publication: 1991

Includes explanations of a retirement plan distribution, options for
rollover or forward averaging, and terms associated with retirement
distributions.

AUDIENCE: Beginning, Individual   RISK LEVEL: Conservative, Moderate
TOPICS: Investment Planning

Merrill Lynch Guide to Collateralized Mortgage Obligations

Merrill Lynch
2000 Premier Place
5910 N. Central Expressway
Dallas, TX 75206

PH: (800) 999-3056
(214) 750-2034
Date of publication: 1993

Covers mortgage backed securities. Includes explanations of the collateralized mortgage obligations, asset collateralization, and terms associated with CMO bonds.

AUDIENCE: Beginning, Individual	RISK LEVEL: Conservative
TOPICS: Bonds	

Mortgage Collateralized Bonds

Prudential Securities, Inc.
10440 North Central Expressway
Suite 1600
Dallas, TX 75231

PH: (214) 373-2700
FAX: (214) 373-2788
Cost: Free
Date of publication: 1991

Covers mortgage backed securities. An investor's guide to MCBs. Gives highlights and features as well as redemption information and explanation of how MCBs work.

AUDIENCE: Beginning, Individual	RISK LEVEL: Conservative
TOPICS: Bonds	

Municipal Bonds Investing for Tax-Free Income

Paine Webber
5151 Beltline Rd.
Suite 101
Dallas, TX 75248

PH: (800) 288-1515
(214) 450-4324
FAX: (214) 450-4350
Date of publication: 1988

Covers municipal bonds and financial planning. Includes advantages of municipal securities, definitions of terms used in bond investing, ratings explanations, and types of municipal bonds.

AUDIENCE: Beginning, Individual	RISK LEVEL: Conservative
TOPICS: Bonds	

Municipal Bonds: Investing For Tax-Free Income

Prudential Securities, Inc.
10440 North Central Expressway
Dallas, TX 75231

PH: (214) 373-2700
FAX: (214) 373-2788
Cost: Free
Date of publication: 1991

Covers municipal bonds and zero-coupon bonds. An informative booklet discussing the "why's" and "how-to's" of municipal bond investing. Gives features of muni bonds, and discusses the different forms and types of muni bonds.

AUDIENCE: Beginning, Individual	RISK LEVEL: Conservative
TOPICS: Bonds	

Municipal Bonds - Now More Than Ever - An Investor's Guide to Municipal Bonds

Smith Barney
12222 Merit Drive
Suite 1250
Dallas, TX 75251

PH: (800) 766-1088
(214) 387-8989
Date of publication: 1990

Covers municipal bonds and financial planning. Includes an explanation of municipal bonds, tax-exempt status, factors determining the price and yield of a bond, taxable equivalent yields, and tax brackets.

AUDIENCE: Beginning, Individual   RISK LEVEL: Conservative
TOPICS: Bonds

Overview: Meeting Your Retirement Objectives

Prudential Securities, Inc.
10440 North Central Expressway
Suite 1600
Dallas, TX 75231

PH: (214) 373-2700
FAX: (214) 373-2788
Cost: Free
Date of publication: 1986

Covers retirement planning. A booklet describing the different types of qualified plans and investment products suitable for these plans.

AUDIENCE: Beginning,   RISK LEVEL: Conservative, Moderate
TOPICS: Bonds, Mutual Funds, Stocks, Investment Planning

Paine Webber Guide to Retirement Plans, The

Paine Webber
5151 Beltline Rd.
Suite 101
Dallas, TX 75248

PH: (800) 288-1515
(214) 450-4324
FAX: (214) 450-4350
Date of publication: 1990

Provides information on general investing and financial planning. Includes an explanation of retirement plan types, maximum contributions, special retirement, plan features, and a chart describing SEP, profit sharing, money purchase, 401K, CODA-SEP, and defined benefit pensions.

AUDIENCE: Beginning, Individual, Professional   RISK LEVEL: Conservative,
TOPICS: Investment Planning, General Reference   Moderate, Aggressive

Paine Webber Retirement Plan Distribution Investor's Guide, The

Paine Webber
5151 Beltline Rd.
Suite 101
Dallas, TX 75248

PH: (800) 288-1515
(214) 450-4324
FAX: (214) 450-4350
Date of publication: 1990

Provides information financial planning. Includes a discussion of distribution tax alternatives, rollover advantages, tax averaging, and IRA explanations.

AUDIENCE: Beginning, Individual   RISK LEVEL: Conservative, Moderate
TOPICS: Bonds, Mutual Funds, Stocks, Investment Planning, General Reference

Professional Portfolio Management - Making the Right Choice

Smith Barney
12222 Merit Drive
Suite 1250
Dallas, TX 75251

PH: (800) 766-1088
(214) 387-8989
Date of publication: 1990

Covers stocks, bonds, and financial planning. Includes a discussion of money managers, selection criteria, risk vs return, and different money manager styles.

AUDIENCE: Beginning, Individual   RISK LEVEL: Conservative, Moderate
TOPICS: Bonds, Stocks, Asset Allocation, Investment Planning

Qualified Retirement Plans for Business

Merrill Lynch
Retirement Builder - Guidebook to
Planning Financial Security
2000 Premier Place
5910 N. Central Expressway
Dallas, TX 75206

PH: (800) 999-3056
(214) 750-2034
Date of publication: 1987/1988

Covers financial planning. Includes explanation of types of qualified retirement plans, their advantages and special factors relating to plan establishment and maintenance.

AUDIENCE: Beginning, Individual   RISK LEVEL: Conservative, Moderate
TOPICS: Investment Planning, General Reference

Retirement Builder - Guidebook to Planning Financial Security

Merrill Lynch
2000 Premier Place
5910 N. Central Expressway
Dallas, TX 75206

PH: (800) 999-3056
(214) 750-2034
Date of publication: 1990

Covers financial planning. Includes retirement planning explanations, financial planning guidelines, income needs analysis, and financial planning calculation charts.

AUDIENCE: Beginning, Individual   RISK LEVEL: Conservative, Moderate
TOPICS: Investment Planning

Retirement Investment Strategies

Dean Witter
530 Providence Towers East
5001 Spring Valley Road
Dallas, TX 75244

PH: (800) 827-2211
(214) 770-9724
Date of publication: 1989

Areas covered by brochure include mortgage backed securities, bonds (corporate, government, and zero coupon), stocks, general investing and financial planning. Includes a discussion of retirement plans and types of investments: money market funds, CDs, mutual funds, bonds, stocks, unit trusts, limited partnerships, covered options, and preferred stocks.

AUDIENCE: Beginning, Individual   RISK LEVEL: Conservative, Moderate
TOPICS: Bonds, Mutual Funds, Stocks, Investment Planning

Retirement Plan Distribution Analysis

Prudential Securities, Inc.
10440 North Central Expressway
Suite 1600
Dallas, TX 75231

PH: (214) 373-2000

A brief booklet that helps calculate distribution tax alternatives.

AUDIENCE: Beginning, Individual   RISK LEVEL: Conservative, Moderate
TOPICS: Investment Planning, General Reference

Retirement Planning - For the Self-Employed Professional and Small Business Owner

Paine Webber
5151 Beltline Rd.
Suite 101
Dallas, TX 75248

PH: (800) 288-1515
(214) 450-4324
FAX: (214) 450-4350
Date of publication: 1987

Provides information on general investing and financial planning. Includes explanations of types of plans including SEP, money purchase, defined benefit, 401K and profit sharing.

AUDIENCE: Beginning, Individual   RISK LEVEL: Conservative, Moderate
TOPICS: Investment Planning, General Reference

Selecting Investments for Safety and Return

Charles Schwab
101 Montgomery Street
San Francisco, CA 94104

PH: (800) 435-4000
Date of publication: 1990

Areas covered by brochure are bonds (municipal, corporate, government, zero-coupon), stocks, general investing, and financial planning. Includes explanations of investment terms, portfolio allocation, goal setting, bond pricing, tax-exempt securities, and mutual fund alternatives.

AUDIENCE: Beginning, Individual   RISK LEVEL: Conservative
TOPICS: Bonds

Short-Term Fixed-Income Investments for Businesses & Financial Institutions

Merrill Lynch
2000 Premier Place
5910 N. Central Expressway
Dallas, TX 75206

PH: (800) 999-3056
(214) 750-2034
Date of publication: 1990

Covers bonds (municipal, corporate, government and zero-coupon), and general investing. Includes explanations of money market instruments, tax-exempt money market instruments, and tax-advantages money market instruments.

AUDIENCE: Professional   RISK LEVEL: Conservative
TOPICS: Bonds

Stock Market Investing - The Definitive Guide for Paine Webber Clients

Paine Webber
5151 Beltline Rd.
Suite 101
Dallas, TX 75248

PH: (800) 288-1515
(214) 450-4324
FAX: (214) 450-4350
Date of publication: 1990

Covers stocks. Includes stock market historical performance, dividend explanation, and a discussion of Paine Webber's research.

AUDIENCE: Beginning, Individual   RISK LEVEL: Moderate, Aggressive
TOPICS: Stocks

Tax Saving Ideas for Investors

Merrill Lynch
2000 Premier Place
5910 N. Central Expressway
Dallas, TX 75206

PH: (800) 999-3056
FAX: (214) 750-2034
Date of publication: 1987/1990

Covers municipal bonds, stocks, general investing and financial planning. 43 tax saving ideas are presented with a focus on personal investing.

AUDIENCE: Beginning, Individual   RISK LEVEL: Conservative, Moderate
TOPICS: Bonds, Investment Planning

Tax-Deferred Annuities

Prudential Securities, Inc.
10440 North Central Expressway
Suite 1600
Dallas, TX 75231

PH: (214) 373-2700
FAX: (214) 373-2788
Cost: Free
Date of publication: 1986

Covers annuities. A helpful guide explaining the benefits and features of annuities. Gives you the when, how-to and why's of buying annuities and discusses the annuitization options.

AUDIENCE: Beginning, Individual   RISK LEVEL: Conservative, Moderate
TOPICS: Bonds, Mutual Funds

Triple Appeal of Convertible Securities

Smith Barney
12222 Merit Drive
Suite 1250
Dallas, TX 75251

PH: (800) 766-1088
FAX: (214) 387-8989

Covers bonds and stocks. A brief explanation of convertible securities and their features, along with a glossary of relevant terms for convertible securities investors.

AUDIENCE: Beginning, Individual   RISK LEVEL: Moderate, Aggressive
TOPICS: Bonds, Stocks

Zero Coupon Bonds

Prudential Securities
10440 North Central Expressway
Suite 1600
Dallas, TX 75231

PH: (214) 373-2700
FAX: (214) 373-2788
Cost: Free
Date of publication: 1991

An informative brochure for zero coupon bond investors. It explains how your money grows, gives a definition of zeros, shows how they should fit in your financial plan, summarizes the different types of zeros and briefly discusses tax implications.

AUDIENCE: Beginning, Individual   RISK LEVEL: Conservative
TOPICS: Bonds

Zero Coupon Treasuries

Smith Barney
12222 Merit Drive
Suite 1250
Dallas, TX 75251

PH: (800) 766-1088
(214) 387-8989
Date of publication: 1988

Covers bonds (government and zero coupon), and financial planning. Includes a brief discussion of U.S. Treasury zero-coupon bonds, an explanation of relevant terms, and a pricing chart.

AUDIENCE: Beginning, Individual   RISK LEVEL: Conservative
TOPICS: Bonds

MAGAZINES, NEWSPAPERS, AND PERIODICALS

This chapter lists the major periodicals, magazines, and newspapers designed to help investors. These publications offer a wide variety in terms of size, content, frequency, and degree of specialization. You are the best judge of which items match the investment areas you need. A phone call to the publication can also help isolate special features and regular investment articles.

Each entry describes the publication's major features, frequency, price, and how to order. Before ordering a financial publication, you may want to preview a copy. Copies are generally available at libraries, bookstores, newsstands, and certain periodical outlets.

Investors who specialize in certain types of investments will benefit from a broad range of specialty publications. Copies may be harder to track down, but again you may want to see an issue before subscribing.

Access Nippon 1994-How to Succeed in Japan

The Reference Press, Inc.
6448 Highway 290 E., Suite E-104
Austin, TX 78723

PH: (512) 454-7778
FAX: (512) 454-9401
Cost: $34.95
Published annually
Date of first issue: 1988
Fundamental Analysis

Profiles of over 200 of the giants of Japanese industry. Each company profile includes an overview of operations, addresses of major offices, sales broken down by products and exports, product names, list of foreign partners, basic financial information, and much more.

AUDIENCE: Individual, Professional   RISK LEVEL: Moderate, Aggressive
TOPICS: Stocks, General Reference

America's Finest Companies

Bill Staton Enterprises
2113 E. 5th Street
Charlotte, NC 28204

PH: (704) 335-0276
FAX: (704) 332-0427
Cost: $32.00 post-paid
Date of first issue: 8/91
Annual periodical
Includes: Earnings Analysis

Over 225 companies with superior records of annual earnings and dividend increases - including 53 with 30 or more years of higher earnings and dividends. Also includes stock symbols, yields, earnings, financial strengths ratings, dividend ratings, dividend reinvestment plan availability, addresses, and phone numbers.

AUDIENCE: Beginning, Individual   RISK LEVEL: Moderate, Aggressive
TOPICS: Stocks

American Small Business & Investors Association

Tim Murray, Publisher
375 Douglas Avenue, Suite 1012
Altamonte Springs, FL 32714

PH: (800) 340-0123
FAX: (407) 788-3933
Frequency: Quarterly
Date of first issue: November 1993
Cost: $49.00/yr
Fundamental Analysis

A magazine geared towards small businesses and investors with the intent of showing how to reduce cost and taxes and how to invest successfully. Gives general financial news and investment tips including spotlights on several different companies.

AUDIENCE: Individual, Professional   RISK LEVEL: Moderate, Aggressive
TOPICS: Stocks

Asia Pacific Securities Handbook

The Reference Press, Inc.
6448 Highway 290 E.
Suite E-104
Austin, TX 78723

PH: (512) 454-7778
FAX: (512) 454-9401
Cost: $99.95
Published annually

Covers the stock markets in Australia, Bangladesh, China, Hong Kong, India, Indonesia, Japan, Malaysia, Nepal, New Zealand, Pakistan, the Philippines, Singapore, South Korea, Sri Lanka, Taiwan and Thailand. Profiles include stock exchange addresses and phone numbers, description of stock market practices, market overview, lists of the top stocks and names, addresses and phone numbers for stock brokerage firms.

AUDIENCE: Individual, Professional   RISK LEVEL: Moderate, Aggressive
TOPICS: Stocks, General Reference

Asia Pacific Securities Handbook Revised

The Reference Press, Inc.
6448 Highway 290 E.
Suite E-104
Austin, TX 78723

PH: (512) 454-7778
FAX: (512) 454-9401
Cost: $99.95
Published annually

Covers the stock markets in Australia, Bangladesh, China, Hong Kong, India, Indonesia, Japan, Malaysia, Nepal, New Zealand, Pakistan, the Philippines, Singapore, South Korea, Sri Lanka, Taiwan and Thailand. Profiles include stock exchange addresses and phone numbers, description of stock market practices, market overview, lists of the top stocks and names, addresses and phone numbers for stock brokerage firms.

AUDIENCE: Individual, Professional   **RISK LEVEL: Moderate, Aggressive**
TOPICS: Stocks, General Reference

Back-up Tables-Statistical Reports-Closed-end and Open-end Investment Companies

Investment Company Institute
1600 M Street, N.W
Suite 600
Washington, D.C. 20036

PH: (202) 293-7700
Cost: $50.00 annually
Date of first issue: 1989
Monthly periodical

Technical analysis. Covers mutual funds and bonds, uses tables and graphs. Monthly closed-end report includes total underwritings and new issues for bond and equity categories. There is also an annual survey of closed-end funds providing outstanding assets, annual volume of underwritings, and selected data on a per fund basis. Monthly open-end fund (back-up) tables include the same data.

AUDIENCE: Beginning, Individual   **RISK LEVEL: Moderate, Aggressive**
TOPICS: Mutual Funds

Barron's National Business & Financial Weekly

Dow Jones & Company, Inc
P.O. Box 7014
200 Burnett Road
Chicopee, MA 01021-9901

PH: (800) 328-6800 subscriptions
(800) 628-9320 info
FAX: (413) 592-4782
Cost: $129.00 annually
Date of first issue: May 1921
Weekly magazine

Special feature issue: Barron's Lipper Gauge - a quarterly report on mutual fund performance, February, May, August, and November. Continual flow of reliable info on virtually all investment areas. Includes facts, figures, exclusive statistics on the whole range of markets and spotlights individual companies and industries. Regular features: company reviews, market update, stock choices, mutual fund review, bond, analysis, money manager interviews.

AUDIENCE: Individual, Professional   **RISK LEVEL: Conservative, Moderate, Aggressive**
TOPICS: All

Blue Sky Guide

Investment Company Institute
1600 M Street, N.W.
Suite 600
Washington, D.C. 20036

PH: (202) 293-7700
Cost: $600.00 initial subscription
$300.00 renewal for updates annually
Date of first issue: 1981
Semi-annual periodical

Fundamental analysis. Covers mutual funds. A two-volume reference compendium of registration and regulatory requirements contained in the 50 states' securities laws offering mutual funds and their sales agents.

AUDIENCE: Individual, Professional   **RISK LEVEL: Moderate, Aggressive**
TOPICS: Mutual Funds

Bond Guide

Standard & Poor's
25 Broadway
New York, NY 10004

PH: (212) 208-8786
Cost: $185.00 annually
Monthly periodical

Bond analysis. 224 page guide with 41 columns of descriptive and statistical data on more than 5,900 corporate bonds, 650 convertibles, and 280 Canadian and foreign issuers. All registered and coupon bonds identified. Features include S&P debt rating, capitalization data, debt to capital ratios and much more. CreditWatch, focuses on fixed income issuers under surveillance for possible ratings changes.

AUDIENCE: Individual, Professional   RISK LEVEL: Conservative, Moderate
TOPICS: Bonds

Brokerage Firm Safety Directory

Weiss Research, Inc.
2200 N. Fla. Mango Rd.
W. Palm Beach, FL 33409

PH: (800) 289-9222
Frequency: Annually
Cost: $189.00

"A listing of major stock brokerage firms with their safety ratings. Contains the only comprehensive ratings on more that 200 securities firms. Includes pertinent information on monitoring the safety of the companies, as well as statistical data on each firm."

AUDIENCE: Beginning, Individual, Professional   RISK LEVEL: Conservative,
TOPICS: All   Moderate, Aggressive

Buhh and Bean Financial Newspaper

Buhh and Bean Financial Newspaper
P.O. Box 4267
Winter Park, FL 32793

PH: (407) 677-7872
Frequency: Monthly
Cost: $19.00/yr
Fundamental Analysis
Date of first issue: 1974
ISSN: 8 0319-1362

David J. Robinson, Editor. Provides a wide range of investment advisory opinion by leading investors, including stocks, mutual funds, precious metals, real estate, currencies, and tax strategies. Recommends and summarizes top investment advisory newsletters.

AUDIENCE: Professional and General Investors   RISK LEVEL: Moderate, Aggressive
TOPICS: Mutual Funds, Stocks, Futures/Commodities

Business Week Magazine

McGraw-Hill
1221 Avenue of the Americas
39th Floor
New York, NY 10020

PH: (212) 512-2511
(800) 635-1200
Cost: $46.95 annually
Date of first issue: 1931
ISSN: 0007-7135

Weekly magazine. Company reviews and stock choices. Departments include: Cover Story, Top of the News, International, Economic Analysis, Government Industries, The Corporation, People, Finance, Science & Technology, Information Processing, Design, Marketing, and Personal Business. Features include: Business Week Index, Reader's Report, Corrections & Clarifications, Books, Index to Companies, and Editorials.

AUDIENCE: Beginning, Individual, Professional   RISK LEVEL: Conservative,
TOPICS: All   Moderate, Aggressive

Canada Company Handbook 1994

The Reference Press, Inc.
6448 Highway 290 E, Suite E-104
Austin, TX 78723

PH: (512) 454-7778
FAX: (512) 454-9401
Cost: $39.95
Date of first issue: 1994
ISBN : 0-921925-45-X
Fundamental Analysis

A reference book providing information on over 1,300 Canadian companies. Profiles over 400 companies on the Toronto Stock Exchange, both current and prior companies. Profiles include a description of the company, performance analysis, stock price performance charts, 5 years of financial data, 2 years of quarterly financial data, stock symbols, and rankings on profit, revenues and assets.

AUDIENCE: Individual, Professional   **RISK LEVEL: Moderate, Aggressive**
TOPICS: Stocks, General Reference

CDA Mutual Fund Report

CDA Investment Technologies, Inc.
1355 Piccard Drive
Rockville, MD 20850

PH: (800) 232-2285
Cost: $275.00 annually
Date of first issue: 1976
Monthly periodical

Technical analysis. Covers mutual funds. This service analyzes the performance, risk posture and percentile rankings of over 4,000 funds. Cornerstone of this report is the "CDA Rating," an overall rating of each fund that takes into account all aspects of performance and risk. Rates of return are calculated for 22 time periods (including bull and bear markets) and each report is mailed 3 days after month-end.

AUDIENCE: Beginning, Individual   **RISK LEVEL: Moderate, Aggressive**
TOPICS: Mutual Funds

Company Handbook Spain-The Maxwell Espinosa Shareholders Directory

The Reference Press, Inc.
6448 Highway 290 E.
Suite E-104
Austin, TX 78723

PH: (512) 454-7778
FAX: (512) 454-9401
Cost: $84.95
ISBN: 8-472092-57-7
Fundamental Analysis

Profiles almost 2,000 Spanish corporations. Information includes: headquarters, industry, phone and fax numbers, major shareholders, recent year's sales, number of employees as well as advertising agency, attorneys, banks, auditors and other communications contacts.

AUDIENCE: Individual, Professional   **RISK LEVEL: Moderate, Aggressive**
TOPICS: Stocks, General Reference

Company Handbook-Hong Kong

The Reference Press, Inc.
6448 Highway 290 E.
Suite E-104
Austin, TX 78723

PH: (512) 454-7778
FAX: (512) 454-9401
Cost: $44.95; published twice/year
Fundamental Analysis

Profiles the 416 companies listed on the Hong Kong Stock Exchange. Includes description of company, major office address and phone number, major stockholders and officers, financial statements, key ratios and profit breakdowns.

AUDIENCE: Individual, Professional   **RISK LEVEL: Moderate, Aggressive**
TOPICS: Stocks, General Reference

Consensus - National Futures and Financial Weekly

Consensus, Inc.
P.O. Box 411128
Kansas City, MO 64141

PH: (816) 471-3862
FAX: (816) 221-2045
Cost: $365.00 annually
Date of first issue: 1971

Weekly newspaper. A unique investment newspaper covering commodities, stock indices, currencies, gold, silver, oil, T-bills. Gives you current market letters of brokerage firms, special reports from brokerage firms, graphic consensus index, weekly price quotes of all major futures markets and comprehensive charting of all actively traded futures. Includes free index hotline.

AUDIENCE: Individual, Professional   RISK LEVEL: Aggressive
TOPICS: Stocks, Options, Futures/Commodities

Debts Outlook

Delta Securities Management
  Corporation
7 Bettlegreen Road
Lexington, MA 02173-6700

PH: (617) 782-1800
Cost: $285.00/yr
Frequency: Quarterly
Technical Analysis

Stock data, charts, ratings for NYSE stocks, includes industry and selected company comments.

AUDIENCE: Individual, Professional   RISK LEVEL: Moderate, Aggressive
TOPICS: Bonds, Stocks

Directory of Companies Offering Dividend Reinvestment

Evergreen Enterprises
Box 763
Laurel, MD 20725-0763

PH: (301) 953-1861
Cost: $28.95
Frequency: Annually
Date of first issue: 1982

A list of companies offering dividend reinvestment plans. Provides names, addresses, phone numbers, charges, eligibility requirements, purchase requirements and more.

AUDIENCE: Beginning, Individual   RISK LEVEL: Moderate
TOPICS: Stocks

Directory of Dividend Reinvestment Plans

Standard & Poor's
25 Broadway
New York, NY 10004

PH: (800) 221-5277
(212) 208-8812
COST: $39.95
Published annually

Includes over 700 companies that offer DRPs in easy-to-read tables. Provides S&P quality rankings, features of each plan, firms which offer reinvestment at a discount, relative values of $1,000 investments made 10 years ago, and more.

AUDIENCE: Beginning, Individual   RISK LEVEL: Moderate
TOPICS: Stocks

Economist, The

The Economist
111 W. 57th
New York, NY 10019

PH: (212) 541-5730
PH: (800) 456-6086;
FAX: (212) 541-9378
Cost: $125.00
Frequency: Weekly
Date of first issue: 1843

Weekly magazine. An international magazine reporting news, world affairs, business and finance.

AUDIENCE: Beginning, Individual, Professional   RISK LEVEL: Conservative,
TOPICS: All   Moderate, Aggressive

Energy in the News

New York Mercantile Exchange
Marketing Department
Four Winds Trade Center
New York, NY 10046-0835

PH: (212) 938-2879
Cost: Free
Frequency: Quarterly
Fundamental Analysis
Date of first issue: 1979

Publisher: Jan Kay, Editor: Louise Burke. Coverage of the New York Mercantile Exchange energy futures, market and options.

AUDIENCE: Individual, Professional   RISK LEVEL: Aggressive
TOPICS: Options, Futures/Commodities

Equities Magazine

Equities Magazine, Inc.
145 East 49th Street
Suites 5B & 5C
New York, NY 10017

PH: (212) 832-7800
FAX: (212) 832-7823
Cost: $36.00
Frequency: Monthly
Date of first issue: 1951

Monthly magazine. "A business and finance magazine featuring investigative reports, company profiles, financial highlights, mergers and acquisitions, foreign investments, statistics and ratings."

AUDIENCE: Beginning, Individual, Professional   RISK LEVEL: Moderate, Aggressive
TOPICS: Mutual Funds, Stocks

European Companies - A Guide to Sources of Information

The Reference Press, Inc.
6448 Highway 290 E.
Suite E-104
Austin, TX 78723

PH: (512) 454-7778
FAX: (512) 454-9401
COST: $89.95
Date of first issue: 1994
ISBN: 0-900246-44-8
Frequency: Annually

"An invaluable guide to information sources for European companies and for doing business in Europe." Covers 35 countries and over 1,500 entries.

AUDIENCE: Individual, Professional   RISK LEVEL: Moderate, Aggressive
TOPICS: Bonds, Stocks, General Reference

Far Eastern Economic Review

Review Publishing Co., Ltd.
25/F Citicorp Center
18 Whitfield Road GPO 160
Hong Kong

PH: (800) 451-3410
FAX: (852) 503-1549
(852) 503-1553
Frequency: Weekly
Cost: $159.00/yr

Provides constant coverage of the stock market around the Asia region. Columns of interest include: business, politics, finance, economics, technology, price and trends, intelligence, defense and international relations.

AUDIENCE: Individual, Professional   RISK LEVEL: Moderate, Aggressive
TOPICS: Stocks, General Reference

Finance and Commerce Daily Newspaper

Finance and Commerce Daily
Newspaper
615 S. 7th St.
Mailing: P.O. Box 15047
Minneapolis, MN 55415

PH: (612) 333-3243
FAX: (612) 333-3243
Frequency: Tuesday- Saturday
Cost: $119.00/yr
Date of first issue: 1887
Fundamental Analysis

General Business, Finance, Banking, Real Estate.

AUDIENCE: Individual, Professional   RISK LEVEL: Conservative, Moderate,
TOPICS: All   Aggressive

Financial Analysts Journal

Association for Investment Management
  Research
P.O. Box 3668
Charlottesville, VA 22903

PH: (804) 980-9775
FAX: (804) 980-9710
Cost: $150.00/yr
Frequency: Bimonthly
Date of first issue: 1945

Fundamental analysis. Covers general investment information. "A practitioner-oriented journal dedicated to the needs of investment professionals....it includes articles describing research in the fields of portfolio management, asset allocation, global investing and security analysis, among others."

AUDIENCE: Professional   RISK LEVEL: Moderate, Aggressive
TOPICS: All

Financial Executive

Financial Executives Institute
10 Madison Avenue
Box 1938
Morristown, NJ 07962-1938

PH: (201) 898-4642
FAX: (201) 898-4649
Cost: $40.00 annually
Date of first publication: 1934
  (formerly Controller)

Bimonthly magazine. Regular specialized features: corporate financing and reporting. An award winning publication in which business executives write articles for senior financial executives in major corporations. Covers cash management, pension fund management, international finance, information technology, new financial instruments, developments at the SEC & FASB, risk management, investment strategy, and more.

AUDIENCE: Professional   RISK LEVEL: Conservative, Moderate, Aggressive
TOPICS: All

Financial Freedom Report

Mark O. Haroldsen, Inc.
2450 E. Fort Union Blvd.
Salt Lake City, UT 84121

PH: (801) 943-1280
Cost: $29.95/quarter
Date of first publication: 1976
Frequency: Quarterly

Quarterly magazine. The magazine for high profit investors. Designed for the highly motivated individual who is seeking to establish his own financial freedom. The main emphasis is real estate and income property, but other areas are also examined. Includes audio report.

AUDIENCE: Beginning, Individual   RISK LEVEL: Conservative, Moderate,
TOPICS: Bonds, Mutual Funds, Stocks   Aggressive

Financial Planning

Securities Data Company, Inc.
40 West 57th Street
8th Floor
New York, NY 10019

PH: (212) 765-5311
FAX: (212) 765-6123
Cost: $79.00
Frequency: Monthly
Date of first issue: 1972

Monthly magazine. Covers stocks, mutual funds, and assorted investments. "A business magazine for professionals in the financial services industry - financial planners, bankers, insurance agents, stock brokers, lawyers, accountants, securities broker/dealers."

AUDIENCE: Professional   RISK LEVEL: Conservative, Moderate, Aggressive
TOPICS: Bonds, Mutual Funds, Stocks, Asset Allocation, Investment Planning

Financial Planning Reporter

Ernst & Young
Box 3337
Washington, DC 20033-0337

PH: (202) 327-9756
Cost: Free to Clients
Frequency: Monthly
Fundamental Analysis
Date of first issue: 1975

Explores current financial planning and investment strategies.

AUDIENCE: Individual, Professional   RISK LEVEL: Conservative, Moderate, Aggressive
TOPICS: Bonds, Mutual Funds, Stocks, Asset Allocation, Investment Planning

Financial World

Financial World Partners
1328 Broadway
New York, NY 10001

PH: (212) 594-5030
(800) 829-5916
Cost: $36.00 annually

Biweekly magazine. Regular features include company reviews, market update, stock choices, and mutual fund review. Departments: Editor Page, Market Watch, Company Watch, Technology Watch, Systems User, Institution Watch, Financial Planner, Mutual Fund Watch. Columns: Economic Currents, Special Situations, and Speaking Out.

AUDIENCE: Beginning, Individual, Professional   RISK LEVEL: Moderate, Aggressive
TOPICS: Bonds, Mutual Funds, Stocks

Forbes, Inc.

Forbes, Inc.
60 Fifth Avenue
New York, NY 10011

PH: (800) 888-9896 subscriptions
(212) 620-2200
Cost: $52.00 annually
Date of first issue: 1917

Bi-monthly magazine. Regular features: company reviews, international news, and government news. Outstanding feature issues: Highest Paid CEOs, Annual Forbes 400 (richest Americans), Special Report on International Business, Earnings Forecast for Forbes 500, Annual Mutual Fund Survey, Annual Report on American Industry, Annual Directory Issue.

AUDIENCE: Beginning, Individual, Professional   RISK LEVEL: Conservative,
TOPICS: All   Moderate, Aggressive

Fortune

The Time, Inc. Magazine Co.
Time & Life Building
Rockefeller Center
New York, NY 10020-1393

PH: (212) 522-1212
(800) 621-8000 subscriptions
Cost: $57.00 one year (26 issues)
Date of first issue: Feb. 1930

Bimonthly magazine. Regular features: company reviews, industry spotlights, market updates, and current news. Outstanding feature issues: Fortune 500 - (April), The Global 500 - (July), Investor's Guide - (Fall), Service 500 (May). Business magazine covering world news, investments business and company reviews.

AUDIENCE: Beginning, Individual, Professional   RISK LEVEL: Conservative,
TOPICS: All   Moderate, Aggressive

Frank Taucher's Supertrader's Almanac

Market Movements, Inc.
5212 East 69th Place
Tulsa, OK 74136-3407

PH: (800) 878-7442
(918) 493-2897
FAX: (918) 493-3892
Cost: $94.00 annually
Published since 1985
Technical Analysis

"The Indispensable Information Source for All Market Traders-From Novice to Seasoned!" Some topics include: The Best 1000 Seasonal Trades of the Last Five Years; Trade of the Year Selection; Over 100 Major Turning Point Dates; Pesavento Index; Divergence of the Year & Slammers, Launchings & Exchange Information.

AUDIENCE: Individual, Professional   RISK LEVEL: Aggressive
TOPICS: Futures/Commodities

French Company Handbook 1993

The Reference Press, Inc.
6448 Highway 290 E.
Suite E-104
Austin, TX 78723

PH: (512) 454-7778
FAX: (512) 454-9401
Cost: $49.95
Date of first issue: 1994
ISBN : 1-878753-34-7
Fundamental Analysis

A reference book profiling major French companies. Includes operations and company history overview, address and phone number, number of employees, names and titles of top management, dates by product line and geographic area, international activities, exports, and much more. Also provides a wealth of information on the French economy.

AUDIENCE: Individual, Professional   RISK LEVEL: Moderate, Aggressive
TOPICS: Bonds, Stocks, General Reference

Futures

Merrill J. Oster/Oster Publications
219 Parkade, P.O. Box 6
Cedar Falls, IA 50603

PH: (800) 635-3931 circulation
(800) 221-4352 ext 645
FAX: (319) 277-7982
Cost: $39.00 annually
Date of first issue: 1981
Changed from Commodities Magazine

Monthly magazine. Regular features: market update. Explores "what, when, & where" of market developments and explains exactly how they will influence future market opportunities. In depth, on-target market news and analysis, to help readers make more informed and profitable trading decisions. Joseph M. Bernado (president).

AUDIENCE: Individual, Professional   RISK LEVEL: Aggressive
TOPICS: Options, Futures/Commodities

Futures Chart Services

Knight-Ridder Financial Information
  Service
75 Wall St., 22nd Floor
New York, NY 10005-2890

PH: (800) 621-5271
Frequency: Weekly
Date of first issue: 1954
Cost: $455.00/yr
Editor: Gerald Becker

Covers 70-80 futures markets and provides high/low/close and weekly range charts.

AUDIENCE: Individual, Professional   RISK LEVEL: Aggressive
TOPICS: Futures/Commodities

Global Finance

Global Information, Inc.
McGraw-Hill
11 W. 19th St., 2nd Floor
New York, NY 10011

PH: (212) 512-2000
FAX: (212) 243-3241
Cost: $10.00/copy; $120.00/yr
Frequency: Monthly
Date of first issue: 1987
Fundamental Analysis

Monthly magazine. An international finance magazine for institutional investors. Covers investing on a large scale. Chapters include: equities, derivatives, mergers and acquisitions, real estate, currencies and more.

AUDIENCE: Professional   RISK LEVEL: Conservative, Moderate, Aggressive
TOPICS: All

Good Money's Social Funds Guide

Ritchie P. Lowry
Good Money Publications
P.O. Box 363
Worcester, VT 05682

PH: (800) 535-3551
(802) 223-3911
FAX: (802) 223-8949
Published annually since 1986
Cost: $29.95

A guide to social and environmental mutual funds. The guide includes descriptions and analyses of the social screens, investor costs and financial performance of socially-screened equity, bond, and money market mutual funds.

AUDIENCE: Beginning, Individual   RISK LEVEL: Moderate, Aggressive
TOPICS: Mutual Funds

Handbook of Dividend Achievers

Moody's Financial Information
  Services
99 Church Street
New York, NY 10007

PH: (212) 553-0435
FAX: (212) 553-4700
Cost: $19.95
Published: Annually

A guide to American companies that have increased their dividends for the past 10 consecutive years. Information includes company overviews, recent developments, prospects, performance statistics, stock movement charts, institutional holdings, price performance statistics, business line analysis, background and financial health indicators.

AUDIENCE: Beginning, Individual, Professional   RISK LEVEL: Moderate, Aggressive
TOPICS: Stocks

Individual Investor's Guide to Computerized Investing, The

American Association of Individual
  Investors
625 N. Michigan Ave.
Chicago, IL 60611-3110

Frequency: Annually
Cost: $24.95 ($19 for AAII members)
Free to all Computerized Investing
  subscribers
Date of first issue: 1994

"The Guide helps steer computer users through the bewildering array of investment hardware, software and databases." It includes in-depth descriptions of our 150 database services and over 500 software programs, analysis of new PC hardware, and an introduction to using computers for investment analysis.

AUDIENCE: Beginning, Individual   RISK LEVEL: Conservative, Moderate,
TOPICS: All   Aggressive

Individual Investor's Guide to No-Load Mutual Funds

AAII
625 N. Michigan Ave.
Chicago, IL 60611

PH: (312) 280-0170
Frequency: Annual
Cost: $24.95

"Provides thorough and up-to-date information on over 600 no-load and very low load mutual funds, including 5 years of returns, NAV's distributions and per share data, fund returns and rankings by investment objective, 3 yr and 5 yr average annual returns, total risk and investment objective risk rankings and performance during bull and bear markets."

AUDIENCE: Beginning, Individual   RISK LEVEL: Moderate, Aggressive
TOPICS: Mutual Funds

Individual Investor-Investing for Maximum Returns

Individual Investor Group, Inc.
38 East 29th St.
4th Floor
New York, NY 10016

PH: (212) 689-2777
FAX: (212) 689-6663
Frequency: Monthly
Cost: $22.95

Each issue offers indepth company profiles. Another section is titled "Focus on Funds" and gives news, performance data, and more on mutual funds. Other features include: Wall Street Wrap-up, investing tools, International financial planning, the Navigator and Insider's Edge and Bulls and Bears.

AUDIENCE: Individual   RISK LEVEL: Moderate, Aggressive
TOPICS: Mutual Funds, Stocks

Institutional Investor

Institutional Investor
488 Madison Avenue
New York, NY 10022-5751

PH: (212) 303-3233
(800) 437-9997
Cost: $375.00 per year
Frequency: Monthly
Date of first issue: 1976
Fundamental Analysis

Focuses on international banking, finance and investing by corporations, governments, and other borrowers.

AUDIENCE: Professional	RISK LEVEL: Conservative, Moderate, Aggressive
TOPICS: All	

Insurance Safety Directory

Weiss Research, Inc.
2200 N. Fla. Mango Rd.
W. Palm Beach, FL 33409

PH: (800) 289-9222
Frequency: 4 issues per year
Cost: $189.00 per issue or $376.00
annually

Contains Weiss Safety Ratings and supporting data on over 1,700 life, health and annuity issuers. Also has detailed explanations of our rating model, component indexes, ratios and what our ratios mean. Multiple listings make it easy to find the strength of your company, the strongest (and weakest) companies in the U.S. as well as the Weiss-recommended companies licensed to do business in your state.

AUDIENCE: Beginning, Individual, Professional	RISK LEVEL: Conservative, Moderate
TOPICS: Investment Planning, General Reference	

Investment Advisor's Guide

Investment Company Institute
1600 M Street, N.W
Suite 600
Washington, D.C. 20036

PH: (202) 293-7700
Cost: $500.00 initial subscription
$200.00 renewals annually
Semi-annual periodical

Covers regulations. A two-volume reference publication containing information relating to regulation of investment advisors by the SEC, under ERISA, and in all 50 states.

AUDIENCE: Professional	RISK LEVEL: Conservative, Moderate, Aggressive
TOPICS: All	

Investment Dealers' Digest

Investment Dealers' Digest, Inc.
2 World Trade Center
18th Floor
New York, NY 10048

PH: (212) 227-1200
Cost: $495.00 annually
Date of first issue: 1935
Weekly magazine

Company reviews, stock choices, bond analysis. Stories about firms and exchanges, and market updates. The Week on Wall Street; Firms and Exchanges; Street Names; The Week in Finance; Corporate Finance; For Reference; Issues in Registration, Securities Registered Last Week; Weekly Review of Offerings; Corporate Monthly Roundup; Municipal Market Data; Corporate Market Data; Calendar of Offerings.

AUDIENCE: Professional	RISK LEVEL: Conservative, Moderate, Aggressive
TOPICS: All	

Investor's Business Daily

Investor's Daily, Inc.
P.O. Box 66370
Los Angeles, CA 90066

PH: (213) 207-1832
(800) 443-3113 subscriptions
East Coast: (800) 831-2525; West
Coast: (800) 831-2525; Midwest: (800)
992-2126; California: (800) 621-7863;
Illinois: (312) 229-0402; FAX: (213)
473-7551; Cost: $169.00 annually.

Regular features: company reviews, market update, stock choices, mutual fund review, bond analysis, and money manager interviews. Date of first issue: April 1984.

AUDIENCE: Beginning, Individual, Professional   RISK LEVEL: Conservative, Moderate, Aggressive
TOPICS: All

Journal of Futures Markets

John Wiley & Sons
605 Third Avenue
New York, NY 10158-0012

PH: (212) 850-6000
FAX: 850-6088
Cost: $459.00 annually
8 issues/yr.

Contemporary articles on the futures markets including practical information, theory, corporate hedging, strategy, tax implications, trading analysis, and commodity portfolio optimization.

AUDIENCE: Individual, Professional   RISK LEVEL: Aggressive
TOPICS: Options, Futures/Commodities

Journal of Portfolio Management, The

Institutional Investor
488 Madison Avenue
New York, NY 10022

PH: (212) 303-3300
(800) 437-9997
Cost: $225.00 per year
Frequency: quarterly
Date of first issue: 1974

Quarterly magazine. An analytical publication focusing on portfolio management and investment systems.

AUDIENCE: Individual, Professional   RISK LEVEL: Moderate, Aggressive
TOPICS: Bonds, Mutual Funds, Stocks, Options, Futures/Commodities

Kiplinger's Personal Finance

The Kiplinger Washington Editors
1729 H Street, NW
Washington, DC 20006

PH: (800) 544-0155
Published Monthly
Annual Subscription $18.00
Date of first issue: 1946

Features regular mutual fund, stock and investment planning articles. Expert recommendations, retirement planning, taxes and real estate.

AUDIENCE: Beginning, Individual   RISK LEVEL: Conservative, Moderate, Aggressive
TOPICS: Bonds, Mutual Funds, Stocks, Investment Planning

Market Chronicle, The

William B. Dana Co.
213 Silver Beach Avenue
Daytona Beach, FL 32118

PH: (800) 962-3262
Cost: $120.00 annually
Date of first issue: 1960

Weekly newspaper. Features company reviews. A 24 page newspaper which covers company reviews, i.e., general press releases. Also discusses new products on the market.

AUDIENCE: Individual, Professional
TOPICS: Bonds, Stocks
RISK LEVEL: Moderate, Aggressive

Money

Time & Life
Rockefeller Center
New York, NY 10020

PH: (800) 633-9970 subscriptions
(212) 522-1212
Cost: $35.96 annually
Date of first issue: October 1972

Monthly magazine, 2 issues in the fall, Outstanding feature issues: Special year end issue (deals with something different each year) November Offers solid investment advice on a wide variety of investments. Gives performance data and helpful how-to's for personal investing.

AUDIENCE: Beginning, Individual   RISK LEVEL: Conservative, Moderate, Aggressive
TOPICS: Bonds, Mutual Funds, Stocks, Asset Allocation, Investment Planning

Money Manager Previews

Wall Street Transcript
Richard Holman
100 Wall Street
New York, NY 10005

PH: (212) 747-9500
FAX: (212) 668-9842
Cost: $2,600.00
Frequency: Weekly
Date of first issue: 1987

Weekly magazine. Covers money manager interviews. Features interviews and discussions with leading money managers and portfolio strategists throughout the world.

AUDIENCE: Individual, Professional   RISK LEVEL: Conservative, Moderate, Aggressive
TOPICS: Bonds, Mutual Funds, Stocks, Options

Moody's Bond Record

Moody's Investor Service
99 Church Street
New York, NY 10007

PH: (800) 342-5647 ext 0435
(212) 553-0435
FAX: (212) 553-4700
Cost: $249.00 annually
Date of first issue: 1969

The most comprehensive and authoritative source of statistical data on 56,000 corporate, convertible, government, municipal, environmental control revenue, and international bonds, plus preferred stocks and commercial paper.

AUDIENCE: Individual, Professional
TOPICS: Bonds
RISK LEVEL: Conservative, Moderate

Moody's Dividend Record

Moody's Financial Information
Services
99 Church Street
New York, NY 10007

PH: (212) 553-0435
FAX: (212) 553-4700
Cost: $595.00 annually
Fundamental Analysis

Quarterly periodical. Outstanding Feature Issues: Tax Status Supplements (Jan-Feb-March). Annual Dividend Record - compilation of full year's dividend information. Detailed reports of current dividend data covering over 17,000 stocks and mutual funds.

AUDIENCE: Individual, Professional   RISK LEVEL: Moderate, Aggressive
TOPICS: Mutual Funds, Stocks

Moody's Industry Review

Moody's Industry Review
99 Church Street
New York, NY 10007

PH: (800) 342-5647
(212) 553-0300
FAX: (212) 553-4700
Cost: $450.00 annually

Biweekly periodical. Regularly features company reviews. Comparative statistics and rankings of 4,000 leading corporations in 145 industry groups. Every two weeks receive approximately 10 industry reviews. Each is a profile on an industry including company's trading symbol and exchange, 52 week stock price range, earnings per share, book value, stockholder's equity, long-term debt, and much more.

AUDIENCE: Individual, Professional   RISK LEVEL: Moderate, Aggressive
TOPICS: Bonds, Stocks

Mutual Fund Encyclopedia, The

Gerald W. Perritt
Dearborn Financial Publishing, Inc.
520 N. Dearborn Street
Chicago, IL 60610

PH: (312) 836-4400 ext. 320
(800) 621-9621 ext. 320
Published 1994 (revised annually)
Cost: $35.95

Profiles 1,100 mutual funds detailing objectives and strategies, financial statistics, current yields, portfolio turnover rate, year by year and 5 year average returns and more.

AUDIENCE: Beginning, Individual   RISK LEVEL: Moderate, Aggressive
TOPICS: Mutual Funds

Mutual Fund Fact Book

Investment Company Institute
1600 M Street, N.W
Suite 600
Washington, D.C. 20036-3265

PH: (202) 293-7700
Cost: $15.00 annually
Date of first issue: 1961
Fundamental Analysis

Editor: Arlene Zuckerberg. Annual periodical. Covers mutual funds. An annual reference guide which includes annually-updated facts, figures, and statistics on the U.S. mutual funds industry, including trends in sales, assets, exchanges, and performance. It also outlines the history and growth of the fund industry and its policies, operations, regulation, services, and shareholders.

AUDIENCE: Beginning, Individual   RISK LEVEL: Moderate, Aggressive
TOPICS: Mutual Funds

Nations Business

Nations Business
1615 H St., N.W.
Washington, D.C. 20062

PH: (202) 463-5650
Frequency: Monthly
Date of first issue: 1912
Cost: $22.00/yr
Fundamental Analysis

Helps owners and/or managers of smaller to medium sized enterprises do a better job of running their business. Provides guidance and advice on effective business management. Business Success Stories, Personal Advice on Health, Investing, Tax Matters, and Information on Washington Developments Affecting Business.

AUDIENCE: Beginning, Individual, Professional　　RISK LEVEL: Conservative,
TOPICS: All　　　　　　　　　　　　　　　　　　　Moderate, Aggressive

Nelson's Directory of Investment Managers

Nelson Publications
One Gateway Plaza
Port Chester, NY 10573

PH: (800) 333-6357
FAX: (914) 937-0727
Cost: $435.00/yr
Published annually
Date of first issue: 1988
Fundamental Analysis

Provides the following information on 2,000 money management firms: firm overview, key investment executives, equity and bond investment approach, decision making process, fees, assets managed, client categories, asset allocation investments by country and performance statistics.

AUDIENCE: Individual, Professional　　RISK LEVEL: Conservative, Moderate, Aggressive
TOPICS: Stocks, Bonds, Asset Allocation, Investment Planning

New York Times, The

The New York Times
229 W. 43rd Street
New York, NY 10036

PH: (800) 631-2500
Cost: $390.00 annually
Date of first publication: 1851

Daily newspaper. Regular features: economic comments, CD and mortgage rate listings, stock market comments and company reviews.

AUDIENCE: Beginning, Individual, Professional　　RISK LEVEL: Conservative, Moderate,
TOPICS: All　　　　　　　　　　　　　　　　　　　　Aggressive

Oil and Gas Investor

Hart Publications, Inc.
1900 Grant Street
Suite 400
P.O. Box 1917
Denver, CO 80201

PH: (303) 832-1917
FAX: (303) 837-8585
Cost: $10.00/copy; $195.00 annually
Date of first publication: 1981
ISSN: 0744-5881

Publisher: Richard Eichler, Editor: Leslie Haines. Monthly full color magazine. Regular specialized features: company profiles, stock choices, oil and gas investments, and interviews. The magazine identifies the trends and where the money flows in the oil and gas industry. Investor covers all the major exploration areas, from Oklahoma, to the Gulf of Mexico, to emerging international plays.

AUDIENCE: Individual, Professional　　RISK LEVEL: Moderate, Aggressive
TOPICS: Stocks, Futures/Commodities

Oil Daily, The

The Oil Daily Co.
1401 New York Avenue, N.W.
Washington, DC 20005

PH: (202) 662-0700
(800) 621-0050
FAX: (202) 783-5918
Cost: $897.00/yr
Frequency: Monday - Friday
Date of first publication: 1951

Covers the energy industry. Includes tables with the Nationwide Rack Price Survey by company, Global Spot Market Price Review and Spot Cash Markets. Also includes world news items relevant to the energy industry.

AUDIENCE: Individual, Professional   RISK LEVEL: Moderate, Aggressive
TOPICS: Stocks, Options, Futures/Commodities

Outlook, The

Standard & Poor's
25 Broadway
New York, NY 10004

PH: (800) 777-4858
(212) 208-8768
Cost: $280 annually

Weekly periodical. Regular features: stock choice and market update. Analyzes and projects business and stock market trends. Brief data on individual securities with buy recommendations. Also includes current S&P market indexes.

AUDIENCE: Individual, Professional   RISK LEVEL: Moderate, Aggressive
TOPICS: Stocks

Pension World

Pension World
6151 Powers Ferry Rd., NW
Atlanta, GA 30330

PH: (404) 955-2500
Cost: $65.00 annually
Date of first issue: 1964

Monthly magazine. This international magazine is directed towards pension Personal Investor fund investors and plan sponsors. Regular features include: coverage of the stock market, employee benefits and more. Comments: 30,000 in circulation.

AUDIENCE: Professional   RISK LEVEL: Conservative, Moderate, Aggressive
TOPICS: All

Pensions & Investments

Crain Communications, Inc.
740 Rush Street
Chicago, IL 60611-2590

PH: (312) 649-5200
(800) 678-9595
FAX: (313) 446-0961
Cost: $135.00 annually
Date of first issue: 1961

Biweekly newspaper. Regular specialized issues include company reviews, stock articles, bond articles, pension funds, real estate, money manager interviews, and stock and bond indexes. The newspaper of corporate and institutional investors. Departments include: Frontlines, P&I Indexes, Valuation Index, Commentary, From the Editor, Letter to the Editor, People, Portfolio Management, Money Movers, Classifieds.

AUDIENCE: Professional   RISK LEVEL: Conservative, Moderate, Aggressive
TOPICS: All

Perspective on Mutual Fund Activity

Investment Company Institute
1600 M Street, N.W.
Suite 600
Washington, D.C. 20036

PH: (202) 293-7700
Cost: $30.00 annually
Date of first issue: 1983

Technical analysis. Covers mutual funds and uses graphs. An annual analysis by the Institute's research department of recent economic trends and their impact on the mutual fund industry. Includes numerous statistical groups.

AUDIENCE: Individual, Professional   RISK LEVEL: Moderate, Aggressive
TOPICS: Mutual Funds

Quarterly Journal of Economics

Quarterly Journal of Economics
Littauer Center Harvard University
Cambridge, MA 20138

PH: (617) 495-2142
Frequency: Quarterly
Institutions $85/yr
Cost: Individual $30/yr
Date of first issue: 1886

Professional economics journal stressing in particular economic theory; banking and finance, money, international trade; industrial fluctuations; economic development, agricultural economics; labor problems.

AUDIENCE: Individual, Professional   RISK LEVEL: Conservative, Moderate, Aggressive
TOPICS: All

Research-Ideas for Today's Investors

Research-Ideas for Today's
Investors
2201 Third St.
San Francisco, CA 94107

PH: (415) 621-0220
Frequency: Monthly
Cost: $35.00/yr
Date of first issue: 1978
Fundamental Analysis

Readers are stock brokers/branch managers.

AUDIENCE: Professional   RISK LEVEL: Conservative, Moderate, Aggressive
TOPICS: All

S.A. Advisory P.R.

S.A. Advisory P.R.
2274 Arbor Lane, #3
Salt Lake City, UT 84117

PH: (801) 272-4761
Cost: $100.00/yr
Published 8-12 times/yr
Date of first issue: 1983
Fundamental Analysis

Specific recommendations and analysis on one stock per issue. Gives extensive financial and corporate data and includes an in depth interview with a principal of the company. Also provides a broker contact for those interested in investing.

AUDIENCE: Individual   RISK LEVEL: Moderate, Aggressive
TOPICS: Stocks

Smart Money

Hearst Publications
250 West 55th St.
New York, NY 10019

PH: (800) 444-4204
Published Monthly
Annual Subscription $24.00
Date of first publication: 1992

Personal finance magazine. Stocks, bonds, mutual funds. Family and personal investment planning.

AUDIENCE: Beginning, Individual   **RISK LEVEL:** Conservative, Moderate, Aggressive

TOPICS: Bonds, Mutual Funds, Stocks, Investment Planning

Spectrum Publications

CDA Technologies
1355 Piccard
Rockville, MD 20850

PH: (301) 975-9600
FAX: (301) 590-1350
Cost: from $250.00

Periodicals: quarterly and monthly depending on publication. Covers stocks and convertibles. Holdings and changes in holdings of common stocks and convertibles as reported to the SEC. Publications include: Investment Company Stock Holdings Survey, 13(F) Institutional Portfolios, 5% Ownership Based on 13D, 13G, & I4D-l Filings, Insider Ownership Based on Forms 3&4, 13(F) Holdings Survey of Convertible Bonds.

AUDIENCE: Individual, Professional   **RISK LEVEL:** Moderate, Aggressive
TOPICS: Bonds, Stocks

Standard & Poor's Credit Week

Standard & Poor's
25 Broadway
New York, NY 10004

PH: (800) 777-4858
(212) 208-8768
Cost: $1,695.00 annually

Focuses on trends and outlooks for fixed income securities including corporate and government bonds and money market instruments. Offers the latest info on S&P's new and changed ratings for corporate, municipal and structured issuers.

AUDIENCE: Professional   **RISK LEVEL:** Conservative, Moderate
TOPICS: Bonds

Standard & Poor's Emerging and Special Situations

Standard & Poor's
25 Broadway
New York, NY 10004

PH: (800) 777-4858
(212) 208-8000
Cost: $195.00 annually
Date of first issue: 1982
Frequency: Monthly

Monthly periodical. Regular features are stock choices and new issues. Points out lesser known stocks which S&P's analysts deem to be overlooked and undervalued. Alerts investors to the growth situations that have appreciation potential. Also provides a regarded analysis of new issues before they go public.

AUDIENCE: Individual, Professional   **RISK LEVEL:** Moderate, Aggressive
TOPICS: Stocks

Statistical Reports - Unit Investment Trusts

Investment Company Institute
1600 M Street, N.W.
Suite 600
Washington, D.C. 20036

PH: (202) 293-7700
Cost: $50.00 annually
Date of first issue: 1985

Technical analysis. Covers investment trusts. Monthly report that includes value and number of deposits of new trusts by type, maturity, and insurance feature.

AUDIENCE: Individual, Professional   RISK LEVEL: Conservative, Moderate, Aggressive
TOPICS: Bonds, Mutual Funds, Stocks, General Reference

Stock Guide

Standard & Poor's
25 Broadway
New York, NY 10004

PH: (212) 208-8786
Cost: $112.00 annually

Monthly periodical. Stock investment data and mutual fund review. Unique 260 page guide to investment data on over 5,400 common and preferred stocks, listed and OTC, providing rapid reviews of all issues with 48 items of data on each. Data include: S&P earnings and dividend rankings, S&P earnings estimates, monthly high/low prices and volume, stock symbol, historical price ranges, summaries of financial positions.

AUDIENCE: Beginning, Individual, Professional   RISK LEVEL: Moderate, Aggressive
TOPICS: Mutual Funds, Stocks

Stocks, Bonds, Bills and Inflation Yearbook

Ibbotson & Associates, Inc.
225 N. Michigan Avenue
Suite 700
Chicago, IL 60601

PH: (312) 616-1620
(800) 758-3557
Cost: $90.00 annually

Shows the growth of a dollar invested in common stocks, small stocks, government bonds, treasury bills, and inflation from 1926, to the most recent year-end. Key historical events are highlighted. Full color, high resolution posters, prints, slides, or transparencies. Other charts available: Stocks, Bonds, Bills, and Inflation, with Real Estate and Gold; Mutual Fund Styles of Investing; Wealth of the World and of the U.S.

AUDIENCE: Beginning, Individual, Professional   RISK LEVEL: Conservative, Moderate,
TOPICS: Bonds, Mutual Funds, Stocks   Aggressive

Taking Stock

Tracy Staton - Editor
Dallas Business Journal
4131 N. Central Expressway
Suite 310
Dallas, TX 75204-9699

PH: (214) 520-1010
Cost: $9.95 annually
Date of first issue: 1989

Annual periodical. Regular features are company reviews. Information about every public company in the DFW Metroplex area that has revenue of at least $10 million. Ranked by revenue (includes earnings, dividend information, number of employees, exchange and symbol, business description and chief executive) also listed alphabetically.

AUDIENCE: Beginning, Individual , Professional   RISK LEVEL: Moderate, Aggressive
TOPICS: Stocks

Technical Analysis of Currencies (Currencies Management)

International Business
Communications
290 Eliot St., Box 91004
Ashland, MA 01721-9104

PH: (508) 881-2800
FAX: (508) 881-0982
Cost: $114/yr
Frequency: Weekly
Date of first issue: 1989
Technical Analysis

Forecasting tool derived from observations of traders and analysts of price and rate trends. Contact: Jonathan Bloch, Publisher.

AUDIENCE: Individual, Professional   RISK LEVEL: Aggressive
TOPICS: Options, Futures/Commodities

Technical Analysis of Stocks and Commodities

Technical Analysis, Inc.
4757 California Ave., S.W.
Seattle, WA 98116-4499

PH: (800) 832-4642
(206) 938-0570
Frequency: 13 times per year
Cost: $49.95 annually
Date of first issue: 1982

Monthly magazine. All about charts and computer applications that can help you profit in today's market. Includes cycles, charts, patterns, systems, real trades, statistics, psychology reviews, indicators and oscillators.

AUDIENCE: Professional   RISK LEVEL: Aggressive
TOPICS: Bonds, Mutual Funds, Stocks, Options, Futures/Commodities

Today's Investor (Penny Stock News)

Forte Communications
111 Broadway
Suite 1900
New York, NY 10006-1901

PH: (212) 406-4466
Cost: $55.00/yr.
Frequency: Monthly
Fundamental Analysis
Date of first issue: 1980

Financial magazine dealing with stocks that sell for $15 per share or less. Profiles of companies which they feel are up and coming issues.

AUDIENCE: Beginning, Individual, Professional   RISK LEVEL: Aggressive
TOPICS: Stocks

Toronto Stock Exchange Review

Toronto Stock Exchange
#2 First Canadian Place
Toronto, ON, Canada M5X 1J2

PH: (416) 647-4655
FAX: (416) 947-4585
Frequency: Monthly
Cost: $14.00/copy, $156.00/yr
   Canada, $219.00/yr foreign
Date of first issue: 1949

Monthly digest of all trading data from the Toronto Stock Exchange. Including stock table, warrants, earning, newly listed companies and statistical events. Cover story and executive profile of TSE listed companies.

AUDIENCE: Individual, Professional   RISK LEVEL: Moderate, Aggressive
TOPICS: Stocks

Trader's Magazine

Trader's Magazine, Inc.
40 West 57th Street
11th Floor
New York, NY 10019

PH: (212) 765-5311
Cost: $60.00
Frequency: Monthly
Date of first issue: 1987

A magazine about people in the investment industry and their personalities.

AUDIENCE: Individual, Professional   RISK LEVEL: Aggressive
TOPICS: Stocks, Options, Futures/Commodities

Trends in Mutual Fund Activity - Statistical Reports - Open End Investment Companies

Investment Company Institute
1600 M Street, N.W.
Suite 600
Washington, D.C. 20036

PH: (202) 326-5800
Cost: $120.00 annually
Date of first issue: 1981

Monthly periodical. Includes technical analysis. Covers mutual funds and uses graphs. Monthly news releases with accompanying tables describing mutual fund sales, redemptions, assets, cash positions, exchange activity, and portfolio transactions classified by investment objective, fund size, and method of distribution. Quarterly sales data for long-term funds is provided on a state-by-state basis. An annual report provides statistics on shareholder accounts, withdrawal accounts, and IRA and Keogh assets and accounts.

AUDIENCE: Individual, Professional   RISK LEVEL: Moderate, Aggressive
TOPICS: Mutual Funds

U.S. News and World Report

Mortimer B. Zuckerman
2400 N. Street N.W.
Washington, DC 20037-1196

PH: (212) 326-5300
(202) 955-2000
(800) 234-2450
Cost: $29.95 per year
Date of first issue: 1948

Weekly magazine. Outstanding Feature Issues: Investment Outlook (December). An independent news magazine serving 12 million readers by focusing on the events and forces that shape their lives. Organized into 6 distinct sections: Outlook, U.S. News, World Report, Business, News You Can Use, and Science and Society.

AUDIENCE: Beginning, Individual, Professional   RISK LEVEL: Conservative,
TOPICS: All   Moderate, Aggressive

USA Today

Gannett Company, Inc.
1000 Wilson Blvd.
Arlington, VA 22229

PH: (800) USA-0001
(703) 276-3400
FAX: (301) 622-6039
Cost: $107.00
Frequency: Daily (M-F)
Date of first issue: 1982

Daily periodical. A national newspaper. The second section is called "Money" and is devoted to financial news. Also gives NYSE, AMEX, NASDAQ, and mutual fund quotes.

AUDIENCE: Beginning, Individual, Professional RISK LEVEL: Conservative, Moderate,
TOPICS: All   Aggressive

VSE Review

Vancouver Stock Exchange
609 Granville St.,
P.O. Box 10333
Vancouver, BC, Canada V7Y1H1

PH: (604) 689-3334
FAX: (604) 688-6051
Cost: $117.00/yr USA & Canada
$145.00/yr overseas
Frequency: Monthly

Provides a complete and official summary on the month's transactions on equities and options; pertinent cumulative figures; recaps details of listing changes; underwritings, options, agency offerings; market commentaries and other topical articles. David R. Morton, Editor.

AUDIENCE: Individual, Professional   RISK LEVEL: Moderate, Aggressive
TOPICS: Stocks, Options

Wall Street Journal, The

Dow Jones & Company, Inc.
World Financial Center
200 Burnett Road
Chicopee, MA 01020

PH: (800) 568-7625
Cost: $149.00 annually
Date of first issue: 10/21/29

Daily newspaper. Regular features: company reviews, market update, stock choices, mutual fund review, bond analysis, and money manager interviews. A daily newspaper of national and international news. Composed of three sections: (1) front-page news; (2) business - economic news - "Marketplace"; (3) money rates, stock quotes, mutual funds, bonds - "Money & Investing."

AUDIENCE: Beginning, Individual, Professional RISK LEVEL: Conservative, Moderate,
TOPICS: All   Aggressive

Wall Street Technology

Gralla Publications
1515 Broadway
New York, NY 10036

PH: (800) 964-9494
(212) 488-9001
FAX: (212) 553-4700
Frequency: Monthly
Date of first issue: 1983

Company reviews. Covers computers, software, on-line services and other technology used in investing. Outstanding Feature Issues: Buying Guide - November or December. Gives readers the latest information on hardware and software developments that are crucial to a strong bottom line.

AUDIENCE: Individual, Professional   RISK LEVEL: Conservative, Moderate, Aggressive
TOPICS: All

Wall Street Transcript

Richard A. Holman
100 Wall Street
New York, NY 10005

PH: (212) 747-9500
FAX: (212) 668-9842
Cost: $1,890.00 annually
Date of first issue: 1964
Frequency: Weekly

Weekly newspaper. Regular features are company reviews and money manager reviews. Reproduces selected brokerage house reports on companies and individuals, discussions on a leading industry or topic by leading analysts, interviews with money managers and top CEOs. Options news, technical analysis.

AUDIENCE: Individual, Professional   RISK LEVEL: Conservative, Moderate,
TOPICS: All   Aggressive

Wiesenberger's Mutual Funds Panorama

Warren, Gorham, & Lamont, Inc.
1355 Piccard Drive
Rockville, MD 20850

PH: (800) 232-2285
Cost: $95.00/yr

Annual periodical. Includes fundamental analysis of mutual funds. A statistical review of pertinent data concerning virtually all mutual funds registered for sales in the United States. Information provided includes year of organization, primary objective, investment policy, statistical data, dividend data, fees and expenses, shareholder's services, information and complete list of addresses and phone numbers for funds.

AUDIENCE: Beginning, Individual	RISK LEVEL: Moderate, Aggressive
TOPICS: Mutual Funds	

Wisconsin Securities Bulletin

Wisconsin State Office of the
  Commissioner of Securities
111 West Wilson Street
Box 1768
Madison, WI 53701

PH: (608) 266-3583
Cost: $15.00/yr.
Frequency: Annually

Walter H. White, Jr., editor. "Contains information on new developments regarding securities-related matters, suggestions on securities, business operations and listings of various securities transactions in Wisconsin."

AUDIENCE: Professional	RISK LEVEL: Conservative, Moderate, Aggressive
TOPICS: All	

Worth Magazine

Capital Publishing Company, Inc.
575 Lexington Ave., 35th Floor
New York, NY 10022

PH: (800) 777-6023
Published Monthly
Annual Subscription: $15.00
Date of first issue: 1991

Focus on individual investors and investment planning with stocks and mutual funds. Regular features are by Peter Lynch and other Fidelity Mutual Fund affiliations.

AUDIENCE: Beginning, Individual	RISK LEVEL: Conservative, Moderate, Aggressive
TOPICS: Mutual Funds, Stocks, Investment Planning	

FINANCIAL TELEVISION PROGRAMS

Television programs that focus on investing and financial news provide an educational insight into the thought processes that drive markets. Broadcast interviews with top money managers offer a rare opportunity to listen in on predictions and beliefs sharpened by experience. In addition, because many of these programs present valuable investment information in an entertaining way, they make it easier to absorb and remember.

You would be hard pressed to find and review each of the available financial programs on your own. Knowing something about most of these programs that concentrate on investing helps you to choose the most appropriate ones.

The financial anchors who have become icons within the investment community include Louis Rukeyser ("Wall Street Week"), Lou Dobbs ("Moneyline"), and Paul Kangas ("Nightly Business Report"). The major anchors have a powerful advantage in their ability to consistently attract influential guests including CEOs, money managers, and successful analysts.

CNBC has developed a program format with "Your Portfolio" catering to individual investors with a concentration on top performing mutual funds.

While all news can be considered relevant to investing, this chapter does not attempt to list all news sources. However, almost all major national programs and networks focused on investment news are listed. Financial programs that center on the investment markets or the impact of news on investments are described. The network phone numbers and addresses are given for more specific program information and local times.

Adam Smith's Money World

Adam Smith's Money World
1329 Braddock Place
Alexandria, VA 22314

PH: (703) 739-5000
Broadcast Times: 8:30 pm
Broadcast Dates: Friday
Cable/Network: PBS

World economy and financial matters.

AUDIENCE: Beginning, Individual, Professional	RISK LEVEL: Conservative, Moderate, Aggressive
TOPICS: All	

Business Day

Business Day
One CNN Center
Atlanta, GA 30348

PH: (404) 827-1503
Broadcast Times: 7:30 am
Broadcast Dates: Monday - Friday
Anchor/Editor: Stuart Varney and
   Deborah Marchini
Cable/Network: CNN

Economy, market activity, international and domestic events relevant to the investment community. Spotlights companies in the news and has special guests addressing specific topics.

AUDIENCE: Beginning, Individual, Professional	RISK LEVEL: Conservative, Moderate, Aggressive
TOPICS: All	

Business Morning

Business Morning
One CNN Center
Atlanta, GA 30348

PH: (404) 827-1503
Broadcast Times: 6:30 am
Broadcast Dates: Monday - Friday
Anchor/Editor: Stuart Varney and
   Deborah Marchini
Cable/Network: CNN

International and domestic general business news.

AUDIENCE: Beginning, Individual, Professional	RISK LEVEL: Conservative, Moderate, Aggressive
TOPICS: All	

CNBC/FNN

Consumer News and Business
Channel/Financial News Network
2200 Fletcher Avenue
Ft. Lee, NJ 07024

PH: (201) 585-2622
(800) SMART-TV
Cable/Network: CNBC/FNN

Ongoing investment programming covering all investment subjects and news. Has constant market updates and non-stop ticker tape. Call 800-SMART-TV to order programming directory.

AUDIENCE: Beginning, Individual, Professional	RISK LEVEL: Conservative, Moderate, Aggressive
TOPICS: All	

Headline News

Headline News
One CNN Center
Atlanta, GA 30348

PH: (404) 827-1500
Broadcast Times: every 1/2 hour -
  15 minutes and 45 minutes after
  each hour
Broadcast Dates: Daily
Cable/Network: CNN

International news summary reports the latest business and financial news. Constant non-stop ticker.

AUDIENCE: Beginning, Individual, Professional   RISK LEVEL: Conservative, Moderate,
TOPICS: All   Aggressive

Market to Market

Market to Market
1329 Braddock Place
Alexandria, VA 22314

PH: (703) 739-5000
Broadcast Times: Check Local Listing
Broadcast Dates: Check Local Listing
Anchor/Editor: Mark Pearson
Cable/Network: PBS

Weekly journal of the farming industry. Gives general economic news and figures also. Discusses current and pending legislation and programs affecting the farming industry. Also addresses current R&D, and gives a market overview and forecast of the commodities and futures markets.

AUDIENCE: Beginning, Individual, Professional   RISK LEVEL: Conservative,
TOPICS: Options, Futures/Commodities   Moderate, Aggressive

McNeil/Lehrer Newshour

McNeil / Lehrer Newshour
1329 Braddock Place
Alexandria, VA 22314

PH: (703) 739-5000
Broadcast Times: Check local listings
Broadcast Dates: Check local listings
Anchor/Editor: Robert McNeil and
  Jim Lehrer
Cable/Network: PBS

General domestic and international news.

AUDIENCE: Beginning, Individual, Professional   RISK LEVEL: Conservative,
TOPICS: All   Moderate, Aggressive

Money Tonight

Consumer News and Business
  Channel/Financial News Network
2200 Fletcher Avenue
Ft. Lee, NJ 07024

PH: (201) 585-2622
(800) SMART-TV
Anchors/Editors: Sue Herera and
  Janice Lieberman
Broadcast Times: Weeknights 7:30
  p.m. EST
Cable/Network: CNBC/FNN

Personal finance issues, mutual funds, stocks, and special features on consumer rip offs. Call 800-SMART-TV to order programming directory.

AUDIENCE: Beginning, Individual, Professional   RISK LEVEL: Conservative,
TOPICS: All   Moderate, Aggressive

MoneyLine

MoneyLine
One CNN Center, Box 105366
Atlanta, GA 30348

PH: (404) 827-1503
Broadcast Times: 5:00 pm & 9:30 pm
Broadcast Dates: Monday - Friday
Anchor/Editor: Lou Dobbs with
  Myron Kandell as an analyst
Cable/Network: CNN

Economy, banking and savings and loan industries, insurance industry, personal finance. Data on major U.S. markets and stock closing prices. International and economic news. Comments: General financial news - both domestic and international.

AUDIENCE: Beginning, Individual, Professional   RISK LEVEL: Conservative, Moderate, Aggressive
TOPICS: All

MoneyWeek

MoneyWeek
One CNN Center
Atlanta, GA 30348

PH: (404) 827-1503
Broadcast Times: 3:30 am - Sunday
12:00 am - Sunday, 7:30 am -
  Saturday
Anchor/Editor: Lou Dobbs
Cable/Network: CNN

Recap of the week's economic activity, indicators, news and market activity and wrap-up.

AUDIENCE: Beginning, Individual, Professional   RISK LEVEL: Conservative, Moderate, Aggressive
TOPICS: All

Nightly Business Report

Nightly Business Report
1329 Braddock Place
Alexandria, VA 22314

PH: (703) 739-5000
Broadcast Times: Check Local Listing
Broadcast Dates: Check Local Listing
Anchor/Editor: Paul Kangas and
  Cassie Siefert
Cable/Network: PBS

Information on the economy, Wall Street, stock market commentary and data. All other major markets including currencies and precious metals and company spotlights in the news.

AUDIENCE: Beginning, Individual, Professional   RISK LEVEL: Conservative, Moderate, Aggressive
TOPICS: All

Wall Street Week

Wall Street Week
1329 Braddock Place
Alexandria, VA 22314

PH: (703) 739-5000
Broadcast Times: 6:30 pm - Friday
  9:30 am - Sunday
Anchor/Editor: Louis Rukeyser
Cable/Network: PBS

Begins with recap of week's economic news and events and market activity. Then panelists and special guests discuss the economy and the markets.

AUDIENCE: Beginning, Individual, Professional   RISK LEVEL: Conservative, Moderate, Aggressive
TOPICS: All

Your Money

Your Money
One CNN Center
Atlanta, GA 30348

PH: (404) 827-1503
Broadcast Times: 7:30 am - Sunday
  1:30 pm - Saturday
Anchor/Editor: Stuart Varney
Cable/Network: CNN

Concerns interest rates, mortgages, loans, education, market data and economic news. Helpful tips and information on all aspects of personal finances. Features question and answer segment for write-in viewers.

AUDIENCE: Beginning, Individual   RISK LEVEL: Conservative, Moderate, Aggressive
TOPICS: All

Your Portfolio

CNBC
2200 Fletcher Avenue
Ft. Lee, NJ 07024

PH:(800) 462-CNBC
(800) SMART-TV
(201) 346-2136
Broadcast Dates: Monday -Friday
Broadcast Times: 7:00 EST TO
  7:30 P.M.
ANCHOR/EDITOR: Bill Griffeth &
Jim Roders

Introduces the viewers to the people who are managing today's mutual fund portfolios and discusses their strategies and philosophies. Viewers have an opportunity to call in and ask questions. Provides a mutual fund ticker on 1,350 open end funds and 100 closed end funds.

AUDIENCE: Beginning, Individual   RISK LEVEL: Conservative, Moderate, Aggressive
TOPICS: Bonds, Mutual Funds, Stocks, Investment Planning

BOOKS AND TAPES ON INVESTING

The wide-ranging list of books and tapes in this chapter should fulfill almost any investment niche with current choices from the largest investment book publishers and audio/video companies. With such a vast selection available, this section has been limited to books and tapes that focus on investment information and strategy.

Each book or tape is listed alphabetically with a description, price, and the publisher's phone number. The target audience, risk level, and investment type are noted where possible.

Most bookstores are now carrying extensive investment book sections and will gladly order titles requested. Rather than simply focus on a single book, the best investors appear to be constantly updating their libraries.

Investors who open this chapter with a specific investment goal in mind will fare the best in building a great investment book and tape library. For example, beginning investors commonly ask generalized questions starting with, "Where do I go to learn about ...?" In order to zero in on the right source of information, they would be better off asking such goal-centered questions as, "Where can I learn more about investing in common stocks for average returns over 10%?"

New investors can quickly benefit by selecting classic investment books. Thousands of investors use William O'Neil's *How to Make Money in Stocks* as both a starting point and ongoing education in common stocks. Graham and Dodd's classic textbook *Security Analysis* is uniformly praised by the greatest sages of stock market investing. Meanwhile, as mutual funds have gained popularity, books such as *The Mutual Fund Encyclopedia* provide an instructional section as well as reference information.

For investors primarily concerned with getting the best fixed rate of interest, Fabozzi's *Fixed Income Handbook* is a comprehensive tool that is designed to educate the beginning investor and advance even the experienced bond portfolio manager.

For the more sophisticated trader, Jack Schwager's *Market Wizards* has become a classic followed by his *New Market Wizards*. Insights into futures, options, and stock trading are given by proven traders in rare interviews.

Note: AFP means Available from Publisher

100 Best Mutual Funds You Can Buy, The

Gordon K. Williamson
Bob Adams, Inc.
260 Center Street
Holbrook, MA 02343

PH: (617) 767-8100
ISBN: 1-55850-856-2
Published: 1990
Cost: $12.95

A guide to selecting the very best mutual funds.

AUDIENCE: Beginning   RISK LEVEL: Moderate, Aggressive
TOPICS: Mutual Funds

100 Best Stocks to Own in America, The

Gene Walden
Dearborn Financial Publishing, Inc.
520 N. Dearborn
Chicago, IL 60610

PH: (800) 621-9621 ext. 320
ISBN: 793107180
Published: 1993 (3rd edition)
Cost: $22.95

Did you know that the single best stock to own in America is Anheuser-Busch, or that 11 million cases of California Cooler were sold in 1987? Here's the Hall of Fame of companies whose stocks have been the best performers year-in and year-out.

AUDIENCE: Beginning, Individual   RISK LEVEL: Moderate, Aggressive
TOPICS: Stocks

100 Best Stocks You Can Own in the World, The

Gene Walden
Dearborn Financial Publishing, Inc.
520 N. Dearborn
Chicago, IL 60610-4354

PH: (312) 836-4400 ext. 320
(800) 621-9621 ext. 320
Published: 1991
Cost: $24.95

Addresses the subject of stock analysis. Rates 100 companies according to earnings growth, stock growth, dividend yield, dividend growth, consistency, and momentum.

AUDIENCE: Beginning, Individual   RISK LEVEL: Moderate, Aggressive
TOPICS: Stocks

100 Minds That Made the Market

Keneth L. Fisher
Business Classics
950 Purisima Road
Woodside, CA 94062

PH: (800) 865-1001
(415) 852-8879
ISBN: 0-931133-01-7
Published: 1993
Cost: $24.95

Fisher explores 100 of the most intriguing innovators of the American financial markets: giants like J.P. Morgan, Charles Dow, and John Maynard Keynes, as well as obscure but important, and often flamboyant financiers such as mining exchange founder E.J. "Lucky" Baldwin, and General George Dorot, "Father of Venture Capital." Each of the 100 cameo biographies teaches lessons in hard work, creativity and dedication and can be enjoyed as a collection or a single bite. Original photos.

AUDIENCE: Beginning, Individual, Professional RISK LEVEL: Moderate, Aggressive
TOPICS: Bonds, Stocks, Futures/Commodities

101 Investment Decision Tools, Barometers, Instruments and Keys (Where to Find Them and How They're Used)

International Publishing
625 N. Michigan, Suite 1920
Chicago, IL 60611

PH: (800) 488-4149 ext. 102
Cost: $19.95
Date of first issue: 1993

"Analyzes various investment vanes from stock indexes to measures of housing affordability to leading economic reports, providing fast and reliable explanations of all the everyday terms and tools investors need, each discussed in an easy-to-follow structured format."

AUDIENCE: Beginning, Individual   RISK LEVEL: Moderate, Aggressive
TOPICS: Stocks, Investment Planing, General Reference

24 Hour Trading - The Global Network of Futures and Options Markets

Barbara B. Diamond, Mark P.
  Kollar
John Wiley & Sons, Inc.
605 Third Avenue
New York, NY 10158-0012

PH: (800) 526-5368 (orders)
(212) 850-6418 (info)
FAX: (212) 850-6088
Published: February 1989
Cost: $29.95

Subjects addressed are futures and options, market strategies, technical analysis; uses charts. A dynamic overview of various futures markets, clearinghouse, and their regulations around the world.

AUDIENCE: Individual, Professional   RISK LEVEL: Aggressive
TOPICS: Options, Futures/Commodities

A-Z of Wall Street: 2,500 Terms for the Street Smart Investor, The

Sandra S. Hildreth
Dearborn Financial Publishing, Inc.
520 N. Dearborn
Chicago, IL 60610

(800) 621-9621 ext. 320
Published: 1988
Cost: $16.95

Definitions. Written for both the individual investor and the investment professional, this book contains over 2,500 clearly written definitions of common investment words and phrases. Readers will find concise explanation of correction, initial public offering and zero coupon bond, as well as many new words tied to current events on Wall Street. Figures and stock pages from The Wall Street Journal and Standard & Poor's give further explanation.

AUDIENCE: Beginning, Individual, Professional RISK LEVEL: Moderate, Aggressive
TOPICS: All

ABC's of Agricultural Options

Commodities Education Institute
219 Parade
Cedar Falls, IA 50613

PH: (800) 635-3936
(319) 277-6341
FAX: (319) 277-7982
Published: 1991 updated
Cost: $55.00
VIDEO

Subjects addressed: trading analysis, options trading. Learn how, when properly managed, options can serve as "price insurance" in your marketing plan. You'll cover terminology, puts and calls, evaluating an options move versus a minimum price contract, and specific ways to determine whether to use options, futures, or the cash market. Available from Publisher.

AUDIENCE: Professional   RISK LEVEL: Aggressive
TOPICS: Options, Futures/Commodities

ABC's of Price Risk Management

Commodities Education Institute
219 Parade
Cedar Falls, IA 50613

PH: (800) 635-3936
(319) 277-6341
FAX: (319) 277-7982
Published: 1990
Cost: $55.00
VIDEO

Learn how to use the marketing system to forward price commodities. Understand the terminology and basic principles behind hedging, futures trading, basis, mechanics of a brokerage account and controlling your pricing decisions.

AUDIENCE: Professional   RISK LEVEL: Aggressive
TOPICS: Options, Futures/Commodities

ABC's of Technical Analysis

Commodities Education Institute
219 Parade
Cedar Falls, IA 50613

PH: (800) 635-3936
(319) 277-6341
FAX: (319) 277-7982
Published: 1991 updated
Cost: $55.00
VIDEO

Subjects addressed are commodities trading, trading analysis, and technical analysis. Technical expert Wayne Purcell shows you how to use price charts and indicators in your trading. He'll help you understand trend lines, support/resistance, gaps, corrections, head and shoulders formations, reversals, RSI and other key tools.

AUDIENCE: Professional   RISK LEVEL: Aggressive
TOPICS: Options, Futures/Commodities

Access Nippon 1994 - How to Succeed in Japan

The Reference Press, Inc.
6448 Highway 290 E.
Suite E-104
Austin, TX 78723

PH: (512) 454-7778
FAX: (512) 454-9401
Cost: $34.95; published annually
Date of First Issue: 1988
Fundamental Analysis

Profiles of over 200 of the giants of Japanese industry. Each company profile includes an overview of operations, addresses of major offices, sales broken down by products and exports, product names, list of foreign partners, basic financial information, and much more.

AUDIENCE: Individual, Professional   RISK LEVEL: Moderate, Aggressive
TOPICS: Stocks, General Reference

Active Asset Allocation: State-of-the-Art Portfolio Policies, Strategies & Tactics

Robert D. Arnott & Frank J. Fabozzi
Probus Publishing Co.
1925 North Clybourn Avenue
Chicago, IL 60614

PH: (800) PROBUS-1
FAX: (312) 868-6250
ISBN: 1-55738-237-9
Published: 1992
Cost: $69.95

Comprehensive overview of the critical issues, theories and portfolio management practices that are successfully employed in today's domestic and global markets. The proven strategies and tactics presented here are the culmination of the expertise of eminent theoreticians and practitioners in the field. The nineteen authors focus on three major areas of asset allocation: policy asset mix and portfolio insurance, optimization and surplus management, tactical asset allocation.

AUDIENCE: Professional   RISK LEVEL: Conservative, Moderate, Aggressive
TOPICS: Bonds, Stocks, Options, Futures/Commodities, Asset Allocation

Active Total-Return Management of Fixed Income Portfolios

Ravi E. Dattatreya and Frank J.
Fabozzi
Probus Publishing Co.
1925 North Clybourn Avenue
Chicago, IL 60614

PH: (800) PROBUS-1
FAX: (312) 868-6250
ISBN: 1-55738-049-X
Published: 1989
Cost: $67.50

Presents guidelines that market participants can employ to enhance returns. Applicable to both active strategies and structured portfolio strategies. The first generation: duration analysis; the second generation: parametric analysis; the other side of the equation: horizon return; making the right assumptions: internal and external consistency; options and their parametric characteristic; analysis of callable bonds; analysis of mortgage-backed securities; using futures and options.

AUDIENCE: Professional   RISK LEVEL: Moderate, Aggressive
TOPICS: Bonds, Stocks, Options, Futures/Commodities, Asset Allocation

Adam Theory of Markets, The

Trend Research Ltd.
J. Welles Wilder, Jr.
P.O. Box 128
McLeansville, NC 27301

PH: (910) 698-0500
Published: 1986
Cost: $65.00

Subjects addressed: commodities trading, stock analysis, market analysis, technical analysis; uses charts. Presents a revolutionary concept about markets... about how markets really work and how they move relative to price and time. Available from Publisher.

AUDIENCE: Individual, Professional   RISK LEVEL: Moderate, Aggressive
TOPICS: Bonds, Stocks, Options, Futures/Commodities

Advanced Strategies in Financial Risk Management

Robert J. Schwartz and Clifford W.
 Smith, Jr.
New York Institute of
 Finance/Prentice Hall
113 Sylvan Aveenue
Route 9W
Englewood Cliffs, NJ 07632

PH: (800) 947-7700
Fax: (515) 284-2607
Published: 1993
Cost: $65.00

Reveals how Fortune 500 companies routinely use risk protection products to better manage asset liability and tap world-wide commercial markets. Discusses interest and exchange rates; systems and credit; tax, legal, and regulatory issues; and more.

AUDIENCE: Professional   RISK LEVEL: Conservative
TOPICS: Bonds, Options, Futures/Commodities

Affluent Investor, The

Stephen P. Rappaport
New York Institute of Finance
113 Sylvan Avenue
Route 9W
Englewood Cliffs, NJ 07632

PH: (800) 947-7700
Published: 1990
Cost: $24.95

Subjects addressed: investing theories, stock analysis, market analysis, bond analysis, trading analysis and investment strategies for all markets.

AUDIENCE: Individual, Professional   RISK LEVEL: Conservative, Moderate, Aggressive
TOPICS: Bonds, Stocks, Options

Analytical Methods for Successful Speculation

James E. Schildgen
Capital Futures Associates, Ltd.
P.O. Box 2618
Chicago, IL 60690

PH: (815) 248-4436
ISBN: 0-939397-00-5
Published: 1986
Cost: $49.95

Offers technical analysis. The complete book of trading systems, comprising all major technical and fundamental analytical methods applied to gold from 1975 to 1985. All methods are briefly yet clearly explained and objectively presented. Choose those that interest you most from over 50 systems. Illustrated with computer studies graphically portrayed.

AUDIENCE: Individual, Professional   RISK LEVEL: Aggressive
TOPICS: Stocks, Options, Futures/Commodities

Analyzing and Forecasting Futures Prices

Anthony F. Herbst
John Wiley & Sons, Inc.
605 Third Avenue
New York, NY 10158-0012

PH: (212) 850-6000
FAX: (212) 850-6088
Published: 1992
Technical and Fundamental Analysis
Cost: $55.00

"Gives a clear explanation of the latest methods for analyzing and predicting futures prices. In addition it explains how these practical techniques can be applied in implementing hedging or speculative strategies. Covers the latest advanced methods such as spectral, array and time series analysis."

AUDIENCE: Individual, Professional   RISK LEVEL: Aggressive
TOPICS: Futures/Commodities

Arms Index (TRIN), The

Richard W. Arms, Jr.
Irwin Professional Publishing
1333 Burr Ridge Parkway
Burr Ridge, IL 60521

PH: (800) 634-3966
(708) 789-5489
FAX: (708) 789-6933
ISBN: 1-55623-101-6
Published: 1989
Cost: $65.00

Covers investing theories and market analysis. An in-depth look at how volume - not time - governs stock price changes. Shows you how the Arms Index helps you make more profitable market decisions. Uses Arms' own system to forecast the price changes of individual issues as well as market indexes.

AUDIENCE: Individual, Professional   RISK LEVEL: Moderate, Aggressive
TOPICS: Stocks

Art of Contrary Thinking

Humphrey B. Neill
Caxton Printers, Ltd.
312 Main Street
Caldwell, ID 83605

PH: (800) 456-8791
(208) 459-7421
FAX: (208) 459-7450
Published: 1993, 5th ed.
Cost: $4.95

Fifth enlarged edition. The originator of the Theory of Contrary Opinion answers the questions: Contrary Opinion - What is it? What will it do for me? This is the workbook of Contrary Opinion for anyone seeking to benefit from the contrary approach in analyzing trends.

AUDIENCE: Individual   RISK LEVEL: Moderate, Aggressive
TOPICS: Bonds, Mutual Funds, Stocks, Options, Futures/Commodities

Art of Wise Investing, The

John Moody
Business Classics
950 Purisima Road
Woodside, CA 94062

PH: (800) 865-1001
(415) 852-8879
ISBN: 0-931133-07-6
Published: 1994 (reprint of 1904 edition)
Cost: Contact Publisher

The subject is stock analysis. Moody, founder of "Moody's Manual of Corporation Securities" and Moody Publishing Company, wrote this petite book of investment values, as the century dawned. He uses colorful, descriptive language to detail today's terms, making for enjoyable and educational reading. Moody's points still ring true, and reading him will help you focus on concepts that have helped investors make money for 90 years.

AUDIENCE: Individual, Professional   RISK LEVEL: Moderate, Aggressive
TOPICS: Bonds, Stocks

Asia Pacific Securities Handbook

The Reference Press, Inc.
6448 Highway 290 E
Suite E-104
Austin, TX 78723

PH: (512) 454-7778
FAX: (512) 454-9401
Cost: $99.95; published annually

Covers the stock markets in Australia, Bangladesh, China, Hong Kong, India, Indonesia, Japan, Malaysia, Nepal, New Zealand, Pakistan, the Philippines, Singapore, South Korea, Sri Lanka, Taiwan and Thailand. Profiles include stock exchange addresses and phone numbers, description of stock market practices, market overview, lists of the top stocks and names, addresses and phone numbers for stock brokerage firms. A.F.P.

AUDIENCE: Individual, Professional   RISK LEVEL: Moderate, Aggressive
TOPICS: Stocks, General Reference

Assessing Risk on Wall Street

Thomas A. Rorro
Liberty Publishing Company, Inc.
440 S. Federal Highway, Suite B-3
Deerfield Beach, FL 33441

PH: (305) 360-9000
ISBN: 0-89709-134-5
Published: 1984
Cost: $19.95

A novel look at investing from the perspective of both risk and profit potential. Starts with basic investment building blocks and progresses to the application of powerful statistical tools. Explains the techniques required to evaluate risk before the investment is made. Uses capital market line to illustrate performance.

AUDIENCE: Beginning, Individual   RISK LEVEL: Moderate, Aggressive
TOPICS: Mutual Funds, Stocks

Asset Allocation: Balancing Financial Risk

Roger C. Gibson
Irwin Professional Publishing
1333 Burr Ridge Parkway
Burr Ridge, IL 60521

PH: (800) 634-3966
(708) 789-5489
FAX: (708) 789-6933
ISBN: 1-55623-164-4
Published: 1990
Cost: $45.00

The first comprehensive, practical book dedicated to Business One-Irwin asset allocation from a nationally recognized authority. Explains how to involve clients in the decision making process. Essential reading for anyone who advises individuals or small institutional clients regarding their investment of money.

AUDIENCE: Individual, Professional   RISK LEVEL: Moderate, Aggressive
TOPICS: Bonds, Mutual Funds, Stocks, Asset Allocation

Barron's Finance and Investment Handbook

John Downes and Jordan Elliot
  Goodman
Barron's Publishing
250 Wireless Blvd.
Hauppauge, NY 11788

PH: (516) 434-3311
Published: 1986, 1990 (updated)
Cost: $26.95

The one indispensable desk reference for all your financial planning and personal investing needs. Dictionary of 2,500 financial and investing terms, name, address, and phone numbers for NYSE, AMEX, OTC stocks, and mutual funds, historical market and economic data, how to read financial news, annual reports, ticker tape and much, much, more. Over 1,200 pages. A.F.P.

AUDIENCE: Beginning, Individual, Professional RISK LEVEL: Conservative, Moderate,
                                                                Aggressive
TOPICS: All

Barron's Guide to Making Investment Decisions

Douglas Sease and John Prestbo
Prentice Hall
113 Sylvan Avenue
Route 9W
Englewood Cliffs, NJ 07632

PH: (800) 947-7700
FAX: (515) 284-2607
Published:1993
Cost: $13.95

Published in association with Barron's National Business and Financial Weekly, a publication of Dow Jones and company, this outstanding investment sourcebook provides sample profiles and illustrated examples that show readers how to assess their tolerance for risk as well as the costs of investing, and discuss asset allocation.

AUDIENCE: Individual   RISK LEVEL: Moderate
TOPICS: All

Basic Gan Techniques

Commodities Education Institute
219 Parade
Cedar Falls, IA 50613

PH: (800) 635-3936
(319) 277-6341
FAX: (319) 277-7982
Published: 1990
Cost: $55.00
VIDEO

Subjects addressed: investing theories, technical analysis. Glen Ring reviews the technical approach to markets and basic Gan tools. Part of a series of 5 tapes available for $233.00.

AUDIENCE: Professional   RISK LEVEL: Aggressive
TOPICS: Stocks, Options, Futures/Commodities

Basics of Investing, The

Benton E. Gup
John Wiley & Sons, Inc.
605 Third Avenue
New York, NY 10158-0012

PH: (212) 850-6418 orders
(212) 850-6233 info.
FAX: (212) 850-6088
ISBN: 0-471-82146-2
Published: 1992 (5th edition)
Cost: $44.95

Reviews securities, options, commodities, tax shelters, works of art, and more. Explains proven methods for analyzing investment opportunities, whether in stocks, oil wells, or diamonds. Examines timing techniques, and considers what to expect from stockbrokers, investment advisors, financial planners, and computer programs.

AUDIENCE: Beginning   RISK LEVEL: Moderate, Aggressive
TOPICS: All

Beating the Dow

Michael O'Higgins
Harper Collins Publishers, Inc.
10 E. 53rd Street
New York, NY 10022

PH: (800) 242-7737
ISBN: 006098404-X
Published: 1992
Cost: $11.00

Subjects addressed: investing theories, stock analysis; uses charts. High return - low risk method for investing in the Dow Jones Ind. stocks with as little as $5000.00.

AUDIENCE: Beginning
TOPICS: Stocks
RISK LEVEL: Moderate, Aggressive

Beginner Guide to Investing in No-Load Mutual Funds, A

J. Stanley Levitt
International Publishing Corp.
625 N. Michigan Ave.
Chicago, Il. 60611

PH: (312) 943-7354
Published: 1991
Cost: $15.95

This book begins with a primer on mutual funds companies, describing what they are, how they work and their safety and cost factors. The author compares mutual funds with other investments such as stocks, bonds, Treasuries and CDs. One chapter is devoted to explaining the six basic types of mutual funds, giving their characteristics and degrees of risk. A separate chapter defines fixed-income funds. The author also discusses the structure of fund families.

AUDIENCE: Beginning
TOPICS: Mutual Funds
RISK LEVEL: Moderate, Aggressive

Behavior of Prices in Wall Street

Authur A. Merrill
3300 Darby Road #3325
Haverford, PA 19041

PH: (215) 642-2011
ISBN: 0-91 1894-49-7
Published: 1966,1984 (revised 2nd edition)
Cost: $38.00

This book concentrates on the profitable study of market timing. The text of this book is addressed to nonmathematical investors. It is a concisely-written volume and is considered the classic guide to typical market behavior. Topics covered include: the Presidential Cycle, monthly, weekly, and daily patterns, holiday behavior, Dow Theory, the influence of Fed policy and much more.

AUDIENCE: Individual, Professional
TOPICS: Mutual Funds, Stocks
RISK LEVEL: Moderate, Aggressive

Best Ways to Make Money Now

Editors of Money Magazine
Money Books
P.O. Box 2463
Birmingham, AL 35201

PH: (800) 765-6400
Published: 1991
Cost: $19.95

Discover the hottest investments of the decade, getting in on the European boom, how to profit from the S & L crisis and how to make sure your money market funds are safe. Also covers college budgeting plans, home selling tips and more.

AUDIENCE: Beginning
TOPICS: Mutual Funds, Stocks
RISK LEVEL: Moderate, Aggressive

Beyond the Investor's Quotient: The Inner World of Investing

Jacob Bernstein
John Wiley & Sons, Inc.
605 Third Avenue
New York, NY 10158-0012

PH: (212) 850-6418 orders
(212) 850-6233 info.
FAX: (212) 850-6088
ISBN: 0-471-82062-8
Published: 1986
Cost: $19.95

The Investor's Quotient unraveled the mystery behind investor behavior; this work takes you one critical step closer to success as a trader or investor. Presents specific methods of self-analysis - proven techniques to help you find your direction, define your objectives, choose your methods, and keep your eye on long-term goals.

AUDIENCE: Individual   RISK LEVEL: Moderate, Aggressive
TOPICS: Mutual Funds, Stocks

Blue Chips and Hot Tips: Identifying Emerging Growth Companies Most Likely to Succeed

W. Keith Schilit and Howard M.
  Schilit
New York Institute of
  Finance/Prentice Hall
113 Sylvan Avenue
Route 9W
Englewood Cliffs, NJ 07632

PH: (800) 947-7700
FAX: (515) 284-2607
Published: 1990
Cost: $19.95

This best seller examines the most and least successful new stock offerings of the past 15 years. Reveals clearly identifiable characteristics that set winning and losing stocks apart, what to look for in an IPO, and key questions to ask before finalizing the deal.

AUDIENCE: Individual   RISK LEVEL: Moderate, Aggressive
TOPICS: Stocks

Blood in the Streets: Investment Profits in a World Gone Mad

James Dale Davidson & Sir
  William Rees-Mogg
Warner Books, Inc.
1271 Avenue of the Americas
New York, NY 10020

PH: (212) 522-7200
ISBN: 0-446-35316-7
Published: 1988
Cost: $6.99

Using straightforward language the authors provide a roadmap to understanding the relationships between politics, the mechanics of markets, and the way people respond to crisis. They uncover the hidden meanings behind current events and make specific recommendations for capitalizing on those events. Replete with revelations. A.F.P.

AUDIENCE: Beginning, Individual, Professional   RISK LEVEL: Moderate, Aggressive
TOPICS: Bonds, Mutual Funds, Stocks, Options, Futures/Commodities

Bond Book: Everything Investors Need to Know About Munis, Treasuries, GNMAs, Funds, Zeroes, Corporates, Money Markets and More, The

Anette Thau
Probus Publishing Co.
1925 North Clybourn Avenue
Chicago, IL 60614

PH: (800) PROBUS-1
FAX: (312) 868-6250
ISBN: 1-55738-248-4
Published: 1991
Cost: $29.95

"The Bond Book" was written and developed for the individual who has some general knowledge in the financial markets but lacks the sophistication and confidence to develop active strategies in fixed income securities. The first section of this book serves as a refresher course, providing a general background of how the debt market works and the various types of risks involved. Part Two is devoted to the major types of fixed income instruments. Part Three shows the reader how to "put it all together" with state-of-the-art portfolio management geared specifically to the individual investor.

AUDIENCE: Beginning, Individual   RISK LEVEL: Conservative
TOPICS: Bonds

Bond Risk Analysis: A Guide to Duration and Convexity

Livingston G. Douglas
New York Institute of
Finance/Prentice Hall
113 Sylvan Avenue
Route 9W
Englewood Cliffs, NJ 07632

PH: (800) 947-7700
FAX: (515) 284-2607
Published: 1990
Cost: $34.95

A seasoned pro explains the basic tenets of bond risk analysis in an easy-to-read work filled with examples. Explains how to use duration and convexity to analyze risk and minimize its impact on any type of bond.

AUDIENCE: Individual, Professional   RISK LEVEL: Conservative, Moderate
TOPICS: Bonds

Brazil Company Handbook 1993

The Reference Press, Inc.
6448 Highway 290 E
Suite E-104
Austin, TX 78723

PH: (512) 454-7778
FAX: (512) 454-9401
Cost: $29.95
Published: 1993
Fundamental Analysis

Includes profiles of 90 of Brazil's major public companies and 60 money managers and investment advisors. Also provides information on the economic climate.

AUDIENCE: Beginning, Individual, Professional   RISK LEVEL: Aggressive
TOPICS: Stocks

Break the Wall Street Rule: Outperform the Stock Market by Investing as an Owner

Michael T. Jacobs
Addison-Wesley Publishing Co.
1 Jacob Way
Reading, MA 01867-3999

PH: (800) 447-2226
Published: 1993
Cost: $24.95

The author proposes an alternative to the current Wall Street rule of selling stock whenever its performance is unsatisfactory. He advocates that investors become effective owners of the companies whose stock they buy. Guidelines for choosing companies structured for the benefit of their shareholders are given. The book describes how to use SEC proxy rules to maximize returns. It discusses how supporting directors and resolutions can help ensure that management works.

AUDIENCE: Beginning, Individual   RISK LEVEL: Moderate, Aggressive
TOPICS: Stocks

Business Barometers

Roger Ward Babson
Business Classics
950 Purisima Road
Woodside, CA 94062

PH: (800) 865-1001
(415) 852-8879
ISBN: 0-931133-10-6
Published: 1994 (reprint of 1909 edition)
Cost: not available

Including both market wisdom and keen analysis of 19th century securities and their evolution, this is one of Babson's finest early works. Babson formed the Babson Statistical Organization, Inc. which later became the basis for Standard & Poor's. This book teaches you to see the market in four phases, instead of just up and down. He clearly explains the phases, shows how you can use them to make forecasts, and links them to other phenomena.

AUDIENCE: Beginning, Individual, Professional   RISK LEVEL: Moderate, Aggressive
TOPICS: Bonds, Stocks

Business One-Irwin Business and Investment Almanac, The

Sumner N. Levine, Editor
Irwin Professional Publishing
1333 Burr Ridge Parkway
Burr Ridge, IL 60521

PH: (800) 634-3966
(708) 789-5489
FAX: (708) 789-6933
ISBN: 1-55623-532-1
Published: Annually
Cost: $49.95

Addresses the subject of market analysis. Uses charts. Contains all new facts and figures on 1992's best investments. The book reviews the significant financial happenings in 1991 and tells what they mean for the serious investor. The 16th edition will save investors valuable time by providing major and group stock market averages, charts for futures-traded commodities, price per earnings ratios.

AUDIENCE: Beginning, Individual, Professional   RISK LEVEL: Moderate, Aggressive
TOPICS: Bonds, Mutual Funds, Stocks, Options, Futures/Commodities

Business One-Irwin Guide to Buying and Selling Treasury Securities, The

Howard M. Berlin
Irwin Professional Publishing
1333 Burr Ridge Parkway
Burr Ridge, IL 60521

PH: (800) 634-3966
(708) 789-5489
FAX: (708) 789-6933
ISBN: 1-55623-048-6
Published: 1988
Cost: $34.95

Covers bond analysis. How to analyze, buy and sell T-bills, notes, and bonds. Details both conservative purchases with minimal risk, and indirect methods, such as futures and options. A.F.P.

AUDIENCE: Beginning, Individual   RISK LEVEL: Conservative
TOPICS: Bonds

Business One-Irwin Guide to Using The Wall Street Journal, The

Michael B. Lehman
Irwin Professional Publishing
1333 Burr Ridge Parkway
Burr Ridge, IL 60521

PH: (800) 634-3966
(708) 789-5489
FAX: (708) 789-6933
ISBN: 0-87094-923-3
Published: 1993 (4th edition)
Cost: $28.00

Covers The Wall Street Journal. Discover how to use the comprehensive information in The Journal to make more profitable business and investment decisions.

AUDIENCE: Beginning, Individual, Professional RISK LEVEL: Conservative, Moderate, Aggressive
TOPICS: All

Business One-Irwin Investors Handbook, The

Phyllis Pierce
Irwin Professional Publishing
1333 Burr Ridge Parkway
Burr Ridge, IL 60521

PH: (800) 634-3966
(708) 789-5489
FAX: (708) 789-6933
ISBN: 1-55623-673-5
Published: Annually
Cost: $20.00

Covers stock analysis. Save time and make more informed investment decisions with all of the statistical information on the year-end closing prices from the NYSE, AMEX, and OTC at your fingertips.

AUDIENCE: Individual, Professional   RISK LEVEL: Moderate, Aggressive
TOPICS: Stocks

Business One-Irwin Guide to Bond and Money Market Investments, The

Marcia Stigum & Frank Fabozzi
Irwin Professional Publishing
1333 Burr Ridge Parkway
Burr Ridge, IL 60521

PH: (708) 789-5489
(800) 634-3966
FAX: (708) 789-6933
ISBN: 0-87094-892-X
Published: 1986
Cost: $42.00

Explores interest-bearing IOUs - under-utilized instruments that offer attractive returns, low risk, high liquidity, and tax advantages. From certificates of deposit to Treasury bills, bond funds, and zeros, this clear treatment of long- and short-term debt securities provides investors with all of the necessary information. A.F.P.

AUDIENCE: Beginning, Individual, Professional	RISK LEVEL: Conservative, Moderate
TOPICS: Bonds, Mutual Funds	

Business One-Irwin Guide to Trading Systems, The

Bruce Babcock, Jr.
Irwin Professional Publishing
1333 Burr Ridge Parkway
Burr Ridge, IL 60521

PH: (708) 789-5489
(800) 634-3966
FAX: (708) 789-6933
Published: 1989
ISBN: 1-55623-126-1
Cost: $70.00

Subjects addressed: commodities trading, analysis, technical analysis. Uses charts. Explains why a mechanical approach is best and teaches you how to choose the right system. You'll become a better system developer and a far more knowledgeable system buyer. Babcock presents historical tests of various trading system approaches in ten markets over a five year period. A.F.P.

AUDIENCE: Beginning, Individual, Professional	RISK LEVEL: Conservative, Moderate,
TOPICS: All	Aggressive

Business Week's Guide to Mutual Funds

J. Laderman
McGraw-Hill, Inc.
11 West 19th Street
New York, NY 10011

PH: (800) 722-4726
(212) 512-4100
Published: 1991
Cost: $24.95

Business Week's annual Mutual Fund Scoreboard combined with complete practical information covering the entire scope of mutual funds. "The result is the most comprehensive and current how-to-guide to mutual funds available today."

AUDIENCE: Beginning, Individual	RISK LEVEL: Moderate, Aggressive
TOPICS: Mutual Funds	

Canada Company Handbook 1994

The Reference Press, Inc.
6448 Highway 290 E.
Suite E-104
Austin, TX 78723

PH: (512) 454-7778
FAX: (512) 454-9401
Cost: $39.95
Date of first issue: 1994
ISBN: 0-921925-45-X
Fundamental Analysis

A reference book providing information on over 1,300 Canadian companies. Profiles over 400 companies on the Toronto Stock Exchange 300, both current and prior companies. Profiles include a description of the company, performance analysis, stock price performance charts, 5 years of financial data, 2 years of quarterly financial data, stock symbols, and rankings on profit, revenues and assets.

AUDIENCE: Individual, Professional	RISK LEVEL: Moderate, Aggressive
TOPICS: Stocks, General Reference	

Candlepower

Gregory L. Morris
Probus Publishing Co.
1925 N. Clybourn Ave.
Suite 401
Chicago, IL 60614

PH: (800) PROBUS-1
(312) 868-1100
FAX: (312) 868-6250
Cost: $50.00
Date of first issue: 1992
Technical Analysis

"Demonstrates what is perhaps the single most important attribute of candlesticks: how candle patterns can be used as a filter, in conjunction with other technical tools to identify high reward/low risk trades."

AUDIENCE: Individual, Professional   RISK LEVEL: Moderate
TOPICS: Stocks, Futures

Capital Ideas: The Improbable Origins of Modern Wall Street

Peter L. Bernstein
The Free Press
866 Third Avenue
New York, NY 10022

PH: (800) 257-5755
FAX: (212) 605-9364
Cost: $14.95 (paperback)
Date of first issue: 1992

"In this lively history of the ideas that shaped modern finance, Bernstein, economic consultant and founder of The Journal of Portfolio Management, tells the story how a small group of scholars revolutionized the management of the world's wealth. He shows how their ideas, by adding a measure of science to the art of investing, enlarged our understanding of capital markets, enabling investors to better manage risk and revitalized economics throughout the world."

AUDIENCE: Individual, Professional   RISK LEVEL: Moderate, Aggressive
TOPICS: All

Cash Book, The—High Yields with Safety

James U. Blanchard III
New York Institute of Finance/
Prentice Hall
113 Sylvan Avenue
Route 9W
Englewood Cliffs, NJ 07632

PH: (800) 947-7700
FAX: (515) 284-2607
Published: 1992
Cost: $19.95

The publisher of the renowned investment newsletter, Louis Rukeyser's Wall Street, tells what to do with cash. Unveils a wide range of strategies—from the ultraconservative to the speculative—for acheiving high yields with maximum safety.

AUDIENCE: Individual, Professional   RISK LEVEL: Conservative, Moderate
TOPICS: Bonds

Chartcraft Annual Long-Term P & F Chartbook

Chartcraft, Inc.
30 Church St.
New Rochelle, NY 10801

PH: (914) 632-0422
FAX: (914) 632-0335
Frequency: Annual
Costs: $49.50

Over 720+ pages, covers 1,200 popular NYSE, ASE and OTC issues. Each chart is a large 4-3/4" x 6-3/4" and most go back 6 - 8 years or more. Each chart lists: full name, symbol, beta, P/E, yield, 30-wk M.A., relative momentum & trend. Featured are Relative Strength and Investors Daily Industry Grouping. Long-term patterns are easily recognized. Updating is easy from your own source or the Chartcraft Monthly Chartbook. The book is updated through each year's end. A.F.P.

AUDIENCE: Individual, Professional   RISK LEVEL Moderate, Aggressive
TOPICS: Stocks

Charting the Stock Market - The Wyckoff Method

Technical Analysis of Stocks and
  Commodities
4757 California Avenue, S.W.
Seattle, WA 98116-4499

PH: (800) 832-4642
(206) 938-0570
Cost: $14.95
Date of first issue: 1987
ISBN: 0-938773-06-2
Technical Analysis

"This book describes and illustrates one of the best pioneering technical analysis methods. Includes price/volume chart reading and analysis, market and industry trend recognition, figure charts, wave charts, relative strength and weakness, stop orders."

AUDIENCE: Individual, Professional   RISK LEVEL: Moderate, Aggressive
TOPICS: Stocks, Futures/Commodities

Closed End Funds

Frank Cappiello, W. Douglas Dint,
  Peter W. Maellem
International Publishing Company
625 N. Michigan, Suite 1920
Chicago, IL 60611

Published: 1990
Cost: $24.95

Covers nearly 200 closed-end funds. Includes address and phone number, transfer agent, background investment objectives, portfolio composition, dividend distribution, management, shareholder reporting, capitalization, year-end and 5 year statistical history and performance ranking. A.F.P.

AUDIENCE: Beginning, Individual   RISK LEVEL: Moderate, Aggressive
TOPICS: Mutual Funds

Commodities: A Chart Anthology

Edward D. Dobson
Traders Press, Inc.
P.O. Box 6206
Greenville, SC 29606

PH: (800) 927-8222
ISBN: 0-934380-02-3
Published: 1981 (2nd edition)
Cost: $29.95

The largest compilation of commodity bar charts available. This collection of 1,107 charts and assorted material dealing with their interpretation is intended to serve as both a convenient reference on what markets have done in past years on a daily basis, and as a concise primer on the use of commodity bar charts. A.F.P.

AUDIENCE: Professional   RISK LEVEL: Aggressive
TOPICS: Options, Futures/Commodities, Asset Allocation, Investment Planning, General Reference

Common Stock Price Histories, 1910-1987

Denis E. Predeville
WIT Financial Publishers
1307 E 74th, Suite 1B
Anchorage, AK 99518

PH: (800) 422-1910
ISBN: 0-9618454-1-4
Published: 1988 (2nd edition)
Cost: $39.95

The first book of its kind to provide long-term price histories of common stocks, some of which date back to 1910. Virtually all stocks on the New York and American Stock Exchanges plus over-the-counter issues are included. Over 4,000 charts - including 2,800 complete histories - are contained in this unique publication.

AUDIENCE: Beginning, Individual, Professional   RISK LEVEL: Moderate, Aggressive
TOPICS: Stocks, General Reference

Common Stocks and Uncommon Profits

Philip A. Fisher
Business Classics
950 Purisima Road
Woodside, CA 95062

PH: (415) 851-3337
ISBN: 0-931133-00-9
Published: 1984 (reprint of 1958
edition)
Cost: $21.95

Features stock analysis. Mr. Fisher tells in detail what to do and what not to do for maximum profits. His 10 "Don'ts" picture the popular regard for mathematical factors such as ratios, percentages, and dividend record. His 15 points to look for in a common stock stress fundamentals such as company quality, management competence, and competitive position - and ways to size up these factors most accurately.

AUDIENCE: Individual	RISK LEVEL: Moderate, Aggressive
TOPICS: Stocks	

Company Handbook Spain-The Maxwell Espinosa Shareholders Directory

The Reference Press, Inc.
6448 Highway 290 E.
Suite E-104
Austin, TX 78723

PH: (512) 454-7778
FAX: (512) 454-9401
Cost: $84.95
ISBN: 8-472092-57-7
Fundamental Analysis

Profiles almost 2,000 Spanish corporations. Information includes: headquarters, industry, phone and fax numbers, major shareholders, recent year's sales, number of employees as well as advertising agency, attorneys, banks, auditors and other communications contacts. A.F.P.

AUDIENCE: Individual, Professional	RISK LEVEL: Moderate, Aggressive
TOPICS: Stocks, General Reference	

Company Handbook-Hong Kong

The Reference Press, Inc.
6448 Highway 290 E.
Suite E-104
Austin, TX 78723

PH: (512) 454-7778
FAX: (512) 454-9401
Cost: $44.95
Published twice/yr
Fundamental Analysis

Profiles the 416 companies listed on the Hong Kong Stock Exchange. Includes description of company, major office address and phone number, major stockholders and officers, financial statements, key ratios and profit breakdowns. A.F.P.

AUDIENCE: Individual, Professional	RISK LEVEL: Moderate, Aggressive
TOPICS: Stocks, General Reference	

Complete Bond Book: A Guide to All Types of Fixed Income Securities, The

David M. Darst
McGraw-Hill Publishing Company
1221 Avenue of the Americas
New York, NY 10020

PH: (800) 262-4729
ISBN: 0-07-017390-7
Published: 1975
Cost: $49.95

Rapidly changing economic pressures and financial concerns require solid advice for investing in all types of fixed-income securities. Valuable step-by-step guidelines, worksheets, charts, simplified formulas, and other aids enable you to devise safe and sound strategies for profitable investments now and in the future.

AUDIENCE: Beginning, Individual, Professional	RISK LEVEL: Conservative
TOPICS: Bonds	

Complete Guide to Closed-End Funds: Finding Value in Today's Stock Market, The

International Publishing Corp.
625 N. Michigan Avenue
Chicago, IL 60611

PH: (312) 943-7354
ISBN: 0-942641-52-3
Published: 1993, 5th Edition
Cost: $24.95

Learn what a closed-end fund is, how to track the discount and utilize trading strategies from three experts. Provides information on more than 400 bond and equity funds, including year-end performance and fund background and investment objective. Participate in the bond and stock market with minimum risk. Jon Chatfield, Editor.

AUDIENCE: Beginning, Individual   RISK LEVEL: Moderate, Aggressive
TOPICS: Mutual Funds

Complete Guide to Convertible Securities, The

Laura A. Zubulake
John Wiley & Sons, Inc.
605 Third Avenue
New York, New York 10158

PH: (212) 850-6000
FAX: (212) 850-6088
Cost: $55.00
Date of first issue: 1991

"Begins with an analysis of a typical U.S. dollar denominated Euro convertible. Goes on to discuss international convertible securities and such related topics as currency fluctuation and foreign currency exposure . . . . Finally, it looks at convertible hedging, breakeven analysis, risk profile and rate of return."

AUDIENCE: Individual, Professional   RISK LEVEL: Aggressive
TOPICS: Bonds, Stocks

Complete Guide to Global Investing, The

Agora, Inc.
824 E. Baltimore St.
Baltimore, MD 21202-4799

PH: (800) 438-1528
(410) 234-0691
FAX: (410) 837-3879
Frequency: Biweekly
Cost: $89
Date of first issue: 1994

Concentrates on emerging markets, worldwide investments and strategies for stock market and currency investing. Also, provides a detailed index on ADRs. A.F.P.

AUDIENCE: Individual, Professional   RISK LEVEL: Moderate, Aggressive
TOPICS: Bonds, Mutual Funds, Stocks

Complete Guide to the Futures Markets Fundamental Analysis, Technical Analysis, Trading, Spreads and Options, A

Jack O. Schwager
John Wiley & Sons, Inc.
605 Third Avenue
New York, NY 10158-0012

PH: (212) 850-6418 (orders)
(212) 850-6233 (info)
FAX: (212) 850-6088
Published: 1984
Cost: $55.00

Covers commodities trading, technical analysis; uses charts. A non-technical book for the intelligent lay person already familiar with the basic concepts of futures trading but interested in more detailed discussion of analytical techniques.

AUDIENCE: Individual, Professional   RISK LEVEL: Aggressive
TOPICS: Options, Futures/Commodities

Complete Guide to Trading Profits, A

Alexander P. Paris
Traders Press, Inc.
P.O. Box 6206
Greenville, SC 29606

PH: (800) 927-8222
ISBN: 0-934380-05-8
Published: 1970
Cost: $19.95

Reap the benefits of short-term trading by learning the most important basic principles of technical analysis and the basic systems of charting. Incorporate these new skills into whatever approach you're accustomed to. Written for the layman.

AUDIENCE: Individual, Professional   RISK LEVEL: Moderate, Aggressive
TOPICS: Stocks, Options, Futures/Commodities

Complete Option Player, The

Institute for Options Research, Inc.
P.O. Box 6586
Lake Tahoe, NV 89449

PH: (702) 588-3590
FAX: (702) 588-8481
Published: 1993
Cost: $19.95

Covers options; uses charts. The book contains over 300 pages full of indispensable tables, charts, investment tools, illustrations and a gold mine of secrets and information on how to win big in the options game. A.F.P.

AUDIENCE: Individual, Professional   RISK LEVEL: Aggressive
TOPICS: Options, Futures/Commodities

Concise Handbook of Futures Markets: Money Management, Forecasting, and the Markets, The

Perry J. Kaufman, Editor
John Wiley & Sons, Inc.
605 Third Avenue
New York, NY 10158-0012

PH: (212) 850-0012
FAX: (212) 850-6088
ISBN: 0-471-85088-8
Published: 1986
Cost: $29.95

Concise paperback version of the definitive Handbook. Retains all of the analytic sections of the larger volume and other important background material. Includes chapters on hedging, options, financial markets, spreads, and technical analysis, as well as regulation, taxation, and computer application. Promotes logic above all.

AUDIENCE: Individual, Professional   RISK LEVEL: Aggressive
TOPICS: Options, Futures/Commodities

Conservative Investors Sleep Well

Philip A. Fisher
Business Classics
950 Purisima Road
Woodside, CA 94062

PH: (800) 865-1001
ISBN: 0-931133-04-X
Published: 1992 (reprint of 1975
   edition)
Cost: $21.95

Covers stock analysis. Fisher shows how conservative investing is more process than type of security. He shows how understanding what you own is truly fundamental to conservativeness, and how, once you do so, you can knowledge to pick good specific securities. Sage advice from one of the pioneers of growth investing, this book helps you reduce risk through knowledge.

AUDIENCE: Beginning, Individual   RISK LEVEL: Conservative, Moderate
TOPICS: Bonds, Mutual Funds, Stocks

Cracking the Pacific Rim

The Reference Press, Inc.
6448 Highway 290 E, Suite E-104
Austin, TX 78723

PH: (512) 454-7778
FAX: (512) 454-9401
Cost: $44.95
Date of first issue: 1994

Profiles the following countries: Hong Kong, Indonesia, Japan, Korea, Malaysia, the Philippines, Singapore, Taiwan and Thailand. Provides market and socioeconomic demographics, policies to attract business, "hot" business opportunities, finance and politics, key business contacts and resources and proper business interaction and etiquette.

AUDIENCE: Individual, Professional   RISK LEVEL: Moderate, Aggressive
TOPICS: General Reference

Cross Currency Swaps

Carl R. Beidleman, Editor
Irwin Professional Publishing
1333 Burr Ridge Parkway
Burr Ridge, IL 60521

PH: (800) 634-3966
(708) 789-5489
FAX: (708) 789-6933
ISBN: 1-55623-316-7
Published: 1991
Cost: $88.00

Written by two-dozen leaders in the industry, "Cross Currency Swaps" gives readers everything they need to effectively manage these complicated, but highly lucrative, instruments. Logically organized, this one-of-a-kind resource includes: the strategies and tactics of prominent international authorities based on their areas of expertise, step-by-step details of each of the various swaps tactics, an historical look at the development of the swaps market, the accounting and taxation treatments of swap transactions, the innovation of swap strategies so readers are prepared for the future.

AUDIENCE: Professional   RISK LEVEL: Aggressive
TOPICS: Bonds, Options, Futures/Commodities

Currency and Interest-Rate Hedging: Options, Futures, Swaps, and Foward Contacts

Torben Juul Andersen
New York Institute of
Finance/Prentice Hall
113 Sylvan Avenue
Route 9W
Englewood Cliffs, NJ 07632

PH: (800) 947-7700
FAX: (515) 284-2607
Cost: $49.95

Explains basic hedging stategies and how they can be used. Covers major market developments and discusses newer instruments such as CAPs, LEAPs, FLEXs, par forwards, and more. Describes how to measure currency and interest-rate exposures and suggests ways to manage these financial risks.

AUDIENCE: Professional   RISK LEVEL: Moderate
TOPICS: Bonds, Options, Futures/Commodities

Cyclic Analysis in Futures Trading: Contemporary Methods and Procedures

Jacob Bernstein
John Wiley & Sons, Inc.
605 Third Avenue
New York, NY 10158-0012

PH: (212) 850-6418 orders
(212) 850-6233 info.
FAX: (212) 850-6088
ISBN: 0-471-01185-1
Published: 1988
Cost: $79.95

Covers commodities/futures trading. This book gives you many of the tips, techniques and tactics you need to develop effective strategies for profiting from cycles in futures markets of all types.

AUDIENCE: Professional   RISK LEVEL: Aggressive
TOPICS: Options, Futures/Commodities

Day Trader's Manual: Theory, Art and Science of Profitable Short-Term Investing, The

W. F. Eng
John Wiley & Sons, Inc.
605 Third Avenue
New York, NY 10158-0012

PH: (212) 850-6000
FAX: (212) 850-6088
Published: 1992
Cost: $60.00

"Offers complete coverage of day-trading methods including price, time and volume analysis techniques, money and position management strategies, trading systems, computerized trading tactics and much more." A.F.P.

AUDIENCE: Individual, Professional   RISK LEVEL: Aggressive
TOPICS: Stocks, Options, Futures

DC Gardner Guide to International Capital Markets, The

The DC Gardner Group PLC
John Wiley & Sons, Inc.
605 Third Avenue
New York, NY 10158-0012

PH: (212) 850-6000
FAX: (212) 850-6088
Published: 1993
Cost: $50.00

A self-study guide explaining how to understand, select and trade the basic instruments in international use including government bonds, commercial paper, asset-backed securities and international equities.

AUDIENCE: Professional   RISK LEVEL: Conservative, Moderate, Aggressive
TOPICS: Bonds, Stocks

Developing an Investment Philosophy

Philip A. Fisher
Business Classics
950 Purisima Road
Woodside, CA 94062

PH: (800) 865-1001
(415) 852-8879
ISBN: 0-931133-06-8
Published: 1980
Cost: $14.95

Covers investment philosophy. This book was originally written at the request of the Institute of Chartered Financial Analysis - in their "monograph" series - aimed at capturing the philosophy, personality and experience of distinguished investors. In it, Philip A. Fisher lays out the lifetime experiences that led to his legendary pioneering work in growth stock investing.

AUDIENCE: Beginning, Individual, Professional   RISK LEVEL:Aggressive
TOPICS: Stocks

Dictionary of Finance and Investment Terms

John Downes & Jordan Elliot Goodman
Barron's Educational Series, Inc.
P.O. Box 8040
250 Wireless Blvd.
Hauppauge, NY 11788

PH: (800) 645-3476
ISBN: 0-8120-2522-9
Published: 1987
Cost: $8.95

Defines new terminology and updates the traditional language of finance and investment. Basic enough for the student, yet comprehensive enough for the professional. Designed for investors of all types, and includes entries from accounting, consumer and business law, economics, taxation, and other related fields. Over 2,500 terms.

AUDIENCE: Beginning, Individual, Professional RISK LEVEL: Conservative, Moderate, Aggressive
TOPICS: General Reference

Directional Movement Indicator (DMI)

Commodities Education Institute
219 Parade
Cedar Falls, IA 50613

PH: (800) 635-3936
(319) 277-6341
FAX: (319) 277-7982
Published: 1990
Cost: $55.00
VIDEO

Covers investing theories, trading analysis, technical analysis. Combines Gann tools with DMI as an overbought/oversold trend indicator and to determine the likelihood of a trending versus a non-trending market. Glen Ring will package these indicators to develop a systematic, technical approach to the markets that will work. Set of 5 tapes in this series.

AUDIENCE: Professional	RISK LEVEL: Aggressive
TOPICS: Stocks, Options, Futures/Commodities	

Directory of Mutual Funds, The

Investment Company Institute
1600 M. Street
Washington, D.C. 20036

PH: (202) 326-5800
Published: 1994
Cost: $8.50

Covers mutual funds. Complete listing of the member 3,000 mutual funds.

AUDIENCE: Beginning, Individual	RISK LEVEL: Moderate, Aggressive
TOPICS: Mutual Funds	

The Disciplined Trader: Developing Winning Attitudes

Mark Douglas
New York Institute of
  Finance/Prentice Hall
113 Sylvan Avenue
Route 9W
Englewood Cliffs, NJ 07632

PH: (800) 947-7700
FAX: (515) 284-2607
Cost: $29.95

Helps traders replace emotional, losing attitudes with iron discipline and responsive behavior. A successful trader shows how to meet the unusual psychological demands of trading in a step-by-step approach to decision-making, implementation, and follow-through.

AUDIENCE: Professional	RISK LEVEL: Aggressive
TOPICS: Stocks, Options, Futures/Commodities	

Dividends Don't Lie: Finding Value in Blue-Chip Stock

Geraldine Weiss & Janet Lowe
Dearborn Financial Publishing, Inc.
520 N. Dearborn Street
Chicago, IL 60610

PH: (800) 621-9621 ext. 320
ISBN: 0-88462-115-4
Published: 1988
Cost: $23.95

Covers stock analysis, market analysis, fundamental analysis; uses charts. Outlines the strategies that give investors excellent returns. Shows how to: spot high quality blue chip stocks, maximize profits and minimize risk, find bargains in the market, identify the 6 criteria for buying stocks and know the right time to buy and sell.

AUDIENCE: Beginning, Individual	RISK LEVEL: Moderate, Aggressive
TOPICS: Stocks	

Divining the Dow

Richard J. Maturi
Probus Publishing
1925 N. Clybourn Ave.
Chicago, IL 60614

PH: (800) 776-2871
Published: 1989
Cost: $22.95

100 of the major stock market prediction systems. A description of each system includes how the system works, who uses it, where to get more information, and what reviewers have said about it. When appropriate, the author provides graphs and charts that demonstrate how the system works. A few of the systems covered in the book include the January effect, the Elliott wave, the contrarian approach, the random walk theory, Barron's confidence index, and best days of the month.

AUDIENCE: Individual, Professional   RISK LEVEL: Moderate, Aggressive
TOPICS: Mutual Funds, Stocks

Do-It-Yourself Investment Analysis

James Burgauer
International Publishing Corp.
625 N. Michigan Avenue
Chicago, IL 60611

PH: (800) 488-4149
Cost: $18.95
ISBN: 0-942641-24-8
Date of first issue: 1990

Subtitled: Practical Guide to Life Cycle Fundamental and Technical Analysis. Provides the quality information necessary to make sound investment decisions. Shows investors the importance of the life cycle of a business, the essentials of fundamental analysis including key investment retiring, technical analysis techniques, wide employed investment strategies and much more.

AUDIENCE: Beginning, Individual   RISK LEVEL: Moderate, Aggressive
TOPICS: Stocks

Don't Sell Stocks on Monday: An Almanac for Traders, Brokers and Stock Market Watchers

Yale Hirsch
Penguin Books
375 Hudson Street
New York, NY 10014

PH: (800) 631-3577
ISBN: 0-14-010375-9
Published: 1987
Cost: $8.95

An insightful, up-to-date collection of prognostic tips based on more than 25 years of research. Theories and advice on investing - day-by-day, week-by-week, monthly-month, and year-by-year - are highlighted by vignettes from stock market history. Includes Hirsch's famous January Barometer Theory and 14 Forecasting Secrets.

AUDIENCE: Individual   RISK LEVEL: Moderate, Aggressive
TOPICS: Stocks

Dow Jones Averages: 1885-1994, The

Phyllis Pierce, Editor
Irwin Professional Publishing
1333 Burr Ridge Parkway
Burr Ridge, IL 60521

PH: (800) 634-3966
(708) 789-5489
FAX: (708) 789-6933
ISBN: 1-55623-512-7
Published: Annually
Cost: $77.00

Covers market analysis. "An essential tool for analyzing financial market history so you can better understand the trends of today's volatile markets. It's a one-of-a-kind compilation of every industrial, transportation, and utility average from the beginning of the 12-stock index through 12-31-92."

AUDIENCE: Individual, Professional   RISK LEVEL: Moderate, Aggressive
TOPICS: Stocks

Dow Jones-Irwin Guide to Stock Index Futures and Options, The

William Nix and Susan Nix
Irwin Professional Publishing
1333 Burr Ridge Parkway
Burr Ridge, IL 60521

PH: (708) 789-5489
(800) 634-3966
FAX: (708) 789-6933
ISBN: 0-87094-482-7
Published: 1984
Cost: $50.00

Outlines critical differences in stock index futures, futures options, and index options on major U.S. exchanges. Contains practical advice for beginning and veteran commodity traders, securities and options investors, financial executives, and institutional money managers looking for alternative risk management strategies.

AUDIENCE: Individual, Professional   RISK LEVEL: Aggressive
TOPICS: Stocks, Options, Futures/Commodities

Dun & Bradstreet: Guide to $Your Investments$ 1994

Nancy Dunan
Harper Collins Publishers, Inc.
10 E. 53rd Street
New York, NY 10022

PH: (800) 242-7737
ISBN: 0062715399
Published: 1994
Cost: $35.00

Explore the new trend toward diversification in investment portfolio and against individual ownership of stock. A new focus on hard assets and the increased attraction of CDs are covered and much more. In its 36th year, it remains a standard source book for both advisors and investors.

AUDIENCE: Beginning   RISK LEVEL: Conservative, Moderate, Aggressive
TOPICS: Bonds, Mutual Funds, Stocks

Dying of Money: Lessons of the Great German and American Inflations

Jens O. Parsson
Wellspring Press
Page Road
Lincoln, MA 01773

ISBN: 0-914688-01-4
Published: 1974
Cost: $18.00

Transforms the dry economic subject of inflation into a white-knuckles kind of blood chiller. Clear and fascinating, yet entirely technically valid, this book applies the lessons gleaned from the German inflation of 1923 to the American inflation that followed 1962. Charts out all possible prognoses for our country's economy.

AUDIENCE: Individual, Professional   RISK LEVEL: Moderate, Aggressive
TOPICS: Bonds, Stocks

Dynamic Asset Allocation

David A. Hammer
John Wiley & Sons, Inc.
605 Third Avenue
New York, NY 10158-0012

PH: (212) 850-6000
FAX: (212) 850-6088
Fundamental Analysis
Published: - 1991
Cost: $55.00

"The author introduces his own proven method of portfolio management and asset allocation strategies. The 'Seven-Step System' using simple statistical techniques to forecast stock, bond, commodity and money market returns."

AUDIENCE: Professional   RISK LEVEL: Conservative, Moderate, Aggressive
TOPICS: Bonds, Stocks, Asset Allocation

Dynamics of Commodity Production Cycles

Denis L. Meadows
MIT Press
55 Hayward Street
Cambridge, MA 02142

PH: (617) 253-5249
ISBN: 0-262-13141-2
Published: 1970
Cost: $32.50

Employs industrial dynamics methodology to develop a general dynamic model of economic, biological, technological, and psychological factors that cause instability of commodity systems. Computer simulation experiments of alternative policies and structural changes reveal surprising implications for stabilization policies.

AUDIENCE: Professional	RISK LEVEL: Aggressive
TOPICS: Options, Futures/Commodities	

Economic Indicators: How America Reads Its Financial Health

Joseph Plocek
New York Institute of
  Finance/Prentice Hall
113 Sylvan Avenue
Route 9W
Englewood Cliffs, NJ 07632

PH: (800) 947-7700
FAX: (515) 284-2607
Cost: $24.95

Demystifies the 20 major economic indicators and explains why markets react so strongly to them. Discusses how to interpret the Consumer Price Index, The Purchasing Manager's Report, Housing Starts and Permits, and more.

AUDIENCE: Individual, Professional	RISK LEVEL: All
TOPICS: All	

Economics of Futures Trading for Commercial and Personal Profit

Thomas A. Hieronymous
Commodity Research Bureau
75 Wall Street
22nd Floor
New York, NY 10005

PH: (800) 446-4519
ISBN: 0-910418-03-9
Published: 1977
Cost: $17.95

A 'how-to' book designed for those in the commodity trades, investors in futures contracts, and students of both. Combines a review of the economics behind the markets with an explanation of the techniques involved in using them. Appraises the performance of the system and presents some startling recommendations for reform.

AUDIENCE: Professional	RISK LEVEL: Aggressive
TOPICS: Options, Futures/Commodities	

Elements for Successful Trading, The

Robert Rotella
New York Institute of
  Finance/Prentice Hall
113 Sylvan Avenue
Route 9W
Englewood Cliffs, NJ 07632

PH: (800) 947-7700
FAX: (515) 284-2607
Cost: $29.95

Charts the way to creating a trading strategy. guides readers on how to combine money-management analysis techniques, established trading techniques (e.g., fundamental, technical, options-based), and the realities of the trading floor (versus trading on paper).

AUDIENCE: Professional	RISK LEVEL: Aggressive
TOPICS:Stocks, Options, Futures/Commodities	

Elliot Wave Educational Video Series, The

Robert Prechter, Jr.
Elliott Wave International
P.O. Box 1618
Gainesville, GA 30503

PH: (800) 336-1618
(404) 536-0309
Published: 1987
Cost: $1,499.00
VIDEO SERIES

Uses charts; addresses subjcts such as Elliott Wave Principle. Set of 10 tapes providing professional instruction on Elliott Wave analysis complete with a set of workbooks containing all of the charts and graphics used during the actual presentation. Comments: taped from a 1987 educational seminar.

AUDIENCE: Individual, Professional   RISK LEVEL: Moderate, Aggressive
TOPICS: Stocks, Options, Futures/Commodities

Elliott Wave Principle, Expanded Edition

Frost and Prechter
New Classics Library
Probus Publishing Co.
1925 North Clybourn Avenue
Chicago, IL 60614

PH: (800) PROBUS-1
FAX: (312) 868-6250
ISBN: 0-932750-17-6
Published: 1991
Cost: $27.50

Learn to apply the principles of Elliott Wave analysis to stocks, bonds and commodities and improve investment returns. The authors cover terminology, rules and guidelines, alternation, correct counting, bear market limitations, charting the waves, wave personality, historical and mathematical background, the Fibonacci Sequence, the Coldel Rectangle, the Golden Spiral, ratio and technical analysis, time sequence, long-term waves, the Grand Supercycle, the Supercycle, Dow Theory

AUDIENCE: Individual, Professional   RISK LEVEL: Aggressive
TOPICS: Stocks, Options, Futures/Commodities

Encyclopedia of Stock Market Strategies

Edited by Investors Intelligence
  Staff
Chartcraft, Inc.
1 West Avenue
Larchmont, NY 10538

PH: (914) 632-0422
Published: 1985
Cost: $60.00 supplements $12.50

Covers investing theories. Newly revised edition of the famous original Encyclopedia, now issued in a 3-ring binder which will be supplemented regularly. The investor, trader or technician now has access to the methods, theories, and thoughts of the world's most noted financial writers; all conceivable investment techniques are covered, in many cases by the originators, with purpose explained and method described.

AUDIENCE: Beginning, Individual, Professional   RISK LEVEL: Moderate, Aggressive
TOPICS: Mutual Funds, Stocks

Encyclopedia of Technical Market Indicators, The

Robert W. Colby and Thomas A.
  Meyers
Irwin Professional Publishing
1333 Burr Ridge Parkway
Burr Ridge, IL 60521

PH: (708) 789-5489
(800) 634-3966
FAX: (708) 789-6933
ISBN: 1-55623-049-4
Published: 1988
Cost: $65.00

Covers market and technical analysis. Separates the myth from reality and shows you the true forecasting value of over 110 indicators. Calculate and interpret scores of widely followed technical market indicators and maximize profit.

AUDIENCE: Individual, Professional   RISK LEVEL: Aggressive
TOPICS: Stocks, Options, Futures/Commodities

Ethical Investing

Amy L. Domini & Peter D. Kinder
Addison-Wesley Publishing Co.
1 Jacob Way
Reading, MA 01867

PH: (800) 447-2226
ISBN: 0-201-10803-8
Published: 1984
Cost: $17.95

How to invest for profit without sacrificing your principles. Traditional sources offer little help in screening companies' activities beyond the balance sheet. This is the first book to show you how you can improve the quality of your life as you improve the value of your portfolio. A practical, profitable, and ethical approach.

AUDIENCE: Beginning, Individual, Professional   RISK LEVEL: Moderate, Aggressive
TOPICS: Bonds, Mutual Funds, Stocks

Eurodollar Futures and Options: Controlling Money Market Risk

Burghardt, Belton, Lane, Luce and
  McVey
Probus Publishing Co.
1925 North Clybourn Avenue
Chicago, IL 60614

PH: (800) PROBUS-1
FAX: (312) 868-6250
ISBN: 1-55738-159-3
Published: 1991
Cost: $65.00

"Learn how to fold futures and options into a portfolio of conventional and derivative interest rate products. Ideal for portfolio managers, traders and bankers."

AUDIENCE: Professional   RISK LEVEL: Moderate, Aggressive
TOPICS: Bonds, Options, Futures/Commodities

European Companies- A Guide to Sources of Information

The Reference Press, Inc.
6448 Highway 290 E.
Suite E-104
Austin, TX 78723

PH: (512) 454-7778
FAX: (512) 454-9401
Cost: $89.95
Date of first issue: 1994
ISBN: 0-900246-44-8
Updated Annually

"An invaluable guide to information sources for European companies and for doing business in Europe." Covers 35 countries and over 1,500 entries.

AUDIENCE: Individual, Professional   RISK LEVEL: Moderate, Aggressive
TOPICS: Bonds, Stocks, General References

Everyone's Money Book

Dearborn Financial Publishing
520 N. Dearborn St.
Chicago, IL 60610

PH: (800) 621-9621
Costs: $24.95
Date of first issue: 1993

A basic book providing financial planning and money management information for all age groups. Covers stocks, bonds, real estate, collectibles and limited partnerships, selecting insurance, tax and general financial advice. A.F.P.

AUDIENCE: Beginning   RISK LEVEL: Moderate, Aggressive
TOPICS: All

Extraordinary Popular Delusions and the Madness of Crowds

Charles MacKay
Buccaneer Books
P.O. Box 168
Cutchogue, NY 11935

PH: (516) 734-5724
ISBN: 0-89966-516-0
Published: 1986
Cost: $36.95

A landmark study of crowd psychology and mass mania throughout history which includes accounts of classic scams such as the Mississippi Scheme, the South Sea Bubble, and Tulipmania. Also deals with fads and delusions such as Alchemy and the Philosopher's Stone, the Prophecies of Nostradamus, the Rosecrucians and astrology. Foreword by Bernard Baruch.

AUDIENCE: Beginning, Individual, Professional   RISK LEVEL: Moderate, Aggressive
TOPICS: Bonds, Stocks

Fibonacci Applications and Strategies for Traders

Robert Fischer
John Wiley & Sons, Inc.
605 Third Avenue
New York, NY 10158-0012

PH: (212) 850-6000
FAX: (212) 850-6088
Published: 1993
Technical Analysis
Cost: $39.95

A new look at the applications and principles of Fibonacci numbers and the Elliott Wave trading system. "Demonstrates how to calculate and predict key turning points in commodity markets, analyze business and economic cycles as well as identify profitable turning points in interest rate movements."

AUDIENCE: Professional   RISK LEVEL: Aggressive
TOPICS: Commodities

Fidelity Guide to Mutual Funds—A Complete Guide to Investing In Mutual Funds, The

Simon & Schuster
1230 Avenue of the Americas
New York, NY 10020

PH: (212) 698-7323
FAX: (212) 698-7035
Published: 1992
Cost: $14.95

"Finding the right type of fund to meet investment goals—from money markets to stocks and bonds, domestic or foreign, taxable and non-taxable—is clarified in this comprehensive guide for the average consumer."

AUDIENCE: Beginning   RISK LEVEL: Moderate, Aggressive
TOPICS: Mutual Funds

Filtered Waves Basic Theory: A Tool for Stock Market Analysis

Arthur A. Merrill
Analysis Press
3300 Darby Road #3325
Haverford, PA 19041

PH: (215) 642-2011
ISBN: 0-911894-36-5
Published: 1977
Cost: $15.00

A simple method of identifying and measuring market swings based on "filtered" analysis - ignoring all shifts below a specified percentage level. Examines every bull and bear market since 1898. Presents charts for the life expectancy of rallies and secondary reactions. Describes applications to individual stocks, and other uses.

AUDIENCE: Professional   RISK LEVEL: Aggressive
TOPICS: Stocks, Options, Futures/Commodities

Financial Analyst's Handbook: Portfolio Management

Sumner N. Levine, editor
Irwin Professional Publishing
1333 Burr Ridge Parkway
Burr Ridge, IL 60521

PH: (708) 789-5489
(800) 634-3966
FAX: (708) 789-6933
ISBN: 0-87094-919-5
Published: 1988 (2nd edition)
Cost: $85.00

Portfolio management and evaluation examined by 48 authorities. Includes sections on Liability and the Analyst, the SEC and Regulations, Investment Vehicles, Special Investment Vehicles, Analysis of Financial Reports, Economic Analysis and Timing, Mathematical Aids, Portfolio Management and Theories, and Information Sources.

AUDIENCE: Professional   RISK LEVEL: Moderate, Aggressive
TOPICS: Bonds, Stocks, Options, Futures/Commodities

Financial Derivatives

Robert W. Kolb
New York Institute of
  Finance/Prentice Hall
113 Sylvan Avenue
Route 9W
Englewood Cliffs, NJ 07632

PH: (800) 947-7700
FAX: (515) 284-2607
Published: 1993
Cost: $14.95

Clear and concise explanations of the developing arena of financial derivatives. Offers a broad overview of different types of derivatives, including futures, options, and swaps, and explores the use of derivatives as tools for risk management in the corporate setting.

AUDIENCE: Professional   RISK LEVEL: Aggressive
TOPICS: Bonds, Options, Futures/Commodities

Financial Engineering: A Guide to the Development and Use of Derivative Products

John R. Marshall and Vipul Bansal
New York Institute of
  Finance/Prentice Hall
113 Sylvan Avenue
Route 9W
Englewood Cliffs, NJ 07632

PH: (800) 947-7700
FAX: (515) 284-2607
Published: 1993
Cost: $14.95

A theoretical and practical framework for understanding financial engineering in detail. Examines the explosive growth of the field; its conceptual tools, products and strategies; and future directions.

AUDIENCE: Professional   RISK LEVEL: Moderate, Aggressive
TOPICS: Bonds, Stocks, Options, Futures/Commodities

Financial Futures Markets

Brendan Brown & Charles R. Geisst
St. Martin's Press, Inc.
175 Fifth Avenue
New York, NY 10010

PH: (800) 221-7945
(212) 674-5151
FAX: (212) 420-9314
ISBN: 0-312-28955-3
Published: 1983
Cost: $25.00

Details the financial futures trading, highlighting the key channels that link this new market and the conventional cash markets. Considers speculation, arbitrage, hedging, scalping, and brokering. Trades in currency, interest rate, and stock futures markets are described within the economics of financial futures trading.

AUDIENCE: Individual, Professional   RISK LEVEL: Aggressive
TOPICS: Options, Futures/Commodities

Financial Marketplace, The

S. Kerry Cooper & Donald R. Fraser
Addison-Wesley Publishing Co., Inc.
1 Jacob Way
Reading, MA 01867

PH: (800) 447-2226
ISBN: 0-201-10548-9
Published: 1986 (2nd edition)
Cost: $23.95

Covers the full range of financial markets and instruments, as well as the most important participants. Emphasizes major innovations, including the financial futures markets. Examines the structure and role of the Federal Reserve System and the goals and methods of monetary control. A balanced blend of description and analysis.

AUDIENCE: Beginning, Individual	RISK LEVEL: Moderate, Aggressive
TOPICS: All	

Financial Options - From Theory to Practice

Stephen Figlewski, William Silber
  and Marti Subrahmanyam
A Salomon Brothers Center Book
Irwin Professional Publishing
1333 Burr Ridge Parkway
Burr Ridge, IL 60521

PH: (708) 789-5489
(800) 634-3966
FAX: (708) 789-6933
ISBN: 1-55623-872-X
Published: 1991
Cost: $25.00

Covers investing theories and options. Focuses on the crucial relation between options theory and actual investing so that you can combine your knowledge of the two and make profitable trades. Explains option valuation theories clearly, concisely and with very little mathematics.

AUDIENCE: Professional	RISK LEVEL: Aggressive
TOPICS: Options, Futures/Commodities	

Finding Winners

International Publishing Corp.
625 N. Michigan Ave.
Suite 1920
Chicago, IL 60611

PH: (800) 488-4149
Cost: $22.95
Date of first issue: 1993

Shows how to find winners from depressed low priced stocks. Tells how to identify these issues based on technical and fundamental viewpoints. A.F.P.

AUDIENCE: Beginning, Individual	RISK LEVEL: Moderate, Aggressive
TOPICS: Stocks	

Finding Your Future

Warner Books
P.O. Box 690
New York, NY 10019

PH: (212) 522-7200
Cost: $10.99
Date of first issue: 1993

Discusses the basics of investing in mutual funds. Explains how and why to invest in particular types of funds geared toward different stages of an individual's life. Rates the 100 top performing funds.

AUDIENCE: Beginning, Individual	RISK LEVEL: Moderate, Aggressive
TOPICS: Mutual Funds	

Fixed Income: A Personal Seminar

New York Institute of
  Finance/Prentice Hall
113 Sylvan Avenue
Route 9W
Englewood Cliffs, NJ 07632

PH: (800) 947-7700
FAX: (515) 284-2607
Published: 1989
Cost: $21.95

This self-teaching guide describes product characteristics of all fixed-income instruments available, discusses the risk/reward of each, and relates the instrument to a particular investor profile.

AUDIENCE: Beginning, Individual   RISK LEVEL: Conservative, Moderate
TOPICS: Bonds

Fixed Income Almanac - 1993 Edition, The

Livingston G. Douglas
Probus Publishing Co.
1925 N. Clybourn Ave., Suite 401
Chicago, IL 60614

PH: (800) PROBUS-1
(312) 868-1100
FAX: (312) 868-6250
Cost: $75.00
Date of first issue: 1993
ISBN: 1-55738-429-0
Fundamental Analysis

Provides over 20 years of historical data, extensive use of charts, bond market volatility, new issue information on CMOs, treasury strips, and high yield corporates, bond upgrades/downgrades, and default rates, historical yield spreads and yield ratios, and Federal Reserve policy.

AUDIENCE: Beginning, Individual, Professional   RISK LEVEL: Conservative, Moderate
TOPICS: Bonds

Fixed Income Analytics

Ravi E. Dattatreya, Editor
Probus Publishing Co.
1925 North Clybourn Avenue
Chicago, IL 60614

PH: (800) PROBUS-1
FAX: (312) 868-6250
ISBN: 1-55738-163-1
Published: 1991
Cost: $69.95

"Fixed Income Analytics" brings a much-needed order to the process of fixed income investment management, beginning with a detailed description of parametric analysis of securities and a discussion of various other advanced valuation technologies, such as yield surface and option adjusted spread analysis. In addition, it shows practitioners the various hedging, arbitrage and portfolio management implications of all new methods of fixed income valuation.

AUDIENCE: Individual, Professional   RISK LEVEL: Conservative, Moderate
TOPICS: Bonds

Fixed Income Arbitrage

M. Anthony Wong & Robert High
John Wiley & Sons, Inc.
605 Third Avenue
New York, NY 10158

PH: (212) 850-6000
FAX: (212) 850-6088
Cost: $55
Technical and Fundamental Analysis
Date of first issue: 1993

"An exposition to the world of relative - value trading in the fixed-income markets written by a leading-edge thinker and scientific analyst of global financial markets. Using concrete examples, he details profit opportunities-treasury bills, bonds, notes, interest-rate futures and options-explaining how to obtain virtually risk-free rewards if the proper knowledge and skills are applied."

AUDIENCE: Professional   RISK LEVEL: Conservative, Moderate
TOPICS: Bonds

Fixed Income Mathematics, 2nd Edition

Frank J. Fabozzi
Probus Publishing Co.
1925 North Clybourn Avenue
Chicago, IL 60614

PH: (800) PROBUS-1
FAX: (312) 868-6250
Published: 1993
Cost: $42.50

Subjects addressed: bond analysis. A complete guide to understanding the mathematical concepts and tools used to evaluate fixed income securities and portfolio strategies. Topics include: the time value of money, bond pricing and return analysis, bond price volatility, applications to bonds with embedded call options. Second edition, revised.

AUDIENCE: Beginning, Individual, Professional   RISK LEVEL: Conservative
TOPICS: Bonds

Fixed Income Synthetic Assets

Perry Beaumont
John Wiley & Sons, Inc.
605 Third Avenue
New York, NY 10158-0012

PH: (212) 850-6000
FAX: (212) 850-6088
Published: 1992
Technical and Fundamental Analysis
Cost: $49.95

Techniques for packaging, pricing and managing CMOS, zero coupon bonds, strips, floating rate notes, mortgage backed securities, T-bills and more.

AUDIENCE: Professional   RISK LEVEL: Conservative, Moderate
TOPICS: Bonds

Flexible Choice: Hedging with CBOT Agricultural Options, The

Chicago Board of Trade
141 W. Jackson Blvd.
Suite 2210
Chicago, IL 60604-2994

PH: (312) 435-3500
Published: 1990
Cost: $3.00

Covers commodities trading. Written for anyone wanting to establish prior to delivery, a selling or buying price for a cash commodity. Ten hedging strategies are described in the 58 page text and each one highlights its market objective, potential outcome, margin requirements, risks and advantages, disadvantages of using a particular strategy. Also included is a glossary of common futures and options terms. A.F.P.

AUDIENCE: Professional   RISK LEVEL: Aggressive
TOPICS: Options, Futures/Commodities

Flexible Choice: Trading with CBOT Agricultural Options, The

Chicago Board of Trade
141 W. Jackson Blvd.
Suite 2210
Chicago, IL 60604-2994

PH: (312) 435-3500
Published: 1990
Cost: $3.00

Covers commodities trading. A 60-page text featuring 12 speculative strategies using CBOT agricultural contracts. Each one highlights its market objective, profit potential, margin requirements and risk. Also includes a glossary of common futures and options terms. A.F.P.

AUDIENCE: Professional   RISK LEVEL: Aggressive
TOPICS: Options, Futures/Commodities

Foreign Bonds - An Autopsy: A Study of Defaults and Repudiations of Government Obligations

Max Winkler
Ayer Company Publishers
P.O. Box 958
Salem, NH 03079

PH: (603) 898-1200
ISBN: 0-405-09308-X
Published: 1933 (1976 reprint)
Cost: $25.50

Classic historical analysis, all the more meaningful in light of today's international financial uncertainty. Retraces the origins of the United States as bankers to the world up to the Depression era. Places modern events in perspective by reviewing default throughout recorded history, from ancient times to the 20th century.

AUDIENCE: Individual, Professional   RISK LEVEL: Moderate, Aggressive
TOPICS: Bonds

Foreign Exchange and Money Markets Guide, The

Julian Walmsley
John Wiley & Sons, Inc.
605 Third Avenue
New York, NY 10158

PH: (212) 850-6000
FAX: (212) 850-6088
Cost: $105.00
Date of first issue: 1992

"Investing in the vital foreign exchange and money markets is introduced. Offers a working understanding of the markets and their respective systems. Describes all aspects of trading calculations including spot calculations, forwards, short dates adjustments and artificial currency option markets to 'third generation' hedge products."

AUDIENCE: Professional   RISK LEVEL: Moderate, Aggressive
TOPICS: Bonds, Options, Futures/Commodities

Foreign Exchange Dealer's Handbook

Raymond G. F. Coninx
Irwin Professional Publishing
1333 Burr Ridge Parkway
Burr Ridge, IL 60521

PH: (708) 789-5489
(800) 634-3966
FAX: (708) 789-6933
ISBN: 1-55623-626-3
Published: 1991, 3rd edition
Cost: $80.00

This third edition takes into account a volatile economic climate and new financial products used in analyzing the many transactions that can now be handled by computer. Coninx gives readers a wide variety of formulas and equations to help avoid the pitfalls of modern trading. Topics include exchange, spot, and forward rates, as well as interest arbitrage, swap transactions, and the calculation of compound interest; step-by-step instructions and detailed examples that show readers how to use valuable formulas and equations.

AUDIENCE: Professional   RISK LEVEL: Conservative, Moderate, Aggressive
TOPICS: Bonds, Options, Futures/Commodities

Foreign Exchange Handbook, The

Julian Walmsley
Wiley-Interscience
1 Wiley Drive
Somerset, NJ 08873

PH: (201) 469-4400
ISBN: 0-471-86388-2
Published: 1983
Cost: $75.00

Designed to help professional traders who are in the international markets. The first edition is on the background of the markets, the second sets out the calculations involved, and the third ties in financial futures and gold markets, payment systems, and exposure measurement and control.

AUDIENCE: Professional   RISK LEVEL: Aggressive
TOPICS: Bonds, Options, Futures/Commodities

Foreign Exchange & Money Markets: Managing Foreign and Domestic Currency Operations

Heinz Riehl & Rita M. Rodriguez
McGraw-Hill Publishing Company
1221 Avenue of the Americas
New York, NY 10020

PH: (800) 262-4729
ISBN: 0-07-052671-0
Published: 1983
Cost: $50.00

Everything you need to know about how the foreign exchange and money markets function in order to successfully manage operations. Includes step-by-step explanations of the basic mechanics and inter relationships, practical business applications, controlling the risks involved, and accounting systems to measure profitability. A.F.P.

AUDIENCE: Professional   RISK LEVEL: Conservative, Moderate, Aggressive
TOPICS: Bonds, Options, Futures/Commodities

Fortune: The Guide To Investing In the 90's

Simon & Schuster
1230 Avenue of the Americas
New York, NY 10020

PH: (800) 223-2348
FAX: (212) 698-7035
Published: 1990
Cost: $14.00

"Answering the most commonly asked questions about the world of investing, this full color, lavishly illustrated handbook will save readers time, money, and frustration as it delineates how to maximize personal investments."

AUDIENCE: Beginning, Individual   RISK LEVEL: Moderate, Aggressive
TOPICS: Bonds, Mutual Funds, Stocks

Fractal Market Analysis

Edgar E. Peters
John Wiley & Sons, Inc.
605 Third Avenue
New York, NY 10158-0012

PH: (212) 850-6000
FAX: (212) 850-6088
Date of first issue: 1994
Technical Analysis
Cost: $49.95

"Peters describes complex concepts in an easy-to-follow manner for the non-mathematician. He uses fractals, rescaled range analysis and nonlinear dynamical models to explain behavior and understand price movements."

AUDIENCE: Professional   RISK LEVEL: Moderate, Aggressive
TOPICS: Stocks, Options, Futures/Commodities

Frank Capiello's New Guide to Finding the Next Superstock

Frank Capiello
McGraw Hill, Inc.
11 West 19th Street
New York, NY 10011

PH: (800) 722-4726
(212) 512-4100
Published: 1990
Cost: $12.60

"Reveals Capiello's method for selecting stocks poised for dramatic price increases - the Xeroxs and IBMs of tomorrow." It also shows you how to rate stocks to discover superstocks before other investors and covers lessons learned in the crash of 1987.

AUDIENCE: Beginning, Individual   RISK LEVEL: Moderate, Aggressive
TOPICS: Stocks

French Company Handbook 1994

The Reference Press, Inc.
6448 Highway 290 E.
Suite E-104
Austin, TX 78723
PH: (512) 454-7778
FAX: (512) 454-9401
Cost: $49.95
Date of first issue: 1994
ISBN: 1-878753-34-7
Fundamental Analysis

A reference book profiling major French companies. Includes operations and company history overview, address and phone number, number of employees, names and titles of top management, dates by product line and geographic area, international activities, exports, and much more. Also provides a wealth of information on the French economy.

AUDIENCE: Individual, Professional   RISK LEVEL: Moderate, Aggressive
TOPICS: Bonds, Stocks, General Reference

Fundamentals of Investments, The

Gordon J. Alexander and William F.
   Sharpe
Prentice Hall
113 Sylvan Avenue
Route 9W
Englewood Cliffs, NJ 07632

PH: (800) 223-1360
Published: 1993 (2nd edition)
Cost: $61.33

Covers investing theories, stock analysis, market analysis, bond analysis, earnings analysis, commodities trading, fundamental analysis, technical analysis, options. Minimal use of charts. Textbook covering the workings of the market, portfolio selection theories, common stock and fixed-income section, taxation and inflation effects on investments.

AUDIENCE: Beginning, Individual   RISK LEVEL: Moderate, Aggressive
TOPICS: Bonds, Mutual Funds, Stocks

Fundamentals of Municipal Bonds

Public Securities Association
40 Broad Street
12th Floor
New York, NY 10004-2373

PH: (212) 440-9430
ISBN: 0-9605198-2-3
Published: 1990 (4th edition)
Cost: $29.95

Covers every aspect of the municipal bond securities market - investor objectives and strategies; the roles of issuers, dealers, and bond brokers; much more. Valuable tables, charts, graphs, and analytical mathematical computations make this reference work for every investor. Revised edition deals comprehensively with recent developments.

AUDIENCE: Beginning, Individual   RISK LEVEL: Conservative
TOPICS: Bonds, General Reference

Futures: A Personal Seminar

New York Institute of
   Finance/Prentice Hall
113 Sylvan Avenue
Route 9W
Englewood Cliffs, NJ 07632

PH: (800) 947-7700
FAX: (515) 284-2607
Published: 1989
Cost: $21.95

This self-teaching guide for novices explains the futures markets. Spells out realistic operating information such as the mechanisms of trading, different types of orders, deliveries, and the role played by the clearing houses; covers market analysis, hedging strategies, and trading techniques.

AUDIENCE: Beginning, Individual   RISK LEVEL: Aggressive
TOPICS: Futures/Commodities

Futures Game, The: Who Wins? Who Loses? Why?

Richard J. Teweles & Frank J. Jones
McGraw-Hill Publishing Company
1221 Avenue of the Americas
New York, NY 10020

PH: (800) 262-4729
ISBN: 0-07-063734-2
Published: 1990, Second Edition
Cost: $26.95

Second edition of the best-selling "The Commodity Futures Game" is an updated reference to the entire field of futures and options trading. New sections on the latest proven techniques for trading in financial futures, as well as the history, mechanics, and use of futures options. Practical features of the original remain intact.

AUDIENCE: Beginning, Individual   RISK LEVEL: Aggressive
TOPICS: Options, Futures/Commodities

Futures Techniques & Technical Analysis

Commodity Trend Service
P.O. Box 32309
Palm Beach Gardens, FL 33420

PH: (800) 331-1069
(407) 694-0960
FAX: (407) 622-7623
VIDEO
Cost: Contact Publisher
Published: 1991

Covers commodities trading, technical analysis. A 2 hour video of Nick Van Nice revealing the latest tricks to profiting in commodities... how to spot "get rich quick" trades using stochastics, RSI, and ADX to spot price trends early and much more.

AUDIENCE: Beginning   RISK LEVEL: Aggressive
TOPICS: Futures/Commodities

Genetic Algorithms and Investment Strategies

Richard J. Bauer
John Wiley & Sons, Inc.
605 Third Avenue
New York, NY 10158-0012

PH: (212) 850-6000
FAX: (212) 850-6088
Published: 1994
Technical Analysis
Cost: $55.00

"Supplies a range of market timing and investment strategies for speculators, hedgers, futures, options, stock and bond traders interested in switching in and out of various asset classes."

AUDIENCE: Individual, Professional   RISK LEVEL: Aggressive
TOPICS: Bonds, Stocks, Options, Futures

Getting Started in Bonds

Michael C. Thomsett
John Wiley & Sons, Inc.
605 Third Avenue
New York, NY 10158-0012

PH: (212) 850-6418 orders
(212) 850-6233 info
FAX: (212) 850-6088
Published: 1991
Cost: $32.50

Covers bond analysis. Complete nontechnical guide to investing at all levels in corporate, federal, and municipal bonds.

AUDIENCE: Beginning   RISK LEVEL: Conservative
TOPICS: Bonds

Getting Started in Futures

Todd Lofton
John Wiley & Sons, Inc.
605 Third Avenue
New York, NY 10158-0012

PH: (212) 850-6418 orders
(212) 850-6233 info
FAX: (212) 850-6088
ISBN: 0-471-61492-0
Published: 1989
Cost: $34.95

Covers commodities/futures, options. How to make money in futures and options. This nontechnical guide shows you how to play the futures markets in commodities, foreign currency, and interest rates, and how to handle options. He explains how to understand the prices in the newspaper and he covers buying and selling "long" and "short," what to expect from your broker, commissions, hedging, trading systems, "technical" tools, and basic trading strategies.

AUDIENCE: Beginning, Individual   RISK LEVEL: Aggressive
TOPICS: Options, Futures/Commodities

Getting Started in Mutual Funds

Alan Lavine
John Wiley & Sons, Inc.
605 Third Avenue
New York, NY 10158-0012

PH: (212) 850-6000
FAX: (212) 850-6088
Published: 1994
Cost: $14.95

Tips for investing wisely for diversification and long-term capital gain. Contents include: What is a Mutual Fund; How to Read a Mutual Fund Prospectus from A to Z; Aggressive Growth and Small Company Stock Funds; Growth Stock Funds; Growth and Income Funds; Managing your Mutual Fund Portfolio, and much more.

AUDIENCE: Beginning   RISK LEVEL: Moderate, Aggressive
TOPICS: Mutual Funds

Getting Started in Options

Michael C. Thomsett
John Wiley & Sons, Inc.
605 Third Avenue
New York, NY 10158

PH: (212) 850-6000
FAX: (212) 850-6088
Cost: $16.95
Date of first issue: 1993

"Using clear, nontechnical language, it explains all the terms and phrases along with strategies, concepts and methods of option investing. Includes 40 graphs and charts, sidebar information, a working glossary plus new and revised case study examples."

AUDIENCE: Individual, Professional   RISK LEVEL: Aggressive
TOPICS: Options

Getting Started in Stocks

Alvin D. Hall
John Wiley & Sons, Inc.
605 Third Avenue
New York, NY 10158-0012

PH: (212) 850-6000
FAX: (212) 850-6088
Published: 1992
Technical and Fundamental Analysis
Cost: $16.95

A concise guide for understanding and investing in stocks. Chapters include: Setting Your Goals; Assessing Risks and Rewards; Common Stock and Preferred Stock; The Basics of Buying and Selling Stocks; Investment Strategies; Fundamental Analysis; Technical Analysis; Warrants; Options and more.

AUDIENCE: Beginning, Individual   RISK LEVEL: Moderate, Aggressive
TOPICS: Stocks, Options

Global Bond Markets

Jess Lederman and Keith K. H. Park
Probus Publishing Co.
1925 North Clybourn Avenue
Chicago, IL 60614

PH: (800) PROBUS-1
FAX: (312) 868-6250
ISBN: 1-55738-153-4
Published: 1991
Cost: $75.00

Provides comprehensive coverage of the world bond markets and related debt instruments. Among the many topics covered are: measuring the risk of foreign corporate and sovereign bonds; measuring global bond portfolio performance; high yield bond investment strategies; hedging global bond portfolios and currency risk; and operational considerations, including clearance and settlement difficulties, the role of the custodian and transactions costs.

AUDIENCE: Individual, Professional   RISK LEVEL: Conservative, Moderate, Aggressive
TOPICS: Bonds

Global Equity Markets

Jess Lederman and Keith K. H. Park
Probus Publishing Co.
1925 North Clybourn Avenue
Chicago, IL 60614

PH: (800) PROBUS-1
FAX: (312) 868-6250
ISBN: 1-55738-152-6
Published: 1991
Cost: $75.00

This book is a thorough examination of the world's equity markets - from New York and London to Paris and Tokyo. Among the many topics covered are: new product innovations and developments in stock markets around the globe, risk reduction through global diversification, the international crash of 1987, corporate accounting practices for different countries, tactical asset allocation, comparison of international indices, hedging global equity portfolios and currency risks.

AUDIENCE: Individual, Professional   RISK LEVEL: Moderate, Aggressive
TOPICS: Stocks

Global Investing

Ibbotson Associates
225 N. Michigan Ave.
Suite 700
Chicago, IL 60601-7676

PH: (312) 616-1620
FAX: (312) 616-0404
Cost: $40
Date of first issue: 1993

Provides data and analysis on today's important U.S. and international investment opportunities. Covering more than 40 countries, it is an invaluable single resource for return data on all major asset categories. Numerous graphs, charts and tables permit a quick comparison of investment choices.

AUDIENCE: Beginning, Individual   RISK LEVEL: Moderate, Aggressive
TOPICS: Bonds, Stocks, Asset Allocation

Global Investing: The Professional's Guide to the World Capital Markets

Ibbotson and Brenson
McGraw Hill, Inc.
11 West 19th Street
New York, NY 10011

PH: (800) 722-4726
(212) 512-4100
Published: 1991
Cost: $39.95

Uses charts. "Sound financial advice on building and maintaining diversified portfolios, based on field-tested economic analysis and historical evidence of capital markets throughout the world - including the boom of 1986-87 and the subsequent crash, as well as recent developments in Europe and on the Pacific Rim." "Incisive, intelligent, and packed with charts, tables and graphs." It shows the reader where money has been made in stocks, bonds, cash, gold and silver, options, futures. A.F.P.

AUDIENCE: Professional   RISK LEVEL: Moderate, Aggressive
TOPICS: Bonds, Stocks, Options, Futures/Commodities

Good Money: A Guide to Profitable Social Investing in the 90's

Ritchie P. Lowry
W. W. Norton & Company, Inc.
500 Fifth Avenue
New York, NY 10110

PH: (800) 223-2584
Published: 1991
Cost: $19.95

Covers investing theories. Is a how-to guide for both individual and institutional investors who want to do good socially while also doing well financially. Shows how socially screened investments can outperform those made only for profit. Illustrates how to match and balance financial goals with social preferences when making investment decisions.

AUDIENCE: Beginning, Individual, Professional   RISK LEVEL: Moderate, Aggressive
TOPICS: Bonds, Mutual Funds, Stocks

Good Money's Social Funds Guide

Ritchie P. Lowry
Good Money Publications
P.O. Box 363
Worcester, VT 05682

PH: (800) 535-3551
(802) 223-3911
FAX: (802) 223-8949
Published annually since 1986
Cost: $29.95

Covers mutual funds analysis. A guide to social and environmental mutual funds. The guide includes descriptions and analyses of the social screens, investor costs and financial performance of socially-screened equity, bond, and money market mutual funds.

AUDIENCE: Beginning, Individual   RISK LEVEL: Moderate, Aggressive
TOPICS: Mutual Funds

Graham & Dodd's Security Analysis

Sidney Cottle, Roger Murray, &
  Frank Block
McGraw-Hill Publishing Company
1221 Avenue of the Americas
New York, NY 10020

ISBN: 0-471-61844-6
PH: (800) 2-MCGRAW
(212) 512-2000
Published: 1962, 1988 (5th edition)
Cost: $59.95

Covers bond analysis, stock analysis, earnings analysis. Provides the principles and techniques to measure asset values and cash flows so that you can sharpen judgments of company earnings, refresh your insight into what individual companies are worth, and evaluate how much debt a leveraged company can service.

AUDIENCE: Beginning, Individual, Professional   RISK LEVEL: Moderate, Aggressive
TOPICS: Bonds, Stocks

Great Cycle, The

Richard Stoken
Probus Publishing Co.
1925 N. Clybourn Ave.
Suite 401
Chicago, IL 60614

PH: (800) PROBUS-1
(312) 868-1100
FAX: (312) 868-6250
Cost: $27.50
Date of first issue:1993
Technical Analysis

"Explains the link between mass psychology and economic performance and shows investors how to profit from swings between optimism and pessimism in the economy and in the financial markets."

AUDIENCE: Individual, Professional   RISK LEVEL: Moderate, Aggressive
TOPICS: Commodities

Guide to Managing Interest-Rate Risk

Donald M. Howe
New York Institute of
  Finance/Prentice Hall
113 Sylvan Avenue
Route 9W
Englewood Cliffs, NJ 07632

PH: (800) 947-7700
FAX: (515) 284-2607
Published: 1991
Cost: $29.95

Presents an integrated overview of interest-rate risk managerial tolls. Covers swaps, floors, caps, and futures. Comparative approach offers a thorough guide for setting up a customized hedge-management program.

AUDIENCE: Professional   RISK LEVEL: Conservative, Moderate
TOPICS: Bonds, Options, Futures/Commodities

Guide to Money Market and Bond Investment Strategies, A

Dr. Carroll D. Aby, Jr.
Chartcraft, Inc.
1 West Avenue
Larchmont, NY 10538

PH: (914) 834-5181
Published: 1989
Cost: $19.95

Covers bond investment, portfolio management, fixed income investments; uses charts. This book aims to acquaint the reader with up-to-date ideas and techniques that will promote financial survival in the current difficult climate. Chapter titles include: Money Market Strategy; Fundamentals of Bond Investment; Taxable Fixed Income Securities; Tax Exempt Bonds; Portfolio Management. Many charts and tables are included to ease comparisons between differing types of fixed income investments and to calculate real returns.

AUDIENCE: Beginning, Individual, Professional   RISK LEVEL: Conservative, Moderate
TOPICS: Bonds

Guide to World Commodity Markets: Physical, Futures, and Options Trading

John Buckley, Editor
Beekman Publishers, Inc.
P.O. Box 888
Woodstock, NY 12498

PH: (914) 679-2300
ISBN: 1-85091-116-9
Published: 1986, 5th edition
Cost: $70.00
ISBN: 0-8464-1361-2
Published: 1989, 6th edition
Cost: $144.00

Sixth edition of this highly acclaimed guide has been thoroughly revised and updated. Provides a detailed survey of the physical and futures markets, and includes more comprehensive exchange details and additional trading members lists. Full information on 18 different commodity markets, in 21 countries and over 60 exchanges.

AUDIENCE: Individual, Professional   RISK LEVEL: Aggressive
TOPICS: Options, Futures/Commodities

Handbook for No-Load Fund Investors, 13th Edition, The

Sheldon Jacobs
The No-Load Fund Investors, Inc.
P.O. Box 318
Irvington-on-Hudson, NY 10533

PH: (914) 693-7420
Cost: $49.00
Published: 1994

This handbook reports on 1,011 no-load mutual funds, 381 low-load funds, and 312 closed end funds. The first section of the book details strategies for investing in no-load mutual funds. The second section contains statistics on each fund, ranking them by objective for the latest one, five and 10 years. Data are included on distributions, yield, net asset value, total assets, beta, management fees and expense ratio. The final section provides contact information for the funds and descriptions of fund objectives and policies. An alphabetical listing of portfolio managers with the funds they manage is also given.

AUDIENCE: Beginning, Individual   RISK LEVEL: Moderate
TOPICS: Mutual Funds,

Handbook for No-Load Fund Investors, The

Sheldon Jacobs, Editor
Irwin Professional Publishing
1333 Burr Ridge Parkway
Burr Ridge, IL 60521

PH: (708) 789-5489
(800) 634-3966
FAX: (708) 789-6933
ISBN: 1-55623-528-3
Published: 1994, 14th edition
Cost: $40.00

A complete text on mutual fund investing, performance data going back 10 years, and a complete directory of toll-free numbers.

AUDIENCE: Beginning, Individual, Professional RISK LEVEL: Conservative, Moderate,
TOPICS: All   Aggressive

Handbook for Professional Futures and Options Traders, A

Joseph D. Koziol
John Wiley & Sons, Inc.
605 Third Avenue
New York, NY 10158-0012

PH: (212) 634-3966
FAX: (212) 850-6088
ISBN: 0-471-87423-X
Published: 1987
Cost: $60.00

Compares trading and hedging techniques for the quantitative edge you need to succeed. Shows how to measure the risks as rewards in virtually every situation. Reviews the myriad forms of analysis - including technical, chart, fundamental, seasonal, cyclical, and spread. Also covers arbitrage, hedging, and foreign exchange.

AUDIENCE: Individual, Professional   RISK LEVEL: Aggressive
TOPICS: Options, Futures/Commodities

Handbook of Asset-Backed Securities, The

Jess Lederman
New York Institute of
   Finance/Prentice Hall
113 Sylvan Avenue
Route 9W
Englewood Cliffs, NJ 07632

PH: (800) 947-7700
FAX: (515) 284-2607
Published: 1990
Cost: $64.95

Brings together the best information on the mechanics and economics of asset-backed securities. Employs the know-how of 25 experts from such top firms as Standard & Poor's and Chemical Bank.

AUDIENCE: Professional   RISK LEVEL: Conservative, Moderate, Aggressive
TOPICS: Bonds

Handbook of Commodity Cycles: A Window on Time, The

Jacob Bernstein
John Wiley & Sons, Inc.
605 Third Avenue
New York, NY 10158-0012

PH: (212) 634-3966
FAX: (212) 850-6088
ISBN: 0-471-08197-3
Published: 1982
Cost: $95.00

Top commodity advisor shows how to use the fundamental but often overlooked principles of cyclic analysis for profitable short and long term trading. Examines the proven repetitive price patterns that can help lower investment risks. Discusses the history, current status, and probable future direction of market cycles.

AUDIENCE: Individual, Professional   RISK LEVEL: Aggressive
TOPICS: Options, Futures/Commodities

Handbook of Currency and Interest Rate Risk Management, The

Robert J. Schwartz and
   Clifford W. Smith
New York Institute of
   Finance/Prentice Hall
113 Sylvan Avenue
Route 9W
Englewood Cliffs, NJ 07632

PH: (800) 947-7700
FAX: (515) 284-2607
Published: 1990
Cost: $65.00

Here 54 of the most respected members of the global financial community show how to apply risk management techniques to prevent or stop loss when currency-exchange and interest rates gyrate. Includes coverage of all major currencies.

AUDIENCE: Professional   RISK LEVEL: Moderate
TOPICS: Bonds, Options, Futures/Commodities

Handbook of Derivative Instruments, The

Atsuo Konishi and Ravi E.
   Dattatreya
Probus Publishing Co.
1925 North Clybourn Avenue
Chicago, IL 60614

PH: (800) PROBUS-1
FAX: (312) 868-6250
ISBN: 1-55738-154-2
Published: 1991
Cost: $69.95

Professionals show how to model and effectively use futures and options to hedge, both interest rates and equities. They also cover the neglected areas of hybrid derivatives, such as convertible bonds, warrants and American Trust Primes and Scores. Also shown is how derivative instruments can be applied to a wide range of real-life hedging and arbitrage situations.

AUDIENCE: Professional   RISK LEVEL: Aggressive
TOPICS: Bonds, Stocks, Options, Futures/Commodities

Handbook of Economic Cycles, The: Jake Bernstein's Comprehensive Guide to Repetitive Price Patterns in Stocks, Futures and Financials

Jacob Bernstein
Irwin Professional Publishing
1333 Burr Ridge Parkway
Burr Ridge, IL 60521

PH: (800) 634-3966
FAX: (708) 789-6933
ISBN: 1-55623-294-2
Published: 1991
Cost: $75.00

Covers commodities trading, stock analysis, trading analysis, currencies interest rates. Uses charts extensively. "Everything you need to use cyclical and seasonal analysis to improve your investment decision-making and results." "Jake Bernstein's comprehensive Guide to Repetitive Price Patterns in Stocks, Futures and Financials."

AUDIENCE: Individual, Professional   RISK LEVEL: Moderate, Aggressive
TOPICS: Bonds, Mutual Funds, Stocks, Options, Futures/Commodities

Handbook of Financial Futures, The: A Guide for Investors and Professional Money Managers

Nancy Rothstein and James Little
McGraw-Hill Publishing Company
1221 Avenue of the Americas
New York, NY 10020

PH: (800) 2-MCGRAW
(212) 512-2000
Published: 1984
Cost: $74.95

Covers commodities trading; uses charts. Designed to explain and illustrate important concepts and methods for the use and analysis of financial futures for hedging and trading purposes.

AUDIENCE: Individual, Professional   RISK LEVEL: Aggressive
TOPICS: Options, Futures/Commodities

Handbook of Financial Market Indexes, Averages and Indicators

Howard M. Berlin
Irwin Professional Publishing
1333 Burr Ridge Parkway
Burr Ridge, IL 60521

PH: (800) 634-3966
FAX: (708) 789-6933
ISBN: 1-55623-125-3
Published: 1990
Cost: $75.00

Covers market analysis. Understand the complex components that make up leading economic barometer and forecast market moves more accurately. Berlin shows you how over 200 major financial market averages and indexes in over 24 countries are constructed. A.F.P.

AUDIENCE: Beginning, Individual, Professional   RISK LEVEL: Moderate, Aggressive
TOPICS: Stocks

Handbook of Financial Markets: Securities, Options & Futures

Frank Fabozzi and Frank G. Zarb
Irwin Professional Publishing
1333 Burr Ridge Parkway
Burr Ridge, IL 60521

PH: (708) 789-5489
(800) 634-3966
FAX: (708) 789-6933
ISBN: 0-87094-600-5
Published: 1981, 1985 (updated)
Cost: $75.00

Covers market analysis. Provides broad knowledge of these 3 financial markets for the experienced and novice investor. Discusses the available instruments in each investment field, the particular risks associated with each trend and the economic and market environments in which trades take place.

AUDIENCE: Beginning, Individual, Professional   RISK LEVEL: Conservative, Moderate,
TOPICS: General Reference   Aggressive

Handbook of Fixed Income Securities, The

Frank J. Fabozzi
Irwin Professional Publishing
1333 Burr Ridge Parkway
Burr Ridge, IL 60521

PH: (800) 634-3966
FAX: (708) 789-6933
ISBN: 1-55623-308-6
Published: 1983, 1991 (3rd edition)
Cost: $85.00

Covers all instruments in the fixed income markets, techniques for evaluating them and portfolio strategies employing them. Fifty leading experts show how to take advantage of new opportunities in the market. Clear cut explanations of complicated bond mathematics.

AUDIENCE: Beginning, Individual, Professional   RISK LEVEL: Conservative
TOPICS: Bonds

Handbook of Municipal Bonds and Public Finance, The

Stephen Boyden Lamb, James
  Leigland, and Stephen P. Rapport
New York Institute of
  Finance/Prentice Hall
113 Sylvan Avenue
Route 9W
Englewood Cliffs, NJ 07632

PH: (800) 947-7700
FAX: (515) 284-2607
Published: 1993
Cost: $64.95

Brings together the top minds in the field on such topics as municipal markets, credit analysis, municipal market techniques, and contemporary public finance issues.

AUDIENCE: Individual, Professional   RISK LEVEL: Conservative
TOPICS: Bonds

Handbook of U.S. Government and Federal Agency Securities and Related Money Market Instruments

First Boston Corporation
Probus Publishing Co.
1925 North Clybourn Avenue
Chicago, IL 60614

PH: (800) PROBUS-1
FAX: (312) 868-6250
ISBN: 1-55738-168-2
Published: 1990
Cost: $32.50

Uses charts. Published biannually since 1922. Contains comprehensive and detailed factual information on the activities, instruments and institutions of the U.S. government securities markets. Covers marketable and nonmarketable securities of the government-sponsored enterprises, such as Freddie Mac; federal agencies, including HUD, SBA and FHA; international quasi-government institutions, the World Bank and Asian Development Bank; and money market instruments.

AUDIENCE: Professional	**RISK LEVEL: Conservative**
TOPICS: Bonds	

Harnessing Profit Through Market Volatility

Kay Angle, John Wiley &
  Sons, Inc.
605 Third Avenue
New York, NY 10158-0012

PHONE: (212) 850-6000
FAX: (212) 850-6088
Date of first issue: 1994
Technical Analysis
Cost: $39.95

How to use market volatility and trading psychology to make money in changing markets. Some topics include: The Volatility Index; Creating and Managing a Portfolio Index; Using the Options Market; Factors Influencing Volatility; Measuring Volatility; the Role and Response of Government; Economic Outlook & Trading Opportunities, and more.

AUDIENCE: Professional	**RISK LEVEL: Aggressive**
TOPICS: Stocks, Options, Futures/Commodities	

Hedging and Options Workshop

Wayne Purcell
Commodities Educational Institute
219 Parkade
Cedar Falls, IA 50613

PH: (800) 635-3936
FAX: (319) 277-7982
Published: 1991
Cost: $198.00 (complete set)
$55.00 (individual tapes -4 total)
VIDEO

Covers commodities trading and technical analysis. Uses charts. All the key pieces to build your own farm marketing plan. Coverage includes ABC's of Price Risk Management - principles of hedging and futures trading; Managing Your Pricing Program; ABC's of Ag options; ABC's of Technical Analysis.

AUDIENCE: Individual, Professional	**RISK LEVEL: Moderate, Aggressive**
TOPICS: Stocks, Options, Futures/Commodities	

Hedging - Principles, Practices, and Strategies for the Financial Markets

Joseph D. Koziol
John Wiley & Sons, Inc.
605 Third Avenue
New York, NY 10158-0012

PH: (212) 850-6418 (orders)
(212) 850-6233 (info)
INFO: (212) 850-6418
FAX: (212) 850-6088
Published: February 1990
Cost: $59.95

Covers investing theories, commodities trading, trading analysis. Guide to successful hedging in financial and commodity markets. It presents an overview of hedging principles and specific applications for investors and portfolio managers.

AUDIENCE: Beginning, Individual, Professional	**RISK LEVEL: Conservative, Moderate, Aggressive**
TOPICS: All	

High Yield Debt Market, The

Edward L. Altman, Editor
Irwin Professional Publishing
1333 Burr Ridge Parkway
Burr Ridge, IL 60521

PH: (708) 789-5489
(800) 634-3966
FAX: (708) 789-6933
Published: 1990
ISBN: 1-55623-235-7
Cost: $55.00

Covers bond analysis. A Saloman Brothers Center Book. The definitive book on high yield debt securities or junk bonds. Eminent authorities show you how to determine to volatility of a junk bond, measure the risk of default, value a high yield portfolio and much more.

AUDIENCE: Individual, Professional	RISK LEVEL: Moderate, Aggressive
TOPICS: Bonds	

High-Risk, High-Return Investing

Lawrence W. Fuller
John Wiley & Sons, Inc.
605 Third Avenue
New York, NY 10158

PH: (212) 850-6000
FAX: (212) 850-6088
Cost: $27.95
Date of first issue: 1994

"Shows how to make unconventional, offbeat but always calculated speculative investments. Contains sound financial planning and prudent investment management guidance. Explores emerging, under valued third-world stock markets, debt/equity swaps and reverse LBO's."

AUDIENCE: Individual	RISK LEVEL: Aggressive
TOPICS: Stocks	

How The Bond Market Works

New York Institute of
  Finance/Prentice Hall
113 Sylvan Avenue
Route 9W
Englewood Cliffs, NJ 07632

PH: (800) 947-7700
FAX: (515) 284-2607
Published: 1994
Cost: $14.95

Based on a popular NYIF seminar. Explains the basics of bonds and their markets; the different bond instruments, including their relative risks and benefits; underwriting, market, listing and quaotations, and the procedures for buying and selling them.

AUDIENCE: Beginning	RISK LEVEL: Conservative
TOPICS: Bonds	

How the Economy Works: An Investor's Guide to Tracking the Economy

Edmund A. Mennis
New York Institute of
  Finance/Prentice Hall
113 Sylvan Avenue
Route 9W
Englewood Cliffs, NJ 07632

PH: (800) 947-7700
FAX: (515) 284-2607
Published: 1991
Cost: $13.95

Explains basic economic principles and relates them to the fundamental concepts of investing. Discusses the key economic indicators, puts them in economic perspective, and explains their relation to the investment problems individuals face.

AUDIENCE: Individual	RISK LEVEL: Moderate
TOPICS: All	

How the Foreign Exchange Market Works

Rudi Weisweiller
New York Institute of
   Finance/Prentice Hall
113 Sylvan Avenue
Route 9W
Englewood Cliffs, NJ 07632

PH: (800) 947-7700
FAX: (515) 284-2607
Published: 1990
Cost: $19.95

Details the most recent developments in the world's largest market, including the entrance of new players, their impact, and what instruments they use. Describes choices confronting investors and offers their expert advice on the best action to take in specific situations.

AUDIENCE: Individual, Professional   RISK LEVEL: Moderate, Aggressive
TOPICS: Bonds, Options, Futures/Commodities

How the Futures Markets Work

Jake Bernstein
New York Institute of
   Finance/Prentice Hall
113 Sylvan Avenue
Route 9W
Englewood Cliffs, NJ 07632

PH: (800) 947-7700
FAX: (515) 284-2607
Published: 1990
Cost: $19.95

In non-technical language, the author gives the reader the information required to understand how futures markets work. Provides a step-by-step account of processing procedures and the paper trail that the process leaves.

AUDIENCE: Individual   RISK LEVEL: Aggressive
TOPICS: Futures/Commodities

How Mutual Funds Work

Albert J. Fredman and Russ Wiles
New York Institute of
   Finance/Prentice Hall
113 Sylvan Avenue
Route 9W
Englewood Cliffs, NJ 07632

PH: (800) 947-7700
FAX: (515) 284-2607
Published: 1993
Cost: $15.95

Explains in detail how funds work and provides investors with the background and tools necessary to analyze mutual funds. Covers equity and bond investing, risk and return, index funds, and different types of foreign equity portfolios.

AUDIENCE: Beginning   RISK LEVEL: Moderate, Aggressive
TOPICS: Mutual Funds

How the Stock Market Works

John M. Dalton
New York Institute of
   Finance/Prentice Hall
113 Sylvan Avenue
Route 9W
Englewood Cliffs, NJ 07632

PH: (800) 947-7700
FAX: (515) 284-2607
Published: 1993
Cost: $15.95

This primer—based on a popular NYIF seminar—explains the workings of the securities industry, including the mechanisms of the market, types of stocks, buy/sell and processing procedures, and the major theories of market analysis.

AUDIENCE: Beginning   RISK LEVEL: Moderate, Aggressive
TOPICS: Stocks

How to Beat the Street with Plan Z

Morry Markovitz and Michael Lam
John Wiley & Sons, Inc.
605 Third Ave.
New York, NY 10158-0012

PH: (800) 225-5945
Published:1993
Cost: $24.95

The author describes an investment program based on the use of zero-coupon bonds. Charts and tables generated by computer simulation show how to plan operates in a variety of scenarios, such as rapidly rising or falling interest rates. Three investment strategies with varying risk and return ratios are illustrated.

AUDIENCE: Beginning, Individual   RISK LEVEL: Conservative
TOPICS: Bonds

How to Forecast Interest Rates

Martin J. Pring
International Institute for Economic Research
P.O. Box 329
Blackville Road
Washington Depot, CT 06794

PH: (800) 221-7514
Cost: Video and free 50 page booklet $95.00
VIDEO

A complete description of the concepts and construction of models and their components used to identify various stages in the business cycle, including barometers for interest rates, equities, and commodities.

AUDIENCE: Beginning, Individual, Professional   RISK LEVEL: Conservative
TOPICS: Bonds

"How to Invest in Mutual Funds"

NBR/Tape
P.O. Box 2
North Miami, FL 33261-0002

PH: (800) 535-5864
Customer Service: (317) 299-9191
M-F 8:30-4:30 PM Eastern Time
Cost: $24.95 + $4.00 Shipping
(Allow 4-6 Weeks for Delivery)
Date of first issue: 3/94

With more than 4,000 mutual funds available, how do you identify those that are right for you?

AUDIENCE: Beginning   RISK LEVEL: Moderate, Aggressive
TOPICS: Mutual Funds

How to Invest Money Wisely

John Moody/Business Classics
950 Purisima Road
Woodside, CA 94062

PH: (800) 865-1001
(415) 852-8879
ISBN: 0-931133-08-4
Published: 1994 (reprint of 1912 edition)
Cost: not available

Stock analysis. A perfect accompaniment to The Art of Wise Investing teaches you about the pre-World War I investment world, especially railroad and utility stocks. He begins by focusing on investors' common mistakes and moves into describing securities. Interestingly, many of the stocks he discusses no longer exist today. Where will today's winners be in 90 years? An insightful introduction helps guide the reader and points out some of the lessons to be applied in today's markets.

AUDIENCE: Beginning, Individual, Professional   RISK LEVEL: Moderate, Aggressive
TOPICS: Bonds, Stocks

How to Make Money in Commodities: The Successful Method for Today's Markets

Bruce G. Gould
Bruce Gould Publications
P.O. Box 16
Seattle, WA 98111

ISBN: 0-918706-05-9
Published: 1982
Cost: $10.95

A respected authority on commodity trading reveals his single most rewarding technique. Concise handbook presents a case-by-case review of actual price moves that offered stunning profits when traded with this remarkable method. He then guides the investor from the technique on paper, to the trading arena.

AUDIENCE: Individual, Professional   RISK LEVEL: Aggressive
TOPICS: Options, Futures/Commodities

How to Make Money in Stocks By: William J. O'Neil

McGraw-Hill
1221 Avenue of the Americas
New York, NY 10020

PH: (800) 2- MCGRAW
(212) 512-2000
Published: 1991 (2nd edition)
Cost: $24.95

Offers a simple, easy-to-use plan for making money in stocks. Drawing on a detailed study of the greatest money-making stocks in the last 33 years, the author gives well-documented guidance in making smart investments. O'Neil's system C.A.N.S.L.I.M. - gives investors an almost foolproof method for evaluating the potential success of a stock.

AUDIENCE: Beginning, Individual, Professional RISK LEVEL: Moderate, Aggressive
TOPICS: Stocks

How to Pick the Best No-Load Mutual Fund for Solid Growth and Safety

Sheldon Jacob
Irwin Professional Publishing
1333 Burr Ridge Parkway
Burr Ridge, IL 60521

PH: (708) 789-5489
(800) 634-3966
FAX: (708) 789-6933
ISBN: 1-55623-574-7
Published: 1991
Cost: $15.00

This introduction to the opportunities and potential pitfalls of mutual fund investing gives readers practical advice on how to build and manage a portfolio of funds. Topics include how to select funds appropriate for meeting or possibly exceeding investment goals, how to evaluate different types of funds, offers model portfolio recommendations for different life cycles, saves readers money by showing them how to manage no-load funds themselves.

AUDIENCE: Beginning   RISK LEVEL: Moderate, Aggressive
TOPICS: Mutual Funds

How to Read a Financial Report: Wringing Cash Flow and Other Vital Signs Out of the Numbers

John A. Tracy
John Wiley & Sons, Inc.
605 Third Avenue
New York, NY 10158-0012

PH: (212) 850-6000
FAX: (212) 850-6088
Published: 1983 (2nd edition)
ISBN: 0-471-88859-1
Cost $27.95
Also available: 3rd edition
Published: 1989, ISBN: 0-471-50745-8
Cost: $34.95

This short, nontechnical guide is designed to help nonfinancial people cut through the maze of accounting information and find out what those numbers really mean. Explains the basics of the three key statements in financial reports - balance sheet, income statement, and cash flow statement - and the relationship between them.

AUDIENCE: Beginning, Individual, Professional   RISK LEVEL: Moderate, Aggressive
TOPICS: Bonds, Stocks

How to Read the Financial Pages

Peter Passell
Warner Books, Inc.
66 Fifth Avenue
New York, NY 10103

PH: (212) 522-7200
Published: February 1986
Cost $4.50

Covers market analysis. Everything you need to master the vital yet often mystifying information published in the financial pages of newspapers and business publications.

AUDIENCE: Beginning, Individual   RISK LEVEL: Moderate, Aggressive
TOPICS: Bonds, Mutual Funds, Stocks, Options, Futures/Commodities

How & When to Buy Stocks, How & When to Sell Stocks, Investing to Win, How to Make Money in Stocks

Investors Daily Library
P.O. Box 24018
Los Angeles, CA 90024

PH: (800) 733-8900
(213) 826-9601
Published: 1989
Cost: $29.95 (all 4); $9.95 (each)
CASSETTES

Over 40 minutes of advice on how to buy stocks and how to protect your profits so you can avoid heavy losses. Listen and learn from the 'best.' These are also available as books by William O'Neill.

AUDIENCE: Beginning, Individual, Professional   RISK LEVEL: Moderate, Aggressive
TOPICS: Stocks

How Young Millionaires Trade Commodities

Futures Discount Group
Zaner & Company
600 W. Jackson
Chicago, IL 60606

PH: (800) USA-MORE
Cost: Free
CASSETTE

Covers investing theories, commodities trading, trading analysis, fundamental analysis, technical analysis and futures. Strategies that helped traders make $1,000,000 each in trading profits. Listen and learn 25 amazing secrets.

AUDIENCE: Beginning, Individual   RISK LEVEL: Aggressive
TOPICS: Options, Futures/Commodities

"If Time Is Money, No Wonder I'm Not Rich": The Busy Investors Guide to Successful Money Management

Simon & Schuster
1230 Avenue of the Americas
New York, New York 10020

PH: (212) 698-7323
FAX: (212) 698-7035
Cost: $20.00

"Quick investing techniques fast formulas for creating a financial plan, strategies for making speedy investment decisions, and much more. Here's the guide for anyone who has cash in the bank but lacks time to manage it."

AUDIENCE: Individual   RISK LEVEL: Moderate, Aggressive
TOPICS: Bonds, Mutual Funds, Stocks, Asset Allocation, Investment Planing

In the Shadows of Wall Street: A Guide to Investing in Neglected Stocks

Peter Strebell & Steven Carvell
Prentice Hall
113 Sylvan Avenue
Route 9W
Englewood Cliffs, NJ 07632

PH: (800) 223-1360
FAX: (515) 284-2607
ISBN: 0-13-455999-1
Published: 1991
Cost: $14.95

The authors show the individual investor, the portfolio manager, and the seasoned professional how to maximize gains from security research. Pointer on how to identify neglected stocks and what kind of research to use in selecting these high-performing shadow stocks.

AUDIENCE: Beginning, Individual	RISK LEVEL: Moderate, Aggressive
TOPICS: Stocks	

Income Investor, The

Donald R. Nichols
Dearborn Financial Publishing, Inc.
520 N. Dearborn Street
Chicago, IL 60610-4975

PH: (800) 621-9621 ext. 320
ISBN: 0-88462-738-1
Published: 1988
Cost: $19.95

Covers bonds, CDs, options, precious metals, mutual funds, stocks, risks and rewards of each. Choosing investments that pay cash today and tomorrow. Nichols explains what income investments are, how they work, and how they can be used to best advantage during both inflation and economic downswings. He also explains why changing tax laws and uncertain equity markets make income investments attractive.

AUDIENCE: Beginning, Individual	RISK LEVEL: Conservative
TOPICS: Bonds, Mutual Funds, Stocks	

Individual Investor's Guide to Computerized Investing, The

American Association of Individual
  Investors
625 N. Michigan Ave.
Chicago, IL 60611-3110

Frequency: Annually
Cost: $24.95 ($19 for AAII members)
Free to all Computerized Investing
  subscribers
Published: 1994, 11th Edition

"The Guide helps steer computer users through the bewildering array of investment hardware, software and databases." It includes in-depth descriptions of our 150 database services and over 500 software programs, analysis of new PC hardware, and an introduction to using computers for investment analysis.

AUDIENCE: Beginning, Individual	RISK LEVEL: Conservative, Moderate, Aggressive
TOPICS: All	

Individual Investor's Guide to Low-Load Mutual Funds, The

International Publishing Corp.
625 N. Michigan Ave.
Suite 1920
Chicago, IL 60611

PH: (800) 488-4149
Cost: $24.95
Published: 1994, 13th edition

"Provides thorough and up-to-date information on no-load and very low-load mutual funds. The guide provides the information needed to make well-informed decisions on mutual fund investments." Also provides information such as: record keeping and tax tips, understanding mutual statements and portfolio building tips.

AUDIENCE: Beginning	RISK LEVEL: Moderate, Aggressive
TOPICS: Mutual Funds	

Individual Investor's Guide to No-Load Mutual Funds

AAII
625 N. Michigan Ave.
Chicago, IL 60611

PH: (312) 280-0170
Frequency: Annual
Cost: $24.95

"Provides thorough and up-to-date information on over 600 no-load and very low load mutual funds, including 5 years of returns, NAV's distributions and per share data, fund returns and rankings by investment objective, 3 yr and 5 yr average annual returns, total risk and investment objective risk rankings and performance during bull and bear markets."

AUDIENCE: Beginning, Individual   RISK LEVEL: Moderate, Aggressive
TOPICS: Mutual Funds

Inflation: Causes and Effects

Robert E. Hall, Editor
University of Chicago Press
5801 Ellis Avenue, 4th Floor
Chicago, IL 60637

PH: (312) 702-7700
Also available in paperback
ISBN: 0-226-31324-7
Published: 1984
Cost: $10.95

Assembled by the National Bureau of Economic Research, the contributors diagnose the problems and describe the events that economists most thoroughly understand. Reflecting a dozen diverse views - many of which challenge established orthodoxy - they illuminate the economic and political processes involved in this important issue.

AUDIENCE: Beginning, Individual, Professional   RISK LEVEL: Conservative,
TOPICS: Bonds   Moderate, Aggressive

Inside the Financial Futures Markets

Mark J. Powers
John Wiley & Sons, Inc.
605 Third Avenue
New York, NY 10158-0012

PH: (212) 850-6000
FAX: (212) 850-6088
ISBN: 0-471-89071-5
Published: 1984
Cost: $49.95

A guide to financial futures contracts and corporate hedging strategies. Revised edition features comprehensive coverage of options contracts on financial instruments and stock index futures. Also examines such established contracts as mortgage certificates, Treasury bills, bonds, notes, Eurodollars, and foreign currencies.

AUDIENCE: Professional   RISK LEVEL: Aggressive
TOPICS: Options, Futures/Commodities

Inside the Yield Book: New Tools for Bond Market Strategy

Sidney Homer & Martin L.
  Leibowitz, Ph.D.
Prentice Hall
113 Sylvan Avenue
Route 9W
Englewood Cliffs, NJ 07632

PH: (800) 947-7700
FAX: (515) 284-2607
ISBN: 0-13-467548-7
Published: 1972
Cost: $22.95

Takes the bond investor behind the scenes and reveals, in non-technical terms, the true nature of bond yields and the ways in which they are often misused. Corrects misconceptions as to bond prices and yields as calculated in the standard Yield Book, and provides a whole new set of tools to aid in bond investment strategy.

AUDIENCE: Beginning, Individual   RISK LEVEL: Conservative
TOPICS: Bonds

Inside Wall Street

Robert Sobel
W. W. Norton & Company, Inc.
500 Fifth Avenue
New York, NY 10110

PH: (800) 223-2584
ISBN: 0-393-00030-3
Published: 1982
Cost: $7.95

Learn how the greatest financial district operates from one who knows the world of finance inside and out. This highly readable account captures the atmosphere, excitement, and personalities of Wall Street. A good guide for both amateurs and professionals.

AUDIENCE: Beginning, Individual, Professional   RISK LEVEL: Moderate, Aggressive
TOPICS: Stocks

Instincts of the Herd in Peace and War

Wilfred Trotter
Omnigraphics, Inc.
2400 Penobscot Building
Detroit, MI 48226

PH: (800) 234-1340
ISBN: 0-8103-4090-9
Published: 1923 (2nd edition), 1975
  (reprint)
Cost: $34.00

Written just following World War I, this fascinating treatise is still remarkably relevant to the modern human instinct. Essays include "Herd Instinct and its Bearing on the Psychology of Civilized Man," "Sociological Applications of the Psychology of Herd Instinct," "Speculations upon the Human Mind in 1915," and "Postscript of 1919."

AUDIENCE: Individual, Professional   RISK LEVEL: Moderate, Aggressive
TOPICS: Stocks, General Reference

Intelligent Investor, The

Benjamin Graham
Harper Collins
10 E. 53rd Street
New York, NY 10022

PH: (800) 242-7737
ISBN: 0-06-015547-7
Published: 1986
Cost: $30.00

Covers stock analysis, market analysis, earnings analysis, fundamental analysis. Guide to sound investing. Main objective is to guide the reader against areas of possible substantial error and to develop policies with which he or she will be comfortable.

AUDIENCE: Beginning, Individual   RISK LEVEL: Moderate, Aggressive
TOPICS: Bonds, Mutual Funds, Stocks

Interest Rate Futures and Options

Mark Pitts and Frank J. Fabozzi
Probus Publishing Co.
1925 N. Clybourn Ave.
Suite 401
Chicago, IL 60614

PH: (800) PROBUS-1
FAX: (312) 868-6250
Cost: $65.00
Date of first issue: 1990
ISBN: 0-917253-95-7

". . . written to provide you with a comprehensive and detailed treatment of all aspects of futures and options on interest rate instruments."

AUDIENCE: Individual, Professional   RISK LEVEL: Aggressive
TOPICS: Options, Futures/Commodities

Interest Rate Spreads Analysis: Managing and Reducing Rate Exposure

Citicorp
Probus Publishing Co.
1925 North Clybourn Avenue
Chicago, IL 60614

PH: (800) PROBUS-1
FAX: (312) 868-6250
ISBN: 1-55738-180-I
Published: 1992, 4th edition
Cost: $65.00

Provides readers with a thorough understanding of how rates react in different economic environments. This book traces the historical movements of key interest rates from 1981 to 1990, including spreads summary statistics for each year during the period as well as for the period as a whole. It also covers: instrument description, computation methodology, absolute rate levels, LIBOR based spreads, treasury based spreads, other money market indices.

AUDIENCE: Professional   RISK LEVEL: Moderate, Aggressive
TOPICS: Bonds, Options, Futures/Commodities

Intermarket Technical Analysis

John J. Murphy
John Wiley & Sons, Inc.
605 Third Avenue
New York, NY 10158-0012

PH: (212) 850-6000
FAX: (212) 850-6088
Published: 1991
Technical Analysis
Cost: Contact Publisher

". . . the author uses years of experience in technical analysis plus extensive charts to clearly demonstrate the interrelationships that exist among the various market sectors and their importance."

AUDIENCE: Individual, Professional   RISK LEVEL: Aggressive
TOPICS: Futures

International Government Bond Markets, The

Frank J. Jones and Frank J. Fabozzi
Probus Publishing Co.
1925 N. Clybourn Ave.
Suite 401
Chicago, IL 60614

PH: (800) PROBUS-1
(312) 868-1100
FAX: (312) 868-6250
Cost: $65.00
Date of first issue:1992
Fundamental Analysis

"Provides an overview and analysis of the world's leading government bond markets and the latest strategies and methods for international fixed income investing, including the spot exchange rate market, controlling exchange rate risk, forward and futures contracts, and currency options."

AUDIENCE: Individual, Professional   RISK LEVEL: Moderate, Aggressive
TOPICS: Bonds, Futures/Commodities

International Investing with ADRs: Your Passport to Profits Worldwide

International Publishing Corp.
625 N. Michigan Ave.
Suite 1920
Chicago, IL 60611

PH: (800) 488-4149
Cost: $24.95
Date of first issue: 1994

A comprehensive guide to ADRs; what they are; types and characteristics; and the benefits of investing in them. Includes pink sheet ADR descriptions covering 1,000 ADRs traded in the U.S.

AUDIENCE: Individual, Professional   RISK LEVEL: Moderate, Aggressive
TOPICS: Stocks

Introduction to Risk and Return from Common Stocks

Richard A. Brealey
MIT Press
55 Hayward Street
Cambridge, MA 02142

PH: (800) 356-0343
ISBN: 0-262-52116-4
Published: 1986 (2nd edition)
Cost: $8.95

A brief, nontechnical review of current research in investment management as well as its implications. Revised, second edition explains the new, unified theory of investment management and presents empirical research to test it. Divided into three parts dealing with market efficiency, valuation, and modern portfolio theory.

AUDIENCE: Beginning, Individual   RISK LEVEL: Moderate, Aggressive
TOPICS: Stocks

Investing Basics

Maria Crawford Scott
The American Association of
  Individual Investors
625 N. Michigan Avenue
Chicago, IL 60611

PH: (312) 280-0170
Cost: $12 for members; $15 for non-
  members
Published: 1993

Teaches the basics of investing without a lot of intricate details. Covers investment principles, your personal investment profile, asset allocation, growth vs. income considerations, selecting an outside advisor and portfolio monitoring and maintenance. A.F.P.

AUDIENCE: Beginning   RISK LEVEL: Conservative, Moderate
TOPICS: Bonds, Stocks

Investing Basics Videocourse

American Association of Individual
  Investors
625 N. Michigan Avenue
Chicago, IL

PH: (312) 280-0170
Cost: $129.00
$98.00 for AAII members
VIDEO

Covers bond analysis, stock analysis, earnings analysis, fundamental analysis, trading analysis, technical analysis. A 6 hour tape focuses on the fundamentals of investing: basic investment concepts; the language of investments, investment choices, stock analysis and research, pooled investment products, developing your financial plan.

AUDIENCE: Beginning   RISK LEVEL: Conservative, Moderate, Aggressive
TOPICS: Bonds, Mutual Funds, Stocks

Investing for a Lifetime: Paul Merriman's Guide to Mutual Fund Strategies

Paul Merriman
Irwin Professional Publishing
1333 Burr Ridge Parkway
Burr Ridge, IL 60521

PH: (708) 789-5489
(800) 634-3966
FAX: (708) 789-6933
ISBN: 1-55623-485-6
Published: 1991
Cost: $27.00

Concerns investing theories. Offers the one thing that nearly every investor wants to learn from a book on investing - how to make successful investment decisions in healthy or weak financial markets. While the book concentrates on mutual fund investing, several different strategies are outlined. Readers will find: ten rules for successful investing; how to distinguish good versus bad advice from brokers, advisors, and newsletters; how to maximize performance from a mutual fund; how to invest for specific purposes, such as retirement or a college fund; how to beat the market using Merriman's own timing techniques.

AUDIENCE: Beginning, Individual   RISK LEVEL: Moderate, Aggressive
TOPICS: Mutual Funds

Investing for Good - Making Money While Being Socially Responsible

Peter Kinder, Steven Lyndenberg,
   and Amy Domini
Harper Collins
10 East 53rd Street
New York, NY 10022

PH: (212) 207-7000
(800) 242-7737
FAX: (800) 822-4090
Cost: $13.00
Date of first issue: 1993
ISBN: 0-88730-662-4

Shows how to build a profitable portfolio consisting only of socially responsible companies. Provides information on researching, selecting and screening potential investments for a wide range of social concerns.

AUDIENCE: Beginning, Individual, Professional   RISK LEVEL: Moderate, Aggressive
TOPICS: Bonds, Mutual Funds, Stocks

Investing in and Profiting from Legal Insider Transactions

Edwin A. Buck
New York Institute of
   Finance/Prentice Hall
113 Sylvan Avenue
Route 9W
Englewood Cliffs, NJ 07632

PH: (800) 947-7700
Published: 1990
Cost: $11.95

Covers investing theories, market analysis, technical analysis. Minimal use of charts. Shows how to legally tap into valuable buying and selling signals from insiders (corporate officers, e.g., stockholders). How to know when to buy, sell, or hold based on insider activity.

AUDIENCE: Individual   RISK LEVEL: Moderate, Aggressive
TOPICS: Stocks

Investing in Call Options: An Alternative to Common Stocks and Real Estate

James A. Willson
Greenwood Publishing Group, Inc.
88 Post Road W
Box 5007
Westport, CT 06881

PH: (203) 226-3571
(800) 225-5800
ISBN: 0-03-059453-7
Published: 1982
Cost: $55.00

Presents a convincing case for selling covered call options instead of investing in realty income property. Illustrates the basic ideas, the opportunities, and the possible pitfalls. Expert information on financing, expenses, tax shelter potential, return on investment, and the ease of dealing with common stock call options.

AUDIENCE: Individual   RISK LEVEL: Moderate, Aggressive
TOPICS: Stocks, Options

Investing in Closed-End Funds: Finding Value and Building Wealth

Albert J. Fredman and
   George Cole Scott
New York Institute of
   Finance/Prentice Hall
113 Sylvan Avenue
Route 9W
Englewood Cliffs, NJ 07632

PH: (800) 947-7700
FAX: (515) 284-2607
Published: 1991
Cost: $29.95

Provides investors and industry professional with direct advice on the hot topic no longer characterized by clear-cut investment strategies. Includes a list of closed-end funds on the market as of fall 1990.

AUDIENCE: Individual, Professional   RISK LEVEL: Moderate, Aggressive
TOPICS: Stocks, Mutual Funds

Investing in Convertible Securities

John P. Calamos
Dearborn Financial Publishing, Inc.
520 N. Dearborn
Chicago, IL 60610

PH: (800) 621-9621 ext. 320
ISBN: 0-88462-736-5
Published: 1988
Cost: $29.95

Written for both investors and professional money managers, the book gives an overview of the various investment strategies and explains how to evaluate the risks and rewards.

AUDIENCE: Beginning, Individual, Professional   RISK LEVEL: Moderate, Aggressive
TOPICS: Bonds, Stocks

Investing in Emerging Growth Stocks

J.W. Broadfoot
John Wiley & Sons, Inc.
605 Third Avenue
New York, NY 10158-0012

PH: (212) 850-6418 orders
(212) 850-6233 info
FAX: (212) 850-6088
Published: 1989
Cost: $29.95

Covers stock analysis. Gives guidance on how to pick stocks that will outperform the market and how to avoid those that will fail. Includes what to look for in small companies, how to analyze them, and how to diversify among them. Shows you how to analyze profitability, competition, and management, with an eye toward when to buy, when to sell, and when to sit on the sidelines.

AUDIENCE: Beginning, Individual, Professional RISK LEVEL: Moderate, Aggressive
TOPICS: Bonds, Mutual Funds, Stocks

Investing in the Over the Counter Markets: How It Works—Stocks, Bonds, IPOs

Alvin D. Hall
John Wiley & Sons, Inc.
605 Third Avenue
New York, NY 10158-0012

PH: (212) 850-6000
FAX: (212) 850-6088
Published: 1994
Cost: $27.95

"Gives investors necessary information in order to understand the risks and realize the rewards of over-the-counter securities investing. Compares the history, structure and function of the OTC and NASDAQ markets and profiles the securities that trade in them. Helps the investor choose among mid-cap, small-cap and IPOs and find strategies for selecting bond offerings from these companies with a potential for profitable, long-term growth."

AUDIENCE: Individual   RISK LEVEL: Moderate, Aggressive
TOPICS: Bonds, Stocks

Investing: The Collected Works of Martin L. Leibowitz

Frank J. Fabozzi
Probus Publishing Co.
1925 N. Clybourn Ave.
Suite 401
Chicago, IL 60614

PH: (800) PROBUS-1
(312) 868-1100
FAX: (312) 868-6250
Cost: $79.95
Date of first issue: 1992
ISBN:1-55738-198-4

"A compilation of Martin Leibowitz's groundbreaking work, is divided into three major parts: Asset Allocation and Pension Fund Strategies, Analysis of Returns for Stocks, Real Estate and Convertibles, Framework for Bond Portfolio Management."

AUDIENCE: Professional   RISK LEVEL: Moderate, Aggressive
TOPICS: Stocks, Asset Allocation, General Reference

Investing with the Best: What to Look For, What to Look Out For in Your Search for a Superior Investment Manager

Claude N. Rosenberg
John Wiley & Sons, Inc.
605 Third Avenue
New York, NY 10158-0012

PH: (212) 850-6000
FAX: (212) 850-6088
ISBN: 0-471-83798-9
Published: 1986
Cost: $29.95

Helps you cut through the confusing hype, marketplace jargon, and misleading claims about performance to find an investment manager who's not only savvy, but also trustworthy. Shows how to evaluate the risks a manager is taking with your money and how to interpret your fees to make sure they're reasonable.

AUDIENCE: Beginning, Individual   RISK LEVEL: Moderate, Aggressive
TOPICS: Bonds, Mutual Funds, Stocks

Investing with Your Conscience: How to Achieve High Returns Using Socially Responsible Investing

John C. Harrington
John Wiley & Sons, Inc.
605 Third Avenue
New York, NY 10158-0012

PH: (212) 850-6000
FAX: (212) 850-6088
Published: 1992
Cost: $24.95

" . . . offers sound advice on both ethical considerations and how-to financial strategies for investing in responsible funds, organizations and managers in global markets, not only to increase your net worth, but to make the world a better place to live."

AUDIENCE: Individual   RISK LEVEL: Moderate, Aggressive
TOPICS: Mutual Funds

Investment Markets

Roger C. Ibbotson & G.P. Brinson
McGraw-Hill Publishing Company
1221 Avenue of the Americas
New York, NY 10020

PH: (800) 262-4729
ISBN: 0-07-031673-2
Published: 1987
Cost: $34.95

Concerns market analysis; uses charts. Shows where and how money has been made in stocks, bonds, cash and cash equivalents, real estate, gold and silver, tangibles, options and futures, and more. Contains more than 80 graphs, charts, and tables containing extensive data and analysis are provided as an invaluable reference aid for both individual and institutional investors.

AUDIENCE: Individual, Professional   RISK LEVEL: Moderate, Aggressive
TOPICS: All

Investment Policy: How to Win the Loser's Game

Charles D. Ellis
Irwin Professional Publishing
1333 Burr Ridge Parkway
Burr Ridge, IL 60521

PH: (708) 789-5489
(800) 634-3966
FAX: (708) 789-6933
ISBN: 1-55623-088-5
Published: 1993, 2nd edition
Cost: $35.00

A fresh approach to professional investment management that involves active client participation. Enables clients to understand the basic nature of institutional investing, formulate specific policies to reach long-term investment goals and objectives, and manage their investment managers in order to achieve their real goals. A.F.P.

AUDIENCE: Professional   RISK LEVEL: Conservative, Moderate
TOPICS: Bonds, Stocks

Investments

William F. Sharpe
Prentice Hall
113 Sylvan Avenue
Route 9W
Englewood Cliffs, NJ 07632

PH: (201) 592-2000
FAX: (515) 284-2607
ISBN: 0-13-504697-1
Published: Dec. 1993 (4th edition)
Cost: $62.00

Comprehensive text provides an overall framework of the subject, discusses taxes and inflation, describes and analyzes various instruments. Covers financial analysis, investment management, performance measurement, and extended diversification. Encyclopedic without excessive detail; rigorous without needless analytic apparatus.

AUDIENCE: Beginning, Individual   **RISK LEVEL:** Conservative, Moderate
TOPICS: All

Investments

Zvi Bodie, Alex Lane, Alan J. Marcus
Irwin Professional Publishing
1333 Burr Ridge Parkway
Burr Ridge, IL 60521

PH: (708) 789-5489
(800) 634-3966
FAX: (708) 789-6933
Published: 1993, 2nd edition
ISBN: 0-256-08342-8
Cost: $62.95

Covers bond analysis, stock analysis, market analysis, earnings analysis, commodities trading, fundamental analysis. Textbook overview of different types of security market operations, portfolio theories, fundamental analysis, security valuation, options and futures, portfolio management and evaluation.

AUDIENCE: Beginning, Individual   **RISK LEVEL:** Conservative, Moderate,
TOPICS: All   Aggressive

Investor's Catechism, The

Marc Reynolds
Business Classics
950 Purisima Road
Woodside, CA 94062

PH: (800) 865-1001
(415) 852-8879
ISBN: 0-931133-09-2
Published: 1994 (reprint of 1908
   edition)
Cost: not available

Covers Wall Street terms. It's difficult to put the lingo of turn-of-the-century Wall Street into context in today's market. This is the translation dictionary you need. You know what "spread" means today, what did it mean in the early 1900s? What is "cutting a melon," a "quintal," or a "by-bidder"? Reynolds explains these and gives you insight into the colorful and, in some cases, extinct language of the early stock market.

AUDIENCE: Individual, Professional   **RISK LEVEL:** Moderate, Aggressive
TOPICS: Bonds, Stocks

Investor's Quotient: The Psychology of Successful Investing in Commodities & Stocks, The

Jacob Bernstein
John Wiley & Sons, Inc.
605 Third Avenue
New York, NY 10158-0012

PH: (212) 850-6000
FAX: (212) 850-6088
ISBN: 0-471-07849-2
Published: 1980
Cost: $19.95

An experienced commodity trader and former clinical psychologist helps you understand how your attitudes and emotional makeup can either contribute to or limit success. Oriented toward the individual investor, shows how to identify, analyze, and correct many of the personal emotional limitations to profitable investing.

AUDIENCE: Individual, Professional   **RISK LEVEL:** Aggressive
TOPICS: Stocks, Options, Futures/Commodities

Investors Guide to Economic Indicators, The

Charles R. Nelson
John Wiley & Sons, Inc.
605 Third Avenue
New York, NY 10158-0012

PH: (212) 850-6418 orders
(212) 850-6233 info
FAX: (212) 850-6088
Published: 1987
Cost: $12.95

Covers market and trading analysis; uses charts. Guide to reading, interpreting, and using economic and financial news reports to make better investment decisions. Shown in plain language and simple charts.

AUDIENCE: Beginning, Individual, Professional RISK LEVEL: Conservative, Moderate, Aggressive
TOPICS: Bonds, Mutual Funds, Stocks, Options, Futures/Commodities

"It's a Sure Thing": A Wry Look at Investing, Investors, and the World of Wall Street

Robert Metz and George Stasen
McGraw-Hill Publishing Company
1221 Avenue of the Americas
New York, NY 10020

PH: (800) 262-4729
Cost: $15.95
Published: 1991

The authors present an amusing slant on the workings of Wall Street in this guide. They examine a range of investment concerns such as how to choose a trustworthy broker, how to spot misleading euphemisms and sweeping generalities, how to tell if your money is working, and why investment charts can appear convincing as they are about to change direction. The book also covers what to look for in analyzing market performance, how to measure your risk tolerance, and how to balance investment risks against opportunity.

AUDIENCE: Individual   RISK LEVEL: Moderate, Aggressive
TOPICS: Stocks

Japanese Candlestick Charting Techniques

Steve Nison
New York Institute of
  Finance/Prentice Hall
113 Sylvan Avenue
Route 9W
Englewood Cliffs, NJ 07632

PH: (800) 947-7700
FAX: (515) 284-2607
Published: 1991
Cost: $65.00

This best seller is the first comprehensive source available to the English-speaking market that describes uniquely incisive Japanese candlestick charting techniques. Makes a breakthrough analytical method—developed over a century before traditional Western methods of chart analysis—available to anyone.

AUDIENCE: Individual, Professional   RISK LEVEL: Aggressive
TOPICS: Stocks, Options, Futures/Commodities

Jake Bernstein's Seasonal Futures Spreads

Jake Bernstein
John Wiley & Sons, Inc.
605 Third Avenue
New York, NY 10158-0012

PH: (212) 850-6418 orders
(212) 850-6233 info.
FAX: (212) 850-6088
Published: July 1990
Cost: $79.95

Covers commodities trading. Uses charts. One of America's leading experts on seasonal futures tendencies explains the seasonal characteristics of commodity spreads and shows you how to use them to tilt the trading odds in your favor.

AUDIENCE: Professional   RISK LEVEL: Aggressive
TOPICS: Options, Futures/Commodities, Asset Allocation, Investment Planning, General Reference

Jesse Livermore: Speculator-King

Paul Sarnoff
Traders Press, Inc.
P.O. Box 6206
Greenville, SC 2960

PH: (800) 927-8222
ISBN: 0-9343800-10-4
Published: 1967
Cost: $17.95

Here is the true story of a man once blamed for causing the 1929 crash, a man blamed for every market break from 1917 to 1940. Here are his trials and triumphs, told with empathy and forthrightness. Here is one of the most legendary figures ever to haunt the annals of the stock market - Livermore brought startlingly to life.

AUDIENCE: Beginning, Individual, Professional   RISK LEVEL: Aggressive
TOPICS: Stocks

Leading Indicators for the 1990s

Geoffrey H. Moore
Irwin Professional Publishing
1333 Burr Ridge Parkway
Burr Ridge, IL 60521

PH: (708) 789-5489
(800) 634-3966
FAX: (708) 789-6933
ISBN: 1-55623-258-6
Published: 1989
Cost: $40.00

Enables the reader to identify trends in the economy at an early stage. Suggests expanding the leading indicators from 11 to 15 and recommends a whole new set of leading indicators that will provide earlier clues to swings that the present set. The essential reference for anyone making investment decisions.

AUDIENCE: Individual, Professional   RISK LEVEL: Conservative, Moderate, Aggressive
TOPICS: Bonds, Mutual Funds, Stocks, Options, Futures/Commodities

Lenox System of Market Forecasting

Radius Press
217 E. 85th Street
Dept. 164MC
New York, NY 10028

PH: (212) 988-4715
Cost: $89.95 + $4.00 S&H
VIDEO

A one hour videotape of the Lenox System tutorial seminar. Learn to compute daily buy and sell market signals based on the principles of pattern recognition, fractal geometry, probability and statistics. This system was developed by Sam Kash Kachigan, a veteran trader and author of one of the nation's leading college statistics textbooks.

AUDIENCE: Individual, Professional   RISK LEVEL:Aggressive
TOPICS: Stocks, Options, Futures/Commodities

Low-Risk, High-Reward Technical Trading Strategies

Glen Ring
Commodities Educational Institute
219 Parkade
Cedar Falls, IA 50613

PH: (800) 635-3936
FAX: (319) 277-7982
Published: 1991
Cost: $233.00 (complete set
   notebook included)
$55.00 (individual tapes - 5 total)
VIDEO

Covers trading and technical analysis; uses charts. A wide range of useful, profit making ideas to help you pinpoint trades with the greatest potential return for the least possible risk. Coverage includes: Personal trading management, ancient Japanese charting techniques, time-based trading, stochastics and directional movement indicator and other directional studies.

AUDIENCE: Individual, Professional   RISK LEVEL: Moderate, Aggressive
TOPICS: Stocks, Options, Futures/Commodities

Lump Sum Handbook, The: Investment and Tax Strategies for a Secure Retirement

Anthony Gallea
New York Institute of
   Finance/Prentice Hall
113 Sylvan Avenue
Route 9W
Englewood Cliffs, NJ 07632

PH: (800) 947-7700
FAX: (515) 284-2607
Published: 1993
Cost: $14.95

This practical handbook cuts through the confusion and addresses the reader's most important fears and questions about lump sum distributions. Suggests tax strategies, discusses IRA rollovers, cites ways to minimize or eliminate estate taxes, and discusses the pros and cons of opting for an annuity or a lump sum.

AUDIENCE: Individual   RISK LEVEL: All
TOPICS: Bonds, Stocks, Asset Allocation, Investment Planning

Major Works of R.N. Elliott, Expanded Edition, The

Robert R. Prechter, Jr, editor
New Classics Library, Inc.
P.O. Box 1618
Gainesville, GA 30503

PH: (800) 336-1618
(404) 536-0309
Published: 1980, 1990 (2nd edition)
Cost: $34.00

The three ground-breaking works by R.N. Elliott - "The Wave Principle" (1938), The Financial World articles (1939), and "The Secret of the Universe" - (1946). Uses charts.

AUDIENCE: Individual, Professional   RISK LEVEL: Aggressive
TOPICS: Stocks, Options, Futures/Commodities

Making Money with Mutual Funds

Werner Renberg and Jeremiah Blitzer
John Wiley & Sons, Inc.
605 Third Avenue
New York, NY 10158-0012

PH: (212) 850-6418 orders
OTHER: (212) 850-6233 info.
FAX: (212) 850-6088
Published: 1988
Cost: $23.95

How to pick funds to fit changing investment needs. A comprehensive portfolio strategy that helps you identify superior funds and control risk at low cost. Allows you to choose your own balance between risk and profitability.

AUDIENCE: Beginning, Individual   RISK LEVEL: Moderate, Aggressive
TOPICS: Mutual Funds

Managing Foreign Exchange Risk

David DeRosa
Probus Publishing Co.
1925 North Clybourn Avenue
Chicago, IL 60614

PH: (800) PROBUS-1
FAX: (312) 868-6250
ISBN: 1-55738-164-X
Published: 1991
Cost: $55.00

Innovative and complex financial instruments and hedging strategies by banking and investment professionals to control the foreign exchange rate risks associated with institutional portfolios. This book contains introductory material about foreign exchange and its peculiar risks as well as descriptions and historical analyzes of the major currencies. It also covers the Interest Parity Theorem, the linkages between the currency and debt markets, the valuation of currency forward and futures markets and currency option pricing, extensive coverage of various hedging techniques.

AUDIENCE: Individual, Professional   RISK LEVEL: Moderate, Aggressive
TOPICS: Bonds, Options, Futures/Commodities

Managing Your Investment Manager: The Complete Guide to Selection, Measurement, and Control

Arthur Williams III
Irwin Professional Publishing
1333 Burr Ridge Parkway
Burr Ridge, IL 60521

PH: (708) 789-5489
(800) 634-3966
FAX: (708) 789-6933
ISBN: 0-87094-723-0
Published: 1986
Cost: $42.50

Shows plan sponsors how to establish a management system for investment capital. Covers how to build a framework for setting goals, how to train managers for achieving goals, and how to set up an information system to provide necessary feedback. Helps build a communications bridge between fund sponsors and investment managers.

AUDIENCE: Professional   RISK LEVEL: Conservative, Moderate
TOPICS: Bonds, Mutual Funds, Stocks

Market Psychology and Discipline

Commodities Education Institute
219 Parade
Cedar Falls, IA 50613

PH: (800) 635-3936
(319) 277-6341
FAX: (319) 277-7982
Published: 1990
Cost: $55.00
VIDEO

Covers market and technical analysis. Glen Ring will help you understand the psychology of the marketplace and of the trader and how this can affect your trading profits. Set of 5 tapes in this series available for $233.00.

AUDIENCE: Individual, Professional   RISK LEVEL: Aggressive
TOPICS: Stocks, Options, Futures/Commodities

Market Wizards: Interviews with Top Traders

Jack D. Schwager
New York Institute of Finance
2 Broadway
New York, NY 10004

PH: (212) 344-2900
ISBN: 0-13-556093-4
Published: 1989
Cost: $19.95

After interviewing top traders in a variety of markets, the author concludes that while method undoubtedly accounts largely for trading success, no one approach is used by all, or even most of the traders interviewed. Some are technicians, others are fundamentalists, some act on personal initiative and intuition, and others rely on automated systems. Glossary.

AUDIENCE: Individual, Professional   RISK LEVEL: Aggressive
TOPICS: Stocks, Options, Futures/Commodities

Markets - Who Pays, Who Risks, Who Gains, Who Loses

Martin Mayer
W. W. Norton & Company, Inc.
500 Fifth Avenue
New York, NY 10110

PH: (800) 223-2584
ISBN: 0-393-02602-7
Published: 1988
Cost: $8.95

Covers market analysis. Sophisticated analysis of the workings and history of the leading securities and common markets of the world. A.F.P.

AUDIENCE: Beginning, Individual   RISK LEVEL: Moderate, Aggressive
TOPICS: Bonds, Mutual Funds, Stocks, Options

Martin Pring on Market Momentum

International Institute for Economic
  Research
P.O. Box 624
Gloucester, VA 23061-0624

PH: (800) 221-7514
(804) 694-0415
FAX: (804) 694-0028
Date of first issue: 1993
Cost: $49.95 Complete coursebook
  with 3 videotapes for $275.00
Technical Analysis

"Covers many of the established indicators as well as new ways of
interpreting old ones." Some of the indicators covered are:
Stochastics, RSI, Commodity Chanel Index, Trix, Ultimate
Oscillator and Accumulation Swing.

AUDIENCE: Individual, Professional	RISK LEVEL: Moderate, Aggressive
TOPICS: Stocks, Options, Futures/Commodities	

Martin Zweig's Wining on Wall Street, Revised Edition

Martin Zweig
Warner Books, Inc.
1271 Avenue of the Americas
New York, NY 10020

Published: 1986, 1990, 1994 updated
Cost: $12.99 (paperback)

Covers investing theories, stock analysis, market analysis, technical
analysis. Uses charts. Zweig clearly explains his proven methods
for avoiding the most common investment errors, preserving capital
and increasing profits.

AUDIENCE: Beginning, Individual, Professional	RISK LEVEL: Conservative,
TOPICS: Bonds, Stocks, Asset Allocation	Moderate, Aggressive

Mathematics of Money Management-Risk Analysis Techniques for Traders, The

Ralph Vince
John Wiley & Sons, Inc.
605 Third Avenue
New York, New York 10158

PH: (212) 850-6000
FAX: (212) 850-6088
Cost: $55.00
Technical Analysis
Date of first issue: 1992

"Permits traders in the futures, options and stock markets to create
profitable trading formulas based on the rules of probability and
modern portfolio theory. Shows how to develop and utilize key
formulas which minimize losses, maximize profits and avoid
excessive risk."

AUDIENCE: Individual, Professional	RISK LEVEL: Aggressive
TOPICS: Stocks, Options, Futures	

Mathematics of Technical Analysis, The

Clifford J. Sherry
Probus Publishing Co.
1925 N. Clybourn Ave.
Suite 401
Chicago, IL 60614

PH: (800) PROBUS-1
(312) 868-1100
FAX: (312) 868-6250
Cost: $55.00
Date of first issue: 1992
Technical Analysis

"The step-by-step examples, explained in non-technical language,
will show you how to apply statistical methods to test and improve
your odds in making investment and trading decisions."

AUDIENCE: Individual, Professional	RISK LEVEL: Moderate, Aggressive
TOPICS: Stocks, Options, Futures	

MESA and Trading Market Cycles

John F. Ehlers
John Wiley & Sons, Inc.
605 Third Avenue
New York, NY 10158-0012

PH: (212) 850-6000
FAX: (212) 850-6088
Published: 1992
Technical Analysis
Cost: $34.95

MESA's (a successful computerized trading system) creator discusses the characteristics of the different market cycles and offers examples of how trading strategies can be altered to increase profitable trades.

AUDIENCE: Professional   RISK LEVEL: Aggressive
TOPICS: Stocks, Options, Futures

Mexico Company Handbook 1993

The Reference Press, Inc.
6448 Highway 290 E
Suite E-104
Austin, TX 78723

PH: (512) 454-7778
FAX: (512) 454-9401
Cost: $29.95
Date of first issue: 1993
Fundamental Analysis

Profiles almost 75 of Mexico's largest public companies and 60 mutual funds. Also provides economic, trade and investment climate information.

AUDIENCE: Beginning, Individual, Professional   RISK LEVEL: Moderate, Aggressive
TOPICS: Mutual Funds, Stocks

Midas Touch: The Strategies that Have Made Warren Buffet America's Pre-eminent Investor, The

John Train
Harper Collins
10 E. 53rd Street
New York, NY 10022

PH: (800) 242-7737
Published: 1990
ISBN: 0-06-091500-5
Published: 1987
Cost: $10.00

Analyzes the investment principles of Warren Buffet, the most successful investor alive—the only one of the Forbes 400 to have earned his fortune entirely through investing, in bull and bear markets. Buffet is a proponent of the value approach, a theory he learned early in his career and one that remains a powerful tool today.

AUDIENCE: Beginning, Individual, Professional   RISK LEVEL: Moderate, Aggressive
TOPICS: Stocks

Mind of the Market: A Study of Stock Market Philosophies, Their Uses, and Their Implications, The

Charles W. Smith
Rowman & Littlefield Publishers, Inc.
4720 Boston Way
Lanham, MD 20706

PH: (301) 459-3366
ISBN: 0-8476-6983-I
Published: 1981
Cost: $12.95

Penetrating view of the investor's mind. A leading sociologist and student of the stock market takes you behind the scenes of formal rules and regulations to reveal those intangible elements that make the market and move its players. A book for all who are fascinated by the world of money and the mysteries of human behavior.

AUDIENCE: Individual, Professional   RISK LEVEL: Moderate, Aggressive
TOPICS: Stocks

Modern Commodity Futures Trading

Gerald Gold
Commodity Research Bureau
75 Wall Street
22nd Floor
New York, NY 10005

PH: (800) 446-4519
Published: 1975 (7th edition)
Cost: $20.00

A practical explanation of the techniques and methods for successful trading in the commodity markets. Also presents the mechanics and background of the markets for those who are new to them. Written by an active commodity market expert and scholar, this book imparts technical knowledge in clear and comprehensible terms.

AUDIENCE: Individual, Professional   RISK LEVEL: Aggressive
TOPICS: Options, Futures/Commodities

Modern Investment Theory

Robert A. Haugen
Prentice Hall
113 Sylvan Avenue
Route 9W
Englewood Cliffs, NJ 07632

PH: (800) 223-1360
Published: 1993
Cost: $61.33

Study guide with questions and answers — provides basics of securities and financial markets, a host of varied investment theories applicable to equities, options, and futures.

AUDIENCE: Beginning   RISK LEVEL: Moderate, Aggressive
TOPICS: All

Money

Lawrence S. Ritter & William L. Silber
Basic Books, Inc.
10 E. 53rd Street
New York, NY 10022

PH: (800) 242-7737
ISBN: 0-45604722-X
Published: 1984 (5th and revised
   edition)
Cost: $15.95

The most authoritative and liveliest guide to the mysteries of money and monetary policy available to the general reader. Thoroughly revised fifth edition considers the financial gyrations that have recently shaken and continue to shake the United States. Provides a clear, complete, accurate, and even amusing analysis of the sphinx-like world of money.

AUDIENCE: Beginning, Individual   RISK LEVEL: Conservative, Moderate, Aggressive
TOPICS: All

Money Dynamics for the 1990s

Venita VanCaspel
Simon & Schuster
1230 Avenue of the Americas
New York, NY 10020

PH: (212) 698-7000
(800) 223-2348
ISBN: 0-671-66158-2
Published: 1988
Cost: $24.50

With the myriad of tax law changes in 1986 and the stock market collapse of 1987, financial planning, personal investing, and asset allocation became a whole new ball game. This dynamic directory to personal investing gives you all the strategies and techniques you'll need to achieve maximum financial gain in the decade ahead.

AUDIENCE: Beginning, Individual   RISK LEVEL: Conservative, Moderate
TOPICS: Bonds, Mutual Funds, Stocks, Investment Planning

Money Game, The

Adam Smith
Random House, Inc.
201 E. 50th Street
31st Floor
New York, NY 10022

PH: (800) 733-3000
ISBN: 0-394-7203-9
Published: 1976 (3rd edition)
Cost: $8.00

About image and reality and identity and anxiety and money, and in that order says the author. This veteran Wall Street observer informs with a thorough knowledge of financial affairs and delights with a keen sense of humor. "None of the solemn sacred cows of Wall Street escape debunking," says Library Journal.

AUDIENCE: Beginning, Individual, Professional   RISK LEVEL: Moderate, Aggressive
TOPICS: Bonds, Mutual Funds, Stocks

Money Management Strategies for Futures Traders

Nauzeri Balsara
John Wiley & Sons, Inc.
605 Third Avenue
New York, NY 10158-0012

PH: (212) 850-6000
FAX: (212) 850-6088
Published: 1992
Cost: $45.00

Offers practical strategies for novice and professional futures traders for limiting risk, avoiding tremendous losses and managing a futures portfolio to maximize profits.

AUDIENCE: Individual, Professional   RISK LEVEL: Aggressive
TOPICS: Futures/Commodities

Money Market Calculations: Yields, Break-Evens, and Arbitrage

Marcia Stigum & John Man
Irwin Professional Publishing
1333 Burr Ridge Parkway
Burr Ridge, IL 60521

PH: (708) 789-5489
(800) 634-3966
FAX: (708) 789-6933
ISBN: 0-87094-192-5
Published: 1989 (2nd edition)
Cost: $60.00

Clearly explains important money market calculations, including those for computing yields to maturity, security prices, accrued interest, and break-even rates, as well as for directly comparing yields on instruments that differ by type and/or maturity. Unique notation system enables anyone to use all formulas and equations.

AUDIENCE: Professional   RISK LEVEL: Conservative
TOPICS: Bonds

Money Market, The

Marcia Stigum
Irwin Professional Publishing
1333 Burr Ridge Parkway
Burr Ridge, IL 60521

PH: (708) 789-5489
(800) 634-3966
FAX: (708) 789-6933
ISBN: 1-55623-122-9
Published: 1990 (3rd edition)
Cost: $80.00

An in-depth look at the money markets. Chapters include Interest Rate Swaps, T-Bonds and Note Futures, Euros, Options in the Fixed Income World, Government and Federal Agency Securities, The Federal Funds Market, Money Market Funds, The Treasury and Federal Agencies and much more.

AUDIENCE: Individual, Professional   RISK LEVEL: Conservative, Moderate
TOPICS: Bonds

Mortgage Backed Securities

Andrew S. Davidson and Michael
  D. Herskovitz
Probus Publishing
1925 N. Clybourn Ave., Suite 401
Chicago, IL 60614

PH: (800) PROBUS-1
FAX: (312) 868-6250
Cost: $65.00
Date of first issue: 1993
ISBN:1-55738-440-1

"A blueprint for the analysis and valuation of mortgage-backed securities....In this groundbreaking book, the authors identify the advantages and disadvantages of each approach, and show investors how to develop an analytical method that is tailored to their own investment objectives."

AUDIENCE: Individual, Professional   RISK LEVEL: Conservative, Moderate
TOPICS: Bonds

Mortgage Securities: The High Yield Alternative to CDS/The Low-Risk Alternative to Stocks

Daniel R. Amerman
Probus Publishing Co.
1925 N. Clybourn Ave., Suite 401
Chicago, IL 60614

PH: (800) PROBUS-1
FAX: (312) 868-6250
Cost: $27.50
Date of first issue: 1993
ISBN:1-55738-477-0

"Covers all the basics: the structure of the products, prepayment behavior, sensitivity to interest rate changes and investment strategies."

AUDIENCE: Individual, Professional   RISK LEVEL: Conservative
TOPICS: Bonds

Municipal Bonds: The Comprehensive Review of Municipal Securities & Public Finance

Robert Lamb and Stephen P. Rappaport
McGraw-Hill Publishing Company
1221 Avenue of the Americas
New York, NY 10020

PH: (800) 262-4729
ISBN: 0-07-036084-7
Published: 1987 (2nd edition)
Cost: $28.50

How municipal bonds originate and are marketed, their advantages and limitations, how to evaluate investment potential, and much more. Presents a clear picture of the market, accounting and legal issues, new bonds, and what the future holds for investors and issuing governments. Revised for the Tax Reform Act of 1986.

AUDIENCE: Beginning, Individual, Professional   RISK LEVEL: Conservative
TOPICS: Bonds

Mutual Fund Encyclopedia, The

Gerald W. Perritt
Dearborn Financial Publishing, Inc.
520 N. Dearborn Street
Chicago, IL 60610

PH: (312) 836-4400 ext. 320
(800) 621-9621 ext. 320
Published 1994 (revised annually)
Cost: $35.95

Profiles 1,100 mutual funds detailing objectives and strategies, financial statistics, current yields, portfolio turnover rate, year by year and 5 year average returns and more.

AUDIENCE: Beginning, Individual   RISK LEVEL: Moderate, Aggressive
TOPICS: Mutual Funds

Mutual Fund Fact Book

Investment Company Institute
1600 M Street
Washington, D.C. 20036

PH: (202) 326-5800
Published: every May for the
  previous year
Cost: $25.00

The book includes facts and figures on mutual fund investing, information on the assets of mutual funds, the sales redemption value, a historical background on mutual funds and recent trends affecting various funds.

AUDIENCE: Beginning, Individual   RISK LEVEL: Moderate, Aggressive
TOPICS: Mutual Funds

Mutual Funds Almanac

Babson-United Investment
Advisors, Inc.
101 Prescott Street
Wellesley Hills, MA 02181

PH: (617) 235-0900
FAX: (617) 235-9450
Cost: $32.00
Date of first issue: 1991

An indispensable reference book of concise, accurate mutual funds information. Include performance statistics for the past 10 years on 2,100 funds, fund objectives, total assets, net asset value, sales charges, expense ratios, minimum investments, addresses and straight talk about the mutual funds industry. A.F.P.

AUDIENCE: Beginning, Individual   RISK LEVEL: Moderate, Aggressive
TOPICS: Mutual Funds

Mutual Funds - How to Invest with the Pros

Kurt Brouwer
John Wiley & Sons, Inc.
605 Third Avenue
New York, NY 10158-0012

PH: (212) 850-6418 orders
Other: (212) 850-6233 info.
Published: 1988
Cost: $19.95

Advice from nine investment pros on how to achieve your investment goals.

AUDIENCE: Beginning, Individual   RISK LEVEL: Moderate, Aggressive
TOPICS: Mutual Funds

Mutual Funds

The Smart BBlockbuster
  Periodicals, Inc.
2131 Hollywood Blvd.
Hollywood, FL 33020-6728

PH: (305) 925-5242
FAX: (305) 925-5244
Cost: $4.95
Date of first issue: Winter 1993

Contents include background of mutual funds, how to read the mutual fund listing, why big investors buy mutual funds, how the funds get paid, how a prospectus can help you, laws that protect you, how to start an investment program, investing the way the pros do, investing for growth, income, etc.

AUDIENCE: Beginning   RISK LEVEL: Moderate
TOPICS: Mutual Funds

Mutual Funds Videocourse

American Association of Individual
  Investors
625 Michigan Avenue
Chicago, IL

PH: (312) 280-0170
Published: 1991 (last update)
Cost: $129.00, $98.00 for AAII
  members
VIDEO

A 4 hour video with workbook. Topics include costs, fees, loads, redemption charges, taxation, cost basis, performance evaluation, risk/return, how to select mutual funds and much, much more.

AUDIENCE: Beginning, Individual   RISK LEVEL: Moderate
TOPICS: Mutual Funds

NBR Video Tape Series

NBR
P.O. Box 2
North Miami, FL 33261-0002

PH: Credit Card Orders 1-800-535-5864
Customer Service (317) 299-9191
M-F 8:30 am-4:30 PM Eastern Time
Video Tapes
Costs: $24.95 for each tape + $4
  shipping and handling

Videotapes, " NBR Industry Watch `92"(Updated annually), "NBR Guide to Wall Street Trading Strategies," "How Wall Street Works," "NBR Guide to Retirement Planning," " NBR Guide to Buying Insurance," "How to Plan Your Estate or Inheritance."

AUDIENCE: Beginning, Individual   RISK LEVEL: Moderate, Aggressive
TOPICS: Bonds, Mutual Funds, Stocks

Nelson's Directory of Investment Managers

Nelson Publications
1 Gateway Plaza
Port Chester, NY 10573

PH: (800) 333-6357
FAX: (914) 937-8908
Published: annually
Cost: $425.00

In depth profiles of over 2,000 money management firms... including 1, 3, 5 and 10 year performance results. Six fact filled sections: Section 1 - In-depth profiles of each money manager; Section 2 - Geographic listing of manager arranged by state; Section 3 - Rankings of all firms by asset size; Section 4 - Listing of firms by type of organization; Section 5 - Index of firms by specialized investment services offered; Section 6 - 1, 3, 5 and 10 year performance rankings of all firms by asset class.

AUDIENCE: Individual, Professional   RISK LEVEL: Moderate, Aggressive
TOPICS: Bonds, Stocks, Asset Allocation

Nelson's Directory of Investment Research

Nelson Publications
1 Gateway Plaza
Port Chester, NY 10573

PH: (800) 333-6357
FAX: (914) 937-8908
Published: annually
Cost: $535.00

Nelson's Directory is published in two volumes. Volume #1 contains expanded research and financial information on over 5,000 U.S. public companies. Volume #2 contains comprehensive information on over 4,000 foreign-based public companies. And, of course, analyst coverage of all 9,000 companies, important stock data and research reports on each company.

AUDIENCE: Individual, Professional   RISK LEVEL: Moderate, Aggressive
TOPICS: Bonds, Stocks, Investment Research

Neural Networks in Finance and Investing

Robert R. Trippi and Efrain Turban
Probus Publishing
1925 N. Clybourn Ave., Suite 401
Chicago, IL 60614

PH: (800) PROBUS-1
Cost: $65.00
Date of first issue: 1993
ISBN:1-55738-452-5
Technical Analysis

"This landmark text not only contains many examples of how neural networks can be used for financial prediction and risk assessment, but provides promising systems for forecasting and explaining price movements of stocks and securities."

AUDIENCE: Professional	RISK LEVEL: Moderate, Aggressive
TOPICS: Stocks, Asset Allocation	

Never Make a Rich Man Poor

Victor Sperandeo
Rand Management Corporation
1 Chapel Hill Road
Short Hills, NJ 07078

PH: (800) 842-RAND
Published: 1990
Cost: $95.00
VIDEO

Victor Sperandeo, a 25 year Wall Street veteran will tell you how to preserve the profits you made in the 1980s and prosper in the 90s, as well as how his exceptional method of managing money has created a 35% plus average annual rate of return for 8 years or more.

AUDIENCE: Beginning, Individual	RISK LEVEL: Moderate, Aggressive
TOPICS: Stocks	

New Commodity Trading Systems and Methods, The

Perry J. Kaufman
John Wiley & Sons, Inc.
605 Third Avenue
New York, NY 10158-0012

PH: (212) 850-6000
FAX: (212) 850-6088
ISBN: 0-471-878790-0
Published: 1987 (2nd edition)
Cost: $65.00

Comprehensive guide critically examines the most commonly used technical trading techniques for determining price movement in today's agricultural, financial and stock market index markets. You'll learn what systems are most profitable under what conditions, why, and how. New edition reflects dramatic changes in the markets.

AUDIENCE: Individual, Professional	RISK LEVEL: Aggressive
TOPICS: Options, Futures/Commodities	

New Contrarian Investment Strategy: The Psychology of Stock Market Success, The

David Dreman
Random House, Inc.
201 E 50th Street, 31st Floor
New York, NY 10022

PH: (800) 733-3000
ISBN: 0-394-52364-4
Published: 1983
Cost: $22.45

Thoroughly updated revision of the highly successful and influential work analyzes the investment climate of the 1980s. Shows how the investor can take advantage of market fluctuations, and gives a personal contrarian assessment of current trends. Demonstrates where the opportunity lies - contrary to the opinion of most experts.

AUDIENCE: Individual, Professional	RISK LEVEL: Moderate, Aggressive
TOPICS: Bonds, Stocks	

New High Yield Bond Market, The

Jess Lederman and Michael P. Sullivan
Probus Publishing
1925 N. Clybourn Ave., Suite 401
Chicago, IL 60614

PH: (800) PROBUS-1
FAX: (312) 868-6250
Cost: $55.00
Date of first issue:1993
ISBN: 1-55738-436-3

". . . the first book to address the new realities of the traditional high-yield markets." Topics include: the corporate debt market, using high-yield bonds to reduce risk without sacrificing return, new opportunities that have emerged since the "junk bond bust," sovereign bonds and mortgage-backed securities.

AUDIENCE: Individual	RISK LEVEL: Moderate
TOPICS: Bonds	

New Market Wizards - Conversations with America's Top Traders, The

Jack D. Schwager
Harper Collins Publishers, Inc.
10 East 53rd Street
New York, NY 10022

PH: (800) 242-7737
FAX: (800) 822-4090
Cost: $13.00
Date of first issue: 1992
ISBN : 0-88730-667-5

". . . offers practical and insightful advice on investing from some of the most prestigious Wall Street professionals in a personal, anecdotal style that makes it both informative and highly accessible."

AUDIENCE: Individual, Professional	RISK LEVEL: Aggressive
TOPICS: Stocks, Options, Futures/Commodities	

New Options Market, The

Max G. Ansbacher
Walker & Company
435 Hudson Street
New York, NY 10014

PH: (212) 727-8300
ISBN: 0-8027-7308-7
Published: 1987 (2nd edition)
Cost: $17.95

Updated and enlarged guide to the options market reveals strategies for profit by trading puts and calls. Describes the advantages and disadvantages of every strategy in easy-to-understand language. Leads you through sample trades and presents everything you need to know to invest and speculate successfully with options.

AUDIENCE: Individual	RISK LEVEL: Aggressive
TOPICS: Options	

New Strategies for Mutual Fund Investing

Donald Rugg
Irwin Professional Publishing
1333 Burr Ridge Parkway
Burr Ridge, IL 60521

PH: (800) 634-3966
FAX: (708) 789-6933
ISBN: 1-55623-045-1
Published: 1989
Cost: $32.00

A strategy for selecting and managing a fund portfolio using current data available by personal computer.

AUDIENCE: Beginning, Individual	RISK LEVEL: Moderate, Aggressive
TOPICS: Mutual Funds	

New Technical Trader, The

Tushar S. Chande and Stanley Kroll
John Wiley & Sons, Inc.
605 Third Avenue
New York, NY 10158-0012

PH: (212) 850-6000
FAX: (212) 850-6088
Published: 1994
Technical Analysis
Cost: $49.95

Discusses new technical analysis methods such as VIDYA, Qstick, new momentum oscillators, linear regression analysis and combines them with strategies for effective risk control and money management.

AUDIENCE: Individual, Professional	RISK LEVEL: Aggressive
TOPICS: Options, Futures	

No Loads - Mutual Fund Profits Using Technical Analysis

James E. Keares
Liberty House
TAB Books, Inc.
Blue Ridge Summit, PA 17294-0214

Published: 1989
Cost: $19.95

Covers market analysis, technical analysis, mutual funds. "A simple, effective system that any investor can use to achieve high profits."

AUDIENCE: Beginning, Individual	RISK LEVEL: Moderate, Aggressive
TOPICS: Mutual Funds	

NYIF Guide to Investing, Second Edition

New York Institute of
  Finance/Prentice Hall
113 Sylvan Avenue
Route 9W
Englewood Cliffs, NJ 07632

PH: (800) 947-7700
FAX: (515) 284-2607
Published: 1992
Cost: $17.95

This revised and expanded primer is an easy-to-understand guide to financial products developing an investment strategy. Beginning with the basics, it explains the merits of full-service versus discount brokers, the full range of products available, and differences between OTC and exchange trading.

AUDIENCE: Beginning, Individual	RISK LEVEL: Moderate
TOPICS: All	

NYIF Vest-Pocket Guide to Stock Brokerage Math, The

William A. Rini
New York Institute of
  Finance/Prentice Hall
113 Sylvan Avenue
Route 9W
Englewood Cliffs, NJ 07632

PH: (800) 947-7700
FAX: (515) 284-2607
Published: 1992
Cost: $13.95

A step-by-step demonstration of how to perform yield, interest, and ratio calculations using a ten-key calculator. Focuses on the math required in the Series 7 exam, as well as the brokerage licensing exams, and includes all math stock brokers require on the job.

AUDIENCE: Professional	RISK LEVEL: All
TOPICS: All	

One Up on Wall Street: How to Use What You Already Know to Make Money in the Market

Peter Lynch
Simon & Schuster, Inc.
1230 Avenue of the Americas
New York, NY 10020

PH: (800) 223-2336
FAX: (212) 698-7007
ISBN: 0671661035
Published: 1989

Cost: $19.95
Covers investing theories, fundamental analysis. The philosophy behind Peter Lynch's Stellar investing record. He shows how to research stocks and analyze financial statements and ignore every influence except the fundamentals of the company you're investing in.

AUDIENCE: Professional	RISK LEVEL: Moderate, Aggressive
TOPICS: Stocks	

Option Market Making

Allen Jan Baird
John Wiley & Sons, Inc.
605 Third Avenue
New York, NY 10158-0012

PH: (212) 850-6000
FAX: (212) 850-6088
Published: 1993
Cost: $55.00

Looks at option trading from the market makers' point of view. Covers risk analysis, spreads, option volatility and pricing, and tactics and strategies for option traders. In depth discussion of synthetic options is included.

AUDIENCE: Individual, Professional	RISK LEVEL: Aggressive
TOPICS: Options	

Option Player's Advanced Guidebook, The

Institute for Options Research, Inc.
P.O. Box 6586
Lake Tahoe, NV 89449

PH: (800) 334-0854 ext. 840
(702) 588-3590
FAX: (702) 588-8481
Published: 1980
Cost: $35.00

Uses pricing tables. An option book which displays when to buy or write specific options and exactly when to take profits. The many pricing tables will stack the odds in your favor - you will never pay too much for an option again.

AUDIENCE: Individual, Professional	RISK LEVEL: Aggressive
TOPICS: Options, Futures/Commodities	

Option Strategies - Profit Making Techniques for Stock, Stock-Index and Commodity Options

Courtney Smith
John Wiley & Sons, Inc.
605 Third Avenue
New York, NY 10158-0012

PH: (212) 850-6000
Published: 1987
ISBN: 0-471-84367-9
Cost: $39.95

Covers all types of options: stock index, stock, and commodity. Bullish and bearish strategies are covered equally. It will be useful to all options traders and hedgers, from novices to professionals. A.F.P.

AUDIENCE: Individual, Professional	RISK LEVEL: Aggressive
TOPICS: Options, Futures/Commodities	

Option Valuation: Analyzing and Pricing Standardized Contracts

R. Gibson
McGraw-Hill, Inc.
11 West 19th Street
New York, NY 10011

PH: (800) 722-4726
(212) 512-4100
Published: 1991
Cost: $50.88

Covers options trading and analysis. "This book presents the option pricing theory not only as a rather complex set of valuation formulas, and as a powerful instrument to help readers understand the basic mechanisms tradeoff." A.F.P.

AUDIENCE: Individual, Professional   RISK LEVEL: Aggressive
TOPICS: Options

Option Volatility and Pricing Strategies

Sheldon Natenberg
Probus Publishing Co.
1925 North Clybourn Avenue
Chicago, IL 60614

PH: (800) PROBUS-1
FAX: (312) 868-6250
ISBN: 1-55738-009-0
Published: 1988
Cost: $47.50

Covers technical analysis. Combines the insights produced by Mr. Natenberg's many years as a professional latest and most advanced option pricing theories with trader to give prospective traders a richer and more comprehensive understanding of the behavior and applications of options.

AUDIENCE: Individual, Professional   RISK LEVEL: Aggressive
TOPICS: Options

Options: The Investor's Complete Tool Kit

Robert W. Kolb
New York Institute of
  Finance/Prentice Hall
113 Sylvan Avenue
Route 9W
Englewood Cliffs, NJ 07632

PH: (800) 947-7700
FAX: (515) 284-2607
Published: 1991
Cost: $34.95

Presents the tools necessary for a dynamic analysis of options evaluation, trading and management. Covers stock options, foreign exchange options, options on futures, and options on stock indexes. Also includes a 5-$\frac{1}{4}$ disk that simulates actual risk and portfolio management options positions and stategies.

AUDIENCE: Individual, Professional   RISK LEVEL: Aggressive
TOPICS: Options

Options: A Personal Seminar

Scott Fullman
New York Institute of
  Finance/Prentice Hall
113 Sylvan Avenue
Route 9W
Englewood Cliffs, NJ 07632

PH: (800) 947-7700
FAX: (515) 284-2607
Published: 1992
Cost: $21.95

This self-teaching seminar explains the fundamentals of options then moves on to more complex topics such as index warrants, arbitrage trading and how to use options when managing a portfolio. Features case studies and charts illustrating different stages of options strategies.

AUDIENCE: Individual, Professional   RISK LEVEL: Aggressive
TOPICS: Options

Options As a Strategic Investment

Lawrence G. McMillan
New York Institute of
  Finance/Prentice Hall
113 Sylvan Avenue
Route 9W
Englewood Cliffs, NJ 07632

PH: (800) 947-7700
FAX: (515) 284-2607
Published: 1993, 3rd edition
ISBN: 0-13-638347-5
Cost: $48.25

Written for investors who have some familiarity with the option market, this comprehensive reference explains both concept and applications of various option strategies - how they work, in which situations, and why. Examples make clear the power of each strategy under carefully described market conditions.

AUDIENCE: Individual, Professional   RISK LEVEL: Aggressive
TOPICS: Options

Options - Essential Concepts and Trading Strategies

The Educational Division of the
  Chicago Board
Options Exchange
Irwin Professional Publishing
1333 Burr Ridge Parkway
Burr Ridge, IL 60521

PH: (800) 634-3966
FAX: (708) 789-6933
ISBN: 1-55623-102-4
Published: August 1990
Cost: $50.00

Covers investing theories and trading analysis. Describes the different trading strategies individuals, institutions and floor traders can use to close the deal. Demonstrates proven options pricing and forecasting theories. Individuals, institutions, and floor traders alike can use these comprehensive trading strategies to work faster and more accurately, predict the winners and avoid the losers and discover practical user-oriented issues and applications for options trading.

AUDIENCE: Individual, Professional   RISK LEVEL: Aggressive
TOPICS: Options

Options on Foreign Exchange

David F. DeRosa
Probus Publishing Co.
1925 North Clybourn Avenue
Chicago, IL 60614

PH: (800) PROBUS-1
FAX: (312) 868-6250
ISBN: 1-55738-249-2
Published: 1992
Cost: $65.00

State-of-the-art theories and strategies for the institutional investor. Aimed specifically at the needs of institutional/bank foreign exchange traders and hedgers who use options strategies and related synthetics. Topics include: currency futures options, mechanics of currency options markets, parity theorems, valuation of European and American currency options, listed currency warrants, OTC options and exotic currency options. Also includes an extensive and useful glossary of related terms.

AUDIENCE: Professional   RISK LEVEL: Aggressive
TOPICS: Bonds, Options, Futures/Commodities

Paper Money

Adam Smith
Summit Books
1230 Avenue of the Americas
New York, NY 10020

PH: (800) 223-2336
ISBN: 0-671-44825-0
Published: 1981
Cost: $14.95

Having interpreted the prosperous 1960s and the stressful 1970s, Smith now tells what has happened since and what to expect next. How the age of paper money has arrived, what it means, and how it has changed our lives. Can there be a real estate crash? Is the stock market safe? Answers to these and many other important questions.

AUDIENCE: Beginning, Individual   RISK LEVEL: Moderate, Aggressive
TOPICS: Bonds, Mutual Funds, Stocks

Passport to Profits: Opportunities in International Investing

John P. Dessauer
Dearborn Financial Publications, Inc.
520 N. Dearborn
Chicago, IL 60610

PH: (312) 836-4400 ext. 320
(800) 621-9621 ext. 320
Published: 1990
Cost: $27.95

Covers international markets, fundamental analysis, currencies, gold, precious metals. Shows investors and money managers how they can enter international markets and play them successfully. Dessauer shows that in the years ahead stock market profits are most likely to be found outside the United States.

AUDIENCE: Beginning, Individual, Professional   RISK LEVEL: Moderate, Aggressive
TOPICS: Bonds, Mutual Funds, Stocks

Personal Financial Planning

G. Victor Hallman & Jerry S.
  Rosenbloom
McGraw-Hill Publishing Company
1221 Avenue of the Americas
New York, NY 10020

PH: (800) 262-4729
ISBN: 0-07-025650-0
Published: 1993, 5th edition
Cost: $40.00

Reflecting the Tax Reform Act of 1986, shows how to set up a coordinated plan for your financial future. Covers every aspect of tax planning, taking advantage of market cycles, selecting and buying the right insurance, planning for retirement, and estate planning. Outlines a simple and practical financial planning process.

AUDIENCE: Beginning, Individual   RISK LEVEL: Conservative, Moderate
TOPICS: Bonds, Mutual Funds, Stocks

Personal Investors Complete Book of Bonds, The

Donald R. Nichols
Dearborn Financial Publishing, Inc.
520 N. Dearborn Street
Chicago, IL 60610

PH: (800) 621-9621 ext. 320
ISBN: 0-88462-627-X
Published: 1989
Cost: $12.95

This book gives comprehensive, up-to-date and clearly written explanations of many investments, including CDs, treasury securities, municipals, zero coupon certificates, corporate convertible bonds and more. Its spells out specific features, advantages and disadvantages of each bond type. Details all types of bonds, assesses risks, and potential yields. Suggests plans for bond use in saving for retirement, college, etc. Beneficial for beginner or sophisticated investor.

AUDIENCE: Beginning, Individual   RISK LEVEL: Conservative, Moderate
TOPICS: Bonds

Point & Figure Constructions and Formations

Michael Burke
Chartcraft, Inc.
1 West Avenue
Larchmont, NY 10538

PH: (914) 632-0422
Published: 1992 (revised)
Cost: $14.95

Uses charts. This all new book modernizes the original P&F methodology first Published: in 1948 by A.W. Cohen. Concepts on constructing P&F charts remain unchanged, but emphasis is placed on relative strength analysis, use of trendlines and support and resistance areas. Several new formations are discussed along with new terminology. This book is designed to be a complete, updated guide to Point & Figure Charting.

AUDIENCE: Individual, Professional   RISK LEVEL: Moderate, Aggressive
TOPICS: Stocks

Practical Asset Allocation and the Business Cycle

Martin J. Pring
International Institute for Economic
  Research
P.O. Box 329, Blackville Road
Washington Depot, CT 06794

PH: (800) 221-7514
Cost: Video and free 80 page
  booklet $95.00
VIDEO

Covers asset allocation; uses charts. During a typical business cycle, the financial markets progress through six stages for which a different portfolio mix of stocks, bonds and inflation - hedge assets is appropriate. With animated diagrams and charts, the course explains when these stages occur, how you can identify them and which asset classes are likely to do best.

AUDIENCE: Beginning, Individual, Professional   RISK LEVEL: Moderate
TOPICS: Bonds, Mutual Funds, Stocks, Asset Allocation

Profit Magic of Stock Transaction Timing, The

J.M. Hurst/Prentice Hall
P.O. Box 11071
Des Moines, IA 50336-1071

PH: (201) 592-2000
Published: 1972
Cost: $15.95

Covers investing theories, market analysis, trading analysis, fundamental analysis, technical analysis; uses charts. "A price forecasting technique that predicts price turns with 90% accuracy. Produces an average net profit of 10% per month and proves your stock market fortune can be built like clockwork."

AUDIENCE: Beginning, Individual   RISK LEVEL: Moderate, Aggressive
TOPICS: Stocks

Profitable Grain Trading

Ralph M. Ainsworth
Traders Press, Inc.
P.O. Box 6206
Greenville, SC 29606

PH: (800) 927-8222
ISBN: 0-934380-04-X
Published: 1933 (1980 reprint)
Cost: $9.95

This classic book on grain speculation was first published in 1933 by a respected grain trader, real estate speculator, and pioneer in the seed industry. Much of his trading philosophy and accumulated market wisdom are revealed in this volume, along with many of the most effective technical trading systems that he discovered.

AUDIENCE: Professional   RISK LEVEL: Aggressive
TOPICS: Options, Futures/Commodities

Profitable Trading with Charts and Technicals

Commodities Education Institute
219 Parade
Cedar Falls, IA 50613

PH: (800) 635-3936
(319) 277-6341
FAX: (319) 277-7982
Published: 1990
Cost: $55.00
VIDEO

Covers investing theories, trading analysis, technical analysis. Glen Ring, editor of Commodity Closeup shows you how to build your own "tool-box" of practical technical analysis techniques. Topics include: market psychology, bar charts, trend spotting, support and resistance, terminal areas, congestion patterns, Elliott Wave applications, Fibonacci numbers, introduction to Gann and RSI, using computerized technical tools, order placement and working with your broker.

AUDIENCE: Individual   RISK LEVEL: Moderate, Aggressive
TOPICS: Stocks, Options, Futures/Commodities

Profitable Trading with Gann and Directional Indicators

Glen Ring
Commodities Educational Institute
219 Parkade
Cedar Falls, IA 50613

PH: (319) 277-6341
(800) 635-3936
FAX: (319) 277-7982
Published: 3/90 redone in March 91
Cost: $233.00/5 tapes and notebook
VIDEO

Subjects addressed are commodities trading, technical analysis. Coverage includes market psychology and discipline, how to improve performance, basic Gann techniques, relative strength index, stochastics, directional movement indicator and specific techniques for combining Gann and directional indicators into a disciplined, profitable, trading plan. Led in front of a live audience.

AUDIENCE: Individual, Professional   RISK LEVEL: Aggressive
TOPICS: Options, Futures/Commodities

Prudent Investing for Safety, Income or Capital Growth

United Investment Advisors, Inc.
1230 Avenue of the Americas
New York, NY 10020

PH: (212) 698-7323
(212) 698-7035
Published: 1983, 1993
ISBN: 0-671-74232-9
Cost: $14.95

An authoritative financial self-help reference on the stock market. Sections include: The Art of Prudent Investing, Your Various Alternatives, How to Make Your Choices, Mastering the Strategies and Tactics, Taking Care of the Housekeeping, Investments and Your Financial Plan, and Speaking the Language of the Bulls and Bears. A.F.P.

AUDIENCE: Beginning   RISK LEVEL: Moderate
TOPICS: Mutual Funds, Stocks

Prudent Speculator, The

Al Frank Asset Management, Inc.
P.O. Box 1767
Santa Monica, CA 90406-1767

PH: (800) 258-7786
Published: 1990
Cost: $27.95

Subjects addressed are investing theories, fundamental analysis, trading analysis. Details the basics of stock investing and shows you how to develop a long-term strategy. By using a combination of investment measurements, Frank shows you how to place your money in the right place at the right time so that it earns the best return for you. A.F.P.

AUDIENCE: Individual   RISK LEVEL: Moderate, Aggressive
TOPICS: Bonds, Stocks

Psychology of Smart Investing: Meeting the 6 Mental Challenges, The

Ira Epstein and David Garfield
John Wiley & Sons, Inc.
605 Third Avenue
New York, NY 10158-0012

PH: (212) 850-6000
FAX: (212) 850-6088
Published: 1992
Cost: $29.95

"Written by a board-certified psychiatrist and the founder of Chicago's best-known brokerage firm, it contains the psychological tools essential to breaking through mental barriers in order to achieve a successful mindset." It discusses poor self-esteem, depression, loneliness, addiction to playing the markets, revenge and more.

AUDIENCE: Individual, Professional   RISK LEVEL: Moderate, Aggressive
TOPICS: Stocks, Options

Quality of Earnings: The Investor's Guide to How Much Money a Company Is Really Making

Thornton L. O'Glove
The Free Press
866 Third Avenue
New York, NY 10022

PH: (800) 257-5755
Published: 1987
ISBN: 0-02-922630-9
Cost: $29.95

A long-awaited guide to maximum-return investment. Learn to spot trouble before the market catches wind of it and recognize the important differences between a corporation's shareholder books and its tax books. Gives the reader the meaningful edge over other investors.

AUDIENCE: Individual   RISK LEVEL: Moderate, Aggressive
TOPICS: Bonds, Stocks

Quantitative International Investing

Brian R. Bruce
Probus Publishing Co.
1925 N. Clybourn Ave.
Suite 401
Chicago, IL 60614

PH: (800) PROBUS-1
(312) 868-1100
FAX: (312) 868-6250
Cost: $69.95
Date of first issue:1990

"Focuses on the foundation needed to manage international funds successfully. Covering international equity and fixed income as well as other pertinent topics relevant to anyone who manages funds, this exhaustive work covers several types of money management for each asset class including both active and passive approaches as well as quantitative strategies which combine variations of the two."

AUDIENCE: Professional   RISK LEVEL: Moderate, Aggressive
TOPICS: Bonds, Stocks

Raging Bull: How to Invest in the Growth Stocks of the '90s

David Alger
Irwin Professional Publishing
1333 Burr Ridge Parkway
Burr Ridge, IL 60521

PH: (800) 634-3966
FAX: (708) 789-6933
ISBN: 1-55623-462-7
Published: 1991
Cost: $27.00

It is widely believed that the 89% of individual investors who own stocks will move from glass ceilinged blue chips to stocks that promise higher growth. David Alger shows investors how to discover the next Apple Computer, Cellular One, or Nike. Strategies for achieving high returns on growth stocks, guidelines for prudent stock analysis that safeguard against risky investments.

AUDIENCE: Beginning, Individual   RISK LEVEL: Moderate, Aggressive
TOPICS: Stocks

Random Walk Down Wall Street, A

Burton G. Malkiel
W. W. Norton & Company, Inc.
500 Fifth Avenue
New York, NY 10110

ISBN: 0-393-02793-7
Published: 1973, 1990, 1991 (5th
   edition)
Cost: $14.95

Subjects addressed are investing theories, stock analysis, bond analysis, fundamental analysis, technical analysis. Beat the pros at their own game and learn a user-friendly long-range investing strategy that really works.

AUDIENCE: Beginning, Individual   RISK LEVEL: Moderate, Aggressive
TOPICS: Stocks

Relative Dividend Yield: Common Stock

Anthony E. Spare
Investing for Income and Appreciation
John Wiley & Sons, Inc.
605 Third Avenue
New York, NY 10158-0012

PHONE: (212) 850-6000
FAX: (212) 850-6088
Date of first issue: 1992

"Offers a conservative investment approach suitable to all market conditions and is especially effective in dealing with uncertain or bear markets." The author explains how to use dividend and price history to screen undervalued blue-chip stocks and how to set up buy/sell ranges.

AUDIENCE: Individual, Professional   RISK LEVEL: Moderate, Aggressive
TOPICS: Stocks

Relative Strength Index: Forecasting and Trading Strategies for the Financial Markets

Andrew Cardwell
John Wiley & Sons, Inc.
605 Third Avenue
New York, NY 10158-0012

PH: (212) 850-6000
FAX: (212) 850-6088
Published: 1994
Technical Analysis
Cost: $55.00

Covers trend analysis and moving averages, Cardwell weekly RSI, positive/negative reversals, 1 time cycles, price cycles and retracement analysis, trading cycle highs and lows, trading bands, trendline analysis, intermarket analysis, RSI and other technical studies.

AUDIENCE: Individual, Professional   RISK LEVEL: Moderate, Aggressive
TOPICS: Stocks

Research, Analysis and Strategies

Frank J. Fabozzi
Probus Publishing Co.
1925 North Clybourn Avenue
Chicago, IL 60614

PH: (800) PROBUS-1
FAX: (312) 868-6250
Published: 1989
Cost: $69.95

Containing chapters by 21 preeminent authorities in the field, this resourceful guide has been assembled to meet the informational needs of portfolio managers and other investment professionals who require the latest methodologies and strategies for staying competitive. This text reviews the investment management process, the foundations of capital markets, and the role of options and futures.

AUDIENCE: Professional   RISK LEVEL: Moderate, Aggressive
TOPICS: Bonds, Stocks, Options, Futures/Commodities

Reuters Glossary: International Economic & Financial Terms

Reuters
Dearborn Financial Publishing, Inc.
520 N. Dearborn
Chicago, IL 60610

PH: (800) 621-9621 ext. 320
ISBN: 0-582-04286-0
Published: 1989
Cost: $12.95

More than 2,000 entries. Concepts such as accelerated depreciation and "zero coupons" explained in full. Originally used as a working tool for Reuters' staff worldwide, it's been expanded and brought up to date. Fully indexed and extensively cross-referenced.

AUDIENCE: Beginning, Individual, Professional   RISK LEVEL: Conservative,
TOPICS: General Reference   Moderate, Aggressive

Risk Based Capital Charges for Municipal Bonds

Robert Godfrey
JAI Press, Inc.
55 Old Post Road
P.O. Box 1678
Greenwich, CT 06835-1678

PH: (203) 661-7602
Cost: $35.10 + 2.50 postage and
  handling
Published: 1987

Written by MBIA executive VP Robert Godfrey, chronicles nation's economic and bond default history from 1869 to present. Offers modern day stress test for bonds to determine whether or not they're likely to default.

AUDIENCE: Individual, Professional   RISK LEVEL: Conservative
TOPICS: Bonds

Safe Investing: How to Make Money Without Losing Your Shirt

John Slattery
New York Institute of
  Finance/Prentice Hall
113 Sylvan Avenue
Route 9W
Englewood Cliffs, NJ 07632

PH: (800) 947-7700
FAX: (515) 284-2607
Published: 1991
Cost: $14.95

Examines the pros and cons of investing in annuities, blue chip stocks, and mutual funds . . . shows how to analyze companies by using S&P ratings, the Value Line Safety Rating, and the price/earnings ratio . . . identifies the most common mistakes and suggests remedies . . and more.

AUDIENCE: Beginning, Individual   RISK LEVEL: Conservative, Moderate
TOPICS: Bonds, Stocks, Mutual Funds, Asset Allocation

Seasonal Charts for Futures Traders: A Sourcebook

Courtney Smith
John Wiley & Sons, Inc.
605 Third Avenue
New York, NY 10158-0012

PH: (212) 850-6000
FAX: (212) 850-6088
ISBN: 0-471-84888-3
Published: 1987
Cost: $80.00

Easy-to-use guide to seasonal price movements provides the statistics you need to time entry and exit points, set stop-loss orders, and establish realistic goals. Offers insight into the profit potential and risk involved at any given time of the year. Charts and tables supply the odds for profit before you put in the trade.

AUDIENCE: Individual, Professional   RISK LEVEL: Aggressive
TOPICS: Options, Futures/Commodities

Secrets of the Temple: How the Federal Reserve Runs the Country

William Greider
Simon & Schuster
1230 Avenue of the Americas
New York, NY 10020

PH: (212) 698-7000
(800) 223-2348
ISBN: 0-671-67556-7
Published: 1987
Cost: $16.00

Chronicles the unseen political struggles that led to financial crisis and the stock market collapse of October 1987. The inside story of how the Federal Reserve, remote and mysterious to most Americans, actually ran things in the 1980s. Explains why politicians of both parties acquiesce to the power of the Federal Reserve.

AUDIENCE: Beginning, Individual, Professional   RISK LEVEL: Conservative, Moderate
TOPICS: Bonds, Mutual Funds, Stocks, Options, Futures/Commodities

Securities Analysis: A Personal Seminar

New York Institute of
    Finance/Prentice Hall
113 Sylvan Avenue
Route 9W
Englewood Cliffs, NJ 07632

PH: (800) 947-7700
FAX: (515) 284-2607
Published: 1989
Cost: $21.95

This self-teaching guide shows the novice how to evaluate stocks in light of individual investment goals and limitations. A hands-on format provides specific situations that develop confidence in analysis and decision making.

AUDIENCE: Beginning
TOPICS: Stocks
RISK LEVEL: Moderate, Aggressive

Security Analysis and Portfolio Management

Donald E. Fischer and Ronald J.
    Jordan
Prentice Hall
Route 9W
Englewood Cliffs, NJ 07632

PH: (201) 592-2000
Published: 1975, 1991 (5th edition)
Cost: $64.00

Covers investing theories, stock analysis, market analysis, bond analysis, earnings analysis, trading analysis, commodities trading, fundamental analysis, technical analysis. Uses charts. Includes investing environment, risk/return analysis, common stock analysis, bond analysis, options, technical analysis, the efficient market theory, portfolio analysis, selection and management.

AUDIENCE: Individual, Professional   RISK LEVEL: Moderate, Aggressive
TOPICS: Bonds, Stocks, Options, Futures/Commodities

Selling Covered Calls: The Safest Game on the Option Market

C. J. Caes
McGraw-Hill, Inc.
11 West 19th Street
New York, NY 10011

PH: (800) 722-4726
(212) 512-4100
Published: 1990
Cost: $24.60

Covers options trading; uses charts. The author shows why covered calls are a good bet in both bull and bear markets. He reviews the entire options market and gives a clear explanation of how this complicated system works.

AUDIENCE: Beginning, Individual   RISK LEVEL: Moderate, Aggressive
TOPICS: Stocks, Options

Selling Short

Joseph A. Walker
John Wiley & Sons, Inc.
605 Third Avenue
New York, NY 10158

PH: (212) 850-6000
FAX: (212) 850-6088
Cost: $42.50
Technical and Fundamental Analysis
Date of first issue: 1991

"Combines a history of short selling with current strategies and applications to present a complete guide to this increasingly popular investment tool. Risks and rewards of short selling are discussed in detail as are short selling as a tool for protecting other investments and for speculation."

AUDIENCE: Individual, Professional   RISK LEVEL: Aggressive
TOPICS: Stocks, Options, Futures

Simulation, Optimization & Expert Systems

Dimitris N. Chorafus
Probus Publishing Co.
1925 N. Clybourn Ave.
Suite 401
Chicago, IL 60614

PH: (800) PROBUS-1
FAX: (312) 868-6250
Cost: $65.00
Date of first issue:1992
ISBN:1-55738-231-X

". . . Brings you up to date with the latest methods, products and firms that are the driving forces behind today's markets. Specific topics include: Preparing for super computer usage, Expert Systems in trust management, computer-based trading, Financial data basis, Statistically valid portfolio diversifications and artificial intelligence."

AUDIENCE: Conservative, Moderate, Aggressive
TOPICS: All

Sooner Than You Think: Mapping a Course for a Comfortable Retirement

Gordon K. Williamson
Irwin Professional Publishing
1333 Burr Ridge Parkway
Burr Ridge, IL 60521

PH: (800) 634-3966
FAX: (708) 789-6933
ISBN: 1-55623-541-0
Published: 1993
Cost: $25.00

Uses charts. Shows readers how to determine a financial plan that will meet their retirement goals. Chockfull of charts, checklists, warnings, pro and con checklists, fill-in timelines, information sources, and a unique ticker system that alerts future retirees of important decisions to be made, this unique and lively book removes the mystique of retirement planing.

AUDIENCE: Beginning, Individual   RISK LEVEL: Conservative, Moderate
TOPICS: Bonds, Mutual Funds, Stocks, Asset Allocation, Investment Planning, General
            Reference

Speculator's Edge - Strategies for Profit in the Futures Markets, The

Albert Peter Pacelli
John Wiley & Sons, Inc.
605 Third Avenue
New York, NY 10158-0012

PH: (800) 526-5368 Orders
(212) 850-6418 Info
FAX: (212) 850-6088
Published: March 1989
Cost: $29.95

Subjects addressed are investing theories, market analysis, trading analysis, commodities trading, technical analysis; uses charts. Covers how to get started in futures trading, market timing, understanding cyclical trends. Shows how to be a profitable futures trader under the basic role of speculator.

AUDIENCE: Individual   RISK LEVEL: Aggressive
TOPICS: Options, Futures/Commodities

Stan Weinstein's Secrets for Profiting in Bull and Bear Markets

Stan Weinstein
Irwin Professional Publishing
1333 Burr Ridge Parkway
Burr Ridge, IL 60521

PH: (708) 789-5489
(800) 634-3966
FAX: (708) 789-6933
Published: 1988
Cost: $17.00

Subject addressed is technical analysis; uses charts. Shows you how to identify predictable patterns in market trends as well as stock and mutual fund movements using techniques developed over the last 20 years.

AUDIENCE: Beginning, Individual   RISK LEVEL: Moderate, Aggressive
TOPICS: Stocks

Starting Out in Futures Trading

Mark J. Powers
Futures Learning Center
219 Parkade
Box 6
Cedar Falls, IA 50613

PH: (800) 635-3936
ISBN: 1-55738-506-8
Published: 1993
Cost: $24.95

An internationally respected expert applies theory and practical experience to commodity futures trading. Evaluates the relative risks/benefits of stocks and commodities. Examines commodity options and futures, as well as stock index futures. Presents valuable trading strategies and price forecasting techniques.

AUDIENCE: Beginning, Individual   RISK LEVEL: Aggressive
TOPICS: Options, Futures/Commodities

Starting Small, Investing Smart - What to do With $5 - $5000

Donald R. Nichols
Irwin Professional Publishing
1333 Burr Ridge Parkway
Burr Ridge, IL 60521

PH: (800) 634-3966
FAX: (708) 789-6933
Published: 1984, 1987, 2nd edition
ISBN: 1-55623-041-9
Cost: $26.00

Subjects addressed are stock analysis, bond analysis, precious metals. For beginning investors, outlines the features, advantages, disadvantages, and returns offered by bank deposits, stocks, bonds, mutual funds, precious metals, and other investments accessible for $5-$5000.

AUDIENCE: Beginning   RISK LEVEL: Moderate, Aggressive
TOPICS: Bonds, Mutual Funds, Stocks

State-of-the Art Portfolio Selection

Robert R. Trippi and Jae K. Lee
Probus Publishing Co.
1925 N. Clybourn Ave.
Suite 401
Chicago, IL 60614

PH: (800) PROBUS-1
FAX: (312) 868-6250
Cost: $60.00
Date of first issue:1992
ISBN: 1-55738-295-6

"Using real-life examples, this rare and readable volume will enable you to realize the benefits of an existing or proposed system, and ultimately how to construct your own system. Topics include asset allocation, timing decisions, pattern recognition and risk assessment."

AUDIENCE: Individual, Professional   RISK LEVEL: Moderate, Aggressive
TOPICS: Asset Allocation

Steidlmayer on Markets: New Approach to Trading

J. Peter Steidlmayer
John Wiley & Sons, Inc.
605 Third Avenue
New York, NY 10158-0012

PH: (212) 850-6000
FAX: (212) 850-6088
ISBN: 0-471-62115-3
Published: 1989
Cost: $34.95

Slow down. Avoid the "kill quick" approach, warns this author, whom Forbes calls "the revolutionary in the pit." Learn to read data from the futures market, and to detect patterns. An inside account based on 25 years of trading on the floor of the Chicago Board of Trade.

AUDIENCE: Professional   RISK LEVEL: Aggressive
TOPICS: Options, Futures/Commodities

Stochastics

Commodities Education Institute
219 Parade
Cedar Falls, IA 50613

PH: (800) 635-3936
(319) 277-6341
FAX: (319) 277-7982
Published: 1990
Cost: $55.00
VIDEO

Covers investing theories, technical analysis. Glen Ring shows you how to use this oscillator as an overbought/oversold and divergent indicator. He also shows how to use stochastics for entry buy and sell signals. Part of a series of 5 tapes available for $233.00.

AUDIENCE: Individual, Professional   RISK LEVEL: Aggressive
TOPICS: Stocks, Options, Futures/Commodities

Stock Market Explained for Young Investors, The

Clayton P. Fisher
Business Classics
950 Purisima Road
Woodside, CA 94062

PH: (800) 865-1001
(415) 852-8879
ISBN: 0-931133-02-5
Published: 1993
Cost: $17.95

Covers market fundamentals. Written by Fisher while he was still a teenager, this book speaks to youth from their own vantage point. Fisher was qualified for this by his regular childhood experiences in his father's large institutional investment firm. Includes sections on compound interest, common mistakes, researching a company, and getting started. Called a "powerful wealth-building tool" and an "easy-to-understand walk around Wall Street," it's an excellent primer for novice investors, or experienced ones needing a quick refresher course.

AUDIENCE: Beginning   RISK LEVEL: Moderate
TOPICS: Stocks

Stock Market Logic

Norman G. Fosback
The Institute for Econometric Research
3471 N. Federal Highway
Ft. Lauderdale, FL 33306

PH: (800) 327-6700
(305) 563-9000
Published: 1971
Cost: $40.00

Covers investing theories, stock analysis, market analysis, earnings analysis, trading analysis, fundamental analysis, technical analysis; uses charts. Should be read by everyone interested in the market. Investors seeking a rational and sophisticated approach to profits on Wall Street will find the answers in this book. Revealed for the first time, all the complete results of a 5 year investigation of stock market behavior conducted at the Institute for Econometric Research.

AUDIENCE: Beginning, Individual   RISK LEVEL: Moderate, Aggressive
TOPICS: Mutual Funds, Stocks

Stock Market Primer

Claude N. Rosenberg, Jr.
Warner Books, Inc.
1271 Avenue of the Americas
New York, NY 10020

PH: (800) 222-6747
(212) 522-7200
Published: 1962, 1987, 1991 (last update)
Cost: $12.99

Covers investing theories, stock analysis, market analysis, trading analysis. Classic guide to investment success for the novice and the expert. Tells you what to buy, when to buy, what to pay, and when to sell to get maximum return on investments.

AUDIENCE: Beginning   RISK LEVEL: Moderate, Aggressive
TOPICS: Stocks

Stock Market, The

Richard J. Teweles and Edward S. Bradley
John Wiley & Sons, Inc.
605 Third Avenue
New York, NY 10158-0012

PH: (212) 850-6418 (orders)
(212) 850-6233 (info)
FAX: (212) 850-6088
Published: 1951, 1992 (6th edition)
Cost: $34.95

Covers investing theories, stock analysis, market analysis, bond analysis, fundamental analysis, technical analysis. Definitive guide to the institutions, principles, and practices of today's market. Covers history, products, and operation of the market to the practical techniques used by seasonal shareholders and traders.

AUDIENCE: Beginning, Individual, Professional   RISK LEVEL: Moderate, Aggressive
TOPICS: Bonds, Stocks

Stock Trader's Almanac

Hirsch Organization, Inc.
6 Deer Trail
Old Tappan, NJ 07675

PH: (201) 664-3400
Published: Annually
Cost: $24.95

The Almanac is an annual appointment calendar that is also considered the "definitive reference work on seasonal trading patterns." Famous for its market lore in the form of daily quotations. In addition, the "Almanac" contains: a directory of Seasonal Trading Patterns, a strategy planning and record section, updates of new techniques and tools, reminders of seasonal opportunities and dangers, monthly almanacs, every form needed for portfolio planning, record keeping and tax preparation. A.F.P.

AUDIENCE: Beginning, Individual, Professional   RISK LEVEL: Moderate, Aggressive
TOPICS: Stocks

Stocks, Bonds, Options, Futures: Investments and Their Markets

Stuart R. Veale
New York Institute of
   Finance/Prentice Hall
113 Sylvan Avenue
Route 9W
Englewood Cliffs, NJ 07632

PH: (800) 947-7700
FAX: (515) 284-2607
Published: 1987
Cost: 6 x 9; cloth, $27.95
Published: 1991
Cost: 6 x 9; paper $18.95

Explore the securities industry, with practical emphasis on the instruments available and how they are used. Explains categories of common stock, exchange and OTC transactions, mutual funds, hedging with options and futures, technical and fundamental analysis, and margin requirements.

AUDIENCE: Individual   RISK LEVEL: Moderate, Aggressive
TOPICS: All

Strategic Currency Investing

Andrew W. Gitlins
Probus Publishing Co.
1925 N. Clybourn Ave.
Suite 401
Chicago, IL 60614

PH: (800) PROBUS-1
FAX: (312) 868-6250
COST: $65.00
Date of first Issue: 1993

"The definitive book on foreign exchange investment, trading and hedging....Specific topics include: advantages and disadvantages of currency investing, diversified currency strategies, foreign currency arbitrage, currency options and option-based risk management, and composite forecasting."

AUDIENCE: Individual, Professional   RISK LEVEL: Moderate, Aggressive
TOPICS: Bonds, Options, Futures, Commodities

Strategic Market Timing

Robert M. Bowker
New York Institute of
   Finance/Prentice Hall
113 Sylvan Avenue
Route 9W
Englewood Cliffs, NJ 07632

PH: (800) 947-7700
FAX: (515) 284-2607
Published: 1989
Cost: $29.95

Demonstrates how to be positioned favorably at all times, and describes practical methods for developing the "ideal portfolio" with the best mix of equity, debt, and other instruments.

AUDIENCE: Individual, Professional   RISK LEVEL: Moderate
TOPICS: Asset Allocation

Super Stocks

Keneth L. Fisher
Business Classics
950 Purisima Road
Woodside, CA 94062

PH: (800) 865-1001
(415) 852-8879
ISBN: 0-931133-03-3
Published: 1992 (reprint from 1982
   edition)
Cost: $28.95

Best-selling stock market book of 1984. It introduces new methods for analyzing and valuing stocks, including the now famous and widely used "Price Sales Ratio." It's on many best-ever lists: Standard & Poor's, Barron's Money, etc. Perfect for beginners or serious professionals interested in learning this unique valuation technique, it covers concepts never before presented in investment literature.

AUDIENCE: Beginning, Individual   RISK LEVEL: Moderate, Aggressive
TOPICS: Stocks

Sure-Thing Options Trading: A Money-making Guide to the New Listed Stock and Commodity Options Markets

George Angell
Penguin USA
120 Woodbine St.
Bergenfield, NJ 07621

PH: (800) 526-0275
Published: 1984
ISBN: 0-452-26110-4
Cost: $9.95

Join the boom in options trading and play the market to your advantage. Learn how to size up an options trade, what to pay, what to select, the advantages of options over stocks, how to trade the new stock index markets, and much more. Straightforward strategies for getting into the hottest investor area today.

AUDIENCE: Beginning, Individual   RISK LEVEL: Aggressive
TOPICS: Options

Swaps Handbook: Swaps and Related Risk Management Instruments, The

Kenneth R. Kapner and
   John F. Marshall
New York Institute of
   Finance/Prentice Hall
113 Sylvan Avenue
Route 9W
Englewood Cliffs, NJ 07632

PH: (800) 947-7700
FAX: (515) 284-2607
Published: 1990
Cost: $110.00

An in-depth discussion of the uses, and practical framework of currency and interest-rate swaps. Details the role of swaps in asset/liability management, swaps accounting, managing a swaps portfolio, and swaps documentation. Plus, step-by-step calculations, a directory of key players. Current supplement FREE with purchase.

AUDIENCE: Professional   RISK LEVEL: All
TOPICS: Bonds, Options, Futures/Commodities

Tax Deferred Investing: Using Pre-Tax Dollars for After-Tax Profit

Michael C. Thomsett
John Wiley & Sons, Inc.
605 Third Avenue
New York, NY 10158

PH: (212) 850-6000
FAX: (212) 850-6088
Cost: $24.95
Date of first issue: 1991

"A quick reference how-to volume on using tax deferral as one means to achieving investment goals. Shows how to establish those goals and then describes all the tax-deferred investment vehicles currently available under the 1986 Tax Reform Act and subsequent changes. Discusses timing of investment strategies and record keeping to avoid mistakes and penalties."

AUDIENCE: Individual   RISK LEVEL: Moderate
TOPICS: Bonds, Mutual Funds, Investment Planing

Technical Analysis: A Personal Seminar

New York Institute of
  Finance/Prentice Hall
113 Sylvan Avenue
Route 9W
Englewood Cliffs, NJ 07632

PH: (800) 947-7700
FAX: (515) 284-2607
Published: 1989
Cost: $21.95

This self-study guide enables investors to benefit from techniques used by the pros. Explains the fundamental assumptions of technical analysis, and shows how charts are constructed, interpreted, and used to forecast price levels.

AUDIENCE: Individual   RISK LEVEL: Aggressive
TOPICS: Stocks, Options, Futures/Commodities

Technical Analysis Explained

Martin J. Pring
McGraw-Hill Publishing Company
1221 Avenue of the Americas
New York, NY 10020

ISBN: 0-07-050885-2
PH: (800) 2-MCGRAW
(212) 512-2000
Publication Date: c. 1994, 3rd
  edition
Cost: $49.95

Covered in detail are such topics as Dow Theory, price patterns, trendlines, moving averages, momentum, cycles, sentiment, speculation, interest rates and the stock market, breadth, volume and technical analysis of international stock markets. This unique guide also features over 130 historical charts, many previously unpublished, and an extensive statistical section.

AUDIENCE: Individual   RISK LEVEL: Moderate, Aggressive
TOPICS: Bonds, Stocks, Futures/Commodities

Technical Analysis of Stock Options and Futures-Advanced Trading Systems and Techniques

William F. Eng
Probus Publishing Co.
1925 North Clybourn Avenue
Chicago, IL 60614

PH: (800) PROBUS-1
(312) 868-1100
Published: 1988
Cost: $60.00

Mr. Eng presents the latest technical analysis systems that are currently being used in the major exchanges around the world. This book includes, among others, the following trading systems: Williams ./.R, Wilder's Relative Strength Index, Lane's Stochastics, Elliott Wave Analysis, plus others.

AUDIENCE: Individual, Professional   RISK LEVEL: Aggressive
TOPICS: Stocks, Options, Futures/Commodities

Technical Analysis of Stock Trends

Robert D. Edwards and John Magee
New York Institute of
 Finance/Prentice Hall
113 Sylvan Avenue
Route 9W
Englewood Cliffs, NJ 07632

PH: (800) 947-7700
FAX: (515) 284-2607
Published: 1983
Cost: $75.00

Covers investing theories, trading analysis, technical analysis; uses charts. Written for informed layman and Wall Street professional in 2 parts: technical theory and trading tactics. The most definitive description of Dow Jones averages and pattern analysis of stocks using Applied Statistical analysis. Considered the trader's "Bible."

AUDIENCE: Individual   RISK LEVEL: Moderate, Aggressive
TOPICS: Stocks

Technical Analysis of the Futures Markets: A Comprehensive Guide to Trading Methods and Applications

John J. Murphy
New York Institute of
 Finance/Prentice Hall
113 Sylvan Avenue
Route 9W
Englewood Cliffs, NJ 07632

PH: (800) 947-7700
FAX: (515) 284-2607
ISBN: 0-13-898008-X
Published: 1986
Cost: $49.95

Logical, sequential reference describes - for beginners and more experienced traders alike - the concepts of technical analysis and their applications. Interprets the role of technical forecasters and explains how they apply their techniques to the futures markets. Includes 400 charts showing how time cycles enhance effectiveness.

AUDIENCE: Beginning, Individual, Professional   RISK LEVEL: Aggressive
TOPICS: Futures/Commodities

Technical Indicator Analysis by Point and Figure Technique

A.W. Cohen
Chartcraft, Inc.
1 West Avenue
Larchmont, NY 10538

PH: (914) 632-0422
Published: 1988
Cost: $15.00

Covers point and figure charts and technical analysis. This book takes 29 of the most widely followed technical indicators and tells us how each is compiled and how to analyze what a point and figure chart of each indicator tells us about a market trend. A.F.P.

AUDIENCE: Individual, Professional   RISK LEVEL: Moderate, Aggressive
TOPICS: Stocks, Options, Futures/Commodities

Techniques of a Professional Commodity Chart Analyst

Arthur Sklarew
Commodity Research Bureau
75 Wall Street
22nd Floor
New York, NY 10005

PH: (800) 446-4519
ISBN: 0-317-03272-0
Published: 1980
Cost: $24.95

Success in commodity trading depends on good price forecasting. Learn to use commodity price chart and other simple technical indicators to time your trades better, spot price trends, estimate the distance a new price thrust will travel, and identify potential trend reversal points. Clear style; practical, original material.

AUDIENCE: Individual, Professional   RISK LEVEL: Aggressive
TOPICS: Options, Futures/Commodities

Techniques of Financial Analysis

Erich A. Helfert
Irwin Professional Publishing
1333 Burr Ridge Parkway
Burr Ridge, IL 60521

PH: (800) 634-3966
FAX: (708) 789-6933
Published: 1994 (8th edition)
ISBN: 0-87094-944-6, Cost: $39.95
Also available in paperback
ISBN: 0-7863-0246-1, Cost: $30.00

The latest techniques and tools, including new material on inflation. Solve typical corporate financial problems by examining three basic financial concepts - operations, investment, and financing. Covers funds flow analysis, ratio analysis, cash budgets, pro forma statements, breakeven analysis, and basic capital expenditure.

AUDIENCE: Beginning, Individual, Professional   RISK LEVEL: Moderate, Aggressive
TOPICS: Bonds, Stocks

Thailand 1994

The Reference Press, Inc.
6448 Highway 290 E
Suite E-104
Austin, TX 78723

PH: (512) 454-7778
FAX: (512) 454-9401
Cost: $46.95
Date of first issue: 1994
Fundamental Analysis

Profiles the 341 companies listed on the Stock Exchange of Thailand, plus 23 unit trusts. Information includes stock symbol, address, phone and fax numbers, company overview, price per share, trading volume, new income, capital, financial ratios, foreign holdings and limits on foreign ownership.

AUDIENCE: Individual, Professional   RISK LEVEL: Moderate, Aggressive
TOPICS: Stocks, General Reference

Theory and Practice of Futures Markets, The

Raymond M. Leuthold, Joan C. Junkus and Jean E. Cordier
Lexington Books
125 Spring Street
Lexington, MA 02173

PH: (800) 235-3565
ISBN: 0-669-16260-4
Published: 1989
Cost: $39.95

An introductory text about commodity and financial futures and options markets. Covers commodity, interest rate, stock index and currency future contracts along with options on these contracts. Many examples on how to use the market for hedging and arbitraging.

AUDIENCE: Individual, Professional   RISK LEVEL: Aggressive
TOPICS: Futures/Commodities

Tight Money Timing: The Impact of Interest Rates and the Federal Reserve on the Stock Market

Wilfred R. George
Greenwood Publishing Group, Inc.
88 Post Road, W
Box 5007
Westport, CT 06881

PH: (800) 225-5800
ISBN: 0-275-91708-8
Published: 1982
Cost: $49.95

Provides the knowledge needed to make money grow in any money climate - tight or easy. Explicit advice in how to recognize tight and easy money signals, draw the appropriate conclusions, and take the correct action to maximize profits in rising and declining markets. A vital asset in today's treacherous investment waters.

AUDIENCE: Individual, Professional   RISK LEVEL: Moderate, Aggressive
TOPICS: Bonds, Stocks

Tools of the Bear, The

Charles J. Caes
Probus Publishing Co.
1925 N. Clybourn Ave.
Suite 401
Chicago, IL 60614

PH: (800) PROBUS-1
FAX: (312) 868-6250
Cost: $24.95
Date of first issue: 1993

"Shows how to make money when stocks are declining in price - without undue risk. This concise volume concentrates on 3 proven strategies: short sales, put buying and call writing to take advantage of inevitable bear runs."

AUDIENCE: Individual, Professional   RISK LEVEL: Moderate, Aggressive
TOPICS: Stocks, Options

Trade Directory of Mexico

The Reference Press, Inc.
6448 Highway 290 E
Suite E-104
Austin, TX 78723

PH: (512) 454-7778
FAX: (512) 454-9401
Cost: $89.95
Date of first issue: 1994
ISBN: 9-686168-26-5

A directory listing over 4,300 Mexican companies involved in foreign trade. Information includes company name, address, phone, fax, export and import products, company size by number of employees and bank references. Also includes a profile of Mexico and the individual states.

AUDIENCE: Individual, Professional   RISK LEVEL: Moderate, Aggressive
TOPICS: Bonds, Mutual Funds, Stocks

Trader VIC II-Analytic Principles of Professional Speculation

Victor Sperandeo
John Wiley & Sons, Inc.
605 Third Ave.
New York, NY 10158

PH: (212) 850-6000
FAX: (212) 850-6088
Cost: $37.50
Technical and Fundamental Analysis
Date of first issue: 1994

"Offers fresh insightful applications to a legion of traditional investment techniques, combining concepts from fundamental and technical analysis, probability and statistics, politics, economics and psychology resulting in a comprehensive and proven trading approach."

AUDIENCE: Individual, Professional   RISK LEVEL: Aggressive
TOPICS: Stocks, Options, Futures

Trader Vic - Methods of a Wall Street Master

Victor Sperandeo
John Wiley & Sons, Inc.
605 Third Avenue
New York, NY 10158

PH: (212) 850-6000
FAX: (212) 850-6088
Cost: $29.95
Technical and Fundamental Analysis
Date of first issue: 1994

"Based on three principles-capital preservation, consistent profits and pursuit of superior returns. "Trader Vic" highlights proven strategies usable by any investor along with exploring the interrelationships between the national and global economics and monetary and fiscal policies, the author describes the psychological barriers which can prevent investors from executing their plans."

AUDIENCE: Individual, Professional   RISK LEVEL: Aggressive
TOPICS: Stocks

Trading and Investing in Bond Options

M. Anthony Wong & Robert High
John Wiley & Sons, Inc.
605 Third Avenue
New York, NY 10158

PH: (212) 850-6000
FAX: (212) 850-6088
Cost: $49.95
Date of first issue: 1991

"To become successful in the bond options market, it is important for professionals to gain a basic, yet thorough understanding of how options are priced, traded and used in interest-rate risk and fixed-income portfolio management....After introducing standard options terminology, it provides background data on U.S. Treasury bonds, bond options pricing models, advanced pricing models, the fundamentals of bond options dealing, strategies driven by interest rate forecasts, the most widely used structured portfolio strategies involving options and more."

AUDIENCE: Individual, Professional   RISK LEVEL: Aggressive
TOPICS: Options

Trading Applications of Japanese Candlestick Charting

John Wiley & Sons
605 Third Ave.
New York, NY 10158

PH: (800) 225-5945
FAX: (212) 850-6088
Cost: $55.00
Date of first issue: 1993

Combines Japanese candlestick charts with a variety of Western technical indicators including Elliot Wave, stochastics, moving averages, oscillators, and more. Provides trading tips based on different markets; equities, grain, energy and foreign currency.

AUDIENCE: Individual, Professional   RISK LEVEL: Aggressive
TOPICS: Stocks, Futures/Commodities

Trading for a Living: Psychology, Trading Tactics, Money Management

Alexander Elder
John Wiley & Sons, Inc.
605 Third Avenue
New York, NY 10158-0012

PH: (212) 850-6000
FAX: (212) 850-6088
Published: 1993
Technical Analysis

Written by a prominent futures trader to enlighten traders on crucial market factors that most experts overlook, such as time, volume and open interest. He also covers all of the well-known indicators: Elliott Wave, moving averages, market logic and point and figure charting.

AUDIENCE: Individual, Professional   RISK LEVEL: Aggressive
TOPICS: Options, Futures

Trading Options on Futures

John W. Labuszewski & John E. Nyhoff
John Wiley & Sons, Inc.
605 Third Avenue
New York, NY 10158-0012

PH: (212) 850-6000
FAX: (212) 850-6088
Published: 1994
Technical and Fundamental Analysis

"A comprehensive introduction to trading options on Treasury securities, currencies and other financial instruments. Features insider insight into pricing concepts and models, sophisticated speculative strategies and risk-management techniques."

AUDIENCE: Professional	RISK LEVEL: Aggressive
TOPICS: Options, Futures	

Trading the Fundamentals

Michael P. Niemira and Gerald F.
 Zukowski
Probus Publishing Co.
1925 N. Clybourn Ave., Suite 401
Chicago, IL 60614

PH: (800) PROBUS-1
FAX: (312) 868-6250
Cost: $37.50
Date of first issue: 1993
Fundamental Analysis

"Explains the significance, reliability and market impact of 23 of the most widely followed economic indicators. More importantly, the authors explain how each indicator behaves through every phase of the business cycle."

AUDIENCE: Individual, Professional	RISK LEVEL: Moderate, Aggressive
TOPICS: Stocks, General Reference	

Trading Using Artificial Intelligence Expert Systems and Neural Network

Mark B. Tishman and Dean Barr
John Wiley & Sons, Inc.
605 Third Avenue
New York, NY 10158-0012

PH: (212) 850-6000
FAX: (212) 850-6088
Published: 1993
Cost: Contact Publisher

"A lucid guide demonstrating how to build and easily use sophisticated market sensitive systems to enhance and streamline financial analysis and boast any trader's day-to-day portfolio management performance."

AUDIENCE: Professional	RISK LEVEL: Aggressive
TOPICS: Stocks, Options, Futures/Commodities	

Trading with the Elliott Wave Principle: A Practical Guide

David H. Weis
Tape Readers Press
P.O. Box 12267
Memphis, TN 38182

PH: (901) 276-0155
Published: October 1988
Cost: $65.00

Covers investing theories, trading analysis, technical analysis; uses charts. Devoted to an extensive trading exercise. Shows how to analyze and trade a market day by day, using Elliott Wave. Weis explains Elliott's system of notation or symbols for labeling waves of different degrees, gives "Guideline for Wave Counting" formulas for projecting tops and bottoms.

AUDIENCE: Individual, Professional	RISK LEVEL: Moderate, Aggressive
TOPICS: Stocks, Options, Futures/Commodities	

Trendiness in the Futures Markets

Bruce Babcock, Jr.
1731 Howe Ave.
Suite 149
Sacramento, CA 95825

PH: (916) 677-7562
(800) 999-CTCR
Published: 1994, 11th edition
Cost: $95.00

Covers trading analysis, futures; uses charts. How to choose the best markets to trade and the best time frames to trade them. Learn how to set trend indicators and oscillators for optimum results based on historical performance. A.F.P.

AUDIENCE: Individual	RISK LEVEL: Aggressive
TOPICS: Futures/Commodities	

Turn in the Tidal Wave (Part I: The Stock Market; Part II: Implications), A

Robert R. Prechter, Jr.
New Classics Library, Inc.
P.O. Box 1618
Gainesville, GA 30503

PH: (800) 336-1618
(404) 536-0309
ISBN: 0-932750-12-5
Published: 1989
Cost: $19.00

An analysis of the predictions made by the author and A.J. Frost in Elliott Wave Principle. "Now, over ten years later, the markets have progressed to a point at which it is prudent, if not crucial, to examine closely our original analysis," says the author.

AUDIENCE: Individual, Professional	RISK LEVEL: Moderate, Aggressive
TOPICS: Bonds, Mutual Funds, Stocks, Options, Futures/Commodities	

Ultimate Mutual Fund Guide, The

Warren Boroson
Probus Publishing Co.
1925 N. Clybourn Ave.
Suite 401
Chicago, IL 60614

PH: (800) PROBUS-1
(312) 868-1100
FAX: (312) 868-6250
Cost: $16.95
Date of first issue: 1993

Combines "....the work of top experts to identify the best mutual funds in various fund categories, including money market, bonds, equity and growth. This easy-to-use guide also provides performance data for each type of fund as well as interviews with fund managers."

AUDIENCE: Beginning, Individual	RISK LEVEL: Moderate, Aggressive
TOPICS: Mutual Funds	

Understanding Corporate Bonds

H. Kerzner
McGraw Hill, Inc.
11 West 19th Street
New York, NY 10011

PH: (800) 722-4726
(212) 512-4100
Published: 1990
Cost: $24.60

Advice for building and preserving wealth by investing in corporate bonds. Shows how to identify high-risk bonds, how to select quality junk bonds, use margin buying to your benefit, how to select a good broker and much more.

AUDIENCE: Beginning, Individual	RISK LEVEL: Conservative, Moderate
TOPICS: Bonds	

Understanding Fibonacci Numbers

Edward D. Dobson
Traders Press, Inc.
P.O. Box 6206
Greenville, SC 29606

PH: (800) 927-8222
Published: 1984
ISBN: 0-934380-08-2
Cost: $5.00

Primer booklet that explains and describes the Fibonacci sequence
and how it is utilized by traders to forecast and interpret price
action.

AUDIENCE: Individual, Professional   RISK LEVEL: Aggressive
TOPICS: Options, Futures/Commodities

Understanding Wall Street

Jeffrey B. Little & Lucien Rhodes
Liberty Hall Press
11 W. 19th Street
3rd floor
New York, NY 10011

PH: (212) 691-8710
Published: 1978, 1987; 2nd edition,
1993; 3rd edition
Cost: $19.95

Covers investing theories, stock analysis, market analysis, bond
analysis, earnings analysis, fundamental analysis, technical
analysis, options. Very basic book for beginners. Begins with
"What is a share of stock?" Covers history of Wall Street, reading
the financial pages, security analysis, growth stocks, and options.
A.F.P.

AUDIENCE: Beginning   RISK LEVEL: Moderate, Aggressive
TOPICS: Stocks

Understanding Wall Street

Liberty Publishing Co., Inc.
440 S. Federal Hwy.
Suite 202
Deerfield Beach, FL 33441

PH: (305) 360-9000
ISBN: 0-89709
Cost: $39.95
Date of first issue: 1990

Based on the book "Understanding Wall Street." Gives basic
information for beginning investors such as; what is a share of
stock?, history of Wall Street, how to read the financial pages, how
to invest and trade, how to select stocks, mutual funds and much
more.

AUDIENCE: Beginning   RISK LEVEL: Moderate, Aggressive
TOPICS: Mutual Funds, Stocks

Using the Relative Strength Indicator (RSI) and High/Low Moving Average Channel

Commodities Education Institute
219 Parade
Cedar Falls, IA 50613

PH: (800) 635-3936
FAX: (319) 277-7982
Published: 1990
Cost: $55.00
VIDEO

Subjects addressed are investing theories, technical analysis. You'll
learn how to use RSI as a directional indicator in conjunction with
the High/Low Moving average channel as a market timing aid. Part
of a series of 5 tapes available for $233.00. A.F.P.

AUDIENCE: Individual, Professional   RISK LEVEL: Moderate, Aggressive
TOPICS: Stocks, Options

Value Averaging

Michael E. Edleson, Ph.D.
International Publishing Company
625 N. Michigan Ave.
Chicago IL 60611

PH: (800) 488-4149
Cost: $22.95
ISBN: 0-942641-24-8
Date of first issue: 1993

Subtitled The Safe & Easy Strategy for Higher Investment Returns. Explains a better technique for investing based on dollar cost averaging-taken one step further. A.F.P.

AUDIENCE: Beginning, Individual   RISK LEVEL: Moderate
TOPICS: Stocks, Mutual Funds

Value Driven Asset-Allocation Plan

International Publishing Corp.
625 N. Michigan Ave.
Suite 1920
Chicago, IL 60611

PH: (800) 488-4149
Cost: $17.95
Published: 1991

The author analyzes good and bad attitudes toward money, how it works, and the dangers of debt and insidious inflation, then goes step-by-step through his wealth building program that employs monthly and yearly monitoring techniques and no-load mutual funds. A.F.P.

AUDIENCE: Beginning, Individual   RISK LEVEL: Moderate
TOPICS: Mutual Funds, Stocks, Asset Allocation

Value Investing: New Strategies for Stock Market Success

Lawrence M. Stein
John Wiley & Sons, Inc.
605 Third Ave.
New York, NY 10158-0012

PH: (800) 526-5368
(212) 850-6000
ISBN: 0-471-62875-1
Published: 1988
Cost: $27.95

Covers stock analysis and market timing. This book offers an honest appraisal of the stock market and shows how individual investors can earn consistently superior profits in both bull and bear markets. Stein explains how to value stocks and the stock market as a whole, use value as a basis for market timing, and implement value into a workable investment strategy that has statistically proven itself in long-term computer simulations.

AUDIENCE: Individual   RISK LEVEL: Moderate, Aggressive
TOPICS: Stocks

Value Investing Today

Charles H. Brandis
Irwin Professional Publishing
1333 Burr Ridge Parkway
Burr Ridge, IL 60521

PH: (708) 789-5489
(800) 634-3966
FAX: (708) 789-6933
ISBN: 1-55623-102-4
Published: 1989
Cost: $30.00

Covers investing theories, stock analysis, and fundamental analysis. Stresses the fundamentals of profitmaking investing and concentrates on what to buy, what prices to pay, when to buy and sell and why. Alerts you to possible errors, and provides ways to select stocks successfully.

AUDIENCE: Beginning, Individual   RISK LEVEL: Moderate, Aggressive
TOPICS: Stocks

Valuing Fixed-Income Investments and Derivative Securities: Cash-Flow Analysis and Calculation

Arnold Kleinstein and Steve Allen
New York Institute of
  Finance/Prentice Hall
113 Sylvan Avenue
Route 9W
Englewood Cliffs, NJ 07632

PH: (800) 947-7700
FAX: (515) 284-2607
Published: 1991
Cost: $34.95

Makes a complicated area of financial analysis intelligible for the novice. Descibes how to value one fixed-income investment against another based on cash-flow analysis. Sample problems and solutions appear throughout.

AUDIENCE: RISK LEVEL:
TOPICS:

Venezuela Company Handbook 1992-1993

The Reference Press, Inc.
6448 Highway 290 E.
Suite E-104
Austin, TX 78723

PH: (512) 454-7778
FAX: (512) 454-9401
Cost: $29.95
Date of first issue: 1992
Fundamental Analysis

Profiles the major companies on the Caracas Stock Exchange. Also gives a comprehensive description of the economy, recent developments in privatization, and accounting rules.

AUDIENCE: Beginning, Individual, Professional   RISK LEVEL: Moderate, Aggressive
TOPICS: Stocks

Wall Street Dictionary, The

R.J. & Robert L. Shook
New York Institute of
  Finance/Prentice Hall
113 Sylvan Avenue
Route 9W
Englewood Cliffs, NJ 07632

PH: (800) 947-7700
FAX: (515) 284-2607
Published: 1990
Cost: $14.95

Complete source of the language of finance and investment for the novice and seasoned professionals. Over 5,000 entries.

AUDIENCE: Beginning, Individual, Professional   RISK LEVEL: Conservative,
TOPICS: All   Moderate, Aggressive

Wall Street Journal's Guide to Understanding Money and Markets, The

R. Wurman, A. Siegel and K.
  Morris
Simon & Schuster
200 Old Tappan Rd.
Old Tappan, NJ 07675

PH: (800) 223-2336
(212) 373-8500
Published: 1989
Cost: $13.95

Addresses investing theories, bond analysis, commodities trading, stock analysis. Covers stocks, bonds, mutual funds, futures, money. A beginner's guide to the financial pages and investing. Covers everything from a CUSIP number to the futures exchanges.

AUDIENCE: Beginning, Individual   RISK LEVEL: Conservative, Moderate,
TOPICS: All   Aggressive

Wall Street Waltz, The

Keneth L. Fisher
Business Classics
950 Purisima Road
Woodside, CA 94062

PH: (800) 865-1001
(415) 852-8879
ISBN: 0-931133-04-1
Published: 1987
Cost: $31.95

Concerns stock analysis. This book gives a clear perspective through the analysis of classical historical charts. By assembling his 90 favorite timeless charts and offering 90 accompanying stories, Keneth L. Fisher, one of America's leading money managers and financial columnists, provides more quick and easy overview and market lore than you are likely to find elsewhere. His readable, conversational style is a breath of fresh air in a world filled with complex concepts and explanations.

AUDIENCE: Beginning, Individual   RISK LEVEL: Moderate, Aggressive
TOPICS: Bonds, Stocks, Asset Allocation

WealthBuilder by Money Magazine

Don and Doris Woodwell
Irwin Professional Publishing
1333 Burr Ridge Parkway
Burr Ridge, IL 60521

PH: (800) 634-3966
FAX: (708) 789-6933
ISBN: 1-55623-441-4
Published: January 1991
Cost: $26.00

This book compliments the New WealthBuilder by Money Magazine financial planning, investment counseling software program. Shows how to draw upon all of the programs features to create a conservative, long-term investment plan. The authors show you how to do more in less time by helping you understand the program better, set and meet savings and investment plans using the software, and become financially secure by diversifying your holdings using WealthBuilder software allocation information.

AUDIENCE: Beginning, Individual   RISK LEVEL: Moderate
TOPICS: Mutual Funds, Stocks

Why the Best-Laid Investment Plans Usually Go Wrong and How You Can Find Safety and Profit in an Uncertain World

Harry Browne
William Morrow and Company, Inc.
105 Madison Avenue
New York, NY 10016

PH: (800) 843-9389
ISBN: 0-688-05995-3
Published: 1987
Cost: $19.95

Study investment techniques from one of America's best-known investment advisors. The author tells why many common techniques fail when they're needed most and how to find safety and profit in the market. Witty and forceful, it has good tips for both the aggressive and passive investor.

AUDIENCE: Beginning, Individual   RISK LEVEL: Moderate, Aggressive
TOPICS: Bonds, Mutual Funds, Stocks, Investment Planning

Winning Investment Strategies: Using Security Analysis to Build Wealth

J. B. Malloy
McGraw Hill, Inc.
11 West 19th Street
New York, NY 10011

PH: (800) 722-4726
(212) 512-4100
Published: 1990
Cost: $22.60

"A successful long-term investment program safe from fluctuations in taxes, inflation, and interest rates."

AUDIENCE: Beginning, Individual   RISK LEVEL: Moderate, Aggressive
TOPICS: Bonds, Mutual Funds, Stocks

Winning Market Systems: 83 Ways to Beat the Market

Gerald Appel
Traders Press, Inc.
P.O. Box 6206
Greenville, SC 29606

PH: (800) 927-8222
Published: 1986 (revised from 1974
  edition)
ISBN: 0-934380-12-0
Cost: $34.95

Encyclopedia of wining strategies and technical indicators. The system strategies and indicators of many well-known market analysts are detailed. The inner workings of the Haurlan Index, the Haller Theory, and interpretation of the A/D line, the McClellan Oscillator as a short-term indicator and many other tools. Strategies include the most bullish trendline formation, how to predict trendline violations, an early warning system, how to interpret the most active, the best hours and months to buy.

AUDIENCE: Individual, Professional   RISK LEVEL: Moderate, Aggressive
TOPICS: Bonds, Mutual Funds, Stocks

Winning on Wall Street

Martin Zweig
Warner Books, Inc.
666 Fifth Avenue
New York, NY 10103

Published: 1986, 1990, update
Cost: $12.95 (paperback)

Covers investing theories, stock analysis, market analysis, technical analysis. Uses charts. Zweig clearly explains his proven methods for avoiding the most common investment errors, preserving capital and increasing profits.

AUDIENCE: Beginning, Individual, Professional   RISK LEVEL: Moderate, Aggressive
TOPICS: Bonds, Stocks, Asset Allocation

Winning the Investment Game - A Guide for All Seasons

James Gipson
McGraw-Hill Publishing Company
1221 Avenue of the Americas
New York, NY 10020

PH: (800) 262-4729
Published: 1987
ISBN: 0-07-023296-2
Cost: $13.00

The author identifies 3 different investment "games" and tells which investment strategies are appropriate (and which are not) for each game. He tells investors how to recognize when the game is starting to change so that they can shift strategies in time.

AUDIENCE: Individual   RISK LEVEL: Moderate, Aggressive
TOPICS: Bonds, Mutual Funds, Stocks, Options

World Futures and Options Directory

Nick Battley
McGraw Hill Book Co., UK
Shoppenhangers Road
Maidenhead, Berkshire SL62QL,
  England

FAX: 0628-770224
Published: 1991
Cost: £75.00 sterling

A comprehensive and up-to-date reference to the futures and options exchanges. Includes details in 48 exchanges, over 350 contracts, in-depth contract specifications, 1989 turnover, and open interest statistics, membership listings of over 30 exchanges.

AUDIENCE: Professional   RISK LEVEL: Aggressive
TOPICS: Options, Futures/Commodities

World's Emerging Stock Markets, The

Keith K. H. Park and Antoine W.
  vanAgtmael
Probus Publishing Co.
1925 N. Clybourn Ave., Suite 401
Chicago, IL 60614

PH: (800) PROBUS-1
(312) 868-1100
FAX: (312) 868-6250
Cost: $60.00
Date of first issue: 1993

"Covers all the important regions, including Asia, Europe, Latin America and South America. This comprehensive guide includes pertinent investment information for each country, such as: market structure and overview, recent stock market performance, international investor issues and tax and foreign exchange regulation."

AUDIENCE: Beginning, Individual, Professional   RISK LEVEL: Moderate, Aggressive
TOPICS: Stocks

Yield Curve Analysis: The Fundamentals of Risk and Return

Livingston Douglas
New York Institute of
  Finance/Prentice Hall
113 Sylvan Avenue
Route 9W
Englewood Cliffs, NJ 07632

PH: (800) 947-7700
FAX: (515) 284-2607
Published: 1988
Cost: $65.00

Addresses the complexities of bond risk and bond return in an easy-to-understand manner. Identifies attractive sectors of the bond market and attractive issues within it.

AUDIENCE: Individual   RISK LEVEL: Conservative
TOPICS: Bonds

You Can Afford to Retire! The No-Nonsense Guide to Pre-Retirement Financial Planning

William W. Parrott
New York Institute of
  Finance/Prentice Hall
113 Sylvan Avenue
Route 9W
Englewood Cliffs, NJ 07632

PH: (800) 947-7700
FAX: (515) 284-2607
Published: 1992
Cost: $14.95

Financial issues associated with retirement planning, including an in-depth study of lump sum distributions. Answers key questions about income needs, taxes, inflation, Social Security, and retirement program options.

AUDIENCE: Beginning, Individual   RISK LEVEL: Moderate
TOPICS: All

GENERAL REFERENCES

The main purpose of the *Sourcebook* is to help you locate sources of information appropriate to your individual investment needs. As such, most of the chapters present specific items geared to specific topics of interest. Of course, there are times when you require much more general information. This chapter contains a variety of general reference sources.

For your convenience the following sources are listed:

Associations

Exchanges

Federal Reserve Banks

Government Agencies and Regulatory Bodies

Investment Information Corporations

Reference Tools

U.S. State Securities Regulators

Associations

AAII
American Association of Individual Investors
625 N. Michigan Avenue
Chicago, IL 60611
PH: (312) 280-0170

Newsletters, books, seminars, tapes

AIMR
Association for Investment Management and
Research
P.O. Box 7947
Charlottesville, VA 22906
PH: (804) 977-5724

Seminars, books, journals, etc.

College for Financial Planning
9725 E. Hampden Avenue
Denver, CO 80231
PH: (303) 755-7101

Commodities Educational Institute (CEI)
219 Parkade
Cedar Falls, IA 50613
PH: (800) 221-4352
(319) 277-6341

Financial Executives Institute
10 Madison Avenue
Morristown, NJ 07960
PH: (201) 898-4600

Future Industry Association (FIA)
1825 Eye Street, NW
Suite 1040
Washington, DC 20006
PH: (202) 466-5460

International Association for Financial Planning
Two Concourse Parkway
Suite 800
Atlanta, GA 30328
PH: (404) 395-1605

Louis Rukeyser's Wall Street Club
P.O. Box 25527
Alexandria, VA 23313
PH: (703) 739-2644

Mutual Fund Investors Association
20 William Street, G-70
Wellesley Hills, MA 02181
PH: (617) 235 4432

National Association of Investors Corporation
1515 E. Eleven Mile Road
Royal Oak, MI 48067
PH: (313) 543-0612

Newsletters

National Futures Association (NFA)
200 W. Madison Street
Suite 1600
Chicago, IL 60606
PH: (312) 781-1300

No-Load Mutual Fund Association
11 Penn Plaza
New York, NY 10001
PH: (212) 563-4540

Public Securities Association (PSA)
40 Broad Street
New York, NY 10004
PH: (212) 809-7000

Research Foundation of the Institute of Chartered
Financial Analysts, The
P.O. Box 3668
Charlottesville, VA 22903
PH: (804) 977-6600

Research, books, monographs

Securities Industry Association
120 Broadway
New York, NY 10271
PH: (212) 608-1500

Exchanges

American Stock Exchange
AMEX
86 Trinity Place
New York, NY 10006
PH: (212) 306-1000
(800) 843-2639

Boston Stock Exchange, Inc.
One Boston Place
Boston, MA 02108
PH: (617) 723-9500
(800) 828-3545

Chicago Board of Options Exchange, Inc.
CBOE
400 South LaSalle Street
Chicago, IL 60605
PH: (312) 786-5600

Chicago Board of Trade, The
CBOT
141 West Jackson Boulevard
Chicago, IL 60604
PH: (312) 435-3500

Chicago Mercantile Exchange
CME
30 South Walker Drive
Chicago, IL 60606
PH: (312) 930-3457

Coffee, Sugar and Cocoa Exchange, Inc.
CSCE
4 World Trade Center
New York, NY 10048
PH: (212) 938-2800

Commodity Exchange Center, Inc.
COMEX
4 World Trade Center
New York, NY 10048
PH: (212) 938-2937
(212) 938-9020 for prices 24 hours a day

Kansas City Board of Trade
KCBT
4800 Main Street
Suite 303
Kansas City, MO 64112
PH: (816) 753-7500
(816) 753-1101 daily closing prices

Mid America Commodity Exchange
MACE
444 West Jackson Boulevard
Chicago, IL 60606
PH: (312) 341-3000
(800) 572-3276

Midwest Stock Exchange, Inc.
440 South LaSalle Street
Chicago, IL 60605
PH: (312) 663-2209

NASDAQ, Inc.
National Association of Securities Dealers, Inc.
1735 K Street NW
Washington, DC 20006
PH: (202) 728-8000
(800) 243-4284

New York Mercantile Exchange
NYME
4 World Trade Center
New York, NY 10048
PH: (212) 938-2222

New York Stock Exchange
NYSE
11 Wall Street
New York, NY 10005
PH: (212) 623-3000
(800) 692-6973

Pacific Stock Exchange, Inc, The
233 South Beaudry
Los Angeles, CA 90012
PH: (213) 977-4500

Philadelphia Stock Exchange, Inc., The
1900 Market Street
Philadelphia, PA 19103
PH: (215) 496-5000
(800) 843-7459

Federal Reserve Banks

Atlanta
Federal Reserve Bank of Atlanta
104 Marietta Street, NW
Atlanta, GA 30301
PH: (404) 521-8500

Boston
Federal Reserve Bank of Boston
600 Atlantic Avenue
Boston, MA 02106
PH: (617) 973-3000

Chicago
Federal Reserve Bank of Chicago
230 South LaSalle Street
Chicago, IL 60690
PH: (312) 322-5322

Cleveland
Federal Reserve Bank of Cleveland
1455 East Sixth Street
Cleveland, OH 44101
PH: (216) 579-2000

Dallas
Federal Reserve Bank of Dallas
400 South Akard Street
Dallas, TX 75222
PH: (214) 651-6111

Kansas City
Federal Reserve Bank of Kansas City
925 Grand Avenue
Kansas City, MO 64198
PH: (816) 881-2000

Minneapolis
Federal Reserve Bank of Minneapolis
250 Marquette Avenue
Minneapolis, MN 55480
PH: (612) 340-2345

New York
Federal Reserve Bank of New York
33 Liberty Street
New York, NY 10045
PH: (212) 791-6134

Philadelphia
Federal Reserve Bank of Philadelphia
100 North Sixth Street
Philadelphia, PA 19106
PH: (215) 574-6000

Richmond
Federal Reserve Bank of Richmond
701 East Byrd Street
Richmond, VA 23261
PH: (804) 643-1250

San Francisco
Federal Reserve Bank of San Francisco
101 Market Street
San Francisco, CA 94120
PH: (415) 974-2000

St. Louis
Federal Reserve Bank of St. Louis
411 Locust Street
St. Louis, MO 63166
PH: (314) 444-8444

Government Agencies and Regulatory Bodies

Commodity Futures Trading Commission
CFTC
2033 K Street, NW
Washington, DC 20581
PH: (202) 254-6387

Department of the Treasury
13th and C Streets, SW
Washington, DC 20228
PH: (202) 622-2000

Federal National Mortgage Association (FNMA)
3900 Wisconsin Avenue
Washington, DC 20016
PH: (202) 752-7000

Government National Mortgage Association
(GNMA)
451 7th Street, SW
Room 6224
Washington, DC 20410
PH: (202) 708-0926

National Association of Securities Dealers, Inc.
NASD
District Office #12
1 World Trade Center
New York, NY 10048
PH: (212) 839-6251

National Association of Securities Dealers, Inc.
NASD
District Office #1
1 Union Square, Suite 1911
Seattle, WA 98101
PH: (206) 624-0790

National Association of Securities Dealers, Inc.
NASD
District Office #2
425 California Street
Room 1400
San Francisco, CA 94101
PH: (415) 781-3434

National Association of Securities Dealers, Inc.
NASD
District Office #2S
727 West 7th Street
Los Angeles, CA 90017
PH: (415) 781-3434

National Association of Securities Dealers, Inc.
NASD
District Office #3
1401 17th Street
Suite 700
Denver, CO 80202
PH: (303) 298-7234

National Association of Securities Dealers, Inc.
NASD
District Office #4
911 Main Street
Suite 2230
Kansas City, MO 64105
PH: (816) 421-5700

National Association of Securities Dealers, Inc.
NASD
District Office #5
1004 Richards Building
New Orleans, LA 70112
PH: (504) 522-6527

National Association of Securities Dealers, Inc.
NASD
District Office #6
1999 Bryan Street
14th Floor
Dallas, TX 75201
PH: (214) 969-7050

National Association of Securities Dealers, Inc.
NASD
District Office #7
250 Piedmont Avenue NE
Atlanta, GA 30308
PH: (404) 239-6100

National Association of Securities Dealers, Inc.
NASD
District Office #8
3 First National Plaza
Suite 1680
Chicago, IL 60602
PH: (312) 236-7222

National Association of Securities Dealers, Inc.
NASD
District Office #9
1940 East 6th Street
5th Floor
Cleveland, OH 44114
PH: (216) 694-4545

National Association of Securities Dealers, Inc.
NASD
District Office #10
1735 K Street NW
Washington, DC 20006
PH: (202) 728-8400

National Association of Securities Dealers, Inc.
NASD
District Office #11
1818 Market Street
12th Floor
Philadelphia, PA 19103
PH: (215) 665-1180

National Association of Securities Dealers, Inc.
NASD
District Office #13
50 Milk Street
Boston, MA 02109
PH: (617) 439-4404

Securities Industry Conference on Arbitration
SICA
New York Stock Exchange, Inc.
11 Wall Street
New York, NY 10005
PH: (212) 656-2772

U.S. Securities and Exchange Commission
(SEC)
450 5th Street, NW
Washington, DC 20549
PH: (202) 272-7450

Investment Information Corporations

Dow Jones and Company, Inc.
200 Liberty Street
World Financial Center
New York, NY 10281
PH: (800) 628-9320

On-line services, publications

Moody's Investor Service
99 Church Street
New York, NY 10007
PH: (800) 342-5647
(212) 553-0300

Research, rating services, on-line services

Standard & Poor's
25 Broadway
New York, NY 10004
PH: (800) 777-4858
(212) 208-8768

Research, rating services, on-line services

Value Line Publishing
711 Third Avenue
New York, NY 10017-4064
PH: (800) 633-2252
(212) 687-3965

Research, performance rating services, on-line services

Reference Tools

Barron's Finance and Investment Handbook
John Downes and Jordan Elliot Goodman
Barron's (Publishing)
250 Wireless Boulevard
Hauppauge, NY 11788
PH: (516) 434-3311
Published: 1990
Cost: $26.95

Business One-Irwin Business & Investment
Almanac
Sumner N. Levine
Business One-Irwin
1818 Ridge Road
Homewood, IL 60430
PH: (800) 634-3966
(708) 206-2700
Published: 1994
FAX: (708) 798-1490
Cost: $40.00

Dictionary of Finance and Investment Terms
John Downes & Jordan Elliot Goodman
Barron's Educational Series, Inc.
P.O. Box 8040
250 Wireless Blvd.
Hauppauge, NY 11788
PH: (800) 645-3476
Cost: $8.95
Published: 1987

Money Encyclopedia, The
Harvey Rachin, Editor
Available through Fraser Publishing
P.O. Box 494
Burlington, VT 05402
PH: (802) 658-0322
Published: 1984
Cost: $26.50

Mutual Fund Encyclopedia, The
Gerald W. Perrill
Dearborn Financial Publishing, Inc.
520 N. Dearborn Street
Chicago, IL 60610
Published: 1990
Cost: $27.95

New Encyclopedia of Stock Market Techniques, The
Michael L. Burke, Editor
Available Through Fraser Publishing
P.O. Box 494
Burlington, VT 05402
PH: (802) 658-0322
Published: 1985 (4th supplement)
Cost: $60.00

Wall Street Dictionary, The
R. J. & Robert L. Shook
New York Institute of Finance
2 Broadway
New York, NY 10004
Published: 1990
Cost: $14.95

Words of Wall Street: 2000 Investment Terms Defined
Allan H. Pessin & Joseph A. Ross
Business One-Irwin
1818 Ridge Road
Homewood, IL 60430
PH: (800) 634-3966
(708) 206-2700
FAX: (708) 798-1490
Published 1983
Cost: $11.95

U.S. State Securities Regulators

Alabama
Securities Commissioner
10th Floor
100 Commerce Street
Montgomery, AL 36130
PH: (205) 261-2984

Alaska
Banking, Securities & Corporations Division
Commerce & Economic Development Department
Pouch D
Juneau, AK
PH: (907) 465-2521

Arizona
Securities Division
Corporation Commission
1200 West Washington
Phoenix, AZ 85007
PH: (602) 255-4242

Arkansas
Securities Commissioner
Suite 4B-206
#1 Capital Mall
Little Rock, AR 72201
PH: (501) 371-1011

California
Securities Commissioner
Department of Corporations
Suite 205
1025 P Street
Sacramento, CA 95814
PH: (916) 445-7205

Colorado
Division of Securities
Department of Regulatory Agencies
1560 Broadway
Suite 1450
Denver, CO 80203
PH: (303) 894-2320

Connecticut
Securities and Business Investments
Department of Banking
44 Capitol Avenue
Hartford, CT 06106
PH: (203) 566-4560

Delaware
Secretary of State
Townsend Building
Dover, DE 19901
PH: (302) 736-4111

District of Columbia
Deputy Mayor for Financial Management
Suite 423
1350 Pennsylvania Avenue, NW
Washington, DC 20004
PH: (202) 727-2476

Florida
Securities Division
Department of Banking and Finance
The Capitol
Tallahassee, FL 32301
PH: (904) 488-9805

Georgia
Securities Commissioner
Suite 802W
2 Martin Luther King Jr. Drive
Atlanta, GA 30334
PH: (404) 656-2894

Hawaii
Business Registration Division
Commerce and Consumer Affairs Department
1010 Richards Street
Honolulu, HI 96813
PH: (808) 586-2727

Idaho Department of Finance
700 West State Street
Boise, ID 83720
PH: (208) 334-3313

Illinois
Secretary of State
213 State House
Springfield, IL 62706
PH: (217) 782-2201

Indiana
Securities Commissioner
Suite 560
One North Capital Street
Indianapolis, IN 46204
PH: (317) 232-6681

Iowa
Securities Division
Insurance Department
Lucas Stone Office Building
Des Moines, IA 50319
PH: (515) 281-4441

Kansas
Securities Commissioner
Suite 501
109 West Ninth Street
Topeka, KS 66612
PH: (913) 296-3307

Kentucky
Financial Institutions Department
Public Protection and Regulation Cabinet
911 Leawood Drive
Frankfort, KY 40601
PH: (502) 564-3390

Louisiana
Department of the Treasury
P.O. Box 44154
Baton Rouge, LA 70804
PH: (514) 342-0010

Maine
Bureau of Banking, Business,
Occupational and Professional Regulations
Department
Suite 36
State House Station
Augusta, ME 04333
PH: (207) 289-3231

Maryland
Division of Securities
Office of the Attorney General
3rd Floor
7 North Calvert Street
Baltimore, MD 21202
PH: (301) 576-6360

Massachusetts
Securities Division
Office of Secretary of Commonwealth
Suite 1719
1 Ashburton Place
Boston, MA 02133
PH: (617) 727-7190

Michigan
Securities Division
Department of Commerce
6546 Mercantile Way
Lansing, MI 48909
PH: (517) 373-0485

Minnesota
Registration and Licensing Division
Department of Commerce
5th Floor
Metro Square Building
St. Paul, MN 55101
PH: (612) 296-2594

Mississippi
Securities Division
Office of Secretary State
401 Mississippi Street
Jackson, MS 39201
PH: (601) 359-1350

Missouri
Division of Securities
Office of Secretary of State
Truman Building
Box 778
Jefferson City, MO 65102
PH: (314) 751-4136

Montana
Securities Division
Office of State Auditor
Capitol Station
Helena, MT 59620
PH: (406) 444-2040

Nebraska
Department of Banking and Finance
P.O. Box 95006
301 Centennial Mall South
Lincoln, NE 68509
PH: (402) 471-2171

Nevada
Securities and Fraud Division
Office of Secretary of State
State Capitol
Carson City, NV 89710
PH: (702) 885-5203

New Hampshire
Division of Securities
Department of Insurance
169 Manchester Street
Concord, NH 03301
PH: (603) 271-2261

New Jersey
Bureau of Securities
Department of Law and Public Safety
Suite 308
80 Mulberry Street
Newark, NJ 07102
PH: (603) 271-2261

New Mexico
Securities Division
Regulation and Licensing Department
Lew Wallace Building
Santa Fe, NM 87503
PH: (505) 827-7750

New York
Bureau of Investor Protection and Securities
2 World Trade Center
New York, NY 10047
PH: (212) 488-5389

North Carolina
Division of Securities
Office of Secretary of State
Suite 302
300 North Salisbury Street
Raleigh, NC 27611
PH: (919) 733-3924

North Dakota
Securities Commissioner's Office
9th Floor
State Capitol
Bismarck, ND 58505
PH: (701) 224-2910

Ohio
Division of Securities
Department of Commerce
3rd Floor
2 Nationwide Plaza
Columbus, OH 43215
PH: (614) 466-3440

Oklahoma
Securities Commissioner
2915 North Lincoln Boulevard
Oklahoma City, OK 73105
PH: (405) 521-2451

Oregon
Division of Securities
Department of Commerce
158 12th Street N.E.
Salem, OR 97310
PH: (503) 378-4385

Pennsylvania
Securities Commissioner
14th Floor
333 Market Street
Harrisburg, PA 17120
PH: (717) 787-6828

Puerto Rico
Securities Commissioner
Department of the Treasury
P.O. Box 3508
San Juan, PR 00904
PH: (809) 723-1122

Rhode Island
Banking Division
100 North Main Street
Providence, RI 02903
PH: (401) 277-2405

South Carolina
Secretary of State
P.O. Box 11350
Columbia, SC 29211
PH: (803) 758-2744

South Dakota
Division of Securities
Commerce and Regulations Department
1st Floor
State Capitol
Pierre, SD 57501
PH: (605) 773-3177

Tennessee
Securities Division
Department of Commerce and Insurance
614 Tennessee Building
Nashville, TN 37219
PH: (615) 741-2947

Texas
Securities Board
P.O. Box 13167
Capitol Station
Austin, TX 78711
PH: (512) 474-2233

Utah
Securities Commissioner's Office
Department of Business Regulation
160 East 300 South
Salt Lake City, UT 84110
PH: (801) 530-6600

Vermont
Securities Commissioner
Department of Banking and Insurance
120 State Street
Montpelier, VT 05602
PH: (802) 828-3301

Virgin Islands of the United States
Corporations and Trade Names Division
Office of the Lieutenant Governor
P.O. Box 450
St. Thomas, VI 00801
PH: (809) 774-2991

Virginia
State Corporation Commissioner
13th Floor
Jefferson Building
Richmond, VA 23219
PH: (804) 371-9967

Washington
Securities Division
Department of Licensing
Highways-Licensing Building
Olympia, WA 98504
PH: (206) 753-6928

West Virginia
Securities Division
Office of State Auditor
W-100 State Capitol Complex
Charleston, WV 25305
PH: (304) 348-2257

Wisconsin
Commissioner of Securities
P.O. Box 1768
111 West Wilson Street
Madison, WI 53701
PH: (608) 266-3433

Wyoming
Secretary of State
State Capitol
Cheyenne, WY 82002
PH: (307) 777-7378

ABOUT THE AUTHOR

Spencer McGowan is a Vice President at Rauscher Pierce Refsnes, Inc., where he serves as an experienced investment advisor. Piloting an innovative series of monthly workshops featuring specialized investment topics, McGowan advises a select group of Texas businesspeople. Previously he was a Vice President of Shearson Lehman and before that an account executive at PaineWebber.

The opinions expressed or derived in this book are those of the individual services and the author and do not necessarily reflect those of Rauscher Pierce or the other entities involved with this book.